Adjustment

Adjustment

The Psychology of Change

WILLIAM R. MILLER
CAROLINA E. YAHNE
JOHN M. RHODES

The University of New Mexico

PRENTICE HALL, Englewood Cliffs, New Jersey 07632

Library of Congress Cataloging-in-Publication Data

Miller, William R.
    Adjustment : the psychology of change / William R. Miller,
Carolina E. Yahne, John M. Rhodes.
        p.   cm.
    Bibliography: p.
    Includes index.
    ISBN 0-13-004342-7
    1. Adjustment (Psychology) 2. Change (Psychology)   I. Yahne,
Carolina Ellen. II. Rhodes, John M. III. Title.
BF335.M54 1990
155.2'4--dc20   89-34685
                                                   CIP

Editorial/production supervision: Marina Harrison
Interior design: Lee Cohen
Cover design: Lee Cohen
Cover Photo: Courtesy Vigeland Museum, Oslo, Norway
Manufacturing buyer: Robert Anderson
Photo Editor: Lori Morris-Nantz
Photo Researcher: Ilene Cherna

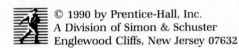

Printed in the United States of America

10 9 8 7 6 5 4 3 2 1

ISBN 0-13-004342-7

Prentice-Hall International (UK) Limited, *London*
Prentice-Hall of Australia Pty. Limited, *Sydney*
Prentice-Hall Canada Inc., *Toronto*
Prentice-Hall Hispanoamericana, S.A., *Mexico*
Prentice-Hall of India Private Limited, *New Delhi*
Prentice-Hall of Japan, Inc., *Tokyo*
Simon & Schuster Asia Pte. Ltd., *Singapore*
Editora Prentice-Hall do Brasil, Ltda., *Rio de Janeiro*

We gratefully dedicate this book to our students and our clients, who have taught us most of what it contains, and

to Sidney Rosenblum, my mentor, and master of the balancing task called adjustment

WRM

to William John Zimmer, with love, for his unflagging faith in my ability

CEY

to my co-authors, for putting up with me through the years of writing this book

JMR

Brief Contents

Contents

PART II Development and the Self

PART III *Challenges of Adjustment*

11. The Addictive Behaviors   286

THE CONCEPT OF ADDICTIVE BEHAVIORS 288

COMMONALITIES AMONG THE ADDICTIVE BEHAVIORS 288

REINFORCEMENT 288 ■ *SOCIAL ACCEPTABILITY IN MODERATION 290* ■ *SOCIAL COSTS 290* ■ *SOCIAL AMBIVALENCE 291* ■ *OVERLAP 291*

CAUSES OF ADDICTIVE BEHAVIOR 293

S: Situational Factors 293 ■ *T: Thought Patterns 294* ■ *O: Organic Factors 298* ■ *R: Response Factors 301* ■ *C: Consequences 303*

CHANGING ADDICTIVE BEHAVIORS 305

SELF-CONTROL SKILLS 306

PREVENTING RELAPSE 309

LIFESTYLE CHANGE 310 ■ *COGNITIVE CHANGE 311* ■ *DEVELOPING NEW SKILLS 312*

SUMMARY 312

12. Sexual Behavior   314

THE CULTURAL CONTEXT OF SEXUAL BEHAVIOR 317

HEALTHY SEXUALITY 317 ■ *SEX ROLES 319*

GENDER SIMILARITIES AND DIFFERENCES 319

SMALL AND INCONSISTENT DIFFERENCES 320 ■ *DIFFERENT REACTIONS 321* ■ *INVISIBLE FEMALES 322* ■ *INDIVIDUAL VARIATION 323*

SEXUALITY AND THE STORC 324

S: Stimuli 324 ■ *T: Thought Patterns 324* ■ *O: Organic Patterns 326* ■ *R: Responses 327* ■ *C: Consequences 330*

SEXUAL PROBLEMS 333

SEXUAL DYSFUNCTIONS 333 ■ *CAUSES OF SEXUAL PROBLEMS 334*

TREATMENT 335

HOW SUCCESSFUL IS TREATMENT? 337

WHEN SEX IS NOT SEXUAL 338

RAPE 338 ■ *SEXUAL HARASSMENT 339*

SEXUAL ABUSE 340

SOCIAL ISSUES 341

PORNOGRAPHY 341 ■ *REPRODUCTIVE FREEDOM 343* ■ *SEX CRIMES 345*

SUMMARY 346

13. The World of Work   348

WHAT IS WORK? 350

CHOOSING ONE'S WORK 350

APTITUDES 352 ■ *ATTRIBUTES 354* ■ *AVAILABILITY 356*

FINDING A JOB 356

JOB SURVIVAL SKILLS 358

PEOPLE SKILLS 358 ■ *TIME MANAGEMENT 359*

THE STORC AT WORK 360

S: WORK SITUATION 361 ▪ T: THOUGHT PATTERNS 361 ▪ O: ORGANIC PROCESSES 362 ▪ R: RESPONSE PATTERNS 363 ▪ C: CONSEQUENCES 363

WORKAHOLISM 363

CHARACTERISTICS 363 ▪ CONSEQUENCES 364 ▪ OVERCOMING WORKAHOLISM 365

WORK AND LIFE TRANSITIONS 366

CHANGING THE SHAPE OF WORK 368

SUMMARY 369

14. The Individual and Society   370

SOCIAL INFLUENCE 372

SOCIAL CONVENTIONS 372 ▪ SOCIAL CONTROL 374 ▪ SHYNESS 376

PARENTING 378

BALANCING EXTERNAL AND INTERNAL CONTROL 378 ▪ EMPHASIZING THE POSITIVE 378 ▪ LISTENING 379 ▪ CONSISTENCY 380 ▪ APPROPRIATENESS 380

ADJUSTMENT AND SOCIAL SYSTEMS 380

AUTHORITARIANISM VERSUS FREEDOM 382 ▪ PERSONAL LIBERTY VERSUS SOCIAL WELFARE 382 ▪ CONSERVATISM VERSUS REFORMATION 383

PEACEMAKING: THE CHALLENGE OF SURVIVAL 384

THE PSYCHOLOGY OF SOCIAL ENVIRONMENTS 386

ENVIRONMENTAL PSYCHOLOGY 386 ▪ ORGANIZATIONAL PSYCHOLOGY 388 ▪ COMMUNITY PSYCHOLOGY 390

PREVENTION IN THE COMMUNITY 390

TERTIARY PREVENTION 390 ▪ SECONDARY PREVENTION 392 ▪ PRIMARY PREVENTION 393

CHOOSING YOUR FUTURE 395

SUMMARY 398

15. Weaving the Tapestry of Meaning   400

HOW IS MEANING RELATED TO ADJUSTMENT? 402

MEANING AS STORY 403

SOURCES OF MEANING 405

DETERMINISM 405 ▪ HUMAN AGENCY 406 ▪ TRANSCENDENCE 406

ISSUES OF MEANING: STRANDS OF THE TAPESTRY 410

QUALITY OF LIFE 410 ▪ UNIQUENESS 411 ▪ UNCERTAINTY 414 ▪ DEATH 416

MAPS FOR THE JOURNEY 418

SOLITUDE 418 ▪ MEDITATION 419 ▪ JOURNAL KEEPING 419 ▪ LIVING IN THE "NOW" 420 ▪ RITUALS AND DISCIPLINES 422 ▪ SOCIAL SUPPORT 423 ▪ LIVING "AS IF" 424

SUMMARY 426

Appendixes   **428**

A. SEEKING HELP   428
B. LEARNING TO RELAX   442
C. A GUIDE TO MORE EFFECTIVE STUDYING   450

Preface

A course in adjustment is a course in human nature. There are many ways to approach this subject. Sometimes the course in adjustment is taught as an introduction to general concepts in the field of human development or social psychology. Sometimes it serves as a lower-level course in theories of personality. Sometimes the focus is mainly on abnormal behavior, on the basics of what can go wrong with human beings.

We believe, however, that the psychology of adjustment is a rich and fascinating area in its own right, and is not just a more elementary version of another specialty area such as personality, abnormal, developmental, or social psychology. Certainly the insights of these fields are vital in understanding human adjustment, as are knowledge and research from learning, physiological, clinical, and counseling psychology. In one sense, the study of the psychology of adjustment is all of these, and in another sense it is none of these. It is an investigation of how people normally cope with the challenges and transitions of life. It is a study of human survival and triumph over obstacles, of growth and adaptation. It is the psychology of normality and of change, of the nature of human nature.

In this sense, adjustment has common ground with many other areas of psychology. It shares *developmental* psychology's fascination with the changing and emerging person and *social* psychology's interest in the influence of group processes on individual behavior. Because people are biological creatures, the insights of *physiological* psychology and neuroscience are crucial in understanding the whole picture of adjustment. The psychology of *learning and memory* is important in helping to comprehend how people acquire and maintain patterns of behavior. Like *personality* theory, the psychology of adjustment attempts to integrate a broad range of information about people. The study of *psychopathology* (abnormal behavior) is the other side of the psychology of adjustment, and sheds light on this field by contrasting what happens when normal adjustment processes fail. Finally, the psychology of adjustment shares with *clinical* and *counseling* psychology a continuing search to understand the processes of change and to identify helpful change methods through the application of general psychological principles. In this way, the study of adjustment is a superb introduction and gateway to the general field of psychology.

Because of this common ground with various areas of psychology, a certain amount of overlap with other psychology courses is inevitable, even desirable. We hope to avoid heavy duplication of other courses, however, and instead to draw together for you a large body of theory and research on how people change or grow. We seek to teach (for newcomers) and integrate (for more advanced students of psychology) some of the fundamental concepts of general psychology into our explanation of human adjustment. Along the way we have also included a substantial amount of interesting and practical information for self-understanding and self-change.

Our goal is to provide you with a balanced view of adjustment. In many cases we will offer you not a finished structure, but rather a set of building blocks along with some ideas for how these blocks of information might be put together. Whether or not you agree with our own views, we hope that you will catch some of our enthusiasm in the search for new knowledge about human nature and that you will continue your own search for how best to put the pieces together long after you have closed this book for the last time.

Our own common approach to the psychology of adjustment (and to the writing of this text) has been a scientific one, broadly defined. We see the scientific method of inquiry through research as a very useful tool for attaining knowledge, though it is by no means the only road to truth. Careful research is a means by which to carve the building blocks, which in turn challenge us to organize them into working structures. Theories *are* those structures, and their usefulness is tested by the extent to which they can incorporate all the available pieces. Sometimes it is necessary to tear down an old structure and build a new one from the ground up; sometimes it is possible just to add on. It is a continuous cycle of new pieces and new structures. You become a part of that process as you read this book.

The special features of this book are designed to make it easier for you to learn the material presented and to challenge you to learn more. Within each chapter we present information in an organized way and provide a summary at the end to emphasize some of the key points. Appropriate references and readings are cited, allowing you to pursue specific topics further according to your own interest. Numerous special interest features are inserted as part of the learning process, including some questionnaires and exercises that you can complete. We encourage you to take the time to do these, because they relate to the material discussed and can help you to apply it more personally. Self-help methods are described throughout the text wherever such methods have been reasonably supported by current research. Three special self-help appendixes have been added, including one on how to study more effectively.

You should be aware, too, that this textbook was written for you by three psychologists with very different training and viewpoints. Dr. Miller's clinical psychology training emphasized cognitive and behavior therapies, which he practices within a broadly spiritual perspective. Dr. Yahne received her Ph.D. from a counseling psychology program emphasizing humanistic and personal growth viewpoints. Dr. Rhodes is a clinical neuropsychologist who is expert in brain-behavior relationships and whose therapeutic training emphasized psychodynamic approaches. Throughout this book we discuss special topics titled "Here We Differ/Here We Agree," at points where in writing we have found a genuine difference of opinion between at least two of us. We include these to illustrate some current points of debate in the field and to remind you that psychology is far from having final "cut and dried" answers to many questions. We also wanted to illustrate how the topics we discuss can have great personal importance and relevance in one's life. At points in the text where we present material that has had special personal importance to one of us, you will find a "Personal Milestone" box describing our own experiences.

The choice of *level* of writing is a difficult one for this type of text, but it is an important choice for the student. At some schools, students enter the adjustment course after having had an introductory course in general psychology. At many others, the course in adjustment represents a first exposure to psychology. For this reason, we have not assumed a prior knowledge of technical psychological terms, and we provide an explanation of new concepts as they are introduced. This is done in the form of a running glossary in the side margin, so that if you are already familiar with a term you need not stop to learn its definition. The glossary is also indexed at the end of this book, to help when you reencounter unfamiliar terms and need a reminder of their meaning. In presenting the psychology of adjustment, we have attempted to integrate some of the essential information for a first exposure to the field of psychology, emphasizing the value of the scientific method in exploring human behavior. We intend, thus, to provide a text that is comprehensible and interesting for the student who is new to psychology.

At the same time we have sought to avoid writing and material that is too elementary. Even in introductory courses, many students these days are returning to college after years of life experiences and do not want texts or instructors that "talk down" to them. Some readers of this book will already have completed several other psychology courses or may have read a variety of books and articles on psychology. We have particularly chosen to focus on aspects of the psychology of change that may be covered less, if at all, in other courses. In this way, we provide a text with fresh material and perspectives appropriate for the student who takes adjustment as one among several psychology courses. We hope to challenge you to stretch your mind and want to learn more.

Since the time of the ancient Greek philosophers, "Know thyself" has been sage advice. In part, that is a good reason for studying the psychology of adjustment, along with the search for a better understanding and compassion for others. The quest for self-understanding is a lifelong journey. It is our wish for you that in the chapters ahead, you will find some knowledge, perspectives, and insights to carry with you and to use on your journey.

■ ACKNOWLEDGMENTS

Many people have contributed to the evolution of this book. We wish to thank those who offered important administrative support in the preparation of manuscript drafts: Erika Love, Judith DuCharme and their staff at the Medical Center Library at the University of New Mexico; the reference librarian staff of the Zimmerman Library; the staff at the Mail Station; Dee Ann Quintanas and Vicki Roberts. T. J. Ferguson was very helpful in keeping the computer and word processing programs running. We also want to thank the editorial staff at Prentice Hall: John Isley, Marina Harrison, and Susan Finnemore.

As we researched and drafted chapters, a wide range of colleagues offered their expertise, comments, ideas, information, and assistance, among them: Gina Agostinelli, Judith Arroyo, Rafael Diaz, Michael Dougher, Mary Dudley, Margaret Earley, W. Sterling Edwards, Henry Ellis, Douglas Ferraro, Steve Gangestad, Therese Goetz, Timothy Goldsmith, William Gordon, Edel Hannemann, Mary Harris, Richard Harris, Reuben Hersh, Gordon Hodge, Robin Smith Jacobvitz, Vera John-Steiner, Georgine Loacker, Vonda Long, Michael Mahoney, Alan Marlatt, Marcia Mentkowski, Kate Noble, Robert Ornstein, James Prochaska, Sheri Pruitt, Mark Rutledge, Jane Smith, Carl Thoresen, Holly Waldron, and Ron Yeo. Successive drafts of the manuscript were reviewed by another group of colleagues, who offered many helpful ideas and suggestions. Paul Zimmer provided a very useful reading through the eyes of a university student.

No one undertakes or completes a project of this size without a very substantial base of social support. The members of our men's and women's support groups have been important sources of laughter, warmth, reality testing, ideas, and inspiration. Other friends helped us keep writing when we felt stuck. The sustaining communities of St. Andrew Presbyterian Church and the Albuquerque Friends' Meeting have been important as well. We have learned much of what we know from our students, who ask thought-provoking questions and seek the answers, and from our clients, who continuously remind us of human resilience and the reality of change. Finally, we are grateful for the love and the models of adjustment provided by our spouses—Kathleen Ann Jackson, William John Zimmer, and Mary Margaret Rhodes, and by our children, who live with us through the very processes of change that are the substance of this book.

■ ABOUT THE AUTHORS

William R. Miller, Ph.D. is Professor of Psychology and Psychiatry at the University of New Mexico, where he has also served as Director of the Ph.D. training program in clinical psychology. He has published 14 books and more than 100 articles and chapters, focusing especially on the treatment of alcohol problems and other addictive behaviors, and maintains an active career of teaching and clinical research. He has held numerous research grants, founded a private practice group, and served as a consultant to many organizations including the U.S. Senate, the National Academy of Sciences, the National Institute on Alcohol Abuse and Alcoholism, and the National Institute on Drug Abuse. Dr. Miller's clinical psychology training emphasized cognitive and behavior therapies, which he practices within a broadly spiritual perspective.

Carolina E. Yahne, Ph.D. is a Clinical Associate in the Departments of Psychiatry and Psychology at the University of New Mexico. She teaches Clinical Psychology and the Psychology of Women, in addition to the Psychology of Adjustment and Interpersonal Relations. Dr. Yahne's independent practice with Health Psychology Associates focuses on consultation with individuals and organizations. As an organizational consultant, her expertise in the psychology of gender aids in implementing affirmative action policies. She earned her doctorate in 1984 from the University of New Mexico in counseling psychology. Her training emphasized a humanistic perspective. Dr. Yahne's publications include reports about the professional responsibility program she designed for the medical curriculum, and about feminist group interventions.

John M. Rhodes, Ph.D. is a diplomate in clinical neuropsychology from the American Board of Professional Psychology. His publications primarily concern neurophysiology, starting when he held a U.S. Public Health Fellowship at the Center for Young Epileptics in Marseille, France. He received his doctorate in 1959 from the University of Southern California, and is Professor Emeritus of Psychology at the University of New Mexico. In addition to therapeutic training in psychodynamic approaches, Dr. Rhodes uses neuroscience to understand the behavioral problems of clients with brain injury and disease. He served on the International Committee for NASA studying brain-behavior relationships in astronauts. He alternates working in his private practice with sailing in the Caribbean.

chapter one

With Navajos . . . the way the Holy People taught us, the goal of life was *yo'zho'*. No word for it in English. Sort of a combination of beauty/harmony, being in tune, going with the flow, feeling peaceful, all wrapped up in a single concept.

Tony Hillerman, *People of Darkness*

Adjustment and Change

OUTLINE

What is **adjustment?** You are about to encounter an entire textbook and course dedicated to this topic. In this chapter we will explore what adjustment is, and we will describe four different approaches for understanding it. We will also take a first step toward the main topic of this book: *how* people adjust and change.

Commonsense definitions of adjustment as well as those found in dictionaries tend to fall into two categories. First, the term "adjustment" refers to a *state of being*, a condition of wellness, of harmonious relationship between the individual and his or her environment. A person who is "well adjusted" is, in this sense, one who is in tune with the world and with other people.

But the word "adjustment" also refers to a *process of change:* people adjust or adapt. In this more active sense of the word, people are always adjusting, growing, changing in search of harmony. In this second sense, a well-adjusted person is one who is capable of constructive change. Such change may be accomplished by changing oneself to fit the environment, by altering the environment itself, or through a combination of these. Adjustment is *both* a state of harmony and the process by which that state is approached.

If this is so, then adjustment is something that concerns us all, for it is what we are constantly seeking and doing. The topics considered in this book are of very personal importance: feelings, values, choices, decisions, relationships, problems. This is one reason why the study of psychology in general and of adjustment in particular is unlike any other field of inquiry. In studying the stars, animals, plants, geologic formations, or even history, you are studying things that are "out there," but when you study people, you do so knowing that *you are one!* The study of adjustment is, in a very real sense, a study of yourself.

Because this subject matter is so personal, you come to it already having many ideas and opinions. All of us constantly observe ourselves and others, and ask the question, "Why?" Aware of it or not, you are often asking yourself the same questions asked by professional psychologists: "How did this happen to me?" "What led him to do that?" "Why did she behave in that way?" "How can one change?"

There are very few simple or totally right answers to such questions. To understand people (and yourself) you must consider a wide range of factors that not only add up, but multiply and interact with each other in complicated ways. Your everyday experience is made up of emotions, thoughts, and actions, all of which influence each other. All of us are biological creatures, and all feelings, thoughts, and behaviors involve physiological events within the nervous system. We are all influenced by what we have learned through experience and by the complex and changing processes of memory through which we stay in touch with our past experiences. Through these and other processes, people change over time, developing ever-different skills, goals, and problems. In addition, all of us live in a social world, influencing others and being influenced by them through a wondrous array of relationships that vary in nature, depth, and importance. Is it any wonder, then, that simple answers to human questions are usually *too* simple?

In the chapters that lie ahead you will find that our approach to adjustment is guided by several basic principles, which we want to acknowledge now. The first of these is our perspective that *adjustment is best understood within the context of human relationships.* Certainly all of us adjust to our physical environment as well: wearing heavy boots to climb a snowy mountain peak and sandals to cross a sunny beach, adjusting our homes as well as our clothing to meet the demands of changing weather. These adaptations, although essential to survival, are not of central concern for the purposes of this book. Rather we

⚓ Adjustment
(1) a state of harmony between the person and the environment; (2) a process of change whereby individuals adapt to variations in the physical and social environment by altering aspects of their behavior and/or the environment.

Adjustment is best understood within the context of human relationships.

will be considering the adjustment processes that allow people to seek harmony within themselves and their social environments.

Second, we work within a framework that might be called **perceptual relativism,** which is the view that in many important ways *reality is in the eye of the beholder.* (Within the discipline of philosophy, this viewpoint is associated with the term **phenomenology.**) Each person perceives the world in a completely original way, unlike that of any other individual. You are unique, and your unique perceptions shape how you think and feel, the information that you receive and reject, and the quality of your relationships with others (Miller, 1985a). An important key to understanding any individual is to appreciate how he or she *perceives* the world—a challenging task indeed.

Finally we maintain that *there is no single "right" way to perceive the world.* We do not endorse any particular theory or viewpoint as "the one true light" for all. Rather, we believe that many viewpoints have light to shed and contain some truth. This is not to say we believe that all ideas are correct or have equal merit from a scientific perspective. Research continues to reveal the nature of human nature, supporting some ideas while disconfirming others. Neither do we mean to say that we have no particular belief systems of our own, because like all human beings we must and do. Rather, it is to say that we intend to present material that provides you with a range of *alternative* views (including our own) along with current scientific evidence on each topic, without insisting that you adopt any one view in particular. At some points the three of us even disagree with each other, and these are noted in the chapters that follow in special boxes titled "Here We Differ/Here We Agree." We include these to illustrate some of the legitimate differences that emerge among psychologists, as among all people. The choice of how *you* will view the world is ultimately yours.

Perceptual Relativism
the view that reality differs from each individual to the next and depends upon one's own unique patterns of perception and thinking.

Phenomenology
the philosophic position that one can never know absolute reality, but only one's own perceptions of it; associated with the writings of Immanuel Kant.

■ ADJUSTMENT: FOUR ALTERNATIVE VIEWS

There are a variety of ways to think about adjustment. We will group them for present purposes into four general categories. Each of these four general models of adjustment includes both a *state of being* ("adjusted") and a *process of change* ("adjusting").

HOMEOSTASIS: ADJUSTMENT BY BALANCE

The **homeostatic** model of adjustment emphasizes balance, drawing on concepts from physics and from physiology. A homeostatic system is one that regulates itself to maintain a balance, to remain close to a standard or **set-point.** A mechanical example would be a household thermostat that regulates temperature, turning on heating or cooling systems to keep the thermometer within a few degrees of the point to which it has been set. Similarly an automatic pilot in an aircraft or boat reads a compass heading to which it has been set and adjusts the steering controls accordingly, thus keeping on course.

Many homeostatic processes occur within the human body in order to maintain life. Your body has its own thermostat in the brain that regulates temperature. The chemical balance or "pH" of your blood is also kept within a very narrow range by such a homeostatic process. In each case, the brain receives information about the present state of the body and then calls into action necessary corrections to return the system back to its natural set-point. If the body drifts too far from one of these healthy set-points, it no longer functions normally, and life itself can be threatened.

Many medical terms refer to these homeostatic processes. The prefixes "hyper" and "hypo" refer, respectively, to a body function that has gone too high or too low relative to a given set-point. After waiting in line on a hot day or being exposed to the desert sun, a person may develop *hyper*thermia (too high temperature). If one is lost in a snowstorm or swimming in frigid water, the danger to life is *hypo*thermia. In both cases the body's temperature has been forced by the elements beyond the normal healthy range within which it functions best. Sometimes the body breaks its own rules in the interest of health, as when a person develops a fever to fight an infection.

There are, then, two crucial concepts to understand in homeostasis. One is the **set-point,** the point or value toward which the system regulates itself. Being at or near the set-point represents the *state* of being adjusted. For body temperature this value is said to be 98.6 degrees Fahrenheit, the point at which the body functions optimally. Maladjustment (or illness, sickness, pathology, abnormality, etc.) is defined as straying too far from this set-point. But how far is "too far"? How far can the system deviate and still function well? This raises the question of optimal or **normal limits,** a second important concept in

Homeostasis
a process of maintaining balance around a central set point, as a thermostat regulates temperature.

Set Point [homeostasis]
a fixed level that is maintained by making adjustments whenever the system deviates from it.

Normal Limits
the boundaries of acceptability, beyond which behavior is judged (relative to a particular value system) to be unusual or problematic.

Homeostasis is the process of maintaining balance.

homeostasis. Changing in order to remain within normal limits represents the *process* of adjustment.

Defining normal limits can be difficult, and often is arbitrary. How high is "high blood pressure" (*hyper*tension)? How low must blood sugar plunge before it is abnormally low (*hypo*glycemia)? On such measures there are general guidelines used by the health professions, but with feelings and behaviors, the answers are much more cloudy. How much activity is "too much" (*hyper*activity) for a four-year-old? How much anger is too much or too little? How much nervous tension is enough to be "psyched" for an exam, and when does it become too high and interfere with performance? The answers to such questions are complicated.

One reason for this complexity is that set-points vary. What is normal for one person may be unusual for another. Normal body temperature differs slightly from one person to the next, and it changes with the time of day. Some researchers believe that each person has a physical set-point for body weight and that at least some "overweight" people are actually at their natural weight set-point (Keesey, 1978, 1986). If such a person tries to look like a slender movie star by undertaking severe diets or other measures to lose weight, then he or she enters an abnormal state that the body fights to correct through homeostatic mechanisms. This is one explanation (though not the only one) for why people quickly regain weight that they have lost during a diet.

Another complexity in understanding adjustment is that "normal limits" and set-points are influenced by those around you. The "system" that determines the ideal set-point for a behavior is, at least in part, the *social* system, and efforts to "correct" behavior may come from other people. Some of the rules for normal behavior are very subtle. How close, for example, is it polite to stand when talking to another person? Each person has an unspoken, learned set-point for this distance. Such rules are learned in the process of growing up within a culture. People in some societies stand very close when talking, whereas in others people are more standoffish. Within a culture there can be large differences among individuals. It can be comical to watch an attempted conversation between two people who have very different set-points for how close to stand. Without being aware of what is happening, they do a dance across the floor, one trying to get closer, the other to keep distance.

What is normal and abnormal in a society has to do with how that culture defines set-points for behavior and how tolerant the culture is of deviations from the set-point (normal limits). Rigid societies and social units (families, groups) are those that specify the clearest set-points and tolerate little variation. More permissive social systems allow greater variation and may not even set "ideal" points or standards. The laws of a society represent a written code of allowed and disallowed behavior. Religious and moral codes similarly promote certain ideals and limits. The homeostatic social control of behavior extends much further, however, to such subtle dimensions as how fast to walk or talk, how loudly to speak, and how much physical contact with other people is allowable. When one's behavior strays too far from the defined set-points, it may be labeled by terms such as "criminal," "immoral," "weird," "inconsiderate," or "sick."

Homeostasis is one very useful way to think about adjustment, and it is especially helpful as a tool for understanding physiological processes (on which behaviors are based). In many ways we seem to adjust and adapt ourselves toward some balance point.

An aspect of this analogy to which one might object, particularly when the model is extended to explain social systems, is that it usually assumes the existence of an *ideal* point or range. A person or group is "adjusted" by remaining within an acceptable range around this ideal point. But who defines this ideal for behaviors, feelings, and thoughts? "Healthy adjustment" to a society

1.1 WHAT IS ABNORMAL?

The term "abnormal" assumes that there is behavior considered to be "normal." Each society and each individual has standards for normality, and these are likely to differ. What is judged to be strange or bizarre by one person or group may be quite acceptable and normal to another.

The following exercise is designed to help you appreciate this perspective and to learn something about your own standards of "normality." For each of the items listed here, first consider how many you would regard to be *enough* for you. Next consider, for each, how many would be *too many* as far as you are concerned. How many would be *too few* for you? Finally, ask yourself how far a person would have to go in each direction before you would consider it to be abnormal. How many would be *abnormally* too many? How few before it becomes *abnormally* too few? Notice that in some cases you may believe that it is *impossible* to have too many or too few.

One way in which we judge what is "abnormal" in others (and in ourselves) is by comparing behavior with our own standards of what is too much or too little.

HOW MANY WOULD BE . . .	ABNORMALLY TOO FEW?	TOO FEW FOR YOU?	ENOUGH FOR YOU?	TOO MANY FOR YOU?	ABNORMALLY TOO MANY?
Cups of coffee per day					
Alcoholic drinks per week					
Hours of watching TV per day					
Hours of sleep per night					
Baths per week					
Friends with whom you can share personal concerns					
Physical fights per year					
Sexual partners in a lifetime					
Children to have in a lifetime					
Visits to church per month					
Hours spent per year seeing a therapist					
Years of education					
Arguments per week					
Hours of exercise per week					
Hours of work per week					
Hours of leisure or recreation per week					

1.2 DO FAMILIES MAINTAIN A BALANCE?

Can a homeostatic model be applied to *social systems*? This is what **general systems theory** attempts to do (Miller, 1978). A popular current outgrowth of this trend is **family systems theory,** which asserts that *families* have certain set-points and that they struggle to maintain a status quo by remaining within a certain optimal distance of these unspoken rules or norms (Ackerman, 1984; Bodin, 1981). Within this view, the **symptoms** of an individual can be understood as serving a purpose within the family, helping to maintain this balance. If, for example, the parents' marriage is in difficulty, a problematic child restores balance by forcing the parents to work together and focus on this new challenge, thus taking their attention away from their own conflicts with each other. Family systems theory would predict that within such a family, if the problem child is "cured," another member of the family will have to develop new problems to restore balance (Haley, 1963; Minuchin, 1974).

Scientific evidence in support of this extension of the homeostatic model is slim at present. There is no central "brain" linking the behaviors of family members, and in some ways homeostasis is too simplistic a model to account for social behavior (Guttman, 1986; Miller & Sobelman, 1985). Yet this theory does provide some interesting hypotheses that remain to be tested, and it offers possibilities for finding new ways to promote better relationships among family members, groups, or even nations (Miller, 1978; Watzlawick, Weakland, & Fisch, 1974).

General Systems Theory
an approach that emphasizes the importance of understanding individual units (of behavior) in the context of larger and smaller systems to which each unit is related. Larger systems, for example, include a family, a subculture, or a society; smaller systems affecting behavior include molecules and physiological systems.

Family Systems Theory
a psychological approach that emphasizes the importance of family interrelationships in understanding and changing human behavior.

Symptom
a characteristic sign that indicates the presence of a larger set or pattern of events.

Self-Actualization
growing toward and developing one's inherent potential, talents, and identity; associated with the work of Abraham Maslow and Carl Rogers.

may not appear healthy to one who perceives the society itself as "sick." Indeed, we honor individuals like Dietrich Bonhoeffer, who at the cost of his own life refused to accept and adjust to the accepted norms in Nazi Germany. Thomas Szasz, a controversial psychiatrist, has argued that there is no such thing as "mental illness," and that this is merely a way for society to control behavior that steps beyond its accepted normal limits (Szasz, 1961, 1978).

Another common criticism is that the homeostatic model places too much emphasis on maintaining the social status quo, while neglecting excellence, individuality, creativity, and justice (all terms that themselves require definition). Furthermore, though set-points and normal limits can change over time as the person or system develops, some view the homeostatic model as too mechanical to account for the complexity and beauty of human growth. Nevertheless it is clear that at some levels people *do* maintain homeostatic balance.

GROWTH: TOWARD SELF-ACTUALIZATION

A *growth* model of adjustment places less emphasis on a state of being "adjusted" and more on the process of changing. Rather than thinking of people as pendulums swinging back and forth about fixed points, the growth model conceives of purposeful movement. The nature of that purpose varies from one theory to another, but generally it is a positive objective of health and one's "natural" or "actual" self. Growth toward this true self (rather than toward what others tell you that you *should* be) is often called **self-actualization.** Just as seeds contain a specific potential to become a particular kind of plant, and just as many living plants turn themselves naturally toward the sun, so people have a natural inner direction toward which they will grow if they are not impeded by the environment.

When Abraham Maslow was developing his theory of self-actualization (Maslow, 1954, 1968), he did a revolutionary thing: he studied people whom he considered to be exceptionally healthy. In the past, theories of human psychology had been developed by studying unhealthy people, or those who were clearly dissatisfied with their functioning. Maslow instead interviewed people whom he considered happier and healthier than the norm. What he found was that this group of people seemed to live in the present rather than spending time regretting the past or worrying about the future. They tended to recognize their own strengths and weaknesses, and to accept themselves for these. They were not critical of themselves or of other people, and they demonstrated what Maslow called a "democratic character structure." They were willing to listen to and learn from others, including others of lower social status. They had escaped rigid social conditioning, and thus behaved in ways that might not be socially approved at times. For example, Ruth Fulton Benedict, one of Maslow's teachers, was a person whom he considered special in this way. As an anthropologist and world traveler in the early twentieth century, she demonstrated an independence of thinking which transcended the limiting social roles assigned to women. Such a self-actualizing person is more fully functioning and lives a more enriched life than does the average person. She or he is seen as developing and using unique capabilities and potentials, free from the inhibitions and emotional turmoil suffered by those less self-actualized (Shostrom, 1966). One goal of humanistic psychotherapy is to help the person become more self-actualized, to develop toward his or her natural potential (Tageson, 1982).

Proponents of a growth model often maintain a strong optimism about human nature and view the person as naturally growing in a positive direction toward his or her best possible self. Change is always possible and always occurring. People are seen as free to change, even in sudden and dramatic ways.

A frequent criticism of the growth model is that it leaves many important terms undefined. Who determines what constitutes "positive growth" or the "natural self"? Who should be the judge of whether actualization is occurring? Again the *ideals* assumed within this model depend upon how one perceives reality. Although profoundly optimistic, this viewpoint is often faulted for being vague and relying on concepts difficult to define or observe.

LEARNING: ADAPTING TO A CHANGING ENVIRONMENT

A **learning** model of adjustment emphasizes still another aspect of human change—our adaptiveness in dealing with a changing world. Here the emphasis is less on set-points or absolute ideals and more on the ways in which people change to cope with their internal and external worlds. Human beings have learned to survive, function, and even thrive in a vast range of environments from tropic to arctic. Likewise the skilled sailor shifts the sails to catch the ever-changing winds. For human behavior, learning and **memory** are the processes by which we accumulate and store information to use later in coping with life's challenges.

A learning model emphasizes how we influence and are influenced by the people and environment around us. To some, this way of thinking about people seems manipulative, but in a real sense we all manipulate (move or influence) each other. A child has difficulty in getting to sleep, and the parent lovingly brings a glass of milk and reads a story until finally the child is fast asleep. Each has influenced the other. The parent influences the child to go to sleep, making some peace and quiet in the house. The child, on the other hand, is influencing the parent to bring milk and stories on request. The very

Learning
the processes whereby behaviors are acquired and changed through experience.

Memory
the processes whereby past experiences can be stored, recalled, and used to change future behavior.

Sailing is the art of catching the ever-changing winds.

Stimulus [pl.: Stimuli]
a change in the external or internal environment.

Respondent Conditioning
a form of learning whereby behavior comes to be elicited by a particular stimulus; associated with the work of Ivan Pavlov, also called Pavlovian or classical conditioning.

Operant Conditioning
a form of learning whereby behaviors are strengthened or weakened by their consequences (see REINFORCEMENT and PUNISHMENT); associated with the work of B. F. Skinner.

Behavior
any response, or set of responses, whether or not overtly observable.

Reinforcement [operant conditioning]
a learning process whereby a behavior is followed by a positive consequence, with the result that the behavior is more likely to be repeated.

Punishment [operant conditioning]
a learning process whereby a behavior is followed by a negative consequence, with the result that the behavior is less likely to be repeated.

same processes of learning that might be labeled "manipulation" can also be seen in another light as cooperation, compromise, and affection.

The ways in which habits develop have been studied extensively by experimental psychologists. During the early twentieth century, emphasis was given to how behavior is influenced by **stimuli,** conditions or changes in the environment. Ivan Pavlov, John Watson, and others clarified principles of **respondent conditioning,** whereby individuals come to behave in new and predictable ways in response to a stimulus. For example, perhaps at some time in your life you ate a certain type of food and soon afterward became nauseous or even violently ill. In such cases it is common for the taste of the food to become aversive, even though the food itself may not have caused the illness. A previously pleasant taste (stimulus) now evokes new responses—disgust and avoidance. Similarly the pairing of a previously neutral stimulus with inherently positive or pleasurable stimuli may increase new positive feelings and responses. This is a central principle in advertising: the product to be sold (toward which one is neutral at first) is associated over and over again with pleasant sights, sounds, images, or fantasies. The advertiser's hope is that the pleasant associations will become attached to the product itself.

Another form of learning through which habits are formed is **operant conditioning.** Research on this type of learning emerged in the 1940s. Here **behavior** is influenced by its result, by what *follows* it (whereas in respondent conditioning the emphasis is on control by what *precedes* the behavior). A behavior that results in a positive outcome will be more likely to be repeated. Thus, in the example given earlier, the child learns that crying or complaining at bedtime will bring some extra attention and perhaps a glass of milk from the parent. The action (crying) achieves a pleasant outcome (milk and attention) and the child is likely on future nights to cry again at bedtime. This process, by which desirable outcomes strengthen a behavior, is called **reinforcement.**

In operant conditioning theory, the opposite of reinforcement is **punish-**

ment. When a behavior is followed by an unpleasant consequence, that behavior is weakened and is less likely to occur in the future. Suppose, for example, that your instructor asked for a volunteer to help with a demonstration to the class. You volunteer. The demonstration turns out to be one that is very embarrassing, and the whole class laughs at you. Probably you would be less likely to volunteer in the future, at least in that class. Volunteering has been punished. If, on the other hand, the demonstration proved to be very interesting, and several students told you after class how much they appreciated your part in it, then you might be more likely to volunteer again in the future. Volunteering would be reinforced.

Both operant and respondent conditioning exert important influences on people's behavior. Human actions are influenced both by what precedes them (stimuli, emphasized in respondent conditioning) and by what follows them (consequences, emphasized in operant conditioning). In addition, other types of learning have been clarified, such as learning by observation (modeling and vicarious learning). These learning and conditioning processes, by which people adapt and acquire new behaviors, will be discussed in greater detail in Chapter 4.

All learning theories, however, emphasize the importance of the *environment* in influencing and shaping people's behavior. Some modern learning theories place greater emphasis on the role of the individual in determining his or her own behavior (see Chapter 5 on self-control). Nevertheless, the emphasis in learning approaches is on the important controlling influences of the environment.

CHOICE: ADJUSTMENT BY SELF-DETERMINATION

Some find that the learning approach, like the homeostatic view, seems too mechanistic for their liking, and choose rather to emphasize *personal choice and responsibility*. Change is seen as determined by the free human will. Each person must choose his or her own path, exercising freedom within whatever natural limits may exist. People are not controlled by the past, and their actions are not solely determined by forces beyond their control or awareness. Individuals may give away their freedom by accepting the beliefs and rules of an external system, but there are no absolutes in the world, and ultimately each person must make his or her own personal meaning. Each person can and does always choose how he or she will *perceive* a situation and the meaning it will have. This became clear to psychiatrist Viktor Frankl during his imprisonment in a World War II concentration camp (Frankl, 1963). Observing his own reactions and those of others, Frankl realized that no matter how oppressive and dehumanizing the conditions, each person still chooses how to respond. His reports include accounts of prisoners who shared their own scarce food and risked their own lives and safety to help others. Though clearly victims, such people chose not to accept a passive victim role in their actions and self-perception.

This inner strength to transcend oppression was expressed dramatically in Alice Walker's (1982) novel, *The Color Purple*. Celie, the main character in the novel, struggles against seemingly impossible circumstances. With love and will she finds her own way to understand and rise above the cruelty and hopelessness of her life. When her husband, who has abused her physically and psychologically for years, tells her she is nothing, she responds by recognizing her own imperfections, while affirming her strength and perseverance.

Within an existential view, you are whatever you choose to be. Personal choice is emphasized above all else—choice of your own reality. A limitation of this view is that in fact one cannot truly choose unless one knows the options and has equal access to the viable choices.

A scene from the movie *The Color Purple*.

Choice and free will are also emphasized in humanistic views, described earlier. An important difference is that the major proponents of humanistic psychology, such as Maslow and Rogers, believed that each person has a natural self, a personal potential toward which she or he may grow. This is like a seed, which contains the potential of a specific full-grown plant. An existential view proposes no such natural plan or identity, but instead asserts that each person chooses somewhat arbitrarily among the alternatives. An image that better reflects an existential view is that of a crossroads with many possible paths that could be followed. The individual continually chooses among roads, thereby forming and defining the self (Yalom, 1980).

INTEGRATION

Each of these four psychological views contains valuable perspectives. Rather than encouraging you to choose among them, we urge you to consider them all in trying to understand your own behavior and that of others. People are biological and social creatures, adjusting at least some of their behavior toward physical and social set-points. Likewise, people are social creatures, influenced by learning and memory processes, which enable a comparison of their present situations with past experiences. People also experience themselves as making choices and as progressing toward goals in a process of continual growth.

You continually choose among roads, thereby forming the self.

For some years it has been fashionable in textbooks of this kind to contrast certain "schools of psychology." Such theoretical and practical differences continue to exist within psychology, and we will consider them later in this chapter. We maintain, however, that if one wishes to approach a fuller understanding of human nature, each of these perspectives must be considered for the truth that it contains. In fact, from a scientific point of view, they can be considered alternative models for organizing information and making predictions about human adjustment.

A majority of modern psychotherapists, when asked what their own orientation is, report that they are **eclectic.** This reflects a shift away from the "schools" approach in which therapists previously identified with one particular view. An eclectic approach is one that entertains a variety of views, considering each for the value it offers. Different theories and perspectives are regarded as alternative lenses through which the world may be viewed. Using more than a single lens affords a broader and richer understanding. However, eclecticism also has its disadvantages. For one thing, the eclectic has more to learn, having to comprehend a variety of different views and approaches. A risk is to know a little about many approaches but to master none. It is also less than clear how to decide which of a range of alternative approaches to adopt in a particular situation. Eclecticism is not in itself a systematic approach to psychology, but rather an openness to possibilities.

■ ADJUSTMENT TO WHAT? CONSTRUCTING REALITY

Having discussed ways of thinking about adjustment, we turn now to look at what people are adjusting *to.* Adjustment does not occur in a vacuum. Each of the four models of adjustment that we have just discussed depends on an interpretation of how the individual uses input from the world around her or him to form a construction of reality. Homeostatic systems function by **feedback** about the organism's present state. A growth model is based on progress toward realizing one's potential, as well as a perception of one's present condition. More recent theories of learning consider that individuals respond to *perceived* rewards and punishments and that learning processes are influenced importantly by the ways in which the individual interprets the environment. Finally, choices can be made only among *perceived* alternatives. This is well exemplified by the *koans* or puzzles used by Zen masters to teach their students to think less rigidly. In one such puzzle the master holds a stick above the student's head and says, "If you tell me that this is a stick, I will hit you. If you tell me that this is not a stick, I will hit you. If you say nothing, I will hit you." Most students wrestle with the obvious alternatives posed by the master, and wind up being rapped on the head. The solution to the koan lies in perceiving yet another alternative: to reach up and take the stick, which the master releases with an approving smile. One chooses only among those alternatives that are perceived to be available and possible.

No one lives in "the real world," or perceives things in a truly objective fashion. Even the most accurate scientific instruments are limited in what they can detect, and are subject to certain kinds of distortion. How much more this is true of people! Individuals respond not to an "actual" world, but to the world as they perceive it. Everything is necessarily filtered through one's abilities and habits of perceiving. For this reason no two people live in the same world. Through language, however, people learn to apply the same names ("chair," "book," "tree") to many objects. This commonality of vocabulary can create the impression that people *do* perceive the same world and share the same reality *in general.* Yet the "mental dictionaries" by which people operate

Eclectic (noun: Eclecticism)
not limited to a single theory or school of thought, but drawing upon multiple perspectives to understand human behavior.

Feedback
information provided to an individual regarding his or her state or performance.

1.3 HERE WE DIFFER/HERE WE AGREE
What *Guides* the Adjustment Process?

LEARNING

I believe that the clarification of principles of learning has been one of the most important historic contributions to a constructive understanding of human adjustment. Much of what people do can be understood through basic learning principles although, to be sure, learning and memory processes are complex. We all are continually *changing* in response to our social environment.

This is a very optimistic viewpoint, because if behavior is learned, then it can be changed through relearning. Modern behavior therapies, often derived from principles of learning that can be observed in both animals and humans, have proved to be helpful in changing a wide range of significant life problems, including depression, sexual dysfunctions, anxiety, insomnia, alcohol abuse, and children's behavior problems.

Contrary to some common stereotypes, a behavioral view of human life does not ignore individual growth. Rather it is a systematic way of understanding development: learning is that by which we will be different tomorrow than we were yesterday, that by which we grow and change and improve. Nor is a behavioral perspective "cold" or "dehumanizing." To the contrary, through well-understood methods of behavior change, it is possible to remove painful problems and obstacles from people's lives. What could be more humane than that? —WRM

NATURAL POTENTIAL

Humanism in psychology appeared as the "third force" due to perceived gaps in traditional psychoanalytic thinking and behaviorism. Humanists believe that human beings are neither ruled by animal instincts (as in Freud's theory) nor are they blank slates awaiting the writing of conditioning (as in learning theory). Humanistic psychologists envision people as basically good, and capable of developing great positive potential if provided with opportunity and support. The method which guides the process of growth involves the continuing awareness of thoughts and feelings in the moment, the present, the here and now. By remaining true to oneself in this way, by trusting one's own intuitive judgment, one can move toward developing full potential. One can also work to alter an oppressive environment, for example, by lobbying for changes in the law. Like many people, I am intrigued by counseling clients who overcome internal and external obstacles to becoming who they fully are. This development toward full potential is the promise of humanistic psychology. —CEY

INTERPERSONAL RELATIONSHIPS

I believe that the interpersonal relationships we experience are the defining characteristics of the adjustment process. We humans start out as relatively diffuse biological entities with a few "hardwired" systems (such as reflexes) and a lot of potential. Anecdotal reports of *feral children* (those raised in the "wild," without parents) suggest the lack of development of humanness without interpersonal interactions. Our relationships allow us to define who we are, what our potential may be, as well as the types of learning to which we will attend. With an interpersonal approach one gets the feedback that can allow (or disallow, since not all relationships are positive) both learning and the development of potential to evolve in the most favorable manner. This approach also allows behavioral scientists to grasp a more consistent understanding of human behavior within its complex contexts, and to build more powerful theories. Although you may prefer the company of your dog or cat to that of some of the people you know, you must still identify and interact with humans because you *are* one! —JMR

INTEGRATION

Although behavioral, humanistic, and dynamic schools of thought have long been rivals in psychology, we believe that they are not necessarily incompatible. Behavioral principles and technologies can, for example, be applied by individuals with humanistic values. Once principles of effective behavior change are understood, it is possible to use them in one's own life. This is at the core of the emerging field of "self-control," wherein the learning of behavioral self-change methods provides the individual with a larger range of alternatives or choices for adjustment. Likewise, there have long been efforts to integrate behavioral and psychodynamic approaches, and learning clearly occurs within an interpersonal context (Arkowitz & Messer, 1984; Dollard & Miller, 1950; Wachtel, 1977, 1982). Neither humanistic nor behavioral approaches deny the importance of interpersonal relationships in forming human character. In sum, human adjustment is guided by a *combination* of the factors emphasized in each of these approaches: learning, inherent potential, and interpersonal dynamics.

1.4   WORD ASSOCIATIONS

Psychologists have long been interested in the processes by which people form word associations. The usual method of study is this: the psychologist presents words one at a time, and as you hear each one, you say the first word that comes into your mind. This word association process is one method for studying human thinking processes and understanding better the individual differences of personality. It also, for purposes of this chapter, illustrates the range of different meanings that people associate with words.

Try this exercise. For best effect, have someone read the list to you, and without giving it much thought, say the first related word that pops into your mind. It is not necessary that the word you say has an obvious or logical relationship to the word you heard. Just give your first association.

It may also be interesting to have your partner write down your word associations, and to compare this list with others. Do you see any consistencies in your associations? What do you think influenced the words you chose? Do you see any cases where your association to one word may have been influenced by previous words in the list? What, if anything, might your word associations tell you about how you think, or the kind of person you are?

WORD ASSOCIATION LIST		
Home	Wooden	Desk
Green	Mountain	A
Enemy	Sister	Lonely
Over	Warm	Gay
Intelligence	Insect	Wall
Blessing	Water	Repair
Field	Psychology	Date
Cat	Close	Angry
Felt	Thunder	Book
Waiting	Naked	Light
Fire	Carpet	Death

are very different when it comes to concepts such as "love," "respect," even "child." (When is a boy or girl no longer a child, but an adult?) The same word used by various people can have very different meanings.

A current **cognitive** perspective in psychology emphasizes this perceptual relativism by pointing to the influence of our hidden beliefs and assumptions. Such assumptions are often unspoken, untested, and unquestioned and usually operate beyond conscious awareness. For example, one person may expect, by virtue of his or her past, to be adored and loved by everyone. This is an expectation that can have disastrous consequences as we shall see later, in Chapter 6. Another person may have learned that people are basically untrustworthy and will take advantage of you if given half a chance. These two individuals bring very different assumptions to a new experience. In meeting a new person, each will react in a manner consistent with prior beliefs.

Psychologist George Kelly developed an entire theory of personality and a system of psychotherapy around the observation that people construct reality in unique ways through their personal processes of perception and thinking. He introduced the concept of **personal constructs** to describe these patterns of perception through which individuals organize their reality (Kelly, 1955). Kelly viewed people as theory builders, constantly forming and validating hypotheses about reality. Like modern cognitive psychologists, he was interested in how people organize information to form categories and rules for classification of new data. Theories are ways of thinking, assumptions about reality, and Kelly proposed that these personal constructs are of profound importance in understanding people and helping them to change.

A graphic example of how assumptions about reality can be limiting is the cattle guard. In New Mexico, where we live, bars are placed across deep troughs in a road, serving to keep cattle from crossing. Presumably the cattle avoid these guards because their hooves slip through the bars. After the cattle have experienced these guards, however, stripes can be painted on the road's surface and will serve the same purpose. People can limit themselves in the same way by perceiving limits where none actually exist.

Another way in which cognitions affect our perceptions is through language. Habitual assumptions and ways of thinking can be buried very deeply in our nature—in language itself. A common example is the existence of several different words for "snow" in the language of Eskimos, each word describing a subtle variation. To the Eskimo, the detection of such differences can be a matter of life or death. To the average English-speaker, however, snow is snow (unless you ski, and begin to differentiate "powder" from "hard-pack," etc.). Having no words for different types, one fails to perceive them.

Language can also influence how people relate to one another. Some languages have a single verb that means both "to teach" and "to learn," suggesting less of a distinction between what teachers do and what students do. In many European languages there are two forms of the pronoun "you": one to use with familiar people and one for more formal relationships—a differentiation that is bound to have its effect on awareness of distance between people. Sex-role stereotypes are often embedded in language, too. In English this appears in the occupational titles of the past: mailman, policeman, chairman, nurse versus male nurse. In old Norwegian the traditional title for a married woman (roughly equivalent to "wife") is *hustru,* which literally means "faithful to the house." In languages where nouns have gender endings, the stereotypes are still more deeply embedded in everyday use, often well below conscious awareness. In German, for example, the words for "leader," "chief," and "doctor" all are masculine nouns. An English language parallel is the use of male nouns for certain occupations or positions, and masculine nouns ("man") or pronouns ("he") to refer to all people—a practice we have tried to avoid in writing this text.

Cognitive Psychology
a psychological approach that emphasizes the importance of mental processes (e.g., information processing, perception, self-talk and thinking) in understanding and changing behavior.

Personal Construct
a pattern by which an individual perceives and organizes reality; this concept was introduced by George Kelly in his Psychology of Personal Constructs.

These illustrations emphasize that reality is primarily in the eye of the beholder and that when you ask someone to "face reality," you are asking that person to see and value the world the way you do. To be sure, people may be able to agree with each other about many aspects of "reality," but no realities are the same for everyone, and many are very specific to a particular society or culture. Not even scientists, the symbols of objectivity in our society, are immune to such processes of bias through perception. Scientists construct reality in the form of a theory and then perceive the world through this perspective. What a scientist concludes or even *observes* is influenced by the assumptions under which she or he entered the process of observation (cf. Denmark et al., 1988).

The social pressure to adjust to reality as defined by a given group can be immense. An important part of growth can be the refusal to adjust to a reality that is oppressive or restricts growth for some members of a group. Some social reformers have succeeded in changing realities to allow members to grow in ways that were forbidden in the past. For example, many women and men worked for suffrage rather than adjusting to the accepted "reality" that women were unfit to vote. As a result, women received the right to vote in the United States in 1920.

■ PERSONALITY THEORIES: HOW PSYCHOLOGISTS CONSTRUCT REALITY

Psychologists use theories as ways of organizing and predicting events. Such theories are a convenience, a kind of shorthand for understanding. A **theory** is a set of working assumptions, of **hypotheses** to be tested through observation, and in this sense theory is vital to science.

Theories are important to scientists and, indeed, to all of us. They are hunches about how the world works, allowing one to organize and deal with reality. It is likely, for example, that you have some implicit theories about how people work and what they are like. When you meet a new person, you observe certain aspects of that individual and begin to form impressions based on your overall ideas about the nature of people. Without a theory, one has no way of organizing observations, or even of knowing what to observe. A theory leads one to attend to certain portions of the available world, and to expect certain outcomes and relationships to appear. This is both the value and the limitation of theory. While theories are helpful in organizing "reality," they also bias that reality in directing one's attention toward certain kinds of events and away from others.

Personality theories are ways of thinking about people. They suggest what is important to observe (often a set of personality "traits"), how human personality is structured (often by breaking it into parts), and how these parts or traits can be expected to interact with one another. Personality theories are designed to help us understand and deal with people by organizing information and predicting events. Whether or not you realize it, you already have a personality theory of your own, because everyone does. Without such an organizing system, you would not know what to look for in people or what to expect from them. A little later in this chapter you will have an opportunity to learn more about your own present view of human personality.

Theory
a general principle or set of related principles intended to explain a pattern of observations.

Hypothesis
a hunch, a working assumption, a temporary explanation to be tested.

SOME LIMITATIONS OF PERSONALITY THEORY

Theories are crucial to the advance of science. Major breakthroughs in the sciences often center on the development of a better theory to explain how the world works. But theories are only ways of thinking (Kelly, 1955) and must be recognized as such. It is very easy to confuse an assumption or hypothesis with a proven conclusion. Having been told that all people of one type (say, one race or one nationality) have a certain characteristic, one tends to notice those individuals who confirm the belief and to ignore those who do not. People have a tendency to confirm their own present beliefs, no matter how incorrect. This tendency is not limited to racial or national prejudices. Once one believes that any two things "go together," it can be difficult to view events otherwise. (Remember the Zen puzzle!) Superstitions are of this nature, being beliefs that certain unrelated events are somehow tied together. In psychology this phenomenon is called **illusory correlation,** the mistaken belief that two events are related to each other when in fact they are not (Chapman & Chapman, 1967). The more general point is that when people set out to test their assumptions about reality, they have a built-in tendency to validate rather than disprove these preconceived assumptions.

A good example of an illusory correlation that is common among students is the belief that "Whenever I change an answer on an exam, I change it from right to wrong. Therefore I should never change answers." This belief is rather unlikely to be true. Most students are just as likely to change an answer from wrong to right as from right to wrong. How, then, does it happen that students come to believe this? How does the illusory correlation occur? Often it happens by **selective attention.** In reviewing an exam, those items that *were* changed from right to wrong answers are likely to be noticed with painful attention ("How could I? I did it again! I had it right and I changed it.") Items that were answered correctly tend to be ignored (selective attention), including those that had been changed from the wrong to the right answer. If you have held this assumption about your own behavior in taking tests, we invite you to check yourself on the next few exams you take. Make note of *all* the answers that you change on your exam. Then when you receive feedback count how many you changed (1) from wrong to right, (2) from right to wrong, and (3) from one wrong answer to another wrong answer. Probably you will find about equal numbers of each of these types of answer changing. (Of course, you may be the exception to the rule, and in any event it will be useful for you to know.)

By selectively noticing and ignoring aspects of the world around you, you confirm (and create) your own reality. This is part of a larger concept in psychology: the self-fulfilling prophecy. In a variety of ways, which will be elaborated in Chapter 2, people cause their own beliefs and predictions to come true.

Illusory Correlation
an incorrect belief that two events occur together consistently, and are related to each other.

Selective Attention
focusing upon certain information while ignoring other information; a psychological process whereby one's present beliefs are defended and maintained.

Generation Effect
a process whereby a theoretical model loses some of the complexity and tentativeness held by those who introduced it, and becomes overly simplistic or rigid as it is adopted by subsequent adherents.

Besides the self-fulfilling prophecy effect of illusory correlation, another danger in theory is the **generation effect.** Often the originator of a theory proposes it as one possible way of organizing observations. With the passage of time, however, the tentative hypotheses can become confused with proven facts, particularly as these ideas are passed on to the next generation. There are many examples of this within psychology. Elisabeth Kübler-Ross (1969), through her work and observations with dying patients, proposed a set of four stages through which people seem to pass in the process of grieving a loss. As these stages became widely known and taught, the next generation of professionals tended to regard these stages as facts. In some cases it was believed that patients were *required* to pass through all the stages in order, as if failing to do so were a sign of poor adjustment. Likewise E. M. Jellinek (1952) attempted to organize his observations of alcoholics into a theory of stages by which alcoholism develops. He presented his ideas as tentative and encouraged that they be tested scientifically. Within a generation, however, his stage theory of alcoholism had been fossilized into the disease concept of alcoholism that many now accept as fact.

Both of the dangers described thus far, illusory correlation and the generation effect, involve the premature acceptance of theory as proven fact. Another risk is the illusion of understanding by naming. The parent distressed because

Johnny cannot read may experience relief when learning that he "has dyslexia," even though this label is nothing more than the Greek term indicating a problem with reading. A person who goes to a physician because of distressing symptoms may feel better if the physician gives a name to the problem, giving the assurance that somebody understands and can help. Personality theories are particularly appealing because they provide sets of labels to use, which can give the powerful impression that one can understand or even predict and control that which is genuinely complex. Students learning psychological theories for the first time sometimes delight in applying their newfound labels by "analyzing" their roommates, friends and family. This is a pattern sufficiently common to have earned a name for itself: "the sophomore-psychology-major syndrome." To be sure, there are good reasons to classify our observations into categories. All of us do, to make sense of the world. Classification is also the first stage of progress for any science. At the same time, however, it is important not to be tricked into believing that one understands something simply because there is a name for it.

FOUR MAJOR PERSONALITY THEORIES

Despite their dangers and shortcomings, theories are essential to any science. They are also inescapable, for it is impossible to function without some sort of framework for understanding and organizing reality. Those who do not take the time to clarify the theory from which they approach reality will necessarily operate with an implicit, unspoken set of assumptions. Coherent theory has always been a vital part of psychology.

With the foregoing cautions in mind, then, we proceed to examine four major types of personality theory that have emerged thus far in the history of psychology. These are not totally separate theories. They overlap with each other, agreeing on certain points while differing on others. Each of these theories corresponds roughly to one of the four views of adjustment presented earlier.

Psychodynamic theories of personality were among the earliest to appear. Most famous of these is Sigmund Freud's complex system of *psychoanalysis*. Many other psychodynamic theories followed, including those of Carl Jung, Karen Horney, Harry Stack Sullivan, Alfred Adler, Wilhelm Reich, and Anna Freud (daughter of Sigmund Freud). These theories vary widely, but they share several common assumptions. One is an emphasis on *unconscious* processes as determinants of behavior and conscious experience. Freud, for example, described powerful biological motivations of sexual energy and aggressive/destructive instincts, and he proposed a system of unconscious processes by which these drives are kept in balance with reality. This concept of balance between conscious and unconscious processes is a common theme in psychodynamic theories and relates closely to the homeostatic view of adjustment described earlier. When forces are out of balance, symptoms of psychological disturbance emerge. William Golding's (1962) popular novel *Lord of the Flies* is a fictional representation of this theme, wherein a group of boys marooned on an island gradually lose the social restraints that have kept their primitive impulses in check. The result is a series of increasingly uncivilized acts driven by aggressive impulses out of control.

Behavioral views, the next to emerge historically, also view behavior as heavily determined. The source of control, however, is not unconscious conflicts and events but rather the physical and social environment. The personality is shaped by learning processes such as operant conditioning (reinforcement and punishment), classical conditioning (learning by association), and vicarious conditioning (learning by observing others). In the earliest behavioral

Psychodynamic Psychology
a psychological approach that emphasizes conscious and unconscious motivations in understanding human behavior, often placing great importance on the influence of experiences during infancy and early childhood; Freud's psychoanalysis is the original and classic psychodynamic approach to psychology

Behavioral Psychology
a psychological approach that emphasizes the importance of environmental influences in shaping human nature, especially through processes of learning and conditioning; typically uses quantitative rather than subjective methods for studying behavior.

models the individual was viewed as passively reacting to the environment, but more recent behavioral approaches have emphasized an interaction between person and situation. Nevertheless human behavior in this view is accounted for largely in adaptive reaction to the changing social environment.

Humanistic approaches have often been called the "third force" in psychology because they arose in reaction to both psychodynamic and behavioral views. Humanistic theorists deny that the individual is primarily determined or controlled by either unconscious or environmental forces. Instead they emphasize purpose and meaning as motivating forces. The individual is seen as engaged in *self-actualization*, a lifelong search for her or his authentic self, the core of true identity. Humanistic theorists maintain profound optimism about the basic nature of humankind, as discussed earlier in regard to the growth model of adjustment. Although not often associated with religion, the humanistic model of personality is most similar to contemporary Western religious systems in its emphasis on lifelong striving toward an inner goal.

An **existential** view of personality is sometimes equated with humanistic approaches, but we believe this to be a distinct view in itself. The existential theorists agree with the humanists on many points, including the individual's freedom to choose. Typically, however, the existentialist denies the existence of any absolute purpose or meaning. Human nature is seen as neither essentially good (as suggested by the humanists) nor driven by dark impulses (as suggested by psychoanalysts). The only given for an individual is that he or she *exists* (thus the name, existential), and beyond this all choices are up to the individual. The only meaning that there is in life is that which one makes for oneself. This recognition can yield a frightening sense of loneliness, but for the existentialist the only life of integrity is one that acknowledges this aloneness and self-directedness through an act of will. The choice model of adjustment is heavily emphasized in an existential approach.

Thus the four personality theories, and the four models of adjustment to which they correspond, differ in their views of the purpose of adjustment. Each has a different answer to the question, "Adjustment toward what?" The *state* of being "adjusted" varies from one view to the next. Is the purpose internal balance, adaptation to the external world, the pursuit of inner purpose and self-actualization, or the recognition that there is no purpose and one must choose a way?

■ TOWARD SELF-UNDERSTANDING AND CHANGE

Humanistic Psychology
a psychological approach that emphasizes the importance of free will, self-direction, and growth toward one's human potential.

Existential Psychology
a psychological approach that emphasizes the centrality of meaning and personal choice in understanding human nature; typically uses introspective self-examination rather than objective approaches in psychological exploration.

Thus far we have emphasized views of *why* people change and of the states toward which individuals strive in the search for adjustment. A somewhat different question is *how* people change, the process by which change occurs. What are the conditions under which change is possible (or impossible)? If you want to make it easier for yourself or someone else to change, what should you do?

First, we would point out that people are *always* changing. No one wakes up the same person he or she was the morning before. Each day brings new experiences, new problems, new learning, new hopes or dreams. Change may be slow, but it is continuous. You can never step in the same river twice, because the water in which you stepped has passed by and the river bottom and bank are ever so slightly changed by each passing second. Most human change, we believe, is like that, although there seem to be exceptions. Some people long for a sudden, dramatic, almost magical change to happen. This is part of the appeal of the ever-popular crash diets, and of clinics promising fast and miraculous cures for various problems. For better or for worse, most lasting change is gradual and continuous.

1.5 | THE PERSONALITY THEORY QUESTIONNAIRE

Name _____

PERSONALITY THEORY QUESTIONNAIRE
William R. Miller, Ph.D.

INSTRUCTIONS: Answer each of the following questions according to whether you *agree more than disagree* (A) or *disagree more than agree* (D) with the statement.

A or D

_____ 1. In attempting to understand human beings one should stick to the observable and avoid theory and concepts that cannot be directly experienced or observed.

_____ 2. Events taking place in the present are systematically linked to events that have occurred in one's past.

_____ 3. A specific piece of human behavior cannot be understood without considering the total person.

_____ 4. People are basically good (as opposed to neutral or evil). If left to a natural state, uncontrolled by external restraints, they seek health and personal growth while respecting the rights of others to do the same.

_____ 5. A person's character is largely determined by the time he or she reaches adulthood. The only real changes that one can expect from an adult occur slowly over long periods of time.

_____ 6. The so-called "laws of behavior" that are intended to apply to all individuals tell us very little about a person.

_____ 7. Much of behavior, both normal and abnormal, is directed by unconscious factors of which we have little or no awareness.

_____ 8. If one is to understand people and their behavior it is important to have a unifying theory of human personality, even though parts of that theory may not at present be based on observable fact or research.

_____ 9. Aggression is an inherent part of human nature, deeply rooted in our basic instincts.

_____ 10. Given alternatives and support, people are capable of making major and enduring changes in themselves, sometimes in relatively brief periods of time.

_____ 11. Much of human behavior is motivated by the continuous attempt to increase pleasure and to avoid pain and discomfort.

_____ 12. People have no inherent values—only those that are discovered or learned through living.

_____ 13. Learning processes play a major role in the formation of personality and the determination of human behavior.

_____ 14. It is an important part of therapy to allow the person to talk and explore his or her experiences without direction or evaluation from the therapist.

_____ 15. Events that occur early in life are more important in determining one's adult personality and behavior than are those occurring after the person has reached adulthood.

_____ 16. Looking within the person (instead of to the social environment) for the causes of behavior is probably more misleading than enlightening.

_____ 17. The idea of self (inner experience) or "ego" is crucial in the understanding of behavior and personality.

_____ 18. Scientific method, in the usual sense of structured observation and experimentation, is not appropriate for the study of psychology in humans.

_____ 19. People are neither inherently good nor basically selfish. Their "human nature" is determined by some combination of heredity and life experiences.

_____ 20. It is important for a therapist to be *personally* involved in therapy, revealing his or her authentic feelings to the client.

_____ 21. Perhaps the most important goal of therapy is to help the individual become aware of and accept his or her own values.

_____ 22. For the most part, therapy should focus on the person's present experiences rather than events from the past.

_____ 23. Human behavior is determined by lawful principles; free will has little or nothing to do with it.

_____ 24. The relationship between a therapist and a client is more than a context within which change happens. It is the relationship *itself* that heals.

_____ 25. A person is free to be what he or she wants to be.

1.5 THE PERSONALITY THEORY QUESTIONNAIRE *(continued)*

SCORING: Indicate below how you answered each item. If you agreed with an item, circle *all of the A's* in that line. If you disagreed, circle *all* of the D's in that line.

Scales

B E H P

1. Ⓐ Ⓐ D D
2. A Ⓓ Ⓓ A
3. Ⓓ A A A
4. Ⓓ Ⓓ A Ⓓ

5. Ⓓ Ⓓ Ⓓ A
6. Ⓓ A A Ⓓ
7. Ⓓ Ⓓ Ⓓ A
8. Ⓓ Ⓓ A A
9. Ⓓ Ⓓ Ⓓ A
10. Ⓐ Ⓐ Ⓐ D

11. Ⓐ D D Ⓐ
12. Ⓐ Ⓐ D D
13. Ⓐ D D Ⓐ
14. D Ⓐ Ⓐ Ⓐ
15. D D D Ⓐ
16. A Ⓓ Ⓓ Ⓓ
17. D Ⓐ Ⓐ Ⓐ
18. Ⓓ A Ⓓ Ⓓ

19. Ⓐ Ⓐ D D
20. Ⓓ A A Ⓓ
21. D Ⓐ Ⓐ D
22. A A A Ⓓ
23. A Ⓓ Ⓓ A
24. Ⓓ A A A
25. D Ⓐ Ⓐ D

55

Next count the number of circles in each of the four columns (disregarding whether it was an A or a D that you circled). Record the totals below, and multiply each total by 4.

TOTALS: B: *16* ×4 E: *16* ×4 H: *12* ×4 P: *11* ×4

= SCORES *64* B *64* E *48* H *44* P

2 *3*

Each of these scores is intended to indicate the percentage of your agreement with a particular viewpoint.

B = Behaviorist
E = Existential
H = Humanistic
P = Psychodynamic or Psychoanalytic

Note that the viewpoints have a certain amount in common. Here are the score profiles for the four most "radical" or extreme positions (100% agreement with one viewpoint):

Radical Behaviorist
B = 100 E = 44   H = 28   P = 40

Radical Existentialist
B = 44   E = 100 H = 76   P = 24

Radical Humanist
B = 28   E = 76   H = 100 P = 40

Radical Psychoanalyst
B = 40   E = 24   H = 40   P = 100

All combinations are possible, however, on the highest two scores. Thus an individual may score as a "humanistic behaviorist" (HB or BH), or as an "existential psychoanalyst" (EP or PE), etc.

Now record your four letters (for tied scores, record in alphabetical order).

Highest score	Second highest	Third highest	Lowest score

1.6 THE PSYCHOLOGY OF RAPID CHANGE

The clock strikes midnight. In his bedchamber the cranky old miser is visited by the ghost of an old friend, beginning a long night of reverie, horror, and regret. When the morning light finally dawns, it finds Ebenezer Scrooge a totally new man.

Within his classic tale, *A Christmas Carol*, Charles Dickens celebrates the possibility of rebirth, of dramatic change in a life gone wrong. But does such transformation actually occur outside the world of drama and fiction? Some religious groups emphasize this kind of dramatic conversion experience, in which the person is suddenly and radically changed. Do such changes last? Some research findings suggest that conversion experiences are usually brief and influence behavior very little in the long run (e.g., Langston, 1970). It is important, however, to distinguish between "programmed" conversion experiences such as those occurring in religious revival meetings and spontaneous individual experiences that often occur outside the context of organized religion and sometimes bring major and lasting redirection of one's life (Oates, 1973).

Indeed there have been carefully documented reports of sudden and radical change. Major personality changes sometimes occur following traumatic events, narrow escapes from death, or other dramatic experiences. Consider this example. Transsexualism is a sexual disorder that is notoriously difficult to change. A transsexual is a man who experiences and believes himself to be a woman in a man's body. Treatment sometimes involves sex-change surgery, but lasting change can also be produced by intensive behavior therapy (Barlow, Abel, & Blanchard, 1979). An early case report recounted months of daily therapy through which painstakingly slow change occurred in one transsexual (Barlow, Reynolds, & Agras, 1973). Another transsexual male had been evaluated and was being prepared for sex change surgery, when he spent two hours with a faith healer. Shortly afterward the research team was surprised to discover that his transsexualism had disappeared almost completely, and literally overnight (Barlow, Abel, & Blanchard, 1977). What routinely requires hundreds of hours of treatment had been accomplished in two short hours.

Can people change suddenly and dramatically? The answer seems to be: Yes . . . sometimes. But how does it happen? The researcher who discovers a therapeutic method by which such changes can be reliably produced will deserve a Nobel prize!

The challenge, then, is one of directing and facilitating change rather than beginning it, of making change purposeful and perhaps easier. Adjustments to major life crises such as the death of a loved one, divorce, or disability are natural processes. Such adjustments occur with time, and often (but not always) follow certain common steps or stages. With proper understanding of the adjustment process, however, it may be possible to assist an individual in the journey through such crises, to make the process a little shorter or at least less painful.

What are some of the basic elements of change and adjustment? Although there are many, we find four common elements, four conditions that seem to facilitate the process of change: awareness, acceptance, alternatives, and access.

AWARENESS

The first important element of change is *awareness* of a need for change. If you are unaware of a problem, you not only won't but can't do anything about it. The situations that often pose the greatest problems are those that one does

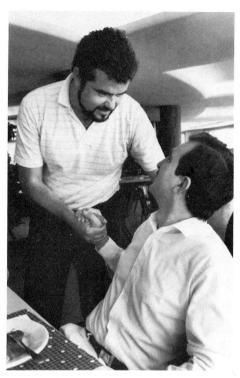

Acceptance is an important condition to aid change.

not understand, such as experiencing a very distressing feeling with no obvious source. It is important to be aware of the problem and also of its basic source or cause.

Awareness is a theme that appears in virtually every theory of change. In psychodynamic theories it has a special meaning in the concept of *insight*, the person's cognitive and emotional awareness of the causes of a problem. Self-understanding is discussed by humanists, and existentialists emphasize the importance of conscious awareness and intentional choice. Behavioral theorists stress clear goals and self-observation as avenues toward awareness. All these theories seem to agree that the process of change begins and continues through the important step of awareness.

Psychologist Michael Mahoney (1974, 1979) has compared the process of self-awareness to that of the scientist engaged in research. As in George Kelly's theory of personal constructs, discussed earlier, Mahoney describes the individual as a **personal scientist** forming hypotheses about himself or herself. Then the person proceeds to check or test these hypotheses to determine whether they are correct, thus increasing self-knowledge. One of our students, for example, complained that he experienced a vague but disturbing kind of anxiety each afternoon he was at school. On other days he seldom had such feelings. With some encouragement he came up with two hypotheses: (1) that he was anxious about examinations, and about being evaluated in general, or (2) that he was suffering from an unconscious conflict that was emerging in this symptom of anxiety (the student had had a course in theories of personality). The first hypothesis was easy to test. If it were correct, the anxiety should decrease after examinations were over and increase as exams approached. It did not. Instead his anxiety occurred in the afternoon regardless of exams. The second hypothesis was much more difficult for him to test alone, and would

Personal Scientist
an "experimental" or scientific approach to life adjustment, in which problems are addressed by forming and trying out hypotheses.

have required professional help. After listening to his descriptions of the "anxiety," however (odd feelings in the stomach, dizziness, weakness, cold chilly sensations), we suggested yet another hypothesis—that he might be suffering from a form of hypoglycemia, because a drop in blood sugar level can also cause such symptoms. Pursuing this possibility, it came to light that he tended to skip lunch on school days, but ate lunch on days when he stayed home. He tested this hypothesis by eating a protein-rich lunch at school, and his "anxiety" attacks disappeared. The diagnosis was later confirmed by a careful medical examination including blood tests. Thus the student became aware of the primary cause of his problem by forming clear hypotheses and testing them until he found the one that worked.

ACCEPTANCE

Many theories of change also discuss the importance of a certain attitude or atmosphere for change, or of a special kind of relationship between a helper and the person who is seeking change. The best word that we can find to summarize this attitude or atmosphere is *acceptance.* This includes both self-acceptance as well as acceptance and support from others.

Here is a puzzling paradox. How can it be that being accepted as one *is* can facilitate change? It would seem more logical that change would occur when one becomes unhappy enough with his or her present state. And if that is true, then the best way to get people to change would be to criticize and shame them into being better people. Similarly if you want to change yourself, it would follow that you would need to feel bad enough about yourself that you would have to make a change.

Part of the problem with this reasoning is that it confuses awareness with acceptance. Awareness of the need for change is important, as mentioned earlier. This kind of awareness is *specific* to the problem, to the need for change in a particular behavior, for example. Acceptance, on the other hand, refers to a more *general* feeling about oneself. It is related to self-esteem, one's overall positive and negative evaluations of oneself, which we will discuss in Chapters 4 and 6. Thus, it is possible to believe that in general you are a worthwhile, lovable, and acceptable person while also recognizing the need for some specific changes. Similarly it is possible to ask a child to pick up the toys more often or to fight with siblings less without pronouncing the child a "bad boy" or "bad girl." Often people fail to make this crucial distinction between specific needs for change and general personal worth.

This, then, is one of the interesting paradoxes of human nature: to the extent that you feel accepted as you are, you are more able to change. To the extent that you feel "not O.K." as you are, it is difficult to change from your present state.

Fortunately not all this acceptance must arise from within, because there are times when everyone feels low self-esteem. Loving acceptance can come from friends and family. Skillful therapists, too, provide an atmosphere of acceptance, acknowledging the basic worth of the individual who is also working toward change. Research based on the ideas of humanistic psychologist Carl Rogers suggests that therapists who succeed in creating this accepting atmosphere for their clients are also more successful in facilitating change (Truax & Mitchell, 1971; Valle, 1981). Psychoanalayst Harry Stack Sullivan (1953) emphasized the importance of relationships that foster tenderness and acceptance, thereby decreasing anxiety, which is a barrier to change. More recent research has shown the importance of social support in helping people to make and maintain personal change (Yahne, 1984; Yahne & Long, 1988). We get by with a little help from our friends!

ALTERNATIVES

Awareness can increase self-understanding, and acceptance can be valuable both in facilitating change and in helping one cope with those situations that cannot be changed. But unless the person also has *alternatives,* change is not possible. In order to become a different person, one needs an alternative toward which to move. Such alternatives may be new behaviors or cognitions, new actions or new ways of perceiving and understanding.

Freedom is the ability to choose among alternatives. If a person continues in a pattern that is obviously problematic and painful, it may be because he or she sees no other choice. It may also be that there is no awareness of the problem, or that it feels too unsafe to change from the known to the unknown. This can be seen in certain kinds of drug dependence. An individual shows **psychological dependence** on a drug when it becomes the only (or easiest) way to cope with a certain type of problem or situation. If a drug is the only means a person has for relaxing, or for getting to sleep, or for loosening up and talking with others, then it is difficult to give it up. Breaking such dependence requires the learning of new alternative ways to meet the important challenges and problems of living (Miller & Pechacek, 1987).

There are several ways to acquire alternatives. In some cases the person already has the needed skill, but is prevented from using it because of anxiety. For example, one may know perfectly well how to start and carry on a conversation when meeting someone for the first time, but may freeze in the actual situation. On examinations a person may know the correct answers but find his or her head so filled with anxious thoughts that the questions seem impossible. In such situations, alternatives can be freed up by dealing with the anxiety-provoking thoughts that restrain and inhibit the person (see Chapter 8).

Sometimes having alternatives means learning new skills. It is possible that a person may need to learn better social relationship skills (Chapter 10) or study skills (Appendix C). People who feel stuck in depression often see no way out, and need to learn skills for recognizing and changing their mood states (Chapter 7). Throughout Part III of this book we will be presenting various alternative strategies for change that have been found, through research, to be helpful in coping with some of life's common adjustment problems.

Another way to acquire new alternatives is to learn them by watching or working with people who present effective models, who are practicing the desirable alternatives. "A picture is worth a thousand words," and seeing a skillful person in action can give life to the principles that look so lifeless and abstract on the written page. This is the basis of apprenticeship training programs, in which a novice works beside a master to learn a trade. All of us learn much, both as children and as adults, by watching those around us, our models of how to cope.

There are times, too, when a person's own resources and alternatives are not enough, and she or he needs to turn to a professional for guidance and alternatives. Recognizing a problem but having no alternatives for solving it is one of several good reasons to seek the help of a competent therapist. In Appendix A we discuss when and how to find professional help.

ACCESS

Psychological Dependence [drugs]
exclusive or preferential reliance upon a drug for coping purposes.

Sometimes a person is able to see alternatives, but does not have access to them. When no access is possible, alternatives seem meaningless or frustrating. Students who are also parents, for example, need access to child care in order to pursue their education. When budgets for day care are cut, many

Alternatives are of little use when one does
not have access to them.

students risk losing access to care for their children. Consequently educational options may be beyond their reach if alternatives are not available. Without access, alternatives are meaningless.

■ SUMMARY

"Adjustment" refers to both a state of being and a process of change. Different theories of adjustment can be grouped into four general themes: the homeostatic model emphasizing balance, growth models emphasizing self-actualization, learning models emphasizing adaptation to the environment, and choice models stressing self-determination by intentional choice. Within each model, the "reality" to which one adjusts is that of one's own perceived world rather than an objective reality.

Personality theories are ways in which psychologists organize data about human nature to understand people better. Four major types of personality theory (psychodynamic, humanistic, behavioral, and existential) correspond, respectively, to the four general models of adjustment.

In the process of change, four common elements emerge as facilitating adjustment: awareness, acceptance, alternatives, and access. Awareness opens the door to change. Both self-acceptance and social support facilitate the change process. Alternatives offer new ways of being and perceiving. Access is crucial to using chosen alternatives.

■ QUESTIONS FOR THOUGHT

?

1. What are the most important adjustment challenges facing you right now?
2. What new major adjustment challenges do you expect to face in the future? What will you need to deal with them?

3. What do you think have been the most important positive influences in your life thus far?

4. In what areas of your life do you need more
- Awareness?
- Acceptance?
- Alternatives?
- Access?

5. Draw a pie chart representing your life at present. First draw an empty circle; then divide it into pieces of various sizes, depending upon how important each piece is. The pieces represent factors that influence your life at present. The more you are influenced by a factor, the larger that piece of the "pie" should be. Here are some of the possible pieces. You may add others. How much is your present life influenced by each of the following?

> Your genetic makeup
>
> Your upbringing during childhood
>
> Your own choices and decisions
>
> The culture and time in which you live
>
> Your parents or family
>
> Chance or luck
>
> Your friends
>
> Your education
>
> Religion and spirituality
>
> Money
>
> Your boyfriend/girlfriend, lover, or spouse

chapter two

Psychological problems are not necessarily the product of mysterious, impenetrable forces but may result from commonplace processes such as faulty learning, making incorrect inferences on the basis of inadequate or incorrect information, and not distinguishing adequately between imagination and reality. Moreover, thinking can be unrealistic because it is derived from erroneous premises; behavior can be self-defeating because it is based on unreasonable attitudes.

—Aaron T. Beck, *Cognitive Therapy and the Emotional Disorders*

Perception and Personality

OUTLINE

■ SENSATION

The human senses are marvelous tools. They bring you the rich experiences of color, sound, aroma, texture, and flavor. Through the senses you enjoy the warmth of an embrace, savor the tastes of a good meal, experience the smells of a fresh spring morning, hear the voice of a friend, study an inspiring work of art.

All such **sensation** begins with special sensors within the body, known as **receptors.** A sensory receptor transforms energy from the *external* world (such as light waves or sound waves) into electrical impulses that can be understood within the *internal* world; namely, within different parts of the brain. The receptors of the eye (called *rods* and *cones*) turn wavelengths of light into signals that go first to the center of the brain and then on to the occipital lobe (at the back of the head) to become the experiences of vision. The ear transforms subtle changes in the vibrations of air molecules into electrical impulses that become the experience of sound. (see Figure 2-1a & b.)

Receptors in the lining of the nose and in the mouth (taste buds) are very sensitive to certain kinds of chemical molecules, producing electrical signals that the brain recognizes as certain tastes and smells. Within your skin are special receptors for temperature, vibration, pressure, and pain. These, too, change information from the external world into electrical impulses that the brain can read. Receptors in your muscles provide information about the

Sensation
the process whereby information is received through stimulation of sensory receptors.

Receptor
a body structure that responds to certain types of stimuli, converting them to information that can be conveyed to the brain.

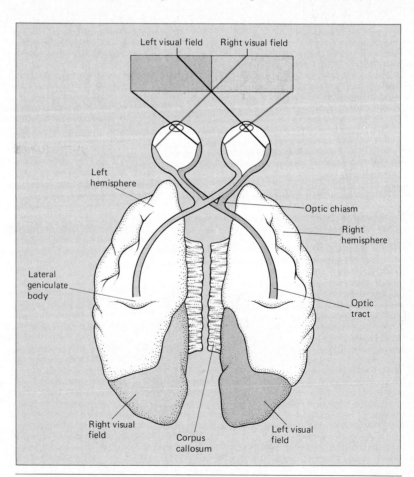

FIGURE 2-1a THE VISUAL SYSTEM

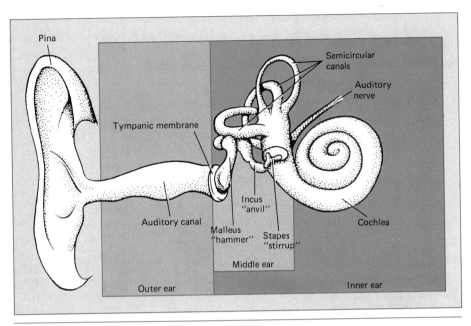

FIGURE 2-1b THE AUDITORY SYSTEM

location and amount of tension in your arms and legs, allowing you to know where your limbs are without looking at them.

The job of every receptor is to convert outside information into these tiny electrical impulses that, for all senses except smell, are sent along pathways to the **thalamus,** an information relay station at the center of the brain. From there the information goes to other parts of the brain, where it is interpreted, experienced emotionally, compared with past events, and finally acted upon or ignored. This next step—the process of organizing and interpreting raw sensory information—is called **perception**, and it represents a vital first link in the complex chains of events known as adjustment. Without perception, there could be no adjustment, no change in response to the external world.

■ PERCEPTION

Perception includes much more than sensation, more than the pure incoming sensory information. What a person perceives is influenced by many other factors: memory and learning from past experiences, present attention, and expectations, for example. This is why four people can all observe the same object or event but still tell quite different stories about what they have seen. All four may be telling "the truth, the whole truth, and nothing but the truth," and yet describe quite different experiences.

To the newborn infant, the world must be a puzzling and fascinating flood of ever-changing stimulation. The philosopher-psychologist William James (1918) described the infant's first view of the world as "a booming, buzzing confusion." The infant seems to stare in wide-eyed amazement, and James assumed that the newborn encounters a world of complete chaos. Current research, however, reveals that the newborn is already equipped with impressive perceptual abilities. Neonates can, for example, differentiate colors, discriminate the mother's face or voice from others, even distinguish the smell of mother's milk from that of other mothers (Walk, 1981). With passing months

Thalamus
a gray matter region near the center of the brain which serves as a relay station for sensory information

Perception
the process of organizing and interpreting sensory information.

2.1 EYEWITNESS TESTIMONY

Eyewitness reports are widely assumed, in courts of law and elsewhere, to be more reliable than other kinds of evidence. It is said that "Seeing is believing," and high credibility is often given to what witnesses report.

Yet numerous studies have shown that eyewitness testimony is remarkably subject to bias and error (Wells & Loftus, 1984). A wide variety of factors can influence people's beliefs about what they "saw." In real life, mistaken identifications from police lineups have resulted in the wrongful arrest and imprisonment of innocent people (Buckhout, 1974). Such mistakes are often made by people who honestly believe, and testify with certainty, that they witnessed something which, in reality, did not occur. How can this happen?

Human perception works, in part, by imposing structure on experience. People tend, for example, to fill in missing pieces that can be "assumed," and to regard similar stimuli as belonging to the same class or to be identical. While these organizing processes are necessary and desirable parts of human perception, given the vast amount of information that the brain must process in an average day, they can yield unreliable results when exact recording of events is essential. Human perception and memory do *not* function like videotape, and it is unrealistic to expect exact and accurate replays of experience.

The procedures that are used to obtain the memories of eyewitnesses can have a strong influence on what is remembered (Wells & Loftus, 1984). In assembling a police lineup, for example, it is important to take perceptual biases into consideration. If a victim reports being assaulted by a white male, it is unethical to show the victim a lineup of one white and five black suspects. It is also possible to create "memories" of details if witnesses are not properly interviewed. Suppose that a witness is asked, shortly after an accident, "How far was the white car into the intersection when the light turned red?" The form of this question suggests that (1) one of the cars was white and (2) the white car was somewhere within the intersection when the light turned red. Once a witness answers such a leading question, he or she may thereafter "remember" that there was a white car in the intersection when the light turned red.

Such biases in perception can apply not only in legal contexts, but in social situations as well. It is not uncommon for two participants in the same social experience to remember and report quite different courses of events. A dorm resident, for example, came to complain to his resident advisor that during a volleyball game, he had been knocked down, turned his ankle, and was left writhing in pain on the court. He described everyone walking

Eyewitness testimony is remarkably subject to bias and error.

off and laughing, leaving him to struggle alone back to his room. When the resident advisor asked several men and women players what had happened, however, a rather different picture emerged. By their report, the student had fallen while running, and at least three players had asked whether he needed help. He told all three that he was fine, and he sat out the last five minutes of play. Was someone intentionally lying? Not necessarily. Perceptions can differ this dramatically.

there is an increasing *organization* of the sensory world. Sensations are grouped, cataloged, associated with pleasant or unpleasant experiences. This developmental process of organizing, of giving *meaning* and structure to experience, is the emergence of perception. Although everyone (except for those born with special handicaps) starts out with the same basic systems available, each individual develops a personal perceptual reality, an organizing system as unique as his or her fingerprints. Although within any group of people there are many common elements of perception, particularly when the individuals have been raised in the same culture, not even identical twins can have identical perceptions. To paraphrase psychologist Henry Murray: every person is in certain respects like all other people, like some other people, and like no other person.

These perceptions, these images in the head, arise from an ongoing interplay of the outer and inner worlds. To be sure, what one sees, hears, smells, tastes, or feels is usually influenced by physical qualities of the "real world." (When they are not, they may be called **hallucinations**). Yet no two people observing the same "real" event can have exactly the same perception, because the physical events of the outer world *must* interact with each person's inner world for a perception to occur.

Consider four people who are taking a tour of a popular spot for visitors, the chapel of the U.S. Air Force Academy at Colorado Springs. One is not a particularly religious person but is awed by the magnificent modernistic architecture and the immensity of the sanctuary. A second is moved to tears by this tribute to the many youth who have died in defense of liberty and the freedom of religion. A third is filled with horror and revulsion at the blending of religious imagery with the instruments of death: a giant cross fashioned from airplane propellers, pew ends carved to resemble the wing tips of bombers. A fourth has been skiing all day, is too tired to pay much attention, and is mostly looking forward to a good meal.

The psychology of perception is a fascinating and complicated subject, and one that deserves an entire course of its own. To help you appreciate the complexity of this process, we will outline six of the factors that influence perception, accounting in part for why people perceive the "same" event differently. (We place "same" in quotations because an event is *not* the same event for different people, precisely because for it to be an event, it has to be perceived.)

SENSORY INFORMATION

Hallucination
a perception that does not correspond to apparent sensory reality.

The factor that is most common across individuals is sensory information, the immediate incoming stimuli from an external event. As an example, consider a bottle of wine. The chemical composition of the wine remains the same (at least for a brief period of time) regardless of who is doing the tasting. Even so, people do not receive exactly the same sensory information from any stimulus.

People's senses differ in **acuity** or accuracy. Some are farsighted, others near-sighted. Some are much more able to hear very soft sounds or high pitches, to taste subtle flavors, to smell faint fragrances. (Most smokers, for example, are less sensitive to many tastes and smells than are nonsmokers.) The minimum amount of a stimulus that is necessary for a given individual to detect its presence is called the **absolute threshold.** People who have a very *low* absolute threshold for the taste of salt, for example, are able to detect even the small amounts of salt in food such as corn flakes. A *high* absolute threshold means just the opposite: a large amount of the stimulus is needed before it can be detected. As people grow older, their sensory thresholds usually increase; they become less sensitive to sounds, lights, tastes, and odors. Some people seem to be completely unable to recognize certain kinds of stimuli and may be called "color blind" or "tone deaf."

Sensory psychologists (and other specialists such as audiologists) can test a person's absolute threshold for a certain stimulus: the smallest amount of a stimulus (a sound, light, touch, etc.) that the person can detect 50 percent of the time. This is what is usually done, for example, when a person has a hearing test. Another interesting measure of sensory acuity is the **difference threshold:** how different (far apart) two stimuli must be before the person can detect that they are different.

SENSORY BACKGROUND

A second factor influencing perception is the present sensory background. Returning to our example of the wine taster, the question here is: "What *other* sensory stimuli are present?" If the person is eating a piece of cheese at the same time the wine is being tasted, this will certainly influence the taste (perception) of the wine (and, for that matter, of the cheese). Likewise incoming information on other sensory channels—music, the odor of perfume, caressing of the skin—may alter perception of the wine. (Notice the pleasant backgrounds presented in advertising for wines and other alcoholic beverages, intended to instill favorable perceptions of the product.)

SENSORY RESIDUAL

A third factor influencing perception is the residual (left-over) effects of recent sensory stimuli. The wine taster who has recently eaten a sweet mint candy or a piece of garlic bread will find that this influences the taste of the wine. After a loud rock concert, the ears are often less sensitive to soft sounds and pitches for a period of time. When driving at night, bright headlights in the eyes cause the pupils to contract, and after the headlights have passed there is a period of time during which the eyes are less sensitive. The presence of alcohol in the bloodstream makes this period even longer, because it slows the eyes' readjustment process. Each of the senses can *adapt* in this way, adjusting the level of sensitivity and therefore influencing perception.

Here is an easy demonstration of the effect of sensory residual on perception. Draw three bowls of water: one hot, one ice cold, and one lukewarm. Thrust one of your hands into the hot water and the other into the bowl of cold water, and hold them there 10 to 15 seconds (the temperature should not be uncomfortable). Then take out both hands and immediately thrust them into the third bowl of water. You will find that while one hand experiences the water as warm, the other experiences it as cool. The perception from each hand is influenced by residual effects from the previous bowl.

Acuity
the sensitivity of a sensory system.

Absolute Threshold
the minimum level of a stimulus that can be detected 50 percent of the time.

Difference Threshold
the smallest change in a stimulus that can be detected; usually measured as the smallest difference that can be detected 75 percent of the time.

ATTENTION

Another factor is **attention**. Each person has the ability to focus consciousness, directing attention to certain aspects of the environment to the exclusion of other aspects. Probably as you have been reading this page you have not been thinking about your scalp, but now that we have mentioned it you can focus your attention there: how your scalp feels, the roots of your hair, whether there are spots that feel tense or itch. (Feel a need to scratch that one little spot?) Perception is influenced by such focusing of attention. The person who absent-mindedly sips a glass of wine in the midst of a stimulating conversation will have a different experience of the wine than does a person who is asked by an entire room full of friends to taste it and offer an opinion. In the latter case, much more attention will be focused on the sensory experience of tasting the wine.

EXPERIENCE

Past experience is an important factor influencing perception. Whenever you encounter something new, be it a strange object or an unfamiliar person, you compare this with what you have experienced before and ask (perhaps consciously or unconsciously), "What (or whom) do I already know that is like this?" Continuing our wine analogy, the experienced wine taster is able to detect much more subtle characteristics of a wine, and tasting itself is a richer perception than for the less experienced individual or for the person who has never tasted wine before.

Memory influences current perception. If, as you grew up, your memory was fed with ideas and experiences that members of a certain racial, national, or religious group are untrustworthy, you may have a hard time allowing trust to develop when you meet such a person. Your past learning affects what you perceive in the present.

Still another aspect of memory and perception is that past experience leads one to certain *expectations* about what will happen. The person who has just paid a large price for a bottle of wine expects it to be good, and this expectancy influences perception. Likewise once a person has formed an initial impression, there is a tendency to retain that opinion, to expect it to be true. A self-perpetuating cycle can occur here because the person then attends selectively to information that confirms the impression and selectively ignores new information inconsistent with his or her opinion. This is one way in which racial and other prejudices are maintained: an individual develops an opinion that all people or objects of a certain group are "that way" (be it lazy, noisy, intelligent, stingy, or jolly) and then notices evidence that confirms the belief while ignoring disconfirming cases (Jones, 1977).

MOTIVATIONAL FACTORS

Attention
the adjustment of the nervous system to sense and respond to particular types of stimulation.

Motivation
factors that elicit, increase, and maintain behavior; a discrepancy between present state and a desired state.

From the foregoing discussion it should be clear that these factors influencing perception do not merely add up, but also interact with each other to influence perception. One final type of influence on perception is found in motivational factors. **Motivation** is sometimes defined as a discrepancy between one's present state and a desired state. Most of what are called "motives" are such states of discrepancy, where there is a desired goal that is at some distance from the present state: hunger, thirst, achievement, frustration (Locke et al., 1981). Research has demonstrated that such motivational states can influence perception. It was shown long ago, for example, that hungry people are more likely, when shown faint or ambiguous stimuli, to perceive them as food objects (Sanford, 1936; Levine, Chein, & Murphy, 1942; McClelland & Atkinson, 1948). In experiments where words are flashed on a screen very briefly, it has been found that hungry people have lower thresholds for food words (can identify them with a briefer exposure) compared with people who have recently eaten (Wispe & Drambarean, 1953).

Effect how we perceives things

■ PERCEPTUAL STYLES

Personality
the cluster of relatively enduring characteristics that forms the unique nature of an individual.

Personality Trait
a relatively consistent characteristic of an individual which persists across time and situations.

Locus of Control
a personality trait proposed by Julian Rotter, consisting of the extent to which an individual perceives his or her life to be under personal control.

External Locus of Control
one end of the continuum of locus of control; the relatively consistent perception that one's life is determined by other people and forces beyond one's personal control.

Internal Locus of Control
one end of the continuum of locus of control; the relatively consistent perception that one's life is determined by one's own choices and actions.

Introversion
the personality trait of being inner-directed; oriented more toward inner processes such as thoughts and ideas than to external reality; opposite of extraversion.

Extraversion
the personality trait of being outer-directed; oriented more toward the reality of the external world than toward the inner world; opposite of introversion.

Thus far we have discussed six factors that influence how people perceive the world around them: sensory information, background and residual sensation, attention, experience, and motivational states. Except for experience, which accumulates over time, all of these are temporary influences that change across times and situations. Are there more permanent influences on perception, individual differences that represent distinctive personal *styles* of perceiving?

Many of what have been called **personality traits** can be understood as relatively enduring patterns or styles of perceiving, of organizing reality. Personality theorists have attempted to identify such traits, dimensions that describe meaningful differences in how people react or adjust to the world around them. In this section we will present four such trait dimensions that have been proposed. Each is a continuum stretching between two opposite poles. Some individuals fall at one extreme or the other, but most lie somewhere in between.

INTERNAL VERSUS EXTERNAL LOCUS OF CONTROL

One of the most studied personality traits in the history of psychology is known as **locus of control.**. This was originally conceived as a generalized expectation about the extent to which one has control over what happens in one's life (Rotter, 1966). At one extreme, the person with a very **external locus of control** tends to perceive things as being beyond his or her personal control, to feel like a victim of external forces such as luck, fate, circumstances, or powerful people. At the other extreme, those with a strong **internal locus of control** believe that they have a great deal of influence over what happens to them, and that the course of their lives is controlled mostly by their own efforts and abilities.

Why is this important? Scores on this scale have been found to predict a wide variety of behaviors (Lefcourt, 1982). Here are a few examples. One study found that people with an external locus of control were less likely to take cover during a tornado alert, believing that God's will or fate would have its way regardless of their actions. In therapy, more external alcoholics tend to respond better to a treatment in which they are told what to do and given outside help for change, whereas internals tend to rely less on outside help and to do better in a therapy that emphasizes self-direction and self-control (Miller & Hester, 1986).

INTROVERSION VERSUS EXTRAVERSION

Perhaps the most popularly known of all personality traits is the dimension of **introversion** versus **extraversion.** Though these terms sound like locus of control, this is a very different dimension. Locus of control is the extent to

2.2 LOCUS OF CONTROL

Here is an opportunity for you to find out where you stand on the locus of control dimension. This scale was developed by a group of researchers at Emory University, as an alternative to the original Rotter scale (Nowicki & Duke, 1974). Rotter's scale has been criticized as confusing a number of different kinds of perceived control including personal, political, and social control. The authors of the Emory scale also attempted to make their scale more readable and less influenced by concerns about "looking good."

Answer the following questions according to the way you *feel*. There are no right or wrong answers. Don't take too much time answering any one question, but do answer them all.

NOWICKI-STRICKLAND INTERNAL-EXTERNAL LOCUS OF CONTROL SCALE

Yes	No		
	✓	1.	Do you believe that most problems will solve themselves if you don't fool with them?
	✓	2.	Do you believe that you can stop yourself from catching a cold?
	✓	3.	Are some people just born lucky?
✓		4.	Most of the time did you feel that getting good grades means a great deal to you?
	✓	5.	Are you often blamed for things that just aren't your fault?
✓		6.	Do you believe that if somebody studies hard enough, he or she can pass any subject?
	✓	7.	Do you feel that most of the time it doesn't pay to try hard because things never turn out right anyway?
	✓	8.	Do you feel that if things start out well in the morning that it's going to be a good day no matter what you do?
	✓	9.	Do you feel that most of the time parents listen to what their children have to say?
✓		10.	Do you believe that wishing can make good things happen?
	✓	11.	When you get criticized, does it usually seem it's for no good reason at all?
✓		12.	Most of the time do you find it hard to change a friend's (mind) opinion?
✓		13.	Do you think that cheering more than luck helps a team to win?
✓		14.	Did you feel that it was nearly impossible to change your parent's mind about anything?
✓		15.	Do you believe that parents should allow children to make most of their own decisions?
	✓	16.	Do you feel that when you do something wrong there's very little you can do to make it right?

✓ ____ 17. Do you believe that most people are just born good at sports?

✓ ____ 18. Are most of the other people your age and sex stronger than you are?

____ ✓ 19. Do you feel that one of the best ways to handle most problems is just not to think about them?

✓ ____ 20. Do you feel that you have a lot of choice in deciding whom your friends are?

✓ ____ 21. If you find a four leaf clover, do you believe that it might bring you good luck?

✓ ____ 22. Did you often feel that whether or not you do your homework had much to do with what kind of grades you get?

____ ✓ 23. Do you feel that when a person your age is angry at you, there's little you can do to stop him or her?

✓ ____ 24. Have you ever had a good luck charm?

✓ ____ 25. Do you believe that whether or not people like you depends on how you act?

✓ ____ 26. Did your parents usually help you if you asked them to?

____ ✓ 27. Have you felt that when people were angry with you, it was usually for no reason at all?

✓ ____ 28. Most of the time, do you feel that you can change what might happen tomorrow by what you do today?

____ ✓ 29. Do you believe that when bad things are going to happen, they just are going to happen, no matter what you try to do to stop them?

✓ ____ 30. Do you think that people can get their own way if they just keep trying?

____ ✓ 31. Most of the time do you find it useless to try to get your own way at home?

✓ ____ 32. Do you feel that when good things happen, they happen because of hard work?

____ ✓ 33. Do you feel that when somebody your age wants to be your enemy, there's little you can do to change matters?

✓ ____ 34. Do you feel that it's easy to get friends to do what you want them to do?

____ ✓ 35. Do you usually feel that you have little to say about what you get to eat at home?

____ ✓ 36. Do you feel that when someone doesn't like you there's little you can do about it?

____ ✓ 37. Did you usually feel that it was almost useless to try in school because most other students were just plain smarter than you were?

✓ ____ 38. Are you the kind of person who believes that planning ahead makes things turn out better?

_____ _____ ✓ 39. Most of the time, do you feel that you have little to say about what your family decides to do?

_____ ✓ _____ 40. Do you think it's better to be smart than to be lucky?

SCORING: Now check your own answers against the following list. Count the number of items on which your own answer *matches* the answer listed.

1. Yes	11. Yes	21. Yes–	31. Yes
2. No	12. Yes	22. No	32. No
3. Yes	13. No	23. Yes	33. Yes
4. No	14. Yes–	24. Yes –	34. No
5. Yes	15. No	25. No	35. Yes
6. No	16. Yes	26. No	36. Yes
7. Yes	17. Yes–	27. Yes	37. Yes
8. Yes	18. Yes –	28. No	38. No
9. No	19. Yes	29. Yes	39. Yes
10. Yes–	20. No	30. No	40. No

Your score is the total number of items on which your answer matches the answer listed. The higher your score, the more *external* your locus of control. The following ranges are based on data collected in 20 different studies, involving more than 1,300 white male and female college students and 2 studies with 172 black students.

	WHITE	BLACK
Strongly external locus of control (more than one standard deviation above the mean)	13–40	20–40
Moderately external locus of control (up to one standard deviation above the mean)	9–12	14–19
Moderately internal locus of control (up to one standard deviation below the mean)	6–8	9–13
Strongly internal locus of control (more than one standard deviation below the mean)	0–5	0–8

Source: *Manual for the Adult Nowicki-Strickland Internal-External Locus of Control*, Department of Psychology, Emory University, Atlanta, GA, n.d.

2.3   INTROVERSION VERSUS EXTRAVERSION

☀ EXTRAVERTS

The afterthinkers. Cannot understand life until they have lived it.

Attitude relaxed and confident. They expect the waters to prove shallow, and plunge readily into new and untried experiences.

Minds outwardly directed, interest and attention following objective happenings, primarily those of the immediate environment. Their real world therefore is the outer world of people and things.

The civilizing genius, the people of action and practical achievement, who go from doing to considering and back to doing.

Conduct in essential matters is always governed by objective conditions.

Spend themselves lavishly upon external claims and conditions which to them constitute life.

Understandable and accessible, often sociable, more at home in the world of people and things than in the world of ideas.

Expansive and less impassioned, they unload their emotions as they go along.

Typical weakness lies in a tendency toward intellectual superficiality, very conspicuous in extreme types.

Health and wholesomeness depend upon a reasonable development of balancing introversion.

Freud
Darwin
Roosevelt
(both Theodore and Franklin Delano)

☀ INTROVERTS

The forethinkers. Cannot live life until they understand it.

Attitude reserved and questioning. They expect the waters to prove deep, and pause to take soundings in the new and untried.

Minds inwardly directed, frequently unaware of the objective environment, interest and attention being engrossed by inner events. Their real world therefore is the inner world of ideas and understanding.

The cultural genius, the people of ideas and abstract invention, who go from considering to doing and back to considering.

Conduct in essential matters is always governed by subjective values.

Defend themselves as far as possible against external claims and conditions in favor of the inner life.

Subtle and impenetrable, often taciturn and shy, more at home in the world of ideas than in the world of people and things.

Intense and passionate, they bottle up their emotions and guard them carefully as high explosives.

Typical weakness lies in a tendency toward impracticality, very conspicuous in extreme types.

Health and wholesomeness depend upon a reasonable development of balancing extraversion.

Jung
Einstein
Lincoln

which you believe you are in charge of your own life, whereas introversion-extraversion has to do with whether one focuses more on internal versus external reality. In everyday language, people sometimes equate introversion with shyness and extraversion with outgoingness, but psychological definitions are somewhat different. Within Jung's personality theory, for example, this dimension describes where a person tends to focus interest and attention. In looking for "reality," an introvert tends to attend to the inner world: to his or her own thoughts, feelings, reflections, memories; to focus on inner experiences, sometimes to the exclusion of the outer world. An extravert, by contrast, tends to look outside for reality and meaning, particularly to other people. When suffering emotionally and struggling with a difficult situation, the introvert is more likely to withdraw, to turn inward for healing, while the extravert is more likely to turn to others for support. Neither preference is more healthy than the other. Each represents a preferred style of coping that may be used in a healthy or unhealthy fashion (Myers & Myers, 1980).

Introverts and extraverts may also differ in how they learn best. Introverts, for example, may learn best by studying with minimal distractions, absorbing material and processing it internally (a style that is much easier to handle for most schools). Extraverts, by contrast, seem to learn better by interacting, discussing, talking through and testing partially formed ideas and skills, and in essence "thinking aloud" (Lawrence, 1979).

Research further indicates that introverts and extraverts respond differently to therapy. DiLoreto (1971) found that extraverts were more successful in a **client-centered** type of counseling based on an interpersonal relationship with the therapist and focusing on feelings. Introverts, on the other hand, benefited more from a **rational-emotive** approach which examined the client's private inner thoughts and beliefs.

AUGMENTATION VERSUS REDUCTION

Client-Centered Therapy
a system of interpersonal therapy introduced by Carl Rogers, whereby the therapist attempts to create an atmosphere of warmth and acceptance in which the client can grow and find his or her own solutions.

Rational-Emotive Therapy
a system of psychotherapy introduced by Albert Ellis, whereby the therapist seeks to identify and change maladaptive beliefs which hinder the client's adjustment and happiness.

Augmenter
in Petrie's theory, an individual whose nervous system tends to amplify or augment sensory input, resulting in a style of avoiding overstimulation.

Reducer
in Petrie's theory, an individual whose nervous system tends to dampen or reduce sensory input, resulting in a style of stimulation seeking.

Another example of differences in perceptual style is found in the work of Asenath Petrie (1967). She hypothesized that people range between two extremes of *augmentation* and *reduction*. **Augmenters** are people who seem to be very sensitive to stimulation, and who (relative to other people) tend to overestimate the magnitude of stimuli. Petrie's original method for measuring this trait was drawn directly from sensory psychology. She blindfolded the person and then presented a sample wooden block, asking the person to feel it and notice its size. Then after a brief pause she asked the person to estimate how large the block had been by adjusting a sliding scale on a tapered block until it was the same size as the original block. Augmenters were those who consistently overestimated the size of the block, who perceived it as having been larger than it actually was. Petrie found that augmenters in general seemed to behave as if their nervous systems "augmented" or amplified stimuli. They enjoyed silence and alone time, and disliked overstimulating activities such as loud rock concerts and roller coasters. If they used drugs, these tended to be substances like alcohol, tranquilizers, and sedatives—drugs that make the world more calm and quiet. By contrast, **reducers,** those who underestimated the size of the block, were found to behave as if their nervous systems reduced the intensity of most stimuli. They enjoyed exciting and stimulating activities, and disliked quiet and solitude. If they used a drug, it was more often something that made the world more exciting or interesting: stimulants or hallucinogens, for example. Augmenters tended to perceive the world as overstimulating and to avoid much risk and excitement. Reducers tended to perceive the world as too boring and to seek out adventure and stimulation. Petrie believed that this personality dimension is fundamentally based in the person's biological makeup.

Sensing Type
in Jung's theory of psychological type, an individual who prefers factual and direct sensory information as a basis for perception; opposite of intuitive type.

SENSING VERSUS INTUITION

One more dimension of perceptual style is Jung's continuum of sensing versus intuition. This describes how people go about collecting information, their preferred manner of perception (Myers & Myers, 1980). **Sensing types,** in

---

2.4   SENSING VERSUS INTUITION

☀SENSING TYPES

Face life observantly, craving enjoyment.

Admit to consciousness every sense impression and are intensely aware of the external environment; they are observant at the expense of imagination.

Are by nature pleasure lovers and consumers; loving life as it is and having a great capacity for enjoyment, they are in general contented.

Desiring chiefly to possess and enjoy, and being very observant, they are imitative, wanting to have what other people have and to do what other people do, and are very dependent upon their physical surroundings.

Dislike intensely any and every occupation which requires the suppression of sensing, and are most reluctant to sacrifice present enjoyment to future gain or good.

Prefer the art of living in the present to the satisfactions of enterprise and achievement.

Contribute to the public welfare by their support of every form of enjoyment, recreation, and every variety of comfort, luxury, and beauty.

Are always in danger of being frivolous, unless balance is attained through development of a judging process.

☀INTUITIVES

Face life expectantly, craving inspiration.

Admit fully to consciousness only the sense impressions related to the current inspiration; they are imaginative at the expense of observation.

Are by nature initiators, inventors and promoters; having no taste for life as it is, and small capacity for living in and enjoying the present, they are generally restless.

Desiring chiefly opportunities and possibilities, and being very imaginative, they are inventive and original, quite indifferent to what other people have and do, and are very independent of their physical surroundings.

Dislike intensely any and every occupation which necessitates sustained concentration on sensing, and are willing to sacrifice the present to a large extent since they neither live in it nor particularly enjoy it.

Prefer the joy of enterprise and achievement and pay little or no attention to the art of living in the present.

Contribute to the public welfare by their inventiveness, initiative, enterprise, and powers of inspired leadership in every direction of human interest.

Are always in danger of being fickle, changeable, and lacking in persistence, unless balance is attained through development of a judging process.

Jung's theory, prefer to stick to facts, to information obtained via the five senses. They believe what they can see, hear, smell, taste, touch. **Intuitive** types, by contrast, tend to perceive the world not in detail but in meaning-filled clusters. They are more interested in ideas and possibilities than in current facts and actualities. They "know" (perceive) things without necessarily being able to indicate how they know, how they observed (a process Jung called "perceiving by the unconscious").

This preference for sensing versus intuition, most often measured by questionnaire, has been found to be strongly associated both with how a person learns best and with the occupation a person chooses. Intuitive people may learn best by reading, by acquiring abstract ideas, whereas sensing people may learn best by hands-on experience (Lawrence, 1979). American school systems (particularly universities) and intelligence tests tend to favor an intuitive style. Even though sensing people outnumber intuitive people by more than two to one in the United States as a whole, this ratio is reversed in college and university populations. Sensing individuals are overrepresented in occupations such as police work, farming, nursing, and factory work, whereas intuitive people are much more common among psychologists, journalists, artists, and actors (Myers & McCaulley, 1985).

UNDERSTANDING PERCEPTUAL STYLES

These are only four examples of ways people may differ in how they tend to perceive reality. For the most part, it is not "better" to be at one extreme than at the other. Unlike certain personality traits (e.g., cruelty), there are no healthy or unhealthy places to be on these dimensions.

Understanding that people do differ on such dimensions may, however, be a key to better communication. A person who does not understand that such differences among people are normal and acceptable may view people at the opposite extreme as being abnormal or misguided. People who are opposite on these dimensions may have difficulty in understanding and communicating with each other. Yet understanding is important, for all kinds of people live in the world. In fact, opposites often do attract, and people who marry each other are frequently opposite on dimensions such as these.

Unless you can manage to associate only with people exactly like yourself, having good relationships requires that you learn ways to live and work with differences. It means learning to appreciate, enjoy, and use differences. On the locus of control dimension, an internal may view the external as pessimistic and defeatist, while the external sees the internal as not facing up to reality. An introvert may view an extravert as "shallow and superficial," whereas the extravert sees the introvert as "dull and withdrawn." An augmenter may call a reducer "foolhardy" and in return be seen as "boring" by the reducer. To the intuitive person, the step-by-step factual process of the sensing type may seem slow and pedantic, while the sensing person complains of the intuitive's mental leaps, "You can't know that! How did you get there?"

Each type of person needs what the opposite has to offer. From the person with internal locus of control, the external can learn that there *are* many situations in which personal effort makes a difference; while the internal can learn from the external how to accept and deal with that which cannot be changed. The introvert can benefit from the extravert's interest in the outer world, from being called to try new things and pay attention to what is happening in the lives of others. The extravert can learn depth from the introvert, being called to take time to pay attention to what is going on inside, to seek meaning and personal identity. If one can get past the discomfort of the opposite, there is great potential for growth.

Intuitive Type
in Jung's theory of psychological type, an individual whose perceptions are heavily guided by ideas, possibilities, and hunches not directly derived from sensory experience; opposite of sensing type.

2.5 PERSONAL MILESTONE
Gifts Differing

I have long been fascinated by what attracts people to one another, and by the complexities of intimate relationships. Treating distressed couples and families is a kind of therapy I find especially rewarding and challenging. After a decade of experience, however, I still sensed that something was missing in my work to heal relationships.

A large missing piece fell into place for me when I first encountered the work of Isabel Briggs Myers. She devoted her life to understanding the how's and why's of differences among people. Her motivation for this search arose in part from witnessing the horrors of two world wars, and from her conviction that warfare is a futile and senseless way to resolve differences. In her search for peacemaking tools, she employed Carl Jung's concept of psychological types as a way of understanding natural style differences. Working with her mother, Katharine Briggs, she developed a practical approach for understanding and working with human differences, culminating in her 1980 book, *Gifts Differing*. Her approach is complex, involving 4 dimensions (2 of which are reflected in Boxes 2.3 and 2.4 in this chapter) that combine to form 16 different personality types.

In a way, her approach offers the same strength of any good personality theory: a system for organizing and understanding human behavior. What I have found particularly refreshing, even inspiring, about her work is the set of implicit assumptions that underlie it. Personality types are natural, preferred styles of perceiving and interacting with others. No type is more normal, healthy, or desirable than any other. In fact, differences are seen as useful, interesting, and essential. Type differences among people form a basis for attraction, cooperation, and mutual growth. Unless one understands this and has a way of recognizing and appreciating types, differences are a source of annoyance and confusion. They become a reason for conflict, for a struggle to determine whose style is "right."

Through the eyes of psychological type theory, I began to recognize processes that had been going on around me all my life. I developed a clearer appreciation of the reasons for conflicts within my family, my social circles, and my department. My closest friends, I discovered, were remarkably similar to me on the dimensions Myers described, and that similarity seemed to be a basis for our intimacy. At the same time, my wife and I found that we differed profoundly on type dimensions, and that those differences were a powerful basis both for our attraction to each other and for the strength of our relationship. People of different psychological types need and benefit from each other.

My therapy with couples changed. Recognizing type differences became a new avenue for understanding and improving communication. I did not abandon the other relationship therapy tools I had learned, but now I use them in a new light. Helping people understand their differences seems to be a key for unlocking those "stuck" struggles. It is no miracle cure, of course. Learning how to live through differences (and similarities) in relationships is a lifelong process. The crucial change seems to come in recognizing, valuing, cherishing, and cultivating our gifts differing.

Thank you, Isabel Myers.   —WRM

MEASURING PERCEPTUAL STYLES

Psychologists measure perceptual styles in many different ways. As mentioned earlier, Petrie (1967) used a simple sensory measurement, estimating the size of blocks, to distinguish augmenters from reducers. Questionnaires have often been used to measure dimensions like locus of control (Rotter, 1966), introversion-extraversion (Eysenck, 1953), or sensing-intuition (Myers & McCaulley, 1985).

Examples from the Rorschach and Thematic Apperception Tests.

The assumption that perceptual styles are very important also underlies a longstanding method in psychology known as projective testing. **Projective tests** consist of stimuli that are vague or ambiguous. The most famous example of these is Rorschach's test, a series of ten inkblots that the person is asked to examine, saying what he or she sees in them. Another common test of this kind is the Thematic Apperception Test (TAT), a series of vague pictures on the basis of which the person is asked to make up stories: What has happened, what is happening, and what will happen next? Because the stimuli *are* quite ambiguous, the person's responses are viewed as projections of his or her own style of perceiving and organizing the world. Since there is little structure in the stimuli themselves, the structure must come from within the person being tested. It has been assumed, by those who use projective tests, that how an individual structures his or her responses to these tests reflects or is similar to how the person will structure and perceive everyday life.

Projective Testing
the use of ambiguous, vague stimuli to learn about an individual's style of perceiving, organizing, and responding to reality.

2.6 HERE WE DIFFER/HERE WE AGREE
The Projective Hypothesis

It was a clever idea: have people look at ambiguous stimuli and then study the creations of their own imaginations. The question is: "What does this tell us about reality?" Most psychologists who employ tests like the Rorschach inkblots and the TAT do so in hopes of being able to predict and understand something else: the person's information processing style and his or her behavior in the real world.

For most of its history, Rorschach's test has been interpreted intuitively, according to beliefs passed down from generation to generation of psychologists. If one traces the history of a particular diagnostic "sign" on a projective test, it is not uncommon to find that experts quote experts, who quote experts, who made it up! It was long believed, for example, that seeing water images (oceans, shorelines, etc.) on the inkblots indicates that the person has a tendency toward alcoholism (Griffith, 1961). This belief was held in spite of a long series of studies providing absolutely no support for the hypothesis. The interpretation of projective tests even today remains mostly intuitive, relying on unreliable standards and illusory correlations (Wiggins, 1973; Ziskin, 1981).

If what one desires to do is to predict behavior (whether or not, for example, a person is likely to be dangerous, to perform well in school, to have alcohol problems), it is best to use much more reliable indicators. A case in point: although projective tests are extremely poor detectors of whether a person has an alcohol or drug problem, there *is* a much more accurate method—to *ask* the person (Miller, 1976). Often the best predictor of future behavior is past history of the same behavior. Contemporary psychologists have much more reliable approaches than trying to explain and predict what a person will do in the real world based on intuitive interpretations of fantasies they create while looking at inkblots.   —WRM

It is *still* a clever idea! When people are exposed to an ambiguous stimulus and are asked to respond, they are essentially forced to use and demonstrate their own unique perceptual organizing systems and learning history. It's true, to be sure, that clinical lore has been passed on, and since we psychologists are human, some of it has been wrong. Current research (cf. Exner, 1986), however, points to considerable consistency in responses to the Rorschach blots, not only between individuals within a culture, but across cultures as well.

In fairness, few people these days would claim to be able to predict dangerousness from projective tests, and there are much better ways to predict school performance. As for alcohol abuse, asking is fine, though self-report of drug use also has its limitations (not that projectives work for this either).

The trouble is that by focusing only on prediction, one misses the whole point of projective testing. Prediction is not what projective tests do best. What projectives *can* do is to give a rich picture of how people tend to organize and view their world when some of the usual social guidelines for perception are removed. A simple example might be a person who denies feeling any depression or hostility, but then gives stories on the TAT that are loaded with depressive themes and aggression.

The projective hypothesis is very much alive, and provides one tool (albeit only one) in the psychologist's armamentarium. The key to understanding projective tests is to focus not on prediction, but on understanding.   —JMR

INTEGRATION

With all their faults, the Rorschach and TAT remain among the most used of psychological assessment tools. While understanding is a major goal in projective assessment, nevertheless the tasks to which psychologists are often asked to apply their evaluations contain significant questions of prediction (e.g., in the courts, the schools, in choosing appropriate treatment interventions). Objective Rorschach-based measures have been found in some cases to be predictive of treatment outcome (e.g., Thornton et al., 1977). Exner's (1986) more recent work provides an alternative system for interpreting the Rorschach by objective criteria. Exner takes a stringent scientific approach, with structured scoring procedures and predictive equations, and has reported greater success in making reliable judgments from Rorschach responses. It appears that a compromise is being worked out between the intuitive value of the projective approach and the need for objectivity and reliability in interpretation.

■ PERSON PERCEPTION

Thus far we have argued that as you perceive the world you are not seeing an objective reality but rather your own reality, perceptions that are shaped both by the real world and by a multitude of factors within you. If this is true for your perceptions of something as simple as a building or a glass of wine, how much more true it is as you perceive people!

SELF-PERCEPTION

One person about whom you have constant thoughts and feelings is yourself. At any given moment you have a certain perception of yourself. This includes both what is usually termed **self-esteem** (your overall evaluation of yourself) and your **self-concept** (beliefs that you have about your own abilities, strengths and weaknesses, and characteristics). These will be discussed more fully in Chapter 4. Notice, however, that there are two elements here. One of them, self-esteem, is mostly an *evaluation*, an emotionally charged judgment ranging from very positive to very negative. It is fairly global, an overall evaluative perception of yourself at a certain point in time. For purposes of discussion in this book, we distinguish this from self-concept, which is more a description of yourself, or how you think about yourself. Self-concept might be reflected in a set of words that you would choose to describe yourself. This difference is exemplified in the questions asked in Box 2.7.

Self-perception is influenced by all the factors discussed earlier: by current incoming information (for example, feedback from other people), by the background (perhaps other people) against which you compare yourself, by memories of what has happened in the recent and distant past, by how much attention you are paying to yourself versus the world around you (self-consciousness), by motivational states (such as desire to achieve or to make a good impression), and by expectations of yourself based in part on past learning. Self-perception, then, is not a solid, unchanging trait but a *perception* that changes over time and situations. In Chapter 6 we will discuss ways in which you can use this fact to change your self-perception.

PERCEPTION OF OTHERS

Similar processes affect how you perceive other people. As you deal with another person you are not reacting to the real person (for no one can ever know completely another's world) but instead you react to your own perceptions of that person. When you realize the truth of this, that what you perceive and believe about others is not necessarily accurate or permanent, you take an important step toward better understanding and relationships.

A good example is first impressions. Aware of it or not, you do form first impressions whenever you meet someone new. This is a process of putting people into categories, ascribing to them goals, motives, and traits (Taylor, 1981; Taylor & Crocker, 1980). Sometimes these first impressions are very strong, particularly if they are negative (Hamilton, 1980); other times they are more tentative. Look at the four pictures on page 51. What are your immediate impressions of these individuals? Think of four words you might use to describe each person. Do you think that you would *like* the person or not? Another interesting exercise of this kind is to go to a shopping center or other busy place (perhaps on campus between classes) and sit down beside an area where people pass. Pick out particular individuals and decide what they must be like. Come up with several adjectives that might describe the personality of each. Also ask yourself, "Do I like this person or not?" Identify why, especially when you have a strong impression. What are the cues, the stimuli that you are using to make your judgments?

As in self-perception, there seem to be at least two dimensions to perceptions of others. One that has been long recognized is a more emotional or

Self-Esteem
evaluative aspects of self-perception; the current overall appraisal of oneself.

Self-Concept
descriptive aspects of self-perception; the current accumulation of beliefs regarding one's own abilities and characteristics.

2.7 | SELF-CONCEPT AND SELF-ESTEEM

"Self-concept," as we are using the term in this book, refers to the *descriptive* aspects of self-perception. Here are some pairs of opposite adjectives that can be used to describe a person. In each pair, the words are intended to be descriptive rather than evaluative, and either extreme could be seen as positive. Where would you classify yourself?

Talkative	Quiet
Cautious	Trusting
Organized	Flexible
Spontaneous	Planful
Religious	Worldly
Ambitious	Modest
Emotional	Logical
Realistic	Idealistic

"Self-esteem," on the other hand, is the term we have used to refer to the *evaluative* aspects of self-perception. Self-esteem scales often consist of True/False items such as "I am a lovable person." Using an approach similar to that above, a measure of self-esteem might contrast pairs of positive and negative evaluation words. Where would you classify yourself on these dimensions?

Good	Bad
Likable	Unlikable
Smart	Stupid
Worthwhile	Worthless
Healthy	Unhealthy
Lovable	Unlovable
Helpful	Useless
Competent	Incompetent

See the difference? The self-concept dimensions contrast equally positive opposites, and help to *describe* who you are. The self-esteem dimensions contrast a positive or desirable description with a negative or undesirable one, and *evaluate* who you are.

evaluative dimension, a "liking" judgment that is either positive or negative (Osgood, Suci, & Tannenbaum, 1981). Research has long shown that this liking factor has a strong effect on overall perceptions of the other person (Asch, 1946; Kelley, 1950). This corresponds roughly to self-esteem, and might even be called "other esteem." A second component in perception of others, corresponding to self-concept, is *descriptive*, involving beliefs about the other person's nature. Two general judgments of this kind that people seem to use in

What is your first impression?

describing others are whether the person is strong versus weak, and whether the person is active versus passive (Rosenberg & Olshan, 1970).

There are, however, several thousand words in the English language that can be used to describe characteristics of people. The words that you choose to characterize another person (or yourself, for that matter) actually reflect both of these dimensions: evaluative and descriptive. People seem to choose adjectives to describe others based on both these factors: what behaviors they observe in the other person (descriptive, or beliefs about their nature) and how they evaluate the person and his or her actions.

Our language contains many synonyms that describe the same behavior but contain different evaluative tones. Consider, for example, one kind of behavior, the extent to which a person is willing to part with money and possessions. If a man spends money or gives it away freely, he could be described as "gener-

2.8 NAMES PEOPLE PLAY

When we choose words to describe other people (or ourselves) we are saying more than simply what they do. We also add, through the words we choose, our own evaluation of the person or action. Social psychologist Dean Peabody (1967, 1984, 1987) has proposed sets of words that differ along two dimensions: a descriptive dimension (high versus low levels of a particular behavior) and an evaluative dimension (positive versus negative value placed on the action or person). Here are some of his word sets, with a few of our own that we have added.

BEHAVIOR:	HIGH		LOW	
POSITIVE EVALUATION	NEGATIVE EVALUATION	POSITIVE EVALUATION	NEGATIVE EVALUATION
Bold	Rash	Cautious	Timid
Uninhibited	Impulsive	Self-controlled	Inhibited
Generous	Extravagant	Thrifty	Stingy
Trusting	Gullible	Skeptical	Distrustful
Idealistic	Unrealistic	Pragmatic	Opportunistic
Confident	Conceited	Humble	Insecure
Consistent	Rigid	Flexible	Erratic
Religious	Pious	Worldly	Godless
Amorous	Lecherous	Chaste	Prudish
Meticulous	Fussy	Relaxed	Sloppy
Outgoing	Gabby	Quiet	Withdrawn

ous" (if you approve) or as "extravagant" or a "sucker" (if you do not approve). Or suppose the opposite is true. Suppose that a woman is very reluctant to part with money. If you like her you might call her "thrifty"; if not, you might term her "stingy."

This principle can be applied to almost any kind of behavior. Is a person who takes risks "courageous" or "foolhardy"? Is one who does not take many risks "careful" or "cowardly"? Hamilton and Zanna (1974) found that the adjective which a person chooses from a pair like this depends upon whether the overall evaluation of the person being described is positive or negative. Your choice might also be influenced by how you feel about the behavior itself, whether *you* like to take risks, for example. Furthermore, extremes of behavior in either direction tend to be judged negatively (Peabody, 1967, 1984, 1987). "Energetic," when taken too far, becomes "frantic." "Leisurely" in extreme becomes "lazy." Box 2.8 shows other examples of sets of words that can be used to describe people based on high versus low levels of a behavior and positive versus negative evaluations of the person.

ATTRIBUTION: EXPLAINING THE CAUSES OF BEHAVIOR

Although there are similarities in how one perceives self versus others, there can also be some interesting differences. One is that many people are more generous with themselves than with others. In explaining one's own successes and failures, there is a tendency to see the successes as being due to internal personal qualities but one's own failures as due to external factors such as bad luck, difficulty of the task, unfairness of others, or extenuating circumstances. This common perceptual tendency, called **defensive attribution,** may also be used when you explain what happens to people you care about (for example, why my child succeeded or failed). Interestingly, some people show precisely the opposite pattern. Depressed individuals in particular tend to view failures as due to personal faults and inadequacies, but see successes as undeserved gifts or accidents (Heimberg et al., 1986; Raps et al., 1982; Seligman et al., 1979). This reversed pattern of attribution may also be used to explain the successes or failures of people one does not like.

One extreme attributional style has been termed **learned helplessness** (Seligman, 1975), which is a general perception that one is unable to bring about any positive change through one's own behavior. Faced with threat or failure, an individual with a learned helplessness perspective may give up easily and stop trying. Research has pointed to a possible gender difference on this perceptual style among school children. Despite their typically superior academic achievement in elementary school, girls have been found to show greater signs of a learned helplessness pattern of attribution. Given failure feedback from adults, girls showed a stronger tendency to stop trying and (more than boys) explained their failure as due to a lack of personal ability (Dweck & Goetz, 1978). Boys, on the other hand, tended to explain their failure

Defensive Attribution
the common tendency to explain one's own successes as due to personal characteristics, but one's failures as due to factors beyond one's personal control.

Learned Helplessness
a state in which the individual makes few or no attempts to adjust, based upon the generalized belief that no response will bring about change; can be induced in animals by repeated exposure to aversive situations from which no response provides escape.

2.9 DEFENSIVE ATTRIBUTION ON THE HIGHWAY

Defensive attribution refers to people's tendency to see their own difficulties and failures as being caused by external forces, by circumstances beyond their own control. Here are some actual statements given to the police by automobile drivers attempting to explain what happened in their accidents. (Reprinted from the *Toronto Sun*, July 26, 1977)

"As I approached the intersection, a stop sign suddenly appeared in a place where no stop sign had ever appeared before. I was unable to stop in time to avoid the accident."

"The other car collided with mine without giving warning of its intentions."

"I collided with a stationary truck coming the other way."

"The guy was all over the road, I had to swerve a number of times before I hit him."

"I had been shopping for plants all day, and was on my way home. As I reached an intersection a hedge sprang up obscuring my vision. I did not see the other car."

"To avoid hitting the bumper of the car in front, I struck the pedestrian."

"My car was legally parked as it backed into the other vehicle."

"An invisible car came out of nowhere, struck my vehicle and vanished."

"The pedestrian had no idea which direction to go, so I ran him over."

"A pedestrian hit me and went under my car."

"The telephone pole was approaching fast. I was attempting to swerve out of its way when it struck my front end."

"No one was to blame for the accident but it never would have happened if the other driver had been alert."

"The indirect cause of this accident was a little guy in a small car with a big mouth."

In a conflict, each individual tends to see the other's acts as unprovoked aggression.

as being due to changeable or controllable factors and responded with increased effort. Bart (1976) has suggested that traditional gender role socialization of females in our society may encourage perceptions of learned helplessness and thereby increase the likelihood of depression in women (see Chapter 7).

Another important dimension of attribution is the perception of whether a behavior occurred in reaction to the external world or because of internal personal qualities. Which of these you believe may depend upon whether you are the *actor* (the person taking the action) or an *observer* (Jones & Nisbett, 1971). The actor tends to experience his or her own behavior as being in response to external events. An observer, on the other hand, may attribute the action to the actor's personal characteristics. An important example is what can happen in conflict situations, whether they be between individuals or between nations. Each party tends to perceive the other's actions as unprovoked aggression occurring because of the other's aggressive or cruel nature. One's own aggressive acts, on the other hand, are likely to be viewed as justifiable reactions, retribution, or self-defense in response to the provocations of the other. When both parties perceive reality in this way, of course, the result is likely to be an escalation of aggression from both sides.

■ PERCEPTION AND PSYCHOTHERAPY

Regardless of their theoretical orientation, most therapists pay considerable attention to perceptual styles and patterns as they try to intervene in helpful ways. There are several major ways in which a client's perceptions play important roles in therapy.

First of all, some of the problems that people bring to therapists *are* perceptions. Among college students, one of the most common requests brought to counselors and therapists is for help in improving self-esteem. "I want to feel better about myself. I'm sick of feeling worthless and put down." As we discussed earlier, self-concept and self-esteem are perceptions, and as such can be changed (see Chapter 6).

Another way in which perceptions play a role in therapy is the "fit" or "match" between the client's perceptual style and the style of therapy. For any given client, certain types of therapy are likely to fit well with her or his perceptual style, while others will not. In discussing perceptual styles earlier in this chapter, for example, we noted that extraverts have been found to respond more favorably to a client-centered approach emphasizing relationships (DiLoreto, 1971). Research on the treatment of alcoholism reveals important benefits from matching individuals with treatments that fit their own preferences and perceptual styles (Miller & Hester, 1986). When a therapy does not match the client's own perceptual style, resistance to the therapy and the therapist may be greater, resulting in less progress and perhaps early drop-out from treatment (Dimond, Havens, & Jones, 1978).

Finally, many therapies focus on helping clients to examine and reevaluate their own perceptions (Beck, 1976; Ellis, 1984; Watzlawick et al., 1974). Perfectionism, for example, often plagues students who return to college while continuing to maintain other roles in a family or career. The unspoken perception is that one must excel as a parent *and* as a student *and* as a worker. To be less than exceptional in any of these roles may lead the perfectionistic person to suffer low self-esteem. A possible therapeutic strategy for such a person would be to examine these assumptions, and perhaps to consider what advice one would give to another person who held such high self-expectations. This returns us to a concept introduced briefly in Chapter 1, that of basic assumptions which influence one's life.

■ BASIC ASSUMPTIONS REVISITED

As an individual develops from infancy to childhood and adolescence and on into adulthood, he or she accumulates a mass of perceptual experiences that are stored in long-term memory. New experiences are continually compared with this **apperceptive mass.** Meeting a new person, entering a new situation, or moving to a new city, the individual searches for the familiar. Is there anything stored in this apperceptive mass that would help him or her to know what to expect, how to react? Judged in relation to this accumulated mass of experience, the new situation is perceived, labeled, interpreted, and given meaning. The new information is understood in relation to the apperceptive mass of past experience.

Through life experiences, each person develops a set of *basic assumptions* about reality. Some of these are shared by almost everyone: for example, that the sun will come up again tomorrow at about the same time that it rose this morning. Other assumptions are more individual, and differ from one person to another; for example, the assumption that other people are (or are not) basically friendly and trustworthy. What you *assume*, your basic expectations about life, very much influence how you act, feel, and think. Often these assumptions are so basic that they are taken for granted, equated with reality, and not questioned unless something or someone calls to attention the need to reexamine them (Miller, 1985a).

Apperceptive Mass
the accumulated memory store of knowledge and experience, against which new information is compared.

Transactional Analysis
a theory of personality and psychotherapy proposed by Eric Berne, which views maladaptive patterns as interactive "games" played to serve individual needs.

BASIC ASSUMPTIONS AND PERSONALITY THEORIES

Many personality theories have pointed to the existence of such basic assumptions and their guiding role in how one perceives and lives in the world. **Transactional analysis,** a popular theory introduced by Eric Berne (1964) in his book *Games People Play,* is designed to help people identify their underlying "scripts," unconscious patterns of expectations that become self-fulfilling prophecies, as if the person were living out the script of a play that has already been written. Alfred Adler (1923) included a similar concept, "style of life," in his theory of personality, and Aaron Beck's cognitive theory of depression (discussed in Chapters 7 and 8) asserts that mood emanates from certain "automatic thoughts" that arise from underlying maladaptive assumptions and styles of thinking (Beck, 1976).

A personal example may help here. One woman whom we treated had grown up with a father who was emotionally distant and never expressed his love for her. "I always had the sense that somewhere inside him was a warm person, but I never got to it," she lamented. What was her reason for seeking therapy? She had suffered a long sequence of disastrous relationships with men, each one following the same pattern. She would fall in love with a man who on the surface seemed cold and distant, but who seemed to show promise of being warm and intimate with her. As time passed, she became more and more insistent in her attempts to "get to" the loving person within, and the man would withdraw more and more into a cold and distant shell. She seemed to be living out a script, choosing men like her father and trying, through them, to realize what she had never completed with her father. Transactional analysts sometimes also refer to hidden assumptions as "tapes," likening them to prerecorded messages that play over and over again until the tape is erased or a new recording is made. For this woman, the tape seemed to be something like, "Men always hold out the promise of love, but never follow through." She was only dimly aware that she had been selecting men who fit and confirmed her basic assumption.

Erik Erikson's (1959) classic theory of personality development was built around the concept of basic assumptions that guide one's life course. Erikson proposed that there are eight developmental stages through which people pass during the course of a normal lifetime. Each one poses a certain challenge, and at each stage the individual makes a crucial decision. The first stage, for example, involves a choice between basic trust versus mistrust, and Erikson believed that this choice begins in infancy. The person who decides in favor of "trust" at this point will go on to develop a deep sense of security, of being able to trust and rely on other people and the world in general, of expecting (or at least hoping for) the best. The person whose early experiences lead to the "mistrust" decision, on the other hand, develops a deep sense of uncertainty, apprehension that the world is an unsafe and risky place to be, and that one must be on guard constantly.

The choices encountered at other stages in Erikson's developmental theory are shown in Box 2.10. Where are you in this growth process, and which way did you decide at each stage you have encountered thus far? As you examine this table, however, realize that these choices are never complete, and that each person is in the process of deciding (or redeciding) *all* of these choices at any point in adult life. Be aware, also, that the stage theories, such as Erikson's, represent only one way of understanding development. In Chapter 4 we will examine some of the shortcomings of and alternatives to stage theories.

There may also be hints about basic assumptions in the favorite sayings or proverbs that you remember from growing up. Some people, for example, are taught that "All things come to those who wait," whereas others are told, "Those who hesitate are lost." The first of these reflects an assumption that it is best to be patient, to delay gratification until later; the second communicates the opposite view, that it is best to act now before the opportunity is gone. What were the favorite sayings in your home? Other ways to discover your underlying assumptions will be explained in Chapter 6 on self-esteem.

2.10   ERIKSON'S THEORY OF PERSONALITY DEVELOPMENT

Erik Erikson proposed a series of eight developmental stages, which he described as "either-or" alternatives. At each stage, an individual would move in one direction or the other. The alternatives at each stage represent opposite life views or positions. The direction taken at each stage in turn influences later developmental stages.

One way to make personal sense of Erikson's stages is to consider what kind of private self-talk might go on inside the head of a person who had moved in one direction or the other. Here are some examples of thoughts and beliefs that might occupy the inner world of a person who took one road or the other at each of Erikson's eight developmental stages. At each stage, which sounds more like what you might be saying to yourself?

oral   *Just feet*

Stage 1:   TRUST versus MISTRUST (Infancy)
           TRUST: The world is safe. I can relax. People will help meet my needs and will help me when I am in pain.
           MISTRUST: The world is dangerous. I must keep my eyes open all the time. People are trying to hurt me, cheat me, take advantage of me.

anal

Stage 2:   AUTONOMY versus SHAME, DOUBT (Early Childhood)
           AUTONOMY: I have a sense of power over my own body. I can handle myself and do things for myself. I can make choices.
           SHAME, DOUBT: I can't take care myself. I am helpless. Other people have to make my decisions and do things for me. I can't stand on my own.

Stage 3:   INITIATIVE versus GUILT (Active Play Age)
           INITIATIVE: I can control myself. I am energetic, and I can go out and get things. I can question the rules openly.
           GUILT: I do bad things and I can't control myself. People are mean and unfair to me, but I'll get even.

Stage 4:   INDUSTRY versus INFERIORITY (School Age)
           INDUSTRY: I can do good work. I can make plans and carry them through. I'm proud of my work. Give me something new to try!
           INFERIORITY: What I produce has no value. People don't care about my work. I'm no good. I can't live up to what people expect of me. I don't want to try.

Stage 5:   IDENTITY versus ROLE DIFFUSION (Adolescence)
           IDENTITY: I am a unique individual, and I know who I am. I have a purpose. It's O.K. that I am different from other people.
           ROLE DIFFUSION: I don't know who I am. I act like whoever I'm with. I don't know what I want, so I'll leave all the possibilities open. I try to be like the people around me.

Stage 6:   INTIMACY, SOLIDARITY versus ISOLATION (Young Adulthood)
INTIMACY, SOLIDARITY: I love you for who you are. You and I are partners
sexually, emotionally, intellectually. I want to share myself with you. I am willing
to make reasonable demands of you, and for you to make reasonable demands
of me.
ISOLATION: You just want to use me. I'm not getting close to you! It's not worth
the risk. Either you guarantee you're completely mine, or forget it.

Stage 7:   GENERATIVITY versus SELF-ABSORPTION, STAGNATION (Adulthood)
GENERATIVITY: You can depend on me. I'm responsible. I can take care of
others. I'm ready to try new things, and laugh at my mistakes. I can be a good
parent.
SELF-ABSORPTION, STAGNATION: I'm not changing for anybody. Don't tell me
about your problems—I've got plenty of my own. I know what's right, and if you
disagree you're wrong. I don't need to try anything new.

Stage 8:   INTEGRITY versus DESPAIR (Maturity)
INTEGRITY: I'm proud of how I've lived my life. No matter how old or sick I may
get, I want to stay involved and useful. Whatever comes, I'll be O.K. I can face
dying.
DESPAIR: Life is meaningless, a bad joke. What's there to live for? It's a lot of
pain and misery with no point, then you die. Nobody cares.

Personality theorists have pointed to yet another interesting way of exploring your own basic assumptions: through early memories. A person's earliest
recollections, it has been suggested, are not accidental or random (Adler, 1937).
People remember from childhood those events that support their own *present*
life view. Freud (1922) believed that people may even manufacture memories of
things that never actually happened. Thus your earliest memories may hold
clues to your own "tapes" or "scripts."

Even recent memories can reflect a person's basic assumptions about life.
Earlier in this chapter (Box 2.1) we presented the example of a student injured
in a volleyball game who perceived that he had been cruelly neglected in his
suffering by the other players. Upon exploration in counseling, it became
apparent that the student had long held a basic assumption that people would
abandon, reject, and abuse him when he needed help. It seemed to him, then,
that there was no point in letting people know that he needed or wanted help.
He consistently perceived others as unsympathetic and uncaring toward him.
As in the volleyball game, then, he would quietly suffer without asking for help,
while bitterly resenting the apparent insensitivity of others toward him. His
basic assumption, that everyone would abandon him, colored his daily perceptions and experiences. These, in turn, led him to behave in ways that made
his gloomy prophecy come true.

SELF-FULFILLING PROPHECIES

There is no escaping from your own apperceptive mass, because you *must* use
your own past experiences in understanding the present. Otherwise you

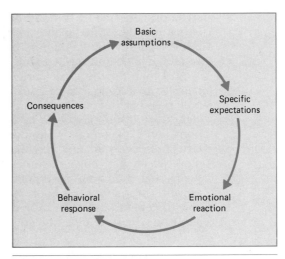

FIGURE 2-2 PROPHECY
THE CYCLE OF SELF-FULFILLING

would be as helpless as the newborn infant facing the "booming, buzzing confusion" of an unorganized world.

Yet is it not necessary to be the victim or captive of your current assumptions. A theme that you will encounter again and again in this book is that to a remarkable extent *you can decide* how to view the world, how you will react, how you will feel. Change is not always easy, of course, but it is always occurring. As you read this page, you are changing: growing a minute older, adding a new concept to your apperceptive mass, perhaps recalling memories or reorganizing your basic assumptions, if ever so slightly.

Being stuck is the opposite of change. How do people get into a rut in their lives? One way is through developing self-perpetuating cycles, basic assumptions that, unquestioned, make themselves come true. As an example, consider Erikson's first choice, that of trust versus mistrust. A basic *assumption* of trust leads to specific *expectations* of what will happen in a certain situation: that people will probably be supportive, helpful, and kind. This in turn leads to *emotional* comfort, and to *behavior* that tends to be relaxed, open, trusting. Seeing such behavior, other people tend to react in supportive, helpful, and kind ways, and this *consequence* serves to strengthen the basic assumption itself. This self-perpetuating cycle is shown in the diagram in Figure 2-2.

The same process can operate to perpetuate a basic assumption of mistrust. Such an assumption leads to specific expectations that people will be cruel and selfish, and will take advantage of any vulnerability shown. This, of course, leaves one feeling anxious, apprehensive, and resentful toward others, and tends toward behavior that is guarded, defensive, and tense. One experiment, for example (Yarkin, Harvey, & Bloxom, 1981), found that people who were given a negative expectation about an individual they were about to meet maintained significantly less eye contact when subsequently talking with this person, whereas those given a positive expectation kept longer eye contact. Seeing apprehensive behavior, other people react in similar fashion, and indeed *look* untrustworthy. Once again the prophecy fulfills itself.

Notice that this cycle works in both directions. Both negative and positive assumptions can be perpetuated by this process. This is, in a way, a homeostatic process (see Chapter 1) that is part of adjustment, and it can maintain either adaptive or maladaptive patterns. Thus the cycle itself is not negative; it is just a part of human nature. Being aware of this process, however, may help you to evaluate how it is working in your own life, and to make positive change.

And that, for the most part, is what the chapters ahead are about: how people can and do change. Current research suggests that such change is not only possible, but can begin at almost any point in the cycle (Kanfer & Goldstein, 1986). One may begin by changing the external environment, assumptions and expectations (cognition), emotional or physiological response patterns (affect), or actions and their consequences (behavior). Sometimes it is more effective or efficient to begin at a particular point in the cycle, but it seems that change at any point can begin to alter other elements of the cycle as well. Throughout this book we will be examining how such change occurs, first in general and then in specific adjustment areas, drawing on modern research where it helps to clarify the processes of change.

■ SUMMARY

One's contact with the external world begins with sensation. Sensory information is in turn interpreted through processes of perception, which is influenced in addition by background and residual stimuli, attention, past experience, and motivational factors. Individuals differ in their characteristic perceptual styles along dimensions such as internal versus external locus of control, introversion versus extraversion, augmentation versus reduction, and sensing versus intuition. One goal of personality testing is to understand the individual's own perceptual style. Just as people perceive the physical world, they also perceive themselves and each other. Self-perception and the perception of others combine processes of description and evaluation. Attribution, a social perception process, involves explaining the causes of one's own behavior and the actions of others. Perceptions and beliefs are a common topic in psychotherapy. Basic assumptions, sometimes held without conscious awareness, can shape a person's perceptions and behavior. Such assumptions can become self-fulfilling prophecies when a person acts in a way that leads to results that confirm the basic assumption.

■ QUESTIONS FOR THOUGHT

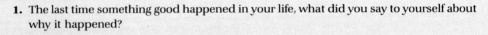

1. The last time something good happened in your life, what did you say to yourself about why it happened?

2. The last time something bad happened in your life, what did you say to yourself about why it happened?

3. When you meet a new person, what factors most shape your first impression?

4. In what areas of your life do you feel helpless, as if there were nothing you could do to improve the situation?

5. When you feel hopeless about some aspect of your life, what helps you to regain hope?

6. In what areas of your life are you a perfectionist? When (if at all) does perfectionism help or hinder your personal effectiveness and adjustment?

7. What are the basic assumptions by which you live? What did you learn as a child about
       Doing better than others
       Making mistakes
       Getting along with people
       Being independent
       Expressing your feelings
       Questioning authority
       Taking risks
       Having fun?

8. What "sayings" do you remember from your growing-up years, that point to basic assumptions?

9. Can you think of an example of a self-fulfilling prophecy in your own life?

chapter three

There were tears and cheers and chants and whistles . . . *kvelling*, that wonderful Yiddish word for emotion so deeply felt that it seems to come out of your pores.
—Geraldine A. Ferraro in *Ferraro: My Story*

Understanding Your Emotions

OUTLINE

*T*he complex phenomena that are called "emotions" play a key role in adjustment. The physiological components of emotions like fear and anger serve important survival functions for all mammals, signaling a need for action and preparing the body to cope with an emergency situation. Profound changes occur in the body when a person is startled. Consider your own reaction to hearing a sudden loud noise, or to encountering a person unexpectedly in a dark place when you thought you were alone. The emotional surge prepares the body to deal with the unexpected.

Emotions play a role in virtually every major area of adjustment. There are significant emotional components to self-esteem, motivation, intimate relationships, work and school adjustment, parenting, and the personal search for meaning. Indeed, a term that people sometimes use to describe personal adjustment difficulties is "emotional problems." Emotion and adjustment are inseparable.

Yet what *is* **emotion?** Though they are the subject of countless poems, songs, books, and talk shows, emotions remain a mysterious force for many people. In this chapter, we hope to help you understand emotions from a psychological perspective.

■ FEELING AND THINKING

Within the English language, the word "feeling" is used to describe many different experiences (von Franz & Hillman, 1979). It can be used to refer to *tactile* (touch) sensations ("Your shirt feels soft") or to **kinesthesis,** one's muscle sensations ("I can feel the tension in my arms"). It is used to describe *intuitions* ("I just had a feeling that something good was going to happen to me that day") and *imagination* ("As the poet read her work, I closed my eyes and I could feel the wind blowing"). People sometimes use the word "feel" when they really mean "think" or "believe," and this is given away when the word "feel" is followed by the word "that" ("Well, I feel that this company should take a more aggressive stance"). Often the meaning here is: "I believe this, and so should you."

All of these are ways in which people use the verb "to feel," but our central concern in this chapter is with still another meaning, perhaps the most common one. For what people most often mean when they say that they feel something, is that they are experiencing emotions. Here the verb "feel" is not followed by "that" but instead by one of the hundreds of adjectives that refer to particular emotions. If a person says, "I feel that . . . ," then he or she is not referring directly to an emotion, but instead is saying "I believe that . . ." or "I think that . . .". Feeling (emotion) statements are simply, "I feel _____ ." Of course one could be sneaky about it and simply drop the word "that": "I feel we are doing the right thing." Still a "that" fits logically in the sentence after the word "feel," and thus indicates a belief rather than an emotion. With emotion statements, the word "that" does not fit. It makes little sense to say, "I feel (that) angry."

Interestingly, although "think" is sometimes considered to be the opposite of "feel," people likewise use "think" to refer to many different experiences, some of which overlap with uses of "feel." It can be used to refer to a logical, reasoning process ("I am thinking it through"), or to less systematic consideration ("I'll think it over"). It can refer to a belief or opinion ("I think that it is wrong to steal"), or to imagination or memory ("I am thinking of the time when we spent the summer on Hudson Bay"). It can also refer to an intuition or

Emotion ✗
a complex state involving cognitive, physiological, and behavioral components, subjectively experienced as feelings.

Kinesthesis
sensations from the muscles and joints, which provide information about the position of one's body and limbs.

prediction ("I think you're going to like her") and even, indirectly, to an emotion ("I am thinking of you," or, "My thoughts are with you"). No wonder people become confused as to what is a thought and what is a feeling!

■ EMOTIONS

How many emotions are there? There is no general agreement. Four commonly recognized basic emotions are (1) fear or anxiety, (2) anger, (3) sadness, and (4) love or joy. There are specific chapters on each of these emotions later in this book.

Yet there are hundreds of emotion words in the English language, and there have been various attempts to classify them. Plutchik (1980) suggested that emotions could be classified much as colors are. Three colors are recognized as "primary" (red, yellow, and blue), while other colors represent mixtures of the primary colors (red + yellow = orange). Colors also differ in their intensity or brightness. "Scarlet" is a very bright, intense red, whereas "brick red" is darker and duller.

Are there "primary" emotions? To answer this question, Plutchik considered a broad range of evidence: animal and human behavior, the physiology of the nervous system, and the language that humans use to describe emotions. He concluded that there are eight primary emotions, each of which can vary in

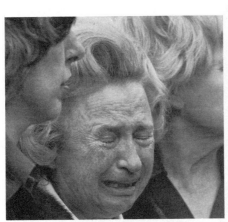

What are the emotions being expressed here?

intensity, and which can be intermixed. These eight primary emotions are shown on the wheel in Figure 3-1. Emotions that are directly across from each other on the wheel (e.g., joy and sadness) are *opposite* emotions. Mixed together, opposite emotions tend to cancel or inhibit each other, just as opposite colors (e.g., green and red) when mixed will neutralize into gray. Emotions that lie *next* to each other on Plutchik's wheel (e.g., anger and disgust), on the other hand, are most similar and blend easily.

One way in which emotion words differ is in *intensity*. There are, for example, a large number of words to describe fear experiences differing in degree: some are mild (uneasy, nervous), some are moderate (afraid, frightened), and some are extreme (terrified, panicked). Similar shades of intensity can be found in words describing anger (annoyed, angry, enraged), sadness (disappointed, blue, dejected), or joy (pleased, happy, overjoyed). Using the color analogy, these differences represent the brightness or intensity of the emotion.

A second way in which emotion words differ, according to Plutchik, is in their *mixture* of the primary emotions. Just as certain colors are very pure or "saturated" (in a box of 128 crayons, those marked simply "red" or "yellow"), it is possible to experience a pure primary emotion such as fear or joy. More often, however, colors are mixed or combined, and particular mixtures or blends are given special names like "mauve" or "magenta." Similarly, primary emotions can be mixed. The open circle at the center of Figure 3-1, marked "C," represents the *conflict* that occurs when different emotions are experienced together. Emotions that are immediately adjacent on the wheel may blend very easily: (Joy + Acceptance = Love; Surprise + Sadness = Disap-

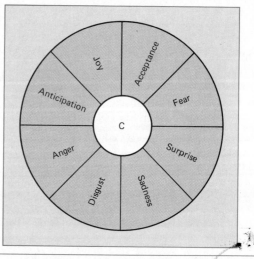

FIGURE 3-1 THE EMOTION SOLID

This wheel diagram depicts Plutchik's eight primary emotions. Those directly across on the wheel are opposite emotions which clash with each other. Each of the eight primary emotions can vary in intensity. The words on this wheel represent medium emotional intensity levels. Anger, for example, could be more intense (rage) or less intense (annoyance). Intensity, thus, forms a third dimension, and in this perspective, the wheel shown here is a cross-sectional cut of Plutchik's "emotion solid," which is shaped like a cylinder. The "C" at the center of the wheel represents the conflict which results when two or more of the primary emotions are mixed together. This conflict is greatest when the intermixed emotions are opposites, lying directly across from each other on the wheel.

3.1 EMOTIONS FROM A TO Z

There are hundreds of words in the English language to describe emotions, how a person feels. Here are a few:

Angry	Irritated	Quiet	Yielding
Bored	Joyful	Resentful	Zestful
Cheerful	Keyed up	Sorrowful	
Depressed	Lonely	Terrified	
Elated	Morose	Uneasy	
Frightened	Nervous	Vulnerable	
Grumpy	Overjoyed	Worried	
Happy	Panicked	Xcited	

pointment; Disgust + Anger = Hate). Emotions more distant from each other on the wheel can also blend, but may evoke greater conflict: (Joy + Fear = Guilt; Anticipation + Fear = Anxiety).

A third way in which emotion words may differ is in the *persistence* they communicate, the sense of how long the emotion is likely to last. Some words imply emotions that are relatively brief (amused, surprised), whereas others imply more enduring emotional experiences (love, depression, resentment). Spielberger (1966b) has distinguished between "state" and "trait" emotions. **State anxiety,** for example, is a momentary and temporary level of anxiousness. **Trait anxiety,** on the other hand, refers to a characteristic level of anxiety, one that persists over time and across various situations. Both kinds of emotions are part of normal human experience, but it is the latter, the enduring patterns of emotion, that tend to present the greater problems and challenges of life.

WHAT DO EMOTIONS MEAN?

Anxiety
emotional fearfulness in anticipation or dread of future events, out of proportion to the actual danger.

State Anxiety
a person's level of anxiety in a particular situation.

Trait Anxiety
a person's characteristic level of anxiety which persists across a wide range of situations.

The physiological systems that are linked to the experiences we call "emotions" are found in the older, most primitive areas of the brain. Similar systems are found in most animals, including all mammals. What we experience as negative emotions are ancient warning and emergency systems that are undoubtedly helpful to survival. The emotions, in this sense, have always been *signal* systems, preparing the individual to take particular kinds of action. One way to understand emotions, then, is to view them as information, as signals of a need for change. Unpleasant emotional experiences such as loneliness, anger, and fear may be messages, indications that it is time for a change of some kind. Positive emotions, too, can call one to change. A feeling of love, for example, may urge one to begin spending more time with the loved person, perhaps to marry.

If a therapist focuses naively on reducing symptoms such as negative emotions, the result is likely to be that the problem will only crop up somewhere else. In effect, if you just reduce symptoms, the client will develop a new set of problems. Unconscious drives have an ingenious way of finding new outlets.

Some say that the research does not support "symptom substitution," and I agree in part. Yet at the very least there *is* one phenomenon that is clear. Very often, the symptom that one was treating comes back! A weakness of many behavioral studies, in fact, is that they haven't followed clients long enough to see the problems return.

I'd like to approach this from a more positive viewpoint, since I'm not sure that the symptom substitution debate ever made sense in the first place. Many of us old-fashioned (some of us just plain old!) psychodynamic therapists have found that when clients achieve some understanding (insight) of the *reasons* for their problems, then symptom reduction occurs rather easily. Some of us even use behavioral symptom reduction techniques at this point. After all, clients need skills to cope with their new insights. But symptom reduction should never be started until some insight has been obtained. It seems to me that behavior therapists are now recognizing this, with their newer emphasis on "cognitive behavior therapy." This certainly sounds to me like an attempt to sneak "insight" in the back door, discovering what psychodynamic therapists have known all along! —JMR

Research that has looked for evidence of symptom substitution thus far has not provided convincing evidence that this is a universal or even common phenomenon in therapy. In studying people whom we've treated for problem drinking, for example, we have found that other life problems tend to *improve* rather than get worse after a "symptom-focused" treatment (Miller, Hedrick, & Taylor, 1983). The very use of the term "symptom" implies some underlying entity that needs to be treated, and perhaps it is better just to talk about problems instead of symptoms.

Now it certainly is true that problems, once treated, often return. Behavioral research in the 1980s took this into account by including longer periods of follow-up. However, this is at least equally true following psychodynamic insight-oriented treatment. "Anna O," the famous case used by Freud as a basis for developing psychoanalysis, continued to suffer the same and worse problems for many years after her analysis (Ellenberger, 1972). There is no persuasive evidence that insight therapies produce more complete or longer-lasting results than would a simpler problem-focused approach, though they may take longer and thus cost more. Neither is there good evidence that insight is necessary before behavior change can occur. Hundreds of outcome studies with behavioral approaches have shown clear (and even lasting) change without an emphasis on insight.

As for the cognitive therapies, these were developed by people (e.g., Beck, Ellis) who were first trained in and then abandoned an insight approach to therapy. These, too, are problem-focused approaches, and are effective in directly relieving human suffering. If it is possible to bring about reasonably rapid and lasting relief from the very problems that bring clients to us, why not at least *start* from that possibility instead of waiting for some kind of insight to occur? Why not relieve suffering first, and then (if it still matters) seek to understand why it occurred? —WRM

INTEGRATION

If "symptom substitution" is understood as a person's replacing one maladaptive way of coping with another, then certainly this occurs at least some of the time. Therapy is, in fact, an attempt to replace one (maladaptive) style of coping with another (more adaptive) one. An important part of therapy, then, is to consider what new coping style the client will use, rather than leaving this to chance. Both arguments seem to recognize this. Change is not only *from* but also *to*. In this sense, therapy includes the planning of *response substitution* (Cahoon, 1968; Kazdin, 1982). If, for example, an individual has relied upon alcohol or another drug to cope with anxiety, simply removing the drug does not provide the person with a new way of coping. Regardless of the theoretical approach, competent therapy includes a consideration of this aspect of change: What is the new pattern toward which the person is changing?

This message value of emotions is recognized by many different psychological viewpoints. An existential psychologist would agree that there is meaning in what a person is feeling, and that the person should listen and attend to emotional experiences for the meaning they contain. The existentialist would even reject the idea that a therapist should work to reduce negative emotions such as anxiety or depression, because this fails to acknowledge the validity of the feeling and to understand its meaning.

A related idea is found in psychodynamic writings that view emotions as symptoms of underlying personality patterns. In this perspective, it is fruitless to try to change surface emotions without restructuring the personality that gives rise to them. A more recent "cognitive" perspective (which will be discussed more fully in Chapter 6) views chronic (trait) negative emotions as the product of particular styles of thinking, perceiving, or information processing. The goal in **cognitive therapy,** then, is to alter the underlying maladaptive thought patterns that are causing the emotional discomfort. What the psychodynamic and cognitive theorists have in common is that both attribute emotional problems to **intrapsychic** factors, enduring patterns within the person that give rise to the negative emotions.

Yet another view is that emotions occur in reaction to events occurring in the environment. This behavioral view is represented by Skinner (1961), who has suggested that experienced emotions are clues to the types of learning experiences which are occurring in the person's life. Positive reinforcement yields pleasant emotions such as joy and happiness. Punishment may yield emotions of sadness, or (especially in the case of negative punishment) anger and resentment. Thus a behavior therapist might use a person's emotions as clues, reflecting the patterns of reinforcement and punishment that are currently influencing the individual.

All these views contain elements of truth. We believe that it is misleading to look *only* inside the person or *only* to the outside world for the causes of emotions. Both internal and external events are important in understanding emotion. Certainly enduring perceptual styles (Chapter 2) can result in characteristic emotional tones (and problems), and therapies that modify underlying cognitive style have proven quite effective in treating emotional problems (e.g., Beck, 1976). Mood is also responsive to external events (Paykel, 1982). Emotions arise from an interaction of the individual with the environment.

Cognitive Therapy
a system of treatment designed to improve adjustment by altering an individual's maladaptive thoughts and beliefs.

Intrapsychic
hypothesized motivational events occurring within the person, not subject to direct observation.

Positive reinforcement typically yields positive emotions.

■ HOW EMOTIONS ARISE: AN INTERACTIVE SYSTEM

These interactions between person and environment can be understood as a five-step process, a process that can be used in understanding (and changing) a wide variety of human experiences, including emotions. This interactive model incorporates the stimulus-response elements of behavioral psychology, cognitive-perceptual processes within the individual, related physiological events within the nervous system, and environmental aspects that are relevant to the person. To help you remember the five elements, we offer a **mnemonic,** an aid in recalling: STORC. The five letters of **STORC** represent the five elements of this system. Where do emotions come from? (Are you ready for this?) The STORC brings them!

In presenting this five-step model, we are indicating that an emotion is not a single isolated event, but rather a sequence of events, a process. One must look at the whole sequence to understand what is happening. To look only at one part of the process is to fail to comprehend the whole picture. This is a bit more complicated than thinking about emotions as isolated events, but then people *are* complicated. And on the bright side, this means that there are at least five different possible places to begin when you are caught in a cycle of negative emotion and want to get out of it. Change can begin at any point along the way. As you read the following explanation, think of a negative emotional experience you have had, and try out the STORC model for yourself.

S—STIMULI (OR THE SITUATION)

We begin the chain of events with an examination of situational or stimulus (S) elements. People often tend to think of their own emotions as caused by events in the external world. ("That really made me angry." "You upset me.") In part this is true. Emotions can indeed be quite influenced by the environment.

A few kinds of situational events are enough to evoke emotions in almost anyone; they have very predictable emotional effects. In Chapter 8 we will discuss "stressors," stimuli that have a high probability of producing stress responses in people. Stressors include stimuli like loud noise, crowding, and physical pain. In his early experiments with animals, Pavlov (1927) demonstrated the stressfulness of another kind of situation: one in which a choice

Mnemonic
a strategy designed to help one remember specific information.

STORC
a method used within this text to analyze emotional and adjustment processes; the acronym stands for stimuli, thoughts, organic events, responses, and consequences.

People tend to think of their own emotions as caused by events in the external world.

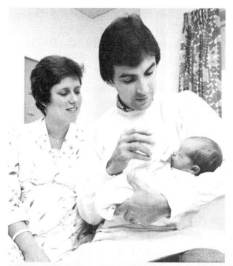

Some situational events are enough to evoke emotions in almost anyone.

must be made between two unclear alternatives. For example, dogs were required to choose between two geometric shapes such as a circle and an oval, and choosing the correct one (the circle) would prevent a painful electric shock. As the two shapes became more and more similar (more difficult to discriminate), the animals began to show clear signs of emotional distress, which Pavlov termed **experimental neurosis.** People, too, tend to show distress if they are forced to make choices when the rules are unclear, or when both choices are likely to be painful. (Have *you* ever felt "damned if you do and damned if you don't"?). Some theorists (e.g., Bateson et al., 1956) have suggested that a long history of such impossible choices ("double-binds") may literally drive a person crazy.

Other kinds of situations frequently lead to sadness or depression (see Chapter 7). Significant losses have long been recognized as causes of depression (Paykel, 1982). Social isolation can likewise lead toward depression. Seligman (1975) has published research indicating that a long series of certain kinds of failures, of experiences in which nothing one does seems to make any difference, can lead to learned helplessness and depression. The individual simply gives up trying and withdraws into a depressed state.

T—THOUGHT PATTERNS

A second element in the chain of emotion is *thinking.* As we indicated in Chapter 2, stimuli are not mere sensations. Rather they are *perceived.* They are interpreted and given meaning. People react not to "the real world" but to their own interpretations of the real world. This fact has been used as the basis for a large number of comic plays and films, in which a foreigner or alien who is not familiar with everyday objects interprets them in unusual ways, yielding amusing reactions.

Psychologist Albert Ellis (1973) has gone so far as to say that *nothing* in this world is inherently upsetting—nothing automatically makes you sad or angry or distressed. Such reactions come only from your interpretations of the world around you. We find this view a bit extreme, in that there are a number of stimuli (such as physical pain, hearing a sudden blast of noise, or witnessing atrocities) that have at least a very high probability of evoking negative emotions in most people. Nevertheless there is some truth in Ellis's assertion: very often people are angry or upset because of how they are thinking about and interpreting a situation.

Early research on learned helplessness led to a more sophisticated understanding of the importance of people's **explanatory styles** (Abramson, Seligman, & Teasdale, 1978). Evidence suggests that a generally pessimistic thought style can have adverse effects on physical health, achievement, mood, and real-life consequences. One team of researchers analyzed the explanatory styles of presidential candidates during their acceptance speeches following nomination at national party conventions from 1948 through 1984. The more pessimistic candidate lost in nine of the ten elections analyzed (Zullow et al., 1988). Within our STORC framework, it is clear that the T (thought) component significantly influences all subsequent links in the chain: organic events (O), responses (R), and consequences (C).

An interesting experimental example of the importance of thought processes comes from research on **perceived control.** Both animals and people show greater distress when exposed to stressors they cannot control and are less distressed when they are in the same "stressful" situation but have a means (or at least an illusion) of control. Not having control makes stress even more stressful. Given a choice, laboratory animals choose a stronger shock that

Experimental Neurosis
a highly emotional state involving repetitive, avoidant, and maladaptive behaviors; can be produced in animals by punishment for incorrect responding to problems which are increasingly difficult or impossible to solve; first demonstrated by Ivan Pavlov.

Explanatory Style
a characteristic style (e.g., optimism versus pessimism) of perceiving the causes of behaviors and events, which remains consistent across a wide range of situations.

Perceived Control
the belief that one has significant control or influence within a particular situation.

is predictable rather than a weaker one that is unpredictable (Miller & Balaz, 1981). Predictability is at least a minor kind of control. Or consider the following classic experiment (Glass, Singer, & Friedman, 1969). College students were placed in a room and given difficult puzzles to solve. Periodically a set of speakers in the room released a loud blast of noise. Half the subjects were given a button and told that if the noise became unbearable they could push it, ending the experiment. The other half, chosen at random, received no button. Even though no one ever pushed the panic button, those subjects who had a button reported being less stressed by the noise and showed significantly better performance on the puzzles, even though all received the same puzzles and the same amount of noise. The perception of control made the difference. (Remember that it was not necessary in this case that the button actually *work*, since no one ever tried it. It was the subjects' *belief* that they had control that made the difference.)

Here is another example of the same phenomenon (Geer, Davison, & Gatchel, 1970). Subjects were told they were participating in a reaction time experiment. They were seated in front of a panel and told that as soon as a light came on, they should press a switch in front of them. They also received electric shocks. One group was told that if they reacted fast enough, they could reduce the intensity of the next shock by one half. The other group was not told this. In reality, both groups received exactly the same shocks, and neither group had any control over the shocks at all. Yet the group *told* that they could control shock intensity by reacting more quickly, perceived the shocks to be less painful and were less distressed by them.

The interpretation of events can also influence which emotion a person experiences. In a famous experiment, Schachter and Singer (1962) found that they could influence the emotion a person would feel by manipulating two factors: physical arousal and context. Being told they were helping to test a strong vitamin, some subjects received, without their knowledge, a harmless dose of the drug **adrenalin,** which produces symptoms of general emotional arousal (rapid heartbeat, sweating, etc.). Others received no drug at all. Then Schachter and Singer exposed subjects to different situations. Some were placed in a room with another "subject" (not really a subject but a part of the experiment) who behaved in an angry and irritated manner. Others were placed with a partner who behaved in a silly, lighthearted manner. Did the subjects themselves experience emotions? Schachter reported that those who received the arousing drug reported stronger emotions, but the particular emotion they reported was determined by the situation in which they were placed. Those in the "angry" room interpreted their arousal as being anger, while those in the "happy" room interpreted their arousal as euphoria. Again it appears that how one feels can depend upon how one interprets or understands what is happening. [Note: Since the time of this study, research with human subjects has become much more carefully controlled. All psychological studies are first reviewed by a human research review committee to ensure compliance with ethical and safety standards.]

Thus far we have been discussing temporary emotional states, but perceptual styles can have more lasting effects on a person's emotional life. A commonly used example is the **Type A personality** (Friedman & Rosenman, 1974). Type A people tend to view the world in competitive ways. They are impatient, time-pressured, achievement-oriented individuals who are more likely to see the world in black-and-white terms. This style of perceiving and thinking has been associated with various chronic stress patterns, including a much higher risk of cardiovascular disease and early heart attack. As we will discuss in Chapters 6 and 7, certain ways of thinking also predispose a person to depression and low self-esteem. It makes a difference what you believe, and how you think about the world!

Adrenalin
a hormone released during emotional states, which prepares the body for emergency responding; also called epinephrine.

Type A Personality
a characteristic set of traits that persist across a wide variety of situations, including a pervasive sense of time urgency, competitiveness, impatience, hostility, and a need for power and control; associated with increased risk of cardiovascular disease.

O—ORGANIC PATTERNS

All emotions are organic events, in that physiological changes in the brain and in other parts of the nervous system are necessary for us to experience *anything*. Feelings, sensations, thoughts, and actions all involve **electrochemical** activity in the nervous system.

Emotions are closely linked to some of the most primitive portions of the brain, and in particular to a circle of structures known as the **limbic system.** The important structures of the limbic system are shown in the sketch of the brain in Figure 3-2. Emotions are related in important ways to behaviors such as aggression and sexual responses, that promote survival of a species.

At the most general level, emotional responding involves arousal of the individual. This arousal can take various forms, and generally serves the function of preparing the individual for self-protection, often described as "fight or flight." The **autonomic** portion of the nervous system, so named because its actions are largely automatic, serves this function of controlling arousal. The autonomic nervous system is divided into two parts, the sympathetic and the parasympathetic, which serve largely opposite functions.

The **sympathetic nervous system** prepares the individual for fight or flight by bringing about a state of emergency in the body. Table 3-1 describes some of the bodily changes that occur when the sympathetic system is activated. The sympathetic system tends to respond as a whole, and is activated by a limbic brain structure known as the **hypothalamus.** Thus the kinds of changes described in Table 3-1 often occur together. A fearful or anxious individual may experience sweating, rapid heart rate, rapid breathing, and a dry mouth.

The **parasympathetic** portion of the autonomic nervous system, by contrast, works less as a whole system, and activates body changes that tend to be associated with states of calm and well-being. Respiration and heart rates decrease, saliva flows in the mouth, digestion is promoted, and muscles relax. Different emotional experiences involve various mixtures of sympathetic and parasympathetic activity.

The autonomic nervous system, centered in the base of the brain and the spinal cord, is controlled by messages from many areas of the brain. Individ-

Electrochemical
the process by which information is transmitted through the nervous system.

Limbic System
a set of structures within the brain that regulates emotion and motivation.

Autonomic Nervous System
a portion of the brain and spinal cord that operates automatically, regulating life-support functions and organ systems; divided into two parts: the sympathetic and the parasympathetic.

Sympathetic Nervous System
a portion of the autonomic nervous system that activates the individual for emergency readiness.

Parasympathetic Nervous System
a portion of the autonomic nervous system that regulates normal, nonemergency functioning of the body's organs and life-support systems.

Hypothalamus
a structure deep in the center of the brain involved in the regulation of hunger, thirst, emotions, and temperature.

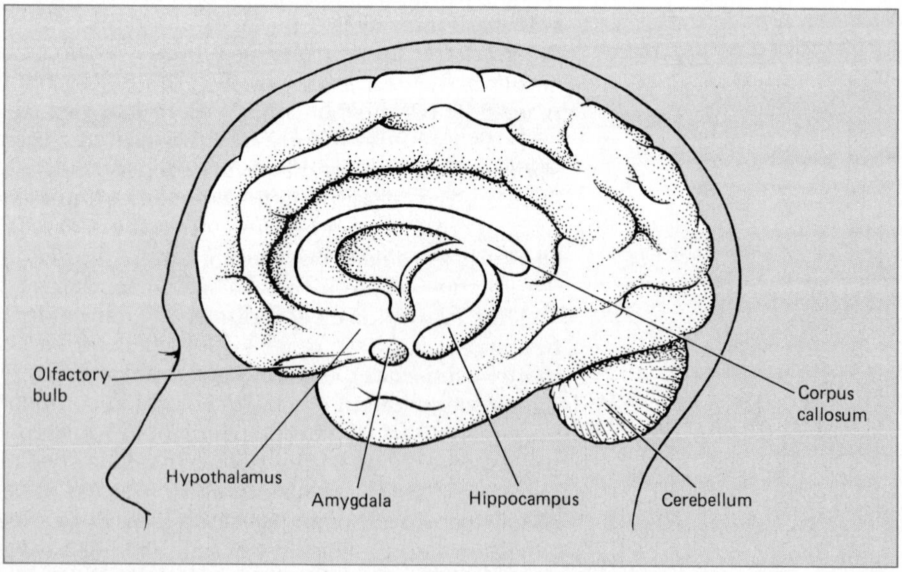

FIGURE 3-2 IMPORTANT STRUCTURES OF THE LIMBIC SYSTEM.

TABLE 3-1
THE AUTONOMIC
NERVOUS SYSTEM

The autonomic nervous system is divided into two parts, the sympathetic and the parasympathetic, which have mostly opposite effects on the body.		
	Effects of Activation in the Sympathetic *Nervous System*	*Effects of Activation in the* Parasympathetic *Nervous System*
Pupils (eye)	Dilated (opened)	Constricted (closed)
Saliva flow	Inhibited (dry mouth)	Stimulated
Heartbeat	Accelerated	Decelerated
Windpipes to lungs	Dilated	Constricted
Digestion	Inhibited	Stimulated
Bladder	Inhibits urination	Promotes urination

uals who suffer injuries to the brain, for example, often show major changes in their emotional experience. Well over a century ago, Harlow (1868) described the case of a well-liked railroad foreman named Phineas Gage, who underwent a major personality change following an explosion in which an iron bar passed through his skull. The most notable changes were that this previously gentle and serious man became irritable, hostile, and profane.

Damasio and Van Hoesen (1983) described a woman who sustained and then recovered from a severe stroke that damaged areas of the brain known to be involved in emotion and speech. During the early months of recovery, the woman showed no distress regarding her inability to speak. Later, when brain functions had recovered considerably, she was able to recall feeling complete indifference to a disability that would be extremely frustrating for most people. Even after recovery, she continued to show a tranquil and carefree nature that had not been characteristic of her before her stroke.

Another demonstration of the importance of the brain in emotion is found in research in which the brain is stimulated electrically. When a very small and brief electrical current is delivered to certain portions of the brain, particularly within the limbic system, both animals and humans show emotional responses. A rage response can be produced in a cat, for example, by sending tiny electrical charges to crucial brain areas. Similar studies have been done with the effects of electrical brain stimulation in humans. Usually this has been done with patients who have had to undergo various types of brain surgery to correct medical problems. Brain stimulation in such patients has resulted in various types of emotional responses, ranging from the recall of clear and emotionally laden memories to the experience of what are called "cold" emotions: physical sensations that are very similar to what one would feel during an emotional experience, but that feel unrealistic because they do not occur in response to an external event.

Such "cold" emotions can also be created by injecting a person with adrenalin, the hormone that is released during emotional and emergency situations. If the individual is aware of having been given this drug, the physical arousal is experienced as *like* emotion, but not *as* real emotion. A number of studies, however, indicate that when a person receives adrenalin without realizing its effects (as in the Schachter and Singer study discussed earlier in this chapter), the resulting arousal may be perceived as true emotion. This suggests that the experience of emotion requires several components: physical arousal (which is remarkably similar across a broad range of emotions) and a situation that is

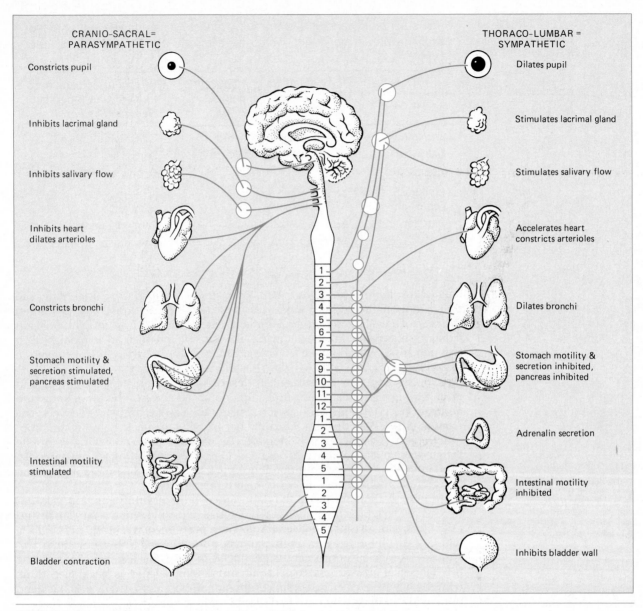

CRANIO-SACRAL=
PARASYMPATHETIC

Constricts pupil

Inhibits lacrimal gland

Inhibits salivary flow

Inhibits heart
dilates arterioles

Constricts bronchi

Stomach motility &
secretion stimulated,
pancreas stimulated

Intestinal motility
stimulated

Bladder contraction

THORACO-LUMBAR =
SYMPATHETIC

Dilates pupil

Stimulates lacrimal gland

Stimulates salivary flow

Accelerates heart
constricts arterioles

Dilates bronchi

Stomach motility &
secretion inhibited,
pancreas inhibited

Adrenalin secretion

Intestinal motility
inhibited

Inhibits bladder wall

FIGURE 3-3

Diagram of the sympathetic and parasympathetic systems, showing their antagonistic effects on various visceral organs. (Figure 15-14 from *General Biology*, by Willis H. Johnson, Richard A. Laubergayer, and Louis E. Delaney, copyright © 1961 by Holt, Rinehart and Winston, Inc., reprinted by permission of the publisher.)

Excitation Transfer Theory X
a theory asserting that the general physiological arousal resulting from an emotional event endures for a period of time and can intensify emotional responding in a subsequent situation.

interpreted in a manner consistent with emotion. These, you will note, are the organic (O), situation (S), and thought (T) elements of the STORC model that we have discussed thus far.

A more recent extension of this line of reasoning is Zillmann's (1984) **excitation transfer theory.** It appears to be true that (1) a generalized kind of arousal underlies a broad range of different emotions, (2) this arousal does not disappear immediately, but diminishes gradually over a period of time, and (3) arousal is interpreted as emotion based upon situational cues. This means that arousal which occurs because of one event will linger for a period of time and can carry over into a subsequent situation. This increased level of arousal may intensify an emotional reaction to the later situation, particularly if the individual does not perceive that the arousal is carried over from the earlier experience. This is an experimental basis for what has sometimes been called **displacement;** for example, getting angry at work, then going home and taking it out on the family or the dog. A substantial amount of research supports the validity of Zillmann's excitation transfer theory. The arousal that results from physical exercise, for example, has been shown to carry over to intensify anger, sexual excitement, or generosity in a situation that immediately follows the exercise. Sexual arousal has been shown to carry over, intensifying anger, humor appreciation, sadness, generosity, even the enjoyment of music afterward (Zillmann, 1979). Whatever situation follows a period of arousal, emotions associated with that situation can be intensified. This appears, in fact, to be an implicit principle in much of advertising, which pairs emotionally arousing scenes with the product to be sold, in hopes of a positive emotional transfer.

Displacement
the transfer of an emotional reaction from its true object to a substitute object.

Premenstrual Syndrome ↙
a hypothesized set of emotional, physical, and adjustment difficulties occurring in women on days prior to and during the onset of menstruation.

Because emotions are directly tied to biological events occurring within the nervous system, it should not be surprising that specific biological changes can also bring major emotional changes. Certain drugs, such as blood pressure medications, can interfere with brain chemistry in a way that induces profound depression in some individuals. The overuse of stimulants such as caffeine and nicotine can bring about increases in anger, irritability, and anxiety. Diet and nutrition can influence emotional health. Hormonal changes such as those that accompany the menstrual cycle may influence emotions, too. Some women experience strong emotional changes a few days prior to menstruation, an observation that has led to the description of a **premenstrual syndrome** (see Box 3.3). Men are similarly susceptible to the emotional effects of hormonal changes, such as those induced by the use of alcohol or steroids. Your physical body, your organism (O), is an important link in the STORC chain.

3.3 IS THERE A PREMENSTRUAL SYNDROME?

Some women experience emotional sensitivity just prior to the onset of their menstrual period. But is this sensitivity a "syndrome" to be diagnosed and treated? The idea of a premenstrual syndrome (PMS) has been controversial ever since it was first suggested to the public by British physician Katharina Dalton in 1964.

Hormonal shifts during the menstrual cycle have been clearly documented, but there is much disagreement as to whether, when, or how these shifts cause negative emotions. Yet negative emotions are the central symptoms of PMS as it is described in the most recent revision of the *Diagnostic and Statistical Manual of the American Psychiatric Association* (1987). This manual gives PMS the lengthy name of "Late Luteal Phase Dysphoric Disorder" and lists among its symptoms sadness,

tearfulness, irritability, anger, anxiety, tension, depression, decreased interest in usual activities, lack of energy, and sleep problems. In recognition of the absence of adequate research at present, it is listed as an "unspecified mental disorder" in the 1987 revision. Yet many believe that even this degree of official labeling of an unproved syndrome is inappropriate, premature, and potentially harmful to women.

Randi Daimon Koeske (1987), a research psychologist, has observed that both physiological and social-cognitive factors may play roles in premenstrual sensitivity. Interestingly, she found that people report *negative* emotions (anger, bad moods) as due to biology, but *positive* feelings (sexual arousal, good moods) as due to personality or situational factors. Such biases in attribution, Koeske warns, may serve to reinforce inaccurate stereotypes and could create the impression of a premenstrual syndrome.

So if a woman feels negative emotions just before her menstrual period, is she the victim of biology? Believing so might lead her to accept her mood as inevitable, or to seek medical solutions to her problem. But what if these moods, like others, are influenced by many factors including the environment, her own thoughts, and her behavior (remember the STORC)? In this case it may not be beneficial for her to see herself as controlled by raging hormones. A broader understanding of emotions might lead her, instead, to find useful coping strategies, and to gain a greater personal sense of self-control.

R—RESPONSES

A fourth link in the chain of emotion is how the individual responds or reacts, how the person shows and expresses the emotion. Given similar internal experiences (similar amounts of pain, for example), people differ in how much they show an external reaction, a behavior change. An ancient philosophy called **stoicism** taught that it is best not to show emotion externally, and people who react very little to painful situations are still sometimes termed "stoic." Is this "strong" or is it unhealthy to hide emotions? Psychologists disagree with one another. In grieving a major loss (such as the death of a loved one), some believe that it is very important for the bereaved person to weep openly and express his or her emotions to others. Research, on the other hand, suggests that many people deal with their grief in a private fashion, and that the overt expression of emotions is not a necessary part of grieving (Clayton, 1979). If anything, it is the person who shows the greatest overt emotionality who may suffer the longest grief reaction (Clayton, 1982).

Still, we all react or respond in *some* way to the events discussed thus far: S, T, and O. Even *not* responding is itself a response. Not showing any overt reaction is simply one way of reacting.

The concern here, then, is how people *react* (R) or cope with situations (S), their perceptions of those situations (T), and whatever physiological changes occur (O). There are many different styles of coping, as many as there are individuals. Some may be labeled "normal" and others "abnormal," according to the standards of the social group in which they occur. Reactions can also be thought of as occurring along a continuum stretching between active and passive coping. **Active coping** generally is an attempt to bring about a change in one's own behavior or in the external world, whereas **passive coping** is characterized by adjusting one's internal subjective state. Passive coping strategies include accepting, withdrawing, avoiding, and using what psychodynamic thinkers have termed "defense mechanisms" (see Box 3.4). Both active and passive approaches are legitimate coping strategies, which may be more or less adaptive depending upon the specific situation.

Consider, for example, a woman who begins to see evidence that her use of alcohol is having negative effects on her health and happiness. Perhaps her physician tells her that her check-up reveals warning signs of alcohol's early effects on the body. Perhaps she is arrested for driving while intoxicated, or wakes up one morning after drinking and realizes that she cannot remember what happened the night before. She may cope with this risk actively, by changing her drinking or getting more information about the extent to which she is, in fact, in danger because of her alcohol consumption. Alternatively, she may cope passively by rationalizing ("I just happened to get caught; it could

Stoicism
an ancient Greek philosophy promoting indifference to emotion and pain; a characteristic personal style of unresponsiveness to emotion or pain.

Active Coping
a style of adjusting by bringing about changes in one's own behavior or in the environment.

Passive Coping
a style of adjusting by bringing about changes in one's own subjective state instead of altering one's overt behavior or environment.

3.4   DEFENSE MECHANISMS

One concept from psychoanalysis that has found its way into popular language is that of "defense mechanisms." In original use (Anna Freud, 1948), these were understood as strategies of compromise between unconscious primitive impulses and the demands of the social environment. Inherently selfish impulses of the individual are transformed into more socially acceptable forms by these defense mechanisms. These are, in Anna Freud's view, unconscious or only partially conscious coping processes. They defend the individual from full awareness of his or her true unconscious impulses. Defense mechanisms, in this view, are used by everyone, and people differ in the number and types of coping strategies used. Problems arise when an individual overuses them or relies heavily upon more immature defenses such as denial or projection. Here are some common defense mechanisms described in psychodynamic writings. Can you think of examples of these coping processes in your own life, or in the life of someone you know?

Anna Freud

Compensation   The person engages or excels in some activity to make up (compensate) for a frustrated wish, a handicap, or perceived inferiority.

Denial   An aspect of reality is rejected, without conscious awareness that one is doing so. The person may disclaim certain motivations, feelings, thoughts, or actions. A portion of external reality may also be denied. The death of a loved one may be denied: "Daddy isn't really dead, he's just away on a trip." This is one of the most immature defense mechanisms.

Displacement   A strong feeling, attachment, or wish is redirected from its true object to a new, more acceptable substitute target. For example, feelings of love or anger, too threatening to experience and express directly, are acted out instead with a different person or object.

Identification   Without conscious awareness, the individual patterns himself or herself after another person. The perceived actions, beliefs, and feelings of the other are taken on as one's own.

Intellectualization   Reason and logic are used as a defense against significant feelings or conflicts. The person seems to have the right words, and can give a logical account of his or her own experience. What is missing is the emotional level. An intellectualizer may, for example, talk analytically and dispassionately about significant losses (such as a divorce, loss of a job) that would be very emotionally distressing for most people.

Projection   The individual's own unacceptable feelings and traits are attributed to ("projected" onto) other people, rather than accepted as his or her own. An angry person, for example, may deny feeling any personal anger but may see others as hateful and revengeful.

Rationalization   The individual finds rational, socially acceptable justifications for his or her own feelings or actions. These rational explanations cover up what are the true, consciously unacceptable reasons for the person's feelings and actions.

Reaction formation   To avoid experiencing a threatening feeling or wish, the individual behaves in a manner that is directly opposite to it. In reaction to strong sexual impulses, for example, a person may undertake a public campaign against pornography. Aggressive impulses may be covered by an excessively sweet, affectionate manner toward the hated individual.

Regression   The person reverts to an earlier, younger style of behavior, as if to retreat to a safer period of development. A teenager may curl up in a ball and suck on a blanket or thumb. An adult may revert to a temper tantrum.

Repression   Threatening knowledge, feelings, or experience are removed from conscious awareness and are relegated or "repressed" to an unconscious level.

Sublimation   Rather than seeking direct gratification of a need or impulse, the individual chooses a more socially acceptable substitute form of fulfillment. Aggressive impulses may, for example, be redirected into competitiveness at work, or might take the form of the satirical humor of the political cartoonist or nightclub comedian.

have happened to anybody.") or denying ("There must be something wrong with the tests. I'm just fine."). In this case, active coping (to reduce risk) would appear a more healthy strategy than passive coping (to reduce perception of risk).

In contrast, consider the case of a man who has tried every reasonable means available to bring about a change he believes is needed in his workplace. He has campaigned for the change with his co-workers, but found no interest. He petitioned his supervisor to make the change and was refused. He appealed to the company manager, who supported the supervisor's view, and then to the board of directors, who similarly rejected his idea. If he believes passionately in the need for this change, he may persist in active coping strategies in his lonely attempt to bring about change. Or he may accept that, although it is not the outcome he wanted, he has done his best, and that the time is not right for change. The latter passive coping strategy—acceptance— may in this case be more adaptive than persisting in an almost certainly fruitless effort to force a change.

What determines whether a person will choose active versus passive coping? One very clear factor turns out to be a belief that Bandura (1982) has termed **self-efficacy.** This is the belief that one *can* do something that will make a difference, that one has available a response that will be effective. People who believe that they can effect a change (high self-efficacy) are likely to try active coping, whereas those who view themselves as helpless or unable to make a change (low self-efficacy) are more likely to use passive coping styles (Miller, 1985b; Rogers, 1975; Rogers & Mewborn, 1976). Once again, a belief or cognition (T) influences how one will respond (R).

C—CONSEQUENCES

Here the cycle of emotion returns to the external world, where it began. Our discussion of this STORC cycle began with stimuli (S), events occurring in the external world. When the person responds (R), this results in certain consequences (C) from the external world.

Operant psychology (Chapter 1), associated with B. F. Skinner (1953), emphasizes the importance of these consequences. Whether or not the person continues to respond in the same way depends upon what consequences occur. Certain kinds of consequences make it more likely that the person will repeat the behavior, will respond in the same way again (reinforcement). Other consequences have the opposite effect, decreasing the probability that the person will continue to respond in this way (punishment). This is relatively easy to see in external behavior. Consider again the example given in Chapter 1 of a family we treated. The parents complained of problems in getting a six-year-old child to stay in bed at night. The child would go to bed, but then would get up repeatedly instead of falling asleep. Asked how they reacted, the parents reported that they had tried everything: holding and cuddling the child, getting a glass of milk, reading stories, promising a special treat in the morning. Clearly it was in the child's best interest to continue getting out of bed! The consequences were very positive, and the parents were unwittingly reinforcing the behavior by their own reactions.

But can *emotions* be reinforced in this same way? Certainly emotional *responses* (R) can. If depressed behavior brings about a desirable change (e.g., more attention and understanding from others), this behavior is likely to continue or increase. Consider a woman who leads a relatively lonely life and slowly becomes depressed. Concerned about her obvious distress, her friends rally around her. They call her several times a day, invite her to lunch, ask if they can give a hand with anything. Experiencing strong social support, she begins to feel better, and at this point her friends go back to their own busy schedules. The lunches stop, the calls become few and far between. Is it surprising, then, if the woman becomes depressed once again?

The same principle can apply to physical problems as well. Wilbert Fordyce (1976) has clearly demonstrated that suffering and pain can be intensified and prolonged if such responses are reinforced, and that pain can be alleviated if the rewarding consequences are discontinued. How is pain reinforced? Think of a typical hospital setting. The nursing staff are usually quite busy with many duties. Who gets the most attention? Often it is the patient who complains the loudest and longest. Pain behavior brings attention from the nurses, perhaps a nice backrub, a conversation. Pain medication is often prescribed on a "PRN" basis, which means "as needed." Thus complaining of pain also results in being given medication, which can be quite reinforcing. Fordyce discovered

Self-Efficacy
the belief that one is capable of accomplishing a particular task or objective.

that by teaching the nursing staff to reinforce active coping behavior instead of pain behavior, patients' suffering and pain could actually be decreased in cases where surgeries and medication had previously failed to do so (Fordyce, 1976).

STORC: AN INTEGRATION

Emotion is not any one of the events just described. Rather it is the entire sequence or chain of events. The relative importance of each link in the chain is very variable. For some emotional problems such as phobias, the stimuli (S) are very important and seem to set off an almost automatic fear response. With such problems, as we shall see in Chapter 8, one key is to break the association between the stimuli (S) and the organic (O) fear response. Other problems such as depression or test anxiety often seem to revolve around thought patterns (T), and change can be brought about by helping the person to alter how he or she perceives and interprets situations. Sometimes organic problems (O) are themselves of central concern, as in asthma, muscle tension, or panic attacks. Here direct physiological changes (such as learning how to relax one's muscles, see Appendix B) may be most helpful. In other cases the "emotional" problem revolves around how the person reacts or responds (R). Depression is often exacerbated by the person's withdrawal from social activity and support. Anger as an emotion is not problematic in itself (see Chapter 9), but angry people sometimes respond in problematic ways (e.g., aggression). Such responses, a part of the cycle of emotion, may also be maintained by reinforcing consequences.

■ EMOTIONS AND SELF-CONTROL

People sometimes see emotions and self-control as being opposites. In the "grip" of emotions, a person may feel out of control, irrational, impulsive. The stereotype of a person with great self-control, on the other hand, is of a very unemotional person, one who is not flustered or upset by even the most frustrating or provocative events. Some people believe that this kind of self-control is just something that certain people *have:* "She has a lot of self-control," or "I don't have much self-control."

As psychologists use the term, however, **self-control** is not so much something that one *has*, but rather something that one *does*. In this sense, self-control occurs through actions that one takes for the purpose of changing another behavior or aspect of oneself. If, for example, you wanted to *increase* the amount of exercise that you get, you might take certain steps to make exercising easier (buying good running shoes or a warm-up suit), or make yourself accountable to someone else (agreeing to run with a friend every weekday morning). If you wanted to *decrease* a behavior such as eating unhealthful foods, you could buy only healthful foods and have nothing else in the house to tempt you. Self-control involves taking specific steps toward change. We will be using this definition of self-control throughout this book.

But how does this apply to emotions? Is it really possible to take steps to change how you feel? Can people exercise some choice about whether, how often, and how strongly they will feel angry, anxious, depressed, or joyful? The answer, we believe, is definitely "Yes!" People are not the helpless victims of their own emotions. To a considerable extent, you *choose* how you will perceive and feel about the world around you and, indeed, about yourself.

The STORC model, by suggesting how emotions occur in steps, also points to a number of ways in which it is possible to *change* problematic emotions. In the remainder of this chapter, we will explain how the STORC model can be

Self-Control X
a change in behavior occurring when an individual engages in actions intended to bring about the change, in the absence of external coercion, and where alternative responses are possible.

Self-control is not something you have, but something you do.

used to discover general principles or strategies of change. In later chapters we will apply these STORC principles to particular life challenges.

S—CHANGING THE SITUATION

Sometimes change can be brought about by changing the *situation*. A high level of stress may be relieved, in part, by decreasing the stressors in one's life. A parent's worry about a small child falling down the stairs may be lessened by installing a gate across the stairtop. Temptation to revert to an undesirable behavior may be lessened by removing, avoiding, and distancing oneself from the sources of temptation.

The approach here is **environmental modification,** to change your physical surroundings in some beneficial way. Most often this involves adding or taking something away from the immediate surroundings. A few examples of adding to your environment are obtaining tapes of favorite music that help you to relax, installing a secure lock or a smoke alarm to decrease worries, or borrowing a self-help book from the library. Some examples of removing obstacles are fixing the annoying leaky faucet, removing pictures that evoke sadness, or moving out of a neighborhood or situation in which you feel constantly in danger.

T—CHANGING THOUGHT PATTERNS

Although distressing situations cannot always be changed, you always have a choice of how you will *think* about your situation. Consider four different ways of interpreting a poor test grade. It might be seen as evidence that you are intellectually inferior, and that you will ultimately flunk out of college and fail in life. On the other hand, it might be thought of as a warning that you need to study a little harder or learn better study skills. It might be seen as a case of bad luck, a temporary setback that just happens now and then. Finally, it might be due to an unfair or unreasonable instructor who writes impossibly difficult exams. These interpretations would all lead to rather different feelings and reactions.

Environmental Modification
making planful changes in one's physical or social surroundings to facilitate adjustment and coping.

3.5	THE GHOSTS IN THE CLOSET A Personal Awareness Exercise on Some Sources of Your Emotions *Al S. Fedoravicius, Ph.D.*

Ghosts! The very image can conjure up disturbed, uneasy, frightened feelings. Ghosts are the lingering, not quite dead remnants of the past. It was this image that Dr. Fedoravicius chose to describe in the following exercise, which is intended to exhume some of the cognitive sources of emotion, the influences of thought (T in our STORC model) on feeling.

Start with a blank sheet of paper, turn it sideways, and then make five columns with these headings:

SITUATION   FEELING   REACTION   PARENTAL   OBJECTIVE

Next think back over the past few weeks and recall some situations in which you felt significant or strong negative emotions. (The exercise can work for positive emotions, too, but for now focus on unpleasant emotions.) Try to come up with at least five. For each one, briefly describe the SITUATION in the leftmost column, then under FEELING describe how you felt. (Remember: Emotions are *not* described by saying "I feel *that* . . .") Next for each situation, write what you *did*, how you responded, under REACTION. These are, roughly, the S, O, and R elements of the STORC model.

What about T? In Chapters 6 and 7 we will describe further how the cognitive or thought (T) elements arise and influence emotion. There are many influences on how a person interprets a situation, and thus on how the person feels and reacts to the situation. The last two columns give you examples of this. Under PARENTAL, write what your *parents* would have said about this situation, how they would have felt or reacted, or how they would have told you to react. Then under OBJECTIVE, write what a completely objective observer, an outsider who is not emotionally caught up in the situation, might say about it.

It is possible to include other columns, too. What might your best friend say or do in this situation? How about a person you look up to as someone you want to be like? What would that person say or do? If you identify with a particular religious or spiritual perspective, what might a leader or founder of your religion say or do in this situation?

All these influences can contribute to your own beliefs about reality, to the ghosts in *your* closet. For each of the situations, consider what important influences in your life may have shaped the way in which you felt and reacted. How much of your feeling and reaction do you think was determined by what was "out there" (in the situation), and how much by the ghosts in your own closet?

The skill of **cognitive restructuring** involves choosing new ways to perceive and interpret what happens to you. It is not necessary to be stuck with one disturbing way of looking at things. Some psychologists and psychiatrists, in fact, believe that thought patterns *are* the reason for emotional upset. Anger, for example, is an emotion that usually needs continual fueling (Tavris, 1982). To remain angry, a person must continue to think about how he or she has been wronged, rejected, or ignored. These thoughts, in themselves, fuel the angry feelings. Alternative ways of thinking (such as forgiving) can alter such feelings.

O—CHANGING ORGANIC PATTERNS

Cognitive Restructuring
a technique of cognitive therapy that changes an individual's thinking and perception of a particular situation or class of situations.

Emotions also involve physiological, organic responses. Problematic emotions often involve excessive arousal of the autonomic nervous system. Another self-control strategy, then, is to change your own level of physical arousal.

One approach is *decreasing overall arousal.* There are a wide variety of skills and methods for calming oneself. These include deep muscle relaxation (Ap-

Biofeedback training.

pendix B), meditation, regular physical exercise, and **biofeedback.** Certain drugs and medications also have a direct calming effect on the nervous system, although there are dangers in relying upon certain chemicals for relaxation (Chapter 11).

Sometimes, through learning, particular stimuli become associated with physical arousal. Phobias, for example, involve strong and unrealistic fear reactions to certain objects or situations. Many people experience physical arousal when they must speak to a large group, even though there is no real danger involved. Another method for changing arousal is **systematic desensitization,** which breaks the association between the threatening situation and physical arousal. The person is literally desensitized to that which was previously threatening, so that the object or situation no longer evokes physical reactions. This method will be explained more fully in Chapter 8.

R—CHANGING RESPONSES

Biofeedback
the use of an electrical or mechanical device to obtain feedback about physiological states and changes that cannot ordinarily be detected consciously; the use of such feedback to bring about changes in physiological states.

Systematic Desensitization
a behavior therapy used to treat fears and phobias, whereby the feared object is associated (either in real life or in imagination) with a response (such as relaxation) incompatible with anxiety.

Still another route for changing emotional patterns is through how you *respond.* Certain ways of responding to negative emotions tend to make them worse. If a person who is feeling depressed also gives in to the tendency to avoid other people and to drop out of activities, the resulting isolation tends to increase the seriousness of the depression. An angry person who behaves aggressively is likely to experience aggression from others, giving further justification for feeling angry.

With regard to fear, *avoidance* is an important contributing response. The old rule, "If you fall off the horse, get right back on," is a good one for this reason. To begin avoiding horses is to invite additional fear. Fear is also likely to increase in a person who feels anxious about public speaking and chooses to avoid having to speak in public. Sometimes the best way to overcome a fear is to practice the very behavior that is feared.

On a larger level, *life-style change* may be necessary to overcome negative emotional patterns. This means changing a broader pattern of behaviors. The "workaholic" executive who allows work to fill every available moment, squeezing out leisure and family time, may have to make major changes in how she or he uses time in order to reduce stress and maintain health (Chapter 8). A life-style that includes very few pleasant activities and social contacts is likely to leave one vulnerable to depression (Chapter 7).

C—CHANGING CONSEQUENCES

Finally, it is sometimes possible to practice self-control by changing the *consequences* of actions. In making any important change, it is helpful to have support and encouragement. Sometimes negative emotional patterns are maintained because, in a sense, they bring a reward or a payoff. Aggressive behavior, for example, may alienate people and bring destructive consequences in the long run, but often it gets the aggressor what he or she wants *immediately*, in the short run.

One way to obtain encouragement for new self-control behavior is through *social support*. Family and friends can be asked to notice and encourage change, and to avoid encouraging old behavior patterns that you are trying to overcome. Special "contracts" can be arranged with friends, agreements to celebrate together when a successful change step is accomplished.

Self-Reinforcement
the use of principles of reinforcement to increase a specific behavior in oneself.

Self-reinforcement is also possible. A person seeking to change may set a series of weekly goals, planning to reward himself or herself when each goal is reached. Planned penalties may also be imposed if one fails to reach a change goal that has been set.

■ SUMMARY

The word "feel" is used in the English language to describe a broad range of responses, leading to a tendency to confuse emotions with thoughts and other experiences. The STORC model is one way of understanding and, if desired, changing emotional patterns. An emotion begins with a situation (S), which is then necessarily interpreted (T) by the person, who shows both an organic (O) and a behavioral response (R), which in turn results in certain consequences (C). These consequences or results become part of the new situation (S), and so the cycle continues. When change is desired, it may be initiated at any point in this cycle: by changing the situation, restructuring thought patterns, altering organic responses, engaging in new behaviors, or altering the consequences of behavior.

In the chapters ahead we will be using this STORC model to discuss specific areas such as mood, stress, and anger. We will explain how this cycle can lead to problems and also how you can use your knowledge of this cycle to help solve personal problems for a more satisfying life. The STORC approach can be particularly useful in developing an understanding of what is happening in your life and why.

■ QUESTIONS FOR THOUGHT

1. Is self-control something you have or something you do? What's your own opinion?

2. Which emotions are easiest for you to express? Which are hardest?

3. Think of a recent experience in which you felt strong emotion. Use the STORC model to examine this experience. What was the situation which led to your emotion? What must you have been thinking? What physical changes did you notice? What did you do? What happened as a result of your response?

4. In our culture, different types and ranges of emotions are "O.K." for men versus women. Which emotions do you think are more acceptable, in our society, for women than for men? For men than for women? What happens when you express an emotion that's "not O.K." for your gender?

5. You see a three-year-old crying. What are you likely to say to the child? Would it be different if it were a boy or a girl? Would it be different if it were your own child, a niece or nephew, or a stranger? Why?

6. In what ways do you hope that your own children might be different from you in how they experience and handle emotions?

7. With whom is it O.K. for you to cry? be angry? be frightened? be joyful? relax and let down your guard?

8. Choose a kind of emotional experience that seems to pose a problem for you. Using the STORC model, generate a list of ways in which you might go about addressing this problem. What changes might you make in the situations or stimuli that lead to this emotion, your thought patterns, your organic patterns, your responses, and the consequences of your responses?

chapter four

O wad some Pow'r the giftie gie us
To see oursels as ithers see us!
It wad frae monie a blunder free us.
—Robert Burns

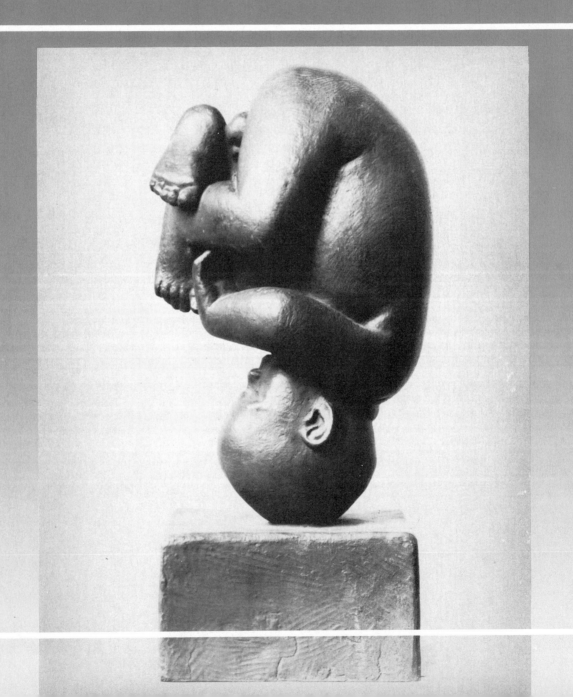

Self and Self-Perception

*T*he concept of "self" has existed for as long as there has been written history. "Self" is an important idea in most personality theories. Asked to describe "yourself," you could easily do so. On the surface, it seems a simple idea. Yet "self" continues to have many meanings. Each personality theory offers a different conception of self.

Once one accepts the idea of self, it is reasonable to ask where it comes from, how the self develops. Some people equate self with "soul," implying that the self exists before and/or after the life of the body. Others regard the self as a blank slate at birth, emerging over the course of development in response to a multitude of influences.

In this chapter we will first examine various conceptions of the idea of "self." Next we will explore two processes related to the concept of self, which are important in understanding adjustment: conflict and self-perception. Then we will turn our attention to theories and research regarding how the self develops. Here we will discuss three major areas: stage theories, life-span development, and processes of socialization and learning. Finally, we will examine the concept of self-ideal, the goals toward which the self develops.

■ WHAT IS THE "SELF"?

The **self** is not a tangible thing, like a chair or this book. It cannot be seen or measured directly. Rather it is an *experience*. Each person has a "sense" of self, experiencing certain feelings, thoughts, beliefs, and actions as being "part of myself" and others as "not me." For this reason, definitions of "self" tend to be stated in terms of experience. There have been many definitions. We will summarize them as falling into four groups:

SELF AS AWARENESS

A philosopher or a neurologist might define self as awareness or consciousness. In this view, the very experience of *being* aware constitutes your sense of self. The philosopher Descartes reflected this view in his dictum, "I think, therefore I am." The self can be experienced as the center of awareness, the "one within, who is aware." Hilgard's fascinating research pointing to a **hidden observer** within the individual is consistent with this view (see Box 4.1).

Self
the experienced sense of being, of uniqueness and separateness from others and the environment; the sum of one's accumulated experience.

Hidden Observer
a portion of the self that continues to monitor events occurring within and around the individual, even when the individual is not consciously aware; associated with the hypnosis research of Ernest Hilgard.

SELF AS SEED

A humanistic psychologist might think of "self" as a kind of blueprint within the person, a seed containing that person's unique, ideal, and natural identity. A person may grow in the direction of this natural self, or may become distorted and misdirected, growing away from his or her true identity. Within this view it can make sense to say, "I am not myself today!" (If self is simple consciousness or awareness, on the other hand, then this statement makes no sense at all. Whatever you are experiencing at the moment *is* your self.) In the "self as seed" conception, a person's behavior at any given time may or may not correspond to "self." The key idea here is of an inherent self that is the person's true nature, whether or not the person realizes or achieves it.

4.1 THE HIDDEN OBSERVER

A part of the self is aware, watching, and listening, even when a person appears to be completely unaware. That was the conclusion of psychologist Ernest Hilgard, based on his explorations of hypnosis. He discovered a kind of "detached witness" within people who were hypnotized. Here's how it happened.

Hilgard had hypnotized a blind man as part of a classroom demonstration. With a good hypnotic subject, it is possible to induce temporary deafness, and this is what Hilgard did. The subject in this state appeared to be completely unaware of what was going on around him. A student in the audience asked Dr. Hilgard whether there might be some part of the man that was still aware of what was being said around him. Curious, Hilgard told the subject quietly that if there were some part of him which could still hear, he should raise his forefinger. To everyone's surprise, the forefinger rose.

What had the subject experienced? He reported that for a period of time, everything was completely quiet. Then he noticed that his forefinger had risen, though he didn't know why. Based on this observation, Hilgard gave the name "hidden observer" to that part of the subject's awareness that had responded.

Is there a hidden observer, a part of awareness that monitors everything even when you aren't aware of it? Have you ever been driving a car while doing something else at the same time—listening to music, talking to a passenger, or just thinking? Suddenly you realize that you have driven for some distance without being aware of either your driving or the passing environment. It's as if you had been on automatic, with some part of you monitoring the road and driving while your attention was elsewhere. Is there a part of the person that is always aware of what is going around her or him, even when the person is in a coma, under general anesthetic, hypnotized, or asleep?

Or perhaps you're a skeptic. How else might you explain Hilgard's observations? If you could account for his findings in another way, could you design a better experiment to determine whether there really *is* a hidden observer?

SELF AS PERCEIVED PERSONALITY

A social psychologist would be more likely to talk about self as a perception. Self is that which you perceive to be consistent in you over time, the inner part of you that endures. What is it about you that is most consistent? Who *are* you? The answers to these questions reflect what you believe about your self, in this sense. Because you may or may not approve of the consistencies that you see in yourself, it makes sense in this way of thinking to make the statement, "I don't like myself." (Notice that in this statement, an "I" is the hidden observer of the self!)

SELF AS WHOLE

Still another view of self, perhaps most consistent with an existential perspective, is that the self is not a *part* of experience but rather the sum of *all* one's experience. Every life experience becomes a part of the whole, of the self. Rather than being a *particular* perception, self is the sum of all the person's systems for organizing and perceiving the world. Put together all your beliefs, your values, your ways of thinking and perceiving, and the result is your "self."

4.2 | HERE WE DIFFER/HERE WE AGREE
The Reality of the Self

Is the self real? Does this entity that I experience as my "self" have a reality of its own that somehow transcends my body? Or is it merely an illusion, the fancy footwork of countless neurons? Does my "self," the very essence of me, cease to exist at the moment my brain dies, or is it what for thousands of years has been called a "soul," a real being that lives on?

For the present, at least, this is a question that eludes science. To be sure, there have been some interesting attempts to study transcendence. Moody (1975), for example, interviewed over 100 people who had been clinically dead and were then revived. He reported that their experiences bore uncanny resemblance to one another, and commonly included feelings of profound peace, an experience of leaving the body and of traveling rapidly through a dark tunnel, and an encounter with a being of brilliant light. Are these common experiences the last gasps of a dying nervous system, or the passage of the self from one existence into another?

There are no conclusive proofs, from a scientific viewpoint, of the reality (or unreality) of the self. Personally, I believe that a core of what we experience as the self lives on after the body dies, that there is an essential self which transcends this biological life. It may be out of vogue within contemporary psychology to talk about the "soul," yet belief in the reality of life after death has been part of our human race for as long as there has been recorded history. My own belief in the reality of the soul (self) is not a conclusion from scientific evidence, but a decision of faith.   —WRM

It seems to me that the question is not whether the self is real, but rather whether it will transcend its own biological life. Science has no answer for this question. For a scientific approach to be used, there are some basic assumptions that must be met. One of these assumptions is that some event must occur in a way that can be observed. Attempting to apply a scientific approach to "life after death" is not something we are currently capable of doing, and I don't expect that to change within my lifetime. To be sure, there are some people who have described experiences that occurred while they were "clinically dead," and most of these experiences appear to have been of a very positive nature. But such stories can hardly be regarded as proof of an afterlife.

Frankly I'm not all that concerned with whether there is a soul that lives on after biological death. What concerns me more is the person who has trouble accepting his or her "real" self *during* biological life! As a pragmatist who lacks a certain romanticism in my soul, I find it difficult to concern myself with something that I cannot know about, and over the years I have found that my patients do not seem to solve their problems very effectively if they don't deal with the here and now. I really have no argument with someone who prefers to believe in the reality of life after death, as long as it does not interfere with his or her ability to function effectively during normal biological life.   —JMR

INTEGRATION

Like all scientists and professionals, psychologists differ with regard to their chosen values and religious beliefs. Some follow Freud's active skepticism and hostility toward religion, regarding it to be a primary source of mental illness. Some retain a personal agnosticism, neither affirming nor denying the reality of spiritual beliefs. Some embrace a personal faith system and participate in organized religion. Recently there has been increased interest in seeking an integration of psychology and religion, and exploring spiritual dimensions of psychotherapy (Bergin, 1980; Miller & Martin, 1988; Stern, 1985). Will psychologists be able to apply their scientific skills in this endeavor, and if so, what will the results be? We anticipate some interesting answers in the years to come.

Each of these four types of definitions has its merits. In this book we will emphasize the last of these definitions, the holistic view. We do so not because we regard it to be the only correct approach, but because it is the broadest view. It can incorporate all the other definitions. "Self," in the sense of all experience, includes (but is not restricted to) the hidden observer, the ideal, and the self-perception.

■ THE DIVIDED SELF

Such a holistic view can also be helpful in understanding an interesting aspect of self, as reflected in everyday language. When people speak about themselves, they often talk as if they were divided. Consider these statements:

> "I said to myself, 'What's wrong with me?'"
> "I wonder what I'll think of myself five years from now."
> "One thing about me that I like is that I am always true to myself."

Who are the different participants in these sentences? It is as though there were a committee making up the self! The members of the committee are not only distinct, but they *interact* with each other ("I could just kick myself").

Personality theories typically suggest how the self (in this holistic sense) is divided. Sigmund Freud proposed three interacting parts of the self: the **id** (primitive desires and wishes), the **superego** (the "conscience" that opposes the id), and the **ego** (the reality-tester that balances the other two parts). Eric Berne's theory of transactional analysis, which became popular in the 1970s, contains three similar divisions of the self: the child, the parent, and the adult. Carl Jung described four primary functions within each person: sensing, intuiting, thinking, and feeling. In describing emotions in Chapter 3, we divided experience into the five elements of the STORC model. The point is that almost every theory of personality suggests a way for making sense of the self by dividing it up into parts that interact with each other. It is not our purpose here to explain all these different ways of dividing up the self, for that could constitute an entire book on theories of personality. One general concept from personality theory is very important in understanding adjustment and growth, however: the concept of **conflict.**

CONFLICT

No matter how a personality theory slices up the self, the parts are usually described as coming into conflict with one another. Consider, for example, a simplistic system that divides experience into feelings, behavior, and thoughts (including values and beliefs). Even within this simple three-part system there are many different possibilities for conflict. A feeling such as anger may conflict with a value or belief that it is not acceptable to feel anger toward another person. The experience of guilt may emerge when a belief conflicts with a behavior (as when a student cheats, but believes that cheating is wrong). Feelings and behaviors can conflict, too, as when a person feels upset about being overweight but keeps reaching into the cookie jar. Conflict is an important concept in almost any definition of the self.

Conflict can be a powerful experience. It may motivate one to change, or leave one feeling frustrated and stuck. It can be challenging, distressing, or depressing. Various factors influence how distressing a conflict will be. One factor is how important the choice is. A conflict in deciding between two different flavors of ice cream is likely to be less stressful than having to choose between two different jobs or lovers.

Id
in Freud's theory of psychoanalysis, the impulse-generating part of the personality which is concerned only with pleasure and gratification.

Superego
in Freud's theory of psychoanalysis, the part of the personality that functions as a conscience, expressing moral values and judgment.

Ego
in Freud's theory of psychoanalysis, the reality-testing part of the personality which forges compromises between the impulses of the id and the moral standards of the superego.

Conflict
the simultaneous presence of two or more mutually inconsistent goals, motives, or desires.

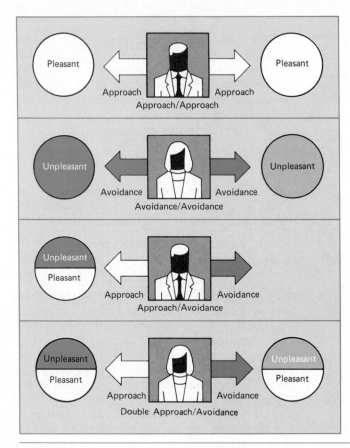

FIGURE 4-1 TYPES OF CONFLICT SITUATIONS

Another factor is the kind of conflict being faced. (See Figure 4-1.) Four different types of conflict are often distinguished. The **approach-approach conflict** requires a choice between positive alternatives: what to order from the menu, which of two attractive job offers to accept. Though they can pose difficult decisions, such conflicts are likely to be less stressful than the other three types which contain negative elements to be avoided. The **avoidance-avoidance conflict** is a choice of "the lesser of two evils," a decision between two undesirable alternatives where one must be faced. A person convicted of drunk driving, for example, may be forced to choose between spending time in jail or enforced alcoholism treatment, both of which he or she would rather avoid. Just as stressful can be the **approach-avoidance conflict.** Here the person experiences both positive and negative feelings about the same thing: the student would like to go see a movie, but fears failing the exam tomorrow without more studying.

Perhaps the most stressful type of conflict, however, is the **double approach-avoidance conflict,** which requires a choice between two different options, both of which contain important negative and positive aspects. An example is the person who is "torn between two lovers." Both are attractive, yet both have their drawbacks. The closer you get to one alternative the more negative that one appears, and the better the other appears. Yet in moving away from the first, the shortcomings of the second become clearer and the first again begins looking more attractive.

Conflicts are a part of everyday adjustment. Some are minor conflicts, whereas others are much more important and stressful. All four types of conflict are typically experienced as internal struggles within the self. There is a

Approach-Approach Conflict
a conflict between two mutually exclusive alternatives, both of which the individual desires.

Avoidance-Avoidance Conflict
a conflict between two mutually exclusive alternatives, both of which the individual wishes to escape.

Approach-Avoidance Conflict
a conflict regarding a single person, object, or situation, which the individual both desires and wishes to escape; a DOUBLE APPROACH-AVOIDANCE CONFLICT involves two such conflictual objects, each of which has desirable and aversive aspects.

need to make a choice, a decision, but any choice that is made involves a losing something positive and/or encountering something negative. Caught in middle of such a conflict, a person may feel unable to move, and may seek a way to avoid choosing altogether. Yet even not deciding is a decision in itself. Dealing effectively with conflict is an important element of adjustment and change.

■ SELF-PERCEPTION

As we consider self in relation to adjustment, another important general process is **self-perception.** Self-perception refers to how you perceive yourself—your own thoughts, beliefs, and feelings about your self. (Notice that self-perception thus corresponds to the third definition of "self" given at the beginning of this chapter.) Self-perception is a very broad term, and it includes three more specific aspects: self-concept, self-ideal, and self-esteem.

SELF-CONCEPT

Think of ten words that describe yourself. As you do so, you are rehearsing one part of your self-perception, your thoughts and beliefs about yourself as you are now. This self-concept is by no means "objective," but rather it is your own present view of how you actually are. Others' views of you may be very different from your own, but it is *your* beliefs about who you are that make up your current self-concept. In pure form, the self-concept is neither good nor bad, positive nor negative. Rather it is a description of what you are like.

SELF-IDEAL

Another important set of beliefs is your **self-ideal:** how you would like to be ideally. These may be stated as "shoulds" (I really should be more patient), as wishes (I wish I were more popular), or just as preferences (I would like to be more relaxed). As with self-concept, self-ideal is a description, not in itself a positive or negative feeling.

SELF-ESTEEM

The term self-esteem refers to how you *feel* about yourself, to positive or negative self-evaluations. It is an overall feeling, in transactional analysis terms, of being "O.K." or "not O.K." (Harris, 1967). Though different from self-concept and self-ideal, it is related to them. Psychologist Carl Rogers argued that self-esteem is proportionate to the distance between self-ideal and self-concept. The bigger the distance (that is, the further you see yourself being from the way you want to be or should be), the lower your self-esteem. To state this as a formula:

Self-Perception
an individual's overall comprehension of self, including self-concept, self-esteem, and self-ideal.

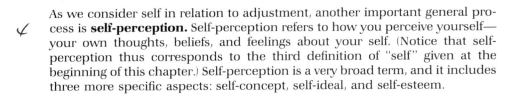

$$\text{Self-esteem} = \frac{1}{\text{Self-ideal} - \text{Self-concept}}$$

Self-Ideal
a description of how an individual perceives he or she should or would like to be.

Self-esteem gets larger as the distance between self-ideal and self-concept grows smaller. According to Rogers, then, self-esteem will increase as the person's actual self (self-concept) and ideal self grow closer. Chapter 6 is devoted to a closer examination of self-esteem and how it can be changed.

Self-esteem suffers when self-concept falls far short of self-ideal. Advertising often offers the promise of magically achieving one's self-ideal.

■ HOW THE SELF DEVELOPS

From where does the self come? Psychologists have put forth many different theories about how the self develops and how people form their self-percep-tions. We will discuss three major approaches to understanding the develop-ment of self: (1) stage theories, which assert that the self develops in discrete and identifiable phases or stages; (2) theories based on life-span development research; and (3) research on socialization and learning processes that shape individual identity. The image that best represents stage theory is that of stairs, which a person climbs one at a time without skipping any. Life-span develop-ment theory evolved as the result of dissatisfaction with traditional stage theo-ries that failed to account for some human experience. Instead of stairs, a woven tapestry is a better image for describing the development of self and self-perception in life-span theories. Stage theorists propose a universal expla-nation for development which is intended to apply to everyone regardless of gender, culture, or historical differences among individuals. Life-span develop-mentalists are more likely to consider the interaction of an individual's devel-opment with various other factors in the environment and the historical con-text. Socialization and learning theories likewise emphasize the importance of the environment, and seek to specify the processes by which identity is shaped through experience.

All three groups of theories can be broadly applied to understand sexual, social, cognitive, and moral development. If these aspects of development are of particular interest to you, consider taking a course in developmental psy-chology or getting an overview of such theories by reading a textbook on human psychological development. Such courses and texts can give you a more complete picture of the field than we can provide in this chapter, al-though many texts still cover mainly stage theories. In this section, we hope to give you a broad appreciation of processes by which the self develops through-out childhood and adult life.

STAGE THEORIES

One strong appeal of a stage theory is that it seems elegant and tidy. As you saw in Chapter 2 where we discussed Erikson's stages of psychosocial development, the qualitatively different steps were neatly delineated by age and task. Freud's psychosexual stages of development are similarly clear-cut. By definition, a stage theory involves universal stages, presumably found among people of all cultures, and the sequence of the stages is invariant, which means that no other sequence in the pattern of growth stages is possible.

Psychosexual Stages.   Freud's notions about **psychosexual development** were revolutionary for his times, the early 1900s, because he believed the development of the personality was influenced by the manner in which the child learned to expend sexual energy from one period of life to the next (Thomas, 1979). It is important to note that Freud deduced his psychology of the child from the psychoanalysis of adults. With the exception of one famous case of "Little Hans," Freud did not study children's development directly.

The idea that children had sexual feelings was novel and threatening to many of Freud's contemporaries in Vienna. Consequently, his theories were not widely accepted during his lifetime. Now, by contrast, many of his insights are taken for granted, accepted as "common sense," and incorporated not only into psychology and psychiatry, but into everyday language and thought.

Freud described birth as a traumatic beginning, followed by an oral period, an anal period, a phallic period, a latency period, and finally, a mature-genital period. These periods were delineated as a prescription for healthy develop-ment, as well as markers for where a person could get stuck, resulting in unhealthy development.

The birth trauma involves the shock of arrival in a glaring, noisy, uncontrol-lable world after spending months in the quiet darkness of the mother's womb. While some births are easier than others, all share a degree of shock and trauma, according to Freud.

The oral stage is said to last from birth to one year of age. It is a time when the infant derives her or his pleasure from sucking, gumming, and mouthing either the mother's breasts or various objects, including the infant's own hands. The infant explores the world through the mouth, taking in experience orally.

Years 2 and 3 of the toddler's life constitute the anal stage. Toilet training focuses on encouraging the child to expel feces and urine at appropriate times and places. The child is believed to derive pleasure from holding onto or letting go of bodily wastes.

Freud named the stage from ages 3 through 6 years "phallic" (phallus means penis), a clear reflection of the male-centeredness of his theory. This is

Psychosexual Development ⅄
a theoretical approach that describes normal development as occurring through a series of crucial stages in which biological impulses are brought into bal-ance with the demands of the environment; typified by Freud's psychoanalytic theory.

Toilet training

the stage in which the **Oedipal complex** is said to evolve, since the boy supposedly directs his phallic strivings toward his mother, but also fears castration by his father. Freud did not find a satisfactory formulation for girls' development during this stage, but speculated that all girls experience "penis envy," a wish that they had genitals like boys.

Latency results from boys repressing or forcing out of consciousness their sexual cravings. Girls' experience remains largely unexplained during the latency stage which is said to last from age 7 to age 12 or puberty. The defense mechanisms, as discussed in Chapter 3, become more clearly established during latency.

The mature-genital period, from ages 14 to 21, is marked by capacity for sexual orgasm, and the primary erotic zone is the male penis or the female vaginal area. Heterosexuality was considered the norm by Freud. He also observed that his society's moral barriers against intercourse between unmarried people and against masturbation created considerable obstacles to satisfying the pleasure needs associated with the mature-genital stage, particularly for adolescents.

Healthy development, in Freud's view, consists of negotiating all these stages successfully. Failing to progress through a stage, or becoming stuck at one stage, leads to personality problems that can persist throughout adult life if not effectively resolved.

Psychosocial Stages. Erikson's theory of how the self develops (see Chapter 2) was an extension and revision of Freud's theory. Erikson accepted most of Freud's view, but made important additions which included more focus on the nature of a healthy personality and identity, stages of social development, and the identity crisis. It is called a **psychosocial** model, because Erikson believed that the process of socializing the child into a particular culture involves passage through a series of innately determined stages which parallel Freud's psychosexual stages. We will briefly trace here how these two theories parallel each other.

Stage I, trust versus mistrust, corresponds to Freud's oral stage. Learning to predict and to depend on one's own behavior and that of others is the key task. The relationship with the main caregiver, usually the mother, is said to be crucial here.

Stage II parallels Freud's anal stage and poses the task of developing autonomy versus shame and doubt. In healthy development, the child here learns to balance a new sense of power with trying too much too soon and risking criticism from others.

Initiative versus guilt (III) is the name Erikson gave Freud's phallic stage because the child is said to struggle with sexual impulses. The child needs guidance in how to pursue life actively, yet in a socially acceptable way.

Erikson's stage IV, industry versus inferiority, coincides with the latency period Freud described. Healthy development means producing something worthwhile which requires perseverance. The child wants to use her or his abilities, and to have achievements recognized by others.

Stage V, identity versus role diffusion, includes the period of adolescence, and was extremely important to Erikson. This is a time of integration of earlier tasks, and of self-definition. Because expectations of childhood and youth are different, it can be a time of role confusion. Erikson's term **identity crisis** is used to characterize the struggle at this stage.

Stage VI, intimacy and solidarity versus isolation, coincides with what Freud called mature genitality. Early adulthood is reached as adolescence is left behind. The person can begin to establish a nonexploitative intimate relationship because she or he has a clear sense of self. Those who do not succeed in

Oedipal Complex
in Freud's theory of psychoanalysis, a normal process of development in which the child (usually used for boys only) is attracted to the parent of the opposite sex and develops hostile feelings and reactions to the same-sex parent.

Psychosocial Development
a theoretical approach that describes normal development as occurring through a series of crucial stages occurring in the context of social relationships; typified by Erikson's theory of development.

Identity Crisis
a disruption of the sense of sameness of self and/or of continuity of one's past and present; a loss of clarity regarding one's own essential nature and roles in society; introduced in the writings of Erik Erikson.

During adolescence, according to Erikson, the central struggle in development is that of identity versus role diffusion.

mastering self-definition later risk becoming self-absorbed, and hence, unable to sustain intimacy with another.

Stage VII, generativity versus self-absorption and stagnation, is uniquely Erikson's, since Freud's stages stopped at mature genitality. This is seen to be a time of productive and creative involvement for self and others, a time when the healthy individual nurtures and guides the next generation. Stagnation keeps a person from such involvement.

Stage VIII, integrity versus despair, is the crisis of late adulthood. A person who negotiates this stage is able to appreciate the continuity of past, present, and future, while accepting life as it is. Healthy development here involves wisdom. A person at the despairing end of the continuum may feel that time is too short, that life is meaningless, and that death is to be feared.

These eight stages have been called Erikson's "eight ages of man's ego development." He attempted to improve on Freud's theory by making the stages more inclusive of a variety of people by basing his theory on a wider geographical sampling in Europe and North America.

Other psychosocial stage models of development have appeared based on male experience (Gould, 1972; Levinson et al., 1974; Vaillant, 1977). Levinson, for example, described a chronological and career progression for males as occurring in the following steps: (1) early adult transition, (2) entering the adult world, (3) age 30 transition, (4) settling down, (5) midlife transition, and (6) restabilization. Vaillant (1977) also studied male adaptation in three spheres (occupational, marital, and medical), acknowledging that these adaptation processes might be different for women.

Cognitive and Moral Stages.   Cognitive and moral development have also been studied as important aspects of how the self develops (Kohlberg, 1969; Piaget, 1932). Piaget studied children's thought processes and was especially interested in intellectual growth. His interest began around 1920 through administering intelligence tests. He was fascinated not with the answers children gave, but rather with the processes they used to arrive at their answers. He saw knowledge as a process rather than a collection of stored information.

Piaget delineated four levels of development of knowledge: (1) the sensorimotor period, (2) the preoperational thought period, (3) the concrete operations period, and (4) the formal operations period. Each of these levels is further divided into stages, but for purposes of discussion here, we will simply summarize the four levels. At level 1 (sensorimotor), the infant senses (sees, hears, feels, tastes, smells) the environment and acts upon it with motor behavior. At level 2 (preoperational), from ages 2 to 7, the child begins to use language in a self-centered, and later, in a social way. From ages 7 to 11 (concrete operations), children can solve problems which involve identifiable objects. At level 4 (formal operations), children from ages 11 to 15 can imagine the conditions of a problem and develop their own hypotheses to test. Piaget's cognitive stages have greatly influenced educational methods used in American and European schools, providing a system for using different instructional approaches at different ages.

Like Piaget, Kohlberg was interested in the *processes* people use to think about their world. He focused on moral development, and the steps by which children grow toward making ethical judgments. Kohlberg specified three levels. The *preconventional* level involves avoiding punishment, seeking reward, and exchanging favors. Level II is called the *conventional* level, and involves conformity to the existing social order through seeking approval and maintaining law and order. Level III is the *postconventional* level, also called principled or autonomous. The person who has developed to this point tries to identify valid moral values regardless of social convention. In identifying his stages, Kohlberg used a method in which he asked subjects their opinion about various hypothetical moral dilemmas, such as the story of "Heinz," whose wife was dying. (Should Heinz steal the drug his wife needs if he cannot afford to buy it?) Kohlberg then observed how the subjects reasoned out their answers and rated their levels of moral development.

In summary, stage theories prescribe steps which a person must climb to reach the more advanced levels of development. The steps must be climbed in order, without skipping any, for normal, healthy development to occur. Later theorists, however, have come to question the accuracy of such stage models in describing human development.

LIFE-SPAN DEVELOPMENT

Life-span development theory and research is a more recent field which addresses gender differences, cultural differences, and individual differences in human development. How the self develops and how humans perceive themselves are seen as still more complex and rich processes, emerging in a wide variety of patterns.

The definition of life span development is fourfold. First, life-span development is a lifelong process in which change can occur at any point in time in the individual's life. Therefore, maturity is not an end state, nor can an ideal end state be determined. Second, it is influenced by the historical time in which it is occurring, so that effects across generations must be considered. Third, it is determined by many different factors and is complex for any one area of behavior, so that an individual exhibits considerable differences over time and across situations. Age is not the primary determinant of change. Fourth, development is best described not in terms of traits or orderly sequences of change, but by a flexibility model in which multiple causes may induce continual change (Baltes, Reese, & Lipsett, 1980).

The first part of this definition means that the self develops throughout the course of life, and does not stop at a certain age, or when a certain point is reached. Children may believe that they will "grow up" some day, and on that day will be mature adults, with the process of growing up completed. What is seen as constituting that day varies, but perhaps it may consist of reaching the age of 18 or 21, having children of one's own, or buying a house, or "settling down." As they approach that day in their lives, they realize that the process is far from complete and that they have a lot to learn and much growing still to do.

Life-Span Development theory and research concerned with understanding how the individual develops throughout childhood and adulthood, influenced by a wide range of personal and social factors.

Stage theories represent development as a set of steps to be climbed; lifespan development theories emphasize the weaving together of threads into a unique tapestry.

Regarding the second point, it emphasizes the unique effects of growing up within particular ages and generations. People who lived through the great U.S. economic depression in the 1930s, for example, developed certain values which may not be shared or understood by those of us who did not experience that historical period. Their moral development may include placing a high value on saving, while later generations may emphasize enjoying earnings now. History plays a crucial role in development, in part because history is what determines what opportunities will be available to a person (Vygotsky, 1978).

Change can occur at any point in the lifespan. Maturity is not an end state, but an emerging process.

The third point, emphasizing differences in behavior across time and situations, calls to mind dating behavior as an example. Adults who find themselves single again, after being part of a couple for many years, are sometimes at a loss as to how to behave socially. They may feel like adolescents again, including all the awkwardness of that period, until they get their bearings and decide how to behave as a single adult. Neugarten (1979) has called our society "age irrelevant," by which she means that "acting one's age" may have less meaning, since people are trying experiences that may not be "age appropriate" by traditional standards. Also, different situations bring out different aspects of the self: one situation can elicit a kind of maturity, while for the same person, another situation may evoke feelings of vulnerability typical of youth.

The final point stresses the role of multiple determinants which induce continual change. You are constantly accommodating, assimilating, and adjusting in the environment. Just when you are comfortable with the status quo, someone or something appears which requires you to rearrange your thinking or behavior. Life-span theorists believe development is much more complex than simply climbing steps in an orderly sequence. Developing the self, according to the life-span development model, involves continuous flexibility in weaving the tapestry of one's life.

Four Themes in Life-span Development.   Four themes regarding women's adult development have emerged from the thinking of life-span development researchers. Their data support the thesis that adult development for women does not follow a sequence of discrete stages, but rather has a fluid quality in which opportunity plays an important role (Neugarten, 1979; Yahne & Long, 1988). The four life development themes include (1) that women develop in a context of relationships, (2) that maturing is often facilitated by the collapse of cherished assumptions, (3) that forging self-perceptions that are both positive and feminine is difficult, and (4) that it is a challenge for women to include themselves as objects of their own care, choice, and responsibility. Whether these four themes also apply to men is a worthwhile topic for future research. Some researchers, however, already question whether traditional stage theories hold even for men, since the evidence for an unchanging sequence of stages is modest and questionable (Anastasi, 1976).

4.3 THEORY VERSUS EVIDENCE

A basic assumption with which we approach our chosen field of psychology is this: that one should place greater value and reliance upon ideas for which there is stronger evidence. This is a central value not only in science, but also in other areas of life such as our legal system.

In this light, it is important to distinguish between theory and evidence. A theory is a plausible explanation of why things are the way they are. It is certainly not, in itself, fact or evidence. The ancient geocentric theory of astronomy, for example, held that the earth lies at the center of the universe, and all other bodies revolve around it. Though it was widely believed to be the truth for centuries,

the observations of Copernicus and Galileo proved this theory wrong, leading to modern theories of the structure and function of the universe. (Incidentally, in 1988 the Public Opinion Laboratory of Northern Illinois University conducted a national survey of basic science knowledge for the National Science Foundation. They found, 450 years after Copernicus, that 21 percent of Americans still believed that the sun rotates around the earth.)

A theory, then, can be quite incorrect, even though it is endorsed by the world's leading authorities or by most or all of humankind. A theory is only a *possible* explanation. Science is the process of formulating and then testing theories. The history of any science is characterized by a series of shifts from one dominant theory to another (Kuhn, 1970). A theory is held as useful until a better one is found which explains more of the available information.

Sometimes it is the introduction of a new way of observing or measuring that permits an advance and change in existing theories. The introduction of the telescope, for example, led to dramatic changes in astronomy. As new and more definitive methods for psychological measurement become available, psychological theory changes, too. For example, the development over the past three decades of better methods for measuring the effectiveness of therapies has been an important advance (Garfield & Bergin, 1986). Rather than arguing about which theory of therapy is superior, it is possible to measure and compare the outcomes of various approaches. In this way, psychologists are gradually clarifying which types of treatment are most effective for which kinds of people with which sorts of problems.

It also happens sometimes that a theory or hypothesis continues to be believed long after the evidence has disproved it. As mentioned earlier, it was once believed that people who reported seeing things having to do with water when they looked at Rorschach's inkblots, had a high likelihood of being alcoholics. The evidence from research simply never supported this belief, yet for decades professionals and textbooks perpetuated the notion and continued to use it in practice (Griffith, 1961). Similarly, certain treatments for alcoholism continue to be used long after they have been found ineffective (Miller & Hester, 1980, 1986a).

Theories are untestable if they cannot be disconfirmed. Consider Freud's assertion that young children are sexually attracted to the parent of the opposite sex (the Oedipus complex). How can this theory be tested or disproved? Suppose one were to ask young children in a variety of ways about their sexual feelings toward their parents. If the children denied such feelings, is this a disconfirmation of Freud's theory? Some might even take it as confirmation of the theory, showing that these feelings are so strong that children repress them.

As you read this book, then, remember that a theory is not a fact. Theories may be fascinating, creative, innovative, interesting, or challenging. They may *sound* quite believable or correct. For the scientist, however, the questions are: What is the evidence? Is the theory testable? Do the data now available support this theory, or does the evidence favor another view? A scientific approach requires that one be willing to give up a theory or modify it once the evidence no longer supports it.

TESTABLE OR UNTESTABLE?

Examine each of the following hypotheses. Which ones are testable, in that they could be disconfirmed by evidence? Which ones are untestable? Why?

Place a "T" by those you think are testable and a "U" by those you think are untestable. For those which are testable, do you think the hypothesis is correct or not? Print T+ next to those you think are testable and correct (that is, the evidence would support the hypothesis). Print T− next to those you think are testable but false (the evidence would disconfirm the hypothesis). What about those that are untestable? Do you think they are true (U+) or false (U−)? Why?

1. Human beings are born good.
2. In conversations, men interrupt more than women do.
3. Blacks earn lower salaries than whites do.
4. There is an unconscious mind that controls people's behavior.
5. As people get older, their bodies process alcohol more slowly.
6. The soul lives on after a person dies.
7. Women form closer relationships with each other than men do.
8. Thinking about getting sick can make it happen.
9. Some people have extrasensory perception (ESP).
10. Having a pet makes people more mentally healthy.

Theme One.   Women develop in the context of relationships. For women, the developmental tasks of identity, intimacy, and generativity (three of Erikson's psychosocial stages) seem to happen together rather than separately. A woman comes to know herself as she is known, through her relationships with others (Gilligan, 1982). Women studied by Hancock (1981) consistently described their lives in terms of relationships with others. They reported that relationships continued as a central focus throughout various life phases, whether work and family responsibilities were separate or combined. The women interviewed shared the assumption that a given relationship would be continuous, and if that proved not to be the case, it led to what has become the second major theme in the new research: the collapse of assumptions.

Theme Two.   Women's maturation process may be furthered by the collapse of cherished assumptions. Women have often reported that unpredictable critical events forced them to rethink values and life direction (Sangiuliano, 1980). Thus, traditional stage theories which address *predictable* changes are incomplete in their attempts to explain women's development. For example, a woman who suddenly learns that her husband has decided to leave the marriage passes through a period of anger, depression, and fear, but then returns for her college degree and makes a new life for herself and her children. Her self-concept now is more positive, she believes, than if her husband had stayed. Contrary to stereotyped beliefs, turning 30 or experiencing menopause do not necessarily result in a crisis. Far more than these predictable events, it is the unpredictable shocks that require adaptation and growth. When cherished or unconscious assumptions (such as the continuity of a given relationship over time) collapse, women are forced to reconstruct new frameworks for living (Hancock, 1981).

Theme Three.   Developing a self-perception which is both positive and feminine is difficult. Women struggle to integrate womanhood and adulthood (J. Miller, 1976). Three interacting components of socialization contribute to early sex-role–related self-perception: (1) parents reinforce children for sex-typed behavior, (2) children imitate the same-sex role model, and (3) self-socialization occurs whereby the child develops a concept of femaleness and adjusts her behavior to match the concept (Maccoby and Jacklin, 1974). Authenticity (being oneself) and subordination (accepting the role traditionally prescribed for females) are incompatible. When women risk moving beyond early socialized role prescriptions, they embark on a crucial developmental journey. Women studied by Hancock (1981) had developed self-perceptions which reflected that they were sensitive to the immediate social context, and adapted their behavior to it. But such flexibility poses a problem for women when negative social stereotypes of females cause them to avoid feminine qualities, or when female sex-role conditioning causes them to avoid behaviors considered to be inappropriate for females (Bem, 1974). Women reclaim a sense of self when they form significant relationships of various sorts. A self-perception that is both positive and feminine sometimes feels impossible to achieve (Notman, 1979).

Chodorow (1978) has speculated on the development of self-perception and masculinity as well, suggesting that since both sexes are usually raised by female caregivers, identification may involve different processes for boys and girls. For boys, issues of separation rather than identification with the caregiver may be crucial to identity. The stereotype of the solitary, "John Wayne" hero in American culture may limit male self-perceptions equally but in a different way than women are hindered in their struggle to develop a sense of self (Lewis, 1978).

Developing a self-perception which is both positive and feminine can be difficult.

Theme Four. Women are challenged to include themselves in the care, choice, and responsibility they have given others. Traditional values of self-sacrifice come to be replaced by recognition of a woman's right to include *herself* among those who deserve care, balancing her rights with the rights of others (Gilligan, 1982).

In 1848, at the Seneca Falls Convention which launched the American suffrage movement, Elizabeth Cady Stanton proclaimed that "Self-development is a higher duty than self-sacrifice." A century and a half later, women are still working on that idea, progressing to interdependence with others which combines self-nurturance and self-responsibility. The idea of **interdependence,** being linked with others in relationships which include mutual help, is being reframed to include the sharing and balance of rights and responsibilities. Many women, believing that others must be cared for first, still have difficulty carving out time and space for themselves. Virginia Woolf addressed this struggle eloquently in her work *A Room of One's Own* (1929), in which one's own room is a symbol for taking one's own life seriously.

Psychosexual Life-span Development. Many of Freud's students and followers have attempted to expand on his stage theory of psychosexual development. He freely admitted that his theory did not adequately account for female development, and he encouraged others to try to do so. Chodorow's (1978) theoretical exploration of gender identity is one attempt to account for differences in male and female development. She suggests that because both male and female children are generally raised by female caretakers, boys develop their sense of self as different from the caretaker, while girls develop in relationship to her. Such a theory may have important implications for how women and men behave in adulthood. Since masculinity is defined through separation while femininity is defined through attachment, male gender identity is threatened by intimacy while female gender identity is threatened by separation. Chodorow speculates that males tend to have difficulty with relationships, while females tend to have difficulty with individuation. Perhaps as more men become primary caretakers of their children, this hypothesis can be tested in different ways.

Interdependence
a sense of the mutual reliance of people upon each other for the fulfillment of needs; an ability to move flexibly between roles of relying upon another and being relied upon.

Psychosocial Life-span Development. As you can see, the life-span development approach is very different in some respects from stage theories which assume that people progress through a standard sequence of stages, and that each stage is characterized by a qualitatively different way of thinking and behaving (Knefelkamp, Widick, & Stroad, 1978). A stage theory typically assumes that all people (males, females, people from all cultures) progress through all the stages in the same order without skipping any step (Stevens-Long, 1979). Furthermore, stage theories have traditionally been based primarily on caucasian male experience. Consequently, they are susceptible to a significant blind spot regarding female experience and development in other racial/ethnic contexts (Hancock, 1981; Weisstein, 1971). According to more recent research, Erikson's model of development as a staircase or a one-way street does not apply well to women, for whom identity, intimacy, and generativity (three *separate* stages for Erikson) seem to develop *simultaneously* (Doherty, 1978; Gilligan, 1982). Erikson's own description of women's identity focused on how it differed from the male norm, reinforcing the idea that women's development is somehow deviant rather than normal. Caring, commitment, attachment, and mastery are indeed key issues in young adulthood, as Erikson and others have indicated (Erikson, 1968; Havighurst, 1972; White, 1975). We question, however, the common assumption that these must be resolved separately or in a fixed order.

An attempt to apply Levinson's psychosocial stage theory to the lives of women similarly resulted in the conclusion that women display less predictability and greater variability than do men. This variability especially involved the *order* in which women accomplished specific developmental tasks, as well as the particular difficulty they faced in doing so (Stewart, 1977; Williams & Long, 1983). For example, developmental tasks of young adulthood such as starting a career and a family, may be undertaken in different sequence by women and men. Because of this different sequence, women in midlife may experience developmental growth, while men in midlife may be evaluating past growth (Neugarten, 1976). Similarly, Radin (1978) found that young women's visions of the future were more likely than men's to include both work and intimacy. Women were also found more frequently to have a mentor relationship and to experience less personality conflict in early adulthood than the men Levinson studied. Thus, stage theories are being expanded, revised, or replaced to account for the broader spectrum of human life-span development.

Cognitive and Moral Life-span Development. Carol Gilligan has made a major contribution to understanding moral reasoning by looking at responses in a different way from Kohlberg, her mentor. Gilligan (1982) identified the development of what she called "the ethic of care." She did so by studying people's moral reasoning in a real-life dilemma as opposed to Kohlberg's imaginary dilemma. She asked women from diverse ethnic backgrounds and social classes how they planned to resolve their current problem pregnancies. By recording their thoughtful answers in this area where women had the power to choose, she obtained fresh insight into the moral reasoning process. The ethic of care, as defined by Gilligan, is marked by three perspectives and the transitional phases between them. First, women were concerned with caring for themselves, with their own survival. That judgment was criticized as selfish in the transitional phase. The second perspective was that of caring for others, taking responsibility for those who are dependent and unequal. This judgment triggered another transitional phase when the women realized that it was illogical to only care for others without regard for self. The third perspective balanced the concerns of selfishness and responsibility by marking the *interconnectedness* between self and other. Self and other are interdependent. The women's moral reasoning seemed to lead them to this point, for which Kohlberg's stage model, with its concern for rights and responsibilities, did not account.

4.4 PERSONAL LIFE THEMES

We asked 140 students in a Psychology of Adjustment class to consider what three major events had most shaped their lives thus far, influencing the development of their sense of self. Seventy-five students indicated that attending or returning to college had a major influence on their lives. Moving, leaving home, or living in another culture impacted 42 students. An intimate relationship or marriage was named by 40 students, with 35 mentioning employment and earning one's own money. Finally, 24 students selected illness or trauma, including automobile accidents and rape, as having a major impact on their lives.

Significant events of this kind can become important personal themes, with impact recurring throughout one's life (Bandura, 1982). These themes can take on great personal meaning, affecting how individuals perceive themselves and how they develop as adults. Such personal themes are part of each and every individual life tapestry. The richness and diversity which result from individual life histories may be underestimated by stage theories of adult development.

Asking the same question of a different group of people might elicit very different answers. If a group other than college students were asked to name their most important life-changing events, for example, the most commonly cited responses would probably be different. It is an important limitation of psychological research that so much of it has been done with college students and generalized to all people. If you chose to do research, what group of people would *you* like to question about events that have shaped their lives?

■ SOCIALIZATION: ADAPTING TO THE SOCIAL ENVIRONMENT

No individual develops in isolation. Rather the self, no matter how it is conceived, develops in relation to the social environment. The course of development is a process of mutual adjustment between the individual and his or her environment. Thus the social environment in which the individual lives and grows will exert important influences on self and self-perception. This process of **socialization** represents a third approach to understanding how the self develops.

Each developmental theory offers its own conceptualization of this socialization process, the adaptation of the individual to the social environment. For Freud, socialization was a lifelong process of compromise between the wholly selfish impulses of the id and the demands of society, with the ego serving as the mediator in negotiating these compromises between the id and the superego (representing society). In many stage theories, the environment is seen as playing a key role by providing crucial experiences or opportunities that permit the individual to progress to the next developmental stage. From a life-span development perspective, which does not assume preprogrammed stages, social experiences are vital in shaping the themes and patterns that characterize the unique individual.

Socialization
the process whereby an individual learns the values, attitudes, norms, and behaviors of his or her social group.

DEVELOPMENTAL CHALLENGES OF SOCIALIZATION

Developmental theories also typically describe particular socialization tasks or challenges that face the individual. Erikson's eight "crises" of development and

Sheehy's (1976) "passages" are examples. Drawing on a broad ethological perspective that considers both animal and human adaptation, Plutchik (1980) pointed to four general types of survival problems that are encountered in socialization: hierarchy, territoriality, identity, and temporality. This is an interesting approach in that both animals and humans face these challenges and must successfully deal with them to survive and grow.

Hierarchy.   In almost any social system, there is a sense of dominance, of higher and lower levels of social power. Within communities of monkeys, for example, each individual has a clear place in the order of dominance, and animals at the top of this dominance order have first choice when it comes to food, choice of a place to sit or sleep, and mating partners. The occurrence of this same phenomenon among birds led to the descriptive phrase, "pecking order." Among people, these hierarchies may be determined by physical strength, wealth, skillfulness, or intelligence.

Like it or not, each individual must recognize the existence of these hierarchies and choose some personal strategy for dealing with them. One may choose a competitive strategy, fighting for higher position. Another may choose a submissive role serving as a helper or "side-kick" to more powerful individuals. Still another may seek to withdraw from hierarchical systems, neither competing nor submitting. The popular **Peter principle** (Peter, 1969) suggests still another strategy: to rise naturally to a level at which you are both comfortable and competent and then to resist and refuse further promotions in the hierarchy that tend to increase stress by pushing you to the limits of your competence and competitive abilities.

Territoriality.   Many animal species have clear methods for marking a physical space, a personal territory that is a safe home base. The invasion of this territory by an outsider results in a struggle for control, sometimes for survival. A human reflection of this is our preoccupation with making maps, drawing and defending local and national boundaries. The maintenance and defense of such territorial boundaries has historically been a primary cause of warfare. Children pass through a process of asserting and learning what is "mine" and what is not. The quest for possessions, for a set of things that "belong to" or are "owned by" the individual, is another example. Human laws are often designed to set clear territorial limits. Possession *is* nine-tenths of the law!

Identity.   Another general adjustment question encountered in the developmental process of socialization (which continues throughout one's life) is: To what (or whom) do I belong? In many animal species, identity with a group is vital to survival, and being separated or alienated from one's group threatens survival. The badge of belonging is a perceived similarity, perhaps superficial (such as racial characteristics), perhaps symbolic (wearing the same uniform, living "under the same flag"), or conceptual (having the same values, ascribing to the same religion).

The formation of "in" and "out" groups appears to be something of a universal tendency among animals and humans. Prejudice and discrimination consist of differential treatment of individuals based on their membership in different groups. Organizations, clubs, religions, and occupational groups often devise overt or secret signs by which the members of the group can be recognized and distinguished from others: a distinctive type of clothing, a secret handshake, a physical mark such as a tatoo, a characteristic pattern of behavior.

The **identity** question, "Who am I?" is difficult to answer without considering oneself in *relation*. Many of the terms we use to answer this question describe roles that one holds in relation to others: mother, son, psychologist,

Peter Principle
a theory, introduced by Lawrence Peter, that within hierarchical organizations, people who perform their jobs competently are promoted until they reach a level of functioning at which they are incompetent.

Identity
the sense of sameness of self, of continuity of one's past and present.

extravert, German, student. In the course of development, one's identity develops in interaction with others. Even deeply personal spiritual questions can be understood as a struggling with the ultimate question, "To whom do I belong?"

Temporality. Life is short. Each individual has a limited time to live, to carry out whatever purpose and goals she or he may choose. Death presents a fourth general challenge of adjustment with which everyone must come to grips. One of the most disturbing and disrupting events that one can experience is the death of a loved one: a parent, one's child, a lifelong friend, one's spouse. Even among higher animals there are clear patterns for dealing with the grief of loss: the cry of distress, comforting, and nurturing from peers.

But we humans have, perhaps, the unique distinction among creatures of being able to contemplate our *own* death. Some cope with this by denying it, by living as if death will never come. Some live with a sense of urgency, as if death were just around the corner and everything had to be done or experienced today. The powerful "death and dying" movement which arose in the 1970s has helped individuals to seek yet another solution: to accept the reality of death, and to live life with joy and appreciation, making conscious choices about how to spend the limited time that is ours.

4.5	**HERE WE DIFFER/HERE WE AGREE** Can Research with Animals Be Generalized to Humans?

Whenever I read about how animals behave and realize the author is generalizing those behavioral observations to human behavior, I question the validity of the generalization. This is especially true since many findings about one group of *humans* do not generalize to other groups of humans. The fact, for example, that findings for white *male* Americans often do not apply even to American *women's* development or to the development of people in other cultures or subcultures makes me wonder how generalizations from dogs to people can be valid. Surely people are more similar to other people than they are to dogs, chickens, or insects! Some sociobiologists (e.g., Wilson, 1975) have taken extreme positions in generalizing animal behavior to humans and have come up with conclusions that I believe could be harmful to human society. Randy Thornhill (1981, Thornhill & Thornhill 1983), for example, is an evolutionary biologist who studies male insects which force copulation with female insects. Based on his findings with insects, he speculates that human rapists of women of reproductive age cannot be distinguished from normal men, whereas men who rape children or women of postreproductive age are abnormal upon psychiatric evaluation. While he admits that these generalizations have yet to be tested, Thornhill asserts that his evolutionary model fits both insects and humans. Unfortunately, his insect observations might be inappropriately extrapolated to conclude that rape is a viable reproductive strategy in humans, and therefore acceptable. Clearly generalizations from nonhuman behavior should be made with caution, taking into account what being human means. —CEY

Caution is certainly appropriate in making any generalization, but one must likewise be careful not to throw out the baby with the bath water. *Of course* there are important differences among species that limit generalization, but there is much to be learned from our similarities as well. Medical research has benefited immensely from commonalities between people and certain animal species. Heart valves, life-saving surgical procedures, and skin grafts are all available because of research conducted first with animals, then generalized to the human body. Similarly within psychology, the basic principles of respondent and operant learning were worked out first through the animal research of pioneers like Pavlov and Skinner. Could these same principles be applied with beneficial results in humans? To a large extent, the answer has been yes, and although human learning is much more complex, the same basic principles of learning have been used to develop effective treatments for alcoholism (Azrin et al., 1982), fears and phobias (Turner, Calhoun, & Adams, 1981), children's behavior problems (Ollendick, 1986), and sex offenders (Adams, Tollison, & Carson, 1981). Lang and Melamed (1969) used their knowledge of operant learning to save the life of an infant who was starving to death because of ruminative vomiting, after all medical interventions had failed. Without the findings of animal research, both medicine and psychology would be far less advanced, and many treatments that now alleviate human suffering might never have been developed.   —WRM

INTEGRATION

Discoveries from animal research can generate ideas about human psychology, but these hypotheses must then be carefully tested with human populations. Certainly generalizability cannot be assumed, and the uncritical application of animal findings to humans could produce harmful results. The use of animal research also raises some difficult questions: How do we decide when generalizing from animal species to humans is appropriate and useful? Are scientists responsible for inappropriate extrapolations from their research by the public? When, if ever, are we justified in inflicting suffering on animals as part of research, to develop more effective treatment procedures for people? Which discoveries merit study and which are more harmful than helpful, especially given limited resources for research?

SOCIALIZATION AND LEARNING PROCESSES

These and other challenges are faced by every individual, who must work out strategies for adjusting, for adapting to the demands and realities of the social world. In the process of maturation, each person develops an individual style, a set of personal strategies and skills for survival and growth. This style emerges through socialization, the process of interaction between the individual and her or his social environment.

How does this socialization process occur? It is here that an appreciation of learning processes is important in understanding adjustment and the psychology of change. Therefore we will describe in greater detail the processes of respondent and operant learning, mentioned briefly in Chapter 1, and some cognitive processes related to learning.

Respondent Learning.   A group of philosophers known as the British associationists began in the early nineteenth century to describe principles by which ideas come to be *associated* with each other (James Mill, 1869; John Stuart Mill, 1865; Spencer, 1855). They maintained that under certain predictable conditions, events come to be associated mentally. Four such principles of association were described: *contiguity* (the two events occur close together in time), *similarity* (the two events resemble each other in some way), *frequency* (the two events occur together often), and *inseparability* (without exception, when one event occurs the other follows). These descriptions by philosophers of mental processes foreshadowed what would later become principles of respondent learning.

The work of Ivan Pavlov, a Russian physiologist, helped to clarify the principles of learning by which associations are formed. Through experiments with animals, Pavlov demonstrated that it is possible to develop strong physiological and emotional reactions to stimuli that previously evoked very little response. A soft buzzer or bell, for example, normally causes little more than mild curiosity in an animal, and after a few soundings, the animal ignores it almost completely. Pavlov demonstrated that if such a sound is paired (followed) with the delivery of meat powder to a hungry animal, soon the animal begins to salivate when it hears the sound. If, instead, the buzzer consistently is paired with a painful shock, soon the animal begins to react emotionally to the buzzer as if it *were* the shock. The buzzer, a previously neutral stimulus, takes on some of the qualities of the stimulus with which it is associated. This process of learning is typically called *respondent* conditioning, though it has also been called *classical* or *Pavlovian* conditioning.

The same process clearly operates in people as well. A single frightening experience (an automobile accident, for example) can leave a person with an enduring fear of similar situations (driving). Becoming ill after eating a certain food can result in a loss of taste for, or even a revulsion to, that particular food. The same process operates with positive emotions as well. Having very pleasant experiences in a particular place often leaves a favorable impression of the place itself, and the person may choose to take future trips or vacations to the same spot. A caretaker who lavishes physical affection and sweets on a child is likely to be welcomed by the child with open arms.

In respondent learning, a previously neutral **conditional stimulus (CS)** is paired with an **unconditional stimulus (UCS)** that evokes a particular automatic or **unconditional response (UCR).** The most powerful arrangement is usually for the CS to occur first, and to be followed very quickly by the UCS. With enough pairings or associations, the CS eventually comes to evoke a **conditioned response (CR)** very similar to the UCR. Thus the once neutral CS now evokes a new response.[1]

Associations that are established in this way also have a way of spreading. A child, frightened by a large and threatening dog, becomes afraid of all dogs. An experience with a very kindly native of Switzerland may leave a favorable feeling for the Swiss in general. A stranger who physically resembles an emotionally significant person in one's life may evoke some of the same feelings and reactions. The process at work here is **stimulus generalization.** Stimuli that are alike in some important way may evoke similar emotional reactions and behavior.

Over time, respondent learning translates into patterns of approach and avoidance behavior. Conditional stimuli that have been paired with a pleasant UCS tend to be approached. Advertisers take advantage of this principle by producing commercials in which their products (which they hope you will approach by buying them) are shown in association with pleasant surroundings, attractive people, or fantasy symbols of success and happiness. On the other hand, a CS paired with an aversive UCS will tend to be avoided. Once frightened by a dog, the child may cry and run away from even the harmless and fun-loving puppy.

Unfortunately such avoidance prevents unlearning of the fear. A respondent conditioning experience does not last forever. If the CS is experienced time after time *without* the UCS following, eventually it loses its emotional impact through the process of **extinction.** The traditional advice of "When you fall off the horse, get right back on," is usually good advice for preventing the development of a lasting fear. If, however, the rider begins avoiding horses, there is no opportunity for extinction to occur, and the fear may continue or even intensify.

Conditional Stimulus
a neutral stimulus that, by respondent conditioning, comes to elicit a conditioned response.

Unconditional Stimulus
a stimulus that automatically evokes a response without requiring a prior period of learning.

Unconditional Response
a response that is automatically elicited (by an unconditional stimulus), without requiring a prior period of learning.

Conditioned Response
a new response to a previously neutral (conditional) stimulus, established through respondent conditioning.

Stimulus Generalization
a process whereby responses learned to one stimulus come to be evoked in whole or in part by similar stimuli.

Extinction
the weakening of a response; in respondent conditioning, the presentation of a conditional stimulus without the unconditional stimulus, resulting in a weakening of the conditioned response; in operant conditioning, the occurrence of a behavior without subsequent reinforcement, resulting in a weakening of the behavior.

---

[1] The CS is more commonly referred to as a "conditioned stimulus," but this term is somewhat confusing, in that the CS begins as a neutral stimulus and only later evokes a conditioned response. We prefer "*conditional* stimulus" as a clearer translation of Pavlov's concept.

Operant Learning.   Another important learning process is *operant* conditioning (also called *instrumental* learning), which was clarified by the research and writings of B. F. Skinner (1948, 1953). The focus here is on the *consequences* of a behavior. Responses that lead to a favorable consequence tend to be repeated; they are reinforced. On the other hand, responses that lead to an unfavorable outcome are less likely to be repeated, they are punished. A central principle in operant conditioning is this "law of effect": that the probability of a behavior being repeated is increased or decreased by the consequences that follow from the behavior. A **reinforcer**, then, is any consequence that increases the probability of a behavior. A **punisher**, by contrast, is any consequence that decreases the likelihood that a behavior will be repeated. There are large differences between individuals in what constitutes a reinforcer or a punisher. In fact, what is a reinforcer for one person can be a punisher for another. The opportunity to sit through a two-hour concert of loud rock music, for example, could be a powerful reinforcer for one person, who would work many hours to obtain a ticket, while the same concert would be a punisher that another person would work to avoid.

This example illustrates two kinds of reinforcement. Both of the individuals in this imaginary example are working (a behavior) to obtain a consequence that is reinforcing for them. For the first person, the reinforcing consequence is to *receive* the concert. This is **positive reinforcement**, in which the individual's behavior results in receiving a reinforcer. For the second person, however, the reinforcing consequence is to *avoid* or *escape from* a punisher. The individual's behavior results in the desirable consequence of having a punisher removed. That is called **negative reinforcement**. Both constitute reinforcement because they *increase* the probability of the behavior occurring in the future. In positive reinforcement, a reinforcer is *presented* or *received* after the behavior. In negative reinforcement, a punisher is *removed* or *avoided* after the behavior.

Similarly there are two kinds of punishment. In one, **positive punishment**, a punisher is presented (received) after the behavior, and as a result the behavior is less likely to occur again. In the other, **negative punishment**, the undesirable consequence is that the behavior results in the loss (removal) of a reinforcer. Consider two ways in which a child's misbehavior might be punished. One way would be that the behavior results in a punisher (spanking, having to wash the dishes). The other would be that the behavior results in the loss of a reinforcer (lost allowance or TV privileges). Again, remember that what constitutes a punisher and a reinforcer varies from person to person.

Box 4.6 summarizes the two kinds of reinforcement and punishment. Remember that reinforcement always *increases* the probability of a behavior, makes it more likely to occur again, whereas punishment always *decreases* the probability of a behavior, making it less likely to occur again. Do not be misled by thinking that "positive" means something pleasant in this case or that "negative" means something unpleasant. Rather, the word "positive" indicates that something is being presented (received) as a consequence of the behavior, and "negative" means that something is being removed (taken away). The term "negative reinforcement" should not be confused with "punishment," since the former *increases* a behavior whereas the latter *decreases* it.

What has all this to do with socialization? Quite a lot. Over the course of years of development, children learn that certain behaviors are likely to result in specific consequences. Some kinds of behavior are reinforced (by parents, friends, teachers), and others are punished. These ongoing interactions between the child and the environment gradually shape how the person will approach the social world.

Reinforcer
a stimulus that, when delivered following a response, strengthens that response.

Punisher
a stimulus that, when delivered following a response, weakens that response.

Positive Reinforcement
the strengthening of a response by contingent presentation of a desirable consequence.

Negative Reinforcement
the strengthening of a response by contingent withdrawal of an aversive consequence.

Positive Punishment
the weakening of a response by contingent presentation of an aversive consequence.

Negative Punishment
the weakening of a response by contingent withdrawal of a desirable consequence.

4.6 REINFORCEMENT AND PUNISHMENT

	AFTER THE RESPONSE, A STIMULUS IS	
AND THE RESPONSE IS THEN	Presented	Withdrawn
Strengthened	Positive reinforcement	Negative reinforcement
Weakened	Positive punishment	Negative punishment

Cognitive Processes in Learning. Early theories of learning tended to be mechanistic, implying a kind of automatic or reflexive response of the individual to stimuli from the environment. More recent writers, however, have placed great emphasis on *cognitive* processes which underlie learning (Gordon, 1989). It appears, for example, that the crucial aspect of a CS in respondent learning is the information it provides about whether a UCS is about to occur. Without such informational value, a CS does not come to evoke a CR.

The concept of "rules" has also become important as a cognitive factor in learning. People respond not to the *actual* world, but to their *perceptions* of the world (Chapter 1). No matter what actual conditions and rules are operating in the environment, a person responds to what he or she *believes* the rules to be. That is, behavior is **rule-governed**, guided by abstractions from experience (Zettle & Hayes, 1982).

A person's values or morals, for example, represent rules for behavior that the person has developed through experience. In Chapter 2 we discussed basic assumptions that guide behavior (called "scripts" in transactional analysis), and these, too, represent abstracted rules about how the world works. As children grow and the brain develops, the **frontal lobes** of the brain become increasingly dominant. As this occurs, the child is more able to behave in accord with abstract rules and principles. This can be seen in age differences with regard to delay of gratification. Given a free choice between studying for a test tomorrow or going out for ice cream, a seven-year-old is not likely to be found at her or his desk. A college student, on the other hand, may elect to study, delaying immediate pleasure in the interest of a longer-term goal.

Another important type of learning that occurs in the course of development is *modeling*. People learn by watching others. This is one way of acquiring new skills. To learn how to scramble an egg or clear a carburetor, one might observe a model, a person who is already experienced in this skill. People also learn about the consequences of behavior and deduce rules by observing others' actions and their reinforcing or punishing consequences.

Rule-Governed Behavior
responses guided by a cognitive principle that the individual derives from experience, then uses to direct future actions.

Frontal Lobes
the upper forward part of the brain, lying behind the forehead, which is associated with tasks of complex learning and reasoning.

Research shows, for example, that children can often overcome a fear of dogs by watching a fearless child have fun playing with a dog, and that adults can overcome a fear of snakes in the same manner (Bandura & Menlove, 1968; Bandura, Blanchard, & Ritter, 1969). Observing others, then, can teach new skills and also can communicate some of the consequences or rules of behavior.

■ THE SELF-IDEAL: WHAT ARE YOU GROWING TOWARD?

Psychodynamic and behavioral theories of development have placed heavy emphasis on the environment and experience as determinants of self. The self is shaped by early and ongoing influences from the social environment. In extreme, this view implies that you are who you are by virtue of the environment in which you happen to have lived. Behaviorist John Watson (1930) became famous for his boast that, if given total control over a child's environment, he could shape that child into any kind of person he might choose.

It is important to understand that this view of the self as a mechanistic product of the environment is a relatively recent and brief one. Prior to the twentieth century, behavior was understood as being strongly influenced by the self as a causal, deciding agent. Indeed, modern legal codes are predicated on the assumption that people willfully decide to commit crimes, and are to be held responsible for their actions. It would be difficult (interesting, perhaps) to build a law enforcement code based on the premise that all behavior results from environmental influences!

There is also evidence that factors traditionally identified with the "self" are being given increasing weight as causes of behavior and change. The contemporary emphasis in learning theory on cognition, information processing, and rule-governed behavior suggests greater interest in the individual as a significant agent. The research of psychologist George Howard (1989; Howard & Conway, 1986) more directly demonstrates the role of volitional processes like "trying" and "choosing" in determining what one will do.

4.7 SELF AS AGENT

Free will. Those two words can conjure up many thoughts, meanings, or emotions. The essential idea is a simple one: that human actions are determined or at least influenced by personal choice and decision processes.

An opposing view is *determinism*, which asserts that human actions are controlled by predictable, specifiable principles, and that personal "will" is an illusion. Determinism is a common assumption in many psychological theories. This view that human behavior is determined by factors other than personal will is shared by groups as diverse as behaviorists (B. F. Skinner) and psychoanalysts (Sigmund Freud).

It is fair to say that most people view themselves and others as having free will. Asked, "Why did you do that?" people are likely to give an answer implying personal volition: "I decided to because . . ." or "I wanted to . . . ." Our nation's legal system is based on this ancient assumption that people act of their own volition. In fact, the law provides that if a person can be shown to have been *unable* to decide rationally or to choose a course of action, this removes or reduces the person's legal guilt for his or her actions. This is the basis of legal concepts such as insanity, capacity, and intent. The idea of personal responsibility for one's actions—that one decides what to do and could have decided otherwise—is a central assumption in much of Western thought and in most world religions.

Yet psychology is the study of the lawfulness and predictability of behavior. A century of research has revealed a broad range of principles of behavior that shape human actions. Is there a place for free will in psychology? How could one ever demonstrate, through properly controlled experiments, that free will exists and influences human action?

Psychologist George Howard of the University of Notre Dame has devised some remarkably simple experiments to demonstrate the role of volition in behavior. Consider, first, the necessary conditions of a proper psychological experiment. One factor (an independent variable) is varied in order to study its effect on one or more behaviors (dependent variables). Ideally, all other factors are held constant, so that if the dependent variable is affected, it can be explained only by the effects of the independent variable. In this case, the independent variable under study is volition—personal choice. But how can you control personal choice as an independent variable? Howard had college students toss a coin daily and record the result of the toss. The instruction was that if the coin came up heads, the student was to *try* that day to change a certain behavior (such as eating of peanuts, the amount of aerobic exercise completed, or the amount of time spent in social interactions). If the coin toss had the opposite result, the student was not to try to control the behavior that day. Nothing else was changed. The only difference between "heads" days and "tails" days (which happened randomly, at the toss of a coin) was personal effort—*trying*. The results of several such studies show a large effect of personal effort (Howard, 1989; Howard & Conway, 1986).

This approach permits one to ask more complicated, and even more interesting, questions. Which behaviors are *more* influenced by personal choice? It seems likely that some behaviors are highly influenced by choice under normal circumstances (for example, what you eat for dinner) and that others are less subject to volition (your heart rate, for example). Some (like the rate of your breathing) are not ordinarily influenced much by conscious choice, but *can* be altered dramatically if the person tries. How much control do you have over a particular behavior? The coin toss experiment is one way to find out. It would also be possible, using this approach, to study individual differences in the overall degree of personal control one has. Do some people, in fact, *have* more "self-control" than others? Why?

Free will or determinism? Our own view is that personal choice is *one* factor influencing human behavior. In some situations, behavior is so automatic, overlearned, or driven by external factors that personal choice seems to have little to do with it. This was part of the humor in "Candid Camera," a popular television series of the 1960s. Unsuspecting strangers were filmed in situations set up by the director, Allen Funt. An elevator door opens, and the car is filled with people facing the *back* of the car. Very often (though not always), a newcomer to this situation also faced the back, a very unusual behavior under normal circumstances. The humor of Candid Camera was how much our behavior is influenced by external factors such as these. In other situations and with other behaviors, personal choice plays a major role. We believe it's not a question of whether there *is* "free will" or personal choice. The question is for a certain behavior and a specific individual in a particular situation, how *much* influence can be exerted by personal volition? Human behavior is complicated!

All of this is to say that there seems to be a renewal of interest in *purpose* as a cause of behavior. Certain learning theorists (Tolman, 1932) and personality theorists (Adler, 1927) have argued that it is impossible to understand behavior without asking what its purpose is, what the individual intended to do. This, again, is a cornerstone of current Western legal codes. For example, to establish guilt for certain crimes, the prosecutor must show that the offender *intended* to commit the act. The inferred intention of the individual (e.g., self-defense versus homicide) often has a major bearing on sentencing. The purpose, intention, and meaning of behavior have always been of central interest within humanistic and existential psychology.

How does this apply to a psychology of self? The implication is that to understand an individual (or oneself), it is vital to know what that person is striving or growing toward. People have not just a remembered past and an immediate present, but also an imagined future. It is here that the concept of the ideal self emerges.

SELF-IDEAL

Think of the people you know whom you would describe as healthy and fulfilled. How do they behave? How do they perceive themselves? What is it about them that makes them seem healthy to you? These are important people to observe, because they may be role models for you, illustrating the kind of person you may want to become.

Returning to the idea of healthy development of the self, one might ask, "What constitutes a healthy person? What are the characteristics of the psychologically healthy adult?" Here are a few historic ideas about ideal adjustment. Love and work have been recognized as crucial components of psychological health in adulthood (Freud, 1964), as have active mastery of the environment and self-acceptance (Erikson, 1968). Existential and humanistic psychologists propose that a fully functioning person is one who embodies a self-actualizing tendency, making conscious choices about behavior and directing her or his own life (Buhler & Allen, 1972; Maslow, 1954; Rogers, 1961). Such a person is described as trusting the self, with a need for positive regard and self-regard. **Congruence** and openness to experience are valued, as is autonomous decision making, regardless of the evaluation of others. The ability to relate to both sexes as people, and to like and accept one's own body, as well as to take responsibility for knowing and managing one's sexual and reproductive life have also been cited as characteristics of a healthy person (Klein, 1976). How do these descriptions compare to your own description of someone you consider healthy?

STUDIES OF IDEAL ADJUSTMENT

If one accepts the notion of an ideal self, then it is possible to conceive of (or even measure) a kind of "ideal adjustment"—the extent to which one is approaching the self-ideal. Recall that, in Rogers's view, people who perceive themselves as being closer to their self-ideal tend to show higher self-esteem. This suggests an interesting approach in understanding ideal adjustment: to study people with positive self-esteem. In one such study, when women with high self-esteem were interviewed about themselves and their upbringing, they described themselves as being *in the process of becoming* their ideal self (Long, 1986). They valued assertiveness and independence, including financial independence. Three "C's" were considered important: congruence (feeling at one with the self), control (over the self and one's own life), and competency (being capable and able). Many of these women with high self-esteem indicated they had been given an empowering message as children: "You can do anything you want to do." They internalized this message and continued to repeat it to themselves as adults, thus strengthening their sense of personal control. Intimacy was reported as important to all of the women, but not at the expense of private time or at the cost of paying insufficient attention to self. In other words, these high-self-esteem women were warm toward others, but not to the point of being self-sacrificing. They struggled for autonomy as individuals, and felt they did not achieve identity and independence until after mar-

Congruence
a psychological state in which a person's feelings, awareness of those feelings, and expression of feelings are consistent with one another; also called genuineness; described by Carl Rogers as a crucial condition for therapeutic change.

riage, rather than during adolescence. Only one woman in the sample judged herself to have married with realistic expectations, and over half divorced, reporting that divorce was an important influence on their growth.

Studying healthy development of the self and self-esteem continues to be important, especially for women, because (as discussed earlier) traditional explanations have included a kind of double-bind that made being both healthy and female difficult. Ironically, both male and female mental health professionals, the very people who are consulted to *help* in the process of developing healthy self-esteem, have been found to judge mental health by how well adjusted the individual is to a social or sex-role orientation or norm (Broverman et al., 1970). The qualities ascribed to psychologically healthy adult females by the mental health professionals surveyed were quite different from those given when the professionals were asked simply to describe "healthy adults" (not identified as being either male or female). Healthy adults and healthy males, by contrast, were described similarly. Thus, it appears impossible for a woman to be a mature and healthy adult, while also meeting traditional sex-role expectations according to the dominant standards. Women are placed in the conflictual position of either exhibiting adult socially desirable characteristics and having their "femininity" questioned, or of behaving in the prescribed feminine manner and thereby judged to be less mature or socially valuable. In your experience is this so? If you are a woman, have you behaved in an assertive way and had others react to you as if you were being "pushy"? What impact might such an experience have on a person's self-esteem?

CROSS-CULTURAL PERSPECTIVES ON SELF-IDEAL

Over 50 years ago, Margaret Mead, an innovative anthropologist, studied development in other cultures, and found that what is considered normal behavior in one culture may be regarded as deviant in another. In a group of people she studied called the Tchambuli, there was a genuine reversal of the gender roles of the mainstream American culture of that day: the woman was the dominant, impersonal, managing partner, while the man was the less responsible and the emotionally dependent person. Mead concluded that human nature is extremely flexible, responding in an accurate and adaptive fashion to contrasting cultural conditions (Mead, 1935).

Just as traditional male theorists have often evidenced blind spots about female experience, so also have white middle-class Americans and Europeans suffered blind spots about the experience of other sociocultural groups. Some attempts have been made to rectify the gaps in psychological theory regarding the experience of peoples from other cultures and subcultures. The growing field of cross-cultural psychology is the result of such attempts. Cross-cultural researchers have sought to discover principles that remain stable over time and across cultures, but studies thus far have largely excluded the great majority of humankind who live in Asia and the southern hemisphere. Concern has been expressed that current theories are merely parochial generalizations, based on ethnocentric constructions of reality (Triandis & Draguns, 1980).

Self and self-perception, the subject of this chapter, may have very different meanings to people who are not part of the Euro-American stream within which most current psychological theories have been developed. The rise of the "me generation," for example, is quite recent, yet is taken for granted today. The current individualism of American society is extreme by worldwide standards (Munroe & Munroe, 1975; Neki, 1976). According to one study conducted in the American Southwest, Anglo homesteaders, Mormons, and Spanish-Americans judged *individual-oriented* relationships to be best, while Native Americans (Navajo and Zuni) emphasized *group-oriented* relations (Kluck-

Over 50 years ago, Margaret Mead, an innovative anthropologist, studied development in other cultures.

hohn & Stodtbeck, 1961). For the Native Americans responding in this study, *self* was less important than the *group*. Asian-Americans likewise have been found to place greater importance on the family or group than on the individual (Sue, 1977). Such cultural differences contribute to dramatically different conceptions of an ideal self, and for this reason have profound implications for programs of education, prevention, and treatment. Current American approaches that heavily emphasize personal achievement, self-fulfillment, and individual rights may be quite inappropriate and maladaptive in other social contexts (Katz, 1985).

From where do ideals come? How do people develop their sense of what it means, for example, to be male or female? In a study of children's behavior in six cultures, Whiting and Edwards (1973) investigated the possibility that psychological maleness and femaleness may be innate. They examined dependency, sociability, nurturance, responsibility, dominance, and aggression. They concluded that the *tasks* assigned to children determine how much they adhere to a masculine or feminine stereotype. When children were assigned the task of being responsible for the care of a younger sibling, for example, both boys and girls behaved in a more nurturing way that might be labeled feminine. The researchers concluded that social expectations may play a larger role than biology in the development of psychological maleness or femaleness.

Cultural norms exert substantial influence over what is regarded to be ideal for the individual. Within current American culture, great value is placed on *assertiveness*, the forthright expression of one's feelings and rights. From the beginning, assertiveness training in the United States has emphasized standing up for one's own rights (Alberti & Emmons, 1986). When transferred to another culture, however, assertiveness takes on new dimensions. In Norway, for example, children are raised to respect and consider the good of the group, of the larger society, and what would be regarded as assertiveness in the United States would communicate rudeness and insensitivity within a Norwegian context. In fact the Norwegian word that has been used to translate "assertiveness," *selvhevdelse*, carries with it the negative connotation of promoting one's own welfare at the expense of others.

Americans also typically place a high premium on independence. Growing up and maturing is thought of as developing from dependence to independence. This view is not shared in all cultures. Neki (1976), for example, contrasts concepts of ideal development in India and the Western world. Within India, according to Neki, dependence is seen as a valued and valuable experience of childhood, and is encouraged and fostered in children. Growing up is seen as moving from dependence to *dependability* (being one upon whom others can rely) rather than to independence. In a society where dependence is seen as a shameful or second-class status, and where independence is the norm, the painful lack is of dependable people. The Indian cultural norms of moving from dependence to dependability and then back into dependence with advancing age, make interrelationships among people more consistent with their expectations. Lacking such a perspective, a society is likely to treat its dependent members with resentment and rejection, a not uncommon experience of the elderly in Western societies.

Looking at psychological development from the perspective of many cultures or of subcultures within a dominant culture can help one gain a broader picture of reality. One of us (CEY), who lived as a white woman on a reservation with Pueblo peoples, became much more conscious of major differences in moral development and valuing. Events that had no meaning for white people were deeply important for the Native American people of the Laguna and Acoma Pueblos. For example, while driving the high school girls' cross-country team to a meet, CEY accidentally ran over a large snake that was stretched across the road. The passengers in the car gasped in horror, since killing a snake was perceived as very bad luck, or even sacrilege. While she felt badly about killing the snake, the experience did not have any special moral meaning for her. Everyone in the car sighed with relief when one of the girls said, "It's O.K., she's white," meaning that moral rules in one culture might not apply to people of another group. The forgiving attitude of the high school students involved recognizing and accepting cultural differences.

Conceptions of what is acceptable or ideal also change over time for given individuals and cultures. The term **acculturation** refers to the process whereby an individual or group comes to share the values and norms of a larger, dominant culture (Leong, 1986). Students who change schools may find themselves in a peer group with values quite different from those of the previous school. Over time, the individual's self-ideal may change to resemble that of the new peer group. The same process can occur for a whole family or cultural group. A generation ago, for example, it was said that direct eye contact with Native Americans was rude and disrespectful. It now seems that may be true with older Native American people, but with today's young adults, direct eye contact may be little different than it is for members of the white culture. Similarly, alcohol use patterns among descendents of immigrants to the United States more closely resemble those of American culture with each successive generation, departing from whatever had been the norm of the culture from which the family emigrated. The ideals against which self may be compared, then, can vary dramatically from one generation or culture to another. These ideals, of the specific time and culture in which one grows up, in turn have a major impact on the individual's sense of self.

■ SUMMARY

The self has been defined in many different ways. Most theories of self include the idea of conflict among various parts of the self. Self-perception includes self-concept (your thoughts and beliefs about yourself as you are now), self-ideal (how you would like to be ideally), and self-esteem (your overall feeling or evaluation of who you are). Three approaches for understanding the development of self are stage theories (Freud, Erikson, Kohlberg, and Piaget), life-span development theories (Neugarten, Gilligan, Vygotsky, and Chodorow), and socialization studies. Socialization is the process by which an individual adapts to the social environment, to cope with common themes such as hierarchy, territoriality, identity, and temporality. Principles of learning are helpful in understanding the socialization process. What constitutes the ideal self varies widely among cultures and subcultures. Generalizations from one group to another must be made with caution.

Acculturation
the process by which an individual or group acquires the values and behavior patterns of a larger cultural group.

■ QUESTIONS FOR THOUGHT

1. Which of the four definitions of "self" offered in this chapter (awareness, seed, perceived personality, or whole) best fits your own sense of what your "self" is?

2. Think of a conflict you have experienced within yourself recently. Did there seem to be different voices arguing against each other within you? Who were those voices? What were the values represented by each voice?

3. Look again at the eight psychosocial stages described by Erikson. Which of these eight basic challenges or conflicts seems to be the one with which you are most involved at this time in your life?

4. Who has had the greatest positive influence on your life thus far? Why? What has this person done to have such an influence on you?

5. Who are your mentors or role models now? What would you like to learn from them? What attributes of these people would you most like to have in yourself? Are there aspects of these people you would not want to have as part of yourself?

6. Are there people you know who represent the kind of person you do *not* want to become? What people have inspired you to say, "I'm *not* going to be like that!" What are the characteristics of these people that you most want to avoid?

7. What examples of *respondent* learning can you think of in your own life experiences? Can you think of ways in which respondent processes have influenced your liking or disliking for certain stimuli?

8. What examples of *operant* learning can you find in your own life? What are the most important reinforcers that motivate you?

9. When you read questions 7 and 8, what happened? Did you want to go back to the text and review respondent and operant learning to understand? Or did you just decide to skip on to the next question?

10. Do you know people who were raised in a culture, subculture, or ethnic group very different from your own? What have they taught you?

chapter five

Things do not change;
We change.
—Thoreau, *Walden*

Self-Control and Change

OUTLINE

*D*o you ever wish you had more self-control? If not, you're unusual. Most often the issue of self-control comes up when you want to make a change in yourself. Perhaps you have some success at first, but then comes a setback. "If only I had more self-control," you say.

Yet what *is* this "self-control"? Where does it come from? Is there hope for people who don't seem to have much of it? That is what this chapter is about. First we will examine the concept of self-control and consider factors influencing its development. Next we will discuss some of the most common obstacles to self-control, and consider what you can do to overcome them. We will explain an interesting theory that describes change as occurring in predictable stages. Then we will turn practical, offering four steps for understanding and dealing with problems. Finally, we will bring back the STORC model as a strategy for finding effective self-control tools to overcome obstacles and problems.

■ SOME DEFINITIONS OF SELF-CONTROL

Perhaps the most common conception of self-control is as a personality characteristic, a trait of which individuals can *have* much or little. This is the definition underlying the statement that a certain person "has a lot of self-control" or the complaint that "I wish he had more self-control." This use of the term is similar to popular concepts of "will power" and "self-discipline." This definition has some merit, in that people do seem to differ from each other on characteristics like **impulsiveness.** As people grow from childhood to adulthood, they normally begin to show more of the characteristics that are usually referred to as self-control: planning ahead, foreseeing consequences, and delaying gratification. This aspect of growing up will be discussed shortly.

More recent psychological conceptions, however, define self-control not as something that one *has*, but rather as something that one *does*. When modern psychologists discuss self-control, they usually are not emphasizing a personality trait but rather a change in behavior. In this view, self-control has to do with changing one's own behavior. And in a way, that is what people mean when they say, "I wish I had more self-control." They really mean, "I would like to be able to change my own behavior."

Not all behavior is self-control. First, self-control can be thought of as a *change* in behavior. A person who has never liked chocolates is not exercising self-control by sitting next to an open box of chocolate candies without eating any. If the person *ordinarily* does not eat chocolates, then refraining is not a change. But suppose it is a different person sitting close to the box of candy, one who dearly loves chocolates and who has almost always eaten them whenever they are available. For *that* person to abstain could be described as self-control, because it is a *change* from previous behavior.

A second characteristic of self-control is the *absence of obvious external controls* that force or account for the change. Suppose that a person who has been a heavy drinker for years goes into a favorite bar but instead of having alcohol, drinks club soda all evening. That is a change in behavior, but is it self-control? It depends. If the drinker is sitting across from a friend holding a gun and threatening to pull the trigger at the first sip of alcohol, it's not exactly self-control. There is a very strong external reason that accounts for the new behavior. It is only in the absence of such external controlling factors that psychologists consider a behavior change to represent *self*-control. Of course

Impulsiveness
the tendency of an individual to act or react with insufficient reflection, planning, or attention to the likely consequences of action.

this is not a simple black-and-white distinction, because there is at least a little external pressure in almost any change that occurs.

A third characteristic of self-control is that the person *intentionally takes steps to change;* he or she *does* something to bring about a change in behavior. A person may, for example, remove all cigarettes from home and work, thus making it less likely that he will smoke. Another may buy a new alarm clock and a warm jogging suit to increase the chances that she will exercise in the morning. Each has done something to help break an old pattern and bring about a new one. Each has practiced one behavior to cause a change in another behavior. If it works, it is an example of self-control (in this more modern sense). If it does not work and there is no change in behavior, then the attempt at self-control has failed (and a different approach should be tried).

We are defining self-control, then, as a change in behavior resulting from an individual taking intentional steps toward change in the absence of strong external control. Self-control is something one *does.* Yet as we mentioned earlier, there are also personal differences in how readily self-control occurs, both between individuals and within the same individual over time. Growing up includes *learning* self-control skills, and some people seem to learn them better than others. We hope that the material we present throughout this book will help you to learn some useful skills for self-control in this sense of self-change. Before we go on to explain some practical tips for self-control, however, it is important to discuss how self-control develops, how these skills emerge as the person grows from childhood into adulthood.

■ DEVELOPMENT OF SELF-CONTROL

As any new parent will attest, the infant and the toddler display precious little that could be called self-control. It is a task that must be mastered in the process of growing up, and a very important one if the individual is to learn to live in society. But from where does it come? How do people acquire the skills that are called self-control?

Claire Kopp (1982) has described some important phases or milestones in the development of self-control. These consist of a set of skills that the child must develop. First, the infant must *attend* to the external world, to focus on certain stimuli and screen out others. This process begins naturally in most children during the first three months of life, through maturation and interaction with caregivers.

Next the child learns to *change behavior* in response to different events in the environment. The child develops behavior patterns such as smiling, crying, reaching out, and grasping, and these begin to occur in response to certain stimuli. As he or she starts to sort out the "booming, buzzing confusion" of the sensory world, the child also learns, during the first year of life, to respond differently to various environmental events.

A third milestone in the development of self-control occurs as the child learns *compliance,* how to change behavior in response to external commands. "Look here!" "Sit down!" "Come to Daddy!" "Take Mommy's hand!" As the second year of life begins, most children are learning to respond to such requests from caregivers. Learning how to respond to instructions from others is a crucial step toward learning how to respond to self-instruction, how to devise and use a plan of one's own. Compliant responses include initiating behavior on request ("Bring it here"), slowing ("Not so fast"), or stopping behavior ("Don't touch").

The fourth phase in Kopp's description involves learning to follow external rules even when the caregiver (or in this case the rule giver) is not present. The rule is *internalized*; control is now emerging within the child. A two-year-old may reach toward a flame, then stop the reach, say "Hot!" and withdraw the hand. Here the child is responding not to an immediate command from the caregiver, but rather to remembered commands and experiences. Children in this phase begin to show an ability to delay gratification: given a choice between getting an attractive treat immediately or waiting a short while and getting a still better one, the child is capable of "resisting temptation" and waiting for the better reward. The development of language seems to be crucial for a child to learn this internalized control (Frauenglass & Diaz, 1985; Luria, 1961; Vygotsky, 1962). Saying "Hot!" is not just an accidental part of pulling back the hand. The learning of language helps the child to remember events and rules, and to change his or her future behavior accordingly, even when adults are not present.

In the final phase, true **self-regulation** emerges as the child learns to evaluate different situations, attach to them different rules for behavior, and thus adjust to the changing environment. Again speech seems to play a key role. Instead of merely repeating external commands, the child develops the ability to engage in private speech that reflects planning and consideration of alternatives. Suppose we could listen in on the thoughts of a child who is trying to build a tall tower from blocks of various sizes: "I want it to be big. What block

Self-Regulation
engaging in flexible, plan-guided behavior in adjusting to changing conditions of the environment.

5.1 DELAY OF GRATIFICATION

One self-control skill that has been studied extensively is the ability to delay gratification or resist temptation. This involves turning down an immediate reward in order to achieve a greater benefit at a later time. In developmental psychology experiments, young children are offered a tempting immediate reward such as two pieces of candy, but told that if they can wait instead of eating the candy, they will receive a better reward, perhaps five pieces. Such ability to wait for a greater reward appears in children as young as two years of age. Needless to say, this is a crucial self-control skill for success in college.

A class of problems known as the "addictive behaviors" (see Chapter 11) have in common the fact that they offer immediate gratification but long-term risk and suffering. Alcohol and drug abuse, gambling, smoking, and overeating all involve immediate pleasurable experiences but a high probability of negative effects on physical and psychological health in the long run. These "short-term-gain, long-term-pain" problems involve one kind of breakdown in appropriate delay of gratification choices.

Developing the ability to delay gratification is highly dependent upon childhood experiences. If children grow up in environments or families where promises of later reward are seldom kept, they may learn to take the immediate gratification instead of the promise. Other families and cultures place great value on the ability to delay gratification, and those who learn this skill are richly rewarded. Some religions teach an even longer form of gratification delay: to decline immediate pleasures of this life in the interest of achieving greater rewards in an afterlife.

Personal and social values regarding delay of gratification can sometimes be detected in favorite sayings or proverbs. What is expressed about the importance of delay of gratification in the following sayings? Which ones do you believe most?

A bird in the hand is worth two in the bush.
All things come to those who wait.
Strike while the iron is hot.
Opportunity knocks but once.
Patience is a virtue.
He who hesitates is lost.

should I use first? I need big ones on the bottom. This one is too small. Here's a good one."

As self-regulation develops, private speech reflects a flexible adaptation to the environment. Rather than having a simple rule for all situations, the child learns to discriminate various situations and behave differently in them. While internalized control is often seen in two-year-olds, children are more likely to be beyond the age of three when they develop this more adaptive type of self-regulation. The child's thinking and behavior become more flexible, changing with different situations. In its fully developed form, self-regulation is the ability to behave in accord with a self-generated plan that is adaptive and responsive to the current condition of the individual's social environment. The five stages of self-regulation development are outlined in Box 5.2.

Each phase in developing self-control depends upon having the skills of the previous phase. Behavior cannot be adjusted to external stimuli (phase 2) if the child does not attend to those stimuli and separate them from the whole perceptual field (phase 1). If behavior cannot be adjusted to external stimuli in general, then the child will be unable to respond to a particular kind of stimulus: commands from the caregiver (phase 3). If the child fails to learn how to

5.2   FIVE PHASES IN THE DEVELOPMENT OF SELF-CONTROL

PHASE	NORMAL AGE	PRIMARY DEVELOPMENTAL TASKS TO MASTER IN THIS PHASE
1. Attention	Birth–3 months	Attend to and focus on certain stimuli; filter out other "background" stimuli; develop organized reflex behaviors
2. Responding	3–9 months	Respond to particular stimuli with voluntary movement; increase awareness of own behavior and of the social world
3. Compliance	12–18 months	Respond to caregiver commands; initiate, increase, decrease, or cease behavior in response to commands
4. Internalization	24 months +	Comply with rules and social expectations in the absence of the caregiver or other external prompt; recall rules; delay gratification
5. Self-regulation	36 months +	Adjust behavior to the social demands of different settings; show flexibility in adopting different rules to govern behavior in different situations

(adapted from Kopp, 1982)

A child develops self-control by learning to plan and consider alternatives.

comply with requests from others, he or she will be unable to internalize those rules (phase 4) and alter his or her behavior in response to the changing conditions of different situations (phase 5). The ability to perform the tasks necessary to each phase depends both upon normal development of the brain (especially increased dominance of the frontal lobes of the brain), and on the availability of necessary social relationships and opportunities that permit learning of the essential skills (Luria, 1973).

Viewed in a larger developmental context such as Erikson's stage theory (see Chapter 4), the development of self-control is just one of a series of tasks or challenges that must be mastered. In American society, at least, it is crucial for a child to develop self-control skills during the preschool years, because entry into the school system requires a great deal of attending, responding to external stimuli and commands, self-initiating, and inhibiting of behavior. A child who enters the school system without such skills is significantly disadvantaged. American adult life, offering a sometimes bewildering range of choices and freedoms, calls for a substantial level of self-control skills. In other societies where external controls are greater and personal freedoms fewer, a relative deficiency in self-regulation might be less disabling, since less internalized control is required (Shipler, 1983).

In this context, the development of self-control depends upon having previously mastered other crucial developmental tasks such as **attachment.** If the child fails to form a significant attachment with a caregiver, he or she lacks the crucial relationship within which self-control skills normally develop. Lacking self-control skills, a child is then less able to cope with later developmental challenges such as the establishment of *competence* in middle childhood, and of *identity* during adolescence.

What happens when self-control fails to develop adequately? The first problems may occur when the child enters school and shows difficulty in coping with these demands for self-regulation. The diagnosis of "attention deficit disorder" (also termed, in the past, "hyperactivity" or "minimal brain dysfunction") seems to center on a failure to develop self-regulatory processes (Douglas, 1983). Children showing such difficulties during elementary school years have been found to have a higher risk of developing alcoholism during adulthood (Jones, 1968; McCord & McCord, 1962). Is alcoholism at least in part

Attachment
a close emotional bonding between two people.

the result of a developmental failure to establish self-control processes? It is intriguing that adult alcoholics rather consistently show a relative inability to learn new rules and to shift their behavior in response to changing environmental conditions (Miller & Saucedo, 1983). While this was once thought to be a *result* of excessive alcohol consumption, evidence now suggests that these deficits may reflect an underlying developmental disorder in self-control abilities that precedes and perhaps causes alcohol abuse (Tarter, 1981). Apparently people do enter adulthood having developed different levels of skills for self-control.

■ OBSTACLES TO EXERCISING SELF-CONTROL

Assuming an individual has developed reasonably normal self-regulation skills during childhood, what stands in the way of *exercising* self-control in specific situations during adulthood? Why do some behaviors seem much more difficult to change than others? Here we begin to explore the basic principles of change, the conditions that seem to be necessary or at least helpful for change to occur. We will discuss five common obstacles to self-control: (1) no goal, (2) no feedback, (3) low self-efficacy, (4) urges and temptations, and (5) no coping response.

NO GOAL

The first barrier to change may be that the person has no clear *goal* toward which to move. This can occur in at least three ways. First, the person may be unaware of a problem, and see no need for change. If you believe that you are already exactly where you should be, then why change? This is, for example, a common barrier to change for problem drinkers (Miller, 1985b). They do not see their drinking as a problem, and so have no desire to change it. The obstacle is lack of *awareness* of the problem.

On the other hand a person may want to change, but may have *no model* for how he or she would like to be after the change. For example, you might wish you were a more confident and self-assured person, but have no realistic conception of how confident people behave, how they act and feel. Here the obstacle is the absence of a clear *model* for behavior.

A third possibility is that the person wants to change and knows how he or she would like to be, but has no clear and specific goal toward which to work. An overweight person, for example, may want to lose weight and know that the needed process is to lose pounds of fat. Yet the person may never have set a specific goal. This could be a long-term goal ("I want to weigh 160 pounds") or, even more helpful in many cases, it can be a short-term goal ("I want to lose 2 pounds this week"). Research indicates that people who set specific goals for themselves are more likely to change than are people who do not set goals, even though they are all working on the same problem (Bandura & Cervone, 1983). The obstacle is the absence of a *specific goal*.

In all these cases, the goal is a desired final state: how the person would like to be after the change. If you do not have a goal toward which to work, you are less likely to change. Specific strategies for goal setting will be discussed later in this chapter.

NO FEEDBACK

Discrepancy
a condition of inconsistency between a goal and one's present state, which tends to motivate change.

A goal alone, however, is not enough. What seems to motivate change is not just a goal, but a perceived **discrepancy.** A discrepancy is the distance between one's goal and one's present state. (Notice the parallel to our discussion of self-esteem in Chapter 4. The difference is that the discrepancy that determines self-esteem is a very general, overall self-perception, whereas here we are talking about a discrepancy on one particular behavioral dimension that may or may not be an important part of self-esteem.) A simple example again is body weight. Suppose a woman weighs 155 (present state) but would like to weigh 120 (goal). The discrepancy is 35 pounds. The larger the discrepancy, the greater the motivation for change (with some exceptions to be discussed later).

To experience a discrepancy you not only must have a goal, but must also know where you are at the present time. If either one of these two pieces of information is missing—a goal or knowledge of your present state—then the discrepancy is unclear (Bandura & Cervone, 1983; Locke et al., 1981). Thus the absence of feedback, of knowledge about your actual present state, is also a barrier to change.

Knowing your present state requires feedback of some kind. In the case of weight, feedback can be obtained by stepping on a scale. On other dimensions, however, feedback can be more difficult. How could you get feedback on your "friendliness," on your mood, or on the strength of your marriage? One basic self-control tool for obtaining feedback is **self-monitoring,** which we will discuss later in this chapter.

Another helpful way to obtain feedback is to ask how others perceive you. New information and perceptions can be gained through feedback from trusted others, especially if such feedback can be given in a caring and usable form. As in goal setting, specific feedback is much more helpful than general or global feedback. "You're a great person" may help you to feel better, but may not be very useful in telling you *what* you do to cause others to see you in a positive light. More specific and usable feedback might be, "I appreciate how you help with little chores around the house." Similarly, global negative feedback such as, "You're lazy and uncaring," is likely to evoke negative feelings,

Self-Monitoring
systematic observation of one's own behavior.

In an attempt to be polite, people sometimes withhold feedback about annoying behaviors, such as talking too much.

but is not likely to inspire behavior change. More specific feedback might be, "I would appreciate your help in doing the laundry and then folding it and putting it away." Here are some suggestions in asking for helpful feedback.

1. Ask for feedback from a person whom you trust, and who cares about you. Over a relaxed lunch, you might ask a co-worker: "Tell me what you thought of my work on that project. What did I do well, and what might I have done differently?"

2. Allow enough time to discuss the feedback. Avoid "hit and run" experiences in which you are given criticism in a hurried way, with no opportunity to talk it over.

3. Choose a time when you feel able to accept feedback, even if some of it is negative. Avoid seeking emotionally charged feedback when you are already feeling especially vulnerable or down, or when the feedback might interfere with an important task you must complete.

4. Ask for *specific* feedback, not only general impressions. If someone offers you generalities, ask them to be more specific or to give an example. "What was it that you liked about what I did?" "Tell me specifically what you would like me to do differently."

Having feedback can increase motivation for change in two ways. First, knowledge of the size of the discrepancy is an incentive for change. Second, if you have ongoing feedback, you can also see the discrepancy shrinking as your self-change efforts succeed, and this feedback of progress can be very encouraging. Change most often comes in small steps rather than large, dramatic transformations. Feedback increases awareness of those small steps toward a goal.

LOW SELF-EFFICACY

As explained in Chapter 3, self-efficacy is an individual's belief that he or she is capable of bringing about a specific change (Bandura, 1982). When a discrepancy exists between goal and present state, the question is: "Is there anything I can do to change it?" This includes at least two parts: (1) "Is there anything that could be done to bring about a change?" and (2) "Am I capable of doing it?" A person who strongly believes that there *is* something that would work to bring about a change, and that he or she could do it, is said to show *high* self-efficacy. *Low* self-efficacy, on the other hand, refers to a belief that one is unable to bring about the desired change.

Suppose you are feeling very down (present state) and wish you were in a better mood (goal). Will you do anything to try to change your mood? It depends in part on self-efficacy. If you believe that there is nothing you can do to improve your mood, that you are the helpless victim of depression and just have to wait for it to pass, then you are unlikely to attempt self-control. If, by contrast, you think (correctly or not), "I know what I can do to start feeling better," then you are likely to try it. (See Chapter 6 for some ideas on this.)

This concept of self-efficacy appears over and over again in popular stories and seems to be an underlying theme of American thinking. It is found in children's stories such as "The Little Engine That Could." In *The Wizard of Oz*, the wizard gives nothing to the lion, the scarecrow, and the woodsman that they did not already possess, except for self-efficacy, the belief that they could do that which they desired. In the second *Star Wars* film Luke Skywalker cries out that he does not think he can lift his spacecraft by mental use of "the Force." To this his teacher, the Yoda, replies, "And *that* is why you fail!" The mysterious Force, we discover, is something very much like self-efficacy.

5.3 GENERAL VERSUS SPECIFIC FEEDBACK

GENERAL FEEDBACK	SPECIFIC FEEDBACK
Gives an overall positive or negative evaluation (approval or disapproval) without being specific	Gives specific information about the effects of behavior
More likely to change feelings than to change behavior	More likely to change behavior without arousing negative feelings
Tends to apply broad labels to the person and his or her actions	Pinpoints actions without labeling the person

Here are ten examples of feedback that one person might give to another. For each one, identify whether it is general (G) or specific (S) feedback. Also imagine how the recipient of each piece of feedback would be likely to respond. How might the person's behavior change, if at all?

1. Professor, your lectures are just incomprehensible!
2. Dad, thanks for the surprise in my lunch bag. I liked it a lot.
3. Sue, you seem to ask questions during class that have already been answered or are about material that was just covered. It often seems like you didn't hear what was happening just before you asked.
4. Joe, these notes are useless. I can't get anything out of them at all.
5. You're such a good friend! I don't know what I'd do without you.
6. Ooh—right there. Rub a little harder. That feels really good!
7. I can't believe how inconsiderate you are. You never think of anybody but yourself.
8. Fran, I'd appreciate it if you would rinse your dishes instead of just piling them by the sink.
9. I think people would see you as less critical if you told them what they're doing *right* a little more often, and focused less on saying what they do wrong.
10. I love you.

1G 2S 3S 4G 5G 6S 7G 8S 9S 10G

What the Wizard of Oz gave to the scarecrow and the tin woodsman was not literally a brain and a heart, but rather the confidence to use what they already had.

Research findings support the importance of self-efficacy in changing behavior. When faced with a discrepancy, people usually do one of two things: either they attempt to change it by an active coping behavior, or they engage in defense mechanisms (see Chapter 3) such as denial ("It isn't really so bad") or rationalization ("I didn't really want it anyhow"). Studies indicate that self-efficacy is a very important influence in determining which of these two ways a person will use to cope (Rogers, 1975; Rogers & Mewborn, 1976). Those showing high self-efficacy try to change the problem, whereas those with low self-efficacy resort to defense mechanisms to reduce their discomfort.

The *size* of a discrepancy may influence self-efficacy and thus one's willingness to try to change. A very large gap between present and ideal states can be quite discouraging. One way around this problem is to set smaller successive goals. When we began working together, the idea of writing this entire textbook seemed overwhelming to us, and quickly plunged us into despair. We dealt with this by setting progressive goals of writing or revising one chapter, which we knew we could accomplish.

Research indicates that self-efficacy influences not only whether a person will try to change, but also whether a change will last or not, once it has occurred. People who believe that a change occurred by accident or because of some other external cause are less likely to sustain that change than are people who believe they brought about the change themselves (Kopel & Arkowitz, 1975).

Before moving on, we would comment that there *are* times when low self-efficacy is appropriate. It is not always possible to bring about change, and sometimes the healthy course is to accept that one has very little control. This truth is captured in the well-known "serenity prayer" authored by Reinhold Niebuhr, now modified and adopted by groups such as Alcoholics Anonymous:

> God grant us grace to accept with serenity the things that cannot be changed, courage to change the things which should be changed, and the wisdom to distinguish the one from the other.

When change is genuinely impossible, acceptance may be more adaptive than continuous efforts to evoke change.

URGES AND TEMPTATIONS

Still another type of obstacle that people encounter when they pursue self-control is commonly described as "urges" or "temptation." Many a New Year's resolution has fallen by the wayside after the person has encountered an urge or temptation to return to previous behavior.

Yet what *are* these urges and temptations? They are difficult to observe directly, yet most everyone experiences them. The "STORC" system that we introduced in Chapter 3 can be helpful in understanding what is happening here. Urges and temptations are events that lead up to a certain response (R), which in turn has its consequences (C). This would suggest that urges and temptations could be thought of as combinations of stimuli (S), thoughts (T), and organic (O) events, since the S-T-O elements precede R and C. Let's examine how well this idea works.

Clearly *stimuli* are important parts of urges and temptations: the tempting odor of a favorite food cooking (like popcorn in the theater lobby), the sight of a favorite old drinking place or of a sexually attractive person. Advertising is based on the assumption that showing you certain stimuli will increase desire and motivation to buy the product. External stimuli, bits of information coming in through the five senses, are important parts of what people experience as urges and temptations. Yet this is not the whole picture. A stimulus that is tempting for one person may be neutral or even aversive for another.

What about *thoughts?* As we pointed out in Chapter 2, stimuli do not have meaning until the brain interprets them, and this often involves conscious thought processes. Looking at a tempting stimulus, the person may begin to think, "Boy, would I like to . . . ." Urges and temptations have very much to do with particular kinds of thoughts such as fantasies, expectations about positive results that would occur, or dissatisfaction with the present (Marlatt & Gordon, 1985). Self-efficacy (a belief) also comes into play here, because urges are only problematic when the person is uncertain of his or her ability to resist. As a person begins to think about stimuli, the urge or temptation may grow stronger (Marlatt & Gordon, 1985).

Urges and temptations can also have definite *organic* components, internal physiological events that the person experiences as urges, craving, or even loss of control. In some cases this is part of the body's normal signal system for reducing important discrepancies. Hunger and thirst, for example, are physical states that are experienced as urges, and motivate eating and drinking. The discomfort of alcohol and drug withdrawal (see Chapter 11) involves physical changes that can be experienced as craving or urges.

These elements—S-T-O—often occur in series or "chains." You see or smell an appetizing food, you think about eating it, you salivate and your stomach growls. Through the learning process of respondent conditioning (see Chapter 4), these chains become linked together. The stimulus (S) automatically evokes certain thoughts (T), organic states (O), or responses (R).

Thus urges and temptations, while emotionally very complicated, can be thought of as chains of events that increase the likelihood of a certain behavior. Although they may be experienced as single events, urges typically consist of sequences of S-T-O elements.

NO COPING RESPONSE

A fifth common obstacle to self-control is the absence of an effective coping response. An individual may have a clear goal and feedback and may even *believe* that she or he can change. Yet if she or he lacks the needed coping skill or knowledge, change is unlikely to occur. Change involves not only wanting to change and believing that you can, but also knowing how.

There are very few simple or single answers where complex human problems are concerned. Despite the many self-help books, advice columns, and how-to articles available, change is not often as simple as 1-2-3. The desire for a simple quick fix can lead to an overly simplistic conception of change and unrealistic expectations, resulting in disappointment and discouragement. Having only one approach, one way to cope with a problem situation, leaves you very limited.

A healthy and optimistic approach to life problems, we believe, is one that draws on a broad range of different coping skills and strategies. Coping usually involves trying various solutions until one (or more often, a combination) works. In the chapters of Part III, as we deal with common adjustment problems, we will be explaining various possible causes and alternative coping approaches. We will use the STORC model as a way of organizing and remembering different coping approaches. We choose this teaching approach (rather than prescribing single solutions) because we know that what is comfortable and effective differs substantially from one person to the next. Part of the satisfaction of coping with life's challenges is weaving new solutions from the various threads of skill that one has acquired along the way.

As discussed in Chapter 1, Mahoney (1974, 1979) describes this as a "personal scientist" approach to life, an experimental approach that in some ways resembles the scientific method. In attempting to understand reality, a scientist manipulates certain factors (known as **independent variables**) to determine their effect on other **dependent variables.** In systematic research, psychologists might study the effect of teacher encouragement (independent variable) on student success (dependent variable) or might compare the effectiveness of two different treatment approaches (independent variable) on depression (dependent variable). In simplified form, the dependent variable is that which is to be changed, and the independent variable is tested to see whether it has an effect. Applied to your own life, dependent variables are behaviors you would like to change (presumably because of a discrepancy). In the search for self-change, you try different methods (independent variables) until you find one that works, thus testing different **hypotheses** about what might effect a change. People may do this without really thinking about what they are doing: applying the scientific method to their own lives, searching for effective strategies for self-control. The personal scientist approach makes this search more conscious and systematic. You become more aware of experimenting with different ways of behaving and being until you discover what works best for you. We hope that as you continue to read this book, you will find some new approaches to use in discovering ways of changing and growing.

Independent Variable

in an experiment, a condition that is systematically manipulated or altered to determine its effects on a specific behavior (dependent variable).

Dependent Variable

in a psychological experiment, a specific behavior being studied for how it is affected by changes in one or more independent variables.

Hypothesis
(plural: Hypotheses)

a hunch or assumption that can be tested by observation or experimentation.

5.4 HYPOTHESIS TESTING

An **hypothesis** is a specific prediction, which follows from one's **theory** or assumptions about reality. To evaluate a theory, it is necessary to form specific hypotheses that can be tested and confirmed or disconfirmed. Hypothesis testing is the formal process by which scientists proceed, but it also occurs in other everyday settings. If you notice an odd smell at home, for example, you are likely to go through a process of forming various hypotheses about what is causing it, and checking each one. Is something burning on the stove? Did I leave the iron on? Has the coffeemaker boiled dry?

Clinical psychologists are often trained in programs that utilize what is known as the **scientist-practitioner model.** This approach teaches students to be both capable scientists and competent clinicians. Scientist-practitioner training programs focus on the *integration* of these two skills. The problems which people bring to a clinical psychologist can be viewed from a scientific problem-solving perspective. An individual's complaints—areas in need of change—can be thought of as dependent variables, which are being influenced by unknown factors. The psychologist's initial task is to generate hypotheses as to which

factors may be causing the problem. These "causes" represent hypothesized independent variables within a scientific view. Once the psychologist has derived hypotheses, she or he can proceed to test them. Any treatment can be thought of as hypothesis testing. The psychologist offers the treatment because he or she has an hypothesis as to the cause of a problem and believes that the treatment will address that cause and problem.

The following are three examples of hypothesis testing. One involves a scientist evaluating a theory. The second is of a clinical psychologist trying to help a client. The third is a college student using a personal scientist approach to solve a personal problem.

	RESEARCH SCIENTIST	CLINICAL PSYCHOLOGIST	PERSONAL SCIENTIST
The Problem	A psychologist is interested in why people seem to be more affected by alcohol when they are at high elevations.	A woman is suffering from recurrent and distressing nightmares and seeks therapy from a clinical psychologist.	A college student is having particular difficulty understanding the material presented in a large chemistry class.
A First Hypothesis	People become more intoxicated at high altitudes because more alcohol gets into the bloodstream when drinking.	The content of the woman's nightmares suggests that depression may be the cause of her problem.	Maybe I am not taking good enough notes in class.
Testing the First Hypothesis	The psychologist conducts an experiment by giving people the same amount of alcohol to drink in an altitude chamber set at either 10,000 feet or at sea level.	The psychologist administers two psychological tests to check for depression, and inquires in an interview whether she is experiencing some of the common signs of depression.	The student visits the campus Study Skills Center to learn about proper notetaking methods, and compares notes with another student who is getting an A in the same class.
Results of First Hypothesis Testing	People drinking the same amount show identical blood alcohol levels at sea level and at 10,000 feet. If there are differences, they must be due to some other factor.	The woman shows no signs of clinical depression. The psychologist does note a high level of anxiety in her test results. She also says that she seems less likely to have nightmares if she takes a hot bath before going to bed.	The Study Skills Center indicates that the student's notetaking skills are basically O.K. In comparison with the classmate's notes, however, the student's own notes contain many factual errors and have entire ideas missing. The A

			student sits in the front row.
A Second Hypothesis	The same level of alcohol in the bloodstream causes greater impairment in behavior at high altitude than at low altitude.	The woman's high level of anxiety during the day carries over into her sleeping hours, and a reduction in her level of anxious arousal at bedtime will reduce her nightmares.	Sitting up front in class will help me be less distracted and will increase my ability to hear, understand, and concentrate in class.
Testing the Second Hypothesis	The psychologist designs a second experiment in which people are given a fixed dose of alcohol at sea level or at 10,000 feet, and then are given a series of tests of speed and memory.	The woman is taught the method of progressive deep muscle relaxation (see Appendix B) and is told to practice it every night just before going to bed.	The student sits in the front row in the chemistry class rather than at the back of the classroom as before.
Results of Second Hypothesis Testing	Again blood alcohol levels are the same at both elevations, but people at higher altitudes are slower on tasks and have more memory difficulties.	After four weeks of practicing deep muscle relaxation at bedtime, the woman's nightmares have decreased from once a night to once a week, and when they do occur they are less frightening.	The student seems to understand the lectures better and gets a much better grade on the next exam.

■ STAGES OF CHANGE

Scientist-Practitioner
an approach to the training of mental health professionals that integrates scientific expertise with clinical skill.

Transtheoretical Approach
a psychological system that cuts across or combines elements from a wide range of different theories; associated with the work of James Prochaska and Carlo DiClemente.

Change does not usually occur all at once, but rather in steps or stages. Before we describe a set of specific methods for self-control, it will be useful to discuss the stages of change, the developmental steps that occur as any change happens. These stages are based on two decades of work by psychologist James Prochaska and his colleagues, who have been studying how change happens both in psychotherapy and in the everyday world (Prochaska, 1984; Prochaska & DiClemente, 1982, 1984).

One conclusion drawn by Prochaska and DiClemente is that change emerges through a predictable set of steps or stages and that these stages are the same whether the change is self-directed or occurs in therapy. Psychotherapy seems to facilitate a natural change process, rather than representing a unique type or process of change. The stages also seem to be similar across a broad range of problem areas and theoretical orientations in psychotherapy, leading Prochaska and DiClemente to call their approach **transtheoretical.**

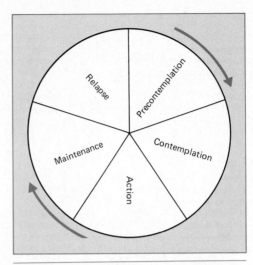

FIGURE 5-1 A STAGE MODEL OF THE
PROCESS OF CHANGE

Adapted from James O. Prochaska and
Carlo C. DiClemente, "Transtheoretical
Therapy: Toward a More Integrative Model of
Change." *Psychotherapy: Theory Research
and Practice*, 19, 1982, 276–88.

Prochaska and DiClemente have described five stages found in this change
process. These five occur in order, although the process is better understood
as a cycle within which the stages are repeated until stable change is finally
accomplished. Each stage may be quite short, occurring in a crucial moment
of change, or may be very long, extending over months or even years. The
stages are shown in Figure 5-1.

In the first stage, called *Precontemplation*, the person is not even considering change. The person has no goal of change, either because he or she sees no
need for it or because there seems to be no way to accomplish it. At the point
where the person begins to consider or think about changing, she or he enters
the *Contemplation* stage. Here the person weighs the costs and benefits of
changing ("I'd like to change, but . . ."). Following this period of contemplation, and sometimes after a critical experience that convinces the person of the
need for change, the *Action* stage begins, during which the person takes
action, trying specific strategies for change. Several different strategies may be
tried. If one of these works and the desired change occurs, then the next
challenge comes with the stage of *Maintenance*, holding onto the new behavior
without slipping back into the old pattern. If this works, then permanent
change has been accomplished. If not, the person enters the *Relapse* stage, a
return to an earlier pattern of behavior.

Relapse is very common as people try to change. It is part of human nature
to lapse back to an earlier way of coping. In extreme forms, a person may
return to a childlike way of behaving when faced with a difficult challenge—
the defense mechanism of regression, discussed in Chapter 3. Within the
transtheoretical model, however, relapse is just another stage of change. The
next step is to return to contemplation of change, then action, and so on.

It is typical for people to go around the circle (shown in Figure 5-1) several
times before they achieve lasting change. Smokers who want to stop, for example, commonly go through these stages several times before finally quitting for
good. Viewed in this way, a relapse need not lead to discouragement. A healthy
approach is to see this as a natural and temporary setback, part of a pattern
that will eventually lead to lasting change.

5.5   TALK AND THE STAGES OF CHANGE

How can you tell where you (or someone else) might be within the stages of change described by Prochaska? One way is to pay attention to what the person *says* about change.

Here are some examples of the types of statements that might be made by a person at each stage of change.

Precontemplation	"I don't have a problem! Leave me alone." "I don't see what's the big deal." "I'm doing fine. *They're* the ones who need to change."
Contemplation	"I am a little worried, but I don't think my problem is really that serious." "I'd like to change, but I don't know how." "On the one hand I like how I am now, but then I can also see that this could get to be a serious problem if I don't change."
Action	"I've decided to quit, and I'm calling that phone number this afternoon." "I don't know how well this will work, but I'm giving it a try." "I'm going to keep at it until I find something that works for me."
Maintenance	"Well, I made the change. Now the big challenge is to keep from slipping backward." "So far, so good. Now I'm just taking it one day at a time." "Sure I'm O.K. right now, but I feel like I could slip right back at any moment."
Relapse	"I feel so discouraged. I really thought I could do it this time, but I blew it again." "I did get careless, but I know how to get back on the track again." "That was really dumb, but I guess there are bound to be some setbacks along the way. Slipping back to my old pattern just reminded me how important it is for me to change."

■ A SELF-CHANGE TOOL KIT

Once a person reaches the point of contemplation and starts considering the possibility of change, what self-control strategies are available to try? There are, in fact, quite a few. As we discuss specific challenges and problem areas in the chapters of Part III, we will be introducing and applying self-control techniques useful in coping with each of these areas. To set the stage, however, we will here discuss a variety of specific strategies for self-control, methods that can be applied to a wide range of life problems and challenges.

Change usually begins with awareness. The move from precontemplation to contemplation involves becoming aware of a problem and of the need for change. Taking action for change is also aided by a clearer picture of the

Self-change is aided by having (and knowing how to use) a variety of "tools."

nature of the problem, the goal for change, and the present state. We begin, then, with four strategies for obtaining information and awareness helpful in self-change.

SPECIFYING THE PROBLEM

Before attempting to change, it is usually helpful to get a clear and *specific* picture of the problem. A vague sense that something is wrong can be a good starting point, but it is not specific enough to allow one to do much about it.

One approach in planning change is to focus on what you *do* rather than what you *are*. We do not mean to say that it is useless to reflect on who and what you *are*. We have devoted all of Chapter 15 to this concern. Rather we are saying that when you want to bring about a change it is helpful to be *specific*. This is true for encouraging change in others as well as in yourself (see Box 5.3). Giving general feedback and labels ("You're too lazy." "You should be more responsible." "You're a wonderful person.") will usually change how a person *feels*, but may not have much of an impact on behavior, on what one *does*. Much more helpful in bringing about change is *specific* information.

One question that can be helpful in specifying a problem is: "If things were 100 percent better, if my self-change program were completely successful, what would be different?" Again, remember to focus on what you would *do* differently, rather than on labels. Instead of saying, "I would be more sociable," consider how your behavior would be different. What do "sociable" people do? What would you do *more* of or *less* of in your daily life? Remember, too, that when broadly defined (as in the STORC approach), behavior includes thoughts and feelings as well as actions. A problem might involve *feeling* more or less of certain emotions or sensations, or *thinking* more or less about certain things.

SETTING A SPECIFIC GOAL

Specifying the problem can lead directly to the next step: setting a specific goal. As indicated earlier, it is important to have a goal toward which to work. A good balance seems to be to pick a goal that is difficult enough to be challenging, but still realistic and attainable (Locke et al., 1981).

When one's goal seems very distant, it can be helpful to break it down into smaller steps or subgoals. A goal of losing 40 pounds, for example, can seem overwhelming. On the other hand, a goal of losing 2 pounds this week seems much more attainable. With steady progressive losses of 2 pounds a week, the larger goal of a 40-pound loss could be completed in just 20 weeks, or less than 5 months. Although it is appealing to imagine change happening rapidly, more often lasting change occurs in small and gradual steps.

SELF-MONITORING

Keeping track of your own behavior (self-monitoring) is an important part of almost any self-control program. There are several possible benefits from doing so. As you begin a self-control program, it gives you a clearer picture of where you are at the present time. This is known as the **baseline**, the starting point. This in turn can serve a motivating function by clarifying where you are relative to your goal, how much you need to change, how far you need to move. As you continue a self-control program, regular self-monitoring provides feedback on your *progress*, the extent to which your self-change strategies are working.

A first step in self-monitoring involves deciding how to observe what you want to change. Usually this means finding something you can count, measure, or rate. A very common form of self-monitoring is keeping a regular *diary* of the behavior (action, thought, or feeling) that you wish to change. Sometimes this diary can be a simple ongoing count, in which you make a mark or note each time the event occurs. Some examples of countables are cigarettes smoked, nightmares, positive and negative things said to others, calories consumed, minutes of study time, or self-critical thoughts. Other things can be measured: body weight, length of fingernails (for those who bite them), dis-

Baseline
the level of a behavior prior to an experimental intervention.

Keeping a diary of behavior helps you keep track of your progress over time.

tance walked or jogged, ounces of alcohol consumed, blood pressure, or test scores. Still other things might best be rated on a scale of 1 to 7, or 0 to 100: daily mood, self-esteem, quality of a night's sleep, personal hygiene, or amount of fun that one had.

Having chosen *what* to monitor, the next step is deciding *how* to monitor. Records can be kept in a wide variety of ways: notes in a notebook, marks on an index card, stars on a chart, coins or buttons switched from one pocket to another, time on a stopwatch, or daily entries on a graph. Practical considerations enter here, too. How can records be kept easily, accurately, and privately?

ANALYZING THE PROBLEM

Once you have a reliable and accurate system for self-monitoring, you can implement one additional method for increasing your awareness: **functional analysis.** This helps you to learn when and under what circumstances the problem tends to occur. Most problems do not occur at random, but rather happen under predictable conditions. Discovering these "high-risk" conditions can be very helpful in planning self-control strategies.

Functional analysis typically is designed to discover two types of environmental conditions related to a behavior: antecedents and consequences. **Antecedents** are those conditions (stimuli) which *precede* the behavior. One person's heavy drinking may, for example, very consistently follow conflicts with other people and feelings of unexpressed anger. For another person, feelings of depression may follow whenever criticism from others is perceived. **Consequences,** on the other hand, happen *after* the behavior. An angry outburst may be followed by family members "backing off" and giving in to the person. Watching television may have the result of helping the person forget other problems for the time being, and eventually to fall asleep. Reinforcement and punishment, described in Chapter 4, have to do with the consequences of behavior.

A functional analysis examines the relationships between a behavior and these environmental antecedents and consequences. You may recognize that the antecedents and consequences here correspond, respectively, to the "S" and "C" elements of the STORC approach. A functional analysis specifically helps to clarify how S and C factors from the environment influence a behavior.

To complete a functional analysis, it is necessary to add to your self-monitoring record some extra information. Each time you record the behavior, also keep a record of what was happening just *before* the behavior occurred (e.g., just before you bit your nails, lit a cigarette, said something critical). (Note that you can do this not only for overt behaviors, but also for covert events such as thoughts, feelings, urges, or feelings of temptation, etc.) Since literally thousands of things will have happened before the behavior, you will have to choose a few aspects of the situation that seem likely to have an influence on the behavior. You might record with whom or where you were, the time of day, what you had been thinking about, what you had been doing, what others said, how you were feeling. Also record what happened *after* the behavior (or thought, feelings, urge, etc): What were the consequences?

After you have kept several days or weeks of records, you can begin a functional analysis of your own behavior. Compare days or times when you showed more of the behavior with other times when the behavior was absent or very low. What is the difference? Does the behavior occur predictably at certain times of day, in certain places, with certain people? Does it seem to be consistently related to certain antecedent feelings or thoughts? Are there consistent consequences that seem to be reinforcing?

Functional Analysis.
the study of a specific behavior to determine its relationships to antecedents and consequences.

Antecedent
a situation that precedes a specific behavior.

Consequence
a situation that follows a specific behavior.

5.6 | AN EXERCISE IN SELF-CONTROL: INCREASING AWARENESS

As you read and study the tools for self-control, apply them to your own life. This can help you to learn by making the material personally interesting and applicable. Think of a part of your own life that you would like to change, one area of your own behavior over which you would like to exert greater self-control. Then apply these four awareness steps:

1. SPECIFYING THE PROBLEM

   What, in general do you want to change?

   If you were 100 percent successful in your self-control program, what would be different?

   > What would you like to do *more?*
   >
   > What would you like to do *less?*

2. SETTING A SPECIFIC GOAL

   What is your general goal for self-change?

   Now be more specific: What is your specific long-term goal?

   > Is this realistic and attainable in the long run?

   What would be a good first step, a short-term goal for this week that would bring you closer to your long-term goal?

3. SELF-MONITORING

   What can you self-monitor in order to specify where you are now and to follow your progress? Is there anything you could

   > Count?
   >
   > Measure?
   >
   > Rate?

   How and where will you keep these records?

   How often will you record?

   What difficulties might prevent you from keeping accurate records, and how can you avoid these difficulties?

4. FUNCTIONAL ANALYSIS

   In examining your self-monitoring records, do you see any consistent antecedents of the behavior? Does it follow predictably from certain circumstances?

   When is the behavior most likely to occur? When does it seem to be least likely to occur?

   Are there any results or consequences that seem to follow consistently from the behavior? Do you think that these reinforce the behavior?

■ ALTERNATIVES: TOOLS FOR PRACTICING SELF-CONTROL

Equipped with clearer awareness of the specific nature of the problem, long-term and short-term goals, self-monitoring, and functional analysis information, you are prepared to begin choosing and trying out some alternative self-control strategies. Here again we will follow the STORC model to help organize the general strategies for self-control.

S—ENVIRONMENTAL PLANNING

Sometimes a problem can be addressed by altering its situational or stimulus (S) aspects. Changes are made in the environment to aid in self-control. Here are several strategies of this type.

Decreasing Temptation. In the interest of self-control, the person avoids or removes from the environment some of the sources of temptation and relapse. A person seeking to lose weight, for example, might decrease temptation by ridding the house of high-calorie snacks and other diet-demolishing foods. Smokers have kept their cigarettes wrapped in aluminum foil and stored in the freezer, increasing the number of steps involved in reaching for a smoke.

Leaving Destructive Situations. It can also be appropriate to remove oneself completely from a relationship or an environment that has a destructive impact. Spouses and children who have been the victims of family violence justifiably leave or are removed from the abusive home. A person may resign from an extraordinarily stressful job or occupation in the interest of personal and family health.

Limiting the Range. When seeking to decrease a problem behavior, the person may limit the situations in which it occurs. (This strategy has also been called "stimulus control.") One who is prone to drinking too much alcohol may place limits on when, where, and with whom he or she will drink. A smoker may decide to smoke only while sitting alone on a certain chair in the backyard.

Extending the Range. When acquiring new and desirable skills, a person often needs to practice them in a wider range of situations. In learning to be more assertive, for example (see Chapter 9), a person may begin by expressing himself or herself in relatively safe and easy situations. As these become comfortable, the new assertive communication skills can be practiced in more challenging settings.

Extending the range can also be used to reduce a behavior. A person who consistently drinks beer to excess may find that by switching to new, less preferred beverages (e.g., dry wine), alcohol consumption is decreased (Miller & Muñoz, 1982).

Environmental Modification. Sometimes making a simple change in the environment can be helpful in altering behavior. Exercising may be promoted by buying a good pair of running shoes and a warm-up suit. Relaxation can be facilitated by arranging a comfortable chair in a quiet and distraction-free room. Roommates with different tastes in loud music may decrease conflicts substantially by purchasing a set of headphones. The stress of supervising a small child can be diminished by "childproofing" the house, placing breakables out of reach, putting locks on cabinets with hazardous materials, and installing a gate across the entrance to a steep set of stairs.

Reminders. New behavior can be prompted by placing reminders in key places. The overly time-conscious person might place a small red dot on the face of a wristwatch, using this as a reminder to relax and slow down whenever she or he anxiously consults it for the time. A colored sticker-dot on the speedometer can similarly serve as a reminder for the time-pressured person to slow down. Many people place a note or picture on the refrigerator door, prompting them to ask, "Do you really need to eat now?" A small alarm on a watch or clock can serve to remind a person to take a crucial medication, or to take a brief nap or rest.

5.7 HERE WE DIFFER/HERE WE AGREE
When Should You "Adjust"?

The term "adjustment" holds negative connotations for those of us who are dissatisfied with the status quo. I do not *want* to adjust to a norm that seems wrong to me, nor do I want to encourage my clients or students to adjust to such norms. Better to be "maladjusted" than to accept conditions that are harmful and hurtful for some groups of people. If anyone has ever told you not to "rock the boat," you know the conflicting feelings of wanting to fit in, to be accepted and liked, while also wanting to change conditions that seem destructive. What would our world be like if no one ever risked rocking the boat? Many important reforms would never have taken place. It takes a lot of courage to rock the boat when surrounded by people who tell you not to do it.

Famous boat-rockers, people who have worked hard for social reform, often pay a high emotional price. Some, like Martin Luther King, have paid with their lives. Knowing the risks, Dr. King told people about his dream, his vision, and asked them not to adjust to the norm of racial inequality. More recently, Bishop Desmond Tutu of South Africa has taken the same risks to oppose racism. When Geraldine Ferraro ran for the office of vice president of the United States, she was rocking the boat of a male-dominated government. Countless not-so-famous boat-rockers have also shown the courage to reject the norm: the wife who refuses to return to a battering husband, breaking with tradition to save her own life; the employee who refuses to participate in activities that violate his or her values, at peril of losing a job or a promotion; the countless people who have risked arrest to shelter and save the lives of refugees, Jews, runaway slaves, or other members of persecuted groups.

The American Psychological Association states that part of its purpose is to use psychology "to promote human welfare." Psychologists have a responsibility to help clients and students, even societies, make moral judgments about their lives. If you feel pressured to behave in a way that seems wrong to you, don't automatically "adjust." Consider rocking the boat! —CEY

It is true that therapists have historically tended to focus on the individual, and in doing so have often ignored the larger social context. If a whole environment is "sick," then in a larger sense it cannot be therapeutic to help a person adjust to it.

In another sense, however, the "adjust to reality" perspective has its merits. *Awareness* of reality, at least, is important for any individual. Although perceptions of reality do differ from one person to the next, there are aspects of the real world that affect us all. A person who does not believe in automobiles will nevertheless be run down by them if he or she attempts to cross the street. Not knowing the local laws does not protect one from being prosecuted for their violation. Reality-awareness, then, has to do with learning how the environment works, what the "rules" (contingencies) are, what consequences are likely to result from different kinds of behavior.

Once you are aware of the reality of your social environment, you can choose how you will respond. You may decide to try to change reality, and indeed you may succeed. But there are also situations in which changing reality is just not possible or feasible; even the largest efforts would yield minimal change. Such situations call for a rather different adjustment strategy, one that accepts reality for what it is and goes on accordingly. There comes a point where continuing to insist that things should be different is of no use, and resolution is found only through acceptance of that reality. Too often those of us who spend our lives helping others to change seem to overlook this side of adjustment. Each of us has only a certain amount of time and talent to use in a lifetime, and it is important to choose carefully those tasks that seem most important, and in which we can make a difference.   —JMR

INTEGRATION

When someone says, "It can't be done," how do you decide whether or not to accept that? History is filled with examples of accomplishments that "couldn't be done": the 4-minute mile, human flight, organ transplants, women voting, racial integration. There is an enduring tension between the desire to bring about change and the acceptance of "reality." When should you "accept with serenity the things that cannot be changed" and when press on with courage in pursuit of change? The wisdom to know the difference between such situations is, indeed, vital.

T—COGNITIVE CONTROL

Even when it is not feasible to alter the external world, it is possible to change the *internal* environment: your own thoughts and interpretations of the external world. Here are four basic strategies.

Discovering Basic Beliefs.   All of us behave as if certain things were true, as if certain rules were automatic. Sometimes these basic beliefs are themselves a source of unhappiness. Discovering the beliefs that are behind your own actions and feelings can be a very helpful kind of awareness. A common method for discovering these beliefs is to keep an ongoing diary (for several weeks at least) of your emotional reactions. When you experience a strong feeling, write it down, and then also record what was happening just before the feeling occurred, which seemed to cause or lead up to the emotional reaction. Feelings do not follow automatically from experiences, however, and so the next step is to ask, "What did I think or say to myself when this happened, how did I interpret it in order to get to this feeling? This is not an easy method, and we will be explaining it in more detail in Chapter 6.

Reevaluating.   Once you become aware of your own thinking, of how your interpretations of situations (S) can lead to negative emotions, it is then possible to consider how you might *reevaluate* a situation in a way that is less upsetting and stressful. It is possible to change your own thought patterns, what you believe and how you interpret reality. This, too, will be discussed further in Chapter 6.

Rehearsal.   It can be helpful to prepare yourself for a challenging situation by mentally rehearsing how you will handle it, what you will say, how you might deal with difficulties or problems. Olympic men's figure skating champion Brian Boitano described, in an interview (Steenman, 1988, p. 110), his use of visualization: "Every day in the car going back and forth to the skating rink to practice, I visualized the skating arena, the audience, my costume and my performance. I saw the standing ovation, heard the thunderous applause raising the roof. . . . I experienced every single emotion I had visualized. . . . It wasn't until the medal presentation when I was standing on the podium that I realized I wasn't dreaming. I knew because 'The Star-Spangled Banner' was being played at a much faster tempo than it had been in my dream. It was then, and only then, that I knew this was the real thing. The dream had finally come true." Imagining yourself successfully coping with an upcoming challenge can increase your comfort and confidence in using your skills in the actual situation.

Self-instruction.   When practicing a new skill, it is helpful to remind yourself of the instructions that you have been given. The novice skier heading down a slope says to herself, "Bend your knees," and the young pianist thinks, "Arch your fingers." The newer members of a marching band or drill team may silently repeat with the rhythm, "Left, right, left, right," to keep their feet moving in step. Giving yourself instructions as you work or play is a natural part of learning a skill. In taking an examination, the anxious student may use the reminder, "Just focus on the questions, and if you don't know one, go on to the next and then come back later if there is time."

O—ORGANISMIC CHANGES

Sometimes bringing about a change in your body can be a helpful part of the solution to a problem. We will offer numerous examples of this in the chapters ahead, but here are some of the basic strategies.

Relax.   Many challenges are met more successfully by the person who is relaxed. Attention, clear thinking, creativity, sports performance, emotional and physical health may all be promoted by relaxation. Though by no means a cure for every problem, relaxation training has been called "the aspirin of psychology." Learning how to relax is an important part of many approaches to self-control (see Chapter 8).

Biofeedback.   As discussed in Chapter 3, biofeedback is the use of a measuring device, usually an electronic instrument, to provide ongoing information about the physical state of a portion of the body. Biofeedback is particularly useful to give information about bodily states that ordinarily cannot be observed directly by the person. Devices are available, for example, to give feedback about small changes in heart rate, blood pressure, skin temperature, and muscle tension. Information about such an organic function is converted into a signal that the person can understand. An electromyographic (EMG) biofeedback device, for example, may signal the level of muscle tension by providing a musical pitch that rises as tension increases and drops as tension decreases. Other devices can provide information about blood flow to particular parts of the body by measuring skin temperature and converting it into an audible sound. Through the use of such a device it is possible to learn self-control of many organic responses not ordinarily under conscious control. This can be beneficial in dealing with a variety of psychological or medical problems. For example, finger temperature biofeedback has been found to be an effective treatment for Raynaud's disease, a painful condition related to inadequate circulation in the hands and feet (Freedman & Ianni, 1986). Tension headaches have also been successfully treated by biofeedback procedures (Holroyd, 1986).

Psychotropic Drug
a medication that affects the person's psychological state or functioning.

Medication.   A wide variety of medications are used to change organic functions directly. One class of medications, known as **psychotropic** drugs, cause physical changes that alter psychological and mood states such as anxiety or depression. Certain drugs, however, particularly some of the psychotropic medications, are potentially addicting or cause other problematic side-effects.

Regular exercise has been shown to have a variety of health and psychological benefits.

Nevertheless, medications, when used properly by prescription, have a legitimate place in managing certain types of problems.

Exercise.   The benefits of regular exercise for physical and psychological health have been increasingly recognized in the past decade. Among the documented benefits are decreases in weight, blood pressure, heart disease risk, and depression.

R—LEARNING NEW RESPONSES

Adjustment and change have to do with learning new ways of responding. This can involve acquiring a completely new skill or altering present behavior in major or minor ways. Again there are some basic strategies.

Modeling.   When acquiring a new skill, it can be very helpful to observe and learn from someone who is already proficient in the skill. This is the principle underlying the ancient "apprenticeship" system for training in crafts and professions. A living picture of how to do it right *can* be worth a thousand words.

Practice.   Any change in behavior is aided by practicing the new behavior pattern. When it is a new skill to be learned, it can also be helpful to have feedback from others about how you are doing, and suggestions or ideas for what you might do differently. Practice makes a new pattern more familiar, until finally it becomes easy and automatic.

Phobia
excessive fear of a specific class of objects or situations, which is out of proportion to any actual threat or danger.

Re-pairing.   Through experience, people learn to respond automatically in certain ways to particular stimuli. Many of these automatic stimulus-response (S-R) pairs are helpful: stepping on the brake when the traffic light turns red, adjusting one's posture to maintain balance when turning a corner on a bicycle. Others, however, interfere with normal adjustment. **Phobias,** for example, are automatic irrational fear responses to relatively harmless stimuli. An elevator, a spider, or an audience may evoke fear reactions that disrupt normal behavior and create discomfort. One method of breaking these S-R pairs and replacing them with new responses to the same stimuli is through systematic desensitization (see Chapter 8). It is, in essence, a systematic approach to establishing and practicing new automatic responses for certain stimuli.

C—CHANGING CONSEQUENCES

Because behavior is also influenced by its consequences, by what follows it, a fifth general self-control strategy is to plan the consequences of behavior that you wish to change.

Self-reinforcement.   As explained in Chapter 4, reinforcement is the process of *increasing* or strengthening a behavior by following it with a rewarding consequence. Self-reinforcement, then, involves planning for yourself a rewarding consequence when you have reached a change goal. A clear goal is set (e.g., the loss of two pounds, two hours of studying, cleaning out the garage) and a reward is planned for when the goal has been reached. The self-reward, then, serves as a kind of celebration of success in reaching the goal. Many different types of self-rewards are possible. Among them are having some free time, spending time with a friend, making a long-distance telephone call, listening to music, buying a special treat, or taking a trip. It is important to have the reward come only after the goal has been achieved. To reward yourself whether or not you reach your goal is to lose the incentive value of this self-reinforcement strategy. This points to a helpful self-control strategy in general: when you plan to do two things in one day, a less pleasant one and a more pleasant one, do the less pleasant task first and then celebrate its completion by doing the more pleasant task (Premack, 1965).

Penalties.   When your goal is to *decrease* a behavior, you may choose to use the principle of punishment by self-imposing a penalty when this undesired behavior occurs. A very simple but sometimes effective example is to wear a large rubber band around one's wrist, and to snap it whenever a certain undesirable behavior (such as fingernail biting) occurs. Penalties can

Simply telling someone else your goal for change makes you more accountable for achieving it.

also be used as a consequence for failing to reach a specific goal, and can in this way be combined with rewards. A student might decide, for example, to set a goal of studying two hours a day for five days. An appropriate reward for accomplishing this might be a whole evening free to go to a movie, attend a concert, or go dancing. A penalty for not accomplishing the goal might be spending the same evening doing difficult chores instead (shampooing carpets, weeding a lawn). A good rule of thumb for choosing penalties is to find something that is unpleasant but also constructive, something that needs to be done, but that you have been putting off because it is unpleasant.

Social Support.   In planning rewards and penalties to help achieve goals, it is also possible to involve others in the process. Simply *telling* another person your specific goal makes you more accountable for achieving that goal. Family or friends can be asked to help you celebrate the accomplishment of a goal, or to help enforce a penalty if you fail to reach the goal. Others can also be asked to help by noticing your behavior change when it occurs and commenting positively on it.

■ SUMMARY

Self-control is something that one does, a change in behavior involving intentional action in the absence of strong external control. Skills for self-control normally develop during the preschool years through learning how to attend and respond to stimuli, comply with requests from others, internalize rules, and finally to adapt one's behavior flexibly in accord with varying situations. Common obstacles to self-control include not having a clear goal, lack of feedback, low self-efficacy, urges and temptations, and the lack of necessary coping skills.

Change occurs most often in gradual steps rather than all at once. One model describes change as occurring in a cycle of stages: precontemplation, contemplation, action, maintenance, and relapse. A broad range of tools can be used in increasing personal self-control. Some of these increase awareness of a problem and the need for change: specifying the problem, setting a specific goal, self-monitoring, and functional analysis. Other strategies were presented within the context of the STORC model: environmental planning (S), cognitive control (T), organic changes (O), learning new responses (R), and changing consequences (C). These self-control tools can be useful in pursuing personal change in a wide variety of areas.

■ QUESTIONS FOR THOUGHT

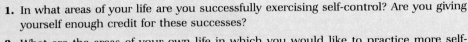

1. In what areas of your life are you successfully exercising self-control? Are you giving yourself enough credit for these successes?

2. What are the areas of your own life in which you would like to practice more self-control?

3. What do you think have been the most important experiences and influences in your own life, through which you have learned greater self-control?

4. How does the idea of "self-control" fit in with your personal values or religious beliefs?

5. Has anyone ever told you that you have "a problem" in an area you hadn't thought of as a problem for you? How did you react?

6. Has anyone ever told you that you have "a problem" in an area where you were already conflicted, and had thought you might have a problem? How did you react? Which way did you lean: toward defensiveness or toward change?

7. What significant changes have you made in your life over the past three years? What steps did you take to accomplish these? What people or conditions made it easier for you to change?

8. What are the most significant temptations for you? How do you deal with temptation?

9. Think of an area in which you were successfully making a change and then relapsed. How did you feel? What did you say to yourself? What happened afterward?

10. Which of the self-change tools described in this chapter are you best at using now? Which ones would you like to learn how to use better?

chapter six

Neither perfect nor contemptible, she discovers the extraordinary power
of her ordinary, unique self and what is truly possible.
—Marcia Westkott, *The Feminist Legacy of Karen Horney*

Self-Esteem

OUTLINE

*I*n Chapters 2 and 4 we introduced the idea of self-esteem as the evaluative aspect of self, how you *feel* about yourself. It is a general, overall feeling, located at any point in time somewhere on a dimension ranging between very positive and very negative evaluation of self. We suggested one way to think about self-esteem is related to the discrepancy between self-ideal (how you think you should be) and self-concept (how you think you are). The larger the difference, the more negative one's self-esteem.

In this chapter we will examine self-esteem more closely, with special focus on how it develops and changes over time. Change in self-esteem is normal and continuous. Although self-esteem shows some consistency within individuals over time, it is also possible to change and improve self-esteem. In fact, a gradual increase in self-esteem is part of normal development (Bachman & O'Malley, 1977). In Chapter 5, we discussed ways to change *behavior*. In this chapter, we will focus on ways to change *thoughts* (cognition) and *feelings* (affect) that are part of self-esteem. Of course behavior, thoughts, and feeling are all interrelated, but sometimes it is helpful to examine them separately to discover how they influence growth and adjustment.

We chose to include this special chapter on self-esteem because, if you are like most college students, there are probably times when the gap between how you *are* and how you *want to be* seems too wide to bridge. The gap between the real and the ideal sometimes seems overwhelming. We will be discussing three general ways to bridge that gap and thereby change self-esteem: through awareness, acceptance, and alternatives. First, however, we will examine in greater detail the nature of self-esteem and how it develops.

■ HEALTHY SELF-ESTEEM

SELF-ESTEEM VERSUS SELF-CENTEREDNESS

What is healthy self-esteem? If one follows the suggestion we made in Chapter 4, the easy answer would be that one has the *highest* self-esteem when there is no gap between self-concept and self-ideal. In this view, the person with highest self-esteem would be the one who sees his or her present self as ideal, presumably with no need for change. One might imagine this to be an ideal state: to see oneself as complete, fulfilled, perfect. But is that in fact a healthy state? Is it possible to have *too much* self-esteem?

Perhaps you can think of people who seem to be too self-centered, who think very highly of themselves, who perhaps ought to perceive a *larger* gap between present self and ideal self. Is there a difference between self-esteem and self-centeredness? The dividing line is not always clear, and will vary considerably from one culture to another. What is regarded as normal, healthy self-esteem in one society may seem boorish and excessively self-promoting in another.

In any culture, though, it is possible to err in the direction of promoting one's own status and interests at the expense of others. The American Psychiatric Association (1987) has described a "narcissistic personality disorder" centering on an extreme self-concern that disregards the worth and rights of others. This narcissistic personality is characterized by an exaggerated sense of self-importance, fantasies of personal power and success, indifference to the needs and feelings of others, and a sense of entitlement to admiration and special favors from others. Thomas Harris (1967), in his popular presentation of transactional analysis, described a personal attitude of "I'm O.K., you're not O.K.," an arrogant life attitude that places self before others. Various psychiatric writers have used such patterns in an attempt to give a psychological definition to theological concepts such as sin or evil (Menninger, 1973; Peck, 1978).

These and other writings imply that it is possible to see oneself as being *too* close to ideal, to have *too small* a discrepancy between self-concept and self-ideal! Where is the healthy balance?

First, it is worth noting that self-centeredness is not equivalent to high self-esteem. One could imagine, for example, a person behaving in a self-centered and egotistical fashion because of a *low* sense of self-esteem. As a coping strategy, a person suffering much self-doubt and negative self-esteem might put up a false front of confidence or bravado, pretending to feel superior to others. In describing the **narcissistic personality,** the American Psychiatric Association (1987) notes that: "Self-esteem is almost invariably very fragile; the person may be preoccupied with how well he or she is doing and how well he or she is regarded by others. This often takes the form of an almost exhibitionistic need for constant attention and admiration. . . . In response to criticism, he or she may react with rage, shame, or humiliation, or mask these feelings with an aura of cool indifference" (p. 350). What appears to be an excessively high self-regard may, in fact, be exactly the opposite.

Second, self-esteem is not to be confused with **perfectionism,** the expectation that you (and others) should be perfect. Burns (1980) has defined perfectionists as people whose standards are high beyond reach or reason, who strain compulsively and unremittingly toward impossible goals and who measure their own worth entirely in terms of productivity and accomplishment. For perfectionists, the drive to excel can be self-defeating. Perceived failure or inadequacy can result for these people in a sudden and dramatic loss of self-esteem. They believe that they must be perfect to be accepted. Consequently, they fear appearing foolish or inadequate and resist sharing their innermost

Narcissistic Personality
a characteristic style of preoccupation with self, with high need for approval and low tolerance for criticism.

Perfectionism
a characteristic style of intolerance for error and shortcomings in oneself or others.

Healthy self-esteem should not be confused with narcissism or perfectionism.

thoughts and feelings with others. This affects interpersonal relationships by inhibiting intimate communication and further deprives them of the acceptance they deserve but cannot earn through accomplishment. Cognitive restructuring, a helpful method for coping with perfectionism, will be discussed later in this chapter in the section on alternatives.

Finally, a person's self-ideal can certainly allow for being less than perfect relative to absolute standards. The philosopher Bertrand Russell (1930) advised, "Nobody should expect to be perfect, or be unduly troubled by the fact that he is not." Even for those to whom achievement is important, it is quite possible to be satisfied with pursuing excellence without tormenting oneself that it has not yet been fully achieved. Some individuals, cultures, and religions place a high value (ideal) on personal qualities such as humility and the recognition and acknowledgment of one's shortcomings. Self-esteem can be founded on pursuing the journey toward an ideal, rather than on having already achieved it. We will explore this further when we discuss self-acceptance.

CORRELATES OF SELF-ESTEEM

How is self-esteem related to other aspects of a person's life? Does level of self-esteem predict anything else about an individual?

Many studies have found relationships between measured levels of self-esteem and other dimensions of adjustment. Low-self-esteem people seem to show greater reliance upon others for identity. In a study of men and women who were romantically involved, Dion and Dion (1975) found that low-self-esteem partners perceived fewer differences between themselves and their lovers, and their romantic emotional attachment was stronger. Individuals with low self-esteem also tend to be more depressed and anxious (Wylie, 1979), less accepting of and more prejudiced toward others (Rubin, 1967), and less able to learn empathy toward others (Miller, Hedrick, & Orlofsky, 1982). High-self-esteem people have been reported to be less affected by failure and negative information (Marcia, 1967) and less susceptible to social influence (Nisbett & Gordon, 1967). Coopersmith (1968) reported that boys with high self-esteem set higher goals for themselves than did boys with lower self-esteem, and were also more successful in achieving their goals.

DEVELOPMENTAL ASPECTS OF SELF-ESTEEM

How does self-esteem develop? Remember that self-esteem is related to the discrepancy between self-concept and self-ideal, both of which are acquired in the process of growing up, and the family is an important influence on this process. Virginia Satir (1972) described the type of family environment in which, she believed, feelings of self-worth are most likely to develop. The optimal family, she hypothesized, is one in which individual differences are appreciated, mistakes are tolerated, communication is open, and rules are flexible. Thus, in addition to influencing the child's self-concept and self-ideal, such a family also communicates acceptance of a gap between the two.

The emergence of self-esteem can also be understood within the classical frameworks of developmental psychology. Recall, from our description of Erikson's theory in Chapter 4, that the establishment of *trust* is the first key developmental issue, which lays the groundwork for healthy self-esteem. Trust emerges in the family context as a result of affection and gratification of the infant's needs. Similarly, Erikson's second stage, *autonomy* is crucial also, with the child learning to view herself or himself as a separate individual apart from parents, though still dependent upon them. White (1975) emphasized the role of a sense of personal **competence** in the development of self-esteem.

In research with boys, Coopersmith (1968) found that for those identified as possessing high self-esteem, a close relationship existed between them and their parents. The parents' love was not necessarily expressed in overt shows of affection or the amount of time they spent with their children; it was manifested by interest in the boys' welfare, concern about their companions, availability for discussion of the boys' problems, and participation in congenial joint activities. According to Coopersmith, the mother and father gave many signs that they regarded the boy as a significant person who was inherently worthy of their deep interest. Growing up with this parental perspective, the boy learned to view himself in a similarly positive light. Parents of these boys were described as strict but fair, and used rewards rather than physical punishment or withdrawal of love as disciplinary methods. The parents of high-self-esteem boys also set definite and age-appropriate standards of performance that enabled the boy to know whether or not he had succeeded in a task, how far he had fallen short when he failed, and what efforts would be required to achieve success.

Hales (1979) reported a similar set of characteristics for the families of high-self-esteem girls. The parents of girls with high self-esteem set clear rules and enforced them consistently, and also encouraged independence and responsibility in their daughter. The overall atmosphere in the home was described as warm and accepting.

To think of self-esteem as a single entity is to oversimplify a complex phenomenon. In early childhood there may be a single global self-evaluation, but as the child develops into adulthood, self-esteem appears to be differentiated into more specific parts, varying with situations (Mullener & Laird, 1971). Epstein (1973) suggested four subcategories of self-evaluation: general competence, personal power, moral self-approval, and love worthiness. The study of more specific dimensions of self-esteem can yield interesting results. Research on gender differences, for example, suggests that while boys and girls do not differ on overall self-esteem, girls do report lower self-confidence regarding tasks they are about to undertake (Maccoby & Jacklin, 1974). Even confidence in one's ability, however, is best judged relative to the particular task at hand

Competence
one's overall ability to cope with a broad range of adjustment tasks and challenges, or specific ability to perform a particular task; White (1975) described "effectance" as a general motivational drive to achieve competence.

Self-esteem is promoted by a close relationship with parents.

(Bandura, 1982). Thus, a person who is extremely self-confident about parenting skills may be quite uncertain regarding academic ability, and the self-assured tennis player may be insecure in socializing. It appears, then, that in studying components of self-esteem, one must take into account the specific task and situation.

You may or may not have come from a family background that nurtured your self-esteem. If you did, congratulations! Whether or not you did, there are steps that you can take to enhance your own self-esteem, regardless of your personal history. We will discuss these now in three major categories: awareness, acceptance, and alternatives.

■ AWARENESS

Change often begins with awareness. With regard to self-esteem, it can be helpful to increase your awareness in three areas: (1) your self-ideal, (2) your self-concept, and (3) the distance or gap between them. Throughout this discussion we will use the example of Linda, a student who explored her self-perception during a series of counseling sessions at a student health center.

BECOMING AWARE OF YOUR SELF-IDEAL

Although your self-esteem probably fluctuates depending on the circumstances of your life, you may have ideals that remain fairly constant. What are the ideals to which you aspire? Are you aware of your self-ideal, or at least parts of it? In Chapter 4 we asked you to think about people who are your role models. What are the ideal qualities you see in these people, which you would like to develop in yourself? What ideals do those role models personify for you? Do you expect to reach your ideals? All these are questions pertaining to awareness of your self-ideal.

> Linda was a "returning" student, entering the university in her mid-thirties while raising a family and working outside the home. She came to the student health center because she felt very unhappy with her life. Self-esteem was a central problem for her. She held very high ideals and daily berated herself for failing to meet them. She expected to maintain an "A" average, to excel at the work, and always to iron her children's jeans. She was, without realizing it, trying to be perfect in every area of her life: an outstanding student, a model employee, an ideal parent, a sensitive partner.

From where does the self-ideal come? Though the sources are many, it is safe to say that it is acquired through experience in the course of child and adult development. Who were the most important influences in your own life, helping you to clarify your own ideals? Significant sources may include parents, grandparents, friends, teachers, religious leaders, authors, or colleagues. You might make a list of those you believe contributed significantly to your own sense of self-ideal, and next to each one note the ideal qualities you learned.

One way in which self-ideal is measured by psychologists is through the semantic differential technique (see Chapter 2). In Box 6-1 you will see an example of this method, a list of pairs of words describing opposite personal characteristics. Between each pair of words is a scale ranging from 1 to 7. For each pair of words, rate where you would *ideally* like to be.

With regard to self-ideal, an important consideration is how realistic or achievable your goals are. To have an ideal exactly the same as your present

6.1 | SELF-CONCEPT VERSUS SELF-IDEAL

On each of the following word pairs, circle the number which represents where you would *ideally* like to be first. Then, with a different colored pencil or pen, circle the number which represents where you *currently* are along the range of each dimension.

Spontaneous	1	2	3	④	⑤	6	7	Planful
Outgoing	1	2	3	4	⑤	⑥	7	Private
Hardworking	1	2	3	④	⑤	6	7	Relaxed
Lenient	1	2	3	4	⑤	⑥	7	Strict
Unattractive	1	2	3	④	⑤	6	7	Attractive
Creative	1	②	③	4	5	6	7	Predictable
Organized	1	2	3	④	5	⑥	7	Flexible
Worldly	1	2	3	4	⑤	6	7	Spiritual
Thinking	1	2	3	4	5	⑥	7	Feeling
Playful	1	2	3	④	5	6	7	Serious
Cautious	1	2	3	4	5	⑥	7	Risk-taking
Warm	1	2	3	④	5	6	7	Cold
Carefree	1	2	3	④	5	6	7	Concerned
Stable	1	2	③	4	5	6	7	Changeable
Reflective	1	2	③	4	5	6	7	Decisive

state is to have no goal at all. On the other hand, goals and ideals can be set so high that they are unachievable, which can result in discouragement and giving up on reaching them. Research on motivation for change suggests that the best goals are those that are challenging but also attainable (Locke et al., 1981).

This is not to say that people should have no lofty goals. Great social reformers have usually lived in pursuit of a dream that seemed well out of reach in the course of their own lifetime. Cervantes's fictional character Don Quixote, in the musical *Man of La Mancha*, urges you "to dream the impossible dream," "to right the unrightable wrong," and "to try, when your arms are too weary, to reach the unreachable star." For those who aspire to such high ideals, however, the question is: "How can I move closer to my goal in achievable steps?" There is truth in the proverb that "A journey of a thousand miles begins with a single footstep." When the ideal is remote, it is helpful to set smaller goals along the way.

BECOMING AWARE OF YOUR SELF-CONCEPT

How would you describe yourself? Accurate self-assessment is often difficult, yet seeing yourself clearly is a crucial component in the development of healthy self-esteem. Where do your current strengths lie? What things about yourself would you still like to change? Return to the semantic differential exercise in Box 6.1 and rate yourself again, but this time describe yourself as you are *at present*, rather than how you would ideally like to be.

> Earning a "B" average, Linda described herself to the psychologist as "not doing very well in school." She felt embarrassed that her children sometimes went to school looking "like nobody cares for them" because their clothes were unmatched or not pressed. Although her evaluations at work had been consistently positive, she saw herself as disorganized. Feeling constantly tired, she also complained of being "unresponsive" sexually.

Techniques like the semantic differential can measure conscious self-concept at one point in time. The self-concept, however, is continually changing. New successes or failures, additional positive or negative information can influence self-concept and thus self-esteem as well (Sigall & Gould, 1977; Solley & Stagner, 1956). Individuals who are depressed or who already have low self-esteem may be particularly vulnerable to further damage to self-esteem from new failures and negative information (Marcia, 1967; Mischel, Ebbeson, & Zeiss, 1973). They also, like Linda, are likely to distort reality by perceiving themselves in an unnecessarily negative light.

An interesting method for tracking ongoing changes in your self-concept is to learn how to monitor your own **self-statements.** Aware of it or not, you are continually "talking to yourself" about what is happening, much as a radio commentator presents a moment-by-moment commentary and interpretation of events in a sports arena. These self-statements are not usually spoken, but rather are very rapidly passing thoughts. Because self-statements are silent and rapid, it takes some practice to become more aware of them.

A useful technique for increasing awareness of your self-statements is the ABC diary described by psychologist Albert Ellis (1984). The ABC diary is used to monitor your own ongoing self-statements. To prepare your diary, make three columns on blank sheets of paper. The left-hand column is headed "A. Situation," the middle "Beliefs," and the right "C. Feelings." To begin, it is usually easiest to make entries only in the A and C columns. An entry is made in the diary whenever you experience a significant emotion: happy, angry, anxious, worried, sad. The particular feeling is recorded in the C column, and in the A column record the antecedent, the situation that occurred just before the feeling occurred, and which seemed to cause the feeling. An example of this type of diary is shown in Box 6.2.

This technique becomes helpful in increasing awareness of self-statements, however, when you begin using the middle (B) column as well. The Beliefs column is used to record your self-statements, your interpretations of situations, the things you say to yourself silently about each situation. Ellis's point is that situations almost never lead *automatically* to a particular feeling. Rather, the feeling results from how one interprets the situation. If you have difficulty filling in the B column, ask yourself: "What *must* I have told myself in order to feel this way about this situation?" An example of a full ABC diary is shown in Box 6.3.

BECOMING AWARE OF THE GAP

Self-Statement
a private thought, spoken or unspoken, regarding oneself or observed events.

As you have described your self-ideal and your current self-concept, what did you notice about the differences or similarities between these two aspects of your self-perception? Is the gap between them large, or does it seem fairly easy to bridge? It is this gap between self-ideal and self-concept that is closely related to self-esteem.

6.2 A TWO-COLUMN DIARY

A. SITUATION	C. FEELINGS
Attractive person did not phone as planned	Disappointed, embarrassed, worthless
Professor praised work	Pleased, proud
Exercised before class	Strong, exhilarated
Burned dinner	Angry, feeling stupid
Big exam coming up	Anxious, helpless

6.3 A THREE-COLUMN DIARY

A. SITUATION	B. SELF-STATEMENT	C. FEELINGS
Attractive person did not call as planned	"I knew it. What an idiot I was even to expect a call. Nobody is interested in me."	Disappointed, embarrassed, worthless
Professor praised work	"I worked hard on that assignment and it really paid off. That just shows I can do well when I try."	Pleased, proud
Exercised before class	"It gets a little easier every time I run. I am taking care of myself."	Strong, exhilarated
Burned dinner	"I can't do anything right. I can't even follow a simple recipe."	Angry, ashamed
Big exam coming up	"I just know I'm going to blow it. I always study my brains out, and then when I get in there I blank out and can't remember a thing."	Anxious, helpless

To Linda, the gap between self-concept and self-ideal was more than apparent, and seemed to her almost impossible to bridge. Consequently she felt discouraged and hopeless. "I'll never be the kind of person I want to be. I'm messing up everything I try. I don't know what's the matter with me that I can't handle my life like other people."

In keeping an ABC diary of self-statements, most people find that there are certain themes that appear again and again, particularly among those self-statements that lead to negative emotions. Sidney Simon (1977, 1978) described such negative self-statements as psychological "vultures," which tear away at self-esteem. According to Simon, vulture food comes in six delicious flavors, six very common areas in which people torment themselves about being inadequate: intelligence, social skills, family, creativity, sexuality, and physical appearance or abilities. Obviously, Linda was tormented by several of these vultures.

Other writers (Ellis & Harper, 1975; Lazarus & Faye, 1975) have described common self-statement themes which reflect unrealistic expectations that are almost guaranteed to produce misery. One of these is the expectation that "Everyone should love me and approve of everything that I do, and if anyone does not love me, it is a disaster that has to be changed as soon as possible." The result of this belief is that the person becomes very upset whenever anyone shows signs of disliking or disapproving of him or her. Because one cannot please all of the people all of the time, this belief results in rather regular emotional upset. Furthermore, the individual begins spending much of his or her time with those who disapprove of his or her behavior, trying to make amends and change in order to suit them. Consequently the individual spends most of her or his efforts "putting out fires," while ignoring those who are already loving and cherishing. A few other common themes of this kind are

* In order to be a worthwhile and acceptable person, you must be totally competent, talented, and successful in everything you do.
* You should never say no to a request, especially from a friend, family member, or person in authority.
* People and things have to turn out the way you want them to. If they don't, you have a good reason to be very upset.
* There are only two kinds of people in the world: good and bad. If you're not good, then you're bad.
* The less you tell others about yourself, the better off you are. If you let people know who you really are, they will judge and reject you.
* When people treat you badly, it is because of something you did. It is vital to find out what you did wrong and to fix it.
* You must be totally self-sufficient and independent. Needing other people makes you too vulnerable.
* You don't deserve happiness unless you have earned it.
* You must accept your life as it is. Nothing you can say or do will make it different, so there's no point in trying.
* It's best to keep things as they are, no matter how bad things get. Change just makes things worse.

Sometimes these limiting beliefs are reflected in common expressions and proverbs, such as "Out of the frying pan into the fire," or "You can't teach an old dog new tricks."

Do any of these sound familiar? Perhaps you even find yourself defending some of these statements as true. Indeed it is possible to think of specific

6.4 HERE WE DIFFER/HERE WE AGREE
Is It Healthy to Hold Absolute Beliefs?

It is not uncommon for psychologists to deride people who adhere to absolute values or beliefs. Watzlawick, Weakland, and Fisch (1974) have denounced belief in an ultimate, all-embracing solution to human problems as "the Utopia Syndrome," speculating that such a belief results in feelings of personal inadequacy for being unable to achieve the ideal. Ellis (1980) has reviled any absolute values or religious belief, proclaiming that "The less religious [people] are, the more emotionally healthy they will tend to be" (p. 637).

My own perspective is quite the opposite. Those who dream no utopian concept beyond the present, who acknowledge no ultimate reality or power higher than themselves, lack the type of vision and meaning that enrich life and inspire major change. Great art and music, humanizing social reforms, the Constitution of the United States, and countless other enduring human contributions have emanated from people with a vision beyond themselves and the present. Self-esteem does not rely upon believing that there is nothing greater than oneself, or upon setting only goals that are within one's reach. It is mundane and limiting to set one's goals and ideals by what has already been achieved, or what seems easy to achieve.

I also question whether it is *possible* to live without absolute values. Each person operates by *some* system of core values, even if it be the absolute belief that there are no absolutes. The difference may be in people's awareness of the core values that direct their lives, of what Paul Tillich (1957) described as one's "ultimate concern."

I do not wish to go so far as to say that those who embrace no absolute values or transcendent reality are thereby maladjusted (though I do believe that they are missing something important). Neither am I equating vision with religious belief. Art, social reform, and utopian visions (e.g., Skinner, 1948) also come from people who affirm no religious precepts. But I do assert the *value* of seeing and pursuing a reality beyond one's own. The poet Robert Frost (1949) exhorted us to "Take something like a star to stay our minds on and be staid." That which is distant and almost unachievable has a way of bringing out the best in people.

                                              —WRM

It seems to me that having strong absolute beliefs can be rather oppressive if not downright dangerous. History is littered with examples of people and nations destroying each other because of their inability to resolve and compromise their unrelentingly absolute beliefs. One need not look very far today to find people tormenting and killing each other over absolute differences in their visions. The world could do with a little more respect and tolerance for different values and a bit less absolutism.

I certainly share the belief that there is value in reaching beyond that which we know, in expanding our horizons. Creativity involves stepping out beyond our normal limits in some way, and integrating reality in an unusual or unique manner. We all have many things we could learn, reach for, and develop in ourselves. I agree that it is exciting, healthy, and beneficial to reach beyond oneself, with or without success. But that doesn't depend on having some absolute or religious system of values and beliefs. In fact, having no-exception views can block one's vision, preventing the person from utilizing all that is available. A big problem with setting absolutes for oneself is that it can limit possibilities, reduce vision, and deprive the person of the full range of experiences that life has to offer. Still, if you choose to live your own life by absolutes, that's your right. Absolutely.

                                              —JMR

INTEGRATION

Whether or not you endorse the idea of "absolute" values, it is important to be aware of the values by which your life is guided. The acceptance of a value as absolute for yourself does not require that you forcefully impose it on others. What are your own core values? What, if anything, do you see as absolute: as constant, larger, more important than yourself?

situations that seem to affirm the truth of beliefs such as these. The problem with these principles, however, is their extremity. Some are overgeneralizations. They may apply in some situations, but not others. As absolute principles they are rigid and unforgiving, hard on self-esteem and relationships with others. Such beliefs may lead one toward behavior patterns that are, in the long run, destructive to self-esteem and to relationships. Later in this chapter we will describe some methods for changing your self-statements.

■ ACCEPTANCE: REDEFINING THE SITUATION

Sometimes people react to the gap between self-concept and ideal self by feeling frustrated, discouraged, or hopeless about it. ("I'll never be the kind of person I want to be. I'll never be good enough.") Here we encounter a fourth aspect of self-perception, in addition to self-concept, self-ideal, and self-esteem. This is **self-acceptance,** which is often confused with self-esteem. At first impression, you might think that a person who is high in self-acceptance is one who has no gap between self-ideal and self-concept, and thus sees no need for change. A self-accepting person, however, may be very aware of the areas in which he or she still needs to change and grow. The acceptance can be a compassionate and forgiving awareness of the gap itself. It is quite possible to experience a gap between where one is and where one would like to be, without feeling great distress or discounting one's own worth. Such self-acceptance is not the same as believing that one has no need for change.

A lack of self-acceptance can, in fact, stand in the way of further growth. What Abraham Maslow (1954) found in studying self-actualized people is that they accept themselves *as they are,* while still working toward their ideal. Does this sound like a contradiction? Some people believe that if they were self-accepting, they would stagnate and lose their motivation to grow. They believe that only by being very demanding can they prod themselves to do better.

> Linda's psychologist chose to begin by helping her to become more accepting of herself and of the gap between her ideals and her present reality. In the fourth session, she reported having been startled by a friend who praised her for carrying a "B" average while managing so many other things in her life. The friend expressed admiration and even envy for Linda's abilities. At first, she couldn't believe that her friend was serious. Several weeks later, however, Linda was able to use this incident to develop an acceptance of her strengths. Though she still wanted to work toward an "A" average, she accepted that she was doing well in light of the many demands on her.

A dramatic demonstration of the power of self-acceptance emerged in a study of male gymnasts (Mahoney & Avener, 1977). All were superb athletes, and all were candidates for the U.S. Olympic team. During final competition, some would make the Olympic team and others would not. What makes the difference? How do those who make the team differ from those who do not? Mahoney and Avener found that the decisive differences were not physical, for all of the candidates had already proved their athletic prowess. Instead they found that those who qualified for Olympic competition were less perfectionistic and more self-accepting than were those who did not qualify. The qualifying group tended to underemphasize the importance of past performance failures, while the athletes who failed to qualify were more likely to rouse themselves into near-panic states during competition through mental images of self-doubt and impending defeat. Self-acceptance for these athletes made

Self-Acceptance
recognition of one's inherent worth regardless of personal strengths and weaknesses.

Self-acceptance can aid performance more than perfectionism does.

the difference. Those whose self-statements reflected acceptance of themselves, including their failures, were more likely to succeed in this new challenge. They were, in essence, acting as kindly coaches for themselves.

What is it that makes self-acceptance so difficult for many people? Although many people can appreciate their own strengths, far fewer accept (though they know) their own shortcomings and weaknesses (Shostrom, 1966). Instead of the compassionate acceptance they might give others, many people continually criticize themselves about perceived shortcomings. Such harsh self-criticism is not helpful. In fact, evidence points to a seeming paradox: those who accept their current shortcomings, their gap, are more likely to succeed in changing and achieving their goals. It is a *lack* of self-acceptance that is associated with stagnation.

■ ALTERNATIVES: PROBLEM-SOLVING STRATEGIES

THREE GENERAL APPROACHES

Thus far we have been discussing *concepts* related to self-esteem. We have related self-esteem to the overall perceived gap between present state (self-concept) and desired state (self-ideal). We have said that awareness is an important first step in improving self-esteem: awareness of self-concept, of self-ideal, and of the gap between them. We have also introduced the concept of self-acceptance, indicating that an accepting attitude toward one's present need for change can, in fact, facilitate that change.

In this section we will suggest a number of alternatives, strategies that can be practiced in working to improve self-esteem. All involve reducing the gap between self-concept and self-ideal, and there are three general approaches for doing so: (1) to reevaluate self-concept, (2) to reevaluate self-ideal, and (3) to change in the direction of the self-ideal. The first two approaches are more *cognitive* strategies and involve changing one's perceptions so that the gap is smaller. The third more often involves change in behavior, moving one's actual state closer to the desired ideal.

Linda's psychologist employed all three of these approaches in working with her to improve self-esteem. First, Linda needed to reevaluate her *self-concept*, because she perceived herself in an inaccurately negative light. The feedback from her friend, expressing admiration for how *well* Linda was coping, proved helpful in reassessing her own good skills. She realized that, in fact, she had been doing a remarkably good job of handling many demands. She also began to reevaluate her own doubts about herself against the fact that others were very happy with her: her supervisor gave her very positive evaluations, and her partner described her as a sensitive, sensual, and caring woman. Second, the psychologist helped Linda to reassess her somewhat unrealistic *self-ideal,* her high expectations of herself. Joining a support group, Linda learned that her problems and frustrations are really quite common. She had held the illusion that everyone else was managing very well, and the support group gave her feedback that others shared the same struggles. She also began to relax her high standards a bit, deciding that it would not be a disaster if her children appeared at school now and then with somewhat wrinkled clothing. Third, Linda planned how she might be more able to pursue her goals and to *close the gap* between where she was and where she wanted to be. She worked on developing better study skills (see Appendix C) and planning her study time more carefully, so that she could have both quality time with her family and friends and efficient periods of study. As she replaced her children's clothing, she bought either no-iron garments, or new fashions that featured a wrinkled look. With the help of her psychologist and support group, Linda also began to explore her own emotions and to increase her self-acceptance as a worthwhile person.

We turn now to a discussion of some specific strategies that can be used in working to improve self-esteem.

LIFE-STYLE BALANCING

Balance is an important key to self-esteem. When self-esteem is too invested in one particular area (in work, or in relationships, or in physical attractiveness, for example), you run the risk of "putting all your eggs in one basket." Consider the example of a person who invests most of his or her time and energy into work and career accomplishments, while doing very little to nurture important relationships (family, friends) or personal (intellectual, emotional, spiritual) growth. For such a person, self-esteem is heavily reliant upon what happens in this one narrow sphere of life. A major setback in that area, then, can take a heavy toll on self-esteem. Can you think of examples from among people you know, or perhaps from fictional literature, of individuals whose whole identity seems to be vested in one area of their lives?

An alternative strategy here for enriching self-esteem is to "spread it around," being careful not to invest too much of one's confidence and competence in any one area. Take a personal inventory of how you are investing your own time and energies. How balanced are you among creative and contributing efforts (work), meaningful relationships, and personal growth? Consider what new skills, interests, relationships, or personal pursuits you might develop. The more areas in which you have a sense of personal involvement and growth, the less the impact of a setback in any one area (Marlatt & Gordon, 1985).

> In one way, part of Linda's problem was that she was already *too* "spread around." As she examined her life, however, she felt a strong desire to spend more quality time in her relationships. She backed off a bit on working long extra hours when, in fact, this was not necessary and she usually accomplished little by working overtime anyhow. Her improved planning and study skills also helped her to use her study time more efficiently, so that she could spend more time with those she loved. As she did this, she found a better sense of balance. Her mind did not drift off so often while studying, wishing that she were somewhere else. Neither did she find herself thinking, while spending time with her family or friends, that she really ought to be studying or working. She felt more balanced.

POSITIVE THINKING

The importance of "positive thinking" has been much discussed and commonly oversold in our society. Thinking positive thoughts is often not enough.

Yet the importance of self-statements should not be underestimated, either. Simply reading either optimistic or pessimistic statements has been shown to have a substantial impact on mood (Velten, 1968). Positive or negative feedback from others tends to influence self-esteem (Ludwig & Maehr, 1967; Sigall & Gould, 1977), and yet individuals differ widely in the extent to which self-esteem is damaged by negative feedback (Marcia, 1967). The difference may well be found, as Mahoney and Avener (1977) showed with male gymnasts, in what people *say* to themselves about the negative feedback.

One simple strategy is to construct and practice positive self-statements. Even writing a positive description of one's own personality has been shown to produce an increase in self-esteem (Mirels & McPeek, 1977). Research suggests that optimistic, positive expectations can increase the probability of a positive outcome occurring (Jones, 1977). There appears to be merit, then, in practicing and intentionally choosing a positive outlook, a strategy that has been commended for centuries (Miller, 1985a). Some possibilities are

1. Write a detailed description of your own strengths, assets, and positive points, as though you were writing a strictly laudatory letter of recommendation for yourself.

2. Think of some positive self-statements and write them down on index cards. Carry these cards with you, and several times a day take them out and read one or two.

3. Set up a special envelope or drawer where you save affirming notes and letters from others. Take them out and read them from time to time.

4. Use positive imagery. In imagination, call "witnesses" to testify to your personal worth. Imagine a person who has loved and cared about you, telling you or others all the likeable things about you.

The point is to *practice* positive self-statements on a regular basis.

> Linda came up with several positive self-statements that she found helpful: "I'm doing fine." "I am happy to have so many people who love and care about me." "I handle a pretty complicated life very well." "I am a worthwhile, lovable, and beautiful person." She chose to write these on small "thank you" cards and carried them in her purse. Once or more a day, she would find a quiet

Choosing a positive outlook is an important element in healthy self-esteem.

moment to sit down, read her cards through slowly and caringly, and accept their truth. She also began saving special loving notes and letters she received, keeping them in a dresser drawer where she would see them regularly.

THOUGHT STOPPING

It can be helpful not only to increase positive self-statements, but to decrease negative self-statements as you work on strengthening your self-esteem. As you become more aware of your own patterns and themes of negative self-statements (your "vultures" or put-downs), catch yourself saying these things and then interrupt the negative thoughts.

The method of **thought stopping** (Wolpe, 1973) is a relatively simple way of doing this. When you are aware of a negative self-statement beginning, say to yourself (perhaps aloud at first), "Stop." This interrupts and interferes with the negative train of thought. If the thought returns, stop it again. Is it surprising that you could have such control over your own thoughts? Try it! After all, they are *your* thoughts! Perhaps you can find an even better phrase to use as your thought-stopper. Some have used words like "Nonsense!" or "Wait a minute!"

COGNITIVE RESTRUCTURING

Stopping negative thoughts as they occur can be valuable in itself, but it is often still more helpful to identify and change the negative thought pattern itself. Cognitive restructuring is the name given to a procedure that involves observing and rearranging thought processes that have been self-defeating. At least three different approaches to cognitive restructuring have been described: the "rational-emotive therapy" of Albert Ellis (1984), Donald Meichenbaum's (1977) "self-instructional training," and cognitive therapy (Beck, 1976; Burns, 1980). All three approaches have many common features, however, and all seek to foster positive adjustment by (1) discovering and detecting maladaptive thought patterns, (2) recognizing their damaging impact, and (3) replacing them with more appropriate and adaptive thought patterns (Hollon & Beck, 1986). According to these approaches, changing the way you think (cognitive restructuring) can improve how you feel about yourself.

Cognitive restructuring begins with self-monitoring, as described earlier in this chapter. Keeping an "ABC" diary clarifies the self-statements that lead to negative emotions and low self-esteem. The key is to become aware of your own negative self-statements, and then to catch yourself when you are saying them. A negative feeling can be a cue to ask: "What am I saying to myself that is causing this feeling? How am I interpreting this situation?" Thought stopping can be used to interrupt the negative self-statement. But then what?

The next step is to start keeping a thought replacement log. An example of this log is shown in Box 6.5. The first column is for recording the negative self-statements that you discover through your ABC diary. The middle column provides a space for writing the logical errors in your negative self-statement. What is *wrong* with the self-statement? Here are some common logical errors in self-statements (Beck, 1976):

* *All-or-nothing thinking.* Acknowledging only two kinds of people in the world (good and bad, smart and stupid, kind and thoughtless, creative and boring), and I must be one or the other.

* *Overgeneralization:* Starting from one experience and expanding it, as if it were true in all situations. Because one person does not like me, I must be unlovable.

Thought Stopping
a self-help technique for ending unwanted thoughts by saying to oneself the word "Stop!" or another interrupting word or phrase.

* *Mental filter:* Ignoring and overlooking the positive, while paying close attention to the negative. In reading through course evaluations, an instructor may flip past all of the positive ones but read the critical ones over and over, in great detail.

* *Disqualifying the positive:* Dismissing one's own positive traits or accomplishments as accident, luck, generosity from others, and so on.

* *Jumping to conclusions:* Assuming the worst before the facts are in, and sometimes thereby causing one's own worst fears to come true.

* *Magnification (catastrophizing):* "Making a mountain out of a molehill"; convincing oneself, based on slim evidence, that things are really terrible.

Having recorded your self-statement and the logical errors in it, your task is to discover a healthy replacement statement and to record it in the third column of your log. After this, the key is to practice your new (replacement) self-statements. One way to do this is to practice them regularly, as positive

6.5 — A THOUGHT REPLACEMENT LOG

NEGATIVE SELF-STATEMENT (SELF-CRITICISM)	COGNITIVE DISTORTION (LOGICAL ERROR)	REPLACEMENT SELF-STATEMENT (SELF-DEFENSE)
"I knew it. What an idiot I was even to expect a call. Nobody is interested in me."	Overgeneralization	"I am a lovable and worthwhile person. Nothing takes that away."
"I can't do anything right. I can't even follow a simple recipe."	Mental filter	"I am a capable person, and there are many things I do very well."
"I just know I'm going to blow it. I always study my brains out, and then when I get in there I blank out and can't remember a thing."	Jumping to conclusions	"Now wait a minute. *Sometimes* I freeze a little on tests, but I know this material, and I will just need to focus on the questions and not let my negative thoughts run wild. I can do it."
I'm never going to be popular. I'm just a social nerd.	All or none thinking	"I'm acting like there are just two kinds of people in the world: popular and unpopular. Sure, I need to learn how to be more comfortable socially, but I'm a worthwhile person just as I am."

self-statements; "I used to believe that _____[old self-statement]_____, but now I know that _____[new self-statement]_____." Another method is to catch yourself when you are saying your old negative statement, use thought stopping, and then practice your replacement statement.

> With the help of an ABC diary, Linda identified several themes that ran through her negative self-statements. These included "You're a failure. No matter how hard you try, it won't be good enough." "You can't cope with everybody's demands." "Be perfect. Don't make any mistakes." As she became aware of these, she started catching herself saying them. At this point she would say to herself, "Now wait a minute . . ." and would counter with a "coaching" statement. When she was berating herself for making a mistake, for example, she sometimes countered with, "It's natural to make mistakes! If I'm not making mistakes then I'm probably not learning and taking enough risks. I'm still an O.K. person, and I get stronger by learning from mistakes." She noticed, when she did this, that she really did *feel* differently. Instead of feeling angry and depressed, she had more of a sense of optimism and acceptance.

SOCIAL SUPPORT

Isolation, real or perceived, is one substantial barrier to learning and using alternative problem-solving strategies. Without feedback and support from others, it is easier to perceive problems as unique, shameful, hopeless, and unsolvable. **Social support**—a little help from your friends—can provide important feedback, information, contacts, and resources. Sharing concerns with supportive others often helps reduce feelings of abnormality, enhancing self-esteem (Barbach & Ayres, 1976; Toth & Toth, 1981).

Social support is the vehicle by which individuals and groups gain access to those resources necessary for problem solving and positive mental health. It is provided by relationships with extended family, friends, acquaintances, and community social service resources. Social support offers tangible resources, information, aid with problem solving, reinforcement, and emotional support (Rowledge, Bond, & Schradle, 1980; Schradle & Dougher, 1985).

Consider your own network of social support for a moment. Whom can you talk to about personal feelings and issues of self-esteem? Who could help you move closer to your self-ideal? Are there people available to help you in reeval-

Social Support
help and encouragement of various kinds, provided through one's relationships with others.

Self-esteem is enhanced by a network of social support.

uating your self-concept and self-ideal? These people and resources are an important part of your social support network.

A study of structured support groups at a university student mental health center demonstrated that such groups can enhance self-esteem (Yahne & Long, 1988). Compared to a control group, the women who participated in this study significantly increased their self-esteem after only six weeks of the support group contact. The women students also reported progress in appreciating their own strengths, in being less critical of their own weaknesses, and in achieving short-term goals. The empowering aspect of the common bond the participants reported is consistent with the findings of Plas and Wallston (1983) regarding reciprocity between women: the more women recognize other females as important and find themselves valuing and encouraging them, the more they see themselves as important. Again, self-regard is linked to one's regard for others.

> Linda participated in a brief structured support group through the student health center, and found that she greatly valued and benefited from the opportunity to talk with others about personal concerns and issues. When the group ended, she and two other women from the group decided to form an ongoing support group of their own. They invited several other friends to join them, and began meeting on a weekly basis. They found that this worked for them much as formal therapy had, helping them continually to reevaluate their own perceptions, feelings, and actions. The group members served for each other as a kind of "reality check," and provided for each other an important extended network of friendship.

6.6 PERSONAL MILESTONE
Social Support

For me, one of the most helpful and stabilizing influences in my life has been my participation in regular support groups. Over the years I have been part of six different groups, all of which met for a year or more. The first three were "sharing" groups of men and women, meeting every week or two to talk about important feelings and changes in our lives. Though I've moved away, I still keep in contact with some of the close friends I made in one of those early groups. I especially valued that group because of the immense diversity. We ranged in age from 18 to 70 and spanned a broad spectrum of occupations and interests.

Then one year I went to a public lecture by a psychologist named Warren Farrell (1974), who was talking about the need for men's "consciousness raising" groups to offer men the same kind of growth and support that was happening among women at that time. A group of us who attended that talk decided to start getting together weekly, and we invited a few other men to join us. We were about 15 in

number, and over the course of a year we grew very close. It took a few months, but after a while we abandoned the usual male defensiveness around other men and started talking about the things we really cared and worried about: our marriages and families, feelings of loneliness and isolation, the stress of competitiveness, our need to look strong and be reliable breadwinners regardless of whatever pain might be in our inner worlds. We found we had much in common, despite our wide political and socioeconomic differences. At the end of the year, when I moved away, it was very hard to say goodbye to some of the first men who had ever truly become my friends.

It wasn't long before I was missing the strong support and caring that I had experienced. I tried several different kinds of support groups, including a couples group and a prayer group. Finally, I decided that what I really wanted was another support group of men. I talked to a few men I knew, and found them equally hungry for a safe place to talk and grow. As I write this, we have passed our ninth anniversary together, meeting every other week. Together we've been through the full span of life's experiences: deaths and births, marriages and divorces, job losses and job changes, the joys and pains of relationships and raising families, devastating memories and uplifting moments. These men *know* me. When I share a new experience, they understand the context of my life into which it comes. They don't let me get away with much, either. I am continually cared for, challenged, called to care for others. In a way, I can't imagine how my life would have been without this group of men, and the other support groups that have been so much a part of my adult growth. Certainly I am healthier, happier, stronger, more feeling, and maybe a little wiser because of these years together.

—WRM

■ SUMMARY

Self-esteem is an important dimension of personality, and is related to a variety of other aspects of adjustment. Self-esteem should not be confused with self-centeredness or narcissism. Low self-esteem is related to a significant gap between self-concept and self-ideal and is importantly influenced by family development. Self-esteem can be increased through at least three general approaches: (1) reevaluating self-concept, (2) reevaluating self-ideal, or (3) changing oneself in the direction of the self-ideal. Specific strategies for improving self-esteem include increasing awareness of self-ideal and self-concept, increasing awareness and acceptance of the gap between them, life-style balancing, positive thinking, thought stopping, cognitive restructuring, and social support.

What you have learned in this chapter about changing self-esteem can be readily applied to dealing with mood and depression, the subject of the next chapter. The adjustment skills discussed in each chapter are intended to build upon each other, helping you to understand and develop a repertoire of strategies for facilitating change and growth.

■ QUESTIONS FOR THOUGHT

1. What is the difference between self-esteem and self-centeredness? How can you tell the difference in your own behavior, or the behavior of others?

2. Do you have perfectionistic beliefs? In what areas of your life do these most get in your way?

3. What types of experiences are most likely to give you a boost in self-esteem? What kinds of experiences harm your self-esteem?

4. The last time you felt supported by another person, what did that person say or do? What kinds of support from others do you most value or need?

5. What people have been role models for you? What ideal qualities do they embody that you may want to emulate?

6. In what areas do you feel the largest gap between where you are and where you want to be? In what areas are you closest to how you would like to be?

7. Do you have personal values that you regard as "absolute" and central to who you are? If so, what are they?

8. Why is it, in your opinion, that self-acceptance is so difficult for many people?

9. What are your strong points? Make a list.

10. What beliefs about yourself have changed the most over the last few years? Fill in the blanks: I used to believe that _____, but now I know that _____.

chapter seven

I do have periods of what to me is incredible depression. As high as I can get, I'm capable of being that low. There are times when I am very sad, times when I'm lonely; there are times when I'm unhappy and when I feel sorry for myself. What have I got to feel sorry for myself about? I have everything. But it has nothing to do with what you've got or where you are. It's the human condition. To run the gamut of these emotions is a great part of the living experience.
—John Denver, December 1977.

Mood, Grief, and Depression

OUTLINE

*T*he words which open this chapter—from an interview with song-writer John Denver—point out that wealth and fame are no insulation from the anguish and richness of human feelings. Emotions, ever changing, are a part of the challenge of adjustment.

The word "emotion" covers a broad and rich array of human experiences. Emotional reactions can be momentary, as when one is startled by a loud noise, or they may last for days, weeks, or even months. They range from the highs of love and joy to the depths of hatred and despair. We devoted Chapter 3 to a discussion of emotions in general, introducing there the STORC model as a tool for understanding these complex experiences.

In this, the first of four chapters on important areas of emotional adjust-ment, we will explore feelings that are often called "down." We will discuss the normal process of grieving that follows a major loss. We will explain how dejected mood differs from depression, a more serious but nevertheless com-mon problem. We will also consider the phenomenon of suicide—why it occurs, and how it may be prevented. In this and subsequent chapters, we will continue to use the STORC model as a way of organizing information on how emotions arise, and how they are changed. We will consider how each element of the STORC model contributes to mood, and how each can be used when one wants to make a change. In the chapters that follow, we will deal similarly with stress and anxiety, anger, joy and love.

■ DIFFERENCES BETWEEN MOOD, GRIEF, AND DEPRESSION

MOOD

The word **mood,** in psychology and in everyday life, is a broad term describing temporary emotional states. The content of a mood might be sad, worried, angry, or merry. A key aspect, however, is that a mood state is relatively tempo-rary or transitory in nature. It is expected to pass in a relatively short period of time: minutes, hours, or at most a few days. Mood, in essence, is normal human emotional change. Mood usually shifts in response to events in the person's world. One who shows unusually frequent shifts among such brief emotional states is said to be "moody."

GRIEF

Grief is also a normal human response, but it differs from mood in three ways. First, it occurs in reaction to a particular kind of experience: a significant loss. Second, it is usually longer lasting than mood. It is not unusual for a major loss, such as the death of one's spouse, to result in a normal grief reaction that persists for more than a year. Third, grief reactions are more specific than mood. They have a particular tone. A grieving person may indeed be moody, with feelings changing widely and even rapidly, but the predominant emotion is sadness. Crying, difficulties in working or concentrating, sleeping problems, fatigue, and restlessness are all typical during major grief reactions.

The line between normal and abnormal grieving is difficult to draw. Kübler-Ross (1969) described five stages through which people typically pass in nor-mal adjustment to a major loss, particularly in grieving a death or in contem-

Mood
an emotional state, usually mild and temporary in nature.

Grief
a normal pattern of emotional and psychological adjustment to a significant loss.

plating their own impending death (see Box 7.1). There is no sound evidence that people *must* pass through these stages overtly or in sequence to grieve "properly." The stages were meant merely to be descriptive of how people *usually* pass through a normal adjustment to loss. The absence of overt emotions and grieving is not, in itself, a reason for concern.

7.1 STAGES OF ADJUSTMENT TO LOSS

Elisabeth Kübler-Ross spent many years talking with terminally ill individuals and their families. Based on her experience, she described the following stages as a normal progression in grieving.

Dr. Elisabeth Kübler-Ross.

1. *Denial.* The initial stage in reacting to a loss is denial. The person may refuse to accept the truth and seek other explanations of what has happened. The diagnosis must be wrong. The names were mixed up. In extreme cases, a bereaved person may deny that the loved one has actually died.
2. *Anger.* The second stage described by Kübler-Ross is anger. Now aware of the loss, the person is resentful, bitter, envious of others, and generally angry: enraged at the world, the doctors, God, or those who do not understand. Plans and dreams have been frustrated, and the person protests that it isn't fair.
3. *Bargaining.* In an attempt to make it more fair, the person may look for options, ways to bargain or negotiate. He or she may try to buy more time, to bargain for relief from the suffering, to make or extract promises.

4. *Depression.* When anger and bargaining fail to change reality, the person may next fall into despair and hopelessness. Mourning comes in full force. The person faces and grieves for the present losses and those still to come.

5. *Acceptance.* Finally, according to Kübler-Ross, one reaches a sense of peace, an acceptance or resolution of the loss. The dying person awaits his or her death with quiet acceptance. Those grieving a loss reach first a resignation, then a more peaceful acceptance of the loss, and move on with the rest of their lives.

There are, however, some experiences that are not usually part of a normal grief reaction, and that signal a need for help (Clayton, 1982). Continued weight loss, pervasive guilt feelings, or persistent slowing of body movement are unusual after the first month, and point to serious depression rather than normal grieving. Suicidal ideas and actions are not part of typical grief, and are always reason for concern. Some individuals try to "keep everything exactly as it was" in the house, or in the room of the person who has died. This compulsion, sometimes called **mummification,** also suggests a failure to resolve the grieving process. The overuse of alcohol or other drugs may complicate a grief reaction (see Chapter 11).

Interestingly, it is not unusual for a bereaved individual to have some direct sensory experience of the one who has died, to hear or smell or see or feel the person's presence. In a survey of people who had recently grieved a death, one person in every six reported having had such an experience (Clayton, 1982).

Friends and family often wonder what they can do to help a loved one deal with grief. Books on "grief counseling" abound, yet despite three decades of attention to this subject, there are still no methods that have been scientifically proven to help a person in resolving grief. Grieving does indeed appear to be a normal process that runs its course with time. Proper help from a friend or counselor could conceivably shorten the process or make it less severe, but few guidelines are available from research for defining what constitutes proper help.

There does seem to be a consensus among professionals in this field that it is helpful for the grieving person to have opportunities to talk about the loss with supportive others. One experienced therapist (Ramsey, 1977) has suggested that those suffering prolonged and unresolved grief will benefit from confronting the emotion-arousing stimuli and memories that they have been attempting to avoid. Still it may be that grieving is a natural process that runs its course sooner or later, with or without the help of others.

Mummification
an abnormal adjustment reaction to the death of a loved one, in which the deceased's habitat and belongings are kept unchanged.

DEPRESSION

In everyday language, people use the word "depressed" to describe normal moods, feelings of being down or blue. As with many other terms, however, **depression** has a more precise meaning within psychology and psychiatry. (One common source of frustration and confusion for the student of psychology is the fact that so many terms that have specific psychological meanings also have different or less precise uses in daily life.)

Depression, like grief, differs from mood in that it refers to a state that is longer lasting. An untreated major depression may persist for months.

Depression
a major emotional disorder characterized by persistent feelings of sadness, accompanied by a variety of other significant changes in functioning.

Depression is a relatively common experience.

Depression is also a **syndrome,** a set of characteristic problems that tend to occur together. The root of the word "syndrome" means literally "to run to-gether." To understand this concept, consider another syndrome: the common cold. This syndrome includes certain typical components or symptoms including stuffy or runny nose, coughing, fever, muscle ache, headache, sneezing, and watery eyes. Not everyone with a cold has *all* these symptoms. The common cold is recognized by observing several of the signs from this syndrome.

Syndrome
a set of symptoms that tend to occur together as a group.

Clinical depression goes far beyond a negative mood. Common components of the depression syndrome are shown in Box 7.2. As with the common

7.2   SIGNS OF DEPRESSION

The American Psychiatric Association (1987) lists the following nine problems as symptomatic of major depression:

1. Persistent feelings of sadness, hopelessness, emptiness
2. A loss of interest and involvement in activities that are usually pleasurable
3. Increased or decreased appetite, with resulting weight gain or loss
4. A change in sleep pattern: either insomnia or increased sleeping
5. A change in body movement: either agitation or a physical slowing of movement and speech
6. A pervasive feeling of fatigue, tiredness, lack of energy
7. Persistent thoughts of personal worthlessness or excessive guilt
8. Difficulty in thinking, concentrating, or making decisions
9. Suicidal thoughts, ideas, intentions, or acts

cold, not every component has to be present. The presence of any four of these nine signs would usually be sufficient for a psychologist to diagnose clinical depression. Like a common cold, depression is recognized as a set of symptoms that vary from person to person.

Another important aspect of depression is that it represents a *change* from the person's previous state. A person who *always* feels fatigued or worthless is not necessarily depressed. Clinical depression is recognized by a change in the person (sometimes gradual) on several of the signs listed earlier. The clinically depressed person may, for example, withdraw from and no longer enjoy activities that were previously regular and enjoyable. He or she may seem uncharacteristically sad, tired, or slow in movement, in contrast to his or her usual style.

In one sense, depression is common because about 10 percent of men and 20 percent of women will experience a serious episode of depression at some time during their lives (American Psychiatric Association, 1987). Yet depression, in another sense, is not normal adjustment. Its severity is out of proportion to the person's life circumstances. Although depressed people can often provide justifications and explanations for why they are feeling so down, their reaction is much more severe and serious than one would normally expect to occur. Most people, experiencing similar setbacks or losses, do not show such disabling depression.

Clinical depression, then, is not the same as mood. It is possible to feel down without being depressed, and some people who are clinically depressed may not realize it because they do not seem to *feel* especially down in mood. Depression is much longer lasting than typical moods, and is recognized as a persistent change from the person's prior state. Unlike a normal grief reaction, clinical depression is out of proportion to the person's life circumstances.

■ CAUSES OF DEPRESSION AND NEGATIVE MOOD

The causes of negative mood and of depression are similar. Many of the factors that can induce a negative mood in the short run may also, if they persist long enough, contribute to a full-blown depression. The severe and disabling condition that psychologists recognize as clinical depression seems, in many cases, to be the result of prolonged exposure to factors that also influence mood. In this view, if a person stays in a down mood long enough, it may turn into clinical depression.

Yet depression is not simply the result of prolonged negative mood or exposure to psychological risk factors. Some people show a remarkable ability to survive psychological hardship, sustaining a positive outlook. There is strong evidence that heredity plays an important role, and that individuals whose biological relatives have suffered clinical depression are at higher risk of developing depression themselves. Personality factors may also play a role in determining susceptibility to depression. For example, people differ in psychological **hardiness,** a personality and attitudinal dimension that has been shown to be a protective factor against physical illness and stress-related symptoms (Kobasa, 1979; Kobasa, Maddi, & Zola, 1983; Weibe & McCallum, 1986).

Hardiness
a personality characteristic associated with the ability to cope with stress while remaining healthy; in Kobasa's definition, it includes a sense of personal control, commitment to life activities, and a view of change as a positive challenge.

Thus it seems that depression, like many other human phenomena, arises from some interaction of heredity and environment, from a mixture of biological and psychological factors. Some people seem to be at higher risk for depression by virtue of their biological and hereditary constitution. Yet many people who have clinically depressed relatives never develop depression themselves, and many others who do become depressed show no family history of such problems. The STORC model can be useful as a way of understanding this complexity of factors influencing mood and depression.

S—SITUATIONAL FACTORS

Not even the most severe of situations has the power in itself to produce depression. Viktor Frankl (1963), describing conditions within the Nazi death camps of World War II, recalled individuals who spent their time encouraging and comforting others. Rather than being defeated by the seeming hopelessness of their situation, they held on to hope and shared it with others.

Nevertheless, certain kinds of situational factors do seem to increase the probability that depression will occur. To be sure, individuals differ in their susceptibility to such situational influence, and the other elements of the model (T, O, R, and C) play a role in determining what impact the situation will have. All else being equal, however, there are conditions that promote negative mood and depression.

As mentioned earlier, one of these is a significant loss. This may be the loss of a loved one through death, divorce, or geographic separation. It might be the loss of one's possessions by fire or theft, or the loss of a job. Some losses are more symbolic: the loss of a dream, or of a certain image of oneself. Certain events, such as moving to a new city, may involve many losses all at once. It is normal to grieve a loss, and as we said, the signs of normal grief overlap with those of depression. In a way, a certain amount of depression is normal and expected for a limited period of time. Sometimes, though, the person continues to be depressed longer or more severely than would be expected. There are no clear guidelines for how long is "too long." In any event, significant losses represent one kind of situational change that can contribute to depression.

Prolonged exposure to stress (see Chapter 8) also increases the risk of depression (Lewinsohn, Hoberman, & Rosenbaum, 1988). The potential sources of stress are many. Some, such as crowding and noise, are environmental. Social and intimate relationships may contribute to stress. Poverty, physical pain, threats to safety, physical illness, and competition all can increase stress and depression.

A third situational factor influencing depression that has been emphasized in the work of psychologist Peter Lewinsohn is the individual's level of social reinforcement (Lewinsohn, 1974; Lewinsohn & Amensen, 1978). Positive rein-

Prolonged stressful conditions, such as unemployment, can precipitate depression.

forcement and pleasant events appear to be important in maintaining a positive mood and outlook, much as vitamins are important in promoting physical health. A sudden drop in reinforcement level can precipitate depression. This may, in fact, be one of the reasons why significant losses (such as moving or losing one's spouse) can invoke depression. Such losses literally involve the death of significant relationships that have been vital sources of positive reinforcement and support. Likewise some people have life-styles or occupations that provide them with very little regular positive input, combined with a rich diet of criticism and negative evaluation. Sometimes (as when a relationship or job is new) reinforcement starts out at a high level but then drops off gradually over time. When such a drop in positive reinforcement occurs, it is described in everyday language as "being taken for granted" or not being appreciated. Continual exposure to conditions of low reinforcement can lead toward depression.

What can be done at the level of *situational* factors in order to prevent or reduce negative mood and depression? The main emphasis here is on planning and arranging for yourself a "balanced diet" in your daily psychological life. One strategy is to plan intentionally for each day to include some *pleasant events*, large or small, that function as "psychological vitamins" to help keep the rest of the day in balance (Lewinsohn et al., 1978). It may be helpful to increase your awareness of your own balance by keeping a daily record of pleasant and unpleasant events that occur. If the unpleasant or stressful events seem to dominate and overbalance pleasant events, it is important to plan time for additional positive experiences. As discussed in Chapter 6, regular social support can be an important source of such positive and balancing experiences. A lack of social support has been found to predict the onset of depression in adults (Phifer & Murrell, 1986).

If your daily diet is heavy with negative and stressful experiences, it may also be important to seek ways to decrease these. Which of them are unnecessary and avoidable? For those that are unavoidable, it can be useful to practice desensitization skills (see Chapter 8) to decrease their negative impact on you. Planning for additional pleasant events and social support can be useful when especially negative experiences are anticipated.

In planning a balanced psychological diet, also try to avoid a common pattern: to have all the negative or stressful events packed together into the daytime, and then a sudden shift to positive time. Marlatt and Gordon (1985) have associated this life-style with a risk for alcohol and drug abuse and propose that instead, it is healthier to distribute positive events throughout the day.

 ## T—THOUGHT PATTERNS

Although situational factors do play a role in mood and depression, there is another sense in which *nothing* in the external situation is *responsible* for your mood. Positive and negative emotions are not direct reactions to the "real" world, but rather are responses to how the person *perceives* that world (Chapter 2). Encountering a rattlesnake along a wilderness trail would evoke considerable arousal for a person who recognized it for what it is, but might result in little more than curiosity for a person who had no idea of the danger it posed. A toy can be a source of fun, fear, jealousy, anger, worry, or sadness, depending upon how it is perceived and used. Similarly, "depressing" events are not inherently depressing, and one's reaction depends upon how one perceives them. In the classic film, *It's a Wonderful Life*, the character played by Jimmy Stewart experiences a sudden series of major setbacks on Christmas eve. Perceiving his situation as hopeless and his life as worthless, he falls into a suicidal mood and wishes he had never been born. In a transforming vision, he gets his wish, seeing life in his town as it would have been had he never existed. Afterward, the same life looks very different to him (hence the film's title). All that has changed is his perspective. Within the context of a positive or optimistic attitude, events which might otherwise be considered stressful or depressing can have a diminished or different impact.

The diary techniques discussed in Chapter 6 are often used as awareness strategies for the prevention and treatment of depression. It is often possible to identify certain themes in the thought patterns of depressed individuals, which predispose them toward negative moods. Depressed people, for example, tend to focus heavily on negative information while overlooking or ignoring positive information, especially about themselves.

Individuals who are achievement oriented or who feel great need for social success and approval may be particularly susceptible to cognitive patterns that lead toward depression (Goodwin & Guze, 1979). College students in particular may fall into this trap. Having been at the top of their high school classes, students enter college along with a large group of other high-achieving students. Faced with more difficult studies and a more intellectually capable peer group, they may nevertheless expect to continue to be at the top of the class. Temporary setbacks, disappointing grades, and a lack of experience in dealing with perceived failure can thus be given exaggerated importance, damaging self-esteem and creating negative moods (Beck & Young, 1978).

Research indicates that depressed people not only show such selective *attention*, but also show selective *memory* for negative events. Consider this from your own experience. When *you* feel down or depressed, what are the things that you are likely to remember? When you feel on top of the world and happy, what memories are clearest? Current evidence suggests that memories may be filed or catalogued according to mood, and that when one is in a particular mood state it is easiest to recall other times when a similar mood prevailed (Bower, 1981). This is termed **state-dependent recall:** What one remembers depends upon one's current state (in this case, mood state). New information is processed differently, and memories are stored differently, depending upon present mood (Ellis, Thomas, & Rodriguez, 1984; Ellis & Ashbrook, 1987). In general, memories tend to be consistent in tone with one's present mood (Blaney, 1986). For example, people who are depressed, in comparison with nondepressed individuals, report that their parents were significantly less loving and more rejecting. Once the depressed state has passed, however, this difference disappears: nondepressed and formerly depressed people are no different in how they recall their parents to have been. This suggests that what people remember is, at least in part, a reflection of their present psychological state. Freud, Jung, and other analysts often asked patients to recount their earliest memories, in the belief that these reflect people's *present* condition in important ways.

In research extending over two decades, Seligman (1975) has identified a particular mental expectancy or attitude that he believes to be an important factor in depression. Called learned helplessness (Chapter 2), it refers to the generalized belief that there is nothing one could do to change one's situation. This phenomenon of learned helplessness can be demonstrated in research with animals. If a laboratory animal is exposed, over and over, to mildly painful electric shocks, it will try everything available in order to escape from the shocks. If nothing works, the animal after a time gives up, no longer trying to escape, and just suffers the pain passively. If such an animal is then placed in a new situation where the shocks could easily be avoided, it still remains passive. It has learned an attitude of helplessness, and behaves as if nothing could be done to change things. A different animal with no previous experience, placed into the same avoidable shock situation, quickly discovers how to turn

State-Dependent Recall
the memory phenomenon in which material that is learned in a certain psychological condition (such as a mood state or a drug state) is best remembered when the individual is in the same condition.

and avoid the shocks. In a wide variety of studies with animals, Seligman and others have demonstrated this phenomenon of giving up, of not trying, of learning to be helpless.

Does a similar phenomenon occur in people? Seligman has drawn strong parallels between the behavior and physiology of helplessness in animals and that of depression in humans. Among the commonalities between experimentally induced learned helplessness and clinical depression are (1) passivity, a failure to initiate responses; (2) loss of appetite and sexual interest; (3) low rate of aggression; (4) social avoidance; (5) belief in personal helplessness, reflected in few attempts to change the environment; and (6) a tendency for the pattern to diminish and disappear over time. These similarities suggest that something like learned helplessness may afflict humans and increase the risk of depression.

Depressed people do often believe and act as if there were nothing they could do to change things. Such a pessimistic attitude serves to immobilize the person, to foster passive withdrawal, thus exacerbating the depression. In this way, learned helplessness exemplifies a more general psychological phenomenon discussed in Chapter 2: the self-fulfilling prophecy. Behaving in a manner that is consistent with a negative emotion tends to amplify that emotion. We will pick up this theme again when we discuss *response* (R) aspects of depression.

A related and rapidly growing area of research is the investigation of **attribution** patterns among depressed versus nondepressed individuals. Attributions are explanations of why things happened (or did not happen), of the causes of life events. One dimension on which attributions vary is *internal* versus *external.* An **internal attribution** is a perception that a particular event was caused by one's own actions. An **external attribution,** by contrast, is a perception that a specific event was caused by factors beyond one's own influence. (Attributions should not be confused with locus of control, a personality trait discussed in Chapter 2. Locus of control is a *generalized* expectancy that events are controlled by internal or external factors. Attributions are explanations of *particular* events.)

Suppose that a friend breaks a lunch date with you. Why did this happen? One possibility is that you have done something to make your friend unhappy with you, or perhaps the friend has decided that you are not a very worthwhile person with whom to spend time. These would be *internal* attributions: it happened because of something about you. On the other hand, the friend may have had something urgent come up, or might not have been feeling well. These are *external* attributions: the cause is something over which you had no control.

Another important dimension on which attributions may vary is *stable* versus *unstable.* Stable attributions explain an occurrence as being due to something that is not likely to change. An unstable attribution, on the other hand, is a cause that is highly changeable. This dimension combines with the internal-external dimensions to form four major types of attributions shown in Box 7.3. If you do poorly on an exam, for example, was it (1) because you just don't have the ability for college work (internal, stable); (2) because you didn't study hard enough (internal, unstable); (3) because the instructor, exams, or course materials are unreasonably difficult (external, stable); or (4) because you were unlucky and just had a bad day (external, unstable)? Depending upon which attribution you chose, you might give up completely (internal, stable), study harder next time (internal, unstable), drop the course (external, stable), or expect to do better next time even without studying harder (external, unstable).

As a general rule, people do not expect change when they attribute a situation to a stable cause, but do expect change when they attribute a situation to

Attribution
an explanation of why an event occurred.

Internal Attribution
a causal explanation of an event that emphasizes personal control.

External Attribution
a causal explanation of an event that emphasizes factors beyond personal control.

7.3	FOUR TYPES OF ATTRIBUTIONS

	STABLE (Unchanging)	UNSTABLE (Changeable)
INTERNAL (It's me)	Personal traits and abilities	Motivation and effort
EXTERNAL (Not me)	Difficulty or fate	Chance or luck

an unstable cause. People normally show a somewhat optimistic style in which they tend to attribute successes to internal causes, but failures to external and/or unstable causes. "My successes are because of my abilities and efforts, but my failures are due to insufficient effort, interference of others, or just plain bad luck." Even psychotherapists tend to see the world this way: "My successes are because I am a good therapist; my failures occur when the case is just impossibly difficult or the client isn't motivated enough" (Miller, 1985b). Though perhaps a bit self-deluding, this normal attributional style is one that encourages a positive outlook and continued personal efforts.

Research indicates that depressed people show a rather different attributional pattern (Peterson & Seligman, 1984; Sweeney, Anderson, & Bailey, 1986). Negative outcomes tend to be attributed to stable, general negative characteristics of oneself: "That's how it always goes, I mess up everything I touch." "I'm a loser in every relationship; who could care for somebody like me?" Positive outcomes, on the other hand, tend to be attributed to external causes: "I just got lucky." "They let me win because they feel sorry for me." "She's nice to everybody." Such attributional patterns also influence ordinary moods. A college study found that students with the depressive attributional pattern were more likely to fall into a depressed mood when later receiving a low grade than were students who attribute negative outcomes to external or temporary causes (Metalsky et al., 1982). In working with humans, it is probably best to understand "learned helplessness" as this kind of depressive attributional style, which blames negative events on generalized, stable, personal characteristics (Abramson, Seligman, & Teasdale, 1978).

Some have argued that such negative thought patterns are common among depressed people because they are the *result* rather than the cause of depression. If that is so, then changing the self-statements and thought patterns of a depressed person should have very little therapeutic benefit. Research shows quite the opposite. Changing self-statements has rather consistently been found to have an impact on mood (Dush, Hurt, & Schroeder, 1983). Cognitive therapies, which focus on altering thought processes, have been found to be quite beneficial in treating clinical depression, and appear to be at least as effective as antidepressant medications (Rush et al., 1977). The amount of

How you explain your own successes will influence how you feel about them.

change in self-statements predicts the amount of improvement in depression (Seligman et al., 1988). The cognitive strategies introduced in Chapter 6, then, appear to be useful not only in increasing self-esteem, but also in preventing and managing depression.

Cognitive therapy for depression typically begins by identifying the individual's thought patterns that may be fostering negative moods (Beck, 1976; Burns, 1980). Some common examples are unrealistically high expectations of oneself or others, hopelessness, pessimism, and excessive self-criticism (see Chapter 6). These cognitive patterns are then challenged and changed, by seeking new beliefs and self-talk that promote healthier functioning. By examining and altering personal beliefs, however, the cognitive therapies raise an intriguing and troubling question (Miller, 1988): Whose beliefs will be used as the "healthy" standard, toward which the "unhealthy" or "irrational" beliefs of others are to be adjusted?

O—ORGANIC FACTORS

Students of psychology are typically taught to look for psychological causes of problems, and often are biased to regard the use of drugs in treatment with something between skepticism and scorn. Yet a serious examination of the literature makes it difficult to dismiss the importance of biological factors in depression.

It is well established, for example, that certain kinds of depression are in part genetically transmitted (Nurnberger & Gershon, 1982). Individuals with close biological relatives showing these types of clinical depression are themselves at higher risk for developing depression. This is clearest for a syndrome known as **bipolar disorder** (previously called manic-depressive illness), in which the person tends to swing back and forth between periods of deep

Bipolar Disorder
an emotional disorder, believed to be biological in origin, in which the individual shows manic states that may alternate with periods of depression.

depression and times of elation, euphoria, and extreme energy termed **manic states.** Among the relatives of individuals with bipolar disorder, there is a high rate of the same condition.

Even in **unipolar depression,** however, heredity appears to play a role, and organic factors are important. One early explanation was that depression results from a certain type of chemical imbalance in the body, from too much or too little of certain *neurotransmitters.* (Neurotransmitters are chemicals which cause electrical impulses to be transmitted from one nerve cell to the next within the nervous system). From current evidence it seems clear that this early hypothesis was much too simple, although clinically depressed people do show abnormalities among neurotransmitter and endocrine systems (Sachar, 1982; Zis & Goodwin, 1982).

Still another important type of evidence is the finding that clinically depressed individuals often respond well to **antidepressant medications.** They show greater improvement than do patients given no medication or a **placebo,** an inert treatment that the patient *believes* to be the effective drug (Mindham, 1982).

How do antidepressants work? The exact mechanisms are still unclear, although it is believed that these drugs work by altering the activity of the neurotransmitters just mentioned. Many mysteries remain, but it is evident that severely depressed individuals often show significant improvement in a matter of weeks on such medications.

Interestingly, individuals with bipolar disorders show profound improvement with a totally different type of medication, a salt known as lithium carbonate (Coppen, Metcalfe, & Wood, 1982). Its effect seems to be to compress mood cycles, so that the lows are not so low and the highs are not so high. It is believed to have this effect not by increasing specific neurotransmitters, but rather by influencing the flow, within nerve cells, of ions of another common salt, sodium. In any event, those suffering from bipolar disorder tend to show major improvement within a few weeks of beginning lithium medication, often after many years of very disabling problems (Fieve, 1976). There is, at present, no other known effective treatment for bipolar disorder.

Other biological factors may play a role in mood and depression as well. Certain undetected physical illnesses (e.g., hormonal imbalances, low-grade infections) can create fatigue or mood fluctuations and mimic the symptoms of depression. Major physical traumas (such as surgery or childbirth) are often followed by a period of clinical depression. Diet and exercise patterns may influence mood. The abuse of alcohol and other psychoactive drugs can produce and increase depression.

We do not wish to convey the impression that depression is *completely* or even primarily a biological problem. All five elements of the STORC model are important to consider in gaining a comprehensive understanding of mood and depression. Nonmedical treatments such as cognitive therapy have been found to be as effective, overall, as antidepressant medications. Yet without a careful consideration of the biological side of depression, the picture is incomplete. Lithium and the antidepressant medications (drugs, incidentally, which have very little effect in a normal individual, and consequently are rarely abused) have an important place in the treatment of clinical depression. Organic balance factors such as a healthy diet, a consistent sleep pattern, and regular exercise may prove of value in preventing negative mood and depression. In an attempt to cope with depression, some individuals also turn to the use of alcohol and other drugs as self-medication. Unfortunately alcohol and other commonly abused drugs are poor choices for relieving depression, and in the long run frequently cause a worsening of the problem, in addition to the other problems that arise directly from alcohol and drug abuse (see Chapter 11).

Manic State
a period of extremely elated mood, high activity, agitation, or irritability.

Unipolar Depression
depression occurring in an individual who does not also show manic states.

Antidepressant
any of several classes of psychotropic medications that are intended to relieve depression by changing chemical balances within the nervous system.

Placebo
a treatment, often a sugar pill, which has no specific effect of its own other than the psychological expectancy effects of being treated.

Exercise can help to maintain positive moods.

Before leaving the organic causes of depression, it is worth mentioning what was once termed "involutional melancholia." It was believed that women entering and passing through menopause (the "involutional" period of life) showed a unique and severe form of depression, and that this was probably attributable to hormonal changes. More recent diagnostic systems (American Psychiatric Association, 1987) have abandoned this notion, however, in that women do not appear to show either a unique kind of depression or a markedly higher rate of depression during menopause. Bart (1969, 1976) in a cross-cultural comparison of women during the involutional years, found no evidence of unique or consistent depression. Instead, in societies where women suffer a significant role and status loss at menopause, depression was more common. By contrast, in societies where women experience an elevation in status during this period of life change, women were much less likely to develop depression. To be sure, significant hormonal changes do occur during menopause. These can be quite dramatic and distressing for a woman, and may be misunderstood by those close to her. The point is that depression during this time of life does not appear to be different in quality, and is not necessarily more common than at other ages.

R—RESPONSE PATTERNS

Once a person begins to experience a negative mood or depression, how he or she responds to this feeling can make a big difference. A common and often unhealthy response is avoidance or withdrawal. The tendency seems natural. Being down, experiencing low self-esteem, the person feels like poor company. He or she may not feel up to usual social contacts or may not want others to see him or her in this dejected state. Feelings of fatigue may contribute to the tendency to avoid and withdraw.

7.4 SENILITY OR DEPRESSION?

When an elderly person begins to have difficulties with attention, memory, social interaction, and mood, those around the person may jump to the conclusion that he or she is "just becoming senile." Symptoms of serious depression may be written off as the effects of aging. Yet deterioration in intellectual, emotional, and social functioning is by no means an inevitable or even typical result of normal aging. When major changes occur, either suddenly or gradually, it is important to determine the cause.

The elderly, like all age groups, are susceptible to depression. The losses of friends, family, health, employment, or certain activities that often accompany aging can contribute to the development of depression. The person may withdraw socially, show a low or flat mood, have difficulties in remembering and concentrating, become irritable, sleep excessively or sit doing nothing for hours or days at a time. Such changes should *not* be blamed on aging itself. Depression occurs at all ages, and can be treated, with the result being a richer and fuller life.

A complication is that similar problems can also result from physical changes in the brain. Some of these involve progressive brain deterioration, the most familiar of which is Alzheimer's disease. A general decline in intellectual functioning (termed **dementia**) can also be caused by physical conditions that are reversible, such as hypothyroidism.

So similar are dementia and depression in the elderly that a careful evaluation is often required to separate them, and the term "pseudodementia" has been applied to a depression-produced syndrome that mimics dementia. A skilled **neuropsychologist** can differentiate the two. A depressed individual, for example, may show improved performance on neuropsychological tests in response to encouragement or other motivation, or may be able to learn and remember when performing tasks that do not require great effort. For those with true dementia, performance on such tests is more consistently poor. Sometimes treatment with an antidepressant medication is tried, to determine whether there is an improvement in functioning within a few months.

A competent evaluation is the key. Depression is very treatable, and should not be ignored or accepted as "senility." The elderly respond well to the same types of treatment that alleviate depression in younger individuals. Detecting and treating depression can restore an incapacitated person to a more healthy and fully functioning life.

Dementia
a general deterioration of the person's prior mental abilities, severe enough to interfere with his or her normal functioning.

Neuropsychologist
a psychologist specializing in the assessment and understanding of behavior as it reflects brain functioning.

Yet avoidance tends to strengthen negative emotions. The person who, once thrown from a horse, continues to avoid horses will experience intensified fear of them. The depressed individual who withdraws from his or her social support network is thereby cut off from important sources of feedback and reinforcement, which in turn amplifies the depression. The general remedy here is to do the opposite of the seemingly natural tendency to withdraw. For the depressed person, it is important to continue seeing friends and engaging in previously pleasurable activities, even though it requires an effort and may not immediately feel pleasant. The same applies to feeling down and low moods, even without full-blown depression.

Low moods and depression may also arise because a person lacks an important coping skill. Deficient social skills, for example, can impede an individual in developing a reinforcing and supportive network of friends, which in turn decreases resistance to depression. Blechman and her colleagues found that depression was highest among elementary school children who lacked in both social and academic skills, whereas none of the children who were above average on both skills showed evidence of depression (Blechman et al., 1986). Social skill deficits can also perpetuate depression in adults. In a therapy group, Dan, an attractive man, spoke movingly about his feelings of loneliness and isolation. After he spoke, several people approached Dan, responding to what he had said. He did not make eye contact with any of them. Something as simple as eye contact is an important reinforcer in social situations. Even people who tried to reach out to Dan found themselves somehow distanced, and they did not find it reinforcing to keep trying. Dan was stuck in a self-perpetuating spiral. He suffered from loneliness, yet his lack of some simple social skills made it unlikely that he would sustain the social contacts he needed to overcome his isolation.

Depression and low moods may also arise from an inability (skill deficit) in dealing with one's own emotions. A classic psychoanalytic view is that depression results from anger (usually narcissistic) which is not appropriately expressed and dealt with, being turned instead against oneself (Freud, 1917). In contemporary psychological terms, this view attributes depression to a lack of appropriate *assertion* skills (see Chapter 9) for expressing emotions. Likewise an inability or failure to grieve a major loss may result in an unresolved grief, contributing to prolonged depression. In these cases it is vital for the person to learn a new skill, a new way of responding that promotes healthier moods and adjustment.

C—CONSEQUENCES

Finally, mood and depression are influenced by how the social environment responds to one's behavior. We have already mentioned that an environment that provides very little positive reinforcement can foster low mood and depression. In such situations, no matter what the person does, very little reinforcement is forthcoming. A prolonged period of this may result in the earlier-mentioned attitude of helplessness and pessimism, which itself feeds depression.

Ironically, some social settings may strongly reward an individual for being depressed. Consider a woman with poor social skills, who consequently had no close friends. Her everyday life was rather uneventful and empty. In time, she became seriously depressed. She confided to several people that she was feeling suicidal and very down. Suddenly the church community of which she was a member came alive for her and rallied around her. The pastor called regularly. Friends began telephoning and dropping in, often bringing food, helping with chores, or even sitting with her through the night. What had been a largely inattentive group of people became, almost overnight, a warm and supportive community. She began feeling better, and as she did, her friends went back to their previous business, leaving her alone again. What would you predict happened next? Yes indeed, she became depressed again. Why? Because for her, in one sense at least, life was more pleasant and bearable when she was depressed. Her friends were compassionate and giving *only* when she was depressed, thereby strongly reinforcing her for being depressed.

Change at this level involves rearranging the social environment, as much as possible, to reinforce healthy behavior instead of unhealthy, disabled behavior. It is not enough just to stop reinforcing depression. Consider again the women just described. Suppose her friends had decided to abandon her in sickness *and* in health! Surely her depression would not have been lessened. Instead she needed to learn (and did learn) better social skills for forming personal and lasting relationships with others. Her therapist also worked with the pastor and her church friends to provide support for her efforts to change, so that she would not be abandoned again as she began to show positive change. A key is to establish a social support network that provides ongoing reinforcement for healthy and adaptive functioning.

Still another possibility is to try new activities, new sources of potential enjoyment and reinforcement. There is a tendency for adults to fall into predictable patterns of social and leisure activities. It usually feels safest to associate with the same people, and do the same familiar things. Some people are reluctant to try new skills because they might not excel at them; consequently they do only what they are sure they can do well. Such limitations unnecessarily restrict a person's possibilities. Exploring new activities, just for the fun of it, can lead to new and rewarding relationships and involvements.

RETURN OF THE PERSONAL SCIENTIST

In Chapter 5 we introduced Mahoney's (1974 & 1979) concept of the personal scientist, of applying the scientific method of inquiry to one's own personal life. The STORC model represents a systematic way of going about this.

No *one* type of cause accounts fully for depression and negative moods. Situations, thought patterns, organic factors, response patterns, and the consequences provided by the social environment all play a role. It is possible, in any individual case, to examine factors at each of these levels in an attempt to discover which might be contributing most to negative mood. Then, one by one, changes can be tried and their effects observed. Is daily mood improved by planning regular daily pleasant events (S)? Is it helpful to identify negative thought patterns and to practice replacing these with more positive self-statements (T)? Does changing to a more healthy diet and regular exercise seem to promote more positive mood (O)? Do negative moods often seem to be preceded by angry feelings, and does it help to learn more assertive ways to express anger (R)? What happens if one's friends are asked to notice and comment on behavior that is more optimistic and positive (C)?

There are a great many strategies to try in order to overcome negative mood and depression. Each step of the STORC model suggests different tactics. Even among severely depressed people, a majority show substantial improvement when treated with methods such as these. Where might *you* begin in working toward a more balanced and positive mood life?

KAREN'S DEPRESSION

Karen had never felt so low in her life. She had been avoiding all her friends for weeks, and when Ron saw her now, he was shocked at how down she looked. "I feel like I'm at the bottom of a deep well with no ladder," she told him. "I can see a little sky way up in the distance, but it seems so far away and it's so dark down here. I'm scared that I'm never going to get out. I think I must be going crazy or dying. I just cry and cry. I don't think I'll ever be done crying." Ron noticed that she spoke very slowly, and in a flat, unchanging tone unlike her usual, lively self. "I shouldn't have called you," she said. "Nobody understands how bad I feel. People just say I should cheer up and look at the bright side. I have to fake being cheerful for *their* sake!"

Ron felt helpless, too. Karen seemed hardly the same person he had known for years. To try to cheer her up would be to do just what everybody else had done. Still he wanted to be helpful. "Maybe you need to get more sleep. You look so tired!"

"Right!" she snapped. "I sleep all day long and it doesn't help. I just feel worse. What do you know!" Then she began to cry. "I'm sorry, Ron. I don't know what's wrong with me. Maybe it's just not worth living anymore."

At Ron's urging and support, Karen decided that day to see someone about her problem. Ron went with her to the student health center on the campus where she was taking classes. Dr. Stillman, a psychologist on the mental health team, saw her right away.

"I just can't think any more. I try to study, but I only stare at the pages and cry. Friends call me to go out with them, but I feel too down to go. I just don't enjoy *anything* I do. My whole life seems gray, empty. I feel so lonely, but I don't want to see anybody."

As they met together several times during the next two weeks, Dr. Stillman sought to understand the sources of Karen's depression. She had been doing well in school, and seemed to have a solid circle of friends who cared about and liked her. Karen couldn't identify any special situations or changes that had occurred in the past few months. A recent physical examination had found her to be in good health. Karen didn't seem to be getting much social reinforcement for her depression. To the contrary, her social contacts had dropped almost to zero.

Asking about family history, Dr. Stillman discovered that Karen's mother had suffered from periods of severe depression several times during her life. Another key seemed to be the extent to which Karen had suddenly withdrawn from her social network of friends, who were very important to her.

After some consideration, Dr. Stillman decided to try two strategies. First, she consulted with a psychiatric colleague to discuss the possibility of an antidepressant medication for Karen. Her hope was that the medication would help Karen to relieve the severe depression in the short run, while they worked together in therapy. Second, Dr. Stillman persuaded Karen that it was important for her to see her friends again and start doing things that used to be pleasurable for her. It seemed likely that Karen's withdrawal when she began to feel down had served to increase and prolong her depression. In addition, they made a special contract that Karen would not harm herself, and would call Dr. Stillman if she felt that she might be in any danger of taking her own life.

Dr. Stillman's plan proved to be a good choice. Within a couple of weeks, Karen's depression began to lift, and she no longer thought of suicide. She slowly resumed her contact with Ron and her other friends, who were glad to see her again. It was quite an effort at first. Dr. Stillman had told Karen she might not enjoy herself to begin with and that she should keep on doing things with friends anyhow. Three months later, Karen was mostly back to her normal self, and the medication was discontinued. She promised herself that if she ever began feeling so down again, she would not fall into the trap of withdrawing from the friends who were so important to her.

7.5 HERE WE DIFFER/HERE WE AGREE
Should Therapists Relieve Depression?

If a depression is incapacitating to the point that the person is unable to get out of bed or go to work, then I believe that providing symptomatic relief is appropriate. However, when feelings of depression are not incapacitating, the client and therapist can work together to *use* the depression. Depression can be helpful because it can lead to a clearer understanding of what change is needed in the client's life. What is the depression communi-cating? Perhaps it is communicating sadness or anger or isolation. Listening to the symptom long enough to hear its message is important in the formulation of a treatment strategy.

If a therapist jumps in with symptomatic relief too fast, neither participant in the therapy has a chance to learn from the symptom. When a person has a runny nose, she or he could take an antihistamine to alleviate the symptom, but the medication does not cure the cold. It merely masks the symptom. I believe a similar phenomenon can occur with depression. Because I believe in an inherent self-healing process in both body and mind, I prefer to listen to and learn from symptoms, rather than masking them.

When a person is depressed, something within him or her is asking for a change. Only by attending to the feeling can the need for change be adequately addressed. Perhaps the depression is the result of grief. Mourning is an appropriate and necessary process. Cutting off mourning prematurely robs the mourner of the valuable experience to heal. Or perhaps the depression is due to unrecognized anger. Allowing time for the anger to surface, to be examined, and to be dealt with constructively is crucial. Perhaps the depression involves isolation. Helping the person recognize her or his loneliness can be the first step in planning various ways to reach out and make contact. Masking the symptoms can be counterproductive in that the depressed person may remain isolated while taking medication.

When I encounter a depressed client, or when I feel depressed myself, I believe the first step is to decipher the message that the symptom is trying to communicate. First, hear the voice of the symptom, and then decide how to deal with it. —CEY

Certainly it is important to consider the causes of depression early in the treatment process. It makes little sense to dispense a standard treatment (be it medication or psychotherapy) without first assessing the factors that have created or maintained the problem.

Yet I cannot see the value of leaving someone in a state of depression. Even if the depression signals the need for a change, is the value of the signal increased by prolonging it? It is quite possible to help the person overcome an acute depression, then work together to sort out its causes and how recurrence might be prevented. To draw on the same analogy, relieving a runny nose in no way prevents one from seeking the causes of

frequent colds. Neither does failure to relieve the runny nose promote discovery of the causes.

Language is important here, because it reflects one's assumptions. To say that it is a "symptom" implies that depression itself is not the problem, but rather that there is some larger underlying entity. Once this assumption is accepted, then it indeed appears fruitless to treat the "symptom." An alternative approach is to start by taking the client's complaints at face value. Perhaps the depression *is* the problem, and its relief is the desired goal.

In any event, I see no point in withholding relief for depression in the belief that this somehow promotes mental health or recovery. The suffering, unhappiness, and suicide risk attached to depression more than offset any motivational or insight benefit that might come from continuing to feel the depression. My inclination is to help the person get past his or her acute depression, and then to consider what meaning it may have. —WRM

INTEGRATION

In practice, relieving depression and sorting out its causes go hand in hand. Sometimes the "cause" of depression is assessed by trying a therapeutic approach that assumes a particular cause and seeing the result. When one treatment strategy fails, the therapist considers that she or he may have been "barking up the wrong tree" and tries a different approach. To overlook an important causal factor in a person's depression is to leave that person vulnerable to future depression. It is important also to look beyond the individual for potential causes, rather than assuming that it lies within the "patient." Marital and family dynamics, work and environmental conditions, social support patterns, and economic hardships, for example, all can be important contributors to depression. The key in overcoming depression is to identify correctly its causes and to address them.

■ SUICIDE

WHO COMMITS SUICIDE?

In one sense, it is extremely difficult to predict suicide. First, it is a relatively rare event. In the United States there are between 10 and 15 suicides annually per 100,000 population. Second, there are many more attempts or suicidal gestures than there are actual suicides, perhaps as many as 50 to 1. Although many people show some of the risk factors for suicide, very few of these individuals actually take their own lives. Even the best psychologists and psychological tests are not very accurate in identifying those who really will make serious suicide attempts, and in separating them from the many others who are at risk.

In another sense, however, suicide is not a random event, and the risk is much higher among certain groups. Men outnumber women among suicides by about three to one, and risk generally increases with age. Ill health and social isolation are also risk factors. Alcohol and drug abuse are associated with increased rates of suicide.

During the 1980s, greater attention and concern was focused on the problem of suicide among children and teenagers. This concern is warranted, because suicide is the third leading cause of death (after accidents and homicides) among people between the ages of 15 and 24 (Pfeffer, 1986). The rate of suicide among adolescents tripled between the 1950s and 1970s and appears to have leveled off in the 1980s (McIntyre, 1980; Pfeffer, 1981, 1986). Over 5,000 children and adolescents are known suicides each year in the United States. As with adults, however, the actual number who die by their own hand may be much higher because many deaths classified as accidental may also have been intentional. With many drug overdoses and single vehicle crash fatalities, for example, it is difficult to know whether the death was suicide or an accident.

7.6 PERSONAL MILESTONE
Adolescent Suicide

My own career was affected deeply and early by suicide. Fresh out of undergraduate training at the University of Michigan, I accepted a job as a high school teacher in New Mexico. Most of my students were Native American. I learned much about their culture, attended the ceremonial dances, and was invited into the homes of my students for meals.

Then I began hearing the stories. On Monday morning, a student would tell me of another student's death over the weekend. Sometimes it was in an automobile crash, after drinking and driving. Sometimes the student was found hanging. Sometimes it was a bullet in the head. I was overwhelmed. My adjustment and coping mechanisms were just not up to the task of dealing with or making sense of these senseless deaths of my adolescent students, some of whom were only four years younger than I.

I spoke with the school counselor about my struggle to make sense of what I saw, and to find some way to help. She suggested that I get more training in counseling. Shortly after that, I returned to graduate school.

Almost twenty years later, I read that the suicide rate for Native American school-aged children is three times greater than that for the American white majority, and that the rate has nearly doubled in the past two decades since my time as a high school teacher (LaFramboise, 1988).

I remain overwhelmed.   —CEY

The strongest risk for suicide, however, is found among those who are clinically depressed. It has been estimated that over the course of many years, about 15 percent of those who suffer from clinical depression die by suicide. Still it must be recognized that *most* of those who become severely depressed do not take their own lives, and that even within this high-risk group, it is extremely difficult to predict which individuals will finally kill themselves (Hankoff, 1982).

A FEW MYTHS

It is important to recognize a few common incorrect beliefs about suicide. One is that *people who are really serious about suicide don't talk about it.* To the contrary, most people who actually take their own lives have previously told someone of their intention, or have made a previous attempt. Those who mention, talk about, hint, or joke about suicide should be taken seriously.

A second misconception is that *once a person has hit bottom and has started to recover from depression, the risk is past.* In fact, suicide can and does occur after people seem to be on the upswing.

A third myth is that *only certain kinds of people commit suicide.* One may have the mistaken impression that only those who are old, or sick, or insane, or poor take their own lives. The truth is that, although certain groups are at higher risk, suicides occur among those in all walks of life.

PREVENTING SUICIDE

In one sense, the prevention of suicide is nearly impossible. If an individual is determined to take his or her own life, even the most coercive measures are unlikely to keep the person alive in the long run.

Often, however, the risk period for suicide is relatively brief, measured in days or weeks. If plans can be made to deter a person from *acting* on suicidal thoughts during this risk period, he or she may emerge from the bleak time and go on to live a healthy and productive life.

What messages might be helpful to offer a person who is contemplating suicide? One is *caring:* to express honest concern and affection for the person, and a desire for him or her to choose life. A second is *optimism:* that although

Many cities have special telephone hotlines for prevention of suicide.

7.7   A RIGHT TO DIE?

Are there conditions under which suicide is justifiable? Szasz (1986) has strongly opposed the use of force or other involuntary measures such as institutionalization to prevent a person from taking his or her own life. He asserted that "although life is precious, disease, disability, and dishonor may render a person's life not worth living and thus may make suicide a blessing for himself or herself as well as for others and society. Nevertheless, we, in the West, impose coercive measures on every would-be suicide (even the hopelessly sick and very aged), as if suicide were never desirable enough to justify it" (p. 811).

The professional and ethical questions are genuinely complex. The modern concept of a "living will" has increased awareness of conditions under which an individual might choose to have his or her life end, rather than endure irreversible pain and disability. On the other hand, temporary coercion might be justified to avert suicide of a person who is severely depressed, but has no enduring catastrophic disability and is likely to view life differently from the other side of the depression. The balance here between personal liberty and the protection of life is a delicate one indeed.

things may seem very hopeless at the moment, change is an inevitable part of human life. At the bottom of depression, the past, present, and future all look bleak. It can be helpful to offer a realistic optimism and a perspective of hopefulness. A third point is that suicide is an *irreversible* decision. There is no changing one's mind later. Because of this, it may be possible to persuade the person to "wait and see," rather than make an irrevocable choice now.

It can also be helpful to work out an agreement that the person will call someone if he or she feels in danger of suicide. The goal is to put a few steps between suicidal thought and action. The arrangement might be for the person to call a particular friend, a pastor, the local suicide prevention hotline, or a professional. It is wise to arrange for several possibilities, in case one person is not available to receive a call.

A person who is distressed enough to contemplate suicide should also be urged to seek professional help. Suicidal thoughts and attempts are not themselves a "mental illness," but definitely indicate the presence of a problem that is serious enough to warrant discussion with a mental health professional.

■ SUMMARY

Mood is a relatively brief emotional state. Grief is a more prolonged but normal reaction to significant loss. Depression, in the clinical sense, describes a persistent and disabling syndrome. The causes of negative moods and depression can be examined using the STORC model. Situational causes of depression include major losses, prolonged stress, and low levels of social reinforcement. Certain cognitive patterns tend to accompany depression, and changing self-statements has been shown to influence mood and depression. Genetic and other organic factors influence risk for depression, and certain antidepressant medications can be effective in treatment. Social withdrawal can intensify depression, and poor social communication skills may interfere with the development of a solid social support system that helps to prevent and decrease depression. Social reinforcement patterns may prolong the problem if depressive rather than healthy and adaptive behavior is reinforced. A "personal scientist" approach seeks the particular factors that influence one's depression, and tries alternative coping strategies to determine what is most effective in preventing and relieving depression. Suicide, a risk for depressed people, is difficult to predict but may be preventable.

■ QUESTIONS FOR THOUGHT

1. What kinds of events in your life have the biggest positive effect on your own mood?
2. What kinds of events in your life have the biggest negative effect on your mood?
3. What things can *you* do to maintain a positive mood and outlook?
4. Which do you need to do more often?
5. What major losses have you experienced in your life?
6. How have you dealt with those losses?
7. Who are the most important sources of positive reinforcement in your life?
8. In what ways do they express their support?
9. The last time you succeeded at something, what did you say to yourself about it?
10. Think of a situation in which you felt "down." Apply the STORC model to analyze your experience.

chapter eight

Fear of danger is ten thousand times more terrifying than danger itself.
—Daniel Defoe, *Robinson Crusoe*

Stress and Anxiety

OUTLINE

Our era has been called "the age of anxiety." The shelves of bookstores and drug stores are filled with promised remedies for stress and anxiety. Any list of challenges of adjustment must surely include these common problems. Yet what *are* anxiety and stress? In this chapter we will explore these complex phenomena as they relate to adjustment and more generally to the field of psychology. After examining various views of the nature of stress and anxiety, we will use the STORC analysis as an approach for understanding some of their causes and also some coping strategies to deal with these modern maladies. Finally, we will explain how anxiety can be important and helpful in adjustment.

■ WHAT IS STRESS?

Stress has become an everyday word, accepted as part of modern life. People talk about being "under stress," "overstressed," "stressed out," and having a "stressful" day. Popular magazines, self-help books, television and radio talk shows, and newspaper stories all discuss the horrors and hazards of modern stress, and prescribe a range of remedies.

The word "stress" was not originally a psychological term. Rather it was and is a concept in physics, referring to the amount of force or strain placed upon an object. In constructing a bridge, for example, engineers must calculate the amount of stress that the structure will have to endure. In this sense, the intensity of stress is measured in units of pressure, such as pounds per square inch. This connotation of "stress" leads us to think of it as exerted from the outside, as arising from an external source.

Some psychological conceptions of stress follow this same thinking. Stress is sometimes thought of in the sense of **stressor,** an external event that places some psychological strain or pressure on the individual. In STORC terms, this is a stimulus (S) conception of stress.

Other uses of the term "stress" focus on the personal experience rather than on an external stimulus. In an attempt to distinguish these aspects, Selye (1974) has suggested using "stress" to describe external stimuli and "distress" to refer to the individual's internal responses. When definitions of stress focus on the subjective experience of distress, they begin to overlap with an older and pervasive concept in psychology: the construct of anxiety.

Stress
a pattern of cognitive, physiological, and behavioral responses to change, which may or may not be experienced as distressing.

Stressor
a particular stimulus or situation that initiates stress responses.

■ WHAT IS ANXIETY?

Anxiety is a good example of what is known as a **hypothetical construct.** It is hypothetical in the sense that anxiety is not tangible, and cannot be directly observed. Instead it is *inferred* from observations. Anxiety is a construct because it is an idea, a perception that is one way of organizing observations. Children do not come into the world aware of the construct of anxiety. They have to learn what it means and to label certain of their subjective experiences as "anxious." The concept of anxiety is so much a part of our everyday language, however, that one easily forgets that it *is* a construct and, instead, thinks of anxiety as an "it," a real thing.

Most people do have experiences that they label as "anxiety." One approach to understanding anxiety, then, is to think of it as a label and to clarify the ways

Hypothetical Construct
an idea or concept that is inferred to explain relationships among observable events, but that cannot be directly measured itself.

in which people use the word. To what experiences do people refer when they apply the term "anxious"?

Words of this sort have long been part of the human vocabulary. In ancient Greek, *merimna* (often translated as "anxiety") referred to a state of distraction, being troubled with cares, having a "divided mind," and being drawn in different directions. In modern popular use, "anxiety" refers to a general state of uneasiness and discomfort (distress), particularly with regard to the future.

In its physical and psychological manifestations, anxiety is essentially identical to fear. Either of two additional characteristics are used to distinguish the label "anxiety" from **fear** in general. First, anxiety is usually experienced in *anticipation* of an event, before it actually occurs. Other words applied to such anticipatory discomfort are "worry" and "dread." Discomfort that is felt *after* an event tend to be given a different label (e.g., guilt, frustration), even though the feeling may be quite similar.

Second, anxiety is judged to be *unrealistic*, out of proportion to the actual degree of danger. A phobia, for example, is an anxiety problem involving a specific fear (such as fear of elevators, harmless snakes, or heights) that is more intense than is warranted by the actual danger posed by the feared object. The person's anxious reaction is out of proportion to what most people would judge to be real threat or danger.

As psychologists began to investigate anxiety, it became apparent that measuring anxiety is not an easy task. Various types of measurement were used. Some researchers used paper and pencil tests or simply asked for self-report of anxiety. Some observed overt behavior, looking for "signs" of anxiety such as trembling, avoidance, errors in speech, or excessive small movements. Still others measured physiological responses to reflect anxiety: heart rate, skin temperature changes, or **skin conductance.** For a time it was assumed that all these measures would reflect true anxiety.

Fear
cognitive, physiological, and behavioral reactions to situations that pose apparent danger.

Skin Conductance
the rate at which the skin conducts small electrical currents; commonly used as a measure of emotion.

But then psychologists began using several of these measures simultaneously, and a problem immediately emerged. These different measures of "anxiety" were only weakly related to each other. Self-report of anxiety might be high without the person showing any behavioral or physiological signs. Large physiological changes occurred in the absence of either self-report or behavioral indicators of anxiousness. And none of these measures seemed to

---

8.1 A PERSONAL DESCRIPTION OF ANXIETY

A medical student who was completing a clinical rotation in pediatrics sought the help of a psychologist to deal with his feelings of intense anxiety. He reported that his continual exposure to sick children was resulting in almost unmanageable anxiety:

> I feel terrified when I see the children on the ward now. I can't stop thinking about my own three-year-old. As soon as I drop him off at the sitter's I start feeling guilty and scared. All day long I see devastated parents and children who are ill or dying. I keep thinking about my own child becoming ill, and I can't concentrate on my work any more. Yesterday I ran into the restroom and broke down in tears. That's not like me. On my other clinical rotations I've done fine, but on this one I feel in a panic all the time. My heart pounds, I find tears welling up in my eyes, and I get this choking constriction in my throat. When that happens I can hardly even speak. I'm afraid I'm going to fail this rotation, and I really feel out of control.

be very highly related to questionnaires that also purported to measure anxiety. Which, then, was the "true" anxiety?

Peter Lang (1969) proposed what is now a widely accepted view within psychology: that anxiety is not a single phenomenon, but rather a label that people apply to a range of different phenomena. At least three different response systems are involved: cognitive, physiological, and behavioral (corresponding to the T, O, and R elements of the STORC model). That is, "anxiety" may be inferred from the person's own subjective experience and self-report, from physiological changes, or from a person's overt behavior. Because these three domains are not strongly linked to each other, there is no one "true" anxiety. Instead there are separate, though interrelated, response systems. Changing any one of these may have little or no impact on another dimension. Helping a person to develop insight into the reasons for his or her anxiety may not, for example, have any impact on phobic behavior. The individual may cognitively understand *why* he or she is afraid, but still avoid the feared object or situation. Likewise, teaching a person to relax physically may not change the cognitive problem of test anxiety, which most often involves difficulties in maintaining attention on the task at hand.

Still another important distinction has been made between *state* anxiety and *trait* anxiety (Spielberger, 1966b). State anxiety is temporary, the level of anxiety experienced in a particular situation. It is a departure from the individual's normal condition. Trait anxiety, by contrast, is the person's characteristic level of anxiousness across a wide variety of situations. State anxiety is transitory, trait anxiety is enduring. To complicate matters further, either one could be defined by physiological, behavioral, or cognitive measures. Some people, for example, experience brief periods of intense physical arousal (state anxiety), but ordinarily do not show a high baseline level of arousal. Others show consistently high levels of response on physiological measures such as muscle tension, suggesting that for them high arousal is more a trait. The term "anxiety" has been used to describe a wide variety of different responses, which may be either temporary or enduring characteristics of the individual.

From this perspective, it is not sufficient to know that a person is "anxious." To understand and change an anxiety problem, it is important to know where the problem is to be found. Is this "anxiety" a problem of too much physiological arousal? Is the problem mainly one of avoidance behavior? Is it a problem of concentration and attention? Does the person experience inhibition and shyness that prevent him or her from using otherwise good social skills? The approach that one would take in pursuing change depends upon the nature of the "anxiety."

This suggests that the STORC model, introduced in Chapter 3, is a helpful tool in understanding anxiety. Rather than being a single "it," anxiety seems to be a series or a set of phenomena that include external stimuli (S), thoughts and perceptions (T), physiological responses of the organism (O), behavioral responses (R), and environmental consequences (C). Stress and distress can similarly be analyzed in this fashion, as can related emotional experiences such as worry and guilt. Before embarking on a STORC analysis of anxiety and stress, however, we will provide a brief history of the concept of anxiety and the role it has played in major personality theories.

■ THE CONCEPT OF ANXIETY IN PSYCHOLOGY

Virtually every major theory of personality throughout the history of psychology has addressed the phenomenon of anxiety. For some it has been a major organizing construct; for others it has been a less central but nevertheless important concern. We will explore the role of anxiety in each of the four major streams of thought discussed in Chapter 1.

PSYCHODYNAMIC THEORIES

For Freud, the concept of *angst* (a German word translated as "anxiety") was central to the entire theory of psychoanalysis. His thinking about anxiety changed substantially over the years, but it remained a key concept throughout his writings. In his later writings on psychoanalysis, Freud (1936) conceived of anxiety as a vital signal, warning of an impending leak in the person's defenses against unconscious material. When the instinctual impulses of the id threaten to break through into consciousness and overt expression, Freud believed, the person experiences anxiety.

This anxiety may not appear as fearfulness, however, but can be transformed into a wide range of forms, called **neuroses.** It might appear as a phobia, as obsessional thoughts, as the compulsion to repeat a seemingly senseless behavior over and over again, as physical complaints, as sexual problems, as panic attacks, or simply as a high level of anxiety that seems to be **free floating.** The anxiety serves as a signal for the person to increase his or her defenses against the basic unconscious conflict(s).

This signal value of anxiety persists as a theme throughout the writings of many other psychodynamic theorists. Anxiety in this sense is healthy and adaptive, preventing a more major breakdown by activating defenses. For this reason, psychodynamic therapists are often critical of those who seek to decrease anxiety directly. Believing that the anxiety is serving a useful and important signal function, psychodynamically oriented therapists instead seek to understand its purpose and then to deal with the underlying conflicts to which the anxiety points. Anxiety is not itself a problem, but signals a need for change at a deeper level.

BEHAVIORAL THEORIES

Neurosis (plural: Neuroses) *one of a group of less severe psychological problems that are assumed to be reactions to anxiety or unconscious conflict.*

The first major departure from psychodynamic views was offered by early learning theorists (Dollard & Miller, 1950; Pavlov, 1927; Watson, 1925), who suggested that anxiety is a product of learning and conditioning. It was demonstrated that patterns of anxiety could be produced in the laboratory through predictable processes of classical conditioning in both animals and humans. Mary Cover Jones (1924) further demonstrated that a child's naturally occurring phobia (a fear of white, furry objects) could be removed through a relearning process.

This gave rise to the development of **behavior therapies** for the treatment of anxiety problems, based on principles of conditioning (Wolpe, 1958). These and other behavioral approaches (to be described later in this chapter) were found to be reliably effective in alleviating problems once believed to require years of psychotherapy (O'Leary & Wilson, 1987). Anxiety was treated directly rather than assuming it to be merely the symptom of a larger personality problem. The success of these early behavioral treatment methods provided an impetus for the development of what is now a major therapeutic orientation: behavior therapy.

Free-Floating Anxiety *persistent and distressing anxiety that is experienced as occurring regularly or randomly, not in response to particular stimuli or situations.*

Behavior Therapy *a problem-solving treatment that focuses on the modification of behavior through the application of principles of experimental psychology.*

HUMANISTIC THEORIES

Rejecting both psychodynamic and behavioral perspectives, Rogers (1959) proposed that human anxiety is the consequence of insufficient acceptance. Indi-

Mary Cover Jones working with the child she helped
to recover from a phobia.

viduals are inherently good and adaptive, but through receiving repeated negative feedback regarding their unacceptability, they come to experience a gap
between how they are and how they believe they should be (Simon, 1978). The
larger this gap, the greater the anxiety.

Rogers proposed that psychotherapy should consist of providing an environment in which anxiety would be minimized by offering acceptance, understanding, and honesty. Given these proper conditions for growth, Rogers maintained, people will overcome their own anxiety and get back on their path
toward self-actualization.

EXISTENTIAL THEORIES

For existentialists like Rollo May (1967), anxiety is a natural and healthy part of
living. The emergence of great anxiety during existential treatment is often
regarded as an encouraging sign of progress. To live honestly and authenti-
cally, people must accept that they are truly alone in the world, that there are
no absolutes to guide them, and that they are totally responsible for making
their own meaning. The emotional crisis that this insight precipitates has been
called **existential anxiety.** Like psychodynamic thinkers, the existentialists
place no premium on reducing anxiety. Whatever the person experiences is a
valid part of his or her existence, and is not to be avoided or suppressed.

SYNTHESIS

Existential Anxiety
anxiety that arises from facing
the true conditions of existence,
particularly from accepting
personal responsibility for
choices.

These four perspectives lead to dramatically different approaches to dealing
with stress and anxiety. Psychodynamic and existential approaches do not
seek to reduce anxiety, which is seen merely as a symptom of the real problem
or as a natural part of existence itself. Behavioral perspectives view anxiety as a
product of learning and seek to reduce it through relearning strategies. Hu-

Within an existential viewpoint, people must learn to accept that they are truly alone in the world.

manistic therapy also regards anxiety reduction as desirable, but the approach is to foster self-acceptance rather than focusing on the anxiety itself.

These theoretical differences are further complicated by the research, described earlier, indicating that anxiety is not a single entity but rather a set of physiological, behavioral, and cognitive phenomena that are, at best, loosely tied together. Because most theoretical discussions of anxiety have assumed it to be a single entity, rather than a label to categorize a set of different responses, the contemporary psychologist faces a confusing challenge in dealing with anxiety problems. The 1980 and 1987 revisions of the psychiatric diagnostic system **(DSM-III)**, reflected this period of transition by departing from the previous unifying notion of "neurosis" and instead describing many separate sets of specific disorders.

Our own perspective is that the optimal approach in understanding and dealing with anxiety is not to be found in endorsing any one particular theory. Instead, one needs a comprehensive approach that embraces and organizes the mass of new available data, rather than defending a single theoretical view.

■ A STORC ANALYSIS OF ANXIETY AND STRESS

DSM-III
the third edition of the Diagnostic and Statistical Manual of Mental Disorders, *a standard reference for the description and diagnosis of psychological problems, published in 1980 by the American Psychiatric Association; revised in 1987 (DSM-III-R).*

Both stress and anxiety can be thought of as chains of interrelated events, interactions between the person and the environment. In this way, the STORC analysis is a helpful approach in understanding these phenomena.

S—SITUATIONAL FACTORS

The first step in a STORC analysis examines situational factors, the stimuli that evoke or initiate the emotional chain. In considering stress, this is an analysis of *stressors*. Which stimuli, which environmental events are distressing the individual?

Some stressors are highly generalizable. They exert stressful effects on many or most people. These include certain environmental conditions (crowding, noise, sensory overload), social contingencies (punishment, deadlines, evaluation), and physical pain. In an era of exceedingly rapid social changes and technological developments, change itself has been identified as a stressor. Toffler's (1970) popular book, *Future Shock*, describes some of the stresses imposed by rapid change and adaptive methods for coping with such transition.

An early attempt to measure the stressful effects of change was the Social Readjustment Rating Scale (see Box 8.2). This scale lists 43 life changes, each of which is assigned a certain number of stress points (Holmes & Rahe, 1967). The authors of this scale asserted that the greater the number of stress points accumulated within a year, the larger the likelihood of developing a stress-related illness. More recent research indicates that the relationship between stressors and illness is not so simple (Feuerstein, Labbé, & Kuczmierczyk, 1986). In part, the stressfulness of an event is determined by how the person perceives the event; for example, as a positive or a negative change (Johnson & McCutcheon, 1980). This factor will be considered shortly, as the "T" element of a STORC analysis. Other research indicates that accumulation of more minor daily annoyances may have a greater impact on illness than do less frequent major life events (Kanner et al., 1981).

Anxiety is often linked to specific classes of stimuli. Phobias, as mentioned earlier, are irrational fears of specific stimuli or situations. Some common phobias involve fear of social evaluation; of snakes, spiders, or other animals; of small enclosed spaces; of heights; of taking tests; or of flying in airplanes. Anxiety can also occur even when one is not in the feared situation, occurring in the form of worry or anxious anticipation of feared occurrences.

Environmental stressors can contribute to anxiety and distress.

8.2 THE SOCIAL READJUSTMENT RATING SCALE

RANK	LIFE EVENT	STRESS POINTS
1	Death of spouse	100
2	Divorce	73
3	Marital separation	65
4	Jail term	63
5	Death of close family member	63
6	Personal injury or illness	53
7	Marriage	50
8	Fired at work	47
9	Marital reconciliation	45
10	Retirement	45
11	Change in health of family member	44
12	Pregnancy	40
13	Sex difficulties	39
14	Gain of new family member	39
15	Business readjustment	39
16	Change in financial state	38
17	Death of a close friend	37
18	Change to different line of work	36
19	Change in number of arguments with spouse	35
20	Mortgage over $15,000*	31
21	Foreclosure of mortgage or loan	30
22	Change in responsibilities at work	29
23	Son or daughter leaving home	29
24	Trouble with in-laws	29
25	Outstanding personal achievement	28
26	Spouse begins or stops work	26
27	Begin or end school	26
28	Change in living conditions	25
29	Revision of personal habits	24
30	Trouble with boss	23
31	Change in work hours or conditions	20
32	Change in residence	20
33	Change in schools	20
34	Change in recreation	19
35	Change in church activities	19

36	Change in social activities	18
37	Mortgage or loan less than $15,000*	17
38	Change in sleeping habits	16
39	Change in number of family get-togethers	15
40	Change in eating habits	15
41	Vacation	13
42	Christmas	12
43	Minor violations of the law	11

Source: Reprinted with permission from *Journal of Psychosomatic Research*, *11*, 1967. T. H. Holmes & R. H. Rahe, The Social Readjustment Rating Scale, pp. 213–218 (Pergamon).
* Adjusted to 1990 dollars.

Several strategies for coping with stress and anxiety focus on change in situational (S) components. One such strategy is *avoidance* of the feared or stressful situation. Individuals who are constantly exposed to a large number of stressors may benefit from reducing such exposure. Vacations, in part, are intended to serve this function, providing at least a brief respite from stressful routines. Many people with phobias cope with their fears by staying away from the objects or situations that terrify them. The snake phobic avoids snake-infested areas and reptile exhibits. Those who fear elevators learn to climb stairs.

Yet avoidance is not always an adaptive strategy in the long run. Those who avoid routine dental care because of their fear will ultimately place themselves at risk of requiring more major and painful levels of the very thing they seek to escape. Bridges are difficult to avoid if you live in San Francisco, as are elevators for the New Yorker. Examinations are difficult to avoid if you want to graduate from college. Avoidance of all situations in which you might be socially evaluated leads to a rather limited life. As a coping strategy, avoidance is limiting and restrictive.

Avoidance also has a way of intensifying fear. That which is avoided seems to gain in its power to evoke anxiety. There are many occasions, as in falling off a horse while learning to ride, where going back and confronting the feared situation will usually decrease fear, while avoiding the situation typically strengthens anxiety. In addition, the habit of avoiding tends to be self-perpetuating, as we will discuss later in this chapter in the section on consequences (C).

An alternative to avoidance, then, is to neutralize or desensitize the stimuli that evoke anxiety. This is the purpose of systematic desensitization, one effective treatment strategy for dealing with phobias. The underlying principle is **reconditioning.** A certain stimulus or class of stimuli evokes anxiety responses, and the goal is to replace these with new responses. This requires practicing the new response (one that is *incompatible* with anxiety) in the presence of the feared stimulus, thus breaking the old S-R tie and substituting a new one (Wolpe, 1973). There are a variety of responses that are incompatible with anxiety, and thus are candidates for use in reconditioning. Eating behavior (Jones, 1924), sexual arousal (Masters & Johnson, 1970), assertiveness (Salter, 1949; see Chapter 9), meditation (Aron & Aron, 1980), and certain drugs

Reconditioning

a process of altering an established stimulus-response pair, so that the stimulus is followed by a new response.

The most commonly used response for displacing anxiety during desensitization is progressive deep muscle relaxation.

(Wolpe, 1973) all tend to suppress anxiety. The most commonly used response for displacing anxiety during desensitization, however, is physical *relaxation.* One method for learning to relax, called progressive deep muscle relaxation training, is described in detail in Appendix B. A number of other ways to induce relaxation will be mentioned later in this chapter (Benson & Klipper, 1975; Walker, 1975).

Having learned a method for relaxing, the person undergoing systematic desensitization next constructs an anxiety hierarchy. This hierarchy is a set of situations that currently evoke various amounts of anxiety, ranging from very little to very much. Box 8.3 shows a sample hierarchy for a student who feared public speaking. The situations are arranged in order, from lowest to highest anxiety, ideally with roughly even steps throughout the hierarchy. The person then works his or her way upward through the hierarchy, starting from the bottom and mastering one step at a time. Usually this is done in imagination, by becoming very relaxed and then imagining a particular scene. The lowest scene in the hierarchy is mastered first, by imagining it repeatedly (while relaxed) until it no longer evokes any anxiety. Then the next scene is imagined until it is neutralized, and so on up through the hierarchy. Mastery of each scene seems to make it easier to go on to the next. Research suggests that, at least for simple phobias and anxieties, systematic desensitization can often be effectively self-administered without the assistance of a therapist, if prescribed steps are followed carefully (Glasgow & Rosen, 1978; Rosen, 1976).

Sometimes desensitization is carried out not in imagination but *in vivo,* in real life. A similar procedure is followed. First a hierarchy of real-life situations is constructed, ranging in small steps from relatively easy to more difficult situations. After practicing relaxation or another skill to displace anxiety, the person then actually performs the lowest task in the hierarchy, repeating it as necessary until it can be done without anxiety. Then the person goes on to the next task in the hierarchy, practicing that task until the anxiety associated with it is neutralized. The hierarchy shown in Box 8.3 could be practiced either in imagination or *in vivo.* Still another alternative is first to master the hierarchy in imagination, and then to practice each step in real life.

An alternative, but somewhat more difficult therapeutic procedure is **flooding.** It is, in a way, the opposite of desensitization, and should only be done with the guidance of a skilled therapist. In flooding, the person is exposed to the *most* feared stimuli, those which would constitute the top of the hierarchy

Flooding
a form of behavior therapy for anxiety disorders, in which the individual imagines or is exposed for prolonged periods to highly feared stimuli or situations.

8.3 A SAMPLE HIERARCHY FOR SYSTEMATIC DESENSITIZATION
Public Speaking Anxiety

Below is an example of a desensitization hierarchy constructed by a person suffering from anxiety about public speaking. The tasks are arranged in order, based on the amount of anxiety each provokes, from lowest (1) to highest (20). In working to overcome this anxiety, the person would progress through these tasks one step at a time, either in imagination or by actual practice. Relaxation or other skills are used to keep anxiety at a low level as each step is mastered.

1. Reading a 2-minute passage to 2 friends.
2. Reading a 2-minute passage to 2 strangers.
3. Reading a 2-minute passage to 5 friends.
4. Reading a 2-minute passage to 5 strangers.
5. Giving a 5-minute practiced speech to 2 friends.
6. Giving a 5-minute practiced speech to 2 strangers.
7. Giving a 5-minute practiced speech to 5 friends.
8. Giving a 5-minute practiced speech to 5 strangers.
9. Reading a 2-minute passage to a class of 20.
10. Giving a 5-minute impromptu speech to 2 friends.
11. Giving a 5-minute impromptu speech to 5 friends.
12. Giving a 5-minute impromptu speech to 2 strangers.
13. Giving a 5-minute impromptu speech to 5 strangers.
14. Giving a 5-minute practiced speech to a class of 20.
15. Reading a 2-minute passage to a class of 50.
16. Giving a 2-minute practiced speech to a class of 50.
17. Giving a 5-minute impromptu speech to a class of 20.
18. Giving a 5-minute impromptu speech to a class of 50.
19. Giving a 5-minute impromptu speech to a class of 20 and seeing 2 people in the back begin to giggle and whisper to each other.
20. Giving a 5-minute impromptu speech to a class of 50 and seeing 2 people in the back begin to giggle and whisper to each other.

in desensitization. Either in imagination or *in vivo*, the person confronts the most feared situations over and over again. At first these evoke great anxiety. Instead of escaping or trying to avoid the anxiety, however, the person perseveres in confronting the harmless but feared situations. With repeated exposure, the stimuli begin to lose their power to evoke fear. This method has been found to be particularly effective in dealing with highly generalized fears such as **agoraphobia,** in which the person becomes increasingly fearful of being alone, away from home, or away from help (Trull, Nietzel, & Main, 1988).

Agoraphobia
fear of being in public places or away from help.

8.4 AGORAPHOBIA: A CASE STUDY

"I don't know what is wrong with me. I feel afraid to do anything anymore. I can't drive. I haven't been out of the city for five years. The thought of being around a lot of other people terrifies me. I can't go near a shopping center or a grocery store. Lately I've just been staying home. I feel safest there. It was all I could do to get myself here to see you. I've been to so many doctors, and they all just tell me there's nothing wrong with me. This isn't like me at all. I'm a strong person, but this is more than I can handle. I live in fear that I'm going to have another attack."

This is what Mrs. S told the psychologist. Her history was typical for agoraphobia. About two years earlier she had begun having panic attacks, frightening periods of high autonomic arousal that seemed to occur at random. "I remember my first attack. I was driving my car, and suddenly I began feeling more and more terrified. My heart was racing and pounding, and I started gasping for air. I nearly had an accident before I could pull over to the curb. I thought I was going to die right there. I sat there until I felt a little better, and then I drove myself straight to the emergency room. They couldn't find anything wrong with me. I've been to four doctors since then, including two heart doctors, but they all tell me I'm fine."

Over the course of a few months, Mrs. S had more panic attacks, which seemed to be coming more often. "Once I was in the middle of the shopping mall and I had an attack. I thought I was going to faint or throw up right there in front of everybody. It was horrible." Gradually, she began to avoid crowded public places. She stopped driving and was afraid to take public transportation. She could ride in an automobile with a friend, but only a certain distance from her home. "I can draw for you on a map where I can go. If I go outside those boundaries, I start having an attack." Mostly she had been staying at home where she felt safe.

The psychologist worked with Mrs. S for three months, first explaining how panic attacks occur. Next they worked together to help Mrs. S develop relaxation skills to give her more control over her level of arousal. Then over a period of weeks, they slowly challenged the boundaries. They went for walks together beyond her "safe zone." They went to shopping centers and other public places. After some successes, Mrs. S began driving again, first for short trips with a friend, then on longer routes with a friend, then alone. The therapist encouraged her not to be stopped by her own fear, but to push past it and stretch her boundaries. She still had panic attacks, but they occurred less often, seemed less intense, and Mrs. S learned that she could survive them and not be stopped by them. Two years later, she still feels somewhat anxious when driving alone or shopping, but she is not restricted by it. She also found a support group of people suffering from agoraphobia, and she enjoys helping others overcome their fears and restrictions.

T—THOUGHT PROCESSES

It is easy to think that anxiety and stress occur in response to what is "out there," to situational aspects of the environment. Yet in another sense, nothing is stressful or anxiety provoking until it is interpreted and perceived by the individual. Major life changes such as those listed in Box 8.2 can be viewed as burdensome afflictions or as challenges and opportunities to find creative new ways of being (Bridges, 1980; Brown, 1980). Stress and anxiety, like beauty, are in the eye of the beholder, the product of cognitive processing.

Some stimuli might be thought to evoke fear automatically: a loaded gun in the hands of an angry person, a coiled rattlesnake. Yet even these have no meaning unless the person perceives in them the potential danger. A firearm, for example, evokes no fear in someone who has no idea what it is.

Most problems classified as **anxiety disorders** consist of a person reacting to a particular situation as if it were much more dangerous than it actually is. One person may, for example, suffer from a **compulsion** to wash his or her hands after touching anything that "contaminates" them: a doorknob, a wall, the handle of a drinking fountain, the railing of a bus seat. Another may feel extremely anxious in crowds, on airplanes, in elevators, or around any kind of dog. Although doorknobs, crowds, elevators, airplanes, and dogs do pose certain minimal risks, the actual likelihood of harm is very small, and the person's anxious reaction is out of proportion to the real danger. Somehow, the individual is interpreting and reacting to these situations as if they were quite dangerous.

One interpretation of how this occurs is that the feared situation may fit into or match a memory of an actual traumatic occurrence in the person's past. The person reacts to this new situation as if it were similar or identical to the previous, traumatic situation. This can occur with or without conscious awareness of the link. One woman, for example, suffered from an intense phobia of wind. Any time she heard the wind blowing, felt it on her skin, or saw it moving the branches of a tree, she experienced terror and ran to take cover under a table or behind heavy furniture. The origin of her phobia was clear. She had been trapped alone in a mountain cabin, eight months pregnant, during a terrible windstorm. The lights went out, a tree fell on the house, and she genuinely thought that she and her baby would be killed. So terrifying was this experience that any sign of wind reminded her of it and revivified the fear, though she knew that her reaction was now irrational. Her phobia was treated very successfully with systematic desensitization (Alperson, 1976).

Psychodynamic understandings of phobia and other irrational anxiety responses also focus on links to the past. The phobia is seen as a representation of a trauma or conflict that is now unconscious. By their actual or symbolic resemblance, the feared situations represent the unconscious material and evoke its emotional charge. A nurse, for example, sought the help of a psychotherapist when she suddenly developed debilitating anxiety and panic attacks at work. She had recently been transferred to "Ward 3B." The therapist uncovered her unfinished grief and anger regarding her father, who had died in another hospital on a ward bearing the same name. The nurse had been quite unaware of the connection.

A related concept from psychodynamic theory is that of **transference.** This is a phenomenon whereby an individual reacts in the present to a person as if he or she were someone else, a significant figure from the individual's past. A physical resemblance of a stranger to one's mother (for example, similar eyes and hair, or a similarity in manner of speaking) may evoke significant emotional reactions, and one may behave toward the stranger (in some ways at least) as if she *were* mother. The resemblance may also be symbolic. Male authority figures, for example, may evoke father images and the resulting feelings and behaviors of childhood. One might experience such reactions to an older male professor or employer, by virtue of his position of authority. The remembered images and emotions from the past are "transferred" onto a person in the present. In essence, the individual is attempting to adjust to a new person or situation by clinging to patterns of perception and behavior that applied in a past setting. For this reason, Peck (1978) has referred to transference as "the outdated map." This phenomenon is most often discussed as occurring within psychotherapy, where the therapist becomes the target of transference, but similar reactions occur in many other relationships. A superficial everyday example is that of meeting a stranger and knowing almost immediately how you feel about him or her. Such reactions are unlikely

✗ Anxiety Disorder
a persistent and maladaptive pattern of behavior related to anxiety (DSM-III).

✗ Compulsion
a persistent unwanted impulse to perform a particular behavior, in which resisting the urge results in anxiety.

✗ Transference
reacting (without awareness) to a person as if he or she were another person who was significant in one's earlier life.

to be based solely on the stranger's behavior. Rather they may be responses to a resemblance between perceptions of this new person and one's memories of past experience with others.

The major point here is that stress and anxiety are responses to the *perceived* situation, and are not inherent reactions to a stimulus in itself. Even physical pain, which most people find quite stressful and anxiety provoking, can be reinterpreted and experienced in a different fashion. Certain religious rites, for example, involve the self-infliction of severe physical pain, which is experienced as spiritually fulfilling and rewarding. In the *sundance* ritual of the Plains tribes of American Indians, young men pierce their flesh deeply with metal hooks that are tied to ropes attached to a central pole. Throughout the day the men dance around the pole, pulling against the ropes and tearing their flesh (Black Elk, 1972). The *Penitentes*, a religious order in the southwestern United States, have for many years subjected themselves to self-inflicted cuts and whipping, and on occasion have practiced actual (though nonfatal) crucifixion of an honored member (Weigle, 1970). To outsiders, these practices appear bizarre, but they exemplify how even physical pain can be approached from a wide variety of perceptions.

The physical sensations of autonomic arousal can themselves be perceived in a variety of ways. We have a colleague who sits in his office before every lecture getting emotionally prepared. To us, his pacing, rehearsing, and hand-wringing look rather like signs of anxiety. Asked about his experience, however, he reports that he is "getting psyched" for his lecture. He perceives and labels his arousal in a positive light.

8.5 PERSONAL MILESTONE
A Terrifying Memory

I was participating in a workshop on eidetic imagery, a particularly vivid type of image by which, according to one theory, psychologically important memories are stored. The leader was conducting an eidetic exercise, instructing us to imagine the home in which we had been raised. "See the furniture in the living room, not as you would now as an adult from above, but as you did then, as a child." I was seeing vividly, at eye level, the old couch, the overstuffed chair, the corner table with pictures. It was very pleasant.

Suddenly the image changed. I was looking up at a ghastly figure. The face was white and menacing, and the figure seemed incredibly tall. Behind him was blue sky. A great wave of terror rushed through me. Then, just as quickly, it was gone. The image had lasted perhaps five seconds in all, and I was back in the old living room again. It took me a little while to register what had happened, and then my question was, "What was *that*?"

Later that evening I reflected back on the image, trying to reconstruct it. I remembered the white face, perhaps with some other colors on it, not a human face. The hair was red and wild. What could it have been? A clown? Also I remembered how unbelievably tall it had towered above me. Even from the perspective of a small child, this figure was too tall to be human. The fear, too, was memorable. I felt an overwhelming panic, gasping for breath. What *was* it?

The next day I called my mother for a chat, and decided to ask whether she could recall any time when I had been frightened by a clown. "Oh, yes," she replied. "I remember that. We were on the boardwalk at Wildwood, New Jersey. You were in a stroller, and there was a clown. He came over to us, but you got really scared. I think probably he frightened you because he was walking on stilts."

Stilts! Of course. "How old was I then?" I asked.

"You couldn't have been much more than a year old."

What an amazing capacity we have to remember!

—WRM

8.6   THE THRILL OF WHITE WATER

The experience of autonomic arousal can be perceived in dramatically different ways. Here is one example from our own lives. One of us loves to kayak through white water. One of us hates to kayak through white water. Why?

"I particularly love the exhilaration of riding the rapids. The water and the rocks go rushing by, and I have a feeling of thrill and excitement. My heart pounds, my whole body is working, and I feel beautiful, sensuous, and alive. When I come out the other side I have this feeling of having come through on my own skill. The rapids provided the challenge, and my part was to meet that challenge."

"I absolutely hate shooting rapids. The water and the rocks are rushing by, and I have this terrifying image of being trapped upside down in my kayak and drowning. My stomach feels queasy and tied in knots, like on the fast rides at an amusement park. What's worse, however, is that I know the rides are safe. This is for *real*. I could *die* out here! My heart pounds, and I feel weak all over. When I come out the other side I am exhausted, thankful just to be alive. I feel like vomiting. I don't ever want to get in a kayak again!"

It is equally possible to misinterpret physical arousal as anxiety. Consider the following example. Before dentists fill a cavity, they normally administer a local anesthetic. It is common practice for this injected anesthetic to be accompanied by a small dose of adrenalin, which is included to prolong the numbing effect. The dose of adrenalin is small enough to have little other effect on most people, but some are more sensitive to this drug than others. One possible effect of adrenalin is an increase in autonomic arousal (see Chapter 3 and the "O" section that follows). A dental patient, injected with anesthetic and adrenalin, may therefore begin to experience rapid heart rate and breathing, sweating, and mild trembling. Not understanding that these result from the drug, the patient asks himself or herself, "Why am I feeling this way?" The waiting dental drill, rack of steel implements, and the sound of drilling from the next room provide an immediate explanation of the experience: it must be fear! Indeed, research indicates that if adrenalin is administered to people without their knowledge, its effects can be interpreted as fear under certain circumstances (Nisbett & Valins, 1971).

Could this process work in reverse? What would happen if people who are genuinely aroused by fear could be convinced that their physical symptoms were actually the effects of a drug? Would they then experience themselves as less fearful? An ingenious series of studies on the **reattribution** of fear indicates that this is quite possible. In these studies, subjects were given a "drug" and then exposed to anxiety-provoking stimuli such as a snake or electric shock. Some were told that the drug would produce certain side effects such as increased heart rate, sweating, or trembling and that these should be ignored as harmless and temporary. Others were given no such expectation. The "drug" was actually a placebo, an inert substance that had no effect whatsoever. The only difference between groups, then, was that one group was led to *expect* to feel signs of autonomic arousal and to attribute these to the drug, whereas those in the other group were "on their own." The prediction of misattribution theory is that those who have an alternative explanation for their arousal will not interpret it as fear, and therefore will behave in a less fearful manner. This hypothesis was confirmed in several studies. Misattribu-

Reattribution
a process of changing one's explanation of the causes of a particular behavior or situation.

Test-anxious students differ from others in what they are thinking about before and during an examination.

tion of arousal has been reported to decrease fear of snakes (Valins & Ray, 1967) and fear of pain (Ross, Rodin, & Zimbardo, 1969), to increase pain tolerance (Davison & Valins, 1969), and even to cause insomniacs to fall asleep more rapidly (Storms & Nisbett, 1970).

Research on test anxiety indicates that thought processes are an important part of the problem (Wine, 1971). On measures of physiological arousal, students who identify themselves as test anxious are no more aroused than other students when taking a test. Most students tend to become more physically aroused when facing an examination. Rather, the difference between test-anxious students and others is most often in what they are *thinking* about before and during a test. Here is an example of what might be going on in the private thoughts of two students starting an exam:

STUDENT A: "Well, here goes. Hope I do well. Hmm. I don't recognize the first question. I'd better skip over it and come back later if I have time. Now the second question . . ."

STUDENT B: "Oh, this is it! I just know I'm going to blow this one. I always blank out when I get to the test, no matter how hard I've studied. I know the material until I get in here, and then it's all a blur. Well, what's the first question? Oh no! It doesn't look familiar at all! Didn't I read the right chapters? I must have missed something. Or maybe I did study it and I'm just not remembering. Oh, this always happens to me. I'm feeling so nervous, I'm probably going to blank out on this whole test. Why don't I know this stuff? I'm going to flunk this course, and then I'll never get a decent job. What am I going to do? I study so hard, and I *just can't think!* What will I do if I flunk out? My whole plan for my life would be ruined."

Student A stays on task and doesn't waste time worrying. Student B, by contrast, is burning up lots of mental time and energy running through unproductive worrying. After more than a full minute of this, student B just feels more anxious and still hasn't gone on to the second question. The difference between student A and student B is in how they are spending their thinking time. The importance of this is seen in the finding that test-anxious students do more poorly than others only on *timed* tests, where such nonproductive thinking wastes important time that should be spent focusing on the task. Strategies that teach better thought-focusing can be very helpful to test-anxious students in overcoming their worry and improving test performance.

Even *imagining* oneself coping successfully can be beneficial in coping with anticipatory anxiety. It is possible in imagination to practice coping in the feared situation and to visualize yourself being successful. In one study, test-anxious students significantly reduced their anxiety by imagining themselves (before the test) coping competently in academic or other situations (Harris & Johnson, 1983).

In a more elaborate approach known as **stress inoculation,** people are taught how to prepare themselves for and then cope with stressful situations. As described by Meichenbaum (1977), stress inoculation has three phases. In the first or *educational* phase, the person is given an explanation in everyday language of how stress and anxiety occur. (The STORC model used in this book could easily serve as the basis for such an explanation.) Presumably this gives the person a greater sense of understanding his or her own negative emotions. Next in a *rehearsal* phase the individual learns specific coping techniques. These include new self-statements to practice before, during, and following a stressful situation. The strategies are not limited to cognitive techniques, however, and often include other methods such as relaxation training. Finally, in an *application* phase the person tries out these new coping skills in planned but stressful situations. After experiencing success in using the new skills in these less difficult situations, the person then begins applying them in his or her more difficult problem situations. (Note the similarity here to the method of systematic desensitization described earlier.) Stress inoculation strategies have been used successfully in helping people prepare for and endure difficult experiences such as painful or frightening medical procedures (Ludwick-Rosenthal & Neufeld, 1988).

One additional cognitive source of stress and anxiety is reminiscent of the thought processes discussed in Chapters 6 and 7 in relation to self-esteem and mood. Certain *beliefs* or characteristic attitudes may predispose a person to harmful effects of stress and anxiety. Kobasa studied a group of executives, all of whom were exposed to high levels of stressors in their daily lives. She found that a cluster of four characteristics, which together she called hardiness (Chapter 7), distinguished between executives with high versus low levels of personal illness (Kobasa, 1979; Kobasa, Maddi, & Zola, 1983). The psychological differences between the high- and low-illness groups are shown in Table 8-1.

Stress Inoculation *training in skills to prepare for and cope with stressful situations.*

TABLE 8-1
ELEMENTS OF
PSYCHOLOGICAL
HARDINESS

Characteristics of Healthy Executives	Characteristics of Executives with High Illness
Clear sense of personal values and goals and a strong *commitment* to them	No clear sense of personal goals and values; sense of *alienation* from self
An *active* coping attitude toward the environment; a vigorous problem-solving approach to life	A *passive*, acquiescent attitude toward the job and environment
A sense of *meaningfulness*	A sense of *meaninglessness*
Internal locus of control—perceived general ability to influence what will happen	*External* locus of control—perceived general inability to influence what will happen

Source: Adapted from Kobasa (1979). © 1979 by the American Psychological Association. Reprinted by permission of the author.

Notice that all of these differences are cognitive factors: attitudes, beliefs, values, or perceptual styles (Chapter 2).

Such cognitive styles and beliefs seem to have an important influence on how well a person copes with stress. One client, for example, complained of extreme stress at work. Fred, as we will call him, reported that he was always "walking on eggshells," afraid that he would make an error that would cause him to be fired. He believed that he was actually incompetent at his job and that his superiors were becoming aware of this. "They're just looking for an excuse to give me my walking papers," he said. In reality, all indications were that Fred was very highly regarded within his company and was viewed as a competent and valuable employee. He had received positive evaluations of his work and had been given raises at the top of the potential range. None of this persuaded him, however. He was so anxious, in fact, that he was beginning to do things that might, in the long run, cause him trouble. Afraid of receiving bad news, he had stopped reading and responding to memos, even though he occupied an important middle-management position where communication flow was vital. He also was becoming so anxious in meetings that he was paying more attention to his arousal than to business. Fred's incorrect perception of himself as incompetent, and his unbased belief that his superiors were evaluating him negatively, left him feeling continually anxious. His beliefs threatened to become a self-fulfilling prophecy.

We will use Fred's situation to provide some additional examples of how cognitive processes can be used to diminish stress and anxiety. After ascertaining that the anxieties were unfounded, Fred's therapist used a variety of cognitive strategies to help him overcome his irrational fears. The first was to have Fred self-monitor his own thoughts that resulted in anxiety. A few weeks of such a diary pointed to some common themes including low confidence and self-esteem and to Fred's tendency to perceive apparently neutral cues and communications as disapproving and threatening. The therapist then had Fred use thought-stopping whenever he found himself thinking such ideas, and to practice thought replacement by altering his self-statements (Chapter 6). The replacement thoughts focused on the strong positive feedback Fred had been receiving, and themes such as "I'm doing fine" and "I'm really pretty good at what I do here."

In therapy it also emerged that Fred's immediate supervisor reminded him a great deal of his father, whom he remembered as stern and constantly disapproving. The therapist worked with Fred to separate in reality the past from the present, to disengage his father memories from actual communications of his boss.

Another strategy that proved helpful to Fred, when he was feeling anxious, was to focus his attention on the task at hand. Like test-anxious students, Fred tended to let his thoughts run wild instead of staying on task. If he felt any physical signs of anxiety, he would focus on these and tell himself, "There, see how anxious you're getting!" His therapist taught him instead to say, "It's only arousal," to remind himself briefly of his true competence, and then to get back on task.

In one session, Fred's therapist also employed the **blow-up technique** (Lazarus, 1971). This involves having the person imagine what is the worst possible outcome, how bad that would really be, and how likely it is to occur in reality. The therapist began, "O.K., Fred, what's the worst thing that could possibly happen?"

Blow-Up Technique X
*a strategy for coping with anxiety
by examining or imagining the
worst feared outcomes (first
described by Arnold Lazarus).*

"Why, I'd lose my job all of a sudden."
"And what would happen then?"
"I'd have to find another one."
"How long do you think that would take?"

"I don't know, maybe a couple of months. I do have some friends who keep telling me to come work for their company."

"So there is at least one possibility right now, and maybe some others?"

"There are two or three places where I've talked to people."

"So you already know some places that might like to hire you, but at worst it could take you a few months to find a new job, if you had no advance notice at all."

"Maybe six months."

"O.K. even six months. How would you live during that six months?"

"Well, we have some savings, and I guess I could get unemployment checks if I had to."

"In other words, you could get by, even for six months, which is the longest it could take for you to get another job, even if you had no warning. But how likely is it really that you're going to get fired from your job with no warning?"

"I worry about it. I really don't know."

"All of your evaluations have been positive, and you've been getting almost top raises. That doesn't sound to me like somebody who is on the verge of being fired. But even if you were, you'd survive it."

"I guess I would, yes."

Working with cognitive strategies such as these, Fred began to build his self-confidence and to overcome his disabling worries about negative evaluation. At the time of this writing, Fred had just been selected, with a generous raise and benefits, to head a new division of his company.

In sum, there are many ways in which thought processes (T) have an important impact on stress and anxiety. This realization has led to the development of various cognitive approaches for reducing anxiety and stress.

O—ORGANIC COMPONENTS OF STRESS AND ANXIETY

There is a physiological side to stress and anxiety, too. The physical symptoms that most people experience as anxiety are primarily the result of arousal of the sympathetic portion of the autonomic nervous system (described in Chapter 3). In response to a perceived threat, the autonomic nervous system prepares the body for an emergency. Heart rate and blood pressure increase, with the resulting sensation of a pounding or racing heart. Glucose (sugar) is released into the bloodstream. Blood flow to the skin decreases, leaving the hands cold. The mouth goes dry, and sweating increases. If such autonomic arousal comes in a large wave, it can be experienced as a **panic attack,** which may also include rapid breathing, dizziness, or nausea.

For reasons that are not yet clear, some people do experience panic attacks in seemingly random situations, and without warning. Not understanding what is happening, such people often believe that they are dying, having a heart attack, or going crazy. Once a person has experienced this panic, the fear of additional attacks may lead the person into the previously mentioned pattern of agoraphobia. They avoid situations in which they might have a panic attack around others, but also avoid situations in which they would be isolated from help. In extreme cases, agoraphobics become housebound, prisoners of fear in their own homes. Though sometimes endured for many years, agoraphobia is very treatable (Emmelkamp, Kuipers, & Eggeratt, 1978; Emmelkamp & Wessels, 1975).

Panic Attack
a period of intense anxiety, especially high autonomic arousal.

Most people, however, experience less intense forms of autonomic arousal. Some suffer chronic moderate anxiety, a feeling of living on the edge of panic. Small stressors may push them to an uncomfortable level of arousal, which they experience as anxiety. In essence, their nervous system is *always* ready for an emergency. Chronic high-level autonomic arousal is one definition of high trait anxiety.

Chronic autonomic arousal takes its toll on physical health. What is a normal and adaptive temporary response to danger becomes an habitual state of alert in the body. Sustained over a long period of time, this chronic stress arousal results in a physical breakdown that Selye (1978) first identified as the **general adaptation syndrome.** Faced with chronic stress, Selye observed, the body eventually depletes its resources for emergency coping, resulting in serious illness or death.

Since Selye's initial work in the 1950s, research has explored in greater depth the detrimental effects of chronic stress on the body. The arousal involved in the body's stress response activates the hypothalamus, a key brain center controlling health and emotional functions. Perhaps through chronic hypothalamic activation, sustained stress can exert very negative effects on health. Stress has been implicated as a causal factor in many specific health problems, including gastric ulcer, hypertension, and heart disease. Stress also has detrimental effects on the body's immune system, its ability to resist disease and infection (Pelletier, 1977).

A variety of strategies exist for decreasing chronic autonomic arousal. Certain classes of drugs, especially tranquilizers, have been widely prescribed to diminish tension and arousal. Unfortunately the regular use of such medications can create problems of another kind, namely, psychological and physical dependence (see Chapter 11). An alternative to the use of medication is the learning and practice of a drug-free skill for relaxing and reducing tension. We have already mentioned progressive deep muscle relaxation as one such alternative (see Appendix B). Other possible alternatives are meditation or prayer (Benson & Klipper, 1975; Emmons, 1978; Shapiro, 1978), yoga, physical exercise, self-hypnosis, imagery, breathing exercises, or biofeedback (Walker, 1975).

Another facet to consider is what other organic factors may be contributing to autonomic arousal. Stimulant medications such as caffeine (in coffee, soft drinks, and chocolate), nicotine (in tobacco products), and amphetamines tend to increase arousal. When used heavily, alcohol, though a depressant medication, affects the brain in a manner that mimics the effects of chronic stress (Noble, 1973). People whose bodies do not regulate blood sugar level properly (as in hypoglycemia or diabetes) may experience fluctuations in autonomic arousal if they do not carefully manage their diets.

Reduction in overall level of arousal may have a number of beneficial impacts. Research with progressive deep muscle relaxation training (Appendix B) has shown beneficial effects of this technique in reducing nightmares (Miller & DiPilato, 1983), blood pressure (Blanchard, Martin, & Dubbert, 1988), insomnia (Bootzin & Nicassio, 1978; Knapp, Downs, & Alperson, 1976), headaches (Andrasik, 1986; Teders et al., 1984), and chronic pain (Holzman, Turk, & Kerns, 1986). Reported beneficial effects of this method have been so pervasive that relaxation training has come to be called "the aspirin of psychology."

R—RESPONSES TO STRESS AND ANXIETY

As mentioned earlier, there is a natural tendency, in response to feelings of stress and anxiety, to *avoid* the situations that one perceives to be threatening. Avoidance behavior, however, quickly feeds into a self-perpetuating cycle. The person who avoids does not diminish his or her own fear, and may even intensify it. To avoid a feared situation is to strengthen the perception that it is indeed something to be feared. It bolsters the belief that "I can't do it," fostering further avoidance and anxiety. Successfully overcoming anxiety more often

General Adaptation Syndrome
a pattern of major and enduring physiological changes that results from prolonged exposure to stress.

involves confronting rather than avoiding that which is feared (Marks, 1978; Weekes, 1972).

The experience of stress and anxiety can be expressed in other behaviors besides withdrawal and avoidance. Some people respond to stress with verbal and physical aggression (see Chapter 9). Others turn to compulsive working in the belief that their stress will diminish if they just work hard enough (Oates, 1971). Still others turn to alcohol or other drugs when faced with anxiety and stress, though ultimately these are more likely to exacerbate the problem.

An effective response to stress and anxiety is to learn an adaptive *skill* for coping with the challenging situation. This may be a skill for mastering anxiety itself, such as relaxation and systematic desensitization. On the other hand, anxiety may be a signal of the need for a change, for more adaptive behavior. After years of struggling with intense test anxiety, one of our students came to this realization: "It finally occurred to me that my fear of examinations had a solid base in reality. It was a message, but I didn't understand it for the longest time. I recognize now that the real problem for me has been deficient study skills. I've been studying long, but not well. My goal was to memorize everything, and that's just impossible. No wonder, then, I was anxious when I faced an exam! How could I possibly remember all that material? Now that I am learning how to study more effectively, I find I am less afraid because I know I can do it." Acquiring needed social or problem-solving skills can be an important step in reducing stress and anxiety (Matheny et al., 1986).

Sometimes the antidote for anxiety is simply to *practice*, to do the very thing that is feared. In one study, male and female college students who were intensely anxious about dating were assigned at random to have "practice dates" with each other (Christensen, Arkowitz, & Anderson, 1975). This simple approach of just practicing what they feared was effective in reducing their anxiety and increasing the frequency of their dates.

The needed skill is not always apparent from the fear itself. Lazarus (1971) reported the case of a client who developed an intense phobia of bridges that prevented him from driving across several long bridges in the city where he lived. A simple behavioral approach would have been to work toward desensitizing the bridge phobia. Curious as to the origins of the fear, however, Lazarus pressed further and asked a fruitful question: What did the fear of bridges prevent the client from doing? As it turned out, the client was unable to get to work, since reaching his place of employment required him to cross a long bridge. What had changed recently at work? The client had received a promotion that required of him managerial tasks which he felt incompetent to perform. For the first time he was in a position of authority and responsibility for others, and he felt anxious and inept in communicating with those he supervised. Lazarus thus decided to teach him some basic skills of assertive communication (see Chapter 9) for making requests, setting limits, and expressing and reflecting feelings. When his skills in this area improved, the bridge phobia disappeared.

C—CONSEQUENCES

Lazarus's case report also exemplifies the importance of the final link in the STORC chain: the consequences of behavior. For his client, the bridge phobia served an important function. It allowed him to avoid his stressful work situation without having to endure direct blame. He was, after all, *unable* to get to work because of his intense fear. Who could find fault with him for this? Without the phobia, he had to cross the bridge, arrive at work, and endure his own anxious behavior and the responses of his co-workers.

People's behavioral expressions of stress and anxiety do not occur in a vacuum. The world reacts. If anxious behavior evokes a positive response, the behavior is reinforced. The fearful behavior of a child or an adult may, for example, prompt others to offer comfort, reassurance, or relief. Friends and relatives may step in and take over for the person who appears too stressed or anxious to perform a task. If the friends and relatives, in turn, find such "rescue" behavior reinforcing, a pattern emerges. The desire of the anxious person for avoidance serves as a perfect complement to their own desire to rescue and feel needed. Each partner is reinforced for his or her role in the dependent relationship.

On the other hand, people can learn not to reveal their anxiety and may be reinforced for this. Facing stressful circumstances without showing any sign of anxiety is sometimes admired as bravery or composure. The ancient Greek philosophy of stoicism placed great value on silent suffering. In our society, men in particular are socialized not to express vulnerable emotions such as anxiety.

Perhaps the most common consequence that *maintains* anxiety is the relief inherent in avoidance learning. Faced with a stressor, the individual feels a building anticipatory anxiety, and dreads the possibility of confronting the feared situation. If the anxious person then finds a way to avoid the situation, this fear subsides. The decrease in fear constitutes negative reinforcement for avoiding. Having once led to a desirable outcome (fear reduction), the avoidance behavior is strengthened and is more likely to be repeated. Thus begins a self-perpetuating cycle of anxiety and avoidance. In agoraphobia, this process can be seen clearly. Feeling the first signs of a panic attack, the person flees the situation to what is perceived to be a safer environment. The fear diminishes, and avoidance is reinforced.

Similarly what has come to be called "math anxiety" is often perpetuated by (and indeed may arise from) avoidance behavior. Current formulations of the

Societal expectations have encouraged the perception that women are less capable at math.

phenomenon of math anxiety emphasize the importance of both cognitive expectations of failure and skill deficits related to selective avoidance of math courses (Tobias, 1978). From the tenth grade onward (but not before) women have shown lower levels of math ability relative to men, coinciding with a tendency of women to enroll in fewer math courses (Meece et al., 1982). Social expectations that women do not enter (or do not do well in) mathematics-related fields may contribute to this self-selection process. Those who are equipped with fewer skills in mathematics, then, are likely to find mathematical tasks more intimidating and are likely to anticipate failure. Again, avoidance and anxiety are interrelated.

Another consequence resulting from behavior is informational feedback. The feedback one receives about one's own ability to handle a situation is an important determinant of future behavior. The experience of successfully coping with a previously feared situation is in itself encouraging, increasing one's self-efficacy—the belief that one can succeed again with this particular behavior in the future (Bandura, 1982). Again, it is the *perceived* consequences of an action, not necessarily the "actual" consequences, to which one responds (Rotter, 1954).

An example of the importance of such self-efficacy feedback is found in another series of studies on misattribution. In these studies, subjects were given false feedback regarding their level of fear. The prediction was that subjects given (false) feedback of a low level of fear would perceive themselves as less fearful in this specific situation, and would show less evidence of fear on subsequent observations. In one such study, subjects were shown slides, and half were given what they believed to be information about their heart rate in response to each, while others received no such feedback (Valins & Ray, 1967). On slides warning of an impending electric shock, their "heart rate" increased. On slides showing snakes, by contrast, their "heart rate" slowed to a calm pace. The final test was of how close each subject was willing to approach an actual (harmless) snake, and how much fear they rated themselves as experiencing. Relative to subjects receiving no feedback, those given false feedback of fearlessness came closer to the snake and touched it more often, even though their ratings of their own fear did not differ from those of controls.

Another study purported to examine pain tolerance (Davison & Valins, 1969). All subjects were encouraged to endure as high a level of finger shock as they could, until they found it too painful to continue. Feedback was given on a volt meter showing how strong a shock had been received. Then all subjects were given a "drug" that they were told would increase their pain tolerance. The drug was actually a placebo. After time for the drug to "take effect," a second pain tolerance test was given. This time, through a secret adjustment in the meter, each shock registered as twice its actual strength, so that subjects believed they were tolerating much higher shock levels. It was after this that the feedback experiment began. Half the subjects were told that the drug had now "worn off." The other half were told that the drug had actually been a placebo, and thereby were led to believe that they had tolerated higher shock levels on their own without the assistance of any drug. This was followed by one final pain tolerance test, on which the latter group tolerated significantly higher levels of shock and rated the shocks as less stressful. In both these studies, false feedback of fearlessness led to less fearful subsequent behavior.

■ FINAL NOTE: ANXIETY CAN BE HELPFUL

As a concluding note, we want to back off a bit from the idea that anxiety is something to be avoided. In fact, anxiety is an important signal system in human adjustment, and in various ways it can be helpful.

Moderate anxiety can serve an activating function, improving alertness and performance.

One perspective to consider here is that the total *absence* of anxiety is in itself regarded as pathological. One normal function of anxiety is as an anticipation of punishment. Anxiety, in this sense, is a restraining influence in society. A characteristic of individuals diagnosed as showing **antisocial personality** (previously termed "psychopaths" or "sociopaths") is their absence of normal social restraint, an apparent deficit in anxiety, guilt, and empathy (American Psychiatric Association, 1987). Hare (1970) has argued that this deficit is based on a type of brain malfunction that makes it difficult for the person to learn restraint through aversive consequences. That is, anxiety is not learned and thereby fails to inhibit antisocial behavior. Others (e.g. Vaillant, 1975) have argued that anxiety is not absent in such people, but only that they conceal and disperse it more readily than others. In any event, anxiety can serve important inhibitory functions in governing social behavior.

Anxiety, in the sense of autonomic arousal, can also serve an activating function. Research indicates, for example, that optimal performance on examinations occurs with a moderate degree of arousal. While very high arousal can interfere with concentration, very low arousal may provide insufficient motivation to perform well (Lundberg, 1982). As mentioned earlier, "test-anxious" students seldom differ from their peers in arousal level. Test anxiety is not excessive arousal, and arousal reduction is not generally effective as a strategy in reducing test anxiety. The learning of more effective study skills, for example, has a greater impact on test anxiety than does arousal reduction (Kirkland & Hollandsworth, 1980). Thus it is not necessarily desirable to have a very low level of autonomic arousal during an examination.

The useful functions of anxiety are exemplified by the fact that several therapeutic techniques actually seek to *increase* anxiety, or regard increased anxiety as a positive sign. Some psychotherapists prohibit their clients from smoking, chewing gum, or engaging in any other behavior that might discharge anxiety. This is done in the belief that anxiety during therapy is both motivating and informative. Existential psychotherapists expect an increase in anxiety as the person confronts his or her previously denied responsibility and

Antisocial Personality
a characteristic pattern of behavior that disregards and is insensitive to the rights of others, without remorse or empathy (DSM-III).

aloneness. Aversion therapies (see Chapter 11) have as their goal the avoidance of a particular response (for example, alcohol and drug use, or socially undesirable sexual behavior). One method for doing this is to associate anxious arousal with the undesirable response (Smith & Gregory, 1976). Even the treatment technique of flooding, which is intended to overcome anxiety, does so by exposing the client to the most feared stimuli and thus first *increasing* anxiety.

Anxiety, then, is not always undesirable. It can be a healthy and adaptive signal. The total elimination of anxiety is not in itself a desirable goal. Rather it is the reduction of *disabling* or maladaptive stress and anxiety that represents a common and worthwhile objective within psychology.

■ SUMMARY

Both "stress" and "anxiety" are hypothetical constructs used to explain portions of human behavior. The concept of anxiety has played a central role in most theories of personality. Research indicates, however, that anxiety is not a single phenomenon but rather a loosely interrelated set of physiological, cognitive, and behavioral responses. Stress and anxiety can be understood as sequences of situational factors, cognitive interpretations, physiological responses, behavioral expressions, and social consequences (STORC). Situational stressors can be dealt with by avoiding them or by neutralizing their ability to evoke aversive reactions (for example, by systematic desensitization). Reattribution, stress inoculation, cognitive restructuring, and the "blow-up" technique represent cognitive strategies for reducing anxiety. Reduction in sympathetic arousal is useful in coping with anxiety problems involving excessive autonomic activation. The learning of effective coping behaviors (such as study skills) is often more adaptive than avoidance in dealing with anxiety. The perceived consequences of one's responses to anxiety and stress influence whether anxious behavior will increase or decrease in the future. The total elimination of anxiety is not a desirable goal, since anxiety plays several useful and adaptive functions in social adjustment.

■ QUESTIONS FOR THOUGHT

1. How did your family deal with stress and anxiety while you were growing up? How is that similar to or different from the ways in which you deal with anxiety and stress now?

2. In what situations do you tend to feel most anxious or stressed? Describe the anxiety-provoking ingredients of these situations.

3. Imagine yourself in a situation in which you feel anxious. What are you saying to yourself? What else could you say to yourself that might help you to feel less anxious?

4. What happens in your own body when you feel anxious? Where do you first notice anxiety? As anxiety increases, what other changes occur in your body?

5. What situations do you avoid? Why? What would happen if you decided not to avoid these situations?

6. Do you agree or disagree with Robinson Crusoe that "Fear of danger is ten thousand times more terrifying than danger itself"? Explain your reasons.

7. When you feel anxious, how much do you talk to other people about it versus trying to hide it? What are the advantages and disadvantages, for you, of hiding versus sharing your anxious feelings?

8. The authors claim that anxiety sometimes can be helpful. Can you think of any ways or situations in which anxiety has been helpful for you? If so, describe how.

9. Do you notice any differences in your anxiety level if and when you use psychoactive substances such as caffeine (in coffee, tea, soft drinks, chocolate), nicotine (in tobacco), or alcohol?

10. Compared to most students in your class, do you think that your own level of test anxiety is higher, lower, or about average?

chapter nine

Violence is the last refuge of the incompetent.
—Isaac Asimov, *Foundation*

Anger, Aggression, and Assertion

OUTLINE

*A*nger: there is perhaps no other feeling about which Americans are so conflicted and confused. The messages one receives about anger are many and mixed:

Anger is natural.

It's best to keep your cool and not lose control.

It is healthy to get your anger out.

Angry people have the highest risk of ulcers and heart attacks.

Expressing anger is likely to lose you friends.

Not expressing anger will make you depressed.

Anger is acceptable for men, but not for women.

One moment we hear a nation denounced for its aggression. The next we hear a businessperson praised for being so aggressive. Battery is a crime, but boxing is entertainment. Several popular comedians have built their careers around an intensely hostile, insulting style that leaves the audience convulsed with laughter. Every weekend throughout the fall, millions are fixed to the television screen to watch football players "throw a bomb," "hit them hard," work "offense" and "defense," and generally defeat (demolish, destroy, run over, crush, beat, massacre) the opposing team. The "new male" is enjoined to be sensitive and caring; yet attractive male stereotypes continue to emphasize aggression, and the epithet of "wimp" discourages men who deviate from the traditional norm. Violence on the evening news is horrifying (but maybe a little fascinating, too?), and the public cries out for swift and severe punishment of the perpetrators of violent crimes. Yet an enduringly popular theme in the entertainment industry is graphic violence, exemplified by over two decades of "teenage slasher" and revenge films. Even in criminal law, violence committed during a "fit of passion" may be regarded as a less serious crime (second-degree murder) than the same act rationally planned (first-degree murder). Is it any wonder that most people are unclear how they feel about anger and aggression?

In this chapter, we will discuss the emotion of anger, distinguishing it from behaviors (such as aggression) that sometimes occur when one is angry. We will explain the concept of assertiveness, which represents a middle ground between being aggressive and being submissive. Next we will consider aspects of human development that influence anger and aggression. We will then apply the STORC approach in analyzing the emotion of anger and related behaviors. Finally, we will explore the concept of the "Type A" personality, a consistent pattern of emotion and behavior that may have a major impact on health.

ANGER, AGGRESSION, AND ASSERTION

As a beginning, we will distinguish among anger, aggression, and assertion. Distinct definitions of these three will be helpful as we consider how they occur, what influences them, and how they are interrelated.

Aggression and violence are deeply embedded in our entertainment and media.

ANGER

Anger is an emotion, a feeling, a private experience. It is a mixture of physiological arousal and a particular mental set. This is not to say that no one else is involved. Because the experience of anger usually includes physical arousal, it may be partly observable to others. Anger also typically occurs in a social setting, rarely in isolation. Anger, in fact, usually derives its meaning from a social context. Anger most often arises in response to what happens (or does not happen) within social interactions. Nevertheless, it must be remembered that anger is an emotion, not a behavior. Angry feelings lead to a wide range of different behaviors (Averill, 1983).

AGGRESSION

Aggression, on the other hand, is behavior, an action which is intended to hurt or harm another. It is one way of expressing angry feelings. The exact behaviors are difficult to specify. A gesture, a smile, a word, a grunt, a silence, an action, or inaction, all can constitute aggression. It can also be expressed indirectly, through inaction or noncompliance—a style called **passive-aggressive** behavior. A student who sits in the front row and sleeps or reads the newspaper during a class may be communicating resentment to the professor passively, rather than telling the professor directly why he or she is angry. An action is understood as aggressive because of its intent or function, the motivation of one individual to hurt or intimidate another.

Aggression is sometimes defined by this underlying motivation: aggressive acts are hostile in intent and hurtful in purpose (Berkowitz, 1962). The inflicting of actual injury is not necessary. An angry child who hurls a block at a playmate has behaved aggressively, even if the block misses its target. Criminal law punishes *attempted* robbery, assault, or homicide even if no actual harm occurred. In one sense, then, aggression is defined by the social interpretation of an act, by the perceived motivation or intent to harm.

Yet aggression can also occur independently of anger, as when a soldier or hired assassin kills a total stranger. Likewise aggressive behavior need not involve a specific intention to harm. Reckless driving, for example, is a punishable aggressive behavior, whether or not the driver intended to harm others.

Anger
emotional arousal that is negative in tone, and cognitively associated with a particular person or situation.

Aggression
behavior that inflicts harm upon another, or is intended to do so.

Passive-Aggressive Behavior
behavior that is intended to frustrate or provoke another, but takes the form of inaction or obstruction rather than overt aggression.

Certain crimes, such as manslaughter, specifically consist of inflicting injury without having intended or planned to do so. Furthermore, certain aggressive acts are carried out not in order to injure, but rather to accomplish a desired result. The belligerent executive who intimidates competitors, the drug addict who robs, or those who plan and carry out warfare may do so not to injure, but rather to achieve a particular benefit or payoff.

Some psychologists (Feshbach, 1970; Hartup, 1974) have attempted to deal with this complexity by distinguishing two kinds of aggression: *hostile* aggression, in which the intent is to injure, and *instrumental* aggression, in which the behavior is directed at achieving a desired outcome other than harming. This differentiation of two types of aggression has yielded some interesting research results. Hartup (1974), for example, reported that although boys and girls did not differ in the amount of instrumental aggression they showed, boys were significantly higher in hostile aggression. The distinction is limited, however, because aggressive acts often serve both instrumental and hostile functions.

Aggression, then, is a complex behavior pattern. It can be an action intended to harm, even though no injury occurs. It also can consist of injurious behavior, even though no hostility was intended. Aggression is defined by a combination of (1) certain actions having a potential or actual result of harm to another and (2) a social judgment regarding the intention of the act (Bandura, 1973).

ASSERTION

Assertion is also behavior. It represents a middle ground between two extremes. One of these extremes is aggression, as just described: promoting one's own interests at the expense of the needs and feelings of others. At the other extreme is unassertive or **submissive** behavior, in which one's own needs and feelings are ignored and suppressed in favor of others (Alberti & Emmons, 1986). Aggressive behavior lacks concern and respect for others. Submissive behavior lacks concern and respect for oneself. Said another way, aggression sacrifices love in the interest of power, while submission sacrifices power and justice in the hope of keeping peace (Augsberger, 1979). It is not uncommon for people (and relationships) to cycle back and forth between these two extremes.

Assertion is behavior in which one's own feelings (angry or otherwise) are expressed in an effective and balanced manner that is respectful both of self and of others. It is the direct, honest, situationally appropriate expression of one's feelings, opinions, or beliefs. It shows consideration, but not deference, for others. It is not intended to harm or intimidate others, but rather to express and assert one's own feelings or rights. Assertive behavior is a middle ground of effective coping, that neither violates the rights of others nor sacrifices one's own dignity.

NORMAL VERSUS ABNORMAL

Assertion
behavior that expresses one's feelings or views without violating the rights of others; a middle ground between aggression and submission.

Submissive Behavior
behavior that acquiesces to the desires of others.

Cultures and societies differ widely in the amount of anger and aggression that they tolerate. Norway and Sweden, for example, are relatively peaceable nations. Violence is not permitted on television, to the extent that many American cartoons are prohibited because of the aggressive content. Behavior that might be acceptably "aggressive" or assertive in a more violent culture is likely to be seen as socially unacceptable in Scandinavian society. Within a more heterogeneous nation, certain subcultures (such as the Amish of Pennsylvania, Ohio, and Indiana) intentionally adopt a pacifist life-style and shun all hostile behavior.

9.1 EXAMPLES OF AGGRESSIVE, SUBMISSIVE, AND ASSERTIVE BEHAVIOR

SITUATION	AGGRESSIVE RESPONSE	SUBMISSIVE RESPONSE	ASSERTIVE RESPONSE
Professor gives you a grade that you believe is unfair.	Write a formal complaint to the university president, without discussing your grade with the professor.	Accept the grade without question.	Discuss the grade with your professor, and explain why it seems unfair to you.
You have parked your car at a curb and return to find someone parked so close to your bumper you can hardly get out.	Let the air out of their tires, and bump the car forcefully several times as you try to get out of the parking space.	Just ease out of the space and drive away.	Leave a polite note on the windshield explaining how their parking so close made it difficult for you.
You buy a gallon of milk and find that it has gone sour.	Complain loudly to the manager in front of other customers about the store's poor health standards.	Pour out the milk and buy another gallon.	Return to the store and ask for a fresh gallon.
At a party, a casual acquaintance rests his arm on your shoulder in a way that feels uncomfortable.	Say, "Keep your hands to yourself," loud enough for a number of others to hear.	Do nothing. Wait for him to move his arm.	Lift the person's arm off your shoulder.

The point is that what is "normal" behavioral expression with regard to anger, aggression, and assertion depends upon the social group within which it occurs and is judged. This is true, in part, because aggression is *defined* in relation to a social judgment of its intent. What constitutes healthy assertive coping behavior in one setting may be maladaptive in another context. Expressing disagreement, for example, may bring about a stimulating discussion in one setting, but cause the loss of a job in another.

Certain types of aggression are regarded as unacceptable in almost every society. Even under conditions of war, aggression against helpless victims is almost universally rejected as inhumane. There are widely recognized psychiatric diagnoses (American Psychiatric Association, 1987) for individuals who are impulsively or unpredictably violent (**explosive disorder**) or who without remorse consistently violate the rights of others (antisocial personality).

✗ Explosive Disorder
a pattern of repeated episodes of serious aggression that is far out of proportion to any provocation that may have been present (DSM-III-R).

9.2   HERE WE DIFFER/HERE WE AGREE
Should Handgun Ownership Be Controlled?

It seems to me that a more fundamental question here is when aggression, even with deadly force, might be acceptable. Certainly my own feelings about this were influenced by the December 7 morning when I woke up at Pearl Harbor to realize that people were dropping bombs on me. I knew it was nothing personal, of course, but I certainly responded on a personal level! In a peacetime society, it is easy enough to talk about aggression as through it is always inappropriate, but I would guess that very few people who have been through an experience like that bombing would reject aggression as a way of defending yourself.

The question, then, becomes: "When is self-defensive aggression warranted?" A relevant case that made national headlines was that of the "subway vigilante," a young man who was accosted by four youths in a New York subway. Perceiving that his life was in jeopardy, he shot and killed one of the youths. Was this justifiable aggression? Every society has to face this question and define for itself what is going to be acceptable and unacceptable aggression. It would be very nice if all governments and all people could come to an agreement that no one would ever engage in aggressive acts again. Given our history, that seems rather unlikely, and instead we had better find realistic ways to protect ourselves. Some states have passed a law that stipulates that if someone enters your home against your wishes and you shoot them, you need not be tried. This has been variously described as self-defense or as the "make my day" law. In any event, it does seem valid to me that people need a safe haven.

So what about handguns? Our nation historically has left it up to the individual whether to own one. If you personally don't wish to have one in your home, that's fine. But should I be prevented from protecting myself in this way if I choose? Those who wish to commit violent or illegal acts have always found a way to do so, even before handguns were invented. I think we have a right to choose whether and how to protect ourselves.

—JMR

In 1989, Sarah Kemp Brady received a "Woman of the Year" award from *Ms. Magazine* for her work against the powerful gun lobby and "for proving the power of personal experience as a catalyst for political action" (Weller, 1989). Her husband, President Reagan's Press Secretary, was shot in the head with a handgun in 1981. James Brady did not die, but requires ongoing supportive care. Ms. Brady has been working for a law that would require those who wish to purchase handguns to wait for approval of their application, while a background check is completed.

Such an approval period, a minimal step toward handgun control, could save many lives. As we were completing the writing of this book, a local example became national news. A man hired an Albuquerque taxi driver to take him to a gun shop. He told the driver he wanted to kill some "Nazis," and his conversation reflected serious mental disturbance. He was able to purchase a handgun, and within hours he used it to kill three innocent people. He then fled to California, where he killed two guards at Universal Studios before he was stopped. A simple background check could have revealed that he had walked away from a mental institution in another state, and the needless deaths of five people could have been prevented.

Self-defense is often cited as an argument for owning a handgun. However, my self-defense teacher at our Rape Crisis Center noted that weapons can be and have been seized and used *against* their owners. I do not recommend carrying a gun for that reason.

Perhaps a cross-cultural perspective can provide insight into this issue. New Zealand, for example, has significantly less violence than the United States. Their laws require the issuance of a firearms license through the local police department. In addition, the purchaser must be over eighteen years of age and must have a specific purpose for ownership of the weapon (such as target shooting). In New Zealand, even police officers do not carry guns.

Handguns invite violence. Their ownership should be carefully controlled.   —CEY

We live in a violent society. According to a recent national survey, about 4 percent—1 in every 25 of us—have lost a close relative or friend through homicide. The vast majority of murders are committed with handguns or other firearms (such as automatic weapons) designed specifically for the taking of human life. We take such weapons (and the "right" to own them) for granted. At least since the invention of motion pictures and television, many of our mythical national heroes have carried and used such weapons.

A waiting period to purchase a gun is a step in the right direction, but only a small one. On January 17, 1989, a young man in Stockton, California, dressed up in army fatigues and went to a schoolyard armed with two handguns and an automatic rifle capable of firing ten bullets per second. He killed five children, aged 6 through 9, and wounded thirty-two others before shooting himself in the head. He had purchased his weapons legally, filling out the required paperwork. His extensive criminal record had not been detected, however, because he had changed his name.

For me, the question is: "Why does any citizen *need* to possess such weapons?" Handguns and automatic weapons are extremely lethal. They can be used to kill rapidly, repeatedly, and from a distance. Their only real usefulness is for threatening, injuring, and killing human beings. Though it can be argued that "Guns don't kill people, people kill people," the truth in our society is that in a majority of cases, people with guns kill people.

I recognize the intent of our constitutional provision of a right to bear arms. I do not believe, however, that the authors of the Constitution could have foreseen the extent to which firearms would be refined and used by our citizens to slaughter each other. Surely there is some middle ground that can be found between an unarmed society and one in which there is free access to Saturday night specials and semiautomatic firearms that are easily converted into automatic weapons. There are entire, modern, civilized, democratic societies in which such weapons are not sold, and where even the police do not carry guns. The founders of our nation intended that our citizenry should be safe.

It takes the most incredible level of denial to believe, today, that we are somehow "safer" by allowing relatively unrestricted possession of handguns and automatic weapons in our society. It would be a very long road from here to an America that shuns such weapons. It's time we started moving in that direction.

—WRM

INTEGRATION

Issues such as this pose complex problems for the makers of social policy. As with other issues (such as mandatory seat belt laws and drinking/driving laws), the rights and freedom of individuals must be weighed against the larger costs and risks to society. Handguns are involved in a major proportion of homicides in the United States. Those most likely to be killed by a handgun are the owner and his or her family members and acquaintances. Yet many individuals and several national lobby groups strongly oppose any regulation of individuals' ability to purchase and own handguns, maintaining that people have a right to defend themselves. What do you think? How should controversial social policy issues of this kind be decided?

One can also imagine circumstances under which the *absence* of anger or aggressive intervention could be regarded as abnormal or unhealthy. Such is the case of bystanders who witness a rape or other violent assault without attempting to come to the aid of the victim. At a societal level, psychologists have described the phenomenon of **psychic numbing,** a passive acceptance of violence and the social conditions that promote it.

■ DEVELOPMENTAL ASPECTS OF ANGER AND AGGRESSION

Psychic Numbing
an acquired insensitivity to threatening conditions or actions.

Perhaps because anger (a largely internal and subjective state) is more difficult to observe and measure than overt behaviors, most developmental studies have focused on aggression rather than anger. The central question addressed in such research is how aggression is learned and encouraged in the course of human development.

INNATE DRIVE

Some theorists have postulated the existence of an innate aggressive drive or instinct. Sigmund Freud (1933) in his later writings proposed a tension within every individual between a life force (*eros*) and an inherent drive toward aggression and destruction (*thanatos*). This model resembles, and was probably influenced by, the insights of energy physics that were emerging in Freud's time, which emphasized opposing and interacting forces.

Some observers of animal behavior (e.g., Lorenz, 1966) have likewise concluded that aggression is inborn throughout the animal world. Predictable patterns of male competitive aggression and social dominance hierarchies are readily observable in many species. Like Freud, Lorenz proposed that aggression arises from a built-in energized behavior pattern that does not require learning or external stimulation to be released.

Taken to extreme, these views breed a certain pessimism regarding the future of humankind. If there is an innate drive toward self-destruction or the destruction of others, the implications are ominous in a world with increasingly devastating weapons. Psychologists, however, have disputed the existence or importance of these hypothesized innate drives or instincts, and have provided persuasive data indicating that the occurrence of aggression is strongly influenced by social learning processes (Bandura, 1973; Parke & Slaby, 1983).

PARENTING STYLE

Research indicates that the *family* plays a key role in determining how aggressively an individual will behave. One study that followed a sample of children through ages 9 to 19 found that more aggressive adolescents came from homes in which the parents were more rejecting, gave less positive attention to the children, used punishment but did not reward prosocial behavior, and experienced more marital conflict (Eron, Walder, & Lefkowitz, 1971; Lefkowitz et al., 1977). This is consistent with more general findings that aggressive children have experienced less affection and more rejection from parents (Parke & Slaby, 1983).

The extent to which children rely upon aggressive behavior is also apparently influenced by the manner in which parents respond to such coercive tactics. Baumrind (1967) classified school children on their level of aggression and then observed parent-child interactions in a standard laboratory setting. The parents of friendly and nonaggressive children, she found, simply did not respond to coercive demands from the child. Instead they responded positively to verbal discussion. The parents of more aggressive children, by contrast, showed the greatest tendency to give in to coercive behaviors from their children and demanded less maturity in problem-solving approaches. In short, parents who reinforced aggressive behavior (by giving in to it) had children who were more aggressive than the children of parents who were unresponsive to coercive behavior. Similar parenting patterns in the families of aggressive children have been reported by Patterson and his colleagues (Patterson, Cobb, & Ray, 1973).

MODELING

Modeling is the process of learning by observing. Research evidence is clear and strong that aggressive behavior is powerfully influenced by modeling. Reviewing a large group of studies on this topic, Bandura (1973) concluded that observational learning influences aggression in at least three important

Parenting styles exert an important influence on how children deal with and express anger.

ways. First, children learn new ways to behave aggressively by observing others. Witnessing live, filmed, or cartoon characters perform novel aggressive behaviors, children subsequently mimic the very actions they saw. Second, modeling has a more general disinhibiting effect, so that children who witness aggressive models are more likely to perform other previously learned aggressive behaviors that were not shown by the model. Finally, children learn by seeing the consequences of the aggressive acts of others. When children observe a model behaving aggressively and then being punished for it, they tend not to copy the behavior. On the other hand, when the model gets away with the aggression, either by being reinforced or by suffering no consequence at all, children who witness the aggressive behavior are likely to mimic it.

These effects are not restricted to children, of course. Individuals who commit antisocial and criminal acts sometimes report having gotten the idea from a television show or a news report of a previous, similar crime. Mob behavior demonstrates the general disinhibiting effect of witnessing aggression in others. Aggressive behavior in adults is controlled, at least in part, by the perceived probability of punishment or adverse personal consequences.

The effects of aggressive modeling can be long-lived. Research indicates that adults who were themselves abused as children are at substantially higher risk for abusing their own children (Silver, Dublin, & Lourie, 1969).

ENTERTAINMENT

If exposure to modeled aggression contributes to actual aggressive behavior, there is much reason for concern about current entertainment programming. Children on average spend over six hours per day watching television—more time than they spend engaging in any other waking activity, including attending school classes, interacting with family members, or playing with other children (Collins & Wiens, 1983; Lyle, 1972). It has been estimated that by the age of 16, the average American child has watched 13,000 homicides on television (Waters & Melamud, 1975). This level of violence on television remained fairly constant through three decades (Gerbner et al., 1980). Male aggression and female deference are the rule during children's commercial television programs, with twice as many male roles portrayed, and with female characters punished for deviance from traditional feminine behavior (Sternglanz & Serbin, 1974).

What effects does TV violence have on aggressive behavior? Many of the studies which have shown a clear modeling effect (seeing and then imitating) in children employed filmed or videotaped models (Bandura, 1973). A federal report on television and violence indicated that extended viewing of violence contributes both to increased rates of aggression and to passive acceptance of aggressive behavior in others (Pearl, Bouthilet, & Lzar, 1982). That is, prolonged exposure to modeled violence not only promotes violence, but also tends to desensitize the viewer to violence in others (Parke & Slaby, 1983). Aggression comes to be seen as normal and acceptable behavior.

It is sometimes argued that violence on television will not promote modeling, because within the plots of programs it is generally punished, leading to negative outcomes. Research on the comprehension of television programming, however, indicates that children do not understand the relationship between the aggressive actions portrayed and the negative consequences that occur (Collins & Wiens, 1983). Often the negative consequences are delayed until the end of the program, well removed in time from the aggression itself. Act and consequences may be separated, as well, by numerous commercials. Collins (1973) found that levels of aggression by children who had viewed aggressive television programming were increased when acts and consequences were separated by commercials. Further, the negative consequences may be portrayed only briefly or indirectly (such as being arrested, with the implication that the perpetrator will be punished by the courts). Consequently, children tend to recall the aggressive scenes but not link such "action" to consequences.

PEER INFLUENCE

Peers likewise exert important influences on aggression through their modeling of aggressive behavior and patterns of reinforcement and punishment.

Children spend about 6 hours per day watching TV and are exposed to thousands of acts of aggression and violence.

9.3 CHILDREN AND TELEVISION

It is clear from current research that television viewing can strongly influence children's attitudes, values, and behaviors. What can parents do to decrease the detrimental effects of television on their children? One approach, of course, is to restrict the amount of time spent watching television and to limit the types of programming that may be viewed. Here are some other ideas that appear promising, based on research evidence:

1. Watch programs with your children, and make evaluative comments about what is happening. This helps children to evaluate what they see, and compare it with parental values.

2. Explain, while viewing with children, how different parts of the plot are related to each other, and how consequences follow from actions.

3. Explain to children the techniques used in making television programs (special effects, stunts, promoting identification with characters, stereotypes), to help them separate fantasy and reality.

4. Discuss the techniques of intentional influencing used in television programming and commercial advertising. Explain why and how such techniques are used, and the effect they are intended to produce.

5. Prepare children for viewing by discussing, before a program, what to expect and what to look for during the program. Give an assignment to remember certain aspects of the plot (what happens to the people who do bad things), or to observe the influencing strategies used in advertising.

6. Discuss with children how what was portrayed on a program compares with their own real-life experience, and what they have learned in other settings.

Source: Adapted from Collins and Wiens (1983).

Children who display aggressive behavior increase the rate of aggression in their peers (Parke & Slaby, 1983). If aggressive behavior is reinforced by peers (by giving in to demands, for example, or by positive attention), the aggression is likely to be repeated (Patterson, 1976; Patterson & Reid, 1970). It appears that peer influence is most potent in the immediate situation, while the effects of modeling from parents and entertainment media are more long lasting. Indirect effects of aggression on peer relationships may, however, result in more enduring effects. Aggressive children may, for example, alienate themselves from their more socialized peers, thereby depriving themselves of multiple opportunities to learn nonaggressive social skills for coping with life problems and challenges (Dodge, 1983). This can become a self-perpetuating cycle, because children who are disliked or rejected by their peers tend to be more aggressive (Dodge, Coie, & Brakke, 1982; Shantz, 1986).

SEX DIFFERENCES

Women and men, despite common stereotypes about sex differences, are more similar than different with regard to situations and stimuli that evoke anger. Both genders feel angry equally often, and for similar reasons (Averill, 1983). Both men and women tend to find it difficult to express anger toward authority figures, people who have more power or status. Both are more likely to vent their anger with a safe person at home. Sex differences have less impact on *feelings* of anger than the situation does (Tavris & Wade, 1984).

When one examines how anger is *expressed*, however, differences emerge. The most consistently documented gender difference supported in the research literature is a higher level of aggressive behavior in males than in females (Maccoby & Jacklin, 1974), especially in hostile (as opposed to instrumental) aggression (Hartup, 1974). These differences emerge very early in life, long before substantial effects from socialization would be expected. Gender differences are consistent across a wide range of aggressive behaviors and have been observed in virtually every culture studied to date. Similar sex differences in aggression are also found in subhuman primates.

Nevertheless, under certain conditions men and women may show equal levels of aggression. This appears to be true in situations where aggression is seen as clearly justifiable or prosocial. Overall the data suggest that men and women experience similar levels of the feelings of anger and hostility, but their behavioral expressions of these feelings may differ. For several reasons, males are more likely than females to express anger as aggression. Boys, more than girls, appear to believe that aggression will lead to positive and desirable consequences (Perry, Perry, & Rasmussen, 1986). There also seem to be important gender differences in the aftermath of aggressive behavior. Following aggression, women consistently show greater anxiety, fear, and guilt, and also evidence substantially greater empathy for the victim (Frodi, Macaulay, & Thome, 1977).

■ ANGER, AGGRESSION, ASSERTION, AND THE STORC

In Chapter 3 we presented the STORC model as one approach to understanding and coping with human emotion. We made specific use of this model in discussing mood and depression (Chapter 7) as well as fear, stress, and anxiety (Chapter 8). In this section we will again use the STORC analysis approach as we discuss anger, aggression, and assertion.

S—SITUATIONAL FACTORS

Situational factors can contribute to angry feelings and aggressive behavior. *Environmental irritants* represent one general type of stimuli that may evoke irritability, impatience, resentment, or other variations of angry feelings. Noise, for example, is such an irritant. Living or working in a noisy environment can promote physiological arousal and anger (Broadbent, 1971; Frankenhaeuser & Lundberg, 1977; Cohen et al., 1980). Furthermore, exposure to noise can increase the likelihood of aggression in angry people (Donnerstein & Wilson, 1976; Konecni et al., 1975). High temperatures may also promote hot tempers. The hottest days of summer have been associated with increased rates of violence and rioting in urban settings (Carlsmith & Anderson, 1979).

Crowding is another environmental factor that invokes anger, or at least discomfort, in many people. Have you ever felt irritated by someone who seemed to be invading your personal space? A chronic lack of sufficient office or parking space around many universities creates friction between people vying for available spaces. Situations that involve prolonged conditions of crowding can result in arousal that may take the form of anger, stress, or aggression. Research with laboratory animals shows that overcrowding, housing too many animals in a confined space, results in increased aggressive behavior.

The concept of **personal space** or territory is, in fact, one that extends to large portions of the animal kingdom. In many species, individuals or pairs of animals establish and mark off a territory as their own. This represents a "home base" where the animal is relatively safe from attack. Other individuals who intrude into this territory evoke threat or attack behavior. Many species also evidence a personal space zone around the individual. As long as others keep this minimum of distance, relations are peaceful. If another individual comes within this minimum distance, however, conflict and protection responses (attack, threat, flight) occur.

Frustration is another commonly cited situational factor contributing to anger and aggression (Feshbach, 1970). Frustration is defined as encountering obstacles which interfere with one's ability to achieve a desired goal. Such obstacles may have a clear physical form (encountering a locked door, or striking a large rock when digging a hole), or they may be more abstract (unrequited love, or failure to receive an expected promotion). There are, of course, large individual differences among people regarding what is perceived as frustrating, and how it is handled. For example, negative feedback from an employer may feel to one employee like an attack and a threat to continued employment, whereas to another worker the same feedback may simply be interpreted as useful information in order to improve job performance.

Even when frustration occurs, it does not dictate how an individual will respond. How you respond to potentially frustrating situational factors depends on you! During World War II, psychologists participated in the selection of military officers who could hold up under stressful conditions (U.S. Office of Strategic Services, 1948). Officer candidates were given a time-limited task to perform, and were told that because it could not be done by one man within the allotted time, they would have two helpers. What the officer candidate did not know was that his two "helpers" were actually psychologists involved in the evaluation. The "helpers" provided intentional obstacles such as incompetent decisions, slow pace, noncooperation, heckling, and mistakes. The real test was not how quickly the candidate performed the problem-solving task (in fact, no one ever finished it!), but rather how the officer candidate handled these frustrating obstacles and the people involved.

Aggression is also a common, though by no means automatic, response when pain is inflicted on a person or animal (Berkowitz, 1983). Aggression is more likely to occur if escape is not an option (as when an animal that normally flees is "cornered"). When aggression is stimulated by pain, it may serve both an instrumental (to stop the cause of the pain) and a hostile (revenge) function.

Other situational factors that influence arousal level can also promote anger and aggression. Overuse of common stimulants, such as caffeine and nicotine, can increase arousal. The sleep deprivation inherent in some life situations, such as medical school training, or the parenting of infants, can promote irritability. Physical pain likewise may increase angry feelings and aggressive reactions. Thomas Gordon (1970) suggested that anger is *always* a secondary emotion, occurring in response to a previous emotional reaction of either pain or fear. Thus, in Gordon's view, anger occurs because the person has first been hurt or frightened in some way.

Social conditions such as modeling and social pressure can also powerfully influence aggressive behavior. Stanley Milgram (1963) provided a dramatic demonstration of this in a widely cited experiment. Ordinary men and women were recruited to participate in what they were told was a study of learning and memory principles. They were shown a shock apparatus with 30 switches, labeled to indicate the intensity of the shock, ranging from mild to extremely

Personal Space
a region of definable distance from the body that, when entered by another individual, evokes specific meaning or emotional response.

Frustration
a condition that prevents an individual from achieving a desired goal.

dangerous. They met a man who was to be the "learner" and saw the man strapped into a chair with electrodes attached. Unknown to the subject, the learner was actually a confederate of the experimenter and received no shocks. The subject's instructions were to deliver a shock every time the learner made an error, increasing the intensity of the shock by one level for each error. As the experimental sessions progressed, the learner made multiple errors and increasingly severe shocks were "administered." As shock intensity increased, the learner began to complain, then to scream in agony. As the subjects became uncomfortable and asked whether they should continue, the experimenter (dressed in a white laboratory coat) insisted that the study must go on. The actual purpose of the study was to determine to what extent subjects would obey the experimenter and continue to inflict extremely painful, even potentially fatal shocks. Under these circumstances, nearly two-thirds of the subjects followed orders to the end of the experiment, delivering what they believed to be extremely painful and dangerous shocks to a helpless victim. They did so despite their own obvious distress. The situational demands for obedience were strong enough to turn these ordinary citizens into apparent torturers.

The modification of situational (S) factors offers one promising route for alleviating excessive anger or aggressive behavior. It would be possible, for example, to keep an ongoing diary of angry feelings, taking notes on the situations in which they occur. As particular situational antecedents of anger are identified, ways can be sought to avoid or decrease these anger-evoking stimuli. Alternatively, by the method of systematic desensitization (see Chapter 8), sensitivity to such situations might be decreased, so that they lead to less arousal. It is possible, for example, for new parents to become desensitized to the higher noise level in their home, so that this somewhat inevitable part of child-rearing is less arousing and aggravating.

T—THOUGHT PATTERNS IN ANGER

In Chapter 2, we noted that the way in which an event is *perceived* plays an important role in how a person reacts. Every event of your life is perceived through your own personal filters of memory, learning, attention, and expectations, by which the event takes on certain meaning for you. An event that triggers anger in one person may seem neutral to another person who perceives it through a different filter.

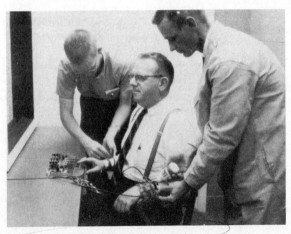

Stanley Milgram's obedience study.

This points to the importance of cognitive factors in anger. Few events, if any, are inherently anger-producing. Anger does not follow *automatically* from a situation, but rather, depends on the *interpretation* given to that experience. Anger is controlled by one's perception and interpretation of events.

Sometimes one additional piece of information can alter an interpretation dramatically, so that anger turns rapidly into another emotional response. Consider two examples. A co-worker or a salesperson may seem to be ignoring you, paying little attention to what you say, and pretending not to hear. This might evoke feelings of anger and resentment toward this insensitive and obtuse person. Then you discover that the person is hard of hearing and wears a hearing aid which, it turns out, needs a new battery. Suddenly the interpretation of the event changes, and with it your emotional reaction. A second example is a woman who observes her husband, over a period of weeks, sneaking out of the house at odd hours, writing notes that he quickly hides away when she comes near, making and receiving telephone calls which he obviously does not want her to overhear. Convinced that he is having an affair, she becomes enraged and decides to confront him with his infidelity. The night before she plans to do so, however, she is startled on entering their home to find a surprise birthday party complete with many friends and special, loving efforts. The meaning of what she has been seeing changes immediately, and her anger turns to joy and appreciation.

The point is that anger is strongly driven by cognitive interpretations. Anger may be evoked suddenly by a situational event. In order to *remain* angry, however, it is necessary to keep rehearsing the perceived injustices or frustrations, to keep the cognitions and images alive by remembering and focusing on them over and over.

For this reason, the cognitive restructuring approach introduced in Chapter 6 can be applied in dealing with anger as well. Current treatment approaches for reducing excessive anger and aggressive behavior often focus heavily on understanding and changing cognitive patterns (Novaco, 1975). The cognitive reinterpretation of events may help to diminish unhealthy anger. New thought patterns, such as forgiveness, may be practiced to diminish angry arousal (Miller & Jackson, 1985).

Just as certain thought patterns may lead toward depression (see Chapter 7), so specific patterns of perception have been associated with anger and with aggressive behavior. More aggressive children, for example, tend to perceive that aggression is easier for them, and that it is likely to lead to positive and desirable outcomes (Perry, Perry, & Rasmussen, 1986). Boys showing high levels of anger and aggression tend to overperceive hostile intentions in the behavior of their peers (Dodge & Frame, 1982). Increased aggressive behavior among intoxicated individuals may be due in part to a similar effect of alcohol on perception: intoxicated people tend to incorrectly perceive others' behavior toward them as hostile and threatening. When the accidental or neutral actions of others are interpreted as intentionally hostile, angry feelings and aggression are likely to result (Dodge, 1980; Dodge & Frame, 1982). Research also suggests that aggressive individuals are deficient in an important cognitive and emotional skill: _empathy_, the ability to take the perspective of another person and imagine or understand how a situation would be perceived from that person's point of view (Chandler, 1973; Feshbach & Feshbach, 1969). Training in empathy has been found to reduce aggression in children (Feshbach & Feshbach, 1982).

Consistent with these findings, research has shown that the teaching of certain cognitive skills may help in reducing anger and aggression. Learning to think through the consequences of aggression before acting it out, taking the perspective of others in the situation, or considering alternative interpretations of a situation can curb impulsive aggressiveness and diminish chronic angry feelings (Camp, 1977; Meichenbaum, 1977; Novaco, 1975).

9.4   FORGIVENESS AND MENTAL HEALTH

Forgiveness is usually thought of as a spiritual issue, and appropriately so. Yet this same concept has important implications for mental health, particularly where anger is concerned. Anger toward a specific person or situation is retained only if it is actively refueled, if the hurts and injustices are continually rehearsed. Chronic anger, in this sense, represents a failure to forgive, a reluctance to let go. Forgiveness is a response to anger.

People sometimes find it difficult to forgive. This arises in part because forgiveness is often confused with five other things. Realizing that forgiveness is not the same as any of these five things can be helpful in finally letting go:

First, forgiveness is not the same as *amnesia*. Forgiving and forgetting are different acts. Forgiveness does not require forgetting. In fact, one can hardly forgive that which has already been forgotten! Forgiveness is given in the face of remembering, and if anything it is forgiveness that enables forgetting. Certainly forgetting is no prerequisite, nor does forgiveness require the promise to forget (which may actually be much more difficult).

Secondly, forgiveness is not *acquittal*. Forgiveness does not mean that the person is found blameless and without responsibility. To the contrary, forgiveness is only required when responsibility of the individual is recognized. One need not deny responsibility in order to be forgiven, nor does forgiveness require later denial by either party. Forgiveness is given in the face of responsibility.

Thirdly, forgiveness is not an *award*. It is not earned, or given to those most deserving. Forgiveness is given freely, without regard for merit.

Fourthly, forgiveness is not *approval*. To forgive an action is not to approve of that action or agree with it. It does not require that the forgiving person say, "I think what you did was OK." In fact, forgiveness is needed only when one does not approve. It is given in the face of disapproval.

Finally, forgiveness is not *acquiescence*. It is not a license to go and do as one pleases in the future. It is not a moratorium on values, a suspension of rules. It is not permission to stay the same, but rather in a very mysterious way forgiveness itself inspires and enables change. Forgiveness is given in the face of the knowledge that the future may or may not be different, but also with the enabling hope that it will. (Miller & Jackson, 1985, p. 252)

Instead of these, forgiveness is a decision, a choice to accept the *person* but not his or her actions. It is a way of letting go of the negative, with a fresh start for the future.

The acceptance that forgiveness requires may also have positive benefits for self-acceptance (Chapter 6). There appears to be a relationship between the ability to accept others and self-acceptance. People with low self-esteem have more difficulty in developing empathy for others (Miller, Hedrick, & Orlofsky, 1982). The practice of extending forgiveness to others may, in the end, enable the experience of forgiveness for oneself.

Holding certain beliefs may also increase the likelihood of feelings of anger and resentment (Ellis & Harper, 1975; Lazarus & Faye, 1975; Novaco, 1975). The narcissistic expectation that "Things should always go as I planned," or that "Others should always give in and do things my way" is very likely to lead to frustration. Later in this chapter we will discuss the "Type A pattern," a set of beliefs and behaviors associated with chronic anger, aggressive behavior, and health problems.

Yet another cognitive factor playing a role in anger is the individual's perception of his or her own physiological arousal. In a classic experiment, Schachter and Singer (1962) injected human subjects with adrenalin. The sympathetic nervous system arousal effects of the drug were explained to some subjects, whereas others were given no expectation of effects from the drug. When they began to feel emotionally aroused, the former group could explain it as a drug effect, whereas the latter group had no obvious explanation of their experience. The experimenters further had each subject interact with another "subject" who, in fact, was a trained confederate. In some cases the confederate behaved in a carefree, euphoric, and playful manner. With other subjects, the confederate behaved in an angry and irritable fashion. The main finding of the study was that subjects *uninformed* of the drug effect reported and showed an emotion consistent with the reaction of their partner-confederate. Those subjects with the euphoric confederate felt happy and behaved playfully. Those subjects with the irritable confederate felt angry and were verbally aggressive. Subjects who knew that their arousal was due to the drug, on the other hand, showed less of this emotional contagion. The usual interpretation of these findings is that general sympathetic arousal is interpreted as any of various emotions (anger, euphoria, fear) based upon situational factors. The arousal underlying these emotions is similar, but the interpretation of the arousal is different depending upon one's social situation.

This socially influenced labeling of arousal may account for one apparent sex difference in emotional responsiveness. Physically arousing situations that evoke anger in men may be more likely to be experienced as anxiety-producing in women (Frodi et al., 1977). For example, imagine two people who have just been involved in a minor automobile accident. Both are experiencing a high level of sympathetic nervous system arousal. One may interpret his arousal as anger, and react with aggression. The other may interpret her arousal as fear, and react accordingly.

Finally, it should be noted that cognitive processes also exert an important influence on how a person responds when angered. What determines whether an angered person will, in a particular situation, remain silent, become verbally aggressive, cry, withdraw, or strike out physically? The person's perceptions and interpretation of the situation are crucial. Few people, for example, physically assault their dentist or physician when he or she inflicts pain as part of a treatment procedure. Thought processes strongly influence how one reacts to pain or anger (Berkowitz, 1983).

O—ORGANIC ASPECTS OF ANGER

In Chapter 3 we discussed the activity of the sympathetic nervous system, and in Chapter 8 we considered some physiological aspects of stress and anxiety. Anger involves many of the same bodily responses. Think about what is happening in your body when you feel angry. Your heart beats faster, you may sweat or feel warm, your muscles may tighten up, your blood pressure rises. All of this arousal is the result of changes in your autonomic nervous system. Although there are some physiological differences among emotions (Ax, 1953), in many ways the autonomic arousal of anger closely resembles the bodily reactions of anxiety and stress, or even of sexual arousal. Thus the factors discussed in Chapter 8 as increasing sympathetic arousal in anxiety (caffeine, for example) may also accentuate anger. General emotional arousal contributes to increased anger and aggressive behavior (Rule & Nesdale, 1976). In this case, however, the "fight or flight" arousal of the sympathetic nervous system (Chapter 3) results in aggressive (fight) rather than avoidance behavior.

The biological bases of "fight or flight" responses can be seen in many animal species.

One organic strategy for reducing anger and aggression, then, is to decrease one's overall level of emotional (sympathetic) arousal. A lowering of overall arousal level may decrease irritability and increase the amount of provocation needed to invoke an aggressive response. Deep muscle relaxation (Appendix B), meditation, or physical exercise, when practiced regularly, can diminish physical arousal.

The physiology of anger and aggression is, however, considerably more complex than sympathetic arousal. The limbic system (Chapter 3) directly controls negative emotions such as anger and channels these emotions into responses such as aggression. The hypothalamus coordinates the activities of the limbic system with regard to emotion and self-preservation. A small electric current delivered to a portion of the limbic system will activate rage and attack behavior in a wide variety of animals ranging from fish to monkeys. More recent research indicates that the right hemisphere of the brain is most closely associated with the experience and expression of negative emotions, whereas the left side of the brain mediates positive emotions (Mesulan, 1985).

The role of brain functions in controlling emotions is clear when one observes the effects of various types of brain injury. Damage to the right hemisphere (as, for example, with a stroke on the right side of the brain, which paralyzes the left side of the body) often results in a somewhat carefree, even jocular attitude, with little apparent upset regarding the disability. Injuries or other abnormalities of the temporal lobe, containing key portions of the limbic system, may leave a person prone to unpredictable outbursts of violence.

It is clear, however, that the brain's role in aggression is strongly affected by learning factors. In a fascinating demonstration of this interaction of organic factors and social influence, Delgado (1963) delivered electrical stimulation to the brains of monkeys focusing on a region associated with rage and attack behavior in various species. The effect of this stimulation was strikingly influenced by the monkey's social position within the colony. The dominant male monkey of the colony, when stimulated, attacked males lower in the hierarchy, but did not attack females or the "number two" monkey with whom he shared leadership of the community. By contrast, when Delgado stimulated the brain of a monkey lower in the social dominance order, the animal showed not rage but fear and cowering behavior. The behavioral expressions of arousal are varied and are strongly influenced by the consequences resulting from such behavior.

R—RESPONSES TO ANGER

It is evident that even when anger is experienced, there are wide individual differences in how people respond to this emotion in themselves. Aggression is by no means an inevitable consequence of anger. It is only one behavioral response to angry feelings. There are many other possible responses to anger.

Some choose to *withdraw and escape* from the anger-provoking situation, rather than to stay and confront it. This is a viable and adaptive strategy in some situations. A person may also withdraw psychologically, becoming silent and passive without actually leaving the situation. Some engage in a distracting, vigorous, or engrossing activity such as running, chopping wood, or playing the piano. Besides withdrawing physically or psychologically, however, some people when angry seek escape through an addictive behavior (see Chapter 11). One research team found, for example, that people who were angered and then given no opportunity to express their anger drank significantly more alcohol immediately afterward, relative to those not angered or those who could express their anger (Marlatt, Kosturn, & Lang, 1975). Others may resort to overeating, or to the use of prescription or illicit drugs.

Submissive behavior is a more general strategy, in which the individual gives in to another at his or her own expense. Rather than expressing the anger directly or behaving aggressively, the person yields and defers to others. Consistent submission, however, may lead to other negative emotional patterns, including depression, anxiety, and low self-esteem. Anger may be expressed indirectly in behaviors such as crying, nail-biting, falling asleep, or even laughing.

Aggression, as defined earlier, consists of behavior that hurts or is intended to harm people or property. Aggressive behavior is substantially more likely to occur in the presence of anger and arousal (Rule & Nesdale, 1976), although some aggression is committed in the absence of anger or hostility. Some have argued that it is beneficial to "get anger out," and have speculated that aggressive behavior serves as a **catharsis,** relieving anger and aggressive impulses. Therapeutic strategies following from this mode of thinking may have clients punch pillows, batter imaginary targets, strike each other with heavily padded soft clubs, or practice other aggressionlike but harmless acts. Still other approaches have sought to induce rage in clients, in the belief that expressing rage is therapeutic. In fact, research fails to support this catharsis model or the therapeutic value of expressing anger through aggression. To the contrary, studies have consistently indicated that aggression breeds aggression, that practicing or even observing aggressive actions increases the likelihood that such behavior will be repeated in the future (Bandura, 1973).

Aggression may occur, in part, because a person lacks appropriate social skills for expressing emotion or having his or her needs met. Lacking alternative skills, the individual resorts to aggression. In his science fiction trilogy, *Foundation,* Isaac Asimov described a culture in which a guiding precept stated, "Violence is the last refuge of the incompetent." Similarly, one psychologist observed, "If the only tool you have is a hammer, you tend to treat everything as if it were a nail."

Research supports this perspective, pointing to a cluster of behaviors in certain children including aggressiveness, negativity, and unpopularity with peers. Such children are characterized by deficits in their social skills for solving problems, for resolving conflicts in nonaggressive ways, and for impulse control (Parke & Slaby, 1983). Deficient in pro-social skills, they rely upon aggressive behavior in an attempt to get what they want, thereby alienating

Catharsis
an experience that releases emotions that were previously repressed.

themselves from their peers and further handicapping themselves for the learning of vital social skills. Aggressive children, in effect, have fewer effective alternatives available for solving interpersonal problems than do nonaggressive children. Retraining aggressive children in more appropriate and effective responses, then, might be expected to diminish their aggressiveness and produce more general positive results. Programs that have modeled and coached nonaggressive problem-solving skills have shown positive results with such children (Camp, 1977; Meichenbaum, 1977; Zahavi & Asher, 1978).

Assertive behavior is a socially adaptive manner of expressing one's own feelings, needs, and rights. As described earlier, it is a middle ground between aggression and submissiveness. The concept of assertiveness has expanded substantially since its introduction in the 1960s (Alberti & Emmons, 1986). Here are some of the social skills included in assertiveness:

Saying no. Refusing a request, turning down an unwanted offer, setting limits.

Making requests. Asking for help, asking others to keep their commitments, standing up for one's own rights and those of others.

Negative feedback. Giving appropriate criticism, receiving negative feedback oneself, pointing out harmful consequences of another's actions.

Positive feedback. Giving appropriate praise or compliments, receiving positive feedback, expressing affection.

Expressing oneself. Giving an opinion, expressing one's feelings, defending a viewpoint.

Accepting responsibility. Admitting fault, openly acknowledging one's own feelings, taking responsibility for one's own part of a problem or conflict.

Assertion skills are, in essence, effective problem-solving skills for dealing with social relationships, conflicts, and problems. The assertive individual need not rely upon submissiveness or resort to aggression in dealing with day-to-day life. He or she has adaptive alternative responses.

C—CONSEQUENCES OF ANGER AND AGGRESSION

Given that an individual has a range of different possible responses to anger, which will he or she choose? In a brand new situation, a person may try out a variety of alternative behaviors. Children entering a new foster or adoptive home, for example, are likely to "test the limits" to learn what happens when different behaviors are tried. In the long run, however, the responses that endure will be those that are reinforced, that lead to desired consequences. How the social environment reacts to a behavior, such as aggression, will determine whether that behavior persists, increases, or diminishes.

Aggression is a somewhat unusual behavior, however, because desired outcomes can be obtained by the aggressor without relying upon the goodwill and willing cooperation of others (Bandura, 1973). Robbers, muggers, and rapists obtain reinforcement for their violent behavior not through the willing cooperation of their victims, but by coercion. Thus it is possible, at least for a time, for the individual to violate social laws and norms while still obtaining coerced reinforcement.

Sometimes aggressive behavior continues within ongoing relationships. Victims appear, at least, to be willing participants in patterns of coercion and violence within families or other social relationships. Do such people have a "need" to be victims? Gerald Patterson, in an influential analysis of aggressive behavior, provided an alternative explanation (Patterson, Littman, & Bricker,

9.5 PERSONAL MILESTONE
Learning to Be Assertive

In the mid-1970s, I attended my first assertion training workshop. It was held in a large meeting room with perhaps fifty women present. I remember only one aspect of the presentation. The workshop facilitator asked us to relax, close our eyes, and simply listen as she read from a document entitled "Everywoman's Bill of Rights."

She read statements such as, "You have the right to have your ideas and opinions respected. You have the right not to be automatically assumed wrong. You have the right to use your own judgment in deciding your own needs." Along with the rest of the workshop participants, I sat quietly, listening as the speaker read.

When she was finished reading, she asked us to continue to sit quietly, giving ourselves time to digest what we had just heard. I realized, sitting there in silence, that tears were rolling down my cheeks.

When I looked around the room, I saw that others had been deeply moved also. The realization that someone thought we had such rights, despite being raised in a culture which continues to deny women's rights, was powerful and hopeful for me.

For months afterward, that experience felt almost like a religious conversion, like being born again.   —CEY

1967; Patterson & Reid, 1970), describing how a pattern of **reciprocity** can develop to maintain the behavior of both the aggressor and the victim.

Consider the example of a day care setting for young children. One child, Robin, sees another, Fran, playing with an attractive toy. Robin asks Fran for the toy, and Fran refuses. Robin then begins throwing blocks at Fran, saying "Give me that toy!" Fran, hurt and frightened, hands over the toy.

What has happened in this situation? Clearly Robin has been reinforced for aggressive behavior. Asking didn't work, but aggression got Robin the desired toy. Fran reinforced Robin for throwing blocks, by giving in to the demand and turning over the toy. The process here is *positive reinforcement*. In the very same interaction, however, Fran was reinforced for submissiveness. The blocks were flying, a scary and threatening situation, until Fran yielded and released the toy. Then Robin stopped this threatening behavior. Thus Robin reinforced Fran for submitting. Fran's submissive behavior ended an aversive situation, the process of *negative reinforcement*. Both participants were reinforced for their reciprocal roles of aggressor and victim: Robin by winning the desired toy, Fran by escaping from a frightening situation. This interlocking pattern of reinforcement is what Patterson referred to as the reciprocity in coercion.

Through this pattern of reciprocal reinforcement, people may shape themselves into coercive relationships that involve family violence, social hierarchies, or even international relations. Those who would intervene to end patterns of violence, then, must attend to and address these powerful payoffs, the patterns of reinforcement that have maintained cycles of aggression. Changing the consequences of aggressive behavior can have dramatic results. When aggression no longer leads to reinforcement, it decreases markedly. Aggressive children, for example, show marked decreases in aggression when parents or teachers are taught not to reinforce it and instead to reinforce alternative behaviors (Patterson, 1971, 1974, 1976).

Through socialization, people differ in their private, internal consequences of aggression as well. As mentioned earlier, research with American adults indicates that women react with greater anxiety, guilt, and fear to aggression

Reciprocity
a pattern in which the behavior of two or more individuals is sustained by mutual reinforcement.

Aggression is sometimes rewarded when a child gets what he or she wants.

9.6   PREVENTING ACQUAINTANCE RAPE

Rape is a frighteningly common act of violence. At least one woman in three is sexually assaulted at some time during her life. Though rape is also committed by strangers, it is most likely to be inflicted by an acquaintance, someone known to the woman. It has been estimated that fewer than ten percent of such rapes are ever reported to the police.

What can a woman do to decrease her own risk of being raped? Warshaw (1988) has compiled an excellent list of ways to prevent acquaintance rape. First, she summarized the behaviors and characteristics that rapists often manifest: being emotionally abusive, insulting, and belittling; trying to control elements of a woman's life; talking negatively about women in general; getting jealous for no reason; drinking heavily or trying to get the woman intoxicated; refusing to let the woman share expenses of a date, and getting angry when she offers; being unable to accept sexual or emotional frustration without becoming angry; being fascinated with weapons; and enjoying being cruel to animals or children. One way to decrease the risk of acquaintance rape is to avoid men who behave in these ways.

Second, Warshaw warned against isolated places where a woman can be easily victimized. It is safer to stay in public places such as restaurants and movie theaters where the presence of other people acts as a deterrent to attack.

Third, it is recommended that women adopt, set, and communicate clear limits regarding their sexuality and be assertive about these limits. Other beneficial strategies for women are staying sober, learning about a new date in advance, paying their own way on a date, educating themselves about self-defense, trusting their own feelings, and taking special precautions in high-risk areas such as a college campus, especially when not yet familiar with the area.

Warshaw's recommendations to women threatened with an attack include running away, screaming, and not giving in to fear. She suggested evaluating the situation, acting quickly, and attacking forcefully, if necessary. Sometimes a potential victim can stall by talking or by spoiling the would-be rapist's fantasy "seduction." Finally, women are reminded that giving in is not consent; rather, it may be a survival strategy. Staying alive is top priority.

Source: Adapted from R. Warshaw, *I never called it rape: The Ms. report on recognizing, fighting, and surviving date and acquaintance rape* (New York: Harper & Row, 1988), pp. 151–160.

9.7   IS IT REINFORCING TO SEE OTHERS SUFFER?

A controversial issue is whether the witnessing of suffering is, in itself, reinforcing. Patterns of American entertainment certainly suggest that people are willing to spend money or go to great lengths for the opportunity of witnessing the suffering of others. Television programming contains an extraordinary amount of violence, conflict, and victimization. News broadcasting focuses on injuries, violence, and loss. Boxing, which clearly inflicts massive damage to the brain over the course of a career, is an enduringly popular sport. Accidents along metropolitan freeways invariably create what is known as a "gapers' block," an unnecessary obstruction of traffic flow as drivers slow to examine the details. Horror films have long been popular, and have increasingly contained vivid violence. The black market periodically offers high-priced "snuff" films that allegedly show the actual rape, torture, and murder of an unsuspecting victim. What is the fascination that attracts people to such forms of "entertainment"? Is it reinforcing, in some sense, to witness suffering, and could this in itself be a motivating factor in aggression and violence, at least for some?

Research suggests that witnessing and participating in aggressive behavior may be reinforcing when the victim is perceived as *deserving* to suffer (Frodi et al., 1977). Until relatively recent history, executions were commonly held in public places and drew large crowds. Preparation for military service, particularly in wartime, typically includes training tactics to depersonalize enemies and to highlight their deservingness of destruction. Bandura (1973) puzzled that so little psychological attention has been paid to military training programs which, "within a relatively short period, transform people who have been taught to deplore killing as morally reprehensible into skilled combatants who feel little compunction or even a sense of pride in taking human life" (p. 99).

Given different learning histories, it is likely that people vary widely in how reinforcing they find the witnessing of suffering in others. Sexual sadism is recognized as a mental disorder (APA, 1987) in which individuals experience sexual arousal in response to seeing or inflicting pain in others. Eric Berne (1964) hypothesized that some individuals become entangled in social "games" wherein they habitually set up circumstances enabling them to experience righteous justification in embarrassing and retaliating against others. The circumstances of Nazi Germany brought to power individuals who reveled in inflicting and witnessing inhumane suffering.

Are all of us or some of us reinforced by the pain of others? Was there some truth to Freud's assertion of an inherent wish for destruction? The question haunts us still.

(their own and others') than do men (Frodi et al., 1977). Women also may experience greater empathy for the victims, which may account in part for their greater anxiety and guilt following aggression.

Finally anger itself has consequences when it becomes prolonged and chronic, taking its toll on relationships, health, and life expectancy. This is well illustrated in research on "Type A" behavior, to which we now turn our attention.

■ TYPE A BEHAVIOR: ANGER AND THE HEART

In 1974, Drs. Friedman and Rosenman published a book entitled *Type A Behavior and Your Heart.* They described a pattern of behavior that they found to be characteristic of their patients who had had early heart attacks. It was the beginning of an important breakthrough in understanding the origins and prevention of heart disease. Subsequent research has confirmed that people who show the Type A behavior pattern are at high risk for coronary disease and that this risk is about equal to the effects of high blood pressure, smoking, and cholesterol *combined* (Cooper, Detre, & Weiss, 1981).

Descriptions of Type A behavior vary, but the essential themes in this pattern are three: (1) an extreme *time urgency:* the person is hurried, impatient, quick to act, tries to do two or more things at a time, moves and talks fast; (2) *excessive competitiveness:* the person views many or most aspects of life as win-or-lose matters, is constantly *proving* himself or herself; and (3) *hostility:* the person shows a quick temper, a short fuse, tends to be distrustful and suspicious, highly critical, showing disgust and contempt for others who do not meet his or her high standards. These elements can lead to a chronic high level of arousal of the sympathetic nervous system. It has been found, for example, that the pupils of the eyes are more dilated (larger) in Type A people, a sign of sympathetic arousal. It is most accurate to think of a continuum between Type A behavior and its opposite (Type B). Rather than there being two distinct types of people in the world (A's and B's), individuals show a full range from one of these extremes to the other.

Some research suggests that the hostility component may be a particularly toxic ingredient of the Type A behavior pattern (Dembroski & Williams, 1989; Matthews & Haynes, 1986). That is, coronary artery disease seems to be closely associated with the degree of hostility shown by Type A males. What *kind* of hostility leads to a coronary? Clive Wood (1986) described it as "cynical contempt." This trait includes deep suspicion, being constantly on guard against others who are viewed as dishonest, antisocial, and immoral. The pattern also includes rage responses and chronic angry feelings. This hostility, expressed predominantly toward others, ultimately destroys the Type A person, too. Type A people apparently do not have permanently raised blood pressure. They let themselves become upset more frequently, however, and drive their blood pressure up more often in a given day. These surges in blood pressure may be responsible for damage to the arteries.

Type A behavior is characterized by time urgency, hostility, and competitiveness.

9.8 SOME SIGNS OF THE TYPE A BEHAVIOR PATTERN

There is no universally agreed-upon definition of the Type A behavior pattern. Often Type A is diagnosed by means of a structured interview. Here are some of the behaviors that an interviewer might ask about in evaluating for Type A patterns:

* The person often feels rushed, pressured, hurried, and hates to wait. Delays of minutes or even seconds are extremely annoying. Waiting (in line, for example) is upsetting. When there are several lines, as at a bank or grocery store, the person watches the other lines and is angered if they seem to move faster. Slow-moving drivers and pedestrians are infuriating. Being late, or having others be late, is very upsetting.
* The person tends to move fast—walks fast or even runs, eats quickly, talks rapidly.
* In conversation, the person is a poor listener, interrupts often, speaks loudly and forcefully.
* The person often tries to do two or more things at the same time. "Doing nothing" is seldom or never pleasant. The person may read during meals or while sitting on the toilet. The person is always working.
* The person is a fast, competitive, angry, and often risky driver.
* Competition is a theme of the person's life. It is terribly important to do better than others. In competitive sports and board or card games, they are angry losers.
* The person is critical toward others, quick to anger at their perceived shortcomings and "failures." Arguments are common and often heated, and the person wants to win regardless of the cost.
* The person is highly sensitive to any perceived criticism from others, and tends to overreact. Perceived injustices are remembered for a long time, and the person thinks about them over and over again, continuing to feel angry and bitter.
* There is a continual sense of physical tension. The person's face appears tense much of the time, movements may be tense and jerky. When talking, the person may use forceful, repeated gestures.

This hostility pattern can also be destructive to interpersonal relationships, leaving Type A people isolated and alone. In this regard, it is interesting that social support appears to be a buffer against the detrimental effects of Type A behavior on health. Research has shown lower rates of coronary artery disease (as measured by angiography—actual measurement of blockage of the arteries) in Type A people with higher levels of social support (Blumenthal et al., 1987). Seeman and Syme (1987) found that in particular the *feeling of being loved* was associated with lower rates of coronary disease among Type A's, whereas the sheer *number* of people in their emotional support network was not a good predictor.

Although the hostility of Type A people may be a particularly lethal factor, it would be premature to claim that this is the *only* hazardous element of the Type A pattern. The time-pressured and competitive aspects may also take their toll on health and relationships. It remains for future research to clarify the ways in which Type A behavior increases risk for heart disease.

How does the Type A behavior pattern develop? Wright (1988) has described a predisposing set of conditions, which set the stage for the emergence of Type A behavior. These include (1) low self-esteem, (2) a high need for competitive achievement, (3) early competitive successes and reinforcement for achievement efforts, and (4) experience with timed tasks (such as examinations) that require performance within a limited time, promoting concern for efficiency. These factors, according to Wright, can lead to a decision to combat low self-esteem through achieving as much as possible. Thus emerges the time-pressured, continuous, and competitive activity of the Type A person.

Like Patterson's work with aggression and Coopersmith's research on self-esteem, most of the original research on Type A personality was conducted with white males (Matthews & Haynes, 1986). A key problem facing psychology today is deciding which findings generalize to females and minority groups, thus requiring replication with these populations. Historically, psychology has been the psychology of Caucasian males. In the 1990s, gender and cultural differences are important considerations in psychological research.

Is the Type A behavior pattern changeable, and does a reduction in Type A behavior result in reduced coronary risk? Happily, the answer to both questions appears to be "Yes." Type A behaviors themselves have been found to change in response to cognitive-behavior therapy (Friedman, Thoresen, & Gill, 1981; Nunes, Frank, & Kornfeld, 1987; Thurman, 1983). Friedman and his colleagues (1986) studied a group of patients who had recently suffered a heart

9.9   A BIT OF ADVICE

This short excerpt of verse, written by Rilke in a letter to a young poet friend, has been used by Dr. Carl Thoresen in programs to help people overcome their Type A behavior.

> Be patient toward all that is unsolved
>   in your heart
> Try to love the questions themselves . . .
>
> Do not now seek the answers,
>   which cannot be given
>   because you would not be able
>   to live them.
> And the point is,
>   to live everything.
>
> Live the questions now.
> Perhaps you will then
>   gradually,
>   without noticing it,
> Live along some distant day
>   into the answers.

Rainer Maria Rilke,
Letters to a young poet, 1934

attack. Part of this group, chosen at random, received cardiologic care plus a special counseling program to reduce Type A behavior. Others received only routine cardiologic care. Over four and a half years of follow-up, the counseled group showed greater reduction in their Type A behaviors. More important, those given only cardiologic care showed twice the rate of subsequent heart attacks and deaths during this period. Apparently, it is never too late to change!

■ SUMMARY

Anger is a complex emotion that can be expressed in a wide range of behaviors. One type of response to anger is aggression, behavior intended to hurt or harm. Assertive behavior, in contrast, seeks a middle ground between aggressive and submissive responses. A variety of developmental factors influence anger and aggression. The STORC analysis can be used to understand components of anger and aggression, and to seek alternatives for dealing with related problems. Situational factors influence anger and aggression, but do not guarantee their occurrence. Thought patterns, perceptions, and interpretations strongly affect anger. Autonomic arousal can intensify anger and aggression. Withdrawal, submission, aggression, and assertion are all possible responses to angry feelings. The likelihood of such responses is influenced by consequences that follow when they occur. The Type A behavior pattern is a cluster of characteristic responses that is predictive of increased risk for coronary artery disease.

■ QUESTIONS FOR THOUGHT

1. What are your favorite TV shows and movies? How much aggression and violence do they contain? In the past month, how many acts of aggression (injury to others) do you think you have witnessed in movies and TV shows?

2. How would you be likely to respond if a man were screaming obscenities at you? How would your response be similar or different if it were a woman screaming obscenities at you?

3. When you feel angry, what do you do?

4. Some people believe that aggression is an innate drive, an inevitable fact of existence. What is your own view about this?

5. While you were growing up, how did the members of your family deal with and express anger? How is this similar to or different from how you deal with and express anger now?

6. If you have children or want to have children, how do you want to deal with your angry feelings toward them?

7. Do you have a friend who deals well with anger? What does he or she do that you admire?

8. What are the main sources of frustration in your life? How much control do you have over them? What could you do to decrease frustration in your life?

9. Thomas Gordon maintained that anger is always a secondary emotion, a reaction to fear or hurt. Do you agree with him? Why or why not?

10. How do you interpret the word "forgive"? Are you aware of issues in your life for which you may need to give or receive forgiveness?

chapter ten

One does not fall "in" or "out" of love.
One grows in love.
—Leo Buscaglia, *Love*

Joy, Love, and Relationships

OUTLINE

Virtually every theory of personality and adjustment has included, as a central life task, the development of significant love relationships. When asked what he regarded to be the most essential ingredients for mental health, Sigmund Freud once answered, "Leistung und Genuss." This has been rendered in English as "to love and to work," although a closer translation of these two German nouns would be "achievement and enjoyment."

In one sense, relationships are the most crucial aspect of the psychology of adjustment, because human beings are social animals, surrounded by relationships throughout life. The topics covered in every other chapter of this book exist within the context of human relationships. Perceptions, emotions, self-esteem, work, sexuality, and change are all importantly shaped by the relationships within which they occur. Some of the highest joys and deepest sorrows of life arise from relationships with others. "Hell," said the philosopher Sartre, "is other people." But in the same sense, paradise is found in others, too.

In previous chapters we have discussed three major classes of emotions: depression, anxiety, and anger. We will begin this chapter with a consideration of a fourth and final class of emotions: joy. Like other human emotions, joy also presents adjustment challenges: to find it, to experience it, to share it, to include it in your life. Then we will turn to a discussion of close relationships: how they begin and develop, what may go wrong in love relationships, and what skills are needed to sustain them. We will discuss when and how to seek help in a troubled relationship. Finally, we will explore the adjustment processes that occur when a close relationship ends.

■ THE EMOTION OF JOY

What is **joy?** There are many synonyms: elation, gladness, delight, cheerfulness, amusement, happiness, bliss, enchantment, pleasure, glee, ecstasy. Just as peace is more than the absence of war, joy is more than the mere absence of negative emotions. Joy is a departure from the ordinary, a change, a lift in mood. As with other emotions, it can be understood not as a single event, but rather as a series of interrelated events. The STORC brings joy, too!

S—SITUATIONAL FACTORS

An interesting exercise is to list the stimuli or situations (S) that evoke joyful emotions in you. What are the things that can "make your day"? Peter Lewinsohn, in developing programs to help people manage their own moods, developed a long list of potentially pleasurable activities called the Pleasant Events Schedule (Lewinsohn et al., 1978). One value of a list such as this is its ability to *suggest* ideas for pleasant experiences: to remind you of forgotten sources of joy, to clarify your present day-makers, to propose new potentially joyful experiences. A shorter list, similar in form to Lewinsohn's, is shown in Box 10-1. Which of these activities do you currently enjoy? Which are activities you might enjoy but have never tried? Which have you enjoyed in the past, but have not done for a while?

Once aware of the kinds of experiences that can bring joy, you can intentionally plan to include such experiences in each day and week. Just as people take vitamins to help maintain a healthy diet, so it is sensible to include

Joy
a highly positive, pleasurable emotion.

What's there to do? Sometimes people fall into such habitual ruts in their daily lives that they forget the range of pleasurable activities available to them. Here is one list of potentially pleasant activities. Some of these will be things you enjoy, and some you may dislike.

Choose from this list at least twenty activities that you would probably enjoy, and that you could do, but have not been doing very often. How many of these could you fit into the next day? The next week? The next month? Give it a try!

Taking a walk	Reading a book or story	Buying a gift for someone
Building something from wood	Watching television	Riding a motorcycle
Going for a swim	Doing housework	Singing
Playing cards	Cooking	Working a crossword puzzle
Going to the library	Going to church	Writing a letter
Having a massage	Building a model	Playing golf or miniature golf
Drawing	Playing with children	Cross-country skiing
Talking with a friend	Visiting people in a hospital	Making something from leather
Taking a hot bath	Gardening	Going out for breakfast
Writing a story	Taking photographs	Riding a snowmobile
Going for a picnic	Caring for a pet	Roller skating
Working on a car	Going to a restaurant	Going for a hike
Window shopping	Sitting in a park	Looking at the stars
Knitting	Going camping	Going to a coffeehouse
Bowling	Going for a run	Potting house plants
Going shopping	Carving or whittling	Collecting stamps or coins
Downhill skiing	Feeding birds	Folk dancing
Going to a play	Square dancing	Taking a nap
Riding a horse	Going for a drive	Ice skating
Hearing an interesting talk	Making jam	Reading a magazine
Praying	Working a jigsaw puzzle	Making a gift for someone
Going fishing	Reading to someone	Planning a trip
Chopping wood	Calling an old friend	Making a tape for a friend
Going to the zoo	Taking dancing lessons	Playing basketball
Baking	Reading a newspaper	Making popcorn
Sewing	Seeing a movie	Looking at pictures
Meditating	Fixing something at home	Taking a bicycle ride
Playing a musical instrument	Looking for a job	Doing nothing for an hour
Reading maps	Making love	Writing in a diary or journal
Listening to music	Painting	Playing a video/computer game
Learning a language	Volunteering time for charity	Trying a new recipe
Going dancing	Going to a sports event	Watching people
Writing a letter	Inviting friends for dinner	Reading cartoons

pleasant events in your life to help maintain a positive mood and outlook (Lewinsohn et al., 1978). These need not be complicated, lengthy, or expensive activities. They can be as simple as stopping to notice the trees or flowers, taking a deep breath, or calling a friend. The point is that you have a lot of choice and control over situations that bring you enjoyment.

T—THOUGHT PATTERNS

Humor
the appreciation of an incongruity, accompanied by playful or otherwise positive emotion.

Joy is also in the eye of the beholder, in how one interprets or perceives a situation. A traffic jam can be experienced as an aggravating, frustrating delay or as an unexpected opportunity to sit quietly and reflect or listen to music. The simple touch of a hand can be filled with meaning, or devoid of it. The fascinating phenomenon of humor is a wonderful example of how a cognitive insight (sometimes called "getting the point") can evoke a joyful emotion.

10.2 THE PSYCHOLOGY OF HUMOR

Two Russians were standing in a three-block line in front of one of the few state liquor stores, waiting to buy vodka and grumbling about Chairman Gorbachev's policy that made alcohol so hard to get. After an hour during which the line barely moved, one of the men became incensed and told the other loudly, "I've had it! This is madness! I'm going to the Kremlin to kill Gorbachev." Off he went, and his friend thought to himself, "Well, that's the last I'll see of Ivan. The KGB will get him for sure." To his surprise, however, an hour later Ivan returned and got back in line. "What happened?" the startled friend asked." "Oh, I gave it up," Ivan replied. "The line over there was even longer!"

Humor. Throughout our lives it brings us joy, provides unexpected moments of mirth in the midst of the gloomiest situations. But what is it that makes **humor** funny? It's a question that has fascinated thinkers since the time of Plato.

One key element of humor seems to be its surprise value, its unexpected or incongruous quality (McGhee, 1979). Jokes commonly set up an expectation, then frustrate that expectation and provide in its place a surprise, an unexpected outcome (Eastman, 1922).

But what is the surprise? "Getting the point" of a joke is a matter of recognizing something hidden within it. In this sense, "Ha Ha" is really a matter of "Aha!" In his extensive writings on humor, Sigmund Freud (1960) described humor as a socially acceptable means for expressing repressed wishes or conflicts. Hostility or sexual content (which account for a majority of the themes in humor) are not stated directly, but are disguised or hidden in the joke. In this way, one person can communicate to another a hostile or sexual theme without doing so blatantly. In addition, the listener has the extra pleasure of discovery, of finding the hidden meaning. This is clear in the classic political joke above. Hostility toward authority figures is a common theme in political humor. During the Watergate era, as revelations regarding President Nixon's involvement were emerging slowly, a distinguished political commentator was asked his reaction to the statement that "Nixon is either a crook or a fool." "Oh," he replied in a tone of admiration, "I think he's much too intelligent to be a fool." And he left it at that.

Sometimes, however, the content of jokes seems much more innocuous, as if the sheer joy of playing with words were the object. Freud called these "innocent" jokes. Puns are often of this sort. They provide the unexpected, requiring the listener to make a verbal connection, as in Steve Allen's classic pun, "One man's Mead is another man's Persian."

Another source of humor is its unexpected appearance in a serious context. The double humor here is not only in getting the point of the joke itself, but in its presence where it is not expected to be. Writing in the usually stodgy *Annual Review of Psychology*, Goldberg (1974) was providing a review of psychological assessment:

> Lewinsohn and his students have tested patients' short-term memory via visual, auditory, and kinesthetic modalities, showing that the test performance of those with anterior damage is worse than those with posterior. Moral: Fall backwards.

Humor sometimes has its effect by suddenly switching the emotional tone. A 1986 *Newsweek* story offered the somewhat disheartening observation that a single American woman over the age of 40 is more likely to be killed by a terrorist than to be married, to which a feminist quipped, "And most would prefer the former." Humor gives us a means to escape momentarily, to cope emotionally with the burdens of life. Lord Byron observed: "And if I laugh at any mortal thing, 'tis that I may not weep."

The mechanisms by which jokes can be made are many: double meaning, absurdity, omission of a logical step, faulty reasoning, or misunderstanding. For any rule that tries to pin down how humor works, there will be exceptions. Jokes are often hostile or sexual, but then again there are many forms of humor that serve to endear, to draw people closer together, to express warmth. Which just goes to show you: all that titters is not cold.

For some people, thinking gets in the way of enjoyment. Masters and Johnson (1970) described the **spectator role** as one of the most common factors interfering with sexual enjoyment and functioning (see Chapter 12). Instead of focusing on and enjoying sensory experiences, the person is busy thinking and evaluating, observing like an outside spectator. Others feel reluctant to give themselves to a joyful experience because of the certain knowledge that it will end. They choose not to enjoy at all, rather than feel joy and then be let down. Still others equate joyful feelings with "bad" behavior, and experience guilt that tempers any enjoyment.

Matina Horner (1972) gave rise to an active and controversial line of research by speculating that women in American society manifest a **fear of success.** Is achievement a desirable, joyful experience for women? Subsequent research has indicated that women may place a higher value on relationships than on success, and as a consequence may avoid or at least not enjoy attainment of success if they perceive that it interferes with significant relationships or other important goals (Dweck & Elliott, 1983).

A corresponding barrier to joy has been described for American men: the **fear of intimacy.** Chodorow (1978) proposed that men experience greater ambivalence about nurturing and intimate relationships because of their developmental history. Because mothers have provided a majority of child care in our society, girls have and can identify with a nurturing role model. Boys, however, develop by distancing themselves and becoming different from this female model. Failure to do so, in Chodorow's view, results in being swallowed up and losing one's identity and separateness. Men, thus, may be left with an enduring anxiety and ambivalence about emotionally close relationships.

Both "fear of success" and "fear of intimacy" are generalizations, and should not be taken as characteristics of all women or men. Any person could be intensely ambivalent about achievement or intimacy, based on her or his own development and perceptions. The point is that the ability to experience

Spectator Role
a process in which direct experiencing is inhibited by the observing and evaluating of one's own reactions or state.

Fear of Success
an hypothetical personality characteristic that predisposes a person to avoid personal achievement and recognition.

Fear of Intimacy
an hypothetical personality characteristic that predisposes a person to avoid close personal relationships.

joy of certain kinds can be constrained by patterns of thought, expectation, and perception.

A vivid example of the impact of experience on intimacy is found in the **post-Vietnam syndrome** suffered by a significant proportion of men exposed to combat during the Vietnam war. The symptoms included a high level of autonomic arousal, nightmares, jumpiness, and sudden outbursts of anger or aggression. Another noteworthy part of the syndrome, however, was a "numbing" of emotional responsiveness, an inability to experience positive emotions and to enter into enduring intimate relationships (Roberts et al., 1982). The trauma of witnessing and participating in so much killing, the sudden loss of combat companions, and the continual threat to life combined to wall off the man's desire and ability to form close relationships. The implicit rule seemed to be, "Don't get attached to anyone." Experiences of this kind can pose enduring barriers to joy and relationships. These problems have been shown to be directly related to combat exposure, and not to problems these men had prior to their military experience (Foy et al., 1984; Roberts et al., 1982).

O—ORGANIC FACTORS

There are clear physiological components of joy, too. Research has identified a family of natural brain chemicals, called **endorphins,** that seem to relieve pain and instill a sense of well-being. Morphine and heroin, highly addicting drugs, act on the brain because of their close resemblance to endorphins, imitating the effects of these natural brain chemicals (see Chapter 11).

It has long been known that certain regions of the brain also produce highly reinforcing and pleasant effects when stimulated. Animals with electrodes implanted in these regions will press a lever up to 7,000 times per hour to obtain electrical stimulation, stopping only in fatigue for sleep (Olds, 1958). In humans as well, stimulation of these brain centers can produce intensely pleasurable experiences (Heath, 1963). Certain drugs, particularly stimulants such as cocaine, appear to have a similarly direct effect on the brain's pleasure centers. Laboratory animals will self-administer such drugs continually, often to the point of physical exhaustion or self-starvation (Wise, 1984). Behaviors (such as drug taking) that elicit such immediate pleasure may override an individual's long-term health and well-being. This is a central problem in the addictive behaviors, to be discussed in our next chapter.

R—RESPONSES

People vary widely in how they respond to joyful feelings. Some, like Kazantzakis's (1971) character Zorba the Greek, enjoy exuberantly and openly by singing, dancing, laughing, and shouting. Some keep joy to themselves, perhaps concerned not to evoke jealousy or resentment in others. One of us, after a move to a new city, was enjoying a new job and the excitement of new colleagues and challenges. Married to a newly unemployed partner who had left a good job to move, however, it was difficult to express this joy at home. Bubbling about the joys of work tended to rub salt on the wounds of unemployment. When, a few months later, both were happily employed, it was easy to share the excitement of new jobs.

Not expressing enjoyment or appreciation has its risks, too. All of us teach others how to love and care for us by how we respond to their efforts to reach out. Consider two people receiving backrubs. One purrs and moans appreciatively, and tells his or her partner which muscles to rub in particular. The other is totally silent, though very much enjoying the backrub. The partner of the latter person has little or no feedback to know which types of massage feel

Post-Vietnam Syndrome
a set of problems observed among veterans returned from combat during the Vietnam war; a specific form of posttraumatic stress disorder.

Endorphins
naturally occurring brain chemicals that reduce pain and instill a feeling of well-being.

Joy can be expressed in many ways.

best, or even whether the person is enjoying it. How good a backrub you receive (and whether you get another one) will depend in part on how you respond. Similarly, it is important to acknowledge the things that others do that bring you joy. This is one function of the words, "Thank you," which appear in virtually every language.

C—CONSEQUENCES

In one sense, joy is often a result of particular consequences. When one's efforts result in the desired positive outcome, the emotional response tends to be satisfaction and pleasure. There can also be, however, a "postsuccess depression" that sometimes occurs after a long-sought goal (such as a college degree) has been achieved. If achieving the goal does not bring the amount of enjoyment and satisfaction that had been anticipated, the person may sink into disappointment and dejection focused on the thought, "Is that all there is?"

The experience of joy can likewise be influenced by how others respond to one's expressions of joy. Some families seem to operate by an implicit rule that "Nobody should have a good time" or "If you feel good you must have done something wrong." In this context, others may respond in a way that encourages the person to keep joy secret. An expression of self-esteem and satisfaction may elicit criticism from a parent or significant other, as if to say, "Don't let others know if you feel good, you might make them feel bad." A long history of such consequences may inhibit a person's ability to *feel* joy.

Most often, joyful experiences occur in the context of relationships. Joyful feelings may reflect a high level of positive reinforcement in one's life. On the other hand, when one's relationships are characterized by very little reinforcement and instead offer mostly punishment and criticism, joy seems harder to find. A key theme in the remainder of this chapter is that you have a great deal of choice about how your own close personal relationships will be, and thus about the amount of joy in your own life.

■ HOW RELATIONSHIPS BEGIN

There are many kinds of relationships: work relationships, love relationships, friendships, parent-child relationships, legal and contractual relationships,

Relationships begin with the first meeting.

and student-teacher relationships. Aspects of these overlap, and any one of these categories will also contain immense diversity. Asked about their "friends," for example, some will describe having dozens of friendships that sound more like casual acquaintances, while others will claim perhaps one or two true friendships, reserving this term for enduring close relationships.

We will not address such a broad range of possible relationships here. Rather we will focus our attention on close, relatively enduring dyadic (two-person) relationships that involve interdependence (Kelley et al., 1983). Notice the four aspects of this definition: the relationships are (1) close, involving personal and usually frequent contact; (2) relatively enduring, lasting over an extended period of time; (3) dyadic, existing between two persons, and (4) interdependent, with each relying upon the other in important ways. In such relationships, the lives of the two people are intimately intertwined. Notice also that it is the presence of all four of these characteristics that sets these relationships apart. People may have relatively enduring, dyadic, and interdependent relationships with their insurance agents, for example, but usually such relationships lack the first quality of being close. A weekend workshop or retreat may bring two people together in a way that fosters temporary closeness and intimacy, but such a relationship lacks the qualities of being enduring and interdependent.

ATTRACTION

One fascinating question is: What draws people together to form close relationships? At the most superficial level, this can be an exploration of what stimuli (S), what aspects of another person, will arouse interest and encourage one to pursue a relationship. Men and women show some similarities as well as some differences in their descriptions of what they find most attractive (Peplau, 1983). Men typically describe physical appearance as most important in women, whereas women more often rate intelligence or sensitivity highest when asked to describe attractive men. Both genders report wanting a permanent relationship, with companionship and affection taking precedence over economic security and social status.

Sociobiologists claim that male animals *fight* and female animals *choose* in the sexual selection process, thus requiring that in order to succeed sexually, males must be able to compete against other males. Females then choose the winner of the competition as the most attractive mate. However, sociobiologists have been justly criticized for selectively focusing only on observations that support stereotypes about human attraction while ignoring observations that run counter to those stereotypes (Hyde, 1985).

Research on **attraction** has contained several important biases that warrant caution in accepting these results at face value. Attraction studies have focused very heavily on white male subjects, on heterosexual attraction, and on college students, leaving it less clear what characteristics foster attraction with women, older adults, and many different sociocultural groups omitted from research. Even within these constraints, studies have severely restricted the types of responses that subjects are likely to give by using sexist and appearance-focused measures. Studies of attraction and preference have, for example, employed nude photographs from *Playboy* magazine and have queried the importance of specific appearance characteristics such as women's breast size (Kleinke & Staneski, 1980; Valins, 1966, Wiggins, Wiggins, & Conger, 1968). Studies focusing on such measures within young college male populations are

Attraction
the process of desiring and seeking a relationship with another person.

10.3 WHAT ARE YOUR PRIORITIES IN AN INTIMATE RELATIONSHIP?

What things are most important to you in an intimate relationship? Which of the following characteristics are highest on your list for an ideal partner? Which are of little importance to you? Are there some that you definitely would *not* want in a partner? Examine this list and pick out the *ten* characteristics that are most important to you in an ideal partner. Write them down in order of importance.

Adventuresome—likes to take risks

Intelligent

Well liked by many people

Independent—doesn't rely on others for identity

Expresses a full range of emotions easily

Has a solid career

Good in bed

Keeps changing and growing as a person

Doesn't make his or her partner jealous

Abstains from alcohol

Has a good imagination

Enjoys touching

Generally positive outlook on life and other people

Wants to have children

Willing to stay up all night to work out a relationship problem

Good cook

Wants to share housework equally

Sociable, enjoys going out to parties

Organized—able to get things done efficiently

Curious—wants to experience life to the full

Has a strong religious commitment

Likes to keep things neat, clean, and in place

Physically strong—likes to exercise regularly

Nonsmoker

Handy around the house—good at fixing things

Enjoys poetry

Dependable and faithful

When you have completed your list, make another one. Which ten items from this list are most characteristic of you? Also, which items are *least* characteristic of you? Compare your self-descriptions with the descriptions of your ideal partner.

likely to result in very limited and misleading conclusions about what is attractive. Many intriguing questions remain unanswered. How do people's preferences and judgments of attractiveness change as they grow and mature? How do these life-span patterns differ for men and women? What attracts *friends* to one another? Are homosexual and heterosexual attraction patterns similar? Is the enduring strength of a relationship influenced by which factors attracted the two people to each other initially?

One issue to which some attention has been given is the question of whether "Likes attract" or "Opposites attract." The answer appears to be that both are true. Studies of **psychological type** have explored the similarities and differences among married couples on four personality dimensions (Myers & Myers, 1980). Not surprisingly, few couples are exactly alike on all four, and few are opposite on all four. The most common pairings are between people who share some important characteristics but differ markedly on others.

It may also be that similarities are more important early in the attraction process, whereas differences are crucial later. One helpful way to think about interpersonal attraction and the forming of interpersonal relationships is as a *process* that occurs at different levels over time (Levinger, 1983).

Psychological Type
a personality classification system based on Carl Jung's theory of individual differences.

1. Acquaintanceship.   The first level of this process of interpersonal engagement is acquaintanceship. At this level, the people might say of each other, "We've met." They interact superficially, and to each the other is more an object than a friend. The factors that influence the occurrence of this level

10.4   MEETING PEOPLE

When we conducted an informal survey of couples we know, asking them how they met, their answers usually involved being introduced by mutual friends, or participating in some activity they both enjoyed. One couple met when the woman invited the man, based on his area of expertise, to come and guest-lecture in a course she taught at a university. Another couple met while enrolled for a class in wind-surfing at a nearby lake. Yet another decided to marry after meeting in an assertion course at a local continuing education program.

One key is to go out into the world, rather than wait for the world to come to you. To meet people, you must come in contact with them. This further involves a willingness to take some risks, to approach others and be approached.

Single people often indicate they dislike the "bar scene," yet do not know viable alternatives for friendly contact. Church groups for singles may offer a less threatening option.

Personal ads in singles newspapers have met with mixed reviews, although the newspapers claim "success" when people who met through the ads marry.

Perhaps the most effective way to meet people with whom you can continue friendships and perhaps more intimate relationships is to participate in those activities that interest you. Do the things that are most interesting and enjoyable to you, but do them around other people. What gives you joy? If you like to read, join a book club that has meetings for discussing literature. If you like to dance, take a dance class. Be open to people who may not seem particularly attractive at first, as well as those who are instantly interesting. Singing harmony with a group transformed one seemingly plain man we know into a suddenly handsome, lively person. Remember, when you are wholeheartedly participating in an activity which you enjoy, you will radiate that joy, and that in itself is extremely attractive.

of interaction are mostly superficial. One is physical *proximity*. People who are in the same class day after day are more likely to meet. Physical attractiveness may increase the likelihood of meeting, as may perceived similarity.

2. Buildup.   Next comes what Levinger calls the buildup phase. Here the people interact with each other more frequently, and they tend to relate to each other mostly within prescribed social *roles*. Advancing from awareness to surface contact (level 1 to level 2) has sometimes been called the process of **affiliation.** This can occur gradually over a span of time, or rapidly in sudden steps. Proximity, attractiveness, and perceived similarity remain important factors, but personal attributes become more important (e.g., basic social skills, shyness, self-confidence, fear of rejection). At this level, it may be *complementary* needs that draw people together, their differences and their need for what the other person has to offer.

3. Continuation.   A relationship may, in turn, progress past the initial buildup phase into continuation, where involvement reaches beyond role behavior. Mutual emotional intimacy develops, and the two people become more interdependent, at some level accepting responsibility for each other. The process of moving from buildup to continuation, which Levinger terms *commitment*, occurs with shared time and experiences. The growth of commitment can be fostered by more advanced communication skills such as empathic listening, acceptance, and self-disclosure (Rogers et al., 1967; Truax & Carkhuff, 1967). Differences and complementary needs remain important, and advancement to mutual commitment and intimacy may depend upon how well people are able to communicate through their differences.

LIMERANCE: THE SWEET GLOW OF ROMANCE

Fairytales, fantasies, romance films and novels, and popular music have often presented very simplistic pictures of attraction and romance. One example is the "one right person" notion: that somewhere in the world there is, for each person, that one perfect partner. Your task is to find that partner. When you finally meet your perfect partner you will *know*, because of how you feel. You will be swept away by romance, lost in the stars, overcome by falling in love. Bells will chime, music will play, lights will flash, and *that* will be the sign that this is your one true love, your perfect mate.

There can be no doubt that falling in love is a genuinely enthralling experience. Though not everyone is so smitten, the period of intense romance that Tennov (1979) has called **limerance** can be among the most exciting, exhilarating, and euphoric experiences of a person's lifetime.

What remains unclear, however, is the *meaning* of this experience. The soaring divorce rate, now approximating 50 percent in the United States, testifies that romantic attraction is no perfect predictor of living happily ever after. Indeed, there appears to be no clear relationship between initial romance and the long-term stability and happiness of a relationship. What is it, then, that causes certain people to ring your chimes? Why are people so powerfully attracted to certain others?

Affiliation
the process of forming a friendly relationship with another person.

One explanation with ancient roots is that the partner is attractive precisely because he or she seems to hold a promise of completing oneself, of finishing some unfinished part of the self. In psychoanalysis, the concept of transference (Chapter 8) describes the process of projecting onto another the characteristics of some significant relationship of the past, based on a perceived similarity. A man may, for example, be romantically attracted to women who

Limerance
romantic attraction accompanied by intensely positive emotion.

Romantic attraction is no perfect predictor of living happily ever after.

remind him in certain ways of his mother. The person may then attempt to resolve in this new relationship the unfinished business of the past.

Patterns of this kind can often be seen in people who become romantically involved over and over again with very similar kinds of partners. We will describe two such people from our own clinical work (Miller & Jackson, 1985). One was Nancy, a woman in her late twenties who sought treatment after the collapse of four romantic relationships in a row. Deeply depressed, she was convinced that she was destined to destroy every love relationship of her life. The pattern was always the same. She would meet a man who overtly gave the appearance of being strong and emotionally distant, but who seemed to show the promise of being warm and loving if only she could reach this inner person. She would fall deeply in love, and for a time the relationship would fulfill her fantasies. Then Nancy would realize that she was not getting the kind of warmth and affection she had hoped for. As she tried harder to reach the "inner man," he would withdraw and show less affection. This led to an escalation of emotionality on her part, and further withdrawal on his part, until finally the relationship ended in a traumatic, sometimes violent fight. Then along would come another emotionally distant but promising man.

"What was your father like?" Nancy's therapist asked.

"He was around a lot, but we could never really get to him," she answered. "I always felt that deep inside somewhere he really loved me, but he never showed it. He never hugged me, never really said, 'I love you.'" Those words contained a key to her pattern. Without awareness, she had been attracted to men who resembled her father's emotional reservedness. Her hope was that *this* time she would get through to him. Yet by choosing men who found it very difficult to express affection, Nancy had stacked the deck against herself every time, and in the new relationship she relived her worst nightmare. This insight did not, in itself, change her pattern, but it was a beginning.

Frank, a 38-year-old man, sought the help of a psychologist just before his sixth wedding. He had married and divorced five times in a decade, and sensed that he was locked into an unhealthy repetitive pattern. He would meet a woman, usually quite a bit younger than himself, who adored him and found him a source of strength and wisdom. She would want to spend every minute with him. Not only did Frank find this flattering, but he would fall madly in love with her. They would marry, but after a few months he started to find his partner too "clinging" and "dependent." He felt trapped, and realized he had made a mistake. Then, either shortly before or shortly after the divorce, along would come another adoring young woman.

For both Nancy and Frank, an important realization was that their romantic attraction, the enchanting feeling of limerance, was no indicator of a solid relationship. In fact, both were attracted to precisely the *wrong* kind of partners. Both escaped from their pattern by dating new kinds of partners, people to whom they did not feel romantically attracted at first.

For others, fortunately, their initial attraction leads them to people who do turn out to be good long-term life partners. Our point here is that, on the whole, the quality and stability of an intimate relationship has very little to do with limerance. Initial romantic attraction predicts little in the long run. Rather, the growth or decay of a love relationship may depend heavily on the skills and expectations with which the individual partners approach them.

■ LOVE RELATIONSHIPS

LOVE

If you had to guess the one subject that has been the theme of more books, poems, songs, stories, art, plays, and motion pictures than any other, love would be a good choice. Love experiences are among the most memorable and meaningful in many people's lives. It is rather remarkable, then, that the subject is so seldom discussed in psychology textbooks (Buscaglia, 1972).

There are many different definitions of love. Where the English language offers one word, ancient Greek contained at least three to denote three different kinds of love: *philios* for the love between brothers and sisters, *eros* for erotic and sexual love, and *agape* for a selfless kind of love that seeks the welfare of the other. A modern English dictionary defines love in at least two dozen different ways. Is love a *state* of being, or is it an act, a *way* of being? How are loving and liking different? Does it mean something different to say, "I love chocolate" and "I love you"?

For purposes of this chapter, we are defining **love** in the same way that we earlier described close relationships: an enduring, intimate, interdependent relationship between two individuals. More than the emotion of joy or the intense attraction of limerance, love is defined by the enduring quality of the relationship.

Love
an enduring, intimate, interdependent relationship between two individuals.

IDEALS

Most people, aware of it or not, entertain an ideal notion of love—how it ought to be at its best. What are the qualities that come to your mind when you think of true love?

One element often mentioned as important in close relationships is **intimacy,** which itself has been defined in various ways. Intimacy has been described as "sustained interest in another person" (Williams & Long, 1983) and

Intimacy
mutual sharing between two people of important personal feelings, thoughts, and experiences.

as the capacity to give to another person without resentment and receive from that person without embarrassment (Klagsbrun, 1985). Erikson (1963) described intimacy as the capacity to make a commitment to another person and to abide by that commitment, even when the going gets tough. Within Erikson's developmental theory (Chapter 4), the establishment of intimacy is an essential task of early adulthood. Failure to master this task results in isolation, or in shallow relationships that afford little satisfaction. Most definitions of intimacy also include the idea that the relationship is sustained over time, allowing for trust to grow and develop.

It is also noteworthy that people's notions of an ideal relationship have shifted substantially over the years. Prior to the 1960s, ideals for marital rela-

---

10.5 CHARACTERISTICS OF A SOUND RELATIONSHIP

There are many definitions of what constitutes a sound or healthy relationship. Here is one set of ideas about prerequisites for a solid intimate relationship (Miller & Jackson, 1985). How do these assumptions compare with your own?

1. A sound relationship is one that occurs between autonomous individuals. Each individual is *capable* of existing independently, and has an identity of his or her own.

2. A sound relationship is one that is chosen. Autonomous individuals can *choose* to depend on others for significant needs, although they do not *have* to. They enter into a relationship out of choice, and they continue in it out of choice.

3. A sound relationship is one in which each individual is committed to the growth and happiness of the other. Each partner in a loving relationship is responsible for supporting the self-esteem and sustaining the positive experiences of the other.

4. A sound relationship is one in which each partner is open to change and in which each partner has positive skills for requesting and negotiating change from the other. People who live together need to be able to change. If positive means for eliciting change from the other are not available, it is likely that negative means will be employed.

5. A sound relationship is one in which each partner shares with the other his or her inner world. This is intimacy. In a context of mutual trust and respect, the partners communicate to each other their ongoing, present reality—perceptions, reactions, emotions, memories, hopes, plans, experiences, and thoughts. Some people mistake intimacy for the sharing of secrets about one's past. History is a part of intimacy, but a more vital (and more difficult) self-revelation is one's immediate reality. This is more difficult than sharing the past because it immediately involves and affects the partner, who in turn reacts.

6. A sound relationship includes commitment. Every relationship is marked by its ups and downs. A sound relationship is characterized by endurance and a commitment to work through the hard times that invariably come as part of a shared life.

Source: Adapted from W. R. Miller & K. A. Jackson, *Practical Psychology for Pastors* (Englewood Cliffs, N.J.: Prentice Hall, 1985), pp. 328–29.

tionships focused on family duties and tasks: having and raising children to carry on the family name and traditions, sustaining the family business and property. The family unit stood at the core, shaping each individual's role. In recent decades, personal fulfillment has come to occupy a more central role, and intimate relationships are often understood as means to this end (Mace & Mace, 1974). An increasing emphasis on the equality of men and women has also engendered a greater sharing of responsibilities. Women are more often found in the workplace, and men more commonly participate in household maintenance tasks and child-rearing. Whereas older marriages assigned greater power to male partners, ideals for intimate relationships are now shifting toward greater equality.

WHAT HAPPENS TO RELATIONSHIPS?

Psychologists and psychiatrists have for decades attempted to understand the normal human personality by studying the abnormal: what goes *wrong* with people. Though this is in many ways a limited approach, it has also been a fruitful one. Can it be applied to relationships? Can one learn something of healthy adjustment patterns in relationships by considering what goes wrong when they fall apart?

At least for a beginning, we will follow this approach, exploring the processes that seem to contribute to the demise of close relationships.

Loss of Novelty.   "The thrill is gone," wails an old B. B. King blues classic, "The thrill is gone away." People who experience an intense period of romance at the beginning of a relationship sometimes expect the same feelings to continue throughout their relationship. When these initial feelings fade, one or both partners may thus be distressed or disappointed. They may even con-

---

10.6 TWO VIEWS OF INTIMACY

Some of our students in the Psychology of Adjustment course have defined intimacy for themselves as closeness which may or may not happen, depending on many factors, including chance. Other students perceive intimacy as requiring effort in a relationship to cultivate the closeness they desire.

Here are examples in the words of four different students:

"I have met several women who were great to be with. Sometimes it works well for a few months, but we part ways. Longterm intimacy may not happen for me, and I guess that's OK."

"My husband and I have been married for ten years, and we are getting closer. We have learned to spend one afternoon together every week as our 'date'. That has helped our relationship grow."

"Working at an intimate relationship sounds like just that: work. I think relationships should be spontaneous and fun. I work enough in other areas of my life."

"My girlfriend and I have built something valuable together."

Which view of intimacy (chance or effort) most closely reflects your own view? What reasons might you give for your view? Do you have an alternative to these two views?

clude, incorrectly, that this means the relationship is no longer worth maintaining or that they have made a mistake and are with the "wrong" person. It was this assumption which had driven Frank through five marriages. George Bernard Shaw (1911), always a skeptic about relationships, once wrote, "When two people are under the influence of the most violent, most insane, most delusive and most transient of passions, they are required to solemnly swear that they will remain in that excited, abnormal and exhausting condition continuously until death do them part."

The problem here is not the fading of limerance, which is inevitable over time, but rather the *expectation* that such feelings should continue at full intensity or increase as the relationship develops. When this unrealistic expectation meets with disappointment, the person may lose his or her desire to persist in helping the relationship to grow. Some people, as a consequence, wander through an extended and often painful series of intense limerance relationships, almost as if they were addicted to the emotional high (Peele & Brodsky, 1975). When partners realize that the fading of limerance is normal (and that, in fact, limerance is not necessary) in healthy relationships, they can continue to work together on their relationship. Often the feelings of intense closeness return in brief periods as a relationship grows.

Disappointed Expectations.   People may carry with them into a close relationship certain expectations about the other, and about how they will be together. During the limerance period when "love is blind," each partner may have projected onto the other these ideal expectations. A tendency during this period is to see your partner as you *wish* your partner were, or as you believe an ideal partner should be. Also, to some extent, people during the initial "courtship" phase of a love relationship tend to be on their best behavior and may avoid showing their less desirable characteristics. Finally, the initial phase of a relationship may provide a very limited amount of information about the partner. Later on, new information becomes available as they confront the routine problems and frustrations of daily life together. One bride, for example, woke up the morning after their honeymoon night to find her new husband in a furious rage about a flat tire on the car. She realized she had never seen him angry before. During their courtship he had controlled his temper, but now, married less than twenty-four hours, she saw a new and somewhat startling side of him.

For these and other reasons, people in close relationships can encounter some significant surprises about their partners. Encountering new situations and behaviors, they may complain, "You're not the person I knew!" Such surprises are likely to be greater if they have not discussed some important issues before sharing a home, and instead have just assumed agreement. These issues include finances, spending time together, jealousy, religious beliefs and practices, whether and when to have children, division of household tasks, friendships, and style of decision making.

Reinforcement Decline.   Positive reinforcement is typically at an all-time high during the early stages of a love relationship. People take special time for each other, exchange gifts, give plenty of positive feedback, are physically affectionate, and acknowledge and respond to each other's needs. Over time, as a relationship develops, these positives begin to decrease. Politeness may wane, and potential shared time is occupied by more of the routine tasks of living: working, taking out the garbage, doing the laundry and dishes, paying the bills. Each person slowly decreases the amount of positive reinforcement and feedback given, often while expecting the partner to maintain the same level of positive support. In everyday language, this situation emerges in the complaint of "being taken for granted."

To make things more complicated, social psychological research indicates that the value or impact of positives from one's partner tends to decrease over time. When a person is consistently positive toward you, there is a tendency to place less value on any given piece of positive feedback from that person. A compliment from an attractive stranger may carry more clout than a similar remark from someone who is consistently complimentary. Thus the ability of partners in a relationship to influence each other with positives may decline over time (Aronson, 1969).

Increased Coercive Control.   When positives decline and lose some of their ability to influence, there is a temptation to resort to negative feedback and coercion to obtain a desired change. This is so, in part, because negative input often gets immediate results within a close relationship. When a person has been consistently positive toward you, criticism from her or him is particularly hurtful. Whereas pleasant requests may not work very efficiently, a "zap" gets attention and gets things done. Intimate partners can thus fall into the trap of using coercive control. As discussed in Chapter 9, each is reinforced for this. The "zapper" gets results and is positively reinforced. The "zappee," by giving in to the coercive demand, turns off the threat or nagging and thus is negatively reinforced for submissiveness.

Unfortunately a prolonged period of low positives and high coercive control tends to destroy a close relationship. As they are used more frequently, the zaps lose their influence and thus provide the temptation to "turn up the volume," using still more painful coercion. Some families escalate into violence in this struggle to influence or control each other. In any event, the result of prolonged negatives is to diminish self-esteem and attachment. Couples who come to psychologists for marital therapy typically show this pattern of exchanging very little positive reinforcement and relying heavily on negative control (Patterson, Weiss, & Hops, 1976). The emotional numbness that can result from zapping each other is reflected in the sad or bitter statement that "I just don't feel anything for you anymore."

When positives decline in a relationship, there is a temptation to resort to negative tactics.

Adjustment Challenges.   In the course of a long-term close relationship, people are bound to encounter many unforeseen setbacks, life transitions, problems, and conflicts. Together they may face the death of parents, rebellious adolescents, loss of a job, major illness, aging, moving away and losing friends. All the other adjustment challenges discussed in this book can and do happen within close relationships.

If the partners have skills to cope with these challenges and transitions, a close relationship can be strengthened. On the other hand, problems and resentments can accumulate if the partners lack the needed skills for negotiating change, making hard decisions, resolving conflicts, and solving problems. This may lead them to use more negatives or simply to avoid spending time together.

Growing Apart.   People change and grow. Change is one of the only things of which one can be sure. In a close relationship, people have the choice of growing together or growing apart. By this we do not mean becoming more similar or different. People in a close relationship may become more similar, but this is not essential or even necessarily desirable. Differences can be a source of attraction, affection, interdependence, and variety. Rather, we are concerned here with the extent to which people in a close relationship remain interested in, aware of, and supportive of each other's growth. In this sense, to love is to be committed to the continued growth and development of the other (Fromm, 1956).

How does it happen, then, that people in close relationships for many years suddenly wake up one morning and find that they are living with a stranger, someone whom they do not really know? The obvious answer is that they have

Love is being committed to the continued growth and development of the other.

been out of touch with each other. Perhaps they drifted into a pattern of sharing too little time together. Perhaps they lacked skills for communicating to each other their changing emotions, values, beliefs, and thoughts. Perhaps, through drifting into a pattern of exchanging zaps, they simply stopped communicating because it seemed too risky to be vulnerable. Whatever the reason, if people do not keep in touch with each other, they grow apart. They continue to grow, but do so apart from their relationship.

Perception Shifts. As problems emerge in a relationship, major shifts can occur in how the partners see each other. Each may begin to blame the other, seeing him or her as responsible for problems in their relationship. "If only my partner would change, things would be better." This perception assigns little responsibility to oneself. It is the *other* person who needs to change. From this perception can flow feelings of anger and resentment, and the partner may be seen as intentionally causing difficulties. Another destructive perception that can emerge is a global pessimism, a sense that the relationship is dead or at least beyond repair. Such a view, in turn, decreases the individual's commitment to the relationship and discourages efforts to make things better.

These shifts in perception are important because some of the assumptions that underlie goodwill within a close relationship are affected. *Trust*, for example, is a perception of the other as one with whom it is safe to be vulnerable and open. *Respect* is likewise a perception that an individual is a worthwhile and competent person, deserving of love (Miller, 1985a). As perceptions of the partner shift toward suspicion, blame, and pessimism, these basic intimacy assumptions are eroded. Each partner may, indeed, complain that "You don't trust me!" or "You don't respect me!"

Isolation. When two people are forming an intimate relationship, it commonly happens that they devote much of their time and energy to each other. One possible result is that they are cut off, in part, from other significant relationships and social support. They form their own world.

Although this is understandable, a loss of social support and feedback from others can intensify problems that emerge within the relationship. This isolation is further promoted within our society by several shared myths about intimate relationships (Mace, 1975). One of these is the myth of *naturalism:* that having a good and healthy relationship is natural, there is nothing you need to do to make it happen. Related to this is the myth of *privatism:* that if problems do emerge in the relationship, one should certainly not talk to anyone else about it. Rather, that's private business, to be kept secret within the relationship. Finally there is a societal *negativism* about relationships: that in general, they don't work out. This is particularly evident in humor and cartoons depicting marriages in a very pessimistic light.

The effect of this is to isolate relationship partners from outside support. Not discussing their problems with anyone else, they gain the inaccurate impression that their problems are unusual. Without support from others, the partners continue to struggle and suffer alone. Perhaps this isolation is one reason for the recent upswing of interest in friendship, extended family, and groups that offer a sense of community or belonging (Peck, 1987).

Before moving on to discuss skills that can be developed to prevent the decay of relationships, we want to point out the applicability of the STORC model in understanding relationships. Did you notice? Though we did not organize the foregoing discussion around the five steps of the STORC analysis, this could be done. Try it yourself! How are each of the five elements— S-T-O-R-C—involved in the development of relationships?

10.7   DANGER SIGNS IN AN INTIMATE RELATIONSHIP

There are no universal signs of trouble in an intimate relationship. The following, however, are changes that often occur when a close relationship is undergoing negative drift.

Increase in arguments or in their intensity.

Decrease in number of social contacts together.

Increased feelings of being deprived, lonely, taken for granted, pessimistic.

Decrease in frequency or satisfaction with sex.

Increase in self-defensiveness and in blaming of partner.

Perceived lack of trust or respect.

Increased reliance on criticism and punishment.

Increase in time spent apart, avoidance of partner.

Decreased consultation of partner on decisions.

Decreased sharing of inner world (feelings and thoughts) with partner.

■ RELATIONSHIP SKILLS

After considering the preceding list of the ways in which relationships can deteriorate, you may be asking yourself how love survives at all. It is true that many close relationships slowly drift into these patterns and ultimately fall apart. It is also true that many relationships endure. What makes the difference?

We believe that part of the puzzle is to be aware of and to guard against these kinds of "negative drift" that can occur in close relationships. The changes described are neither inevitable nor irreversible. They are natural changes, in the sense that they do tend to occur in relationships where the partners do nothing to prevent them. A useful analogy is a greenhouse with thriving plants. Given regular sunlight, warmth, and water, the plants continue to grow. Ignored for a period of time, however, the plants begin to brown and droop, and the greenhouse loses its healthy, vibrant appearance. If regular care is resumed, the greenhouse can be restored to its green and optimal condition. If the neglect continues for too long, however, the plants begin to die. We will discuss now some ways in which to maintain healthy relationships and help them to grow.

COMMUNICATION SKILLS

One characteristic of growing relationships is healthy habits of communication. As mentioned earlier, growing apart occurs when people stop communicating effectively. Growing together involves regular, two-way intimate communication. Learning better skills for communication has been found to be an important process in healing troubled relationships (Jacobson, 1984).

Time.   The "regular" aspect of healthy communication requires some planning. For many people in our society, the time demands of work, study, child care, and household maintenance easily crowd out time for intimate communication. Early in a courtship relationship, people often make "dates" with each other, setting aside special time for them to get to know each other better. As a relationship grows, this process remains important. Quality communication does not occur without setting aside time for it to happen. In some relationships, the problem is not an *inability* to communicate, but merely the fact that the participants do not take special time for sharing with each other their inner worlds.

Listening.   One of the most important skills needed to build close relationships is the skill of good listening. A person who is a good listener has a rare and valuable gift to offer others. Think about an average week in your life. How many minutes of true, high-quality listening would you say you receive from others in the course of a week? To listen is a gift.

Yet what *is* good listening? It is not the same as keeping quiet, because people may be silent and also not listening. Silence is a beginning, however, because it does provide one essential condition of listening: to allow the other person to pursue his or her own direction without interrupting with your own material. An interesting exercise that can be used to practice this is "silent partner," in which one person talks and the other listens. The speaker has five minutes of uninterrupted time to talk. The listener's job is to remain completely silent, but nonverbally to communicate that he or she is listening with full attention and understanding. The roles can then be reversed. During the process, the listener often becomes aware of how many things he or she would have said. Most often, the listener would have inserted his or her own material, drawing attention away from what the speaker had been saying. These interruptions detract from good listening and serve as roadblocks to communication. They place an obstacle in the way of the speaker, who must detour around it to keep going in the same direction.

Thomas Gordon (1970) described "the typical twelve" ways in which people ordinarily respond when someone is talking to them. All twelve of these are *not* listening. Although they may be intended as helpful, they serve as roadblocks. Their effect is clear: they stop the person from talking and divert the speaker in a different direction. Good listening, then, also involves avoiding these responses and, instead, allowing and helping the person to express her or his own feelings and thoughts.

After examining the list of roadblocks in Box 10.8, you may be thinking, "That's everything I do! What else could I possibly say if I want to be a good listener?" Notice that we have said that good listening is not just silence, and also is not putting up the roadblocks in Box 10.8. Good listening is *not* approving or disapproving, giving advice or criticism, questioning or probing, interpreting or reassuring. It *is* giving your whole attention to what the other person is saying, and at least one thing more.

This additional quality of a good listener has been called understanding, **accurate empathy,** or reflective listening. In this sense, understanding is something that the listener *does*. First described by Carl Rogers (1957), this skill of accurate empathy involves reflecting back to the speaker what he or she has said. Though this may sound easy, in fact it is a skill that takes time and practice to develop.

Why would a listener reflect back what the speaker has just said? The purpose is to promote understanding. In any communication, there are at

Accurate Empathy
the skill of correctly identifying and reflecting back another person's subjective meaning and feeling states; associated with the counseling theory of Carl Rogers.

10.8   ROADBLOCKS TO EFFECTIVE COMMUNICATION

When someone talks to you, how do you respond? Are you a good listener, or do you rely on these roadblocks to communication? The twelve roadblocks below, adapted from Thomas Gordon's *Parent Effectiveness Training,* have in common the underlying message, "Listen to me!" They also tend to have the effect of interrupting the other person, derailing them from what they would otherwise have said. Which are your own favorite roadblocks?

1.   *Ordering, directing, or commanding.* Here a direction is given with the force of some authority behind it. There may be actual authority (as with a parent or employer) or the words may simply be phrased in an authoritarian way. Some examples:

Don't say that!
You've got to face up to reality.
Go right back there and tell her you're sorry!

2.   *Warning or threatening.* These messages are similar to directing, but they also carry an overt or covert threat of impending negative consequences if the advice or direction is not followed. It may be a threat that the individual will carry out, or simply a prediction of a bad outcome if you don't comply.

You'd better start treating him better or you'll lose him.
If you don't listen to me you'll be sorry.
You're really asking for trouble when you do that.

3.   *Giving advice, making suggestions, providing solutions.* Here the individual draws on her or his own store of knowledge and experience to recommend a course of action. These often begin with the words:

What I would do is . . .
Why don't you . . .
Have you tried . . .?

4.   *Persuading with logic, arguing, lecturing.* The underlying assumption in these is that the person has not adequately reasoned it through and needs help in doing so. Such responses may begin:

The facts are that . . .
Yes, but . . .
Let's reason this through . . .

5.   *Moralizing, preaching, telling them their duty.* An underlying moral code is invoked here in "should" or "ought" language. The implicit communication is instruction in proper morals. ("Preaching" here is used in its more negative sense, of course.) Such communications might start:

You should . . .
You really ought to . . .
It's your duty as a ____ to . . .

6.   *Judging, criticizing, disagreeing, blaming.* The common element here is an implication that there is something wrong with the person or with what he or she has said. Note that simple disagreement is included in this group.

It's your own fault.
You're being too selfish.
You're wrong.

In this group as in most of the others, the same message can be implied without using these exact words.

7. *Agreeing, approving, praising.* Some people are surprised to find this included with the roadblocks. This kind of message gives a sanction or approval to what has been said. This, too, stops the communication process and may also imply an uneven relationship between speaker and listener. True listening is different from approving and does not require approval.

I think you're absolutely right . . .
That's what I would do . . .
You're a good boy . . .

8. *Shaming, ridiculing, name-calling.* Here the disapproval is more overt, and is directed at the individual in hopes of "correcting" a behavior or attitude.

That's really stupid.
You should be ashamed of yourself.
How could you do such a thing?

9. *Interpreting, analyzing.* This is a very common and tempting one for counselors: to seek out the hidden meaning for the person and give your own interpretation.

You don't really mean that.
Do you know what your *real* problem is . . . ?
You're just trying to make me look bad.

10. *Reassuring, sympathizing, consoling.* The intent here is usually to help the person feel better. What's wrong with that? Nothing, perhaps, but it's not listening. It meets the criterion as a roadblock because it interferes with the spontaneous flow of communication. Examples:

There, there, it's not all that bad.
Things are going to work out all right.
Don't worry, you'll look back on this in a year and laugh.

11. *Questioning, probing.* People also mistake asking questions for good listening. Here the intent is to probe further, find out more. A hidden communication from the questioner, however, is that he or she will be able to find a solution as soon as enough questions have been asked. Questions interfere with the spontaneous flow of communication, diverting it in directions of interest to the questioner but not, perhaps, to the speaker.

What makes you feel that way?
How are you going to do that?
Why?

12. *Withdrawing, distracting, humoring, changing the subject.* Finally, this very direct roadblock is an attempt to "take the person's mind off it." It directly diverts communication, and underneath implies that what the person was saying is not important or should not be pursued.

Let's talk about that some other time.
That reminds me of the time . . .
Hey, what's all the fuss about?
You think *you've* got problems, let me tell you . . .
I hear it's going to be a nice day tomorrow.
Oh, don't be so gloomy. Look on the bright side . . .

Source: W. R. Miller & K. A. Jackson, *Practical psychology for pastors* (Englewood Cliffs, N.J.: Prentice Hall, 1985), pp. 35–37.

least three places where misunderstanding can arise. The speaker begins with an intention, a private thought, something that he or she means to say. This meaning is coded into words that are spoken, and in this process of *encoding* is the first place where miscommunication can happen. The speaker may not say what she or he really means. Second, the spoken words must be heard by the listener, and this *hearing* process is a second potential point for break-down. The listener may not hear the words correctly. Third, the listener has to decode the words that were heard, to figure out what they mean. This *decoding* process is a third point where miscommunication readily arises. Thus, by the time the listener interprets a meaning from the words, three translation processes have occurred: coding, hearing, and decoding. Little wonder, then, that the meaning that the listener receives can be very different from the meaning that the speaker intended.

The process of reflective listening attempts to avoid such miscommunication by checking the listener's interpretation against the speaker's meaning. Consider this conversation between a student and a professor:

STUDENT: I'm trying to figure out what courses to take next semester. There are so many possibilities!

PROFESSOR: And you want to sort out which courses make the most sense for you.

S: Right. Really, though, I guess I'm trying to decide where I'm headed, what I want to do after I graduate.

P: So until you figure that out, it's hard to think about what courses you should take. It sounds like you're feeling a little confused about that.

S: Well, not confused so much as curious. There are so many things that interest me. I really like psychology, and I can imagine myself going into that. I enjoy being around people, and I've thought about working in personnel, or even being a tour guide for travelers. I love to travel. Business kind of interests me, too.

P: You're a little like the kid in the candy store: so many tasty possibilities!

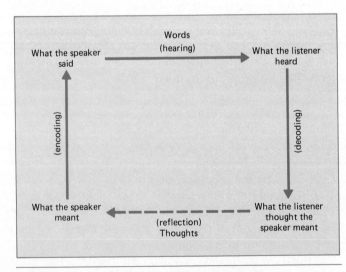

FIGURE 10-1   A MODEL OF COMMUNICATION

Adapted from Thomas Gordon, *Parent Effectiveness Training.* (New York: Wyden, 1970).

S: Exactly! I could probably do well in any of these. But which one? I don't know how to decide.

P: Part of the problem, then, is figuring out *how* to decide among all these attractive choices.

S: I want to know what it would be like actually to be working at these jobs.

P: "Curious," you said a moment ago. You really want to find out what it's like to be out there working in jobs, so you could get a better sense of how much you might like them.

S: Well, I think I'd really like any of them. The question is more which one is *right* for me.

P: Where you belong.

S: Yes. I have a sense that one of these is the right one for me, but I'm not sure how to find out which one.

In Chapter 13 we will discuss some of the ways in which this student might begin sorting out a career direction. For now, however, our focus is on the way in which the professor listened to this student. Look closely. Notice that every one of the professor's responses was a reflection of what she thought the student was saying. She wasn't right every time, but always the student responded by saying more, by exploring further. What sounded like a request for academic advisement turned out to be a much larger question of the student's life direction. Had the professor whipped out the class schedule and started advising after the first question, she would not have learned what the issue really was.

Reflective listening is an important therapeutic skill. Therapists in training are often taught how to respond in this way. Therapy usually involves much *more* than reflective listening, but research indicates that clients' improvement is greater when they work with therapists who are skillful at accurate empathy (Garfield & Bergin, 1986; Miller, Taylor, & West, 1980). In therapy, as in other settings, understanding builds stronger relationships.

Intimacy.   Unlike most therapy, however, close relationships usually involve two-way intimacy, with both partners sharing their inner lives with each other. Listening is not enough for forming an intimate relationship. Close relationships are built on the regular mutual sharing of feelings, thoughts, values, interests, and affection. Assertive communication (Chapter 9) is an important adjustment skill within relationships. From a nine-year longitudinal study of 487 couples, Gottman (1979) concluded that good "arguing" skills are very important in helping couples stay together in the long run.

Marriage enrichment groups have sometimes used a method known as "love letters" to encourage intimate expression within relationships (Doherty, McCabe, & Ryder, 1978). In this approach, a topic for discussion is chosen or assigned, and each partner sits down alone for a designated period of time (perhaps ten minutes) to write down his or her thoughts and feelings on the topic. Then the partners exchange their writings, each reading the other's. Finally, they talk together about the topic, starting from what they have written and read. By starting with individual reflection and writing, this process is sometimes helpful in facilitating mutual expression.

PROBLEM SOLVING

Besides listening and expressing feelings, it is important that the partners in a relationship have skills for solving problems that arise. Otherwise, they may reach an impasse whenever dissatisfaction is expressed, having no adequate means to resolve the problem.

A first step is to agree to work on solving the problem. Frustration and misunderstanding can arise if one partner is simply wanting to express feelings while the other is trying to solve the problem. There is a time for each, but it is best to be clear which is happening: expressing or problem solving? Reflective listening is an appropriate response to expressing. When problem solving is the goal, however, then suggesting possible solutions is appropriate. (Remember that making suggestions constitutes a roadblock when the goal is listening.)

A second step is to clarify the problem. Usually it is helpful to state the problem in brief, specific, nonblaming terms. Another important guideline is that an issue is a problem even if only one partner is upset about it (Kelley et al., 1983).

A third step in problem solving is **brainstorming.** This involves generating as many different solutions as possible, without stopping to criticize or evaluate them. All possible solutions count, no matter how unrealistic or unacceptable they may seem at first. The purpose here is to come up with a number of possibilities.

Next comes the process of choosing (and in the case of relationships, negotiating) an acceptable solution. Possible alternatives are discussed and evaluated and then a mutually agreeable choice is found. (If this fails, return to brainstorming to seek additional alternatives.) Sometimes such solutions involve a kind of trading, in which each agrees to one solution in exchange for another desirable change. Several successful approaches to marital therapy have been based on the teaching of such negotiation skills (Jacobson & Margolin, 1979; Patterson, 1976; Stuart, 1980).

Finally, there is an ongoing evaluation of how this solution is working. Most decisions are reversible, and a decision to *try* one solution is usually just that. Experience may indicate that the chosen solution is not working well, and that the problem-solving process should be renewed.

BALANCING OF POSITIVES AND NEGATIVES

Brainstorming
generating ideas freely, without censoring or criticizing them.

Dissatisfaction in relationships often arises from what one or both partners may perceive to be an unfavorable balance of positives and negatives. For

---

10.9 FIVE STEPS IN PROBLEM SOLVING

1. Focus on problem solving.
2. Clarify the problem to be solved.
3. Brainstorm potential solutions.
4. Choose the best solution.
5. Try it and evaluate.

reasons discussed earlier, close relationships can drift away from early patterns of affection and positive exchanges, toward the use of negative control tactics. When punishments outnumber rewards in a relationship, dissatisfaction arises. Indeed, by the time couples seek help in their relationship, they often have deteriorated to the place of exchanging mostly negatives, while offering each other very few positives.

A protection against this negative drift is intentionally to increase positives expressed within the relationship. This means that each partner needs to know what *is* positive for the other. That which is positive and important for one may not be so for the other. For this reason, acknowledgment and thanks are important in order to let the other person know what is positive and appreciated (Remember our earlier comment about backrubs. Have you ever given a backrub to someone who gives no clue about what feels good or even whether the backrub is appreciated at all?) With this knowledge of what is positive for the other, each partner can strengthen the relationship by increasing positives.

The other side of avoiding negative drift is to resist the temptation to rely upon punishment and negative feedback. Again it is important for each partner to understand what *is* negative for the other. With this knowledge, each can strengthen the relationship by intentionally avoiding these negatives when possible, and finding alternative methods for communication and problem solving. Each partner has a responsibility to let the other know what is especially negative, and to ask for and negotiate change. Maintaining a healthy balance of positives over negatives is an important process in keeping close relationships strong (Levinger, 1983).

■ SEEKING HELP

When problems arise or negatives outweigh positives in a relationship, one option is to seek outside help. Marital and family therapy has been a rapidly growing specialty for several decades. In addition to traditional therapeutic settings, an increasing variety of relationship enhancement workshops have appeared (Guerney, 1977). The common goal is to help people improve their close relationships.

When is it appropriate to seek outside help in a relationship? In general, we would answer that it is appropriate when the relationship shows signs of negative drift (see Box 10.7) and the partners' own efforts have been insufficient to improve the relationship. Many of the issues involved in seeking individual professional help (see Appendix A) also apply here. Yet there are some important differences as well.

One unique aspect is that one partner in the relationship may perceive a problem while the other does not. One may want to seek help, while the other is reluctant to go. Unrealistic expectations about relationship therapy may be part of the problem. For example, a partner may be reluctant to seek help because of the perception that therapy involves determining which partner is to blame for the problem. Given that perception, it is understandable that therapy would be seen as threatening. Another possibility is that the reluctant partner fears changing what seems an acceptable or advantageous state of affairs in their relationship.

These concerns in turn point to other unique aspects of relationship therapy. Ideally, the focus is on the *relationship* rather than on individuals. There is no attempt to assign blame; rather the partners work together with a therapist to bring about a positive change in their relationship. Effective therapies

The common goal in couple therapy is helping people to improve the quality of their relationship.

focus on areas reviewed earlier: patterns of communication, problem-solving and negotiation skills, and positive and negative exchanges in the relationship (Gurman, Kniskern, & Pinsof, 1986; Jacobson & Margolin, 1979).

AN IDEAL RELATIONSHIP

An important issue is that relationship therapy necessarily rests upon a model of what an "ideal" relationship should be. In seeking help, it is important to consider the goals or ideals toward which one wishes to work. A particular therapist's approach may be guided by what have been very powerful stereotyped roles of how men and women should be within relationships. Studies of how power is shared in relationships reveal that a strong imbalance of power is the norm, with males holding more power than females in a number of overt and subtle ways. Traditional feminine contributions to relationships tend to be valued less (Sprecher, 1985), and models of mental health tend to be oriented toward stereotyped male characteristics (Broverman et al., 1970; Long & Heggen, 1988). During conversations, wives propose twice as many topics for discussion as their husbands, yet succeed in having their topics actually discussed only half as often (Fishman, 1983). This parallels more general research on male-female dialogue, showing that 96 percent of interruptions in opposite-sex conversations are from men interrupting women. This is strikingly different from what occurs in same-sex pair conversations, where interruption rates are approximately equal (Zimmerman & West, 1975; West & Zimmerman, 1983). These data indicate that within our society men take and are given "conversational authority" when communicating with women. Both men and women contribute by their behavior to men's control patterns in conversation, even to the detriment of effectiveness on team problem-solving tasks (Newman, 1984). The impact of such authority and control on love relationships may be that mutuality and efficient problem solving are sacrificed.

The implicit model of an "ideal" relationship, however, is undergoing change. Today's couples differ in significant ways from past generations. More than 20 percent of baby boom women will remain child-free, in contrast with only 10 percent three decades ago (Naisbitt & Auburdene, 1985). Their choice to forgo biological mothering has implications for their intimate relationships. Couples without children report more satisfaction with their marriages than do couples with children during the child-rearing years (Campbell, Converse, & Rogers, 1975), perhaps because child-free couples have more time to devote to developing their own relationship. With the current norm of dual-career couples, people also spend more time working outside the home, further altering traditional conceptions of the nuclear family. As mentioned earlier, expectations are also shifting in a direction of greater equality within close relationships. In seeking help in a relationship, it is wise to discuss what are the therapist's own goals and ideals for relationships.

■ WHEN RELATIONSHIPS END

Sometimes, despite the best efforts, relationships deteriorate. Between a third and a half of all marriages now end in divorce. Some view divorce as a normal and healthy part of life-span development. Others are concerned that we have entered an era of the "disposable relationship." In any event, the ending of intimate relationships is a common and usually painful adjustment process, though one that can be accomplished with dignity and reasonable harmony for all involved.

THE DECISION TO STAY OR GO

How do people decide whether to end a relationship or to persist? The balance of positives to negatives is one factor. Also important is what a partner may see as *alternatives.* A very difficult relationship may nevertheless be tolerated if it is seen as better than the alternatives (financial insecurity, fear of growing old alone, etc.). On the other hand, the development of an "affair," a new and attractive intimate relationship, provides a positive alternative that may tip the balance in favor of dissolving a marriage. For some, strong personal values lead them to endure extreme adversity with hope that the relationship will improve. Others are inclined to end a relationship at the first serious disappointment of their expectations.

It is indeed difficult to judge when endurance is justified or when ending the relationship might be the best course. Prolonged conflict and physical and psychological abuse in a continuing relationship can take a greater toll in the long run than separation. Indeed, one's very life may be jeopardized by staying with an abusive partner. On the other hand, we have seen couples, in our own therapeutic work, who have rebuilt their intimate relationships from a point of deterioration that even we regarded as nearly hopeless. The decision to stay or go is an intensely personal and difficult one.

ADJUSTMENT TO SEPARATION

As with any major loss, the loss of a significant intimate relationship poses a heavy adjustment challenge. Johnson (1977) proposed that adjustment to divorce involves a series of stages, similar in some ways to the process of grieving a death. Whereas our society provides a clear set of rituals for the bereaved, no such social rituals have existed to help mark and ease the transition of the death of a relationship.

The early stages of separation are often characterized by intense and rapidly changing emotions, a period that Johnson (1977) called "separation craziness." It is relatively normal for a person in this phase to undergo wild mood changes, feeling elated and confident at one moment, helpless and dejected in the next. This emotional roller coaster seems to be most severe during the period of decision to separate, and in the weeks immediately following. Uncertainty about the decision, vacillating between staying or ending it, can intensify and prolong this emotional turmoil. This is a classic example of the difficulty of an approach-avoidance conflict (Chapter 4).

Once the decision to separate is made and the initial emotions subside, the grieving and adjustment processes begin. An early challenge is how and when to tell people what has happened. The individual comes to a personal explanation of what happened, and then begins sharing this story with others. In the process of telling others, these relationships are reaffirmed and social support can be increased. Without this contact, friends may stand by, not knowing what to say or do. It can be useful to tell friends how to help, what is needed.

The person's social circle also is likely to change. Some previous friends may back away, through discomfort or loyalty to the other partner. A friendship circle that consisted mostly of couples may no longer be comfortable. New friendships emerge, and the person is again part of the "single" world, which can be a shock in itself. A temptation at this point is to jump immediately into a new primary relationship, in an attempt to fill the emotional void.

Separation from a close relationship may also require the development of new skills. To the extent that household maintenance tasks were divided, the person may not know how to change a tire or a diaper, balance a checkbook, use a washing machine, cook a meal, or open a bottle of wine. If the person has been out of the single world for a long time, skills for meeting people and socializing may be very rusty. There may also be other major transitions that accompany the separation: finding a place to live or a job, negotiating finances, dividing property, and arranging child custody.

In the longer run, intimacy may pose special challenges. The traumatic end of a relationship may leave the person with a fear of intimacy, a reluctance to trust or commit to a new relationship. The emotional impact of separation and divorce can be long-lasting. One research team studied families over a span of ten years following divorce. At eighteen months after separation, unresolved issues continued to torment both parents and children, including feelings of anger, humiliation, and rejection. With time, however, the emotional turmoil normally heals, and people find themselves capable of rebuilding close relationships and a satisfying life-style (Wallerstein & Blakeslee, 1989).

Remarriage and the new "blended" families that follow are receiving increased study. Most divorced people remarry. Visher and Visher (1988) have predicted that by the year 2000, the *majority* of families in America will be stepfamilies.

Additional alternative life-styles seem to be growing in popularity. Some Americans remain unmarried or do not remarry, but live with intimate partners. Some couples choose not to have children. It is estimated that between 5 and 10 percent of ever-married women in the United States will choose not to reproduce (Macklin, 1987). Voluntary childlessness is, however, very difficult to measure, because it requires one to determine *motivation*. It overlaps with other reasons for childlessness including fertility difficulties, the decision to delay marriage or having a family, and the disruption of relationships that might otherwise have included children. Houseknecht (1987) indicated that the 1970s trend to postpone child-bearing may have subsided in the 1980s, and that young women may be returning to more traditional values and life-styles.

■ SUMMARY

Joy is a complex emotion and can be understood as a sequence of events (STORC) rather than a single occurrence. Although some think of them as "natural" events that occur spontaneously, both joy and intimate relationships can be cultivated and nurtured. Intimate relationships are defined as close, relatively enduring dyadic relationships that involve interdependency. In the process of attraction, relationships are formed in an evolution that has been described as including acquaintance, building-up, and continuation stages. Romantic attraction is an intense emotional experience, but does not necessarily indicate the long-term stability or strength of a relationship. Notions of what constitutes an "ideal" relationship vary widely across time and cultures. As relationships develop, certain types of problems are common and predictable. Although such problems are inevitable in any relationship, they can often be anticipated and overcome. Developing specific coping skills can be helpful in building and maintaining intimate relationships. The ending of an intimate relationship is a difficult transition that requires its own unique set of adjustments.

■ QUESTIONS FOR THOUGHT

1. Think of three different times in your life when you have felt especially joyful. Describe them. Do they have anything in common?

2. What are some ways in which you might make your life more joy-filled?

3. What relationships in your life have been most joyful? Why?

4. Do you have a friend or acquaintance who often makes you laugh? What does this person say or do that appeals to your sense of humor?

5. What activities are there that you really *enjoy* doing, yet rarely do?

6. How did you meet your best friend? Were you immediately attracted to each other? How did that particular person come to be your best friend?

7. Think about the people to whom you have been romantically attracted. What have they had in common? What attributes do you find especially attractive?

8. What kinds of people are you very *unlikely* to meet because of how and where you spend your time?

9. What are the most important ingredients for you in an ideal love relationship?

10. When do you tend to feel jealous? How do you handle your feelings of jealousy?

chapter eleven

That humanity at large will ever be able to dispense with artificial paradises seems very unlikely.
—Aldous Huxley, *The Doors of Perception*

The Addictive Behaviors

OUTLINE

■ THE CONCEPT OF ADDICTIVE BEHAVIORS

Chemical Dependence
problematic involvement with and reliance upon alcohol and/or other drugs.

Substance Abuse
pathological or problem-producing patterns of eating, drinking of alcohol, or other drug use.

Addictive Behaviors
repetitive responses that yield short-term reinforcement but also actual or increased risk of harm.

Addictionology
the study of addictive behaviors; professional specialization in research or treatment in this area.

Anorexia
a condition in which the individual avoids normal intake of food, resulting in perilously low body weight and related physical and psychological problems; also called anorexia nervosa.

Bulimia
a pattern of periodic eating binges, sometimes accompanied by induced vomiting or the abuse of laxatives to purge the excessive food and weight; may occur in association with anorexia.

During the 1970s psychologists began recognizing and discussing the commonalities among a set of problem behaviors which previously had been viewed as rather different: alcohol abuse, drug abuse, cigarette smoking, and overeating. Social views of these behaviors would not suggest a great deal of similarity. In popular conceptions, alcoholism is a disease, drug abuse is a crime, gluttony is a sin, and smoking is a bad habit. What do they have in common?

The first links were made between alcohol and other drug abuse, and in the 1960s and 1970s these problems came to be seen as similar enough that alcoholics and drug abusers were sometimes treated within the same programs. The concept of **chemical dependence** combines alcohol and other drug abuse into a single construct. This remains a controversial issue today. Should there be separate treatment programs, or should alcohol and drug abuse be treated similarly and together? The same issue faces researchers. The federal government maintains separate research agencies: the National Institute on Alcohol Abuse and Alcoholism and the National Institute on Drug Abuse. Periodically the government considers whether these should remain separate institutes or should be combined.

As the social acceptability of cigarette smoking decreased through the 1980s, tobacco (and its active ingredient, nicotine) was increasingly recognized as a drug. The concept of **substance abuse** emerged, referring initially to the harmful use of chemicals such as alcohol, street drugs, tobacco, and prescription medications, but then, coming to include overeating as well.

By the late 1970s, a still broader concept had emerged: **addictive behaviors.** A journal with this title began publication in 1976, and professional books on the subject began to appear (e.g., Donovan & Marlatt, 1988; Miller, 1980). A Society of Psychologists in Addictive Behaviors was formed, organized in 1975. In various nations including the United States and the Soviet Union, a professional specialty in **addictionology** emerged.

The concept of addictive behaviors, from its beginning, encompassed a broader range of problems. Eating disorders—first obesity, then also **anorexia** and **bulimia**—were incorporated. Within this concept, a still wider range of compulsive behaviors has come to be seen as related. Sexual compulsions, "workaholism" (Oates, 1971), pathological gambling (Volberg & Steadman, 1988), and even certain types of love relationships (Norwood, 1985; Peele & Brodsky, 1975) have been described as "addictive."

■ COMMONALITIES AMONG THE ADDICTIVE BEHAVIORS

What could such a broad range of problems have in common? Though there is no generally agreed-upon definition of addictive behaviors, here are some of the characteristics shared by these problem areas.

REINFORCEMENT

A central and distinguishing characteristic of the addictive behaviors is that they are driven by fairly immediate incentives, but result in negative consequences that are more delayed. This can be described as "short-term gain, long-term pain." Unlike the immediate reward of the addictive behavior, its

11.1 IS LOVE ADDICTIVE?

Listen to the lyrics of songs about love, especially blues or country music. There are some common themes: "I've got to have you;" "Since you're gone, I feel like I'm about to die;" "The thrill is gone since you went away." The singer could equally be talking about a narcotic drug. Some lyrics even make the direct analogy, as in "Baby, don't get hooked on me."

Social psychologist Stanton Peele has argued that at least certain types of love relationships bear all the hallmarks of addiction (Peele & Brodsky, 1975). Such a love relationship rivets the person's attention, so that it becomes difficult to think about anything else. It produces a "high" during early stages, which fades over time as if tolerance were developing. People run to love to fill a felt void in their lives. An intense love relationship can be so engrossing that other aspects of life suffer: personal growth, work, studies, friendships. As a love relationship goes "out of control," erratic behavior often emerges. When love ends, a period of intense suffering (withdrawal) often follows. Peele describes such a case:

> Since Linda left, I mainly just lie in bed. I'm just too weak to move, and I have the chills all the time. . . . I've been crying a lot. . . . I try to calm myself by drinking the scotch my sister left here. . . . I feel so horrible, so dispossessed—like the real me doesn't exist anymore. (p. 69)

In her best-selling *Women Who Love Too Much*, Norwood (1985) describes a pattern (not restricted to women) of addiction to partners who are emotionally unavailable. The addiction, she maintained, is to trying to reform the partner through love and caregiving. In Norwood's view, this represents an attempt to relive and correct the emotional pain suffered in one's own family.

When is it love and when is it addiction? Peele proposes six questions for distinguishing between a healthy love relationship and one that is addictive in quality (pp. 83–84):

1. Does each lover have a secure belief in his or her own value?
2. Are the lovers improved by the relationship? By some measure outside of the relationship are they better, stronger, more attractive, more accomplished, or more sensitive individuals? Do they value the relationship for this very reason?
3. Do the lovers maintain serious interests outside the relationship, including other meaningful personal relationships?
4. Is the relationship integrated into, rather than being set off from, the totality of the lovers' lives?
5. Are the lovers beyond being possessive or jealous of each other's growth and expansion of interests?
6. Are the lovers also friends? Would they seek each other out if they should cease to be primary partners?

Addictive behaviors are alike in bringing an immediate payoff, but with a long-term cost.

negative consequences are usually more remote. The rapid reinforcement that results from engaging in the behavior seems to override prudent restraint to protect oneself against later adverse outcomes. Subjectively, this can be experienced as a compulsion to engage in the addictive behavior, which may persist despite obvious and serious negative consequences. Most people can think of clear examples from among those they know: the drinker who continues to get drunk even though it endangers his or her job and family, the person who continues smoking after a heart attack or the removal of a cancerous lung, the gambler who loses devastating sums of money again and again in hopes of "hitting the big one." What examples can you think of among those you know?

SOCIAL ACCEPTABILITY IN MODERATION

Another interesting similarity among the addictive behaviors is the fact that they are, for the most part, socially acceptable behaviors in moderation or under certain circumstances. Eating, drinking alcohol, gambling, having sexual and love relationships, using drugs (at least prescription or over-the-counter medications) to feel better—all these are accepted as normal behavior up to a point. Cigarette smoking is tolerated as a personal choice, though decreasingly so. It is when one of these reinforcing behaviors seems to go "out of control" that it is described as addictive. The behavior accelerates to the point where it creates significant risk or damage, and it persists despite these adverse consequences. Jogging or other exercise, for example, is widely regarded as a healthful activity. Some individuals, however, press themselves to the point of physical damage and persist in strenuous running despite painful injury and serious risk to their health. For them, exercise has become addictive in this sense.

SOCIAL COSTS

Another striking feature of the addictive behaviors is their immense cost to society. By a 1983 estimate, alcohol abuse alone inflicts more than $117 billion in annual social costs within the United States, in addition to the roughly $67 billion spent each year to purchase alcoholic beverages (National Institute on

Alcohol Abuse and Alcoholism, 1987). Alcohol abuse is directly linked to about 100,000 premature deaths per year in the United States, and may contribute indirectly to as many as 100,000 more. Cigarette smoking contributes to approximately 300,000 premature deaths per year (Surgeon General, 1984). Gambling and drug abuse provide multibillion-dollar markets for organized crime. Even legalized gambling, however, absorbs astounding wealth. A freeway billboard for one casino, for example, advertised $880 million paid out in one year through their slot machines. If one assumes at least a two-to-one profit margin, then the patrons of this single hotel casino put nearly $2 billion per year into the slot machines alone! Smoking, alcohol abuse, and overeating account heavily for the two leading causes of death in our society: heart disease and cancer. Alcohol-related fatalities (including deaths from falls, drowning, injuries, homicide, suicide, freezing, cirrhosis of the liver, and automobile accidents) represent the number one cause of death for people under the age of 40.

SOCIAL AMBIVALENCE

It is not surprising, then, that the addictive behaviors are also typically behaviors about which we as a society are profoundly ambivalent. They are accepted in moderation, but can inflict terrible tolls in excess. On one hand, we extol, through advertising and social communications, the attractiveness and virtues of drinking, smoking, working, eating, sexuality, using "proper" drugs, and gambling. Although some of these behaviors are rejected and prohibited by some parts of our society (such as certain religious groups), they are widely regarded as acceptable and enjoyable. In many ways, society is structured to encourage these behaviors. Yet there is no one who does not witness the devastating effects when these behaviors become excessive and addictive in their friends, family, or themselves. We strike out periodically through social prohibition, a "war" on drugs, raids on gambling operations, or aggressive educational campaigns. But the behaviors themselves remain deeply embedded within our society.

OVERLAP

One last noteworthy point is that there is substantial overlap among the addictive behaviors. They often occur together. Smoking and drinking behavior, for example, are highly correlated. Heavy drinkers also tend to be heavy smokers (Bobo et al., 1987; Klatsky et al., 1977). Among women, heavy drinking also

There is much social ambivalence about alcohol.

overlaps with a wide range of dieting behaviors (Van Gelder, 1987). Alcoholism treatment centers, upon closer examination, are finding that a majority of their patients also abuse other drugs. It is no coincidence that casinos serve free drinks to their "high rollers," for with intoxication comes increased (and often foolish) risk taking.

11.2   IS THERE AN "ADDICTIVE PERSONALITY"?

Early psychological theories of alcoholism, drug abuse, and other addictive behaviors viewed them as symptoms of a disturbed personality. The belief was that a certain *type of personality* was inclined toward addictive behaviors. Following this line of reasoning, researchers began the search for unique characteristics of "the alcoholic personality" or "the addictive personality."

There were many hypotheses. Alcoholism, for example, was claimed to be symptomatic of neurosis, of sex-role ambivalence, of abnormal needs for power and control, of passive dependence, and of latent homosexuality. Yet four decades of searching have failed to yield any consistent personality picture that is unique to alcoholics. Commenting on the conflicting and contradictory findings of studies in this area, Miller (1976) observed: "One could conclude from this research that the average alcoholic is a passive, overactive, inhibited, acting-out, withdrawn, gregarious psychopath with a conscience, defending against poor defenses as a result of excessive and insufficient mothering" (p. 657).

When consistencies do emerge, they appear to be more the damaging *effects* of overdrinking than personality prerequisites for alcoholism. Alcoholics, for example, commonly show an abnormally strong pattern of a behavior pattern known as **field dependence.** This means, essentially, that their perceptions are more strongly dominated by the environment around them (the field), and they are less able to separate their own reality from the world around them (Barnes, 1979). Other evidence, however, indicates that this is the result of alcohol-inflicted damage to the brain, and when alcoholics recover they tend to become less field dependent (Miller & Saucedo, 1983).

Perhaps there is not *one* alcoholic personality, but rather a set of personality subtypes.

It might be that several different personality types are predisposed toward problematic drinking. Research on this topic has, indeed, pointed toward four major personality subtypes found among people with diagnosed alcoholism (e.g. Løberg & Miller, 1986). These four profiles, however, very strongly resemble the four types of personality clusters found within a normal population. The overall implication is that there is no unique alcoholic personality (or set of personalities) and that people who abuse alcohol are about as different from one another as the general population. It is not surprising, then, that the search for a still more general "addictive" personality (held in common by alcoholics, drug abusers, gamblers, overeaters, etc.) has not proved very fruitful.

One line of research has produced some interesting evidence of what may be characteristics of a prealcoholic personality, of individuals with higher than average risk of developing alcohol or other drug problems. Several research programs have studied children from birth or a very young age, and followed them through adolescence or adulthood (Jones, 1968; McCord & McCord, 1962), or have examined childhood records (Robins, Bates, & O'Neal, 1962). Children who would later become alcoholics differed from others, showing a pattern of greater aggressiveness, overactivity, and antisocial behavior. Said another way, the prealcoholic children showed signs of poor development of self-control skills. Beyond this, no personality characteristics stood out as risk factors. A major thirty-year follow-up study of adults (Vaillant, 1983) yielded a similar conclusion: no particular personality type is predominant among alcoholics, except for the expected effects of excessive drinking itself. Rather than a unique personality, wide individual differences characterize those we call "addicted" (Peele, 1985).

■ CAUSES OF ADDICTIVE BEHAVIOR

Conceptions of the *causes* of addictive behavior have been a subject of much confusion and transition. *Moral* models emphasize the personal responsibility of the individual for choosing and engaging in the behavior. Within this perspective, appropriate responses might be criminal sanctions, spiritual exhortation, or values education. *Disease* models, by contrast, view the individual as "sick" and not morally responsible for his or her problem. The emphasis here is often on biological or genetic factors. Other models emphasize the influence of *psychological* factors such as social learning, intrapsychic conflicts, dysfunctional family systems, personal needs, and motivations. If such are the causes of addictive behaviors, then it is appropriate to offer psychological interventions such as behavior therapy, family therapy, or other forms of psychotherapy. Finally, *sociological* models emphasize the role of the environment in causing addictive behaviors, examining factors such as availability, social expectations and sanctions. Those emphasizing sociological perspectives might favor measures to restrict availability, to reeducate society as to risks and dangers, and to alter patterns of social sanctions for addictive behavior.

Attempts to address or prevent addictive behaviors have often relied upon simplistic models and approaches. It has been common, for example, to emphasize one of the foregoing causes to the exclusion of others. Drug abuse interventions in our society have relied heavily upon moral approaches, emphasizing values education and criminal legislation intended to restrict the supply and use of drugs. Alcohol abuse is now popularly conceptualized as a biological aberration, a mysterious disease with genetic roots (Milam & Ketcham, 1983).

Our own perspective is that *all* the causal factors listed are important influences on addictive behavior and that a truly comprehensive view is required to address these problems effectively. In fact, another commonality of the addictive behaviors has been the failure of any single causal theory to account for and alleviate them. Approaches that emphasize only one causal aspect invariably fail to address the larger problem effectively. In discussing the addictive behaviors, then, we will again employ the STORC model, which takes into account a broad range of causal factors.

S—SITUATIONAL FACTORS

Suppose you were challenged with a bet (speaking of gambling). Suppose you were offered a thousand dollars if you could correctly choose a person with an alcohol problem from among total strangers. You could know nothing about the person's own drinking habits, family history, health, or social problems. That is, all the *direct* markers of alcohol abuse (health problems, social problems, heavy drinking) are unknown to you. How would you choose the person most likely to have an alcohol problem?

First, it would be prudent to choose a person who lives in an environment where alcohol is freely available at low cost. It would be unwise to choose someone from an area where alcohol is banned or relatively unavailable. Your chances of a correct choice would also be increased by selecting a person from a social group in which heavy drinking and alcohol problems are common. In the United States, for example, a population with a rather high rate of alcohol consumption and problems in general is found on military bases, where alcoholic beverages are readily available at low cost. Because smoking and drinking are highly correlated, it would also be wise to choose a heavy smoker. A young male would be a good choice, since men have substantially higher risk for problem drinking than women do, and the peak risk period is during their twenties.

Field Dependence
a consistent personal pattern in which perceptions of objects are highly influenced by the background or environment surrounding them.

All these are *risk factors*, markers of a person at higher risk of developing alcohol problems. Those to whom alcohol is readily available and whose friends practice heavy drinking are more likely to consume larger quantities of alcohol. In most societies, young males are at higher risk, perhaps because male sex-role behavior favors heavier consumption (though one could also posit a biological explanation of the sex difference). Those who consume large quantities of alcohol are, in turn, at higher risk of experiencing alcohol-related problems and health damage.

Besides these general social risk factors, an individual's addictive behavior changes in response to specific situational factors. Most drinkers, for example, are likely to consume more alcohol in some situations than in others. Place, companions, time of day, day of the week, activities happening around the person, even the type or pace of background music may influence alcohol consumption. *Modeling* by others is also a powerful influence on addictive behaviors. The sight of another person having a drink, lighting up, shooting up, or eating large quantities of high-calorie food can have a facilitating effect on the same behavior in the observer.

T—THOUGHT PATTERNS

Cognitive factors can also play a powerful role in addictive behaviors. One important type of cognition is the individual's **expectancies** about the behavior. If a person expects beneficial effects and has positive associations from using a certain drug, for example, then use is more likely to occur. Positive expectancies are reflected in statements such as "I need a _____," or "I'd feel better if I just had a _____." So powerful are expectancies that they shape the actual effects that are experienced.

This has been demonstrated in a large number of studies employing a research method known as the **balanced placebo design** (see Figure 11-1). In this design, people are assigned at random to one of four groups. Half are told that they are receiving the drug (alcohol, for example), and the other half are told that they are receiving no drug at all. Each of these two groups is in turn split in two, with half actually receiving the drug and the other half actually

Expectancy
the anticipated result or outcome of an action.

Balanced Placebo Design
an experimental procedure used to separate the effects of a drug from the expectancy effects associated with knowing one is taking the drug; the balanced placebo group in this design is administered the drug without being told that they are receiving it.

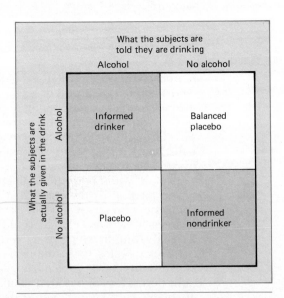

FIGURE 11-1 THE BALANCED PLACEBO DESIGN

receiving no drug. These, then, are the four groups: (1) the drug group, which expects and receives the drug; (2) the placebo group, which expects the drug but does not receive it; (3) the drug-free group, which does not expect the drug and does not receive it, and (4) the balanced placebo group, which receives the drug without expecting it. The value of this research design is that it allows one to separate the effects of expectancy from the effects of the drug itself.

When this design is used to study the effects of drinking, all participants receive a flavored "cocktail" which may or may not have alcohol in it. The cocktail is mixed in such a way that drinkers cannot detect the presence or absence of alcohol. Some are told they are drinking alcohol, while others are told their drink contains no alcohol. Such studies have shown that many of the effects attributed to the drug alcohol are, in fact, the result of the drinker's expectations (Marlatt & Rohsenow, 1980). *Believing* that one is drinking alcohol (whether or not the alcohol is there) has been shown to increase sexual arousal, alter anxiety, make humor seem funnier, and increase aggression. Several studies of alcoholics have found that subjective craving and "loss of control" behaviors occur when alcoholics *believe* they have consumed alcohol, whether or not they actually received alcohol. In fact, the only effects that have been found thus far to be purely the result of the drug alcohol are changes in performance measures such as reaction time, memory, and concentration abilities. In the case of sexual arousal, the actual effect of the drug alcohol is a sedative effect, decreasing arousal. Sexual arousal and excitement that occur with drinking appear to be purely expectancy effects (see Chapter 12).

It is not irrelevant, then, what people *expect* to happen when they engage in an addictive behavior. Accurate or not, the expectancy of an immediate positive effect serves as a strong incentive for engaging in addictive behaviors. Furthermore, the expectancy can become a self-fulfilling prophecy because it influences what the person actually experiences. With certain drugs such as marijuana, a new user often must be "educated" as to the expected positive effects in order to experience them.

Many of the "effects" of drinking and other drugs on social behavior result from expectations, and not from the drug itself.

11.3   EXPECTATIONS ABOUT ALCOHOL

What do Americans expect to happen when they drink? Sandra Brown and her colleagues (1980) explored this question in a series of studies. A questionnaire originally developed with a large group of normal college students revealed six major themes:

1. *Perception.* Alcohol transforms experiences and makes them seem more positive.
2. *Pleasure.* Alcohol increases social and physical pleasure.
3. *Sexuality.* Alcohol increases sexual performance and enhances sexual experiences.
4. *Power.* Alcohol makes you feel more powerful and behave more aggressively.
5. *Sociability.* Alcohol increases social comfort and enhances social assertiveness.
6. *Relaxation.* Alcohol reduces tension.

While people overall had positive expectations about alcohol's effects on behavior, the expectancies held by *heavier* drinkers were still more positive, particularly with regard to sexuality and power themes. That is, people with more positive expectations about alcohol's effects also tended to drink more of it and to have more alcohol-related problems (Goldman, Brown, & Christiansen, 1987). This research group also showed that young adolescents who held more positive expectancies about alcohol were more likely, one or two years later, to be problem drinkers (Roehling et al., 1987; Smith et al., 1986). Having positive beliefs about the effects and benefits of drinking, then, is not a harmless matter.

The advertising of alcoholic beverages, of course, is designed precisely to create positive associations and expectations with regard to alcohol. Ads associate alcohol with fun and pleasure, sexual eroticism, social success, physical strength and attractiveness, personal power, and wealth. This is not unique to alcohol advertising. Similar tactics are used to sell clothing, automobiles, and a wide variety of other products. In the case of alcohol, however, the truth is often precisely the opposite of what is implied in advertising. Consider these contrasts:

WHAT PEOPLE *EXPECT* ALCOHOL TO DO (ALSO THEMES IN ADVERTISING)	WHAT ALCOHOL *REALLY* DOES
Alcohol relaxes you and makes you feel better.	Alcohol has no beneficial effect on mood. Pleasant feelings sometimes associated with the first few drinks are probably the result of expectations and social factors. Having more than a few drinks has been shown to *increase* anxiety and depression.
Drinking gives you social ease and status and places you with the successful people.	Drinking is not associated with any particular social class. Heavy drinking is associated with social and economic failure, divorce, job loss, and poor social judgment.
(For men): Drinking alcohol makes you more masculine and is the pastime of men who are physically strong and successful.	Although alcohol increases *fantasies* of being masculine and powerful, in fact the opposite is true. Heavy drinking has been shown to decrease male sex hormones and to "feminize" the male

(For women): Drinking alcohol makes you more feminine, and is the pastime of beautiful and desirable women.

body by promoting hair loss, breast development, and shrinkage of the testicles. Although alcohol increases *fantasies* of being feminine and attractive, in fact the opposite is true. Heavy drinking has been shown to interfere with female sex hormones and is associated with sexual, menstrual, gynecological, and infertility problems.

Drinking is part of a healthy life-style and is good for your heart.

It has never been proved that moderate drinking is good for the heart. It *is* clear, however, that heavy drinkers have much higher overall rates of death and disease (including heart disease) than do non-drinkers. Heavy drinking compromises the body's immune system and is specifically related to high blood pressure and weakening of heart muscle.

Drinking makes you sexy.

In fact, the actual drug effect of alcohol is to *reduce* sexual arousal. Any feeling of being more sexy while drinking is psychological, the result of expectations. Intoxication makes both men and women less able to respond sexually. Over time, heavy drinking decreases sexual desire and sex hormones. Intoxication is also linked to poor judgment, unsafe sex practices, and increased risk of AIDS and other sexually transmitted diseases.

Drinking makes you more friendly, witty, and sociable.

Alcohol does not improve social skills, though intoxication may cause a person to *perceive* himself or herself as smooth and witty. Changes in social behavior arise mostly from expectations. Alcoholics typically show poor social skills. Heavy drinking has been clearly linked to a predictable pattern of brain damage.

Drinkers are cool, even-tempered, and relaxed and lead exciting lives.

Heavy drinking is associated with poor judgment, foolish risk taking, overreaction, aggression, and violence. Over half of all violent crimes are committed by people under the influence of alcohol. About half of all deaths by fire, drowning, falls, suicide, homicide, and automobile crashes are associated with alcohol.

Abstinence Phobia
feared negative consequences of stopping an addictive behavior.

Another type of expectancy that can play an important role is the person's expectations about what would happen if he or she refrained from the addictive behavior. People suffering from anorexia or bulimia commonly fear that they would become obese if they refrained from their habitual starving or self-induced vomiting. Users of alcohol, tobacco, or other drugs may fear the suffering they expect to experience if they give up the drug. Psychologist Sharon Hall (1979) has termed this the **abstinence phobia.**

An intriguing cognitive phenomenon known as the **abstinence violation effect** may also play a role in maintaining addictive behaviors (Marlatt & Gordon, 1985). Imagine the following situation. You're an ex-smoker who hasn't had a cigarette for three months. You've struggled with the desire to go back to smoking. At a party where many people are smoking, a friend takes out a pack, taps it to expose the filter of your favorite brand, and offers you one. Five seconds later you are smoking. What happens next in your thoughts? Might it be something like this?

> Wow, this tastes great! But now I've done it. I'm a smoker again. All my hard work for three months down the drain! I didn't plan to smoke, but I guess this addiction of mine is just too strong for me. Now that I've started again, I'll never beat the craving. Well, I've got nothing to lose now. Might as well have another one.

The same inner monologue, with minor variations, could well occur for the abstinent problem drinker having one drink, the dieter breaking a diet, or the recovering gambler who has just placed a bet. The **slip,** which in itself need not turn into a full-blown **relapse,** suddenly takes on monumental importance. All the credit for months of "good behavior" is seen as lost. The person expects and fears craving, loss of control, being overpowered. The person's whole identity shifts, with one act, from "nonsmoker" to "smoker," from "on the wagon" to "off the wagon," from "straight" to "junkie," or from "on the diet" to "off the diet." The person's thoughts transform a simple slip into a major relapse (Marlatt & Gordon, 1985). Such "all or nothing" thinking is an extreme view that precludes seeing a range of intermediate possibilities. Cognitive restructuring (see Chapter 6) of such thoughts, then, may help to prevent a slip from turning into a full relapse (Cummings, Gordon, & Marlatt, 1980).

O—ORGANIC FACTORS

Organic factors in addictive behaviors tend to fall into two general classes: genetic risk factors that predispose a person toward the problem behavior and biological aspects of the addictive behavior itself. We will begin our discussion with the latter.

Some behaviors are inherently reinforcing. Obvious examples are eating and sexual behavior. As discussed earlier, certain drugs have a powerful reinforcing effect, such that laboratory animals will work to the point of exhaustion in order to receive small doses. Morphine and heroin, for example, directly stimulate reinforcing channels in the brain that are normally served by the endorphins (Chapter 10). The "high" that runners experience from long-distance running may occur through stimulation of the natural production of these same endorphins. A puff on a cigarette delivers a stimulating dose of nicotine directly to the brain within a matter of seconds. A drink of alcohol on an empty stomach reaches the bloodstream within a matter of minutes, and from there immediately affects the brain. Through organic effects such as these, addictive behaviors can be strongly reinforced.

Another important phenomenon in understanding addiction is **tolerance.** Stated simply, tolerance is a relative insensitivity. As tolerance for a drug is acquired, for example, the effect of a given dose decreases. Larger and larger doses are required to yield the same effect. With a drug, this can happen in several ways. The person's **metabolic tolerance** may increase, so that the body becomes more efficient at eliminating the drug. In this case, lower levels of the drug would be found in the body at a fixed time after a certain dose. **Cellular tolerance,** on the other hand, represents a change in cells and or-

---

Abstinence Violation Effect
cognitive changes that follow the breaking of a personal prohibition (e.g., breaking a diet or having one drink after going "on the wagon") and that increase the risk of this slip turning into a full relapse; associated with the work of Alan Marlatt.

Slip
a single violation of a self-chosen rule for one's own behavior.

Relapse
return to a previous pattern of behavior that one has attempted to avoid.

Tolerance
decreased sensitivity to a drug, such that a certain dose produces less effect than before or than would be expected in most individuals.

Metabolic Tolerance
decreased sensitivity to a drug, resulting from a higher rate of elimination of the drug from the body.

Cellular Tolerance
decreased sensitivity to a drug, such that bodily tissue or organs show less change in response to the drug.

gans so that they show less of a response to the drug. A heavy dose of alcohol, for example, commonly disrupts the electrical control pattern of the heart, as reflected on an electrocardiogram (EKG). Over time, however, heavy drinkers show less of this effect. The heart seems to become less sensitive to alcohol's disrupting effects. Finally **behavioral tolerance** represents a learned ability to resist the behavior changes that normally accompany a drug dose. The person is, in fact, intoxicated (as measured by level of drug in the body), but does not appear to be so. All three types of tolerance have this in common: their effect is to decrease the apparent impact of a certain drug dose.

Contrary to common belief, tolerance is not a good sign. The ability to "hold your liquor" and not feel or appear to be intoxicated is, in fact, a risk factor for developing alcohol problems. The insensitivity of tolerance amounts to the absence of normal and vital warning signs. A normal drinker (or eater) reaches a point of feeling that he or she has "had enough" after moderate intake. Some drinkers, however, are insensitive to the effects of moderate blood alcohol levels. Consequently they drink to relatively high levels of intoxication, with the mistaken notion that they are not being affected. The alcohol damages the brain and other organs of the body, but the person has no built-in warning signal. A reasonable analogy is a person who lacks all pain sensations. Rather than a blessing, this is a curse. The person without pain easily sustains serious burns, wounds, and injuries with no warning that it is happening. Typically such pain-free people do not survive.

With tolerance often comes the development of **withdrawal** symptoms, whereby the person becomes so accustomed to the drug that he or she experiences discomfort (or even severe illness) when it is withdrawn. Abstinence from the addictive behavior results in discomfort, and a return to it brings relief. Drugs vary widely in their ability to produce physical withdrawal. Heavy use of alcohol, nicotine, barbiturates (sleeping pills), or heroin can produce potent withdrawal symptoms. The severity of withdrawal symptoms also varies from restlessness and agitation (nicotine), to flu-like symptoms (heroin), to severe hallucinations, seizures, and life-threatening delirium tremens (alcohol and barbiturates). Still other drugs, such as hallucinogens, seem to have little potential for producing physical withdrawal symptoms.

Tolerance and withdrawal symptoms in turn can form part of a larger **dependence syndrome,** a cluster of behaviors that reveal increasing attachment to the drug. As dependence emerges, the person experiences increasing urgency and compulsion to engage in the behavior, commits ever more time and resources to the addiction, and returns rapidly to an addictive pattern after periods of abstinence (Gross & Edwards, 1976). Degree of dependence appears to be a useful index for judging the severity of certain addictive behaviors and for predicting relapse and recovery.

Beyond these characteristics of drugs themselves, individuals may possess certain biological or genetic characteristics that predispose them to addictive behavior problems. Evidence is strong that the children of alcoholic parents are themselves at higher risk of developing alcohol problems (Institute of Medicine, 1987). Several lines of research now indicate that genetic factors contribute to this risk. Alcoholics' children, adopted shortly after birth and raised by nonalcoholics, nevertheless show a higher risk of alcoholism than do other adopted children (Goodwin, 1976). Other studies have found that monozygotic (identical) twins of alcoholics are at significantly higher risk for developing alcoholism themselves, relative to the dizygotic twins of alcoholics (who do not share the same genetic structure). But genetics cannot be the whole story. Most children of alcoholics do not develop alcoholism themselves, and most people with alcohol problems did not have alcoholic parents. Even among the identical twins of alcoholics, who share 100 percent of their genetic material, only about half develop alcohol problems.

Behavioral Tolerance
decreased sensitivity to a drug, reflected in less change in observed responses to the drug.

Withdrawal
a set of physical symptoms that occur when an addictive drug is discontinued suddenly.

Dependence Syndrome
a set of physical and psychological changes that emerge as a person becomes addicted and the individual's life begins to center on the addiction.

Know Stimulant or Depressiant

11.4   THE PHARMACOLOGICAL EFFECTS OF ADDICTIVE DRUGS

All of the following drugs are "psychoactive"—they can alter human psychological states such as mood, motivation, and perception. This is one reason they are potentially rewarding drugs, and are prone to be abused. But what other effects can they have? The following table, adapted from Nahas and Frick (1981), summarizes other known characteristics of these drugs and their effects. Six characteristics are displayed: (1) whether the drug has been shown to be neurotoxic—damaging to the central nervous system; (2) whether it is a drug that nonhuman primates will self-administer; (3) whether it is possible to develop a tolerance to the drug; (4) whether withdrawal symptoms can occur when drug-taking is stopped; (5) whether use of the drug has been shown to cause somatic illness—damage to the body; and (6) whether users can self-administer a lethal dose. A + sign indicates "Yes", and ++ indicates a strong potential for tolerance or withdrawal symptoms. Where current information is unclear, a ? is indicated.

Drugs	Neuro. Psych. Toxic.	Reinforce (Self-Adm.)	Toler-ance	With-drawal Sympt.	So-matic	Lethal Over-dose
Opiates						
Opium	+	+	+	++	+	+
Morphine	+	+	+	++	+	+
Heroin	+	+	+	++	+	+
Synthetic agonists	+	+	+	++	+	+
Major psychostimulants						
Cocaine	+	++	++	+	+	+
Amphetamines	+	++	++	+	+	+
Psychodepressants						
Ethyl alcohol (50 ml a day)	+	+	+	++	+	+
Barbiturates	+	+	+	++	+	+
Benzodiazepines	+	+	+	++	+	
Methaqualone	+	+	+	++	+	+
Cannabis						
Hashish, marijuana (THC)	+	+?	+	+	+	
Hallucinogens						
LSD	+		+			+
Psilocybine	+		+			+
Mescaline	+		+			+
Phencyclidine	+	+	+	+	+	+
Solvents						
Benzene	+		+		+	+
Toluene	+		+		+	+
Acetone CCL$_4$	+		+		+	+

Trichloro-	+		+		+	+
ethylene	+		+		+	+
Ether, N_2O, $CHCL_3$	+		+		+	+
"Minor" psychostimulants						
Tobacco (nicotine)		?	+	+	+	
Cola			+			
Khat		+	+	+		
Caffeine			+		?	

Source: Adapted from G. G. Nahas & H. C. Frick II (eds.), *Drug abuse in the modern world* (Elmsford, N.Y.: Pergamon, 1981), Table VII, p. 23.

Other biological characteristics may influence risk for addictive behavior. As mentioned earlier, tolerance for alcohol and insensitivity to its effects can increase risk. Studies with obese people have similarly found that overweight individuals may be less sensitive to internal cues of hunger and satiation (Schachter, 1971). Their eating behavior appears to be more under the control of external, situational factors, and less regulated by internal need states.

Individuals also differ widely in their response to particular drugs. Research with animals, for example, has shown wide variation in brain sensitivity to alcohol. Some animals are heavily sedated by alcohol and fall asleep at relatively low doses, whereas others with similar history of exposure to the drug show little sedating effect at the same dose levels (Tabakoff et al., 1980). Petrie (1967) described a biologically based dimension of sensitivity to stimuli, ranging from extreme *augmenters* who are easily overwhelmed by stimulation, to extreme *reducers* who are frequently in search of stimulation (see Chapter 2). She reported that augmenters who use drugs prefer sedating chemicals (such as alcohol or barbiturates), whereas reducers prefer drugs that make the world more exciting (stimulants or hallucinogens).

Organic factors cannot be ignored in understanding addictive behaviors. Individual biological differences seem to bestow higher or lower levels of personal risk. Yet this risk may never be realized unless the individual encounters environmental conditions that favor the development of problem behavior. Likewise, addictive behaviors in themselves have powerful reinforcing properties, often with clear biological roots. Yet if this is so, why don't *most* people develop addictive patterns when dabbling with these behaviors? Eating, drinking, and gambling are common behaviors, yet most people who engage in them do not become addictively enmeshed with them. Furthermore some addictive behaviors (e.g., gambling) involve no drug and no clear physiological mechanism for addiction.

R—RESPONSE FACTORS

An addictive behavior is, by definition, a response, a behavior. One topic of interest, then, is the level and pattern of the behavior itself. For several addictive behaviors, there is evidence that engaging heavily in the response for a period of time creates a pattern likely to sustain itself. Heavy use of alcohol, tranquilizers, or barbiturates can result in increased tolerance and withdrawal signs. The person then experiences discomfort on reducing use and consumes fairly large doses to retain the desired effect and stave off withdrawal. An extended period of overeating and resulting weight gain may stretch the stomach and alter metabolism in a way that favors continued excess. A person who begins smoking in response to peer pressure can become dependent upon nicotine, eventually smoking to maintain a certain nicotine level in the bloodstream (Schachter, 1977, 1978). Thus, beyond a certain threshold of moderation, the addictive behavior may drive itself.

An interesting aspect of many addictive behaviors is the development of patterns of **binges.** Periods of abstinence or moderation alternate with binges, in which the person indulges with little restraint. Some view this as an alternation between "being good" and "being bad." Alcohol and other drug abuse, bulimia, gambling, and sexual compulsions all can follow this pattern. Apter's theory of psychological reversals (see Box 11.5) addresses such patterns in particular. Addictive behaviors can also occur as steady excess, to the point of risk or harm. This is an equally common pattern of alcohol abuse and is more characteristic of obesity and smoking.

To the extent that an addictive behavior is used as a coping skill, the availability of *alternative* responses is an important issue. Psychological dependence is usually defined as heavy or total reliance upon a response or drug for a particular kind of coping. A person might, for example, cope with nervous or depressed feelings by engaging in an addictive behavior. If this is the *only* means the person knows for coping with anxiety or depression, then he or she

Binge
a period of unrestrained indulgence.

11.5   PSYCHOLOGICAL REVERSAL THEORY

Throughout this text we have described behavior as occurring on a continuum. Depression, aggression, joy, anxiety, and behavior in general have been discussed as occurring on a more-or-less scale, as changing gradually in degree rather than suddenly.

British researcher Michael Apter (1982), however, points out that this approach to understanding behavior has its limitations. Some behaviors seem to show more a pattern of alternating between two extremes, almost in an all-or-none fashion.

Imagine a long hollow tube with both ends sealed, inside which is a rubber ball that can roll freely from one end to the other. If the middle of the tube is placed on a fulcrum, one end of the tube (where the ball is) will rest on the ground and the other will be up in the air, much as a seesaw. This is one of two stable positions in which the tube can rest. If you apply downward pressure to the upper end, the other end will slowly rise. Just after you pass the horizontal position, the ball will suddenly roll from one end to the other, and the

tube now comes to rest in its other stable position. These two positions are mutually exclusive: the tube cannot rest in both positions at once. The tube demonstrates a condition that Apter calls *bistability*. A typical light switch is another example of bistability.

Are there human behaviors with bistability? From fiction we have the example of Dr. Jekyll, who drinks a potion and is dramatically transformed into his brutal opposite, Mr. Hyde. The addictive behaviors sometimes appear to follow this pattern as well, alternating between two stable states: "being good" and "relapse." The switch from one pattern to the other is what Apter calls a *psychological reversal*. Psychologists are now seeking to understand the conditions that influence a person to undergo such a reversal, to relapse (Marlatt & Gordon, 1985). Is this, perhaps, what the addictive behaviors have in common: that they tend to flip-flop back and forth between extremes, rather than changing gradually and smoothly?

is, in this sense, psychologically dependent. (This should not be confused with the physical dependence syndrome, discussed earlier, which centers on tolerance and withdrawal symptoms.) Another person may be painfully shy and feel incapable of socializing without having had several drinks. The key here is the absence of alternative coping behaviors. Faced with the difficult situation, then, the person is likely to resort to the addictive behavior as a coping response.

C—CONSEQUENCES

Why do people drink too much? Why do people smoke, or use other drugs, or become entangled in one destructive relationship after another? Why do they gamble away their money, eat too much, or exercise themselves to death's doorstep? One obvious answer is that they find it more reinforcing than the alternatives (assuming they *know* alternatives and have access to them).

As discussed earlier, the powerful reinforcing nature of many addictive behaviors is well understood. Most drugs that are abused act directly on the brain to produce effects that are immediately reinforcing. Eating and sexual behavior are also inherently reinforcing.

But what about gambling? Here an understanding of principles of reinforcement is helpful. The reinforcer for which a gambler works in most cases is money. The gambler is not reinforced for every gambling response (which would be **continuous reinforcement**). Instead the reinforcement is periodic and unpredictable, an arrangement that is termed a **variable ratio (VR)** schedule of reinforcement. One characteristic of a behavior maintained by a VR schedule is that it is steady and very resistant to extinction. That is, the individual will keep on responding in a steady and long-lasting fashion even when no reinforcement is received. Every now and then, unpredictably, reinforcement occurs, and keeps the behavior going. The VR schedule is thus a very efficient way of maintaining a behavior. Relatively little reinforcement is needed to maintain steady and durable responding. Gambling is built completely around the principle of a VR schedule of reinforcement.

Neither the inherent brain effects of drugs nor the VR reinforcement schedule of gambling can account, however, for why some people succumb to their addictive qualities and others do not. The addictive behaviors can also yield a

Continuous Reinforcement
a schedule of reinforcement in which a behavior is rewarded every time it occurs.

Variable Ratio
a schedule of reinforcement in which a behavior is rewarded on a periodic, unpredictable basis.

All forms of gambling rely on variable reinforcement schedules.

broad range of other positive (and negative) consequences. Among these are social reinforcement for use (or nonuse), access to other desired behaviors (e.g., permission to behave in certain ways because one is "drunk"), avoidance of or escape from unpleasant consequences, and relief of unpleasant emotional states. Continued addictive behavior can be understood, within the broader context, as a preponderance of positive over negative consequences. That is, the reinforcing consequences of continuing the behavior outweigh its negative consequences and the potential positive consequences of alternative behaviors. This balancing of negative and positive incentives is diagrammed in Box 11.6. As long as the reasons favoring the behavior remain "heavier" than the perceived benefits of change, the addictive behavior continues.

11.6 THE DECISIONAL BALANCE

How do people make important life decisions? Social psychologists have discussed decision making as a process of balancing the pro's and con's of each alternative (Janis & Mann, 1977). As new factors are added to one side or the other of a personal conflict, the balance may be tipped in favor of one particular course of action.

This view of decision making may be particularly useful in understanding addictive behaviors (Appel, 1986). The following diagram illustrates a decisional "seesaw" with regard to use versus nonuse of alcohol or another drug. The "pro-use" side is weighed down by two kinds of factors: the perceived benefits of using (e.g., feeling good) and the perceived costs and risks of not using (e.g.,

being rejected by friends). On the other side are factors weighing against use: the perceived costs and risks of using (e.g., expense, brain damage) and the perceived benefits of not using (e.g., clearer thinking, improved health).

As weights are added to or removed from one side or the other, the balance can shift. Notice also that all of the weights are *perceived* benefits or costs. The balance shifts as a person's *perceptions* change. A decision to change an addictive behavior occurs as the person perceives more risks and fewer benefits associated with the behavior. Can you think of examples from your own life to which this model applies?

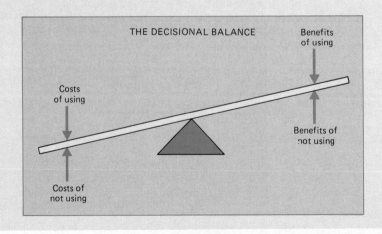

THE DECISIONAL BALANCE

Benefits of using

Costs of using

Benefits of not using

Costs of not using

■ CHANGING ADDICTIVE BEHAVIORS

In Chapter 5 we discussed a model of change which proposes that people pass through predictable *stages* as they undergo the process of change: precontemplation, contemplation, action, maintenance, and relapse. This model was developed through the study of addictive behaviors (Prochaska & DiClemente, 1986), and so it is appropriate to reconsider the model here.

The contemplation stage describes well the reinforcement balance just discussed. In the contemplation process, the individual is weighing the positives against the negatives. A drinker in the contemplation stage might say something like this:

> I think I probably do drink too much, but I really don't drink *that* much more than my friends do. Sometimes I do overdo it, though, and the next morning I can really feel it. I might not even remember what happened the night before. I do *enjoy* drinking, though, and I don't know what I'd do to loosen up if I couldn't go out drinking with my friends. Still I worry that maybe I'm hurting myself in the long run, maybe damaging my body.

The back and forth, the "Yes, but . . ." is clear. In contemplation, the person sees both the positive and the negative, and struggles to decide how much importance to give to each.

11.7   AM I DRINKING TOO MUCH?

How much is too much? How can you tell if you are overdoing it and harming yourself, or at least running a significant risk of doing so? A consensus in the field at the moment seems to be that the line between "safe" and "hazardous" drinking is best drawn between two and three drinks per day, with one "drink" being equal to 10 ounces of beer, 4 ounces of table wine, or one ounce of 100-proof distilled spirits (Gross, 1983).

Yet amounts alone can be misleading. A small woman will be substantially more affected by two drinks than will a large man. Another approach is to watch for danger signs, indications that one's drinking is getting out of hand. With a little modification, most of these signs can apply to almost any addictive behavior. Here are some of the classic warning signs, any one of which can be reason for concern:

Tolerance.   Larger doses are required to feel the effects.

Subjective Compulsion.   There is a sense of desire or need for a drink, a sense of importance or urgency about having alcohol available.

Social Problems.   Drinking begins to be associated with social problems: impaired work or study, accidents, fights, embarrassing indiscretions.

Concern of Others.   Other people express concern about the person's drinking and its negative effects.

Defensiveness.   The drinker becomes defensive in response to expressions of concern and defends the justifiability and harmlessness of drinking.

Decreased Control.   The person becomes less able to make decisions about drinking and to control the occasions and amounts of drinking.

Invariance.   The drinking pattern becomes more and more predictable, unchanging, and occupies an increasing amount of the person's time.

Memory Blackouts. The person is unable to remember all or part of what happened during a period of drinking.

Psychological Dependence. The person experiences a need for alcohol in order to cope with a particular life challenge or situation.

Withdrawal. The person experiences discomfort when *not* drinking. This can vary from mild agitation and anxiousness to extreme dependence signs such as hallucinations and delirium. Drinking relieves the discomfort temporarily.

At some point, the balance (shown in Box 11.6) tips, when the negative costs outweigh the positive benefits. At this point the person reaches a decision or determination to change and begins seeking strategies for action.

There are many different approaches for changing an addictive behavior. Although recently there has been increased emphasis on obtaining formal treatment, the fact is that most people who change an addictive behavior do so on their own, with no professional help whatsoever. Their reasons and their methods for change are quite varied (Prochaska & DiClemente, 1986). Research with these self-changers and with formal treatment methods, however, does point to some commonalities. It seems important, for example, for the individual to reach a point where the balance tips from positive to negative. In treatment, this is often termed "motivation" (Miller, 1985b). With self-changers, this may occur with a sudden crisis or scare, though the balance may also just tip slowly over time.

Another common theme is the development of *skills* for dealing with (abstaining from or controlling) the addictive behavior. Early in the change process, people often use a general strategy of *avoidance,* staying away from temptation. The new ex-smoker removes all cigarettes and ashtrays from the house and avoids friends who are smokers and situations in which smoking is more likely to occur. Later in the change process, the person may use more *active coping* strategies, exposing himself or herself to more difficult situations without relapsing.

SELF-CONTROL SKILLS

From research on how people change their behavior, it is possible to describe a set of self-control skills that can be useful in pursuing change (see Chapter 5). In a series of studies at the University of New Mexico, we have explored the effectiveness of teaching these skills to problem drinkers. To our surprise, we found in study after study that people working on their own using a behavioral self-control instruction manual (Miller & Muñoz, 1982) were just as successful in changing their drinking as people coming in for therapist-directed treatment (Buck & Miller, 1981; Miller, Gribskov, & Mortell, 1981; Miller & Taylor, 1980; Miller, Taylor, & West, 1980). Research teams in other countries have reported similar success in teaching self-control skills to problem drinkers (Alden, 1988; Berg & Skutle, 1986; Brown, 1980; Sanchez-Craig et al., 1984). These same principles have also been applied in the treatment of drug abusers (Wilkinson & LeBreton, 1986), smokers (Lichtenstein & Brown, 1980), and overeaters (Wilson, 1980).

Behavioral self-control strategies for changing addictive behaviors have commonly included six elements. First is *goal setting*, the establishment of

11.8 CONTROLLED DRINKING: A CONTINUING CONTROVERSY

When British researcher D. L. Davies reported, in 1962, that several alcohol addicts in his study had returned to stable, normal drinking, he did not expect the storm that was to follow. His study was met in the United States with an angry and distressed outcry among alcoholism professionals, who adamantly maintained that it had to be false because no true alcoholic can ever return to drinking safely. It was the beginning of what has come to be called "the controlled drinking controversy" (Marlatt, 1983).

Reports of return to moderate drinking are controversial if one accepts the assumptions of "the American disease conception of alcoholism" (Miller, 1986). The central tenet of this view is that alcoholics are qualitatively different from normal people, having an irreversible disease that renders them incapable of controlling their own drinking behavior. Based in the philosophy of Alcoholics Anonymous (1955), this view remains scientifically unproven and has been increasingly questioned (Peele, 1985).

What has been shown beyond reasonable doubt, however, is that *some* individuals, diagnosable as "alcoholic" by any modern criteria, can and do reestablish moderate and problem-free drinking, maintaining this stable pattern over a period of years (Heather & Robertson, 1981). This occurs whether the individuals received treatment intended to produce controlled drinking (Miller, 1983a), abstinence-oriented treatment (Polich, Armor, & Braiker, 1981), or even no treatment at all (Vaillant, 1983).

This finding need not be understood as threatening to traditional abstinence-oriented approaches, or even to biomedical views of the causes of alcoholism. No one asserts that moderation is an appropriate or feasible goal for everyone with alcohol-related problems. Indeed, the percentage of treated individuals who succeed in sustaining moderation over long spans of time typically ranges between 5 and 20 percent (Miller, 1983a). For others, complete abstinence from alcohol is the most successful and stable approach. The ultimate goal, regardless of approach, is to alleviate the problems and suffering that accompany excessive drinking.

Is it possible to predict who will succeed through abstinence and who will sustain problem-free moderation? Although findings thus far are mixed, one general predictor seems to be the severity of alcohol problems or alcohol dependence. Those with more severe problems are most likely to wind up abstaining, and are less likely to sustain moderation without problems. Less severe problem drinkers, on the other hand, are more likely to moderate their drinking successfully (Miller, Leckman, & Tinkcom, 1989; Polich et al., 1981). Peele (1987) maintained that a person's beliefs about alcoholism are also important predictors of outcome. Those who accept assumptions of the traditional disease view of alcoholism tend to become abstainers, whereas those who reject this view are more likely to become moderate drinkers (cf. Miller et al., 1989).

For those who embrace a traditional disease view, "controlled drinking" remains an emotionally charged issue. Critics argue that the recovering person who never drinks will never have alcohol-related problems, whereas those who resume drinking take a chance of slipping back into old patterns. It is also worth asking, "Why is it so *important* to drink? Why not just quit?" What do you think about this issue?

During the American prohibition era, it was believed that no one could drink alcohol in moderation and that any drinker was doomed to become a drunkard. In the current disease era, this status is reserved for those labeled "alcoholic." Yet alcohol problems occur along a full continuum of severity, and it is likely that a variety of alternative treatment and prevention approaches will be necessary to deal successfully with such a range of individuals. For some, abstaining from alcohol is the only real option. For others, practicing moderation is a successful strategy for preventing future problems.

clear goals toward which to direct one's self-change efforts. These can include an ambitious long-term goal of major change, as well as short-term, week-by-week goals that represent steps toward major change. Some examples of clear long-term goals are a specific ideal body weight, a "quit date," or a moderate use level that poses no important problems or health risks.

Self-monitoring is a second common element in self-control programs (see Chapter 5). Clear records of one's own behavior provide feedback about progress toward the goal. In addition, keeping records can in itself have a suppressing effect on an addictive behavior. People who self-monitor their own drinking or food intake, for example, often report that the recording process increases their awareness of the behavior and decreases their consumption.

11.9   NEW ROADS: ALTERNATIVES TO PSYCHOLOGICAL DEPENDENCE

To the psychologically dependent person, an addictive behavior is not a problem, it is a solution. It represents a way to get from one point to another. It is a vehicle used to travel from an undesirable place to a desired goal. It is a means to an end (Miller & Pechacek, 1987).

Consider the following lists. On the left are some situations and feelings that sometimes trigger an addictive behavior (or a relapse). On the right are some of the perceived positive effects which people seek from addictive behaviors, such as drinking. The two lists are arranged in such a way that each desired effect on the right corresponds to a "trigger" situation on the left. See if you can match them up:

TRIGGER SITUATIONS	DESIRED EFFECTS
Insomnia	Feel socially at ease
Feeling angry	Forget
Tension	Courage to say true feelings
Frustration with problems	Feel more powerful
Social pressure	Get to sleep
Feeling helpless	Relax
Depression	Feel better
Shyness	Be accepted by the group

In each case, the addictive behavior represents a *road* from left to right, from perceived negative to perceived positive. It may not be a very effective road. Alcohol, for example, is a very poor way to get from feeling depressed to feeling better. Nevertheless, it may be the only road a person knows.

Overcoming psychological dependence involves finding new roads, new ways to cope with the undesired "trigger" situations without relying upon an addictive behavior. Look again at the two columns. Based on what you have learned in this course thus far, can you think of new roads, alternative ways to get from left to right, without using drugs?

Examples of self-monitoring include keeping records of alcohol consumption, counting calories or cigarettes, and weighing oneself.

Rate control is a third strategy for change. This involves changing the behavior itself in a way that decreases it or slows it down. Drinkers may take smaller and less frequent sips, "nursing" each drink to make it last longer. Smokers may gradually reduce their total number of cigarettes per day and switch to low-nicotine brands. Dieters switch to low-calorie foods and practice slowing strategies such as carefully chewing each morsel or putting the fork down after each bite. This can be done either as a way of tapering down in preparation for stopping (as in preparing to quit smoking) or as an ongoing discipline for maintaining moderation (as in weight control).

Self-reinforcement is often included in self-control programs as a way of consolidating gains. When rate control strategies are used successfully, self-monitoring reflects progress toward the goal. At this point, it can be useful to celebrate the progress (though not by engaging in the problem behavior!) Through a prearranged plan, one can give oneself a reward for reaching a short-term goal that is one step toward larger change. The reward is delayed until the goal is reached, and then functions as a reinforcer for progress. An overweight person might plan to purchase new clothes as each progressive weight loss goal is met, for example. Those who have smoked or abused alcohol or other drugs sometimes talk about having "turned my habit into furniture," by saving the money they would otherwise have spent on their habit and then buying special things for themselves.

A *functional analysis* of the addictive behavior is a fifth part of most self-control programs. As indicated earlier in this chapter, such behaviors commonly occur in predictable situations. That is, a person is more likely to engage in the behavior when in certain situations, with certain companions, at certain times of day, or in association with certain activities. Careful self-monitoring records can reveal these patterns if, along with the behavior, the person records the situation in which it is occurring. Through this process, one can become aware of high-risk situations, those in which the addictive behavior is most likely to occur. Strategies can be devised, then, either to avoid them or to cope with them actively.

Psychological Dependence *reliance upon drug use or another maladaptive behavior as the primary means for coping with problems.*

When an active coping approach is chosen, then the sixth element of behavioral self-control comes into play: the need for learning *alternative coping skills*. If one has been depending upon the addictive behavior as a way of coping (**psychological dependence**), then new adjustment skills must be developed for dealing with life challenges. Without such skills, the individual is likely to resort to the addictive behavior as a known and familiar way of coping, despite its negative consequences.

■ PREVENTING RELAPSE

In addition to the commonalities discussed at the beginning of this chapter, the addictive behaviors also show another common feature: a remarkable tendency for relapse (Brownell et al., 1986). If one were to choose at random a person being discharged from alcoholism or drug abuse treatment, or a person who had just quit smoking or lost weight, the prediction most likely to be accurate is that the person would relapse within six months. Within the first six months, over 80 percent typically relapse to the addictive behavior (Hunt, Barnett, & Branch, 1971). One might conclude from this observation that the addictive behaviors are hopeless conditions. Yet that conclusion would be wrong, for over the long run most people overcome these problems. A more accurate and optimistic understanding is that the change process for addictive behaviors *normally* includes one or more relapses. This is emphasized by Prochaska and DiClemente (1982, 1984) in their transtheoretical model of stages of change (Chapter 5). Relapse is simply one stage of change, after which the person again passes through contemplation and action processes. This cycle is repeated until finally the person succeeds in maintaining the change.

Recent research suggests that relapses to addictive behaviors seldom occur "out of the blue." Relatively few people are overtaken by what they experience as an irresistible craving or by an internal, physical state that causes them to relapse. Rather, the precipitating factors are most often found in certain types of situations (S) or thought patterns (T) that place the person at higher risk of relapse. Negative emotional states are the most common antecedents of relapse: feeling depressed, angry, or anxious. These unpleasant emotional states account for about one-third of relapses to alcohol, tobacco, and excessive eating (Cummings, Gordon, & Marlatt, 1980). Social pressure and interpersonal conflicts also rank high on the list of relapse risk situations, together accounting for at least another one-third of relapses. Other commonly identified risk factors include being in a situation of temptation (passing by my favorite bar) or thought patterns that bring the person closer to relapse ("What could it hurt to have just one?") (Litman, 1986). Contrary to popular conceptions, then, relapses seem to occur in response to emotional or social events for which the person does not have an effective coping strategy (Annis & Davis, 1989).

Once a person has "slipped" and broken his or her rule for self-control, the abstinence violation effect (discussed earlier) may begin. A simple slip then can turn into a full-blown abandonment of self-control. It is important to distinguish here between a slip (a simple violation of a self-control rule) and a relapse (a full return to the previous behavior pattern). One swallow does not a relapse make! If the rule violation is given great importance, however, it may be followed by what has been called **loss of control,** a binge of the previously forbidden behavior.

Relapse risk is a highly individual matter. What poses a significant risk for one person will not for another. Consequently the prevention of relapse also requires individual planning, and there is no single prescription to follow which works for all or even most people. Relapse prevention became a very active topic of research during the 1980s. Here are three themes that have emerged thus far (Annis & Davis, 1989; Marlatt & Gordon, 1985).

LIFE-STYLE CHANGE

To escape from a destructive behavior pattern, it may be helpful or even necessary to change significant parts of one's life-style. An addictive behavior may have occupied substantial amounts of time that need to be directed in other ways. It may have been a primary source of recreation or excitement, for which a healthy substitute needs to be found (Glasser, 1976). Life-style or occupation may bring one into frequent contact with people or situations likely to increase the risk of relapse. It may be necessary to replace one's primary circle of friends. A life-style that is out of balance, dominated by stress or negative events or overworking, can predispose one to seek escape. One step in a personal relapse analysis, then, is to examine such life-style factors that regularly increase some of the most common risk factors: negative emotions, social pressure, and interpersonal conflict. Ordinary health considerations of life-style (sleep patterns, diet, exercise) can also be important.

Loss of Control
a subjective sense of being unable to restrain oneself from engaging in a particular behavior.

A lifestyle which includes regular enjoyable activities is helpful in preventing and overcoming addictive behaviors.

COGNITIVE CHANGE

For some people, impending relapse can be detected from their private thought patterns. Several common themes are inability to cope ("I can't handle this without . . ."), testing of personal control ("I could just have a few . . ."), and positive expectancies for the addictive behavior ("I'd feel so much better if I . . ."). Another potentially important cognitive phenomenon is the making of decisions which move the person closer to a relapse. These often begin with the words "It couldn't hurt if I . . .". Members of Alcoholics Anonymous refer to such thought patterns as "stinking thinking" and recognize the role these thoughts can play in returning a person to a previous harmful behavior pattern.

DEVELOPING NEW SKILLS

A third common theme in relapse prevention work is the development of new skills for coping with high-risk situations (see Box 11.9). Alternative skills for dealing with depression (Chapter 7), anxiety (Chapter 8), or anger (Chapter 9) may prevent reliance upon an addictive behavior for escape. Social pressure can be countered if the individual is skilled in assertive communication (Chapter 9). This was a central theme during the 1980s in the U.S. campaign to "Just say 'no' to drugs." Likewise research indicates that relapse is decreased by the teaching of positive skills for dealing with interpersonal conflict (Miller & Hester, 1986a).

■ SUMMARY

Although in popular thought they may seem quite different, the addictive behaviors show many commonalities. They involve engaging in behaviors that are immediately reinforcing, at the cost of long-term negative consequences. Addictive behaviors tend to be socially acceptable in moderation, but inflict immense social costs that follow when they are practiced to excess. As a result, the addictive behaviors are the subject of profound, and often emotionally intense, societal ambivalence. The causes of addictive behaviors have been the subject of debate for centuries, with moral, disease, psychological, and sociological models all having their advocates. One's understanding of the causes of addictive behaviors strongly guides the measures one is likely to favor in addressing and preventing these problems. The STORC model can again be applied as a tool for behavior analysis, emphasizing the roles played by risk factors, cognitive expectancies, physiological addiction, response patterns, and reinforcing consequences. The stages-of-change model, introduced earlier in this text, can be particularly helpful in understanding the change process with addictive behaviors. Behavioral self-control strategies for change include goal-setting, self-monitoring, rate-control, self-reinforcement, functional analysis, and alternative coping skills. Relapse, a common phenomenon in the addictive behaviors, can be prevented through understanding its causes and addressing these by learning effective coping strategies for dealing with life challenges.

■ QUESTIONS FOR THOUGHT

1. What are your own "addictions"? What is it about these behaviors that fits the label "addictive"?

2. Apply the STORC analysis approach to the behavior you chose as an answer to question 1.

3. For the behavior you chose in answering question 1, what factors (if any) encourage you to make a change? What factors favor your continuing this behavior?

4. Some argue that the government's "war on drugs" has failed to control drug use, and has further encouraged organized crime. One alternative is simply to legalize drugs that are currently illegal (marijuana, cocaine, heroin, etc.). What do you think about this idea?

5. People sometimes experience difficulty in controlling their own behavior (for example, their drinking, smoking, or sexual behavior), and find themselves doing what they know to be harmful or risky. What parts of your own life are like this? Where do you wish you had more control over your own behavior?

6. If you were placed in charge of our nation's efforts to decrease and prevent problems related to smoking and drinking, what five changes would be your highest priorities? Why?

7. Do you think that alcoholism is a "disease"? Why or why not? How about cigarette smoking? The regular use of cocaine or marijuana? Compulsive gambling? What factors decide, in your own perceptions, what constitutes a "disease"?

8. Imagine yourself in a situation where you are feeling bad. How might you complete this sentence: "I'd feel better if I just _____"?

9. Have you ever made a New Year's resolution, or made a commitment to change a certain behavior? What happened the first time you violated your resolution? What thoughts probably went through your mind at that moment?

10. Do you think there should be special restrictions on the advertising of potentially addictive drugs such as alcohol and tobacco? What restrictions (if any) do you favor? Why?

chapter twelve

I have a brain and a uterus, and I use them both.
—Patricia Schroeder, U.S. Congresswoman from Colorado

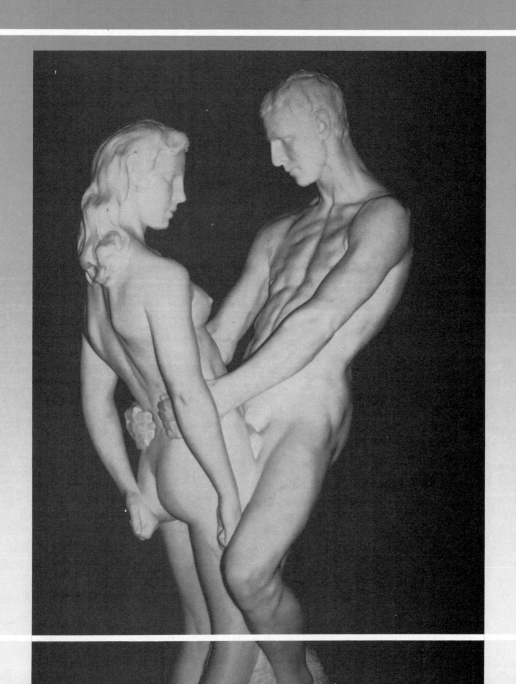

Sexual Behavior

OUTLINE

*T*his is the sex chapter. As you begin reading it, you doubtless have some expectations, hopes, fears, or imaginations about what it will contain. Within our culture, sexuality is a highly charged subject. It can evoke laughter, tears, fascination, anxiety, joy, guilt, relaxation, or anger. Sexuality is a common theme in the advertising of everything from alcohol to automobiles, from fashions to fragrances. Like aggression, sexual themes dominate the entertainment media, while sex crimes command news headlines. Sexual satisfaction is the enduring and elusive promise of a plethora of self-help books and of feature articles in nearly every popular magazine. From childhood onward throughout the life cycle, sexuality is a major theme among the challenges of adjustment.

College students, regardless of age, frequently express concern about their sexuality. They ask themselves whether they are normal, if sex plays too great or too small a role in their lives, whether they are sufficiently attractive or sexually proficient, or if something is "wrong" with them. Many struggle with misinformation, or with a sense that there is no truly safe place to discuss their concerns. In this chapter, we will describe a variety of sexual experiences and provide some information to help you make more informed choices about your own sexuality. We do so within the larger perspective that every human being has the right to make decisions about his or her own body and how best to care for it.

Before beginning, we would also state the obvious: that sexuality is not separate from the rest of life, from what we discuss in the other chapters of this book. Sexuality has emotional and value dimensions as well as physical aspects, and is but one part of the complex picture of human adjustment. It cannot be fully understood by itself, out of this context. Sexuality is a great deal more than genital stimulation. The material discussed in our chapters on joy, love, and relationships (Chapter 10) and on meaning (Chapter 15) is, therefore, integrally related to sexuality in human life.

Sexuality is not separate from the rest of life.

■ THE CULTURAL CONTEXT OF SEXUAL BEHAVIOR

HEALTHY SEXUALITY

Our current culture defines healthy sexuality very differently from how it has been (and will be) understood in other cultures and at other times. Seeking a general definition with cross-cultural validity, the World Health Organization described healthy sexuality as integrating somatic, emotional, intellectual, and social aspects of sexual being which enhance and enrich personality, communication, and love (Miller, 1987). Other definitions have emphasized the negative, conceptualizing sexual health as the absence of sexual problems, diseases, and unwanted pregnancies. Some cultural definitions understand love and sex as inseparable, whereas others regard it as common to have sex without love, or love without sex (Sullivan, 1953). In Victorian culture, sexual pleasure for women was neither expected nor approved. In modern popular culture, superorgasmic sexuality is an implicit prerequisite for self-esteem. Attitudes about nudity, masturbation, adolescent sexual behavior, and homosexuality vary widely from one culture, subculture, or time to another.

All of this is to say that sexual health is a relative matter, highly dependent upon personal and societal expectations. What seems optimal sexual health for some will seem "sick" to others. Sexual behavior can be viewed as duty or recreation, affection or competition, pleasure or performance.

Human sexuality, like other human behavior, is largely based on what is socially acceptable and culturally learned. Though there is a natural and inherent physiology of sexuality, sexual behavior is heavily influenced by learning. Consequently it can also be unlearned or relearned, which is one reason why sex therapy (to be discussed later) can be quite effective.

One common source of misery, as people perceive and think about their own sexuality, is an "either/or" dichotomy, an absolute all-or-none way of thinking about sexual health. This dichotomy can take on many forms. One is the notion that there are only two kinds of people in the world: those who are sexually adequate and fulfilled and those who are sexually inadequate and unfulfilled. The truth is that sexual concerns and problems are virtually universal; yet either/or thinking leaves one distressed with anything short of the imagined ideal. This in turn can translate into extreme expectations about sexual performance: feeling totally responsible for the success of the sexual encounter, or being "swept away" by accepting no responsibility for the experience (Cassell, 1984).

The very language used to describe sexual behavior, even among professionals, bespeaks dichotomous thinking reminiscent of the Type A personality (Chapter 9). A man or woman is said to "achieve" an orgasm. A man who does not maintain an erection long enough for "successful" sexual relations is described as having "erectile failure" or as being "impotent" (literally meaning, "powerless"). Women experiencing sexual difficulties have been labeled as "frigid." Inhibition of orgasm in men has been called "ejaculatory incompetence" or "retarded" ejaculation. Even Masters and Johnson (1970) described sexual problems as "inadequacy." Such performance-oriented language, we believe, is not a cause so much as a reflection of our society's dichotomous and power-oriented view of human sexuality (Farrell, 1974; Millett, 1970).

All-or-nothing perceptions can foster a lack of natural enjoyment of sexuality and, ironically, can contribute both to a fear of sexual problems and to their creation. If there are only two kinds of people, those who are sexually adequate and those who are not, then any occurrence of a sexual problem implies that one is in the latter category. Dichotomous thinking likewise places undue focus and emphasis on "achieving" an orgasm, often missing the broader nature and pleasures of sensuality and sexuality.

An alternative way to understand sexual health is as a *continuum* (or a set of continua) along which experience varies in the course of a lifetime. It is quite natural for sexual desire, attractions, and behavior to fluctuate over time. Such change is, in fact, guaranteed to occur. Human sexuality changes with mood, health, pace of life, fatigue, distractions, self-esteem, drug states, environment, affection, age, relationship factors, and general happiness. In such a complex picture, it is grossly oversimplifying to think in terms of all-or-none categories.

12.1 SEXUAL MYTHS

In a society where sexuality is a highly emotionally charged subject, open discussion is often inhibited, and misinformation abounds.

Here are a few common myths about sexuality.

1. *Loss of sexual interest and ability is normal with aging.* The physical changes of aging do influence sexuality, and sexual frequency tends to decrease with age. Nevertheless the societal notion of older adults as asexual is an unfounded stereotype. Sexual desire and normal sexual functioning occur at least well into the eighties.

2. *Women have two kinds of orgasms.* Freud contributed to the myth that women have two types of orgasms: a clitoral orgasm (e.g., from masturbation) and a vaginal orgasm (e.g., from intercourse). The clitoral type has been described as a less mature form, inferior to the "first-class" vaginal orgasm. Masters and Johnson (1966) dispelled this myth, demonstrating no physiological differences between female orgasms from masturbation or intercourse (except that the former tend to be more intense). Indeed, male and female orgasms are strikingly similar in their physiological pattern.

3. *Penis size is related to sexual enjoyment.* This myth is perpetuated by films and fiction. In fact, penis size is unrelated to sexual functioning and enjoyment. The outer one-third of the vagina accommodates to the penis during intercourse, regardless of size.

4. *To experience orgasm, a woman has to surrender control.* The "swept away" myth has more to do with our societal hang-ups about power and control than with sexual enjoyment. In fact, becoming orgasmic usually involves a woman taking a certain amount of control and responsibility for her own sexuality (Barbach, 1975).

5. *Sexual problems are rare and point to deep-seated problems.* As we will discuss later in this chapter, sexual dysfunctions are really very common. A conservative estimate is that, at any given time, at least 50 percent of all couples are experiencing sexual dissatisfactions and problems. The myth is promoted by our social taboo against admitting or talking about having sexual problems. Sexual problems are rarely linked to physical or deep personality problems, and their treatment can be brief and quite successful.

SEX ROLES

Many societies have strikingly different standards and expectations for males and females with regard to sexual behavior. Sexual initiation, aggression, and responsibility for the sexual fulfillment of both partners have been stereotypically associated with the male role in current Western society. Females have been consigned more passive or flirtatious roles, often given the responsibility for resisting the aggressive sexual overtures of males and for practicing birth control. These interlocking aggressive versus passive roles have shaped our societal concepts and expectations of sexuality (Farrell, 1974; Greer, 1971).

One reflection of this is in the relative acceptability of sexual behavior among males or females. A number of popular films (such as one entitled *Private Lessons*) have centered on the sexual tutoring of a young boy by an adult woman. The societal attitude implied in these films is that the boy in question is very fortunate, to be initiated to healthy sexuality by an experienced older partner. The reverse situation of an older man with a female minor is obviously viewed rather differently as a criminal offense to be severely punished.

Imbalanced sex roles with regard to sexual behavior are apparent in many other areas of our society. Beauty contests, advertising, entertainment, pornography, and behaviors for attracting partners all reflect double standards and imbalance of male and female roles in sexuality. This polarization of sex roles can be understood as harming both men and women. Women are relegated to passive roles, waiting to be picked or pleased, victimized by sexual aggression, viewed as sexual objects. Men's sexuality is distorted into performance pressure, where power and penis are equated, sexual relationships sacrifice closeness for control, and men are confined to sexual bragging or silence. Said another way, women's roles relinquish power for love; men's roles shortchange love in favor of power.

An alternative to such sex-role stereotyping is **androgyny,** a psychological trait in which the individual possesses the positive characteristics of both traditional male and female roles (Bem, 1985; Kaplan & Bean, 1976). The androgynous person can be both analytical and affectionate, competitive and compassionate, strong and sensitive. She or he can take risks and take care, show both love and leadership, balance independence with loyalty. In the realm of sexual behavior, the androgynous person is free to pursue or be pursued, to give and to receive, to say yes or no.

■ GENDER SIMILARITIES AND DIFFERENCES

Related to the topic of sex roles and stereotypes is a large body of psychological research on how men and women are similar and different. Rather than writing a separate chapter on gender, we have discussed these issues where they arise throughout this text. However, there are some important general points to consider in understanding gender research.

First, it is worth noting that gender differences receive an unusual amount of attention. Few studies have been done of psychological differences between tall versus short people, or of blue-eyed versus brown-eyed individuals, but much effort is devoted to the search for differences between males and females (Jacklin, 1989). How important are such differences?

After reviewing over 1,200 books, chapters, and articles, Margaret Matlin (1987) drew four general conclusions:

Androgyny
a personality construct in which traditionally male and traditionally female psychological characteristics are both incorporated and integrated.

1. Actual gender differences on psychological dimensions "are generally small and inconsistent" (p. 16), but

Androgynous behavior is appropriate to the situation, regardless of the gender of participants.

2. People do *respond* differently to women and to men.

3. In the psychological literature, women have been mostly "invisible"—ignored and unstudied—and minority women are particularly so.

4. Both male and female individuals vary widely, making it difficult to generalize about all women or all men.

These four themes from Matlin's review will serve as an organizing focus for the discussion that follows.

SMALL AND INCONSISTENT DIFFERENCES

Jacklin (1989) commented that our society seems preoccupied with gender differences. Americans place great importance on gender, starting from a child's birth. The first question often asked at a birth is "Is it a boy or a girl?" instead of potentially more important questions, such as "Is the baby healthy?" or "Is the mother all right?" In part because our culture tends to focus on gender, its importance is often exaggerated (Bem, 1985). In socialization, for example, differences are reinforced and exaggerated each time a child is rewarded for "gender-appropriate" behavior and scolded for "gender-inappropriate" behavior.

In light of this amount of attention, it is remarkable how few reliable gender differences have been found. Matlin's first conclusion, in reading hundreds of studies in this area, is that genuine differences between males and females tend to be small and inconsistent. The term "inconsistent" here means that existing studies are contradictory. One study may find a difference between boys and girls, while another piece of research on the same topic finds no differences. This is both confusing and challenging. Which study, you may ask, is to be believed? One guideline for critical thinking is to ask which study was better controlled against bias. For example, Benbow and Stanley (1983) reported that boys were better at math than girls, and speculated on a biological basis for this difference. However, their studies failed to control for different amounts of math-related experiences. The observed difference, then, may be attributable to the fact that boys are typically encouraged to take more math coursework and to play more games which require math, rather than to any innate difference in ability (Lips, 1988). In evaluating research, it is important to consider what uncontrolled factors may be biasing the findings.

Consider another reported finding, from the field of human sexuality. Women's reactions to first heterosexual intercourse have been reported to be guilt, sorrow, and disappointment, whereas men's reactions are found to be significantly more positive (Lips, 1988). Why? These differences could be an **artifact** of the self-report measure used, or the sample of respondents chosen. For social reasons, men may be more likely than women to *describe* their sexual experiences as positive. Furthermore, social expectations may shape behavior in such a way that intercourse is, in fact, less physiologically pleasurable for women than for men. The "missionary" (male superior) position in intercourse, for example, provides substantially less direct stimulation to the woman's clitoris than to the penis. When the clitoris is appropriately stimulated, women achieve orgasm as quickly as men: within three minutes (Tavris & Wade, 1984). Furthermore, intercourse may not be women's preferred method of sexual expression, but traditional sexual relations, and research about such experiences, have focused almost entirely on intercourse. Lesbian women, whose sexual expression does not include heterosexual intercourse, report more frequent orgasms than do their heterosexual counterparts, giving some support to the notion that kissing and other lovemaking activities may be more satisfying to women than intercourse (Blumstein & Schwartz, 1983; Peplau & Amaro, 1982).

Another potential source of bias in the study of gender similarities and differences is the publication process. For example, the math study just reported received a great deal of coverage in the popular press, but criticisms of its shortcomings and limitations did not. Thus readers, including the parents of daughters, were left with the mistaken impression that girls should not be encouraged to *pursue* math (Eccles & Jacobs, 1986). Findings of sex differences are more likely to be published (and reported in the popular press) than research which finds males and females to be similar (Hyde, 1985). Thus, readers may get an exaggerated view of the role gender plays in behavior.

Although most gender differences are small and inconsistent, there are some exceptions. One clear sex difference, reflected in many studies, is found in health and illness (Strickland, 1988). Females, across the life span, appear to be at a biological advantage over males. Women live longer than men, despite the fact that their nutritional and health needs may be given lower priority. Women are less likely to die by suicide and accidents. However, women are at risk for forcible rape and battering. Violence against women includes 70,000 reported rapes and 2 million cases of battering by husbands annually in the United States (Strickland, 1988). The mental health of men and women is different in that women are more likely to report problems and are more often diagnosed as depressed. Men, conversely, are more often engaged in acting-out behaviors, consistent with the traditionally prescribed male role.

DIFFERENT REACTIONS

Artifact
in psychological research, a finding that is produced inadvertently by specific conditions of the research.

As indicated earlier, differences that are found between males and females may not be due to inherent gender differences. Rather, they may arise from differences in how people respond and react to males and females. Consider the differences in how friends and family may react when a boy versus a girl joins a softball (or football) team. Would men and women get different reactions on taking a class on cooking, sewing, or aerobic dance? In judging desir-

Men and women get different reactions from others when participating in the same activity.

ability, much more emphasis is placed on physical attractiveness for women than for men in our society (Matlin, 1987). Thus the same behavior or attribute in males and females often receives very different responses from society, and these, in turn, have an important influence. Remember the C in STORC! In other words, men and women may be similar, but still be *judged* differently.

Because American culture is preoccupied with gender differences, it has been suggested that the belief in differences becomes a self-fulfilling prophecy, especially in our child-rearing practices (Jacklin, 1989). Less reinforcement for male aggression might lead to fewer heart attacks, accidents, and suicides among men. Less reinforcement for female passivity might lead to less depression in women.

Males and females may even respond differently to *themselves*, and to cues from their bodies. In a study of sexual arousal (Lips, 1988), the self-reports of women and men were contrasted with physiological measures (penile enlargement and vaginal moisture). Both women and men reported sexual arousal and showed parallel physiological changes in response to erotic tapes. A discrepancy was found, however, in that at earlier stages of physiological arousal, women were less likely to detect and report their own arousal. What would you conclude? Are women more modest or ambivalent about their sexual feelings? A simpler explanation is that an enlarging penis is more easily noticed than early moistening of the vagina. Is this a real gender difference in arousal?

INVISIBLE FEMALES

Matlin's third observation is that women are often "invisible." That is, our language, culture, and research often proceed as if women did not exist. Much of psychological theory is based on work by and about males. When findings about women are presented, it is often as the exception to or difference from the norm.

Invisibility is especially challenging for women. Laurel Kessell, a champion volleyball player on the American Olympic team in Seoul, received less media coverage in her hometown of Albuquerque than did the males on the local losing college football team. Being competent is not newsworthy enough for women to receive representative coverage.

Similarly, in psychological theory and research, women are frequently underrepresented. Rape and pregnancy, important issues for women, were given less than one sentence each in a leading introductory psychology text, which gave REM sleep seven pages! Until recently, women's perspectives on sexual satisfaction received relatively little investigation.

The invisibility of women has even been embedded in our language, which has referred to all people as "men" or "mankind" and used "he" as a generic pronoun. As a partial remedy to this language bias, the American Psychological Association (1983) published guidelines for the use of nonsexist language in its journals: "the use of *man* as a generic noun can be ambiguous and may convey an implicit message that women are of secondary importance" (p. 44). In the past, generic male pronouns were considered correct grammar, yet readers became confused, thinking that only males were being described (Spender, 1980). By using female and male pronouns, writing is more accurate and women become more visible. We have made a special point in this textbook to use inclusive language throughout and to recognize work by and about women whenever possible.

Another attempt to remedy women's invisibility in psychology includes guidelines for avoiding sexism in psychological research (Denmark et al., 1988). Whether in question formulation, research methods, data analysis and interpretation, or conclusions, steps can be taken to delete the kind of bias psychology has permitted in the past. For example, in formulating a research hypothesis that aggressive stimuli enhance sexual arousal, it is important to be aware that previous results have been based on male subjects only. Therefore, the researcher should formulate the question so that any subsequent findings can be accurately generalized to females as well (Denmark et al., 1988).

INDIVIDUAL VARIATION

While it is tempting to generalize about "all women" or "all men," individual variation is so great that many generalizations are misrepresentations of the truth. Matlin's (1987) fourth theme emphasized that within-sex variability is typically much greater than differences between groups of men and women. In other words, women may be very different from one another in choices, personal characteristics, and reactions to life events, just as men may be different from one another.

Both men and women, for example, vary widely in specific abilities in subjects such as math, language, or psychology. Given this fact, it is easy to find examples from either gender at either extreme. Once one forms the impression that there is a gender difference in one of these abilities, the process of illusory correlation (Chapter 1) may draw upon specific examples to maintain the stereotype. In fact, strong and consistent gender differences are few, and variation is much greater within each gender.

Thus, when you consider sex differences, remember gender similarities, as well. Critically read any research, and ask yourself how bias may have influenced the findings. Could an observed difference be due to something other than an inherent difference between males and females? Are the samples representative of both genders, and of diversity on other dimensions (e.g., racial/ethnic background)? Are the conclusions supported with adequate evidence? Consider what means you would use to remedy possible bias problems in gender research.

■ SEXUALITY AND THE STORC

The STORC model can be applied in understanding sexual behavior. The model is particularly helpful in understanding and remembering the complexity of human sexuality.

S—STIMULI

The S in STORC, as you recall, stands for the stimulus or the situational component. What functions as a sexual stimulus for people can vary very widely. Masters and Johnson (1966) found in their laboratory studies of sexual response that basic physiological patterns in sexual responding are similar for men and women and are not changed in form by the type of arousing stimulation (intercourse, masturbation, genital stimulation by the partner or by a vibrator, or fantasy). Forms of genital stimulation do vary, however, in the *intensity* of resulting sexual response. Masturbation typically produces the most intense experiences, with partner manipulation second, and intercourse third in intensity (Belliveau & Richter, 1970).

Learning is unquestionably a major influence on what a person finds to be sexually arousing. Almost any stimulus that is repeatedly associated with sexual arousal (e.g., during masturbation fantasies) can, by processes of respondent conditioning, acquire the ability to induce arousal itself. Thus the sound of a lover's voice, the smell of a perfume, particular clothing or tastes can take on sexually arousing qualities of their own.

For this reason, it is of concern what is associated with sexual arousal. It is possible, by masturbating to certain fantasies, to establish a pattern of arousal to the stimuli or situations imagined. This is one explanation of how deviant patterns of arousal come to be established or maintained. Men who sexually molest children (**pedophilia**) or who publicly expose their genitals to strangers (**exhibitionism** or "flashing") commonly practice masturbation with fantasies of these behaviors. This conditioning pattern is also one reason for concern about the clear trend in motion pictures toward pairing sexual eroticism with violence.

Because the stimulus (S) elements of sexual arousal are learned and can be relearned, it is possible to change what a person finds to be sexually stimulating. Research on the treatment of sex offenders has demonstrated dramatic changes in arousal patterns; for example, eliminating sexual arousal to children and increasing arousal to adults (Adams, Tollison, & Carson, 1981). Similarly dramatic reversals in arousal have been reported in the treatment of **transsexualism** (Barlow, Reynolds, & Agras, 1973).

Pedophilia
a psychosexual disorder involving sexual activity of an adult with children.

Exhibitionism
a psychosexual disorder of males, involving uninvited exposure of the genitals to others, for the purpose of personal sexual arousal.

Transsexualism
a psychosexual disorder involving lifelong discomfort with one's gender and a desire to be of the opposite gender.

T—THOUGHT PATTERNS

Thought patterns (T) also are important in human sexuality. It has been said that the most important sexual organ is found between the ears.

Expectations do play a large part in sexual behavior. For example, in a study we described in Chapter 11, people who *believed* they were drinking alcohol showed increased sexual arousal, whether or not the beverage they were given actually contained alcohol (Wilson & Lawson, 1976). The subjects' degree of physiological arousal was determined by a thought, the expectation of sexual feelings as the result of drinking alcohol. Such expectations are, of course, themselves the product of social learning.

The importance of thought processes is illustrated by the situation of a college man who sought treatment for problems in maintaining an erection

12.2 REVOLUTIONARY RESEARCH

As you can imagine, research on human sexuality poses a variety of methodological, ethical, and political problems. Only a few decades ago, there was little or no accurate scientific information about human sexual functioning, simply because such research had never been conducted. Some pioneers in this field deserve credit for their work to understand and accurately describe human sexual experiences.

In the 1940s, Alfred Kinsey surveyed Americans for the first time about their sexual lives. Asking thousands of people to describe how they experienced their own sexuality was a revolutionary undertaking. He discovered, for example, that only about half the married women surveyed experienced orgasm with intercourse. He also found, however, that sexual responsiveness increased with years of marriage (Kinsey et al., 1953). It would seem that practice improves performance, or at least enjoyment!

Kinsey, using survey methods, relied exclusively on self-report measures. Later researchers built on his ideas, but incorporated laboratory measures. William Masters and Virginia Johnson, beginning in the 1960s, conducted their ground-breaking work, which included direct observation and measurement of sexual behavior. It was at their laboratory in St. Louis, Missouri, for example, that they observed and described—for the first time in history—the four phases of the normal human sexual response (Masters & Johnson, 1966).

These advances in fundamental scientific knowledge were not achieved without cost. The early researchers in this area struggled against a tide of political pressure and adverse publicity. A debt of gratitude for knowledge of human sexuality is owed to these three revolutionary researchers, who provided a strong foundation for subsequent research and understanding.

Kinsey, and Masters and Johnson provided a strong foundation for research and understanding of human sexuality.

during intercourse. He had had several prior sexual partners without experiencing this problem. One night, however, he was invited by a young woman to come home with her. He was not accustomed to women being so aggressive about sex, and he felt somewhat uneasy. They began drinking, and he consumed five beers. As they began lovemaking, he learned that she lived with her parents, who might be coming home at any moment. Minutes later he found that he could not maintain an erection. He felt humiliated and worried that something was wrong with him.

The next time he was about to have sexual relations with a woman, his mind began racing. "I wonder if it's going to happen again. Maybe I'm impotent. What will I do if I can't get it up?" The result, of course, was quite predictable. After several such experiences, he referred himself to the Psychology Clinic, believing that he must have a serious personality problem. His treatment was quite simple. After he saw his physician to rule out a medical condition, we explained to him that anxiety and alcohol easily accounted for his first erection problem. After that, it was his anxious thoughts, distracting in themselves, that probably caused his continuing difficulties. We assured him it was very unlikely that his problems were the result of any major personality or physical problem, and we advised him to be more moderate in his occasional use of alcohol. Finally we advised him, if he experienced his anxious thoughts again, just to let the thought go rather than following it and to focus instead on his pleasant physical sensations. This advice proved sufficient to solve his problem.

The main point here is that how you think about sex will affect the experience for you. If you assume that sex with the same partner over time will become stale and boring, that assumption can become a self-fulfilling prophecy. Thought patterns can be changed and hence your experience may change as well. As we will discuss later, gaining new information and cognitive perspectives is an important part of sex therapy, whether from a self-help or a professional source. New information about sexuality can be liberating for people who have learned misinformation.

O—ORGANIC PATTERNS

The O in STORC, as you will recall, refers to the organism (not to be confused here with orgasm), to organic or physiological patterns. The pioneering work of Masters and Johnson (1966, 1970) provided a clear picture of physiological changes that occur in the body during sexual experiences. The *pattern* of these physiological responses is remarkably similar for men and women, and (as mentioned earlier) for different types of sexual stimulation. Masters and Johnson described the normal human sexual response as consisting of four phases: excitement, plateau, orgasm, and resolution.

The first or *excitement* phase for both women and men occurs as a stimulus triggers sexual excitement. It can last from a few minutes to several hours, depending upon stimulation. During this phase a variety of physical changes occur, with wide individual differences. There is a flushing (reddening) of the skin, particularly on the stomach, breasts, throat, and neck. Muscle tension increases throughout the body. Both heart rate and blood pressure increase. Blood flow to the genitals causes erection of the penis in men and a swelling of the labia and clitoris in women. Erection of the nipples of the breasts often occurs in both women and men. In women, both the uterus and the inner portion of the vagina expand, and the walls of the vagina are lubricated.

As sexual tension rises, these physical changes increase and then level off for a brief period known as the *plateau* phase. In essence, the physiological changes of the excitement phase reach a peak. The increases in skin flushing, muscle tension, heart rate, blood pressure, erection of the nipples, and blood flow to the genitals reach a maximum. There are also some unique organic changes during the plateau phase. In women, the outer third of the vagina contracts, and the clitoris draws back underneath a hood of skin just before orgasm. In men, the testicles are enlarged and are drawn up closer to the body during the plateau phase.

The *orgasmic* phase is brief and intense, lasting on average between five and seven seconds. The physiological changes of the plateau phase are maintained during orgasm, with some intensification of muscle tension, heart rate, and blood pressure. In both men and women the orgasm consists of a series of muscle contractions in the genitals, varying in number from three to ten or more, each lasting less than a second. In men, these contractions are accompanied by **ejaculation.** Women may experience multiple orgasms, several sets of orgasmic contractions spaced very closely together in time. The uterus contracts immediately after orgasm.

Following orgasm, the body enters the fourth phase of human sexual response, called the *resolution.* This consists mostly of a reversal of the physical changes which occurred during the first two phases. The muscles relax, blood pressure and heart rate return to normal, the red flush disappears from the skin, and the genitals return to a non-swollen state. Sweating often occurs, sometimes over the whole body, during the resolution phase. Men experience a **refractory period** following orgasm, during which it is difficult or impossible to experience erection and another orgasm. The refractory period lengthens with age, varying from a few minutes to a few days.

There are many misconceptions regarding the effects of aging on sexual response. There are no inherent changes due to normal aging that cause a man to lose the ability to maintain an erection or that remove the ability of a man or woman to experience orgasm. Sexual desire and the frequency of sexual behavior do tend to decrease with age. There are also normal changes in the intensity and speed of sexual response. A longer period of stimulation may be necessary for a man to experience erection, for example. These physical changes are often offset, however, by an increased comfort with one's own sexuality. Women typically report greater orgasmic frequency and more satisfaction with their sexuality during their late thirties and forties than during their twenties (Hite, 1976). The female **menopause** has no inherent effect on sexual desire or behavior. In fact, the absence of pregnancy fears may have a liberating effect on sexuality.

R—RESPONSES

Sexual responses (R) or behaviors vary widely. The means by which people seek sexual expression differ among individuals, cultures, and times. Each society offers norms and taboos for sexual expression, designating some behaviors as acceptable and others as unacceptable or illegal.

Masturbation is a very common form of sexual behavior in younger men and women. The frequency of masturbation among men tends to decrease after their teens, whereas among women masturbation becomes more frequent before leveling off in the late thirties. There are no known harmful effects of masturbation, except when it is practiced to the exclusion of other forms of sexual expression.

Women and men may need and desire different things in sexual expression. When asked about their preferences in foreplay, intercourse, and afterplay, men in one survey rated intercourse as most important, while women rated foreplay and afterplay as most important (Denney, Field, & Quadagno, 1984). The authors suggested that these differences might be due to women valuing verbally and physically affectionate behavior more than men do. Men and women also tend to place different emphasis on the meaning of touch, with women preferring to be touched on the hands or face (rather than breasts or

Ejaculation
in males, the release of semen from the penis through rhythmic muscle contractions.

Refractory Period
a span of time following orgasm in which sexual arousal is inhibited in males.

Menopause
in women, the ending of menstruation, usually occurring in the late forties.

Masturbation
sexual self-stimulation.

genitals) as a way to communicate warmth and love (Nguyen, Heslin, & Nguyen, 1975).

Homosexual behavior involves sexuality between two persons of the same gender. (The term "lesbian" refers to relationships between women, and "gay" usually refers to male homosexuals.) In Kinsey's extensive surveys, 37 percent of men and 13 percent of women reported having had at least one adult

---

12.3 SEXUAL BEHAVIOR AMONG COLLEGE STUDENTS

The following are some questions asked of 500 students at the University of New Mexico. See how closely you can guess the percentage who answered each question in specific ways.

1. Having intercourse on a one-night stand is good
   a. Often.
   b. Hardly ever.
   c. Occasionally.
   d. Never.
2. Couples should have sex
   a. On the first encounter if they feel like it.
   b. Wait at least a week (after meeting the person).
   c. Wait until they know they are serious about each other.
   d. Only after marriage.
3. Sex for me is
   a. For pleasure only.
   b. A statement of love for someone, as well as pleasure.
   c. A commitment to be loyal to one person, as well as pleasure and a statement of love.
   d. For reproduction only.
4. Extramarital sex is
   a. Always wrong.
   b. All right as long as both the husband and wife consent to look elsewhere.
   c. All right if you don't get caught.
   d. All right for the husband but not for the wife.
   e. All right for the wife but not for the husband.
5. The person I have sex with
   a. Must have sex with me only.
   b. Has made no commitment to have sex with me only.
6. I first had sexual intercourse
   a. Before 16.
   b. 17.
   c. 18.

d. 19.

e. 20.

f. 21 or over.

g. I haven't yet.

Responses

1. a. 7%   b. 9%   c. 50%   d. 33%
2. a. 53%   b. 6%   c. 35%   d. 7%
3. a. 5%   b. 39%   c. 33%   d. 1%
4. a. 40%   b. 38%   c. 10%   d. 0.4%   e. 0.2%
5. a. 44%   b. 50%
6. a. 25%   b. 17%   c. 17%   d. 7%   e. 4%   f. 6%   g. 14%

Responses may total less than 100 percent because some students left specific questions unanswered.

Source: Adapted from the *New Mexico Daily Lobo*, November 29, 1977, pp. 1–3.

homosexual experience resulting in orgasm (Kinsey et al., 1948, 1953). Nearly one man in five (18 percent) reported at least an equal preference for homosexual as for heterosexual behavior during some significant portion of adult life, and 4 percent reported exclusive lifelong homosexuality. Whereas homosexuality was once regarded as a form of mental illness, the American Psychiatric

Touch can communicate affection, warmth, and love.

Association (APA) in 1973 officially abandoned this view. By 1980, the only remaining diagnosis, "ego-dystonic homosexuality," was reserved for those who desired to change their sexual preference from homosexual to heterosexual (APA, 1980). In response to protests from gay and lesbian groups, this diagnosis, too, was removed in the most recent revision of the psychiatric diagnostic manual (Franklin, 1987). This normalizing view of homosexuality is supported by a large body of research indicating no consistent significant differences between homosexual and heterosexual adults on measures of psychological adjustment and psychopathology (Diamant, 1987).

C—CONSEQUENCES

Like all behavior, sexual behavior results in certain consequences (C) in the outside world that, in turn, affect behavior and overall adjustment. Sexual fulfillment is itself a **primary reinforcer;** it is inherently rewarding in itself. Nevertheless sexual behavior is shaped by a complex set of consequences, including inherent pleasure. Among other consequences that influence sexual behavior are its cognitive and emotional effects (self-esteem, guilt, joy, etc.) and social effects (affection, approval, punishment, etc.). Both types of effects can be either positive or negative.

In one's private world, sexual experiences may have profound consequences. One's sense of self-esteem (Chapter 6) may be increased or diminished as a result of sexual expectations and behavior. If there is a large discrepancy between what one expects and what one experiences, self-esteem may suffer. On the other hand, joyful and comfortable sexuality can enhance an overall sense of self-esteem. If sexual performance and personal worth are closely linked for an individual, self-esteem is particularly vulnerable to being affected by sexual experiences. Depending upon what one has learned and come to believe, sexual behavior can also have powerful emotional after-effects ranging from elation and satisfaction to despair and guilt.

Fear of negative consequences also shapes sexual behavior. In recent years, awareness and fear of sexually transmitted diseases have increased markedly. The alarming upsurge in cases of **AIDS** has had a special impact. The increasing incidence of less serious but very unpleasant (syphilis, gonorrhea, chlamydia) and even incurable infections (such as genital herpes) has also created caution. Unwanted pregnancy represents yet another potential negative consequence of unprotected sexual contact. Precautionary measures can decrease risk of both pregnancy and sexually transmitted diseases. Nonoxynol-9, an ingredient in most commercially available spermicides, also kills many organisms that cause sexually transmitted diseases, including the AIDS virus, gonorrhea, syphilis, chlamydia, and herpes ("Can you rely," 1989). Latex condoms, combined with a spermicide containing nonoxynol-9, may be the best preventive measures at this time for those who choose to be sexually active.

Needless to say, the potential negative consequences are not the whole picture. Beyond its immediate physical pleasures, sexual behavior can have powerful positive effects. The addition of sexual intimacy may deepen an already close relationship and increase the partners' joyful attachment. Survey results reflect a substantial (though far from complete) overlap between sexual satisfaction and overall marital happiness. For adolescents, engaging in sexual behavior may represent an attempt to establish personal identity as an adult and independence from parents (Jessor, 1984).

Homosexuals face special negative consequences and problems as a result of societal fears and hatred. Public expression of affection is severely restricted for gays and lesbians. Homosexuals often encounter special barriers to hospital visits, employment, and access to public services. Lesbians and gays may

Primary Reinforcer
a stimulus that functions as a reinforcer by virtue of its inherent rather than acquired properties.

AIDS
Acquired Immune Deficiency Syndrome, a disease that destroys the body's immune system; usually contracted through sexual intercourse or sharing of contaminated needles.

12.4 SEXUAL GUILT

According to a recent article (Sex Cools, 1989), chastity and commitment are returning to popularity with college students. However, students still practice risky birth control, with 50 percent reporting the use of withdrawal or the rhythm method, both notorious for leading to pregnancy. Why do otherwise bright and responsible people resort to shoddy contraception? Could it be that part of the answer lies in guilt about sexuality? Preparing responsibly for sexual activity by purchasing birth control devices does require premeditation, which may trigger guilty feelings.

For several decades, researchers have been exploring the impact of sexual guilt on adjustment. Establishing a means for measuring sex guilt has led to the construction of sentence completion, forced-choice, and true-false guilt inventories (e.g., Mosher, 1968, p. 692). Sample questions include such items as

"Prostitution makes me sick when I think about it." (true/false)

or

"If in the future I committed adultery . . .

a. I hope I would be punished very deeply.

b. I hope I enjoy it."

Obviously, guilt scores on such measures vary widely among individuals. But do these scores mean anything?

In one study using the balanced placebo design (see Chapter 11), subjects were given drinks that they were either told contained or did not contain alcohol. Effects on sexual arousal were examined. The "loosening up" effect of *believing* they were consuming alcohol was significantly greater for people who had scored high on sexual guilt, whether or not the drink *really* contained alcohol (Lang et al., 1980). Thus, for individuals with high guilt, drinking "alcohol" seemed to free them from inhibitions they had learned about sexual expression, and to give permission for greater sexual arousal.

Morokoff (1985) showed erotic videotapes to women who had scored high or low on a measure of sexual guilt, and rated sexual arousal both by self-report and by direct physiological measurement. Women who were high in guilt about sex *reported* less arousal, but showed significantly more arousal on the physiological measure, in comparison to women who scored low in sex guilt (Morokoff, 1985). The researcher's conclusion was that forbidden material such as the videotapes might be more arousing to women who had actively avoided such material in the past; yet these women were unwilling or unable to recognize their own arousal due to their guilty feelings.

How do you interpret these findings? The pattern in high-guilt individuals appears to be one of physical readiness to respond, but psychological inhibition from doing so. Such conflicts between values and experience may interfere with sexual enjoyment and adjustment. Perhaps this is the truth underlying the old joke about a guilt-inducing religion: it doesn't keep you from sinning, but it sure keeps you from enjoying it! What kind of "therapy," if any, might you prescribe for a person with high sexual guilt? What value and ethical issues are involved here?

As this textbook goes to press, there is no known cure for Acquired Immune Deficiency Syndrome. We hope that as you read this page, a cure has been found.

Until a cure is found, health scientists, including psychologists, continue to work toward education about and prevention of the disease. One important form of education and prevention includes behavior-change programs to limit the spread of the epidemic. Such programs must be based on accurate information about AIDS and sexual behavior.

Five kinds of sexual behavior appear crucial to study and target in the prevention of AIDS: extramarital sexual interactions, anal intercourse, sex with prostitutes, sexual interactions "across nominally distinct sexual orientation groups" (p. 922), and sexual contact with people in cities where the incidence of AIDS is already high (Reinisch, Sanders, & Ziemba-Davis, 1988).

Extramarital sexual relations are relevant to study because risk increases with the number of sexual partners. Anal intercourse is a high-risk activity and may be more prevalent than previously thought in heterosexual relations. Males are more likely to infect females than the reverse, but sex with prostitutes can provide a channel for transmitting AIDS to the heterosexual population. Bisexuality represents another avenue for such transmission across groups labeled "homosexual" and "heterosexual." Research indicates that despite their labels, "heterosexuals" may engage in sexual activities with partners of the same sex, and "homosexuals" may have opposite-sex partners. Thus, sexual-orientation categories may not be as distinct as has been believed. Finally, New York, Newark, San Francisco, Los Angeles, Houston, Washington, Miami, Chicago, Philadelphia, and Dallas are, at the time of this writing, the ten American cities with the highest numbers of reported cases of AIDS. Unprotected sexual contact during visits to or with residents of these cities puts individuals at greater risk.

Intravenous drug use is another major risk factor, largely because of the sharing by users of contaminated needles. Alcohol and other drug use, however, are more general risk factors because of their association with unprotected and high-risk sexual practices.

AIDS represents an ominous threat, which has already claimed thousands of lives and may well claim millions. It is fast becoming the leading killer of younger adults. It is also a cause of death that is almost completely preventable, given proper precautions.

12.6 PERSONAL MILESTONE
Writing About Sex

When my twenty-year-old son returned from college for Christmas vacation, he was curious about how this text was progressing. I described the current chapter, and he indicated that he was willing to proofread the rough draft. After going over the outline, and what I had written so far, he said that it seemed so negative, like sex was all problems. I realized that his criticism was valid, that I had said very little about pleasure or fun or healthy sex. I also realized that writing about positive aspects of sex was not easy. I ran an on-line computer search seeking research about "healthy sexuality," "marital satisfaction," and so on, and found almost nothing. Apparently the main focus of research has been dysfunction. There seems to be a great deal in the media about current "epidemics," like AIDS and teen pregnancy, but little about happiness that is not romanticized to the point of ridiculousness. My son said, for example, that he has recently learned from his intimate relationship that sex is much more satisfying with someone he cares about deeply. I was moved by his candor, and I felt very happy for him. I also realized that poets may do a better job of writing about positive aspects of sexuality than do psychologists!
—CEY

become the target of discrimination, ridicule, or violence. Constant exposure to these social conditions can take its toll on self-esteem, exacerbating anxiety, depression, or addictive behaviors.

Finally, each society defines certain sexual behaviors as criminal offenses and responds with punishment or mandatory treatment. In Western cultures, sexual acts with children, exhibitionism, prostitution, and public nudity are illegal behaviors in most settings. The persistence of such behaviors despite substantial punishment attests to the powerful offsetting positive reinforcement attached to sexual behavior.

■ SEXUAL PROBLEMS

Sexual problems are very common, although openly admitting and discussing them are not. **Sexual dysfunctions** can be thought of as inhibitions of what is a normal human response process. As will be noted in what follows, the four-phase model of sexual response, described earlier, provides a useful basis for understanding sexual difficulties (Masters & Johnson, 1970).

SEXUAL DYSFUNCTIONS

The most common complaints include inhibited sexual desire, erectile dysfunction, premature ejaculation, organismic dysfunction, vaginismus, and dyspareunia. We will describe each of these difficulties, discuss sexual problems in general and their causes, and then comment on treatment.

Inhibited Sexual Desire.   One of the most common sexual complaints has been called **inhibited sexual desire.** The problem here is distress over a perceived lack of sexual desire or interest, either in oneself or one's partner. Approximately 30 percent of sex therapy referrals involve inhibited sexual desire (Pietropinto, 1986).

> Helen found herself so tired from caring for a small child as well as working full time outside the home, that she rarely felt any interest in having sex. Mostly what she felt was exhaustion. When her husband wanted intercourse, she wanted to sleep. She felt guilty about not meeting his sexual needs, and fearful that he would find another woman to fulfill them. But neither guilt nor fear relieved her fatigue, and her disinterest in sex persisted. She loved her husband, but found herself keeping her distance from him, because any closeness might lead to arousing his desire for sex, which she felt unwilling or unable to fulfill.

Sexual Dysfunction
an experienced problem or dissatisfaction in sexual responding.

Inhibited Sexual Desire
a sexual dysfunction involving difficulty in experiencing sexual arousal and excitement.

Erectile Dysfunction
a sexual dysfunction involving difficulty with experiencing or maintaining an erection.

This problem amounts to an inhibition of the *excitement* phase of sexual response, discussed earlier. In a study of normal couples, 48 percent of women reported difficulty in getting sexually excited, and 35 percent of women and 16 percent of men reported disinterest in sex (Frank, Anderson, & Rubenstein, 1978).

Erectile Dysfunction.   Difficulties with experiencing or maintaining an erection are reported by about one man in ten (Frank et al., 1978). This problem again involves inhibition at the *excitement* phase of normal sexual response.

An important distinction is between total and situational **erectile dysfunction.** In the former case, the man does not have an erection under any circumstances, even during sleep. It is normal for men to experience several erections during the night, typically at 90-minute intervals associated with periods of dreaming sleep. The total absence of erections often points to an organic problem and the need for medical consultation. Situational erectile dysfunction, by contrast, refers to difficulties with erection only in certain situations or with certain partners. Normal sexual response during masturbation but not during intercourse, for example, suggests a psychological basis for the problem and predicts a good outcome with proper sex therapy.

A corresponding problem for women is difficulty with vaginal lubrication. This is usually overcome with the use of an artificial, water-based lubricant. Oil-based lubricants like petroleum jelly may damage condoms and diaphragms (Sanford, Hawley, & McGee, 1984).

Premature Ejaculation.   By far the most common sexual problem among men is **premature ejaculation.** In essence, the problem is that the man reaches orgasm and ejaculates too soon by his own or his partner's estimation. Most commonly this means that the man ejaculates and begins to lose his erection before his partner has experienced sexual satisfaction. This can occur anywhere along a continuum, ranging from the man who ejaculates before the penis is inserted to one who may reach orgasm only after a prolonged period of intercourse, but still before his partner is satisfied. In an interview study, 36 percent of men complained of ejaculating too quickly (Frank et al., 1978).

According to interview data (Kinsey et al., 1948), the average length of time from erection to ejaculation is about five minutes, and 75 percent of men ejaculate within two minutes of intromission (inserting the penis). The problem is that this period of stimulation is insufficient for the majority of women to reach orgasm.

Orgasmic Dysfunction.   Besides inhibited sexual desire, the most common sexual complaint among women is difficulty in reaching orgasm (**orgasmic dysfunction).** About 15 percent of women report that they are unable to experience orgasm, and 46 percent report difficulty in reaching orgasm (Frank et al., 1978). This mirrors the diagnostic distinction between *primary* (never experienced an orgasm) and *secondary* orgasmic dysfunction (currently not experiencing orgasm in some or all situations).

Though it is much less common, men also experience inhibited orgasm. Like women with orgasmic dysfunction, they show normal arousal during the excitement phase, but sexual response is inhibited before reaching the plateau or the orgasmic phase.

Premature Ejaculation
male orgasm that occurs too early during sexual relations, in the judgment of one or both partners.

Vaginismus.   **Vaginismus** is the name given to a problem that prevents sexual intercourse. In some women, the muscles around the vagina contract tightly and involuntarily, preventing entrance by the penis. These muscle contractions can be quite painful. Vaginismus can result from a painful or traumatic sexual experience, such as rape, or in reaction to a variety of other sexual difficulties.

Orgasmic Dysfunction
difficulty or inability to experience orgasm in response to sexual stimulation.

Dyspareunia.   Sometimes pain occurs during sexual relations, interfering with normal sexual responding and pleasure. Called **dyspareunia,** this problem usually arises from a physical problem such as an infection, inflamed or torn tissue, or insufficient lubrication.

Vaginismus
a sexual dysfunction in which sexual intercourse is prevented by muscle spasms of the vagina.

CAUSES OF SEXUAL PROBLEMS

Dyspareunia
painful intercourse.

Although each of the problems just described has its own set of common causes, there are some similarities in the factors that contribute to sexual dysfunctions. We will discuss several of these common factors.

First, it is worth noting that most sexual problems amount to disappointment of *expectations*. What constitutes a "dysfunction" or a "problem" is very relative to what the individual, couple, or society expects. For example, neither "premature" ejaculation nor female orgasmic dysfunction is considered to be a problem in cultures and eras where sexual satisfaction of women is not expected. A "problem" emerges when at least one partner is distressed about the situation, that is, when reality does not match up to his or her expectations. Sexual behavior is not a problem if it is not distressing or harmful to the consenting partners involved.

Masters and Johnson (1970) pointed to two other common causes of the sexual dysfunctions they studied. One of these they called the **spectator role,** in which the person mentally "steps out" of his or her body and begins observing or evaluating what is happening. Juan reported exactly this:

> I'm in the middle of having sex with my wife when I start thinking to myself, "How am I doing? I wonder if she's enjoying herself, or if she's faking it? I don't know how much longer I can hold out. How long has it been now? Maybe seven or eight minutes?" As soon as I get to thinking like that, I start having problems.

By taking on this role as an observer and evaluator, the person usually becomes distanced from her or his own sexual pleasure and focuses on thoughts rather than the immediate physical sensations that form the human sexual response. The result is a disruption of the normal pattern, resulting in inhibition of excitement.

A second and related problem emphasized by Masters and Johnson is **performance anxiety.** Earlier in this chapter we described a man whose anxiety about his sexual adequacy turned a single instance of erectile difficulties into "impotence." Anxiety and sexual arousal are incompatible; they inhibit each other. Being anxious or concerned, then, is likely to prevent the normal human sexual response from following its course.

Many other factors can interfere with normal sexual responding. Alcohol and drug intoxication, fatigue, fear of disease or unwanted pregnancy, anger, or distraction can get in the way. Sexual problems may arise from larger areas of conflict within the relationship. Physical problems can be a source of sexual dysfunctions as well, particularly in dyspareunia and total erectile dysfunction. Sexual misinformation or lack of knowledge can, in itself, be a source of problems. Unpleasant or traumatic early sexual experiences (such as incest), guilt about sexual feelings or behavior, or fear of intimacy can also be involved.

Finally, we would add that sexual problems occur in the context of relationships and seldom is it useful to think of them as belonging to one person. Successful sex therapy is greatly aided by, and often requires, the involvement of both partners. Sexual problems often interact with each other, forming interlocking patterns. For example, premature ejaculation and secondary orgasmic dysfunction complement each other, with each partner "giving up" and thus exacerbating the problem. The placing of blame or responsibility on one partner is unhelpful in working out a solution to sexual problems.

Spectator Role
being distanced from immediate experience, as if observing one-self as an evaluator.

Performance Anxiety
focus on and concern about the quality of one's behavior.

■ TREATMENT

The good news is that modern sex therapy has a very good track record. The techniques of treatment developed by Masters and Johnson (1970) have been further refined and tested by more recent researchers (Wincze, 1981; Wright, Pelrreault, & Mathieu, 1977) and have been translated into self-help programs for women (Barbach, 1975; Heiman, LoPiccolo, & LoPiccolo, 1976) and for men (Schover, 1984; Zeiss & Zeiss, 1978; Zilbergeld & Ullman, 1978).

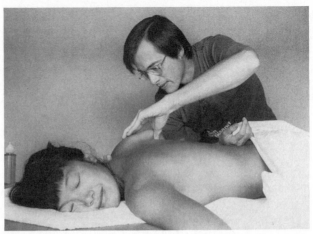

Massage can restore positive physical experiences to a couple's sensual life.

To understand sex therapy approaches, it is useful to remember that many of the causes of sexual problems are, in essence, factors that inhibit what is otherwise a natural response. They get in the way of normal responding. The four phases of sexual response described by Masters and Johnson (1966) are not learned, but occur naturally. Sexual dysfunctions, then, can be understood as obstacles blocking this natural response pattern. Sex therapy is the process of removing these obstacles.

The methods originally developed by Masters and Johnson focus heavily on overcoming the spectator role and performance anxiety. These elements have been retained in more recent sex therapies. The obstacle of taking a spectator role is most often overcome by an approach called **sensate focus.** Partners are taught to give and receive sensual pleasure through touch, massage, and caresses. Emphasis is placed on experiencing the pleasures of touch, and genital sex is initially deemphasized or even forbidden. The purposes are several. First, sensate focus is meant to restore positive physical experiences to the couple's sex life, while initially keeping clear of the anxiety-provoking problem areas. It also is meant to expand each partner's concept of sexuality to one of sensual pleasure, taking the focus away from achieving a particular experience, such as orgasm or prolonged intercourse without ejaculation. Sensate focus also redirects the person's attention to her or his own body and away from the evaluative and distanced perspective of a spectator.

A common element of sex therapy techniques is their gradual approach through **successive approximations.** In working toward a goal of becoming orgasmic or maintaining erection, the partners move at a pace that is comfortable for them both. Intercourse is often prohibited during the early phase of sex therapy to remove the anxiety and performance pressure that have contributed to the problem. A specific series of assignments is often used to overcome the anxiety that is inhibiting normal sexual arousal. You may recognize that successive approximation is also an important element in the method of systematic desensitization, described in Chapter 8.

For certain sexual problems there are uniquely effective methods of treatment. Men can learn to delay ejaculation, for example, through the use of a method known as the **squeeze technique** introduced by Semans (1956). Like many sex therapy methods, this involves both partners. The man's penis is stimulated until he reaches a point very near ejaculation. At this moment, the partner gently but firmly squeezes the head of the penis between thumb and forefinger, causing an inhibition of ejaculation. This procedure is repeated

Sensate Focus
a sex therapy strategy involving the centering of attention on immediate sensory experiences.

Successive Approximation
working in small, gradual steps toward a desired goal.

Squeeze Technique
a sex therapy strategy used to treat premature ejaculation.

over and over in "stop and go" fashion for about 20 minutes. Through practice sessions such as this, most men are able to learn greater voluntary control over ejaculation (Zeiss & Zeiss, 1978).

Vaginismus can usually be treated successfully with a relatively simple de-sensitizing strategy. The woman is given a set of dilators of varying sizes which are gently inserted into the vagina to stretch contracted muscles. Masters and Johnson (1970) reported virtually 100 percent success in using this method to overcome vaginismus.

HOW SUCCESSFUL IS TREATMENT?

The Masters and Johnson sex therapy methods have been evaluated by several research groups (Lobitz & LoPiccolo, 1972; Mathews et al., 1976; Zeiss, 1978), with generally very favorable results. Orgasmic dysfunction, erectile problems, premature ejaculation, and inhibited male orgasm have all been treated quite successfully, with favorable outcomes reported in 70 to 80 percent of cases on average. Although skeptics have claimed that these figures are overly optimistic (e.g., Zilbergeld, 1983), in general the outlook for overcoming sexual problems with proper help is very good indeed.

One source of disagreement has been the definition of what constitutes a cure in sex therapy (Wade & Tavris, 1987). If the definition of cure is complete elimination of sexual problems for both partners, then sex therapy may not appear to be so successful. What does seem to be a realistic goal is the alleviation of most of a couple's sexual problems most of the time. Because sexual problems are defined in relation to the dissatisfaction of the partners, the ultimate criterion for "cure" must also rely upon the partners' reported happiness with the outcome.

Because the Masters and Johnson methods for overcoming sexual dysfunction can be clearly specified, they have been described in a variety of self-help books. A treatment that is effective when administered by a therapist, however, may or may not be useful in self-administered form (Rosen, 1976a). Initial evaluations of self-help (minimal therapist contact) programs for sexual dysfunctions have provided encouraging results (Kass et al., 1976; Zeiss, 1977, 1978).

Last, we would advise caution when seeking sex therapy, to ensure that the therapist is properly qualified. The practice of "sex therapy" is uncontrolled in most states, so that almost any person can advertise the offering of such services, regardless of his or her training and competence. Needless to say, the opportunity to explore people's private sexual lives can attract a variety of unqualified individuals with unprofessional motives. Before seeking or referring someone for the help of a sex therapist, carefully inquire as to the helper's professional background and certification, and the specific training and supervision which qualifies her or him to offer such services. Finding a therapist through the Yellow Pages or advertisements is particularly hazardous in this area. Call the office of your state psychological association, or consult the department of psychology or medical school of a local university and ask for the names of properly qualified sex therapists. Finally, realize that there is no profession of "sex therapy" per se. Professionals who are qualified to offer sex therapy are first broadly trained in one of the major helping professions (psychology, psychiatry, social work, nursing, etc.) and then receive special training and supervision in the treatment of sexual dysfunctions. Thus a qualified sex therapist should be licensed or certified by the state in his or her chosen profession, in addition to having specific credentials of training for treating sexual problems. (In Appendix A we offer more general advice for seeking professional help.)

■ WHEN SEX IS NOT SEXUAL

Power, violence, force, and coercion can masquerade as sexuality in our culture. Hostility and dominance over people with less power is often confused with sexuality, perhaps in part because of the blending of these themes in entertainment and pornography media.

RAPE

Rape is sexual penetration that is forced upon an unconsenting victim. Rape is much more a violent crime than a sexual one, and recent changes in language help to identify it as such by terming it sexual assault. Current research indicates that about 25 percent of women are sexually assaulted at least once during their lives (Matlin, 1987).

Because women under the age of 25 are the most common victims, college women (many of whom are in this age range) are particularly at risk. In campus settings, a common and underreported form of sexual assault is *date rape* (Barrett, 1982; Warshaw, 1988). Although the stereotype of rape is that the assailant is a stranger, in fact the rapist and the victim often know each other and may have known each other for some time.

> Sheila thought of Mark as a friend. She enjoyed talking with him, and often had coffee with him after class. They discussed what they were learning, and also talked about their personal lives, their feelings and hopes. One evening they were both at a party, and after having a couple of drinks, they went out for a walk together. In a nearby park they sat down among some trees and talked. It was quite dark, and after a while they kissed for the first time. Sheila enjoyed the kiss, but began feeling uncomfortable as Mark kept kissing her and pulled her down onto the grass. When he began unbuttoning her blouse, Sheila protested, "Don't, Mark!" But Mark continued despite her protests, holding her down and telling her that she really wanted to make love. When she struggled to get away, Mark pushed her back down hard, saying "I don't want to hurt you." Afraid of being hurt, she stopped resisting. During intercourse, she cried quietly. Afterwards Mark walked her back to the party in silence.

Date rape, or acquaintance rape, is particularly difficult for the victims, because in addition to the suffering of being sexually assaulted, victims of date rape also may begin questioning their own judgment and perceptions regarding the people they choose as friends and companions.

Victims of rape, like those subjected to other traumatic experiences, frequently suffer some long-term consequences (Matlin, 1987). Immediately following the assault, it is common for the victim to experience a period of emotional shock. This may be expressed as intense anxiety or depression, but other victims show a calm and controlled exterior while suffering inwardly. A very frequent experience is *self-blame*. The victim, almost always without cause, believes that she may have done something to provoke the attack or could and should have prevented it. This may be one reason why only a minority of rapes are ever reported to the police. Although depression normally subsides within a few months, anxiety may persist for much longer, evidenced in feelings of jumpiness and vague uneasiness. Sexual relationships can also be disturbed, and some women find all sexual activity to be aversive, painful, or at least unpleasurable for a period of time. The victim's spouse, family, and friends may react in ways that increase her depression, self-blaming, and loss of self-esteem. Some of the symptoms of this **rape trauma syndrome** (Burgess & Holmstrom, 1974; Matlin, 1987) may persist for five years or more after the assault. This period of suffering and adjustment may be short-

Rape Trauma Syndrome
a pattern of psychological disturbance that follows sexual assault.

Immediately following sexual assault, it is common for the survivor to experience a period of emotional shock.

ened and eased by competent rape crisis counseling (Becker & Abel, 1981). Review the box on acquaintance rape in Chapter 9 for additional methods for dealing with this important problem.

SEXUAL HARASSMENT

Sexual harassment is a term used to describe sexually exploitive behaviors that may fall short of sexual assault. According to the Equal Employment Opportunity Commission (1980), it consists of "unwelcome sexual advances, requests for sexual favors, and other verbal or physical conduct of a sexual nature." Sexual harassment may occur in any setting, and often occurs within ongoing relationships where the offender has a power advantage over the victim. This leaves the victim in conflict, because confronting the offender with his conduct may lead to adverse consequences or the loss of positive out-

Sexual Harassment
unwanted verbal or physical approaches of a sexual nature.

12.7   WHAT ARE THE ISSUES HERE?

After a supervisory session at the student's practicum site, the supervisor walked her to the parking lot, where he kissed her as she got into her car. She was surprised, shocked, and she began to cry. She also quickly realized that her evaluation for the practicum was in the control of the supervisor. The parking lot kiss was confusing because although the student had no sexual feelings for the supervisor, she liked him very much and respected his clinical judgment. Their sexual relationship ended a few months later with the supervisor's marriage intact, when he accepted a better job in another state. The student's mar-

riage ended in divorce; she had no letter of recommendation from the supervisor and no job. While the sexual contact clearly affected the student adversely, the adverse effects on the supervisor were less clear. Years later, however, he did comment that he had never allowed himself to accept another teaching position where sexual contact was possible.

What are the issues here? Where does the responsibility for this situation lie? When sexual relations emerge within an uneven power relationship (such as supervisor/supervisee), what are the relative risks for each person? What would you do in this situation?

comes. This is so common as to be seen as acceptable or even humorous in some situations. The "casting couch," for example, is a metaphor from the entertainment industry for extorting sexual favors in exchange for a promise of employment or promotion.

Sexual harassment of college students by professors is another common abuse of power. Twenty-five percent of recent women graduates of psychology programs reported in a survey that they had experienced sexual contact with a psychology educator during their training (Pope, Levenson, & Schover, 1979). Because of the power imbalance between a student and a teacher, the risk of coercion is clearly present. Sexual harassment is unethical behavior and is specifically prohibited by the code of ethics of the American Psychological Association (1981). A case filed in 1977 (*Alexander* v. *Yale University*) involved an undergraduate woman who charged that she received a lower grade on a paper and in a course because she refused a professor's sexual overtures. The significance of the case is that the court decision indicated that sexual harassment is a form of sex discrimination and therefore is prohibited under Title IX of the 1972 Education Amendments (Dzeich & Weiner, 1984).

Another setting in which sexual harassment and assault may occur is of special concern to psychologists. This occurs when a therapist makes sexual overtures to or becomes sexually involved with a client. There are no circumstances under which sexual harassment or a sexual relationship is regarded as acceptable or ethical behavior, according to the professional ethical standards of the American Psychological Association (1981). Sexual involvement with a client is regarded to be an abuse of power and a distortion of a relationship that is intended to be helping and professional. This violation of a professional relationship is not, of course, limited to psychology, but may occur as well in any profession, including medicine, dentistry, law, the ministry, or sales.

■ SEXUAL ABUSE

One of the early shocks of Sigmund Freud's career was his observation that many of the female patients he treated for psychological problems reported that they had been sexually abused by their fathers or other males close to them. In the Victorian society in which Freud worked, this revelation was horrifying indeed. In his early writings, Freud hypothesized that the emotional distress which he called "neurosis" resulted at least in part from the trauma of sexual molestation.

As Freud's theories developed, his thinking about reports of childhood sexual molestation shifted, and he began to reconstrue these reports of abuse as fantasy manufactured by the unconscious mind. Children, Freud maintained, *desire* sexual contact with the opposite-sex parent, and out of this unconscious desire they create memories of events that never actually occurred. "If in the case of girls who produce such an event in the story of their childhood the father figures fairly regularly as the seducer, there can be no doubt either of the imaginary nature of the accusation or of the motive that has led to it" (Freud, 1966, p. 370). Contemporary writers argue that by invalidating women's experience in this way, Freud laid the groundwork for continuing harm to girls and women, both in their families and in psychotherapy, for decades to come (Masson, 1984; Rush, 1980; Westerlund, 1986). In fairness, it must be acknowledged that despite social pressure, Freud did continue repeatedly to acknowledge the reality of incest. A few lines after the foregoing quote, Freud wrote, "You must not suppose, however, that sexual abuse of a child by its nearest male relatives belongs entirely to the realm of phantasy" (p. 370).

It was not until the 1970s, however, that child sexual abuse and **incest** came to be recognized as disturbingly common, and as contributing to long-term emotional adjustment problems. Current studies estimate that 15 to 19 percent of women and 6 to 9 percent of men were victims of sexual abuse before the age of 17 (Peters, Wyatt, & Finkelhor, 1986; Finkelhor, 1984). The emotional problems of adults who were sexually victimized as children resemble, in some ways, those of adult rape victims. Anxiety, depression, guilt, and low self-esteem are prevalent. The stigma, shame, and fear involved, particularly with repeated sexual abuse, may contribute to a social isolation that persists into adulthood, creating disturbed social relationships and a poor social support system. Sexual disinterest, dissatisfaction, and dysfunction may also result (Finkelhor & Brown, 1985; Johnson & Shrier, 1985; Tasi, Feldman-Summers, & Edgar, 1979). Again, proper psychotherapy may be quite helpful in overcoming these difficulties.

■ SOCIAL ISSUES

Sexual behavior poses adjustment challenges not only to individuals, but also for social systems. How much personal freedom should be allowed to individuals in expressing their sexuality? What controls should be exercised by the government? Virtually all cultures provide controls over sexual behavior, although the nature and extent of these controls vary widely. We will consider here only a few of the perplexing social issues posed by sexual behavior.

PORNOGRAPHY

One issue facing any government is the extent to which it will permit the publication and distribution of sexually explicit material in print (books, magazines) and electronic media (films, television, videotapes). For several decades, a debate has raged regarding the true effects of **pornography** on society. Some view pornography as a safety valve, a less harmful outlet for sexual energies and interests. Others maintain that pornography promotes sexual victimization, and more generally a societal view of women as sex objects.

To address this controversy, the Attorney General of the United States appointed a special commission to investigate the effects of various kinds of pornography. In its final report, the Attorney General's Commission (1986) concluded that pornography emphasizing themes of violence materially increases the likelihood of aggression against women. Child pornography, already illegal in the United States, is also believed to contribute to sexual abuse of children. Other categories of pornography, such as nonviolent materials depicting degradation, domination, subordination, and humiliation, or nonviolent and nondegrading materials, or materials depicting nudity, appear to have less clear-cut effects on adults. One psychologist member of the commission who dissented from the general conclusions emphasized that adolescents and young adults are large consumers of pornographic materials and little is known about the impact of such materials on young people. She strongly recommended relevant school sex education programs as a way to

Incest
sexual abuse of a child by a relative.

Pornography
sexually explicit material, intended to arouse sexual desire.

12.8   REFLECTING ON PERSONAL CHOICES

Here are some serious personal choices that face individuals in contemporary society. If you have not yet made these choices, we encourage you to give them serious thought and consideration and to talk them over with others you trust. If you have already experienced these choices, reflect on how your thinking on these issues has changed over time.

1. Would I like to have children one day?

2. How old would I like to be when I have my first child?

3. How many children would I like to have?

4. How sad would I be if I were not able to have any children?

5. What would happen and how would I feel if pregnancy came before marriage?

6. If my partner or I were to become pregnant before I wanted to, would an abortion be a way I might approach the situation?

7. Would I like to wait until I'm married to start having sexual intercourse?

8. At what age would I like to be married if I could have this happen whenever I wanted it to happen?

9. How many years of formal education would I like to complete?

10. At what point during or after this educational process would I like to be married?

11. How do work and child-rearing fit into the plans my partner and I have?

12. Of all the things I could do in my life, probably the most important to accomplish would be _____.

13. This life goal would be affected by child-bearing in the following ways: _____.

14. What would it mean to me if my marriage were to end in divorce?

15. Would I like to have sexual intercourse with the person I marry before that marriage occurs?

16. How would I feel if my partner were to have sexual intercourse outside of our marriage?

17. How would I feel if I were to have sexual intercourse outside of my marriage?

18. How does my life plan thus far fit with my religious beliefs or with my personal value system?

inoculate children against the potential damage from early exposure to negative sexual images.

The issues regarding pornography remain complex, and experts in the field disagree about the seriousness or nature of its effects. A crucial balance is sought between protecting society against potential adverse effects of pornography and protecting freedom of expression.

REPRODUCTIVE FREEDOM

Reproductive freedom refers to the individual's right to make choices about having children. In one sense these are private matters, but in various times and cultures they have also taken on intense social dimensions. Again a balance is sought between individual liberty and societal values.

Birth control is one issue of reproductive freedom. For some, because of moral or religious convictions, the use of birth control in itself is unacceptable. On the other side, proponents of birth control argue that without it, the world will quickly be devastated by overpopulation and that family planning promotes the physical and mental well-being of both children and parents. The alarming rise in sexually transmitted diseases, including AIDS, has added another reason for the use of condoms, which are fairly effective in preventing both unwanted pregnancies and the spread of diseases.

The availability of effective birth control methods raises other issues. How should partners share the responsibility for practicing birth control? What are the long-term risks in using particular birth control methods? The availability of birth control has also caused young people to be faced with a choice that, only a generation ago, was not considered to be a choice: Should we have children, and if so, when? This has been called "the most fateful decision of your life" (Whelan, 1976), and the pro's and con's involved can be perplexing indeed. This decision can be intertwined with considerations of personal career (Fabe & Wikler, 1979). Should one develop a career before having a family, have a family first, or start family and career at the same time?

A related personal and social issue is **abortion**. In our society, two polarized groups have arisen, "pro-life" and "pro-choice," equally impassioned in their arguments. A 1973 Supreme Court decision made abortion available to women choosing it, within certain constraints. Opponents of abortion seek an amendment to the U.S. Constitution to illegalize abortion. In July of 1989, the U.S. Supreme Court upheld a Missouri statute that prohibited public hospitals or public employees from performing abortions. Furthermore, the statute prohibited counseling a woman about the option of abortion unless her life was endangered.

The opposite side of this coin is **infertility,** a problem of increasing frequency in our society. Infertility refers to difficulty or inability to become pregnant and give birth to a live baby when one wants to do so. A somewhat arbitrary but often used standard is that infertility is a problem when a couple has tried without success for at least a year to become pregnant. Infertility is common. It has been estimated that about one couple in six experiences problems with infertility (Menning, 1977). The cause is usually physical rather than psychological and is often curable with proper diagnosis and treatment. About half the couples experiencing infertility problems do eventually have biological children. Others choose to adopt children already born.

Abortion
the termination of problem pregnancy.

Infertility
difficulty in establishing or maintaining a pregnancy.

12.9   HERE WE DIFFER/HERE WE AGREE
Abortion Choice and Reverence for Life

It would be difficult to find a contemporary issue over which people differ more impassionately than that of the human rights involved in decisions about abortion. For myself, I choose reverence for life as a guiding principle: that human life is of special worth and is, in a real sense, sacred. Applied to the issue of abortion, this belief leaves me troubled. It is very clear that near the end of pregnancy, an unborn child is alive in every sense, and an act of violence (such as a violent assault or a drunk driving accident) that ends the child's life is criminal. I also clearly believe that contraception is vital in controlling world population and thereby preserving human life.

Between these two extremes lies the controversial terrain of abortion. Some maintain that termination of pregnancy is justifiable during the first trimester, but unacceptable once the fetus is viable (i.e., could survive outside the womb). I find this an empty distinction. If human life is sacred, surely this is so before as well as after any arbitrarily chosen point during gestation. From this perspective, abortion constitutes the termination of a human life.

It seems to me, further, that one who takes this stand is obliged to honor the sanctity of life consistently on other issues. It makes little sense to me, for example, to oppose abortion on grounds of the sanctity of life while favoring capital punishment, or supporting the stockpiling of a nuclear arsenal capable of ending all human life. The absurdity of bombing abortion clinics on behalf of the sanctity of life is likewise apparent.

Given my reverence for life position, another crucial issue immediately presents itself. Am I so certain of the rightness of my own view that I would impose it on all others by criminalizing medical abortion? Here I must answer, "No," although I understand the conviction of those who oppose choice. "Pro-life" does not automatically require

"antichoice." On a moral issue of this complexity, I am inclined to have each person weigh the alternatives and decide in personal conscience. For me, a reverence for life position seeks and actively promotes alternatives to abortion. These include strategies for preventing unwanted pregnancies and sound alternatives (such as adoption) to terminating them when they occur. As the father of two adopted children, I am grateful for those who make this choice.   —WRM

Writing as a woman who has had a legal abortion, I feel very strongly that abortion needs to be kept a safe and legal option for women. Prior to the U.S. Supreme Court decision (*Roe* v. *Wade*) in 1973, American women faced tremendous hardship with problem pregnancy: they could risk illegal abortions from possibly unqualified people; they could present to physicians as mentally ill, and therefore qualify for therapeutic abortion if a second physician agreed with the diagnosis; they could attempt to abort themselves, often with fatal results; they could bear a child they did not want. A few women with access to financial resources could travel to foreign countries where abortion was legal to obtain the medical care they needed. Clearly, all those approaches violate the rights of a human being who has autonomy over her own body.

I am currently the president of the New Mexico Religious Coalition for Abortion Rights, an interfaith group that supports a woman's right to choose about her reproductive life. Quakers, Jews, Presbyterians, Lutherans, Methodists, Episcopalians, Unitarians, and Catholics recently worshipped in an interfaith religious service in my neighborhood to celebrate the sixteenth anniversary of the Supreme Court decision that upheld a woman's right to choose. Religious freedom and reproductive freedom go hand in hand, although there is a minority that believes that it should impose its religious beliefs on all citizens. Since this country was founded on the premise of separation of church and state, however, that minority would be violating our constitution if it insisted that its religious beliefs become law: "Congress shall make no law respecting an establishment of religion, or prohibiting the free exercise thereof . . ." (First Amendment to the U.S. Constitution).

Equality under the law must provide women with the same rights as men. Forcing women to bear children they do not want would be a violation of our civil rights. Like men, we deserve to live undivided lives, lives in which we are not forced to choose between child-bearing and career, for example. Our quality of life should be equal to that of men, in that we should be treated as equally sound in judgment. Reverence for life includes reverence for a woman's life.

While I am sincerely happy for my colleague's adopted children, as well as my own children, contraception and abortion need to be available choices as well. Every woman deserves the right to use her own best judgment about her body and her life.   —CEY

INTEGRATION

On issues of great disagreement it can be useful for advocates of diverse positions to seek points of agreement, common values on which they can concur. Several seem possible here. One point of agreement is the desirability of access to alternatives to abortion, so that fewer women must face this difficult choice. Another possible agreement is the value placed, in American society, on individual freedom. Where opinion is divided and large elements of society genuinely disagree, the principle of freedom constrains one segment of society from imposing its beliefs on all of society. Those who oppose abortion are not required to undergo or to participate in abortions under the current system. Criminalization of abortion would, however, delimit the liberty of those who now make this choice. Another likely agreement is the adverse effects of criminalizing abortion. Finally, it is a potential point of agreement that the same fervor and compassion that is expressed on this issue should also be manifested in our concern for the welfare of people already born.

SEX CRIMES

Each society also faces issues of how to define and deal with criminal sexual behavior. One test of the criminality of an act is the extent to which those involved willingly consented. We have already discussed sexual assault as a violent crime in which the victim is forced to participate in a sexual act without her or his consent. A related issue is the legal "age of consent." Most societies punish sexual behavior of adults with *minors*, those under a specified age at which the individual is deemed able to give consent. In dealing with sex offenders, society faces another important balancing of interests: protecting society from harm and securing the rights and treatment of the individual. Happily, these interests can coincide. Effective methods are available for treating at least some types of sex offenders (Adams et al., 1981). Such treatment may serve as a better protection for society than long-term imprisonment, which often results only in a hardening of the offender without treating the problem and deterring future offenses.

Many societies also, however, define as criminal certain sexual behaviors between consenting partners. Prostitution is an example. But how far should such controls go? Some states define particular sexual behaviors as punishable offenses, even when occurring between consenting marital partners in the privacy of their own homes. Many states define any homosexual intimacy as criminal. Though such statutes may be seldom enforced, the right of a government to prescribe and proscribe private sexual behavior is a controversial matter. In Chapter 14, we will examine further the balancing of individual freedom and the collective interests of society.

■ SUMMARY

Sexuality is best understood in relationship to other dimensions of human adjustment. What constitutes "healthy" sexuality varies widely from one culture or group to another, and sexual "dysfunction" is defined by the distress or dissatisfaction of sexual partners. A STORC analysis can be used to understand sexual stimuli (S), the influence of thoughts (T) and expectations, the organismic (O) physiology of sexuality, sexual responses (R), and their consequences (C). Homosexual behavior is no longer officially regarded to be abnormal, and psychological adjustment measures do not show significant differences between heterosexual and homosexual individuals. Sexual problems are very common, affecting more than half of all couples at any point in time and are also highly treatable. Performance anxiety and the spectator role are two common factors contributing to sexual dysfunctions. Rape is a crime of violence and not predominantly a sexual act. Victims of both rape and child sexual abuse show posttraumatic stress reactions. Sexual harassment, pornography, reproductive freedom, and sex-related crimes all pose enduring and challenging issues for any society.

■ QUESTIONS FOR THOUGHT

1. The World Health Organization (WHO) defined healthy sexuality as integrating somatic, emotional, intellectual, and social aspects of sexual being which enhance and enrich personality, communication, and love. Using your own words and experience, paraphrase and comment on the WHO definition. Is the definition relevant for you? Why or why not?

2. What aspects of your "appropriate" sex role were you taught as a child? List specific messages you were given about how to behave in a way that complied with your gender. Were the messages spoken or nonverbal?

3. What is an early sexual memory for you? What feelings were/are associated with that memory?

4. How did you learn about sexuality? Who gave you the information you first received? Was it useful? Was it accurate?

5. What religious beliefs were you taught about sexual behavior? Do you practice what you were taught? Have you chosen different values?

6. How does your sexuality diminish your self-esteem? How does your sexuality increase your self-esteem?

7. When people experience sexual problems, what keeps them from seeking help, in your opinion?

8. What is the policy on your campus about sexual harassment of students? If a student were sexually harassed by a professor, what would you advise the student to do?

9. Do your sexual feelings or behavior change in any way when you use alcohol? How does your own experience fit with the research reported in the text about alcohol and sexual behavior? What conclusions have you drawn from your own experience?

10. How would you respond if a close friend were diagnosed as having AIDS? What would be the best response in your opinion?

chapter thirteen

I have learned that to get a job done and have fun in it is about all you can get out of life.
Jessie Tarbox Beals:
First Woman News Photographer, by Alexander Alland 1978

The World of Work

OUTLINE

What is there to do?" It is a common and plaintive cry of boredom often heard during middle childhood and adolescence. After retirement, adults sometimes complain of "having nothing to do." Throughout the life span, human beings want to be *doing*.

Psychologists often recognize three major areas or challenges of life adjustment (Gilmore, 1973). In Chapter 10 we explored the challenge of *loving*, of relating to other people. In Chapter 15 we will discuss the challenge of *being*, of finding personal meaning and purpose in one's life. In this chapter, we deal with the challenge of *doing*, of contributing in a meaningful way to the world around us (Gilmore, 1973).

■ WHAT IS WORK?

In our society, the word "work" has many meanings. It can refer to exerted effort or to the results of that effort, to a means of earning income, the type of occupation one pursues, or even the place where one pursues it. It carries some emotional connotations, too, attached to the anxiety of being "out of work" or "behind at work," and to the American "work ethic" that places a high moral value on personal effort and achievement.

We wish to suggest a broader conception of work, captured well in the question, "What do you do?" A person's work is that which occupies her or his time, energies, and imagination. It is by no means restricted to that for which a salary is received. In this context, it is incorrect to answer, "I don't work." The question is, "What do you *do*?" Your work is that which occupies your time, consumes your energies, captures your imagination. Play is the work of children. Pursuing an education, volunteering services in the community, holding down a full-time job, managing a household and caring for children, writing a book, traveling the world in search of experiences—any of these could be one's "work." In this larger sense, a person's work *is* never done; it merely changes in nature throughout the life span.

■ CHOOSING ONE'S WORK

The choice of your work is a choice of how you will spend your time and your life. This is a decision in which most people in our society have considerable freedom, although in a desperate search for work individuals may lose track of some choices they have.

One consideration here is the amount of time you will devote to various areas of your life. As we are writing this chapter, the covers of popular magazines (particularly women's magazines) every month feature articles on "Balancing work and relationships," "Making time for yourself and your social life," and "Juggling career and family." This reflects what seems to be a national frustration with the difficulty of balancing the three life areas just outlined: work, relationships, and meaning. Later in this chapter we will discuss the problem of "workaholism," devoting excessive amounts of time to one sphere of life, and will provide some helpful guidelines on time management.

Another important perspective is the fact that most people now undergo several important changes in work and career in the course of a lifetime. A few

It is often difficult to combine work and child care.

decades ago, it was reasonable to expect that a male would choose one occupation, pursue it throughout life, and retire from it with the gift of a gold watch. This pattern is now the exception rather than the rule. Each year, one-third of Americans change jobs (Naisbitt & Aburdene, 1985). The world of work is changing so rapidly that jobs and even entire occupations become obsolete in relatively short spans of time (see Box 13.1). It is commonplace for people to change not only their workplace and job description, but also their career direction several times during adulthood.

13:1   THE CHANGING WORLD OF WORK

Each decade now brings a dramatically changed world of work. The present nature of employment, jobs, and careers is strikingly different from what the prior generation knew only thirty years ago. Observers of social trends predict that still greater changes are to come in the twenty-first century (Naisbitt, 1984; Toffler, 1980). Here are a few of the changes already apparent in work patterns within our society:

WORK FORCE

An increasingly large proportion of job seekers and workers are women. Most women now choose (or are forced by economic necessity) to seek salaried employment. Revisions in retirement standards and laws have also lengthened the typical work career by several years, and this trend is likely to continue as the average age of the U.S. population increases. These and other factors are increasing the number of available workers.

WORK TIMES

As the number of potential workers increases and people combine jobs with family and other personal pursuits, the demand for part-time jobs is on the increase. Typical work hours are also shifting and becoming more flexible. A four-day workweek is increasingly common, either with longer daily hours (10- to 12-hour days) or fewer total weekly hours. Employers more often offer "flex time," giving employees a choice about the hours they will work. In metropolitan settings, traffic problems are prompting variations from the traditional 9-to-5 workday.

WORK DIVISION

Another effect of changes in the work force is the availability, though still small, of shared jobs. One full-time position may be shared by two workers.

WORK PLACES

There is a shift away from centralization of work in large factories and agencies. Developments in telecommunications and computers are enabling people to do an increasing amount of their work at home, on the road, or in smaller satellite locations (possibly at the cost of greater isolation). Work sites are more often accommodating to the needs of workers in areas such as child care, providing on-site care facilities.

WORKER HEALTH

Recognizing that it is economically advantageous to promote the health of employees, work sites are devoting increased attention to prevention and health maintenance efforts. Smoking cessation treatment, diet and exercise programs, regular health check-ups, and on-site "employee assistance" counseling are becoming commonplace in larger work settings.

WORK PARTICIPATION

Following radical trends in Japanese industry, American workers are increasingly encouraged to participate in the planning and quality assurance processes of the workplace. Many companies have shifted away from a centralized hierarchical organization to an emphasis on smaller work teams and "quality circles." In these smaller groups, individuals retain a greater sense of personal responsibility for their work. Whereas product assembly was once accomplished by a long line of individuals each performing one special operation, it is increasingly common for small teams to conduct the assembly process (e.g., for an automobile) from beginning to end.

WORK TYPE

Although the manufacture of products is still a vital part of the national economy, there is a clear shift from products to services and, most recently, to an information economy (Naisbitt, 1984; Naisbitt & Aburdene, 1985). A rapidly increasing percentage of available jobs involve the provision of services, conveying of information, and management of data. The demand for certain types of employees (e.g., steelworkers, farmhands, secretaries) can change dramatically with market fluctuations, the availability of natural resources, and advances in technology.

DUAL-CAREER FAMILIES

It is now typical for both husband and wife to have active careers while also raising a family (Naisbitt & Aburdene, 1985). The work and job satisfaction of employees is thus affected by additional factors such as children's illnesses, school hours and vacations, and child care. At home, dual-career families must often deal with difficult challenges of dividing responsibilities for child-rearing and household maintenance.

How, then, does one choose a career direction? Of the literally thousands of alternative occupations available, what factors should be considered in deciding what to do with one's life? We suggest "three A's" to consider: aptitudes, attributes, and availability.

APTITUDES

Aptitude
a specific ability or talent.

Your **aptitudes** are your special abilities, areas in which you are particularly gifted or talented. Everyone has them. Some are already realized, reflected in past work experience. Others are potential but still undiscovered talents.

Work-related skills have sometimes been divided into three general categories: data, people, and things (Bolles, 1989). *Data* skills focus on facts, numbers, information, and ideas. They include tabulating, computing, analyzing, and interpreting data, as well as inventing and innovating. Dealing with *people* requires skills such as communicating, serving, persuading, teaching, entertaining, following instructions, supervising, and negotiating. Still different skills are needed for working with *things* such as machines, tools, and raw materials. Here some important skills are assembling, repairing, operating, monitoring, handling, cutting, and lifting.

One approach to discovering your aptitudes—what you are "good at"—is to examine your past experience, and not only your work experience. What do you do well? Skills in organizing data, for example, may be reflected in pastimes such as stamp collecting or working puzzles, or in service activities such as being librarian or secretary for a club, committee, or organization. The skill of instructing may be reflected in one's parenting, coaching, tutoring of fellow students, or writing of recipes. Skill in working with things may be evident in people who are "handy" around the house; repair their own automobile or bicycle; play musical instruments; or enjoy fishing, building models, painting, or gardening.

Another approach to discovering your special abilities is **aptitude testing,** in which specific skills and potentials are evaluated. Aptitude tests range from focused, objective tests (such as a typing test) to more complex measures of a broad range of abilities. Tests designed for screening applicants to college, graduate school, or professional training are of this kind. Many colleges and universities have a career advisement office to help students in evaluating their own aptitudes.

Although present aptitudes are important to consider, the skills and abilities needed for many jobs require specific types of training. Such training can be obtained in a variety of ways. One approach is formal education, through coursework at a college of university, or specialized training at a technical or vocational school. Another traditional approach is **apprenticeship** or on-the-job training, where the emphasis is more on learning by observing and doing. Volunteer service is still another way in which people obtain job-relevant experience and skills.

An important message here is to plan ahead. A common frustration of those who staff career advisement centers at colleges and universities is that stu-

Aptitude Test
A measure of a specific ability or talent, often used in occupational counseling.

Apprenticeship
a period of training in which a novice learns a new task or trade by observing and working with an experienced person who has mastered it.

Seek advice early from a mentor or role model about a career direction.

dents appear for guidance in the middle of their senior year. By this time, it is too late to shape their course of studies to prepare them for the career directions they desire. A wiser approach is to seek advice early, and to plan one's education in advance so that it supports a career direction.

This is not at all to say that education should be aimed solely at preparation for a particular occupation. In the rapidly changing world of work, narrowly specialized training is risky. A balance is needed between training in the specialized skills needed for particular employment and a general education that provides broader perspectives and adaptability. The value of coursework cannot be judged solely by asking, "How will this help me in my job?" or "How much will this increase my income?" Even within one's training for a particular career, it is wise to develop a broad range of competencies rather than learn only a specialized skill. In our doctoral training program for clinical psychologists, for example, all students are required to develop competency not only in psychotherapy, but also in psychological assessment, teaching, research, and general psychology. We require this range of competencies to prepare our students for a changing professional world. The demand for psychotherapists fluctuates over time, and in this specific area psychologists compete with other professionals such as social workers, psychiatrists, and counselors. A broadly trained clinical psychologist, however, is prepared to offer a variety of professional services: consultation, education, evaluation, psychotherapy, expert testimony in the court system, writing, and research. A broad education that develops a range of knowledge and competencies is a good preparation for the changing world of work.

The necessary *styles* of learning are also changing. Rote memorization is no longer adequate in a world of rapid change. Specific knowledge is quickly outdated. Instead it is vital, in the course of education, to learn how to learn, how to think, how to acquire, assimilate, and accommodate to a continual flow of new information. This further changes the nature of education. It is no longer feasible to expect to "get an education" and be done with it. Rather it is clear that lifelong learning and continuing adult education are already essential realities (Naisbitt & Auburdene, 1985).

ATTRIBUTES

Work satisfaction (and ultimately work quality) depends importantly on a good match between the job and the person. Individuals sometimes worry about

Lifelong learning and continuing adult education are essential.

13.2   PERSONAL MILESTONE
Choosing a Career

Choosing one's life work often comes about in strange ways. In my case, one man in particular set me on the road toward psychology. I should add that I had lots of help from other men and women later on, but it was Clarence Fylling who got me started. He was the Superintendent of Schools in the small northern California town of Oroville when I first met him.

I had been trying to find my way in the radio business after being discharged from the military at the end of World War II. I had been kicked out of a number of colleges, usually for poor attendance and/or poor grades. (I was disenrolled from one college even before I had a chance to attend a single class, when my friends and I were accused of tearing up a bar.) I had worked at a number of small radio stations, and as a flunky at ABC in Hollywood. Usually, I felt it necessary to tell my bosses how to run their businesses, and because of this immature behavior, I continued to find new jobs and lose them.

One year I got a job as the program director for another small radio station in Oroville. Soon the usual happened, and I was fired. I happened to be dating Mr. Fylling's daughter at the time. I never really knew whether he saw some potential in me, or just got tired of feeding me, but he hired me as a teacher for the seventh grade. I was to teach mathematics, health, and physical education.

Never having finished more than a year of college, and never having had one education course, I didn't have the faintest idea how to teach. Mr. Fylling and the principal showed me the textbooks and the material to be covered. They also explained that this school system gave achievement tests every year and students were expected to make, on average, a year's progress. That made sense. However, as we were walking down the hall to my first class, I nervously asked Mr. Fylling, "What do I do?"

"Walk in with a baseball bat in your hand and don't be afraid to use it," he responded. *This* I could understand! Then, after a pause, he added, "And don't forget, every student in that room is an individual, and deserves to be treated as one!" I had never thought of such a combination before. I have spent more years than I care to count trying to match that blend of awareness of one's own strength with respect for other people as individuals. Ultimately, I went on to earn a Ph.D. in clinical psychology. I learned a great deal about psychotherapy, neurophysiology, and neuroanatomy. I taught university students for many years. Through it all, I never forgot what Mr. Fylling had tried to teach me that day about the psychology of being both a teacher and a human being.   —JMR

---

fitting themselves to a particular job or occupation. A better question is: "What jobs or occupations fit *me* best?" Considerations here extend well beyond aptitudes or skills, to include the person's **attributes:** his or her own values, preferences, needs, and characteristics.

Within each of these three broad spheres—data, people, and things—there are many choices to be made. With what *kinds* of people would you like to work: babies, the elderly, students, laborers, the handicapped, women, or men? What *types* of things do you enjoy using: tools, machines, cloth, computers, typewriter, cameras, vehicles? What varieties of data would you find stimulating in your work: numbers, news, blueprints, ideas, catalogs, facts? The possibilities are endless. Materials have been developed specifically to help college students and others find their preferences among these many options (Bolles, 1986).

A different approach for person-job matching is the **interest inventory.** Several instruments of this type are available, usually in paper-and-pencil form (e.g., Hansen & Campbell, 1985). Your campus may have a career counseling

Attribute
a personal characteristic, trait, or value.

Interest Inventory
a test designed to measure the similarity of a person's values and preferences to those of individuals working in specific jobs and occupations; used in career counseling.

service where such tests are administered. These tests provide information about how the individual compares, in interests and values, with people *already working* in a variety of occupations. A high score on a "librarian" scale from one of these tests, for example, would indicate that the individual shows a pattern of personal attributes similar to people who are already working as librarians. This should not be confused with *aptitude* for a particular kind of work. Rather it indicates similarity to the type of people who have previously chosen the particular occupation.

Is it good to be similar in personality to others in one's occupation? Such similarity could make it easier to like, get along with, and agree with one's co-workers. A twenty-year longitudinal study of medical students found that the selection of medical specialty is predictable from personality type and that those who initially select a specialty atypical for their type tend to change specialties in the long run (McCaulley, 1977, 1978). *Satisfaction* with one's employment, then, may be influenced by similarity to co-workers.

On the other hand, individuals with "atypical" values, perspectives, and attributes may be particularly valuable to a company or profession. Such a person may question standard practices, suggest unaccustomed solutions, or point to previously unconsidered aspects of the work. A very people-oriented individual working in a job that usually attracts very data-oriented or thing-oriented workers may raise important questions about the impact of the work on people, or find ways to make a system or machine more "user-friendly."

AVAILABILITY

A third consideration in choosing a career direction is the availability of work in this area. This should not be an overriding concern, and it is unwise to select a career solely on the basis of the current "market" or demand. The availability of work in specific specialties will fluctuate over time. Nevertheless, this is one important factor to consider.

It is possible to begin by narrowing down the areas of interest. Are there particular geographic restraints, areas where you know you want to live, or where you would most like to live? Given your own aptitudes and attributes, what general types of work would you be good at and enjoy? What kind of work environment would be best for you? Then comes the next step: What types of work are possible and available within these guidelines, given your own strengths and personality? The task, now, becomes that of job-hunting, tracking down the possibilities.

■ FINDING A JOB

After narrowing the field of search according to your aptitudes, attributes, and preferences, how is it best to proceed? Contrary to common impressions, there is no single, particularly effective method for finding a job. Instead, an optimal approach is to pursue many different possibilities, and to use a variety of strategies. Box 13.3 lists fifteen different methods for finding job possibilities. According to Bolles (1986), people who are looking for jobs use, on average, fewer than two of these alternatives. The more options one pursues, the greater the likelihood of finding the right job.

In this regard, two perspectives are important. The first is that finding a job is itself a full-time job. Most people spend far too little time and effort when they are looking for new employment. Given how important it is, the search for suitable work deserves full attention. The second important perspective is

13.3 FIFTEEN AVENUES FOR JOB-HUNTING

In hunting for a job, it is useful to pursue as many different avenues as possible. The typical job hunter uses only one or two of the following possible approaches suggested by Bolles (1986):

1. Send out your resume to possible employers.
2. Get in touch with people and agencies (sometimes called "headhunters") who search for employees to match with job openings.
3. Respond to job announcements in newspapers, journals, or other trade publications.
4. Advertise your availability in a "work wanted" announcement in newspapers, journals, or other trade publications.
5. Use private employment agencies.
6. Use public employment services provided by local, state, and federal governments.
7. Use your college placement office.
8. Consult employment registers, which announce openings in a centralized fashion.
9. Ask everyone you know to tell you about any job openings where they work or other jobs they have heard about.
10. Visit potential employers at their offices.
11. Apply for governmental jobs through "civil service" channels.
12. Consult local unions, hiring offices, or agencies that provide businesses with part-time or temporary help.
13. Enroll in a formal job-search program provided by a local or out-of-town agency.

To these we would add

14. Register with the personnel offices of major employers in the area, and check regularly for new job postings.
15. Consult the Yellow Pages of the telephone directory under subject titles related to the types of work you might like to do; then call these places of business to set up a visit or just to inquire about current or future openings.

Source: Adapted from Richard Nelson Bolles, *Newsletter about life/work planning*, 1986, p. 2.

personal power. You have something good to offer: *yourself*! Employers seldom come to you with job offers. Rather you will need to seek and create your own opportunities, to present yourself in a positive and persuasive way.

Psychologist Nathan Azrin set out to discover how people get jobs, and how he could help others find employment (Azrin & Besalel, 1980, 1982). In asking people who already had jobs how they had gotten them, he discovered that very few had learned about the job by reading a job listing. Rather a majority had heard about the job opening from a friend or relative. This suggests one relatively simple strategy: tell everyone you know that you are looking for a job, and ask for their help in finding the kind of work you want. After several years of exploration, Azrin developed an approach called the **job-finding club** for helping people find work. The essential elements of this approach are these:

1. Commit substantial time to job finding. Participants come to the job club five days a week and spend the entire morning there making contacts and practicing skills. Each afternoon is spent in following up on leads and interviewing.

2. Make use of all available sources of potential job leads: friends, relatives, newspapers, job postings, public listings.

3. Don't be restricted to positions that are currently "open" or posted. Many jobs are never announced as "openings." After clarifying the kinds of work you would enjoy, identify potential employers and call them. (The Yellow Pages of the telephone directory are an excellent source of ideas.) If possible, go to visit the potential employer face to face, whether or not there are any current job openings.

4. Practice interviewing skills. Personal presentation is a very important factor in hiring. Specific elements such as dress, eye contact, communication skills, positive outlook, politeness, assertiveness, and persistence can make the difference.

5. All efforts count, and should be encouraged. The group support of a "buddy" system can be helpful in sustaining effort and avoiding discouragement. "The story of most people's job hunt is: NO NO NO NO NO NO NO NO NO NO NO NO NO NO NO NO NO NO NO NO NO NO NO NO NO YES" (Bolles, 1989).

In several evaluations of the job club approach, Azrin has found that it is substantially superior to traditional methods for finding employment (Azrin & Besalel, 1982).

■ JOB SURVIVAL SKILLS

Once people land a job, what determines whether they keep it? Johnson (1978) described three sets of skills that determine job survival: (1) *technical* skills that are required to do the job; (2) *organizational* skills such as being on time, not missing workdays, managing one's time, and doing reliable work; and (3) *interpersonal* skills for communication, cooperation, negotiation, assertiveness, leadership, and conflict resolution. Johnson maintains that the last of these, *people* skills, are usually most important and determine whether otherwise skillful people will retain their jobs and gain promotions. Technical and organizational skills are important, but are insufficient for getting along in many occupational settings.

PEOPLE SKILLS

Job-Finding Club
a structured daily group approach for finding employment, originally designed and tested by Nathan Azrin.

Skills in interpersonal communication can be the deciding factor in who is *hired* for a job in the first place. Azrin's highly successful job-finding approach emphasizes basic communication skills for effective interviewing. Once hired, an employee's job retention, adjustment, and satisfaction can be influenced strongly by interpersonal skills.

Nonverbal behavior can communicate a substantial amount of information. Ineffective communicators may maintain relatively little eye contact, speak in a soft and unassertive tone of voice, and show a slumped posture that expresses dejection, defeat, and the expectation of rejection. At the opposite extreme, nonverbal behaviors can be offensive. An unrelenting stare, loud tone of voice, and intrusion into the other's personal space (see Chapter 14) can be as much a put-off for potential employers as an unassertive nonverbal style. Effective communication involves a middle ground between these two extremes, as discussed in our consideration of assertiveness in Chapter 9.

Another interpersonal skill important to job survival is good listening. Many problems and misunderstandings can be averted by avoiding the communication "roadblocks" discussed in Chapter 10 and instead practicing reflective listening. Conflicts in the workplace often arise in part because people react to too little information, not taking time to ask for and listen to the whole story. As emphasized in Chapter 2, people respond to their own perceptions and interpretations of the situation, often without trying to get the whole picture.

An important companion skill for listening is verbal assertiveness, expressing one's own feelings, needs, and rights (Chapter 9). An unassertive person may not even ask for clarification, and thus will not have the opportunity to listen to what significant others have to say. An aggressive individual, on the other hand, may intimidate and alienate others, and thus likewise be cut off from hearing honest feedback. Employees who lack assertiveness skills may vacillate between these two extremes, suppressing personal assertion until frustration reaches a peak, then reacting in a hostile manner, then returning to a more submissive style. In jobs that involve interaction with the public (as many do), interpersonal communication skills are crucial for maintaining positive relations with current and potential customers, service personnel, clients, and colleagues.

Because conflicts invariably arise in work settings, employees also need skills for pinpointing, expressing, and resolving interpersonal problems (Johnson, 1978). Reaching a clear and agreed-upon definition of the problem or conflict is a good first step. Possible paths to resolution and cooperation can then be sought, discussed, tried, and evaluated (Chapter 10).

TIME MANAGEMENT

Another key skill area in job survival and satisfaction is effective time management. It is a common complaint that "I don't have enough time," but the fact is that everyone has exactly the same amount of time: twenty-four hours a day. The difference is in how that time is used. A common piece of advice from time management experts is: "Don't work longer or harder, but work smarter!"

That can be more easily said than done. The fruitful management of one's own time is an enduring life challenge. Here are a few general tips and guidelines, distilled from a variety of time management sources (cf. Lakein, 1973).

List.   A first step is to keep a list of work to be done. Not to do this often means moving from one crisis to another, doing whatever seems urgent at the moment. A clear work list enables better planning of one's study or work time.

Prioritize.   The hero of Kenny Rogers's hit song, "The Gambler," offers this advice:

> Every gambler knows the secret of surviving
> Is knowing what to throw away and knowing what to keep.

An essential element of time management is the setting and following of priorities. When there is too much to do, it is vital to decide what really needs to be done and what can wait (or not be done at all). A simple system is to arrange a work list into three categories of importance. Priority 1 jobs are those which are most important. Those in category 2 are important, but not as vital or pressing as those with top priority. Category 3 is for those jobs that are worthwhile but not essential or highly important. Specific jobs may move from one category to another as deadlines approach or as other events increase or decrease their importance.

Dismantle.   A common obstacle to accomplishing larger jobs is that they seem overwhelming. Consequently, they are put off ("procrastinating") in favor of other important but more readily accomplished tasks. The result can be an intimidating backlog of large unaccomplished jobs. For us as authors, the writing of this textbook often seemed an impossibly huge task. An alternative to despair and procrastination in such circumstances is to break the job down into smaller component parts. "Finding a job" can be dismantled into more easily accomplished tasks such as asking one friend for help in making contacts, placing one contact call, filling out one application form, or scheduling one interview.

Allocate.   Once you have set priority categories and dismantled larger jobs into component parts, give time to those jobs that you assigned to categories 1 and 2. Plan the day in terms of what can realistically be accomplished. Stick to this plan, and avoid temptations to do other things because they are more fun or easier.

Schedule.   Many people find that it is best for them to do specific types of work during certain hours of the day. A person who does his or her best creative work in the morning, for example, might reserve the hours before lunch for doing tasks that require this kind of special or sustained attention. Afternoons might then be used for other more routine tasks such as returning telephone calls, responding to mail, and attending to details. If flexibility is available, specific days might be set aside for working on jobs that require sustained attention. This textbook was completed, in part, because we devoted specific times and "writing days" to it.

Another scheduling issue is the intermixing of work time and other time. Suppose that you had four hours of work to do and also planned to go shopping. A temptation is to do the more enjoyable task first, putting off the harder work until later. In general, it works better to do the harder task first and then to "celebrate" by using the more enjoyable task as a reinforcer. Planning specific times for work and leisure ("I will work for four hours, and then I will go shopping") can also help to prevent them from interfering with each other. Without a plan for how to intermix them, your work time may be filled with thoughts of what you would rather be doing, and your leisure time with thoughts of the work you really ought to be doing.

■ THE STORC AT WORK

By this time, you should be getting good at applying the STORC approach in analyzing and understanding personal adjustment situations. We will suggest just a few ways in which a STORC analysis can be applied at work, and we invite you to think more specifically about STORC elements of your own present or planned work experiences.

Remember that one central point in a STORC analysis is the realization that the experience—in this case, work—is not a single element, but rather a process. Stress is not merely stressors from the environment (Chapter 8). Anger is not just a thought process (Chapter 9). Relationships involve more than behaviors and consequences (Chapter 10). Sexuality encompasses far more than the physiological reactions of the organism (Chapter 12). All of these, and work as well, can be understood as cycles of events.

S—WORK SITUATION

Work occurs in a context, an environment. Perhaps when you think of work you think of the place where it happens—being "at work." Psychologists who specialize in **human factors** devote attention to the impact of the work situation on the adjustment and productivity of workers. Work quality and satisfaction can be importantly influenced by environmental factors such as lighting, crowding, temperature, noise, and the length and timing of shifts (Saal & Knight, 1988).

The work environment is also a social environment. The interpersonal atmosphere in a work setting affects morale and productivity. The health, happiness, and effectiveness of workers can be increased in work settings that provide opportunities for social support and attend to personal needs such as security, safety, and child care.

T—THOUGHT PATTERNS

As in all other adjustment areas we have discussed, the work environment is a *perceived* situation. Cognitive factors such as attitude and expectations toward work are important influences.

A good example of the importance of cognition in work is the influence of *goals*. Research shows that having one or more clear, achievable goals is a vital element of work motivation (Locke et al., 1981). A goal provides something to work toward, to achieve.

A common source of worker dissatisfaction is the perception of being powerless or manipulated—of not having a "say" in work conditions, patterns, or goals. Motivation is increased by a sense of personal control, choice, and involvement (Deci & Ryan, 1985). Workers' unions arose to provide this sense of influence over one's own work conditions, and strikes often occur in response to perceived inequities or insufficient responsiveness to workers' needs.

The beliefs or assumptions of managers also exert a major influence over the work environment and over **organizational behavior.** McGregor (1960) contrasted two different manager belief systems about what motivated workers. **Theory X** is the belief that people are inherently unmotivated to work and have to be forced and controlled in order to produce. This belief system has also been called "scientific management" (Taylor, 1911). Aversive control strategies such as threat, intimidation, and punishment are often used by Theory X managers. Theory X organizations are structured as power hierarchies, with each level exerting control over lower levels through direct reward and punishment. McGregor's **Theory Y** starts from a very different set of assumptions about workers. Work is seen as a natural and potentially satisfying part of life. It is assumed that workers will be responsible, motivated, creative contributors if they are given the proper work environment and if their own needs and goals are considered. Theory Y organizations operate more by collective effort, goals, and responsibility, with less emphasis on hierarchical power control—a style more characteristic of Japanese industry. These represent two extremes and other possibilities exist. Ouchi (1981) suggested the possibility of a Theory Z,

Human Factors
a specialization within psychology focusing on the design of machines and work environments to fit the needs and abilities of workers.

Organizational Behavior
a specialization within psychology that focuses on behavior processes (e.g., motivation, satisfaction, decision making, leadership) within organizations.

Theory X
the belief that workers are inherently unmotivated and must be controlled by external reward and punishment.

Theory Y
the belief that workers are internally motivated and can be responsible and self-directed without coercion.

Theory Y organizations operate by collective effort, goals, and responsibility.

which would combine the individual incentives and initiatives of Theory X with Theory Y's emphasis on shared goals and attention to the needs of workers. The point is that the assumptions with which management operates are important influences on the work environment.

O—ORGANIC PROCESSES

Certain occupations pose high risks for detrimental physical effects. Air traffic controllers, for example, work in a high-stress environment where any small error or period of inattention could result in catastrophe. In such occupations, special attention must be paid to physiological aspects of the job, and work conditions are often adjusted to diminish long-term detrimental health effects.

Human Factors research applies knowledge about human abilities to specific tasks and work settings. A human being, for example, is limited in how rapidly he or she can react to a change, or in how many different stimuli can be attended to at the same time. Special work situations must take into account natural organic processes such as fatigue. Engineers on Australia's railways encounter long straight stretches of track that continue for hundreds of miles with very little variation in the environment. The danger of dozing off in such a situation is high. One simple device used on these trips requires the engineer to hit a lever at least once every 30 seconds, thus signaling awakeness. If the lever is not tripped, a loud alarm is set off waking the engineer. A similar device might be useful to long-distance truck drivers. The National Institute for Occupational Safety and Health has conducted research to determine if there is a link between prolonged use of video display terminals and pregnancy problems (Reynis, 1987).

R—RESPONSE PATTERNS

All work involves behavior. The kinds of skills discussed earlier in this chapter are important elements of effective work adjustment. Work effectiveness can be defined, in fact, as how well one responds to the S, T, and O elements of the work environment.

People adapt different strategies for dealing with any work setting (including studying for college courses). Some seek to get by with the minimum required to pass or get a paycheck. Others seek to achieve and impress by working very hard and may be satisfied with nothing short of perfection (straight "A's"). Most work situations require attention to a variety of different tasks, and each worker must decide which tasks get top priority, and which can wait. Some use a strategy of giving full attention to one task at a time, while others seek to make a little progress on multiple tasks at the same time.

All work environments also provide stresses and problems. Work skillfulness is reflected not only in how one performs the routine tasks, but how well one responds to the unexpected, to interpersonal conflicts, to pressure, and to new problems.

C—CONSEQUENCES

Schedule of Reinforcement
the plan by which a behavior is reinforced, either at predetermined intervals or after a specified number of responses.

Fixed Interval Schedule
a pattern of reinforcement in which a reinforcer is given regularly, after the passage of a specific period of time.

Fixed Ratio Schedule
a pattern of reinforcement in which a reinforcer is given regularly, after a specific amount or number of responses.

Work is performed for the rewards it brings. Sometimes these rewards can be counted in dollars, in a living wage. The rewards that keep a person involved and motivated, however, may be considerably more complex than salary. Incentive and motivation have to do with the consequences that one receives for one's work.

Consider your own situation. Why are you taking college courses? What are the incentives for which you are working? What rewards do you receive or hope to receive from this effort?

Employers and managers struggle with the question of how to motivate good work performance. Incentive systems may operate very differently in Theory X versus Theory Y organizations. **Schedules of reinforcement** are also likely to influence work performance. Some organizations may pay by the hour, a **fixed interval** schedule of reinforcement. Others pay on a **fixed ratio** schedule, according to the amount of work completed—a pay system sometimes called "piece work." In managerial and professional positions, salary is most often paid on a longer periodic (e.g., monthly) basis, rather than rewarding smaller amounts of time or work completed.

■ WORKAHOLISM

CHARACTERISTICS

Workaholism
a term used to describe a pattern of excessive or compulsive devotion of one's time and effort to work, at the expense of other areas of one's life.

Time problems are not always due to a lack of organizational skills. Some who are relatively efficient users of time chronically overload themselves, placing excessive emphasis on the importance and value of working. Work, for them, bears all the marks of an addictive behavior (Chapter 11). Here are some of the central characteristics of what has come to be called **workaholism** (Hodgson & Miller, 1982; Oates, 1971):

Long Hours.   The workaholic arrives early and leaves late. Evenings, weekends, and holidays are often filled with working. Though he or she may believe and say that such hours are "necessary," the pattern of overworking relative to others is clear, and the heavy work load is in fact chosen and self-imposed.

Discomfort with Leisure.   Play, relaxation, recreation, vacations, and doing nothing are not part of the workaholic's life. Being away from work is uncomfortable. If he or she takes some "time off," it is often spent thinking and worrying about work, feeling guilty or vaguely anxious, checking in by telephone, or actually doing work. Even days off and vacations are scheduled and packed full of busyness.

Time Pressure.   The workaholic shares some characteristics with the Type A personality (Chapter 9). One common element is the continual sense of urgency about time. There is frequent anxiety or resentment about "wasting time," "deadlines," and "not having enough time." This is accompanied by an impatience with perceived irresponsibility or inefficiency in oneself or others.

Overcommitment.   The workaholic typically overcommits his or her work time, planning and agreeing to do far more than is realistic to accomplish well within an ordinary work span. The concept of "time management" is immensely appealing to the workaholic because it suggests that still more work could be crammed into less time.

Competitiveness.   There is an unmistakable sense of workaholics "trying to prove something" to self or others. They are often viewed as highly competitive, aggressive, and serious.

In short, the lives of workaholics are out of balance. The time and effort devoted to working grows and grows, displacing time for relationships, personal growth, and fun. The result is often chronic stress, impaired health, and shallow relationships. We hasten to add that this "overwork" pattern need not occur within traditional work settings. Workaholics often find ample opportunities for overcommitment in community service settings, churches, college coursework, and volunteer work as well.

CONSEQUENCES

Ironically, such a pattern eventually undermines the security and quality of the person's work. Chronically overextended, the workaholic is unable to cope with unforeseen setbacks or additional adjustment demands. There is no slack, no room for error. The self-imposed quantity of work compromises its quality. Work competence is further undermined by the side-effects of this pattern. Little time is devoted to developing supportive relationships with co-workers; family and friends are neglected. Consequently the social support network of the workaholic may be sparse indeed. The chronic stress of a workaholic life-style also contributes to the deterioration of the person's health over time. If unchanged, it may lead to an early heart attack or other serious health impairment.

Addictive behaviors, you may recall, are characterized by the fact that the behavior's long-term destructive consequences are overridden by immediate reinforcement. One difficulty in overcoming workaholism is that this behavior pattern is strongly reinforced in many segments of society. The workaholic is commonly praised as "conscientious," "committed," and "productive." Indeed, until the pattern becomes self-destructive, the workaholic may be invaluable to an employer, breaking records and exceeding expectations. Admiration is given for how hard a person works, but seldom for how well a person relaxes or plays. In certain occupations (e.g., middle-management executives,

13.4 CONFESSION OF A WORKAHOLIC

The following is a self-description written by a workaholic. Writing this story and sharing it with others has been part of his own progress in overcoming his pattern.

I am a workaholic, a person who is a compulsive worker. I cave in readily to the idolatrous idea that I am indispensable. No matter how hard or how long I work, I feel as though it's not enough. I choose to get too little rest, and I ignore God's commandment to observe a sabbath. In fact, about the only time I rest is when I am ill, and even then I am likely to do work while I'm sick in bed. Faced with a problem, I seek to solve it by working harder. I choose to believe that there are never enough hours in the day or days in the week.

I don't have trouble saying "No" when I want to say "No." My trouble is learning to say "No" when I want to say "Yes" to more responsibilities, more work. I willingly seek to work harder than anybody else, then feel sorry for myself and wonder why there is a sense of emptiness in my relationships. I enjoy my work, but I get work mixed up with my whole life, until they start to seem the same. As a result, I miss so many opportunities for closeness with others. I hardly know the people with whom I have worked for years. I spend too little time with my family and my friends, and when I do I am still thinking about work. Most of all, I take no time for myself; I am forgetting who I am.

I am a workaholic. I am encouraged in this addiction by people who express their admiration for my energy, my commitment, my devotion, my ceaseless efforts. They are amazed at how much I get done and help me continue my illusion that I am indispensable. Mine is a socially acceptable and a life-threatening compulsion. I have decided that it is time for me to change. I have only glimmerings of how to do it, of a way out. But it is time, long past time, to begin.

pastoral ministers) the seventy-hour workweek can be a common expectation. A workaholic pattern may also, in the short run, generate a higher income and standard of living, and in this way may be valued by family and friends. In short, many around the workaholic may have a vested interest in maintaining the compulsive working pattern and can powerfully reinforce it.

OVERCOMING WORKAHOLISM

Although a number of books have been written to help individuals overcome workaholism (Are, 1985; Hodgson & Miller, 1982; Oates, 1971, 1978), no systematic research on the effectiveness of such approaches has been published to date. Nevertheless the strategies proposed overlap with those used effectively in treating other addictive behaviors (Hester & Miller, 1989) and focus on restoring a balance between work and other important spheres of one's life. Here are some elements that can be useful in escaping from a pattern of compulsive working.

1. *Set clear limits.* Choose a fixed number of hours or set of times for working, and abide by these limits despite the inevitable feeling that "There's still more to do." Gradually reduce the amount of time spent working, and establish definite "work-free zones" in each day and week.

2. *Reduce amount of work.* Decide what jobs are truly important and have top priority; then start saying "No" to everything else until life and time feel more manageable. To reduce total work time (step 1) without also reducing work expectations is to increase anxious and frantic feelings during work hours. Delegate work to others wherever it is possible and appropriate. (Workaholics tend to try to do everything themselves so that it is done "right" and "on time.") Ask for help!

3. *Practice incompatibles.* Spend work-free times in activities that are incompatible with working or worrying about work. These vary widely for individuals, but can include activities such as listening to music, meditating, fishing, playing with children, doing nothing at all, getting away from telephones and pagers, reading for pleasure, hiking, exercising, gardening, or building. Be careful not to turn these leisure activities into new work projects, new demonstrations of competence, competitiveness, tirelessness, or admirability.

4. *Develop relationships.* Devote intentional time to building close relationships. Spend time with friends, family, or co-workers with the sole purpose of sharing the time and getting to know each other better.

5. *Cultivate acceptance.* Pursue a sense of self-worth that is not tied to accomplishments and achievements (Chapter 6). Accept that you are acceptable, lovable, and worthwhile just as you are, without continually having to prove or demonstrate it. Practice this same acceptance toward others, encouraging and acknowledging their efforts without expecting perfection. Self-acceptance and acceptance of others seem to go hand in hand.

6. *Let go of time urgency.* Leave for appointments early instead of at the last minute, and when arriving early use the extra time to relax and have a small calm space in the day. Walk at a relaxed pace, and speak in a slower and softer fashion. When driving, don't shift lanes and speed to arrive a few seconds or minutes faster. When faced with a choice among several lines (at a grocery store, bank, or highway toll booth), avoid trying to find the shortest and fastest line. Instead, intentionally choose the line that looks longest. Such behaviors act against the destructive assumption that everything must be done as quickly and efficiently as possible.

Making changes such as these may increase not only the person's life satisfaction but also, paradoxically, the quality of his or her work. A chronic compulsive work style leads, in the long run, to burnout, illness, depression, and impairment. A more balanced lifestyle, giving work proper perspective and priorities, can actually improve productivity, although this is not the only or most important benefit. Workaholics usually don't work better, just harder.

■ WORK AND LIFE TRANSITIONS

Earlier in this chapter we noted that it is now normal for people to undergo several changes in career during the course of a lifetime. Individuals change jobs, shift to an entirely new career, and alternate periods of full-time work with years of education, part-time employment, volunteer service, or child care.

Not infrequently these career changes correspond with other major life transitions. A "midlife crisis" may include extensive reevaluation of one's own purpose, skills, and identity and part of the readjustment that occurs may be entry into a new job or occupation. Conversely, the midlife loss of one's job

The average age for retirement is on the increase, with people working longer than ever before.

may precipitate a crisis of economics, identity, and meaning. A specialty service known as "outplacement," sometimes provided by employers, involves counseling with those whose employment is ending, to help them identify and find new and meaningful employment.

As it has become normative for women to develop occupational careers, a common question is whether and when to have children. Women and men who commit their early adulthood to the development of their careers find themselves, in their thirties, aware of the ticking "biological clock" that limits the span in which women can become pregnant more easily and safely. For those who have children, further issues arise as to whether and how long to interrupt one's career to raise children, and (in two-parent families) which parent would do so.

Because people's lives increasingly reflect periods of "time out" from full-time employment (whether for education, military service, child rearing, geographic relocation, voluntary or involuntary unemployment), more individuals face adjustment problems associated with reentry into the work force. (Similar adjustments face the worker who reenters higher education.) As discussed earlier, such persons often have highly transferable skills from previous life experiences, although they may not recognize these as work-relevant skills (Bolles, 1989).

The process of aging likewise brings transitions in one's work. With increased age certain skills expand, while others diminish. New employment becomes more difficult to obtain in later adult life, and opportunities may become more constrained. On the other hand, the average age for retirement is on the increase, with people working longer than ever before. As the average age of the population continues to increase during the 1990s, society may find new and more creative ways to use the unique skills and experience of more senior employees.

Retirement itself poses a major life transition, which can be viewed in widely different ways. Some view retirement as the end of productive life, others as liberation to pursue new or long-delayed interests. Some people never retire, but continue to work throughout their life spans. Others undergo "psychological retirement" years before the official termination of their employment (Kanter, 1977). Still others, after retiring formally, pursue a new career or volunteer their skills in new ways. Retired executives, clergy, and craftspeople now frequently contribute their experience and services to the betterment of their communities, professions, and fellow human beings.

One clear direction that emerges from writings on retirement is the wisdom of advance planning for it. Those who come upon retirement as if it were a sudden, unforeseen event, may find themselves feeling lost and useless. The transition to a happy and productive later adulthood depends, in part, on preparing for continued "doing" after formal retirement. Work, in this broader sense of doing, is an important component of healthy adjustment throughout the life span.

■ CHANGING THE SHAPE OF WORK

It is important to realize that workers and work environments exert mutual influences upon each other. While a person's work can have a major impact on his or her personal adjustment, work settings and organizations are also susceptible to change by the individuals within them.

Sometimes such changes can be made in a relatively simple manner. The University of New Mexico School of Law, experiencing an increasing number of students in need of child care during their graduate education, provided a solution by setting aside a room for this purpose near the students' classrooms. The parents themselves shared the cost of child care workers to staff the room. This simple solution proved very helpful, and women are now able to nurse their infants between classes if they wish. Even small changes of this kind within an organization can sometimes have a major impact on personal and social adjustment.

One factor to evaluate, in considering employment opportunities, is the extent to which a work environment provides opportunities for personal growth and is responsive to employee needs and requests for change. What chances are afforded for individual development and advancement? Do cur-

Changes in an organization, such as providing on-site child-care, can sometimes have a major impact on personal and social adjustment.

rent employees seem to be growing or to be "stuck"? A major source of employment satisfaction is the perceived availability of opportunities and challenges. Perceived opportunities for growth and advancement are important determinants of self-esteem, achievement motivation, commitment to one's work, and personal involvement in work and in relationships with co-workers. The phenomenon of feeling stuck and reaching a plateau in work (Near, 1985) is associated with disengagement, lack of commitment, and low achievement.

Organizations vary in their amenability to change and sensitivity to employee needs. Some jobs are, indeed, a "dead-end." Yet all social systems are comprised of individuals, and do change in complex ways in response to the initiatives and actions of those individuals. It is to this complicated interaction of person and system that we turn in Chapter 14.

■ SUMMARY

Throughout the life span, work represents one major area of life adjustment. The choice of work is influenced by one's aptitudes, personal attributes, and the availability of different types of work. In seeking a job, many people unnecessarily limit themselves by using too few of the broad range of strategies available. In maintaining employment, interpersonal skills often prove to be at least as crucial as technical and organizational skills. Time management is a lifelong challenge to make intentional use of the time one has. For some individuals, work occupies an excessively large amount of life time and energies, approximating an obsession or addiction sometimes called "workaholism." Maintaining a single career throughout one's lifetime is now the exception rather than the rule, and midlife changes in career direction are quite common. Retirement also poses a major adjustment challenge for many people. Individuals and their work environments exert important mutual influences upon each other.

■ QUESTIONS FOR THOUGHT

1. What was the first work you ever did? How old were you? Were you paid for the work? Did the work experience affect your self-esteem?

2. What do you do well? What are you "good at"?

3. What did your family or friends want you to do when you grew up? Did you concur?

4. Have you visited the career planning and placement service on your campus? What resources are offered there?

5. How do you plan to pursue "lifelong learning"? What does that phrase mean to you?

6. What is your favorite question to be asked during a job interview? Why?

7. Do you subscribe to Theory X or to Theory Y? What are the reasons for your choice? Is Theory Z possible?

8. If you won enough money so that you could live comfortably without working for pay for the rest of your life, how would you spend your time on a daily basis?

9. Have you ever observed someone retire well or gracefully? What did he or she do that seemed well-adjusted to you? When you retire, what aspect of that person's behavior do you want to emulate?

10. If a friend asked you for help in finding satisfying work, what advice would you give?

chapter fourteen

We Americans have a chance to become someday a nation in which all racial stocks and classes can exist in their own selfhoods, but meet on a basis of respect and equality and live together, socially, economically, and politically. We can become a dynamic equilibrium, a harmony of many different elements, in which the whole will be greater than all of its parts and greater than any society the world has seen before. It can still happen.
—Shirley Chisholm, *The Good Fight*

The Individual and Society

OUTLINE

*I*n Chapter 10 we commented that nearly all adjustment occurs within the context of relationships. In this chapter we will take a still broader view, examining how individuals adjust to and are shaped by the larger social environment. We will discuss the nature and mechanisms of social influence and explore some specific social adjustment issues such as shyness, parenting, dealing with authority, and aging. Then we will turn our attention to the work of community and environmental psychologists, those who seek to bring about constructive changes in social systems. Finally, we will consider how entire social systems adjust and change, the processes that influence the ultimate survival of a society and, indeed, of human life itself.

■ SOCIAL INFLUENCE

There is no question that society exerts enormous influence upon an individual's behavior and adjustment. Aggression is significantly shaped by observing such behavior in others, and by the ways in which the social environment responds to aggressive acts (Chapter 9). Love relationships are influenced by social expectations of what love is, and by notions of appropriate role behavior within relationships (Chapter 10). Peer influence substantially affects whether and how a person will use alcohol and other drugs (Chapter 11).

The role of the social environment has been emphasized throughout this book, whenever we have employed the STORC model as a tool for behavior analysis. Social influence is directly represented within this model by the S and C components. Stimuli (S) represent input to the individual from the environment, situational factors evoking behavior. Consequences (C), in turn, represent the ways in which the social environment responds to behavior, influencing the probability that the behavior will be repeated. The STORC approach depicts the endless dance between individual and environment, their mutual control and influence. The individual is shaped by society, but likewise a society consists of individuals and their actions. Each alters the other.

SOCIAL CONVENTIONS

Much of social control is subtle. The members of a society learn complex patterns of behavior that become accepted as ordinary, normal. Through learning and following these social norms, a certain predictability is achieved. Within a culture there are established (though usually unspoken) norms for how close to stand to another person when talking, how long to maintain eye contact, how loudly and rapidly to speak, and even what to say. The polite, "How do you do?" is not expected to elicit an elaborate explanation of one's current psychological state. It is merely a convention of speech, adding predictability when meeting someone new. It is the taken-for-granted quality of such a greeting that provides the humor in the old joke about two psychoanalysts who pass on the street, "Hello, how are you!" says one. The other nods and smiles, then silently puzzles, "I wonder what he meant by that!"

The unspoken rules of a culture serve to increase predictability of behavior. Within spoken or written language, it is essential to insert marker statements that increase predictability, that help the listener or reader follow transitions. When an individual violates these subtle, unspoken rules of convention, others

Individuals adjust to and are shaped by the larger social environment.

14.1 POLITENESS AND CULTURE

It is in stepping outside one's own accustomed culture that the usually comfortable becomes awkward. Visitors to the United States are often startled, sometimes delighted by Americans' outgoing nature, their willingness to talk to almost anyone. In another culture, initiating a conversation with a complete stranger might substantially violate social rules of propriety.

At the end of an excellent meal in a restaurant in rural Germany, one of us grew impatient with the fact that the server had not returned with a check. Seeing the signs of getting ready to leave, a Bavarian friend quickly intervened, advising that it would be a great insult to the restaurant owner for us to get up from the table. It would communicate disrespect and express the opinion that this was a "fast-food" restaurant. Behavior that is polite or meaningless within one culture can carry an entirely different significance within another.

These cultural differences are particularly apparent in social norms for conversing. Direct eye contact, which is common in European cultures, can represent an impolite and embarrassing intrusion within other cultures. Relative to Americans, Arabs tend to stand closer, speak more loudly, and practice even more eye contact and physical contact during conversations (Watson & Graves, 1966). Within

Europe, people from southern and Mediterranean nations more resemble this Arabian style, whereas northern Europeans are characteristically more subdued and maintain greater interpersonal distance (e.g., Little, 1968).

A dramatic demonstration of this can often be found by visiting the international departure lounges of JFK airport in New York City. Each lounge is assigned to a particular airline and is contained behind relatively sound-proof glass walls and doors. Waiting for a flight, one of us recently ventured into the departure lounge of a southern European airline. Opening the door, a wall of loud conversations emerged: a pandemonium of shouting, expressive gesturing, spirited arguing, and agitated tongue-lashing of children. The glass wall to the next lounge revealed that it was likewise filled with people, awaiting departure for Scandinavia. The glass door opened to what seemed, by comparison, a monastic silence. Adults and children were reading, speaking softly to each other, waiting quietly for the flight home.

Normal, polite behavior varies widely from one culture to another. These learned norms of conduct are often taken for granted, unless one is exposed to cultures, individuals, or groups who do not share the same standards of conduct.

Unspoken cultural norms control social behavior such as how close it is polite to stand.

may react with discomfort or alarm. Consider how you might react to the following:

A person sitting alone at a restaurant table next to yours, carrying on an animated conversation with an empty chair.

A person stepping out of an elevator in a crowded bank building during office hours, wearing a fake rubber nose and a party hat.

Someone walking down the street backward.

Someone next to you muttering obscenities during a funeral service.

Or consider your reaction to a stranger who would walk up and say to you:

> Do you like bing cherries? That Bing can sure sing! Cross, boy, cross the street! In the cross I trust. God be with you! Good boy. Good bye.

None of these people has broken a law, but each is likely to evoke caution and emotion from others. They are violating social customs. Persistent deviation from norms may result in a person being regarded as "mentally ill" and separated from society (Szasz, 1961).

If too great a premium is placed on social convention and predictability, the result can be an inflexible and overly restrictive society. As we shall discuss shortly (notice the marker statement for transition!), social conformity pressures can exert a frighteningly powerful influence over individual behavior. Novelists Orwell (1949) and Huxley (1946), among others, described future societies in which behavior is so totally prescribed that individual differences and freedoms are eradicated. Nations, and regional cultures within nations, differ widely in the extent to which deviance is tolerated. Within the United States, for example, states, regions, and cities vary with regard to their rigidity of norms and pressure for conformity.

SOCIAL CONTROL

Conformity
behaving in accord with the actions and expectations of others.

At several earlier points we have discussed research on **conformity** and obedience. Asch (1956) demonstrated that individuals will agree with judgments that are obviously wrong, (such as which of two lines is the shorter) if a number of others have previously and uniformly endorsed the wrong answer. The presence of one or more heavy drinkers has been shown to increase the alcohol consumption rate of others in a group (Chapter 11). Stanley Milgram's (1963) research (Chapter 9) provided the startling finding that two-thirds of normal subjects, under pressure from a white-coated experimenter, were willing to deliver extremely painful and potentially fatal electric shocks to a helpless victim. Another surprising experiment attempted to simulate the conditions of a prison environment and study the effects of this environment on the behavior of normal individuals (Haney, Banks, & Zimbardo, 1973; Zimbardo, 1975). Stanford University undergraduate students were assigned at random to roles as prisoners or guards, were uniformed accordingly, and were placed in a prison setting constructed in the basement of a university building. The experiment had to be ended early because of the alarming brutality that emerged between the "prisoners" and "guards" after just a few days.

The weight of the experimental evidence is substantial. Normal human beings are quite capable of being induced by social pressure to violate their better judgment, abandon normal social constraints, and engage with chilling conformity in acts of violence. The history of humankind in itself provides ample evidence of this capability, most recently in the slaughter of Jews in Nazi Germany, the massacre of innocent Vietnamese at My Lai, and the mass homicide/suicide of the People's Temple community at Jonestown.

What factors favor or constrain such extreme conformity? One important factor is the extent to which the victim is personal or impersonal. An important element of the psychology of enmity (Keen, 1988) is that the enemy be perceived as inhuman, insane, evil, depersonalized. The "basic training" preparation of soldiers for killing commonly involves dehumanizing images of (and names for) the enemy. Acts that ordinarily would be considered evil are redefined as good.

Another important factor is obedience to authority. Milgram's (1963) classic study dramatically demonstrated the extent to which an authority figure (in this case, an experimenter in a white coat) can elicit an amazing degree of obedience. This obedience effect has been replicated in several other studies. Female college students participated in a study in which they were told to teach a puppy a discrimination task by punishing errors with electric shock (Sheridan & King, 1972). (The shocks were, in fact, mild, but just uncomfortable enough to cause the puppy to jump and squeal.) Subjects complained verbally, but continued to administer what they believed were extremely painful shocks. Partway through the study, a harmless anesthetic gas was released into the puppy's chamber, causing the puppy to falter and then fall asleep. The appearance was that the puppy had been killed by the shock. Yet the experimenter insisted that the subject continue shocking the cuddly puppy for not responding. Three quarters of the subjects obeyed. In a still more distressing replication, nurses in an actual hospital received a telephone order from a staff physician to administer 20 milligrams of a drug, "Astroten" (actually a harmless substance), to a patient. The drug label clearly warned that the maximum safe dose was 10 milligrams. Contrary to medical standards, twenty-one of twenty-two nurses poured out the medication in preparation to administer it (Hofling et al., 1966).

In studies subsequent to his classic study on obedience, Milgram (1974) searched for ways to decrease subjects' conformity. What would increase their resistance to the experimenter's demand to keep on administering painful and dangerous shocks? One change which decreased obedience was direct personal contact. Milgram studied four different degrees of contact with the victim. In the most remote, the victim was in another room and could not be seen or heard (except for pounding on the wall). In a second, the victim was unseen (in the next room) but could be heard protesting, screaming, or pleading. In a third condition, the victim was in the same room and could be both seen and heard. Finally, in the condition of highest contact, the subject actually had to force the victim's hand down onto an electric plate before administering the shock. With each degree of increased contact with the victim, subjects were more likely to refuse to continue with the experiment. To be confronted directly with the human suffering inflicted by one's own actions may serve as a deterrent. In an age of weapons designed to kill at great distance, such a deterrent may have little impact.

Another deterrent factor that reduces conformity is the presence of another person who resists. In Asch's studies of verbal conformity, subjects went along with a plainly incorrect answer if everyone else before had indicated it to be the right answer. If even one prior person had disagreed with the incorrect consensus, however, then the real subject (who was last in the chain) was more likely to affirm the right answer, too. Similarly, Milgram found that if another "subject" in the room (actually a confederate working for Milgram) refused to continue shocking the victim, the actual subject was considerably more likely to resist authority pressure as well. The refusal of one person to conform made it easier for the subject to do so as well, whereas a subject who was alone with the experimenter was more likely to give in to authority pressure. The likelihood of resisting blind obedience to authority was also increased if the subject was not under direct observation by the experimenter, and if the subject was the final person in a "chain of command" (actually delivering the shocks) rather than being an intermediary in the chain.

SHYNESS

Why is **shyness** included as a topic in this section on social control? We have included it here both because it is a very common adjustment problem, and because shyness represents excessive social inhibition. It is also a good example of a seemingly individual problem which is importantly influenced by social conditions. The shy person seems to have *introjected* extreme social control, to have adopted overly restrictive rules for his or her behavior.

In surveying over 5,000 people, Zimbardo (1977) found that more than 80 percent reported that they had been shy at some time in their lives. Half of these, over 40 percent of the sample, said they considered themselves to be shy people. Contrary to the social stereotype, Zimbardo found no difference between men and women in the proportion reporting themselves to be shy. Within a college student population, in fact, slightly more men identified themselves as shy people.

In attempting to understand the phenomenon of shyness, Zimbardo further studied differences between shy and nonshy people. Among the characteristics of shy people which he reported are these:

* Shy people tend to have lower self-esteem; their thoughts commonly include many negative self-statements: "I'm hopeless," "Nobody likes me," "I'm not good looking," "I'm stupid."

* Shy people are much more self-conscious, focusing their attention on themselves, with great concern for how others see them.

* When they experience physical signs of anxiousness, shy people focus on them and imagine negative outcomes. Nonshy people notice physical anxiety, but take it in stride and are more likely to imagine positive outcomes of their behavior.

* Shy people suppress enormous amounts of their experience: words, thoughts, feelings, behaviors. "While publicly the shy person seems to be going nowhere quietly, inside is a maze of thought highways cluttered with head-on collisions of sensations and noisy traffic jams of frustrated desires." (Zimbardo, 1977, p. 29)

Shyness
excessive social inhibition.

Just how people come to be shy is a matter on which psychologists disagree. Some emphasize genetic factors, others stress childhood experiences, and still others understand shyness as a behavior pattern shaped by learning processes throughout the life span. Shyness is much more common among school children than among adults. That many people overcome their childhood shyness is reflected in the fact that 40 percent of Zimbardo's sample reported they once were shy people but no longer are.

How do people overcome shyness? The prescriptions provided by Zimbardo emphasize several processes which we have discussed in previous chapters. Low self-esteem (Chapter 6) appears to be a key issue, maintained perhaps by continual negative self-statements. In this regard, cognitive restructuring (focusing on the "T" element of STORC) may be helpful. As self-esteem improves, shyness diminishes.

The issue of avoidance, discussed in relation to anxiety (Chapter 8), also plays an important role in shyness. Avoidance behavior is a central characteristic of shy people, and avoidance tends to increase anxiety. The result is a self-perpetuating cycle of avoidance and anxiety. Shy people, for example, are likely to establish and maintain less eye contact with others, and as a consequence attract less social contact. As with many anxiety disorders, shyness can be effectively reduced by practicing the very behaviors that are being avoided. In this process, it can be helpful to use a healthy and nonshy person as a model, to suggest new behaviors to practice.

Among the behaviors commonly avoided by shy people are *assertive* responses (Chapter 9), those which involve expressing one's own feelings, desires, and rights. Practicing assertive behavior can be particularly powerful as a method for overriding shyness.

Finally, the excessive **self-consciousness** of shyness can continue to be an obstacle, even when practicing new behaviors. Continual and critical self-evaluation ("Am I doing it right? Oh, I just know I look stupid! What will people think of me?") is a substantial obstacle in developing new and natural social skills. The key here seems to be to focus attention outward, to appreciate the positive experiences of the outer world and to become fascinated with learning about other people. Nonshy people focus less anxious attention on themselves, and look to the outer world with the hopeful expectation of positive and rewarding experiences.

Zimbardo called for a larger view of shyness, which takes account of the extent to which it is influenced by conditions in society. If a full 40 percent of the adult population is afflicted with shyness, one must begin to ask what are the social conditions that create such a widespread inhibition. An approach that understands shyness only as an individual problem is, then, much too limited. As an example, he cites his discovery that the student health center of his university was seeing about 500 students a year whose primary complaint was loneliness (which is commonly related to shyness). Students were being treated with individual psychotherapy, assuming the problem to be individual. "But what would you do if all 500 came to the health center at once, complaining of loneliness?" he asked a colleague on the staff. If that happened, he was told, they would call the university administration to find out what was happening, and why there was such an epidemic of loneliness.

Zimbardo speculates that a high rate of shyness within a society is the product of (1) excessive emphasis on individual achievement and success, prizing competition rather than cooperation; (2) discouraging the open expression of positive and negative feelings; (3) making acceptance contingent upon unrealistic, inconsistent, and/or severe performance standards; (4) regarding failure as shameful; and (5) weakening identification of the individual with the larger social group. Children in shyness-producing societies "learn to live too much within a private world of their own thoughts, devoid of action"

Self-Consciousness
focusing attention on oneself and one's behavior or performance.

(p. 221). In this perspective, shyness is a by-product of the continuing social search for a balance between individual liberty and the common good.

■ PARENTING

Parents provide the environment in which children learn how social systems work. Within the family, children first learn to modify their behavior in response to external stimuli (such as parental requests), then to exercise self-regulation, directing their behavior in response to internal cues (such as plans or values). The family provides children with their basic preparation to cope with the larger social systems. In the family context, children learn about communication styles, negotiation, mutual support, dealing with authority, and sharing responsibility.

As with close and intimate relationships (Chapter 10), there is a great myth about parenting: that it is a natural skill that one acquires automatically. The fantasy is that good parenting is somehow inherent, built into us as human beings, or perhaps graciously bestowed upon us when children arrive. Increasingly, however, it has been recognized that parenting skills must be learned, and as a consequence a variety of parent-training approaches have emerged (Gordon, 1970; Krumboltz & Krumboltz, 1972; McGinnis & McGinnis, 1983; Wagonseller & McDowell, 1979). They vary in content, but share the assumption that good parenting involves a difficult but learnable set of skills. Here are a few of the common themes from these programs.

BALANCING EXTERNAL AND INTERNAL CONTROL

For children to learn self-control, they must gradually transfer from externally controlled to internally controlled behavior. Earlier in development, children need more limits, more prompts, more direct "showing how." In adulthood, people rely less upon such external controls and govern their own behavior according to internalized rules. In between these two extremes lie years of childhood and adolescence, during which time this transition occurs gradually and sometimes turbulently.

There is some consensus in the field that problems arise if parents do not facilitate this transition toward internal control, but instead persist in imposing rigid external controls. Gordon (1970) asserted that adolescent rebellion is not an inevitable part of development, but rather occurs in response to excessively controlling parenting. Behavior change approaches are more successful, particularly with older children, when they are flexible and involve the child in negotiation and alternative choices (e.g., Miller & Danaher, 1976). On the other hand, children flounder if given too little external structure too soon. Parents who are more successful in teaching self-control have been observed to practice a balance between external direction and self-direction in their parenting. They show what developmental psychologists have described as a "dance" back and forth between providing guidance or direction and allowing the child to try on his or her own (Stern, 1977).

EMPHASIZING THE POSITIVE

Teachers of parenting skills also commonly emphasize the importance of positive reinforcement. "Catch them doing something right" is a key piece of advice. Although punishment has an impact, and is invariably part of almost any relationship, parents are advised to rely much more upon noticing and affirm-

Teachers of parenting skills recommend catching your child doing something right.

ing the child's positive behaviors. A family that relies heavily upon punishment is like a city traffic system with all red lights and no green. Such a system communicates "Stop!" but seldom "Go!" Using the traffic analogy, the result is great congestion and confusion. The cars ultimately pass through the red lights, though erratically and sometimes aggressively. Similarly, children who receive mostly punishment are given guidelines for many things *not* to do, but may not learn a flexible range of socially appropriate behaviors.

Remembering to reinforce can be difficult. It is easier to attend to the "squeaky wheel," to pay attention only when something is going wrong. A challenge in parenting (and indeed in all relationships) is to acknowledge and affirm good efforts, positive behaviors. In working with parents, we often ask what they would like to change in the family. The list usually consists of a long set of behaviors they would like for the children to stop, avoid, or decrease. Administration of a general anesthetic would accomplish such goals! We encourage parents also to consider what they would like their children to do *more* of, to increase. The teaching and encouragement of positive alternatives is, in fact, a sound approach to decreasing undesirable behaviors. (We discussed this same principle in Chapter 11 on addictive behaviors. Merely suppressing a behavior is often insufficient. The to-be-avoided behavior must be replaced with more positive alternatives.)

LISTENING

Yet another nearly universal theme in parenting skill programs is the vital importance of *listening* to children. It is easy for a parent to fall into the trap of always telling, teaching, correcting, and ordering (external controls). Listening takes time. It requires devoting all of one's attention to the other person, if only for a few moments. Gordon's (1970) "Parent Effectiveness Training" program focuses almost exclusively on teaching parents how to listen to their children.

As discussed in Chapter 10, good listening means avoiding roadblocks to communication, and responding in a way that encourages the person to keep talking.

CONSISTENCY

Children are most likely to learn when they live in an environment that is consistent, predictable. When the rules shift from one day to the next, children are likely to be more anxious. It is unclear which behaviors are encouraged and which are not allowed. One disadvantage of growing up in a dysfunctional family is that the parents' behavior and rules may fluctuate greatly from day to day. An alcoholic parent, for example, may behave very differently when drinking and when sober. Although children show a remarkable ability to adjust and survive even in chaotic homes, the absence of consistency can take its toll.

For this reason, parenting skill programs often encourage parents to make their rules and guidelines very clear and explicit. For some children it is helpful to have these written down on a chart or checklist. Children who know and understand the family's rules are, of course, more likely to follow them. It is normal for children to "test" the rules periodically, to determine whether they are still in effect. Consistency provides a clear and predictable environment in which to grow.

APPROPRIATENESS

Parents should also take into account the child's abilities and developmental level. In Puritan America, children were viewed as miniature adults and were expected to behave accordingly. It is inappropriate, however, to expect young children to perform with the same degree of coordination, motor skill, or intelligence as an adult. Depending upon the extent to which a child's attention span has developed, certain situations (such as sitting through a long lecture or church service) are likely to be difficult.

Parental tolerance for normal child behavior is also a factor here. In a study of children referred to a clinic for treatment of "hyperactivity," Johnson and his colleagues (1973) observed the children in their home environment. They also observed a sample of ordinary children who were not being referred for any behavior problems. From the latter sample, they determined "normal" ranges of activity, noncompliance with parental requests, and other behaviors that might cause a child to be labeled as hyperactive. Applying these norms with the referred sample, they found that many of the supposedly hyperactive children showed quite normal behavior for their age. The problem appeared to be more one of parental comfort with normal child behavior. Had they launched a behavior modification program with these children, they would have been attempting to suppress normal and ordinary responses for children of their age.

■ ADJUSTMENT OF SOCIAL SYSTEMS

Throughout this book we have been discussing the adjustment of individuals, the processes by which persons change. Social systems, constituted of individual members, also undergo continual change. In fact, many of the processes and factors considered in the study of individual adjustment are also helpful in understanding the adjustment of social systems.

The behavior of societies and organizations has historically been the province of sociology. Over the past few decades, however, psychologists have become increasingly interested and involved in the study of social systems. An important advance in this area has been the emergence of general systems theory (J. G. Miller, 1978), which was mentioned in Chapter 1. From this perspective, life can be understood as the interaction of hierarchically organized levels of systems. Although we typically think of individuals and societies, in fact there are more levels of systems. A human being is constituted of systems of molecules organized into cells. Cells in turn are systematically organized to form the major organs of the body. The brain, the liver, the heart, the blood, the skin, all are composed of specialized cells that work together to form a functioning system. At the next highest level, the organs interact systematically to constitute the human body. Diseases of the body usually involve a breakdown in this systematic organization at some level. Cells or organs fail to function in harmony, resulting in abnormal states and often the destruction of parts of the system.

Human beings, in turn, organize themselves into hierarchically arranged social systems. Family systems consist of individuals who are interrelated, and who interact with one another according to prescribed (though perhaps unspoken) rules. Families interact with each other to form neighborhood groups. Along with other social systems (such as work groups, school groups, and church groups), these interact to constitute a community. A still larger system level is the society, defined by residence or heritage within certain geographic boundaries. At the highest level of social interaction (barring contact with extraterrestrial life), societies interact to form the system that is the family of humanity.

As with the human body system, maladjustment occurs at all levels of social systems. Family members may interact with harmony, form alliances against one another, or even commit violence toward each other. The members of a community implicitly agree to abide by prescribed rules, enforced informally by social sanctions and formally by a police agency. Community politics involve interaction and competition among the lower-level social systems that constitute the community. At a societal level, constituency systems (exemplified by special interest lobbies in the Congress) interact and compete for resources. Similarly, nations form alliances, compete, do violence to one another, and expand or disintegrate within the large system that is international relations. All these system levels interact with each other, as well. Individuals are elected to leadership roles within societies. International warfare yields injury to individual bodies, disrupting the balance among cells and organs, leading to death or readjustment. The death of an individual alters family functioning, which in turn has an impact on the community.

Within a general systems perspective, a discipline that studies only one system level is extraordinarily limited. Indeed the trends in our society are toward recognizing the interdependence of systems levels. In medicine, there has been an increasing call for a **holistic** perspective that looks not just at cellular and organ systems, but also the individual and the social systems within which he or she exists. In addictive behaviors, the field is shifting away from a focus on the individual, toward perspectives that acknowledge and address the role of family and social systems. The STORC analysis employed throughout this book emphasizes the interaction between individual (including human biological systems) and environment.

The discipline of psychology itself is undergoing change as a result. As we shall discuss later in this chapter, new disciplines of community psychology and environmental psychology have emerged to study and impact larger social systems. Family systems theory has become a significant psychological perspective, yielding new forms of therapy that attempt to improve adjustment by

Holistic
including a broad range of perspectives or factors.

altering the structure and interactions of the family. A specialty in organizational behavior (Chapter 13) has likewise emerged, focusing on adjustment processes within social organizations such as companies and agencies. Whereas psychology was once associated with the study of individuals, and clinical psychology with one-to-one therapy, the nature of the discipline and profession has changed dramatically. Before we examine these important changes within psychology, however, we will discuss three enduring themes that recur in the adjustment of social systems.

AUTHORITARIANISM VERSUS FREEDOM

Social systems vary in the extent to which they emphasize and enforce conformity to existing authority. At one extreme are **permissive** families, subcultures, organizations, and societies, which provide relatively few constraints on individual behavior. At the opposite extreme are **authoritarian** systems in which individual behavior is extensively prescribed, and compliance is enforced through social controls typically reliant on punishment. Individuals also vary along this dimension of authoritarianism, ranging from those who routinely question and resist authority, to those who favor an unquestioning obedience to those in power.

In political language, the underlying issue is that of individual freedom. Governmental systems differ widely along this continuum. Dictatorships and other totalitarian systems maintain a police state in which conformity to authority is maintained by force. Democracies seek to maximize personal freedom, providing individuals with greater access to those in authority and to mechanisms for social change. Nevertheless all democracies enforce compliance with specific rules of conduct, and a certain degree of respect for and obedience to duly constituted authority. Anarchy, the complete absence of government and law, is seldom regarded as a desirable goal.

It is worth noting that each extreme has its attractions. Freedom is highly valued for the choices that it affords to individuals. Yet Fromm (1963) and others have observed that with freedom comes increased responsibility and anxiety, and there is a human tendency to avoid and escape from freedom. The continual emergence of authoritarian governments and religious cults exemplifies the potential appeal of a system that provides the absolute rules, the standards for right and wrong.

PERSONAL LIBERTY VERSUS SOCIAL WELFARE

A related issue is the balance between individual liberty or initiative and the common good of the social group. A central question here is the extent to which individual prerogatives are limited in the interest of the overall welfare of all members of the system. This issue interacts with authoritarianism, in that subjugation of individual liberty may be established by common consent (as in a democratic or socialist system) or by totalitarian edict (as in a dictatorship or many communist societies). Some of the most hotly debated social issues center on this essential tension, where individual choices may negatively impact the welfare of other individuals or of the entire social group. Some examples are given in Box 14.2. Socialist societies lean toward sacrificing total individual liberty and economic enterprise on behalf of social equality and the common good.

In smaller social systems such as families and organizations, this same issue is important. Organizations and industries must decide the extent to which they will tolerate individual differences or require conformity to com-

Permissive
oriented toward minimal restrictions and rules.

Authoritarian
oriented toward unquestioning obedience to authority and rules.

14.2 INDIVIDUAL LIBERTY VERSUS SOCIAL WELFARE: SOME ISSUES

As a major adjustment theme for social systems, the tension between individual prerogative and the common good poses enduring challenges for social decision makers. Here are some examples. Consider discussing one or more of these issues in class, to exemplify the trade-offs between these two values, and then seek common ground between the extreme positions. What points of agreement are possible?

Seatbelts and helmets. Should drivers of automobiles be required to wear seatbelts and motorcycle riders be required to wear helmets?

Pollution. Should industries be required to pay the costs of clean-up for environmental pollution resulting from their operations?

Gun control. Should individual citizens be permitted to purchase handguns? Machine guns? Explosives?

Alcohol. Should government increase taxes on alcoholic beverages? Should there be greater restrictions placed on the hours of sale, and on the number and types of places that may sell alcoholic beverages?

Drinking and driving. Should the sale of alcohol be permitted at drive-up windows? At gasoline stations? At major sporting events where everyone will drive away? At bars that can be reached only by private automobile?

Television. What restrictions should be practiced with regard to the portrayal of sex and violence on television? Would it make a difference if you had clear and convincing evidence that exposure to TV violence increases the rate of actual violence in a society?

AIDS. Should individuals with AIDS be permitted full and free access to work and school settings? When exposure to the AIDS virus has been diagnosed, should notification of the person's sexual partner(s) be mandatory, potentially violating the individual's right to privacy?

Smoking. What restrictions should be placed on where smoking is allowed?

---

mon standards in the interest of the larger group. Families vary in the extent to which each member pursues his or her own individual interests or participates in the common work and welfare of the family.

CONSERVATISM VERSUS REFORMATION

Yet another theme in social adjustment is the tension between status quo and change. Political conservatism favors the status quo and resists change, except perhaps to reverse an already accomplished change and return to what is viewed as a more desirable prior state. This expresses, at a social system level, the human tendency to hold onto what is good, to retain the known present state of affairs rather than risk change.

At the opposite extreme are the social reformers, ever seeking new ways of doing things and agitating for change in the system. The yearning here is to try what is new, to risk change in the hope that a new state of affairs will be better.

Families vary in the extent to which they will tolerate individual differences.

■ PEACEMAKING: THE CHALLENGE OF SURVIVAL

Each of the foregoing themes of social adjustment represents a tension between opposites. Not only do social systems and their members differ along these dimensions, but over time there tends to be a pendulum effect of swinging back and forth between extremes. As we enter the 1990s, for example, the U.S. population seems to be moving toward a greater willingness to constrain individual options on behalf of societal welfare. Legislation and social pressures increasingly constrain drunk driving, smoking in public places, child abuse, and pornography. Lawmakers mandate the wearing of seatbelts and motorcycle helmets, place return deposits on beverage containers to decrease litter, and require parents to restrain small children in car seats. This follows a period of more than two decades in which individual freedom was maximized at the expense of societal costs. Rank (1936) observed that this same pendulum swing occurs within the life of each individual, who seeks a balance between isolation and belonging.

Differences within and between systems along these and other dimensions invariably lead to conflict. The issue of how to resolve such conflict poses a major adjustment challenge that may ultimately determine the survival or demise of the human race. Human ingenuity has devised the means whereby massive populations may be destroyed, and the prospect of "omnicide" has become a credible and chilling reality. Never before has the urgency of peacemaking and successful conflict-resolution skills been so apparent.

Ironically, people have learned much more about how to wage war than about how to make peace. It was not until 1986 that the Congress created a National Peace Academy, a relatively tiny parallel to the Army War College and the national military academies. The discovery and development of methods for the peaceful resolution of conflict represents a vital first step. Conflicting interests are inevitable, and in the absence of effective means for compromise and resolution, a resort to violence is common. Competence in resolving conflict is an important factor in the prevention of violence.

Peace, however, is more than the absence of violence. The nonviolent resolution of conflict is more a precondition for peace, rather than its essence.

Peace is promoted by personal contact, and international student exchanges are one method for facilitating such contact.

People differ widely in their notions about what constitutes peace. Here are a few of ours:

1. *Peace is promoted by personal contact.* It is much easier to hate and harm someone who is faceless, nameless, distant, and depersonalized. Peacemaking involves resisting the natural temptation to withdraw into ghettos of agreement, associating only with those who hold similar views and values. Coming face to face with diversity is a beginning condition for peaceful understanding.

2. *Peace is promoted by valuing differences.* Human beings manifest immense diversity. If differences between individuals and groups are seen as reason for rejection, avoidance, and fear, then peace becomes difficult, a tense "cold war" standoff. On the other hand, human differences can be understood as valuable, interesting, useful, the essence of human nature (Myers & Myers, 1980). The suppression of dissent and differences breeds discontent. Peaceful understanding requires learning how to value and use human differences.

3. *Peace is promoted by seeking commonalities.* Consider what you do when meeting someone new. The initial conversation typically involves a searching for common ground, common experiences or acquaintances. Discovering such commonalities provides a basis upon which to begin a relationship. This search for commonality is in no way inconsistent with our previous point about valuing differences. Rather it involves seeking common ground in the midst of differences. Working together toward a common objective is a step toward peace. This avoids the opposite trend toward polarization, which promotes conflict. It would be possible, for example, for "pro-life" and "pro-choice" advocates, who differ adamantly on views about abortion, to work together in promoting positive alternatives to abortion (such as contraception and adoption).

4. *Peace is promoted by pursuing the welfare of the other.* Peace is not a vacuum. Actions that promote the other's welfare and interests are peace-making and can insulate against the inclination to aggress. This works best, of course, when the effort is mutual, bilateral.

The fact remains, however, that knowledge and understanding about peace and peacemaking are at a relatively infant stage. It is important that potential strategies for peacemaking be studied and evaluated. Strategies that are *intended* to promote peace can have exactly the opposite effect. An often-cited example is the strong British popular movement for disarmament and negotiation during the rise of Nazi Germany. With the intention of avoiding war, some advocated a conciliatory stance toward Hitler. German intelligence interpreted this as a lack of resolve on the part of the British people and as permission to invade surrounding nations without British opposition. A strategy that was meant to prevent war thus may have hastened it.

Peacemaking, then, remains an exciting new frontier to be explored by future psychologists. What approaches prevent the transformation of conflict into violence? Once violence has begun, what methods may stop its escalation? What factors promote a stable state of peace that is resistant to violent flare-ups? In the answers to such questions lie important keys to harmony within future relationships among individuals, groups, and nations.

■ THE PSYCHOLOGY OF SOCIAL ENVIRONMENTS

Although many people think of psychologists as involved in individual, one-to-one work with people, there has been a growing trend toward larger interventions. Psychologists are increasingly involved as consultants in industry, architecture, engineering, and environmental design. In working within social systems, psychologists may have as their "client" not an individual, but rather an entire community, school system, company, church, hospital, or organization.

The challenge is exciting. When intervening at this level, one has the opportunity of providing a beneficial impact on many people. A constructive psychological change within a school system or university may impact hundreds or thousands of students. Psychological consultation in industry may produce management changes that benefit a large number of workers. System interventions of this kind are opportunities to pursue one of the key purposes of psychology, as stated by the American Psychological Association (1981): "the promotion of human welfare."

There is another side to this coin, however. Precisely *because* a large number of people are potentially impacted by intervention with a system, there is a great responsibility to ensure that this impact *will* be beneficial rather than detrimental. The implementation of system changes that are purported to be "progress" or "prevention" *can* yield harmful results. The professional oath of physicians charges, "First, do no harm." This responsibility is still greater when an intervention will affect hundreds or thousands of people.

We will discuss three specialties that have arisen within psychology, all of which are intended to intervene at a system level. They have in common the desire of psychologists to promote human welfare, but differ in the types of change they pursue.

ENVIRONMENTAL PSYCHOLOGY

Throughout this book we have emphasized the interaction of the individual with the social environment. Individual behavior, personality, and adjustment

14.3   HOW DESIRABLE IS "PROGRESS"?

They seem like folk out of a storybook. Dressed in plain clothing, shunning the automobile in favor of the horse and buggy, the Amish people of Pennsylvania, Ohio, and Indiana are a stark contrast to the high-tech culture around them. So different is their lifestyle that they attract thousands of tourists every year, who come mostly to look and to sample the legendary Amish cooking, sometimes asking awkward questions like, "How can you be so backward?"

The intentional and practiced isolation of the Amish has contributed to the fact that they are so misunderstood. A stereotype is that they have odd superstitious beliefs that cause them to avoid automobiles and other technological advances. In fact, the shunning of "progress" is a conscious and well-reasoned choice. "Automobiles," we were told by an Amish leader, "have a fragmenting effect on society. They give people the hurry-up sickness. The family and the community begin rushing off in a hundred different directions, losing track of each other and of what really matters. We choose not to have our community broken in this way. We prefer to keep life simple, slower; to enjoy and appreciate the gifts we have been given."

Two thousand miles away is another community. The Pueblo of Taos has been in the same location and continuously inhabited for nearly 700 years. In this century the white population has grown up around it, an art-conscious city and one of the country's best ski areas. Taos is a short distance from Los Alamos, where the atom bomb was created during World War II, and where nuclear weapons research continues actively today. But the pueblo and its native people continue much as they have been for centuries. There are no paved roads, no electricity, no modern appliances.

The cold mountain stream still flows quietly in an open channel through the center of the pueblo. The Taos Indians, too, have intentionally chosen to shun the world's "progress." The people don't talk much to outsiders about their values and religious beliefs. One woman put it simply: "We believe that this hectic rush to make more *things*, to build bigger and stronger machines and weapons, is crazy. The world seems to be rushing toward destruction. We hold to the old ways, the traditional values of our people. We believe that if we are faithful to these ways, when all else is gone, we will still be here."

are affected in important ways by the environment in which the person lives. In this light, psychologists have become increasingly interested and involved in the *designing* of environments.

The underlying goals of environmental design vary. A waiting room may be designed to promote comfort and patience. Any visitor to Disneyland can appreciate the care taken to design this environment so that those waiting in long lines have a clear sense of movement, and have interesting and varied stimuli to occupy them while they wait. In designing hospital rooms, attention to simple details (such as the view a patient will have out the window) may promote recovery (Ulrich, 1983). Work areas may be designed to facilitate efficiency and minimize distractions. Major casinos are commonly built so that gamblers have no windows, doors, or clocks in sight, presumably to increase their stay by decreasing thoughts of leaving and awareness of the passage of time.

One environmental variable that has been the subject of much research is exposure to noise. Animals and humans subjected to noise in experimental settings show predictable physiological changes that are characteristic of stress responses (see Chapter 8). Social behavior can also be substantially affected. Several studies have shown that background noise decreases people's willingness to engage in helping behavior (Mathews & Canon, 1975; Page, 1977) and increases the likelihood of interpersonal aggression (Donnerstein & Wilson, 1976; Geen & O'Neal, 1969; Konecni, 1975). Living on a noisy street can decrease the amount of social interaction that occurs in the neighborhood (Appleyard & Lintell, 1972). Even long-term constant exposure to noise does not necessarily diminish its detrimental effects (Cohen & Weinstein, 1981).

Personal space is a psychological variable of importance in architectural planning. Hall (1966) identified four spatial zones that influence social behavior. The *intimate* zone extends from physical contact to a distance of about 18 inches from the person, and movement into this personal space is typically associated with intimacy. From 18 inches to 4 feet is the *personal* zone, the characteristic distance for personal conversations among friends and acquaintances. From 4 to 12 feet is the *social* zone, typical for less personal interactions such as those between business associates. Very formal exchanges, such as those between seated students and a professor at a podium, involve a separation of 12 feet or more, encompassing the *public* zone.

Intrusion into the personal zone can have important effects on social behavior. One study found that subjects were less willing to help a stranger in need if that person had intruded into their personal zone (Konecni et al., 1975). There are interesting cultural as well as individual differences in the size of one's personal space, which influence how readily an intrusion is perceived. Kinzel (1970), for example, found that the personal zone for prisoners convicted of violent crimes was about four times larger than that for nonviolent prisoners. That is, violent prisoners felt uncomfortable when others approached within distances that, for others, were well beyond their normal personal space. Such findings suggest potentially important considerations in the design of public and living spaces (e.g., offices, prison cells).

Environmental psychologists seek to apply psychological knowledge in the design, planning, and modification of the physical environment. By taking into account factors such as noise exposure, lighting, temperature, personal space, and crowding, it is possible to design environments that promote physical and psychological health.

ORGANIZATIONAL PSYCHOLOGY

A second specialty focusing on system-level interventions is that of organizational psychology (Howell & Dipboye, 1986; Schultz & Schultz, 1986). Whereas environmental psychologists and experts in human factors focus more on the design of aspects of the *physical* environment, organizational psychologists concentrate more on the *interpersonal* environment. Organizational psychology includes research, theory, and application in areas such as (1) employee recruitment, selection, and placement; (2) motivation and job satisfaction; (3) group dynamics; (4) leadership and supervision; (5) work description and performance evaluation; and (5) training and development. An organizational psychologist might, for example, be called in to consult with a large company or agency, to help improve management styles and employee satisfaction. Such a consultant would be likely to explore areas including

* How are decisions made within the organization? Who makes them? Who is involved in the decision process? How are others informed of decisions?

* How are the personnel organized? Who reports to whom?

* What are the formal as well as informal channels of communication within the organization?

* Where do workers socialize? What opportunities are there for informal communication?

* How do people at each level of the organization understand their jobs? How satisfied are they with their jobs? What changes would they like to see?

These and other questions would be explored in a series of interviews conducted with a representative sample of workers at each level of the organization. Protection of confidentiality is important here, so that individuals can express their views openly without fear of recrimination. Based on what is learned during the sensing interviews, the consultant would then recommend possible changes that could be made within the organization, to promote specific goals.

Organizational psychologists face some of the same problems encountered by clinical psychologists. As in individual therapy, there is the initial challenge of developing rapport with client organizations, except here the "client" is a conglomeration of people. Once problems are identified, there is the challenge of how to move beyond this insight into the source(s) of the problems and to effective solutions. It is important, also, that the psychologist intervene in a way that the new behaviors of the organization will persist after he or she has left the picture. Managers and employees need to be taught problem-solving skills to use on their own, instead of instilling a dependency on the psychologist for solutions. Recommendations need to be made in a way that they are likely to be implemented, rather than being filed away in a drawer unused. All these problems parallel similar challenges faced by the clinical psychologist in treating individuals.

The psychological assessment skills of clinical psychologists also parallel an important function of organizational psychologists. Concerned to improve their procedures for selecting and training supervisors and managers, large companies are developing assessment centers with the help of organizational psychologists. At such centers, supervisory personnel are typically evaluated by being presented with a series of **behavioral simulations** of actual day-to-day management problems and responsibilities. They are given practice exercises in which they must make management decisions. Performance in such situations can be used to select the best candidates for management positions or to train current managers in better supervisory skills. Organizational psychologists participate in assessment centers by selecting and developing exercises to represent a broad sample of realistic management challenges. They also develop reliable and valid measures to assess the performance of managers participating in the exercises.

Behavioral Simulation
a test in which an individual is exposed to an artificial situation intended to reproduce real-life conditions.

An organizational psychologist might also evaluate the effectiveness of the assessment center itself. Does the center in fact improve the selection of managers? Does the training provided by the center improve the work of supervisors? Is the center a good investment; are the costs involved justifiable from the demonstrated benefits to the organization? Knowing how to ask and answer such questions is the expertise of **program evaluation,** another important skill of organizational psychologists. In general, program evaluators face the challenge of determining whether an organization or specific program is meeting its intended goals. This, too, parallels the challenge to the clinical psychologist of determining whether her or his therapeutic interventions are having the intended effects.

Program Evaluation
specialized skills in assessing the effectiveness and impact of interventions.

Psychologists can also participate in the development and administration of an **employee assistance program (EAP)** for the employees of an organization. The typical EAP provides brief counseling and referral services for troubled employees, who may either be referred by their supervisors or may seek assistance on their own. EAP personnel help employees to identify the prob-

Employee Assistance Program
a service intended to help employees deal with personal problems, and thereby improve their performance on the job.

lems they face, consider possible solutions, and find the resources necessary to help resolve the problems. Sometimes this can be accomplished in a few counseling sessions within the EAP, and sometimes the employee is referred to other professionals for assistance.

Interpersonal relations can be closely tied to aspects of the physical environment. Within our own Department of Psychology at the University of New Mexico, for example, we have consistently assigned faculty offices so as to intermix individuals with different specialties and interests. We have intentionally avoided placing all psychologists of the same specialty in close proximity. Some other departments assign faculty from each specialty area to separate areas, floors, or even to different buildings. Our office plan is specifically designed to encourage conversation and interaction among professors with different interests and to discourage the often tempting division of the faculty into specialty factions.

COMMUNITY PSYCHOLOGY

The field of community psychology dates back at least to the 1960s, and focuses on change at the level of an entire community. Historically, the focus of community psychology has been on the **prevention** of psychological problems, although more recently the emphasis has shifted to the more positive and general theme of health promotion.

Like Caesar's Gaul, prevention efforts have traditionally been divided into three parts: primary, secondary, and tertiary prevention (Caplan, 1964). The last of these, **tertiary prevention,** involves providing services to individuals who have already developed problems, in hopes of diminishing their disability and preventing future relapses (Marlatt & Gordon, 1985). This overlaps with what is usually thought of as treatment or therapy. **Secondary prevention** focuses on early identification and intervention. As in tertiary prevention, individuals are singled out for special intervention. The difference is that they are selected not because they have fully developed problems, but rather because they show early signs or high risk of developing problems. **Primary prevention,** by contrast, does not single out certain individuals for special treatment. Instead intervention is done on a mass scale, targeting an entire population: a school system, a factory, a community, even a nation. The goal is to reduce the occurrence of problems and to promote positive adjustment within the whole target population.

Prevention *efforts designed to reduce the occurrence of a particular problem within a population;* **Primary Prevention** *efforts are designed to reach and impact the entire group or population;* **Secondary Prevention** *efforts are designed to detect and impact high-risk individuals;* **Tertiary Prevention** *efforts impact individuals already showing the problem, to reduce the occurrence or severity of future problems.*

■ PREVENTION IN THE COMMUNITY

TERTIARY PREVENTION EFFORTS

Until relatively recently, the long-term maintenance of treatment gains was largely ignored within psychology. Studies reported the improvement of treated individuals immediately after therapy, but seldom included adequate follow-up to determine the extent to which changes were sustained or lost in the long run. As treatment research began to include long-term follow-up, however, a common picture emerged. The impressive success rates reported at the end of treatment often were not maintained over long-term follow-up (Brownell et al., 1986b). In alcoholism treatment, for example, brief follow-ups typically suggest that about two-thirds of clients are doing well (Emrick, 1975). When only studies with at least one year of follow-up are considered, however, the typical success rate shrinks to about one-fourth of the treated population

(Costello, 1975). Relapse after treatment is a major problem, both in psychology and in medicine (Marlatt & Gordon, 1985).

As this somewhat discouraging picture became clear in the 1970s and 1980s, psychologists began reevaluating traditional models of treatment, seeking approaches to decrease relapse and improve the maintenance of treatment gains. "How could we change our approaches to treatment," they asked, "so that people will *stay* well in the long run?" Several interesting answers have emerged.

One very clear trend has been a move away from the traditional model of treating psychological problems in a hospital setting. In the 1950s, it was widely accepted that treatment for "mental problems" involved going away to a special institution, where one was kept until the problem was resolved. The assumptions underlying this approach suggest a "repair shop" mentality. The problem is presumed to reside within the individual, who can be taken out of the environment, treated, and then returned to the environment intact. Though appropriate for treating certain medical conditions, it is now widely questioned whether this approach should be used in dealing with psychological problems. With great consistency, controlled research has shown no superiority of residential (inpatient hospital) treatment over less expensive and less intrusive outpatient approaches that treat the person in the community (Kiesler, 1982; Miller & Hester, 1986b). Though certain behaviors (e.g., violence, suicide attempts) still warrant the protective supervision of a residential setting, psychological treatment has rapidly moved toward community-based outpatient approaches. Similar trends, though slower in coming, are emerging within the U.S. correctional system, as it is realized that imprisonment often leaves offenders more, not less, dangerous to the community (Menninger, 1968), and constructive alternatives to prison are being explored. Nonviolent offenders may be offered alternatives to incarceration, whereby they can perform community service or make restitution to their victims. Intensive treatment programs that effectively change the behavior of offenders can better protect the public welfare than can spans of imprisonment that release offenders back into society unchanged or more hardened.

Another important realization has been recognition of the importance of the individual's *social* adjustment in recovery from psychological problems. Unemployment and family discord have long been recognized as predictors of poor treatment outcome. Yet until recently, surprisingly few treatment programs have taken direct steps to help their clients obtain gainful employment or improve family relations. Placing a troubled person in a hospital for a course of intensive individual treatment is likely to do little good in the long run if the person is then returned to the same circle of friends, troubled family, social isolation, discrimination, unemployment, and economic distress. Treatment programs which address these social adjustment problems have proven far superior to traditional approaches focusing on the individual alone (e.g., Azrin et al., 1982).

A third theme is the importance of *attribution* of change (see Chapter 7). Individuals who attribute their change *internally* (i.e., believe that they accomplished it through their own efforts and abilities) are more likely to sustain the change. When change is attributed externally (i.e., to the influence of another person, to a drug, or to a situation), it is less likely to last (Kopel & Arkowitz, 1975). Similarly, motivation for change can be influenced by the extent to which the person perceives a problem and believes that he or she has freely chosen to pursue change (Deci, 1975; Miller, 1985b).

All three of these themes emphasize treatment of the individual within his or her natural community context, rather than removing or coercing the person into a specialized treatment setting. For treatment (tertiary prevention) to be successful, these social adjustment variables should be addressed.

SECONDARY PREVENTION

To succeed at secondary prevention, it is vital to identify accurately those individuals who are at risk, and to intervene before they develop serious problems. There are at least two approaches for such early identification. One is to discover the *early signs* of the problem, and to intervene before it progresses. The "warning signs of cancer" education program takes this approach: if cancer can be found in its early stages, the chances of curing it are much better. The same appears to be true of many other problems as well: alcohol and other drug abuse, depression, hypertension, anxiety, and stress. Early intervention is often more effective and less expensive than tertiary prevention.

A second early identification approach relies not on the beginning signs of problem development, but rather on *risk factors* that increase the person's chances of eventually developing the problem. Among the important risk factors for certain conditions are genetic history, gender, age, occupation, personality type, stress level, poverty, alcohol and other drug use, diet, and exercise patterns. Based on these or other factors, individuals can be identified as being at high risk for developing specific types of problems. A family history of certain problems (e.g., alcoholism, hypertension, depression, schizophrenia) is associated with an increased personal risk for the problem.

Once a person or group of people has been identified as being at risk (i.e., showing early signs or having significant risk factors), the challenge of secondary prevention is to intervene in a way that will reduce risk. Here research is essential to determine whether a particular intervention strategy is effective in decreasing risk. R. A. Brown (1980), for example, compared two educational approaches in working with a group of individuals convicted of driving while intoxicated. He found that an approach that taught skills for managing one's own drinking behavior was superior (in producing behavior change) to a traditional lecture program focusing on the dangers of drinking and driving. Similarly, several experimental recovery programs have now demonstrated their ability to extend the life span following a heart attack (e.g., Friedman et al., 1986).

Unfortunately, many secondary prevention programs have never been subjected to this type of systematic evaluation. Once identified as being "at risk," children or adults may be subjected to well-intentioned but ineffective interventions. A distressingly large proportion of current "preventive," "correctional," and "remedial" programs are supported only by tenuous anecdotal evidence.

An often-ignored but very exciting side of secondary prevention research is the study of **resilience.** Why do many who are subjected to high risk factors emerge intact? It is commonplace to hear of individuals who have been marred by violence, dysfunctional families, exposure to combat, or conditions of deprivation. Some writings on the "adult children of alcoholics" have mistakenly claimed that nearly all children of alcoholics are scarred in predictable ways. Yet many, perhaps most individuals who are exposed to difficult or deplorable circumstances somehow come through them relatively well adjusted. Some, in fact, overcome their deprivations and handicaps to achieve greatness. The backgrounds of great political leaders, for example, are sometimes characterized by seemingly insurmountable privations, abuses, and tragedies (e.g., Elizabeth I of England, Abraham Lincoln). A worthwhile question to explore, in pursuit of secondary prevention, is how these remarkable survivors differ from those who, exposed to similar risk factors, suffer lifelong disability (Garmeczy & Tellegen, 1984; Rutter, 1984). What are the protective factors that distinguish resilient children and adults from those who suffer adverse consequences in similar circumstances? Such explorations could yield new knowledge that could be used to construct "psychological inoculations" against the adverse effects of stressors (Kobasa & Puccetti, 1983).

Resilience
ability to endure difficult conditions and to resist their adverse effects.

14.4 HUMANIZING MEDICAL EDUCATION

Surviving in medical school has historically been a key challenge for medical students. Humiliation, sleep deprivation, and isolation from family have, for some reason, been viewed as essential facets of preparation to be a physician. Such stressors take a toll on the physical, mental, and family health of American medical students.

Recently, a number of medical schools have been questioning what constitutes effective medical education and have been experimenting with alternative approaches. These programs are a combination of primary and secondary prevention. They are implemented with an entire population of medical students (primary prevention), who also constitute a group at high risk for stress problems (secondary prevention). The intent of these alternative training programs is to reduce unnecessary stress and enhance learning.

Two such programs have been implemented at the University of New Mexico School of Medicine. One of these, the Primary Care Curriculum (PCC), represents an alternative to the traditional emphasis on passive learning through lectures. Students trained through the PCC spend their first two years in active, problem-centered learning. Assigned a particular case problem, the students are responsible to draw upon available library and faculty resources to obtain relevant information and develop a competent diagnosis and treatment plan. Greater emphasis is also placed on an apprenticeship model of training, learning through active work in clinical settings, supervised by mentors. The intent of this approach is to reduce evaluation stress typically associated with medical education and to humanize medical training further by emphasizing personal contact with patients, faculty, and other students during the early years of training. Recent comparisons of the two approaches to medical training indicate that the groups show equal competence in medicine as reflected on board examinations, but that the PCC students are less stressed and maintain a more positive outlook (Moore-West et al., 1986).

A second approach has been the addition of a seminar on professional responsibility to the medical school curriculum, for all third-year students. In this seminar, students and faculty discuss the meaning of professional responsibility to patients, colleagues, community, significant others, and self. "Responsibility to self" includes practicing good self-care for physical and mental health. The seminar also makes use of natural helping networks of peers, faculty, and staff within the medical school. An initial evaluation of this new program (Yahne & Edwards, 1989) indicates that not only do the students perceive the benefits, but the volunteer faculty members describe benefits to themselves as well. Social support from within the medical school community has a stress-buffering or stress-reducing effect for participating students and faculty alike. Social support in natural settings (primary prevention) can reduce the need for professional help (Hunter & Riger, 1986). One hope for both PCC and the seminar on professional responsibility is that this learning environment will encourage future physicians to treat their patients in a less stressed and more caring way. Also, hopefully they will turn to their peers for support rather than viewing them as adversarial competition.

PRIMARY PREVENTION

Most challenging of all, perhaps, is the task of primary prevention. The goal is similar to that of secondary prevention: to reduce the occurrence of specific problems. Instead of targeting particular "at-risk" individuals, however, primary prevention interventions are aimed at an entire population. The preventive intervention may be offered to all members of a workplace, a school system, a health maintenance organization, or an entire community. It might be

Just the process of *treating* psychological problems in our society is more than enough to keep mental health professionals busy. Relatively little professional time and effort have been devoted to preventing these problems. Yet, in the long run, prevention is the key to overcoming such widespread problems as alcohol and other drug abuse, depression, physical abuse, and stress.

It seems clear that prevention efforts that encompass a whole community or society will require the involvement of a much broader range of intervention agents. Health professionals—the psychologists, psychiatrists, social workers, nurses, and counselors—are simply too few in number to carry out needed treatment and prevention efforts.

Fortunately, help is available. A variety of adjunctive agents can be included in prevention efforts. Christensen and his colleagues (1978) described five possibilities.

1. *Paraprofessionals.* Paraprofessionals are specially trained individuals who work under the supervision of health professionals. Though they do not hold professional degrees (such as Ph.D., M.D., or M.S.W.) themselves, paraprofessionals learn specific skills that can be employed in prevention programming. They might, for example, learn and teach stress management, job-finding skills, healthy dietary patterns, or good listening skills.

2. *Partners.* Even without specific paraprofessional training, people can be helpful in prevention efforts simply by applying the skills they already possess. Individuals being discharged from institutions (such as prisons or hospitals), for example, may need to learn everyday living skills: how to use the bus system, how to cook for themselves, how to use a laundromat. People who are naturally skillful at certain tasks (which is just about everybody!) can volunteer their time to be partners with those who need this kind of support. Sometimes, too, the simple companionship of such a relationship can be important in preventing future problems. This is an underlying idea in formal partnership programs such as Big Brothers and Big Sisters.

3. *Peers.* People struggling with the same difficulties and problems can often be supportive and helpful to each other. In this case, the relationship is that of peers, instead of one person being identified as the helper (as with partners, just described). Each person is dealing with his or her own adjustment challenges, while offering companionship and support to others facing the same or a similar situation. A large network of mutual help organizations has arisen, including the many "anonymous" groups, support groups for families of people with Alzheimer's disease or other major illnesses, and widow-to-widow programs. Still less formal support networks often arise in neighborhoods or among groups of friends.

4. *Paraphernalia.* A growing array of health promotion devices and tapes can be obtained by the general public. It is possible to purchase biofeedback devices, exercise aids, dietary supplements, videotapes, and instructional audiotapes. The effectiveness of many such devices is unknown, but this is a medium through which prevention efforts can be extended.

5. *Print.* Finally, the written word remains an important medium for promoting prevention. The U.S. government in 1988 distributed preventive information regarding AIDS to every household in the country. Books are available to help people learn meditation, relaxation, anger management, and communication skills and to promote moderate drinking, weight loss, better moods, and more fulfilling sexuality. Again, the effectiveness of such advice is often unknown.

The point is that there are many ways in which prevention efforts can be extended to reach a broader segment of the population. Once effective prevention strategies have been identified, there are many ways to communicate them.

possible, for example, to devise an annual "mental health check-up" as a routine voluntary evaluation of an individual's psychological health, relevant risk factors, developmental changes from previous years, and status on key dimensions of adjustment.

One of the most strikingly successful primary prevention programs to date is the Stanford Heart Disease Prevention Project (Maccoby et al., 1977; Williams et al., 1981). Remarkable in its scope, this program studied three entire communities in the state of California. One community was subjected to an intensive blitz of media programs, educational events, and distributed literature, all designed to teach and promote healthy life-style patterns associated with lowered risk of heart disease. A second community was given only media presentations. And a third received no intervention at all. Over several years of follow-up, randomly chosen residents of the two communities receiving intervention showed significantly better cardiovascular health, and heart disease indicators in these communities were significantly lower than in the control community. It had been demonstrated that the health of an entire community could be improved through planned intervention. This study is being repeated with five new communities (Fortmann et al., 1986).

As with secondary prevention approaches, however, the vast majority of current primary prevention programs have never been subjected to adequate scientific study. Entire communities and school systems are subjected to unevaluated "prevention" programs focusing on alcohol and other drug abuse, sexual behavior, marital and family relations, physical diseases, and safety. With the best of intentions, administrators adopt prevention strategies without requiring reasonable evidence that they in fact prevent the problem of concern. Hundreds of public school curricula of this kind are available from publishers, videotape manufacturers, and consultants.

Yet the available research on such educational strategies is less than encouraging, and there are striking examples of "prevention" programs that have actually backfired, increasing the problem of concern (e.g., Kinder, Pape, & Walfish, 1980; Stuart, 1974). In our view, it is unethical to implement a primary prevention program unless (1) it has previously been subjected to adequate scientific tests to determine its effects, or (2) it is accompanied by an adequate evaluation component that will reveal its effects in the target population. The very fact that an *entire population* is targeted increases the potential for impact, be it beneficial or detrimental, and thus increases the responsibility of planners to know the effects of their programming.

Primary prevention is, in a way, the richest fruit of a mature psychology of adjustment. As the study of adjustment reveals how people change, it becomes possible to translate the knowledge and principles into programs to benefit the larger population. There remains much to be done. Despite the many ideas and findings presented in this book, we believe that the field is only beginning to develop a comprehensive understanding of the complexity that is human change. Many basic questions remain unanswered. There are still many hidden keys to discover, opening new doors for the promotion of human welfare.

■ CHOOSING YOUR FUTURE

Throughout this chapter we have been discussing some of the processes by which society chooses its own future. It is easy to feel caught up in the dizzying pace of social change, to feel swept along by social forces toward an unknown destination.

In a very real sense, however, you are currently creating your own future. A crucial part of this process is your own vision of your future, your expectations

"I have a dream" were central words in the life of Martin Luther King. In affirming your own dream, you create your future.

about what is to come. In subtle, sometimes eerie ways, people have a propensity for fulfilling their own prophecies (Jones, 1977; Miller, 1985a). The dream is the beginning of a reality. "I have a dream" were central words in the life of Martin Luther King. During his lifetime, King's dream of racial equality seemed distant indeed. It was a time of almost totally segregated housing, schools, transportation, restaurants, and employment. Blacks were excluded from voting, and political power was uniformly white. Yet three decades later the dream is becoming reality. To envision a future is the first step in creating it.

14.6   REHABILITATION FOR CRIMINALS?

When someone breaks the law, what should be our response as a society? There are at least three approaches underlying any correctional system: (1) *removing* the offender from society, (2) *punishing* the offender, and (3) *rehabilitating* the offender. All three approaches may have a common goal: to protect society by reducing future criminal offenses. But how effective are these three approaches in protecting society?

Confinement in a jail, prison, or penitentiary is now the customary approach in U.S. correctional systems, serving both as punishment and removal of the offender from society. Though costly, imprisonment does restrain the person from most offenses during the period of confinement. Eventually, however, all but the most violent offenders are released back into society, usually after a few months or years of incarceration. The removal goal of imprisonment, then, is achieved only temporarily, and some believe that offenders are returned to society as *more* dangerous individuals, by virtue of their experiences during incarceration.

Since the code of Hammurabi, introduced almost 4,000 years ago, punishment in proportion to the offense has been a principle of law. Because imprisonment is costly and may be ineffective in deterring future crime, some have argued for the use of corporal punishment (such as electric shock) as a just, less expensive, more humane, and no less effective approach (Newman, 1983). The infliction of pain and suffering was the main form of punishment for offenses against society until the 20th century, during which there was a rapid expansion of prisons, and incarceration became the most common penalty.

What about rehabilitation? How effectively can offenders be given *treatment* instead of (or in addition to) punishment, and thus changed in a way that reduces future crime? Although there is a stereotyped pessimism that criminals cannot be treated, research clearly shows otherwise. Gendreau and Ross (1987), reviewing over 300 studies, concluded that "It is downright ridiculous to say 'nothing works' " (p. 395). Among the effective rehabilitation strategies they found are:

> community-based behavioral therapies
>
> family therapy
>
> treatment of alcohol and other drug problems
>
> early information (e.g., parenting skill education)
>
> self-control training
>
> individual tailoring of treatment
>
> cognitive and client-centered therapies

These rehabilitation approaches have been found more effective than the usual legal sanctions alone. In contrast, they found little or no evidence to support brief educational strategies, psychoanalysis, wilderness experiences, or shock incarceration programs such as "Scared Straight."

This is not to say that all offenders could be treated effectively. For some, rehabilitation does not work, and unless better approaches can be found there are few alternatives to incarceration. For most offenders, however, treatment and rehabilitation are more effective (and less expensive) than prolonged imprisonment. In the long run, rehabilitation appears to offer greater reduction in crime and thus better protection of society.

But a dream is not enough. Until it is expressed in action, the dream remains a private experience. Visions and expectations of the future become reality as and because they inspire actions. Change occurs as people begin to live as if the dream were real, to act on the vision (Kelly, 1955). The accomplishment of change often requires much more than a temporary effort, but rather a sustained and consistent pursuit of the new. Enduring change, both personal and social, emerges as behavior shifts consistently in a new direction. Without the dream, action becomes directionless and empty of purpose. Without enactment, the dream remains an unfulfilled promise. Together, vision and consistency of action craft the future.

For this reason, your expectations, hopes, and dreams are matters of great consequence. In choosing and affirming them, you guide and create your own future. To be sure, each of us lives within many constraints. No one is limitless. No one has complete control of his or her life. Adjustment sometimes requires acceptance of these limits and a recognition of what is beyond one's own control. Yet most people live far within their limits and do not explore many possibilities that are available to them. To see the possibility, to dream it, is the beginning.

It is to these issues of personal vision and meaning that we turn in our final chapter.

■ SUMMARY

Social norms and pressure exert substantial but not insurmountable influences on individual behavior. Tendencies toward conformity and obedience to authority are counteracted by direct personal contact and by the presence of others who resist conformity. Shyness represents excessive internalization of social control, and is related to low self-esteem. The family is the context within which individuals normally learn skills for dealing with others, for balancing internal control with external influence. Society consists of multiple levels of social systems including families, neighborhoods, and communities, each of which is comprised of individuals. Thus individuals and society (comprised of individuals) exert significant influences upon each other. Like individuals, social systems are constantly changing, seeking balance along dimensions such as authoritarianism versus freedom and personal liberty versus the social welfare. Peacemaking involves finding common ground and effective methods for resolving the conflicts that invariably arise in human interactions.

Three specialties within psychology focus in particular on larger social systems. Environmental psychology is concerned with the effects of the physical environment on individuals and groups. Factors such as personal space, noise, lighting, temperature, and crowding are considered in designing optimal human environments. Organizational behavior focuses more on the interpersonal environment within social systems. Specialists in this field study how systems are organized, how decisions are made, and how power is distributed. Community psychology is concerned with the prevention of psychological problems and the promotion of health within larger social systems. Tertiary prevention involves providing services to individuals who have already developed problems. Secondary prevention emphasizes early identification and intervention. Primary prevention focuses on direct interventions within entire social systems, rather than targeting particular "at-risk" individuals. Prevention is still a relatively young field, and it is vital that programs intended to prevent problems be carefully evaluated to determine their actual effects. In a very real sense, people choose their own future, individually and collectively, through their vision of the future and the actions they take in pursuit of that dream.

■ QUESTIONS FOR THOUGHT

1. How would you describe the social environment in which you have lived? Have you ever lived in a different society from the one you live in now?

2. When you meet an international student on your campus, do you notice or discuss cultural differences in social conventions with her or him? If you have not had contact with international students, how do you explain that lack?

3. In what ways do you consider yourself a conformist; a nonconformist?

4. What images do you see when you hear the term "the enemy"? How have you been trained to treat enemies? Under what circumstances do you disobey and obey that training?

5. Would you describe yourself as shy? Does your experience fit with the research done by Zimbardo?

6. Have you received any training in parenting skills? What kind of parenting skills do you use currently, or do you hope to use if you plan to have children?

7. Have you ever acted as a mediator or peacemaker between people who had strong differences? Have you observed someone else serving as a peacemaker? What are key conflict resolution skills for you?

8. In what ways does your physical environment affect your psychological well-being? When you are outdoors, what kind of environment do you prefer? When you are indoors, what kinds of factors are most important to your sense of comfort?

9. If an organizational psychologist were to consult with employees at your workplace, what would you suggest to that consultant about improving employee satisfaction there?

10. When you read about groups that have chosen to avoid "progress," such as the Amish or the residents of Taos Pueblo, what, if anything, do you appreciate about their views?

chapter fifteen

Everywhere the sun, moon and stars, the climates and weathers, have meanings for people. Though meanings vary, we are alike in all countries and tribes in trying to read what sky, land and sea say to us. Alike and ever alike we are on all continents in the need of love, food, clothing, work, speech, worship, sleep, games, dancing, fun. From tropics to arctics humanity lives with these needs so alike, so inexorably alike.
—Carl Sandburg, prologue to *The Family of Man*

Weaving the Tapestry of Meaning

OUTLINE

The winds blew cold around and through the flimsy dormitories built to house the exiles. By day the exiles endured forced labor outside in subzero temperatures. At night they returned to their squalid quarters and meager rations. So it went day after day, year after year. It was common, in the course of a winter, for twenty to die in each dormitory of a hundred prisoners.

But there was an exception. To the work camp there came a new exile, a storyteller. Every night in her dormitory, after a cold day's labor, the prisoners gathered around her in anticipation of her remarkable tales. So greatly did they value her sagas that the exiles of her dormitory agreed to divide up her assigned tasks among themselves, so that she might conserve her health and strength to continue telling them her stories at night. They clung to her words, waited eagerly for the day to end so that they might hear her spin new tales or continue a saga from the night before. All that winter, while many died in the camp, everyone in the dormitory of the storyteller survived.
(Adapted from Eliade, 1978)

■ HOW IS MEANING RELATED TO ADJUSTMENT?

Psychological adjustment poses many challenges throughout the course of a lifetime. Each person faces the challenge of making and sustaining relationships with others (Chapter 10). Each must find the ways in which he or she will "make a living," working and contributing to the larger social world (Chapter 13). In addition to loving and working, there is another enduring life task. It is reflected in the history of humankind since the beginning of written records, and before that in the oral traditions passed in stories from generation to generation. This life task lies at the heart of many human endeavors that endure from century to century: art, religion, stories. It is the search for meaning.

Meaning has to do with a sense of one's identity and purpose. Though often aided and enriched by one's family and culture, the search for meaning is an intensely personal task. The inner struggles that begin in adolescence and reemerge throughout adulthood center on questions of meaning, purpose, identity (Erikson, 1959). Fowler (1981) has posed a set of such questions:

What are you spending and being spent for? What commands and receives your best time, your best energy?

What causes, dreams, goals, or institutions are you pouring out your life for?

As you live your life, what power or powers do you fear or dread? What power or powers do you rely on and trust?

To what or whom are you committed in life? In death?

With whom or what group do you share your most sacred and private hopes for your life and for the lives of those you love?

What *are* those most sacred hopes, those most compelling goals and purposes in your life? (p. 3)

In the answers to such questions are the beginnings of one's meaning. The answers are necessarily personal, different for each individual. Although it is tempting at times to look to others for the answers and to adopt others' values, each person ultimately chooses and discerns his or her own meaning. According to a Quaker belief, each human being is a unique, irreplaceable person who has never been on earth before and never will be again. In the words of Charles Schultz's comic strip character Charlie Brown, "In the book of life, the answers are not in the back."

The search for meaning is a key issue within existential psychology, one of the four perspectives introduced in Chapter 1. Existentialists emphasize the aloneness of each human being: we enter the world alone, leave it alone, and in between are responsible to find our own meaning. During childhood and adolescence the values of one's parents and peers tend to be seen as absolute reality. As the person matures, these familiar values and beliefs usually begin to crack, and it becomes apparent that they are not absolute. The result can be a loss of meaning or identity. The person may encounter an **existential crisis,** the frightening experience of no external givens, no absolutes, no meaning except that which one makes for oneself. The feeling is that of being in a small open boat, adrift on a vast uncharted ocean, with no moorings and no land in sight. An existential crisis of this kind can evoke a deep sense of loneliness, emptiness, and anxiety. From here, the person begins (or, more accurately, resumes) the process of weaving her or his own tapestry of meaning.

■ MEANING AS STORY

Meaning is elusive, often difficult to describe. Those who seek to express meaning often do so in the form of a story. Ask a question of an existential therapist, a rabbi, a Zen or Sufi teacher, and you may well be answered with a story. The vital, life-giving quality of story is reflected in the tale which opened this chapter. Because meaning is notoriously difficult to describe in scientific terms, this chapter may seem different from all the others. We will use stories at various points to capture and emphasize our meanings.

The storytellers of a society are its meaning-bearers. Before there were any written records, storytellers preserved the meanings and identity of a culture through their tales and songs. Alex Haley's (1976) engrossing saga, *Roots*, represents the product of his search for his own heritage, the story of his ancestry. For Haley, the discovery and retelling of the story was part of his own search for meaning and identity. A society retains, renews, and celebrates its own collective identity through its stories.

At Acoma Pueblo, a special mesa in New Mexico where a group of American Indians has lived for centuries, the Governor's Feast is a time of dancing and gift-giving. Because the pueblo is on a mesa very elevated from the plain from which it rises, Acoma is called the "Sky City." It is reached on foot, ascending

Existential Crisis
an anxiety-laden experience associated with confronting conditions of existence such as aloneness, finiteness, or the unknown.

Acoma Pueblo, New Mexico.

the mesa either on a path or by climbing the rock by steps and handholds that have been used for hundreds of years. Witnessing the dancing at Sky City is, itself, a special gift. The dancers are regaled in skins and colorful costumes of the buffalo, eagle, butterfly, and deer. The drummers and singers fill the air and seem to shake the ground with their rhythmic chants. The unique worship and celebration of the dances evokes a deep sense of connection with the traditions of countless generations of the Acoma people. Even the visitor is caught up in the search for and celebration of identity.

Just as a culture experiences its identity in story, so do individuals. Ask a person, "Tell me who you are," and if you will take the time to listen you may hear a story, or a series of them. The person's own life story is woven from the strands of countless memories, shaped into patterns that give them form and order. Ask a person to tell you his or her life story and you can learn much, not only from the particular content given, but by noticing *which* of millions of details the person recalls and emphasizes, and how the person patterns them and gives them form. One's identity is held both in the particular strands that make up the fabric and in its pattern. At times of great change, the pattern may unravel, requiring the person to reweave a new tapestry from the many-colored yarns available.

The importance of this tapestry is poignantly apparent in the experiences of people who suffer major neurological impairment, as from a serious brain injury. Sacks (1985), a neurologist, offered a moving account of the world of the neurologically impaired. Patients who have lost their memories have an especially painful time in struggling to establish meaning and identity in their lives. Having few remembrances from which they can construct a tapestry of meaning, they seem to float unanchored and "de-souled" in a world that is confusing, fragmented. In a desperate attempt to give their experiences meaning and structure, they **confabulate,** filling in missing pieces with manufactured details, and literally *making* sense. Sacks describes some of these patients as engaged in "a veritable delirium of identity-making and -seeking" (p. 115).

Confabulation
manufacturing information or details that are missing because of memory deficits.

The discovery of meaning in one's life is like the work of a weaver.

Yet from these people, Sacks maintains, we have much to learn. They can teach others about meaning, how people make it for themselves to enhance their quality and understanding of life. One patient, named Rebecca, suffered from a congenital condition which left her mentally handicapped. Her intelligence quotient (IQ) was measured as less than 60, far below normal. Though she could not read, she had always loved to hear stories and would listen intently as her grandmother told them. She hated the remedial classes which constantly highlighted her deficits. Rebecca explained to Dr. Sacks: "I'm like a sort of living carpet. I need a pattern, a design, like you have on that carpet. I come apart, I unravel, unless there's a design. . . . The classes, the odd jobs have no meaning. . . . What I really love . . . is the theatre" (pp. 184–185). Sacks removed her from the remedial classes and enrolled her instead in a theater group. She became quickly involved in theater and "If one sees Rebecca on stage," Sacks remarks, "one would never even guess that she was mentally defective" (p. 185). The theater provided the design that she needed to make sense of her life.

■ SOURCES OF MEANING

From where do the patterns come, which form the tapestry of meaning in one's life? We will explore three different interpretations, three views of the source of meaning patterns. These three views are determinism, human agency, and transcendence.

DETERMINISM

The first of the three views is that a person's meaning is determined by experience. A seventeenth-century root of this view is the assertion of philosopher John Locke that the newborn is a *tabula rasa*, a blank slate upon which experience writes. Locke rejected the notion that any ideas or meanings are innate in human experience, and argued instead that they arise from sensory experiences and reflection.

Psychodynamic perspectives have emphasized the formative developmental influences of early life experiences in determining adult personality. Early childhood experiences are seen as determining the person's relatively fixed patterns of perception and functioning. These patterns and their determinants remain largely unconscious, shaping and guiding future experience. Memories themselves are selectively forgotten, recalled, altered, even manufactured to support basic unconscious motivational patterns set by early experience. This emphasis can be seen in the writings of Freud, and those of neo-analytic theorists such as Erik Erikson, Harry Stack Sullivan, Anna Freud, Wilhelm Reich, Otto Rank, Margaret Mahler, and others.

This essentially deterministic view is retained in a variety of more recent psychological theories. Transactional analysis (Berne, 1964) postulates the existence of unconscious "life scripts" which people act out, reliving expectations set by early experience. Some cognitive therapists like Albert Ellis (1984) emphasize the role of "irrational beliefs" which shape perceptions and emotions. Janov's (1970) "primal therapy" assigns a central role to very early (infancy) experiences in determining basic patterns of thought, feeling, and action.

Determinism
the view that all behavior has specific causes and that, if these causes could be fully known, behavior would be completely predictable.

Behaviorism likewise embraces **determinism,** maintaining that one's identity can be understood as the product of experience through processes of learning. Behaviors (as well as thoughts and feelings) are controlled by their consequences. Those which are followed by reinforcement are strengthened;

those which are not reinforced or lead to aversive consequences are weakened. Skinner's (1971) radical behaviorism, as a view of human nature, is considerably more complex than this, however. He recognized that from experience, individuals can abstract rules about behavior and its results. These rules can then govern future behavior, even overriding changes in the actual environmental contingencies. Such rules may remain relatively resistant to change from disconfirming experience. (The phenomenon of illusory correlation, discussed in Chapter 1, is an example.) Behavioristic formulations nevertheless remain deterministic, because even such behavior-governing rules are themselves the product of experience and learning processes.

Still another deterministic view is **sociobiology,** a development within the field of biology arising in the 1980s, which stresses the determinant power of one's genetic makeup. Animal and human behavior is seen as primarily promoting the propagation of one's own genes. Experience interacts with this overriding motivation for self-propagation. Behavior is seen as purposeful, driven and determined by the goal of genetic survival.

HUMAN AGENCY

A second view of the source of meaning patterns is that they are *chosen* by each individual. This raises the familiar "free will" alternative to a classic deterministic position. Existential psychologists have strongly espoused this view, maintaining that people are not mere products of experience but exert **agency** of their own (May, 1967, 1969). They are free agents, able to act and choose of their own volition. Human beings are seen as capable of rising above their own learning and experience.

Psychodynamic and cognitive therapists, though espousing a developmental determinism, do imply the possibility of rising above one's past. Both attempt to make conscious the unconscious patterns that have motivated the individual's perceptions and actions. In so doing, the hope is to increase awareness of prior determinism and thereby to enable new, conscious choices about one's own life. This common goal of psychotherapy—to wake up, become aware, and consciously choose a new direction (Prochaska, 1984)—has also been a central goal of most world religions (Watts, 1975).

In a human agency view, then, people have the meaning that they make for themselves. Although they may choose to adopt the meaning and values of an outside agent—a parent, peer group, religion, political party, cult, or teacher—nevertheless it is still the individual's *choice* to do so (Fromm, 1963).

TRANSCENDENCE

A third perspective on the source of meaning in human life is that it arises from a **transcendent** source, one that lies beyond human agency. In this view, meaning and purpose are innate, or independent of the individual's particular experiences or choices.

This view is expressed in a variety of forms. The most general of these is the view of humanistic psychologists that human worth is inherent, and that human life is innately meaningful in itself, regardless of the individual's developmental history, perceptions, or decisions. An implicit assumption of some humanistic psychologists goes a step beyond this to postulate an individual, inherent personal nature. In Chapter 4 we likened this concept of human nature to a seed, which contains the blueprint or "intention" of a particular full-grown living being. The innate "purpose" or plan of the seed remains unchanged, although the plan may be frustrated by poor environmental conditions. Psychological perspectives that exhort a person to "become your natu-

Sociobiology
a theoretical perspective within biology that maintains that behavior is best understood as determined by and promoting the survival of the individual's genetic structure.

Agency
active control, power, or influence.

Transcendent
that which lies beyond and exists apart from ordinary human control and experience.

Awakening and choosing a new direction are central themes not only in psychotherapy, but also in most world religions.

ral self" or to "find out who you really are" imply this sort of built-in intention or nature.

With one additional step, this view takes on theological proportions. Most religions include certain assumptions about the inherent nature of human beings. These are often understood as having been created, ordained, or intended by a higher power which transcends human nature. Some religions, for example, frame the search for meaning as seeking "the will of God," which can be understood both as a general intention for all people and as specific purposes for individuals. Some religions envision a state of perfection (such as *nirvana* in Hinduism or Buddhism), which represents an ultimate intention

15.1 HERE WE DIFFER/HERE WE AGREE
The Role of Religion and Spirituality in Psychology

This issue obviously is a complicated one. Many psychologists are indeed skeptical of spiritual beliefs and have difficulty with religious institutions of any kind. My own position on this has been to accept in my patients whatever spiritual beliefs they wish to follow, so long as their belief system is not causing them to be maladjusted in life. My personal view, however, is that reliance on a religious institution or belief system tends to take away some of the freedom and creativity that life has to offer.

Religion is an easy way to escape from one of the major issues facing all of humankind: that of loneliness. It is usually a startling realization when people finally see that they are really, absolutely alone. Yet accepting this, I believe, brings a person an important new level of responsibility and freedom. They can short-circuit this if they reach out to find a "greater meaning" in some spiritual or religious belief system. It is an understandable response to the terrifying experience of aloneness, to be sure. It offers the security of a life hereafter or of being assured of being a "good" person by some absolute standard.

But the fact is that we are all alone. The very nature of consciousness and the way the brain operates ensures that we have always been alone since birth, and always will be to the moment of death. No one can get inside anyone else's head. That's just how it is. When you recognize this fact and see it not as a devastating rejection but as a reality of life, then you can get along quite nicely in life. It is still necessary to get along with other people, of course, and this happens best through some consensus about ethical behavior. From this viewpoint, however, I find most spiritual or religious beliefs to be rather irrelevant to life.

Well, not quite irrelevant. Religious and spiritual beliefs have often been used to disagree with or demean others, to try to gain an upper hand and control others. Throughout the history of humankind, religious institutions have functioned to control people, and have perpetrated some immense atrocities and violence upon others. There can be positive values in religion, too, but it is possible for people to adopt these without buying into religious systems and institutions. It is when religions formalize their structure and start imposing this on others that I object.

I am not convinced that religious and spiritual belief systems contribute greatly to helping people grow in a positive fashion. They seem to me more likely to restrict and control people, and to give them a false sense of security. To be yourself is harder. It requires you to become aware of your own uniqueness without buying your meaning from someone else. In doing that, you're on your own. You can never truly understand anyone else, nor can they really understand you. Once you accept that, paradoxically, you can establish fantastic intimate links with other people.   —JMR

I've always wondered why psychologists in general have tended to be so antagonistic toward religion. Psychologists in their work and writings tend to disavow spiritual beliefs and shun religion (Bergin, 1980). There is no denying that religious beliefs and systems, like any element of society, can be misused and applied toward inhumane ends. Though religion has a terrible track record with regard to war, violence has also been motivated by patriotism, economic interests, pride, political ideologies, geographic boundary disputes, and family ties. Historian G. K. Chesterton once observed, "It is not that Christianity has been tried and found wanting, but rather that it has never been tried at all." The potential for control and misuse is not unique to religious systems.

What is unique and interesting is the extent to which human beings have always been drawn to a search for that which transcends us, for what we call God. More than 90 percent of Americans profess a belief in God (Bergin, 1980). Spiritual beliefs and participation in religious institutions are significant if not central to the lives of many people. Religious communities have survived, adapting and embracing the same essential tenets for thousands of years. How odd that psychology, scarcely a century old, should pronounce all this irrelevant if not pathological! At the very least, the psychology of religion should be seen as a fit and interesting subject for study!

But intriguing though it is, putting religion

under the microscope misses the point. For all of recorded history, including today, many (in some nations most) people have said that their decisions and actions are guided in vital ways by their spiritual beliefs. To ignore or merely tolerate this as an "irrelevant" factor in, for example, psychotherapy, is to overlook what people indicate, loudly and clearly, to be a major driving force in their lives. Some therapists, like Albert Ellis, have even pronounced most religious beliefs to be pathological, and have sought to disabuse clients of these "mistaken" and "irrational" views.

Ultimately, the importance that one places upon spirituality and religion depends in large part on the extent to which one believes in the reality of God, of the transcendent. If God is a reality, then seeking greater consciousness of and closeness to God is a natural pursuit for humankind. If God is a reality, then it is unthinkable to exclude from psychology the consideration of spirituality. If, on the other hand, one views God to be fictitious, then spiritual functioning is of interest, if at all, in the same way that fairytales and fantasies are.

For myself, as a believer, I am at least as interested in spiritual functioning as in cognitive and emotional functioning. I find my own spiritual and religious life to be wholly compatible with and complementary to my work as a psychologist. Each adds depth to the other. Likewise I find that incorporating a client's own religious beliefs into the process of psychotherapy can facilitate healing. In the first study of its kind, Rebecca Propst (1980) found that therapy which included the client's own religious imagery was more effective in treating depression than the same therapy conducted without religious imagery.

Though they serve different purposes, religion and science (including psychology) are not incompatible. It is, in my view, arbitrary and limiting to regard all of religion and spirituality as "off limits" or irrelevant to psychology and psychotherapy. We have expended great efforts to understand human behavior, thought processes, and emotions. The spiritual side of people deserves the same curiosity and understanding as we seek to comprehend the science of psychology and to alleviate human suffering.   —WRM

INTEGRATION

Though slow in beginning, psychology is showing increased interest in and openness to religion and spirituality. In 1975 the American Psychological Association officially added a new division of Psychologists Interested in Religious Issues. An empirical psychology of religion is growing, and a new crop of textbooks on this subject makes it easier to offer courses in this area (e.g., Spilka, Hood, & Gorsuch, 1985). The Association for Advancement of Behavior Therapy has an official special interest group on Spiritual and Religious Issues in Behavior Change. Several journals now publish research and articles on the integration of psychology and religion. Contemporary psychology is increasingly integrated into textbooks on pastoral psychology (Collins, 1980; Miller & Jackson, 1985). Popular books, including some best-sellers, are exploring the interface of psychology and religion (e.g., Campbell, Watts, & Miller, 1988; Peck, 1978; Watts, 1979). It appears that psychology, like medicine, is slowly entering an era of a more "holistic" approach which seeks to encompass the whole person in the process of healing.

and meaning for human beings, toward (or away from) which they may move. In spiritual and religious forms of transcendence, the individual sorts out the meaning of her or his life in relation to a higher power.

Transcendent views themselves differ in the extent to which they emphasize determinism versus human agency. Certain religions view the course and purpose of human life as preordained, determined by fate or a higher power, which can be influenced little if at all by human agency or experience. Other views understand the transcendent sources of meaning as more responsive to human experience and initiatives. Greek mythology, for example, is filled with tales of the gods being influenced and swayed by human actions.

On the island of Cyprus there lived a talented sculptor named Pygmalion. He hated women, perceiving them as hopelessly flawed. Yet he labored to produce a statue of a woman that would be perfect. In this he was successful. His statue was so artful that an onlooker would easily mistake it for a live maiden, temporarily posed. Strangely, Pygmalion found himself falling in love with his statue. He kissed her, brought her gifts, dressed her in rich garments, embraced her, and gave her a bed of her own where he placed her each night. He became obsessed with her, driven nearly mad with frustration that she could never respond to him. The goddess of love, Venus, saw all of this. On the day of the feast honoring her on Cyprus, Venus heard Pygmalion's plea to find a woman like his statue. When he returned home, he went to the statue and, as he had done so many times before, he kissed her. To his astonishment, he felt the marble lips grow soft. He embraced her, and the stone turned to warm flesh. Then she smiled. The statue had become a living woman. It is assumed that they lived "happily ever after." (adapted from Hamilton, 1942)

■ ISSUES OF MEANING: STRANDS OF THE TAPESTRY

Life meaning is difficult to describe, and is highly individual. Still there are some common issues that arise in human development, which center on questions of meaning. Virtually all of Erikson's developmental stages (Chapter 4) involve value choices between two extremes on a meaning dimension. This is particularly apparent in the stages from adolescence onward: identity versus role diffusion, intimacy and solidarity versus isolation, generativity versus stagnation, and integrity versus despair (Erikson, 1963). In this section, we will highlight some of the general issues of meaning likely to arise in each human life, forming strands to be woven together. We will focus in particular on issues of quality of life, uniqueness, uncertainty, and death.

QUALITY OF LIFE

In every age, it has been recognized that the perceived *quality* of one's life is not driven or guaranteed by what society values as the signs of success. The experienced quality of life does not depend upon the accumulation of possessions. Within many religious views, in fact, the pursuit of meaning is promoted by the renunciation of wealth and external comforts.

The more general meaning issue here is: "What is the *Good?*" What is that toward which you strive? What is worth attaining? What has lasting meaning? Every culture expresses a collective view of the "Good" toward which its members strive. In the age of mass media, this is contained within what has come to be called the "pop culture" (Fishwick, 1974; Nelson, 1976). The pop(ular) culture is expressed in media such as films, television, advertising, sports, games, music, and best-selling books. In these media, which convey the culture's shared implicit values, can be found messages about the Good to be desired and pursued. In what has been called "the 'me' generation," contemporary American culture emphasizes hedonism—the pursuit of personal pleasure in dimensions of economics, health, sexuality, and popularity. Pleasure is cast as the ultimate Good, with life consisting of something like a board game in which you accumulate as much of it as possible before the game ends. Other times and cultures have promoted different popular values, placing prime importance on working, military conquest, or cooperation in the interest of the larger social welfare.

A personal definition of the Good is likely to be reflected in how one spends one's time. Here we return to the first of Fowler's (1981) questions: "What are you spending and being spent for? What commands and receives your best time, your best energy? What causes, dreams, goals, or institutions are you pouring out your life for?" Implicit in the devotion of one's time is the value placed on that which is being pursued with that time. Similarly, the uses of discretionary financial resources reflect that which the person regards to be Good, worth promoting or having. What values are you affirming *now* in your life, through the ways in which you spend your time and resources?

A related issue from pop culture is: What is the *threat* to the Good? In Fowler's terms, "What power or powers do you fear or dread?" In recent popular U.S. culture, several themes represent the threat to happiness. These include growing old, poverty, physical unattractiveness, and social rejection. Advertisements for products commonly present or imply a supposed threat to happiness, and then promote the product as a solution to that threat. Prejudice and discrimination, enmity, persecution, and warfare are often driven by the perception that the "other" or the "enemy" represents a threat to the Good (Keen, 1988).

One important issue of meaning, then, is found in what a person perceives to determine the quality of life, and to threaten it. Once these values are set, they become important directives, and may guide much of a person's behavior even without his or her awareness.

UNIQUENESS

A second common issue of meaning is that of uniqueness, of separateness from others. Uniqueness is the realization of being unlike *anybody* else, of having a design in one's living tapestry that has never been woven before. In developmental terms, this is the differentiation of "me" from "not me" (Sullivan, 1953), the emergence of a sense of unique identity. Each person is different from any other human being who has ever lived, but the question of uniqueness is: "*How* am I different?"

15.2 | WHO AM I?

Here is an exercise to help you reflect on your own sense of identity. You will need to have about 30 index cards or slips of paper to begin.

1. On each card, write one description of yourself. It might be an adjective ("gentle" or "ambitious"), a noun naming a role you have ("student" or "daughter"), a verb ("working" or "struggling"), or even your name or nickname. Keep writing descriptions until you seem to reach the end, to run out of major aspects of yourself.

2. Next lay the cards out on a flat surface and rearrange them in a particular order. On top, place the card which describes the most important or essential aspect of who you are as an individual. Continue arranging cards in order of decreasing importance, until at the bottom you place the description that is least central or important to who you are.

3. When you have completed this, pick up the stack of cards. Starting with the card on the bottom, read each card, one at a time, and ask whether this is an aspect of yourself which you could give up and still be "you." If so, lay that card down and go on to the next card from the bottom of the stack. Keep laying down cards until you come to the descriptions which you regard to be *essential* to your identity, to who you are.

4. If you're an introvert: Think about it. If you're an extravert: Discuss it with a friend.

Creativity
the capacity to generate new ideas, solutions, products, or possibilities.

Convergent Thinking
a deductive pattern of reasoning in which multiple sources of information are organized to reach a new conclusion or insight.

It is here that **creativity** emerges, the making of something new. The domains in which one can express creativity are many: art, ideas, literature, science, cooking, management, teaching, and inventing are but a few examples. Efforts to measure creativity have indicated that there is no single trait, but rather that there are various forms of creativity. One example is the difference between convergent and divergent thinking. **Convergent** (or deductive) thinking integrates many elements to reach a single conclusion. It starts from many and works toward one. Arthur Conan Doyle's fictional detective, Sherlock Holmes, was a master of this creative skill. He observed large sets of facts, perceiving relationships among them and deducing the truth. Convergent

15.3   RIGHT BRAIN, LEFT BRAIN

Neuroscientists have known since the late 19th century that somehow the left and right sides of the brain are different. Patients with strokes in the left hemisphere often have difficulty with understanding language. People with strokes in the right hemisphere often have difficulty with nonverbal functions, like learning positions and finding their way in three-dimensional space. Einstein is said to have visualized his theory of relativity and then had to translate the vision (right hemisphere) into mathematical logic and language (left hemisphere).

The two halves or hemispheres of the brain are connected by a large group of nerve fibers known as the corpus callosum, and by smaller bands of fibers (commissures) deeper in the brain. The roles of the two hemispheres became clearer through classic experiments in which these connections between the hemispheres were cut in the brains of animals (Myers & Sperry, 1953). The same was done with some human patients during the 1960's, in an attempt to treat uncontrollable epilepsy, which was believed to be caused by the spread of abnormal electrical activity from one hemisphere to the other (Bogen & Vogel, 1962). These patients understood the purpose of this "split brain" surgery, and were also willing to participate in later studies to compare the work of the right and left hemispheres.

From studies of these patients, it was possible to demonstrate that the left brain, when separated from the right hemisphere, tends to emphasize verbal, sequential, temporal, and logical or rational thought—the kind of thinking strongly emphasized and valued in Western cultures. The right hemisphere, when isolated, functions more by nonverbal, visual and spatial conceptions, intuition, and holistic thought—the kind of thinking often emphasized and valued in Eastern cultures. Similar findings emerged from the animal studies, confirming that the hemispheres of the brain, when separated, do function independently to a great extent.

The publication of results from these early studies led to a great increase of interest in the different functions of the right and left brain (Springer & Deutsch, 1981). The right brain came to be described as a center of creativity and intuition, with the left brain tending toward rigid logic and analysis. When information is presented just to the left hemisphere, people tend to use a logical language type of analysis. When information is presented just to the right hemisphere, people have more difficulty attaching language to their understanding, but seem to have more of a spatial and holistic appreciation of the information they have received.

Further research revealed that the right brain plays a greater role in awareness and expression of emotions (Tucker, Watson, & Herlman, 1977). One study, for example, indicated that emotions are expressed more intensely on the left side of the human face, which is controlled by the right brain (Sackheim, Gur, & Saucy, 1978). Emotional problems such as depression, thus, may be related more closely to the right hemisphere, whereas problems of disordered thought (such as schizophrenia) may be centered more in the left hemisphere. It is also clear, from infant development, that emotional expression appears long before language emerges. It is not surprising that human emotions often prove difficult to express in language, and fail to obey the rules of logic. Some forms of psychotherapy have attempted to give people better language systems for expressing their emotions, or greater rational control over emotions (e.g., Ellis & Harper, 1975).

The right brain controls the left side of the body, and therefore right-hemisphere-dominant people tend to be left handed. Are left-handers, then, more creative than right-handers? To answer this question, one of our students studied a large number of art (painting) students at the University of New Mexico. Interestingly, she found that over 20% were left-handed, as compared with 10–12% of the general population. When this hypothesis was further tested, however, by comparing painters who had shown their work at the Museum of Modern Art in New York City and a group of lawyers selected from a reference manual for the American Bar Association, both groups had the same, normal percentage of left-handers. Creativity is not restricted to those with right brain dominance.

The truth is that, except in people whose corpus callosum has been severed, the hemispheres work together. Effective human adjustment usually requires a balancing and integration of left and right hemisphere functions.

thinking combines elements in new ways. **Divergent** (or inductive) thinking, by contrast, represents a different kind of creativity. It starts from a common point and then moves out in different directions. It starts from one and works toward many. For example, How many uses can you think of for a brick? Both types of thinking involve creativity, but require different skills.

Related to creativity is the desire to contribute something unique, something that will endure beyond one's own lifetime. Erikson described this in his developmental choice between "generativity versus stagnation." The person who successfully resolves this life task in the direction of generativity is freed to change, to try new ways of doing things, to innovate, and also to support and encourage others in their own unique efforts. There are, of course, many ways to express generativity: through parenting, teaching, writing, painting, sports, or volunteer service. The figures pictured at the beginning of each chapter in this book are among the hundreds which are found in Frogner Park of Oslo, Norway, which contains the life work of sculptor Gustav Vigeland. Vigeland envisioned the sculpture park as encompassing the full life span, from infancy to old age. He convinced the city of Oslo to commit Frogner Park to this purpose and spent 30 years carving the 650 figures that now stand there as a gift to future generations.

Another side of creativity and uniqueness is the motivational issue of independence, of being clearly separate from others. In adolescence, this issue is manifested in breaking away from the family and identifying one's own separate values and life-style. In the United States, independence is highly prized, and "No one's going to tell me what to do" is a common theme. Other cultures foster greater *inter*dependence, placing less importance on the independent rights and actions of individuals (Neki, 1976).

The process of aging also impacts issues of uniqueness and independence. A friend who is a few months from retirement is expressing concern that he will not have an identity away from his lifelong work. His career has been his meaning. Retired from it, he is unsure how to behave and how others will act toward him after his change in roles. Likewise, in a society that so greatly prizes independence, any increased dependence upon others that comes with aging may be experienced as shameful and humiliating. Growing older requires both some new skills and a more graceful sense of self that continues to seek and find meaning and identity (Erikson, 1963; Skinner & Vaughan, 1985).

Divergent Thinking
an inductive pattern of reasoning in which, faced with a single task or problem, multiple possibilities are generated.

15.4 PERSONAL MILESTONE

It seemed like a great evening to make the five-hour sail to Catalina from San Pedro. I had read a few weeks before that Sterling Hayden had thrown a $10,000 diesel engine overboard so that his South Sea trip would be in the purist spirit. In a burst of male ego, I had thrown my own broken-down outboard over the side and was priding myself on being able to sail in and out of my slip, and pick up a mooring with my 26-foot sea bird yawl.

The weather had been nasty but the skies had cleared. My companion and I were happily leaving the harbor and had passed the San Pedro light and breakwater when it became obvious that we had made a terrible mistake. Though the skies had cleared, the waves were still up. We had just turned the corner of the breakwater when we took a huge wave over the bow. At the same moment the jib pulled loose and the forward hatch blew open. We stopped dead, and without a jib we started being driven toward the rocks of the breakwater. I told my companion to take the tiller and, if possible, steer toward the harbor mouth. She refused. In disbelief, I asked again, and she just sat there, frozen. I realized then that we were both going to die. If we didn't sink from the water we were taking through the hatch, we would be dashed on the rocks. There would be no help, as no one could possibly see us, and there was no way we would survive the waves and currents.

In desperation, I let go of the tiller, dashed forward and latched the hatch back down. I grabbed the jib and tied it down with a knot that to this day I cannot describe. I back-winded the jib, and the bow came around just enough to head us toward the harbor mouth.

We surfed into the harbor, just scraping the last rock between us and safety.

We sailed back into the slip where I furled the sails, tied up, and stalked off the boat to the nearest bar. Not a word had been spoken since her last refusal to help. Over a bourbon I tried to regroup from my combination of anger and fear. It occurred to me that I had just experienced a truly remarkable event in my life. I had fought a battle for my life and won, but no one else had to be hurt or defeated for this to happen. Further, I wasn't going to receive any recognition or praise for this victory. My trophy was my life.

I came to my senses and began feeling better—better, in fact, than anything I had ever felt before. Concerned about my companion, I went back and found her, and we talked it through. She likened the experience to hurling down a freeway in heavy traffic, with the gas pedal stuck down, and not knowing how to drive, when the driver says, "Oh, the brakes have gone out. Here, take the wheel while I fix them!" I realized that she had never before taken the tiller, even in good weather. The next day, she began learning.

For myself, I learned quite a bit from this experience. I found I could trust and believe in myself. Though I continued to be competitive afterward, I have never since taken competition totally seriously. There is something important about being tested for your life (accidentally, in this case) and finding you can survive and still function under such severe stress. It brings a level of confidence which nothing can take from you, and it puts both success and failure in new perspective.

—JMR

UNCERTAINTY

Obsessive-Compulsive Personality
a consistent personal style of perfectionism, rigidity, and preoccupation with order.

Another issue of meaning is uncertainty, and how to deal with it. This issue emerges early in development, as the young child realizes that the world is not always as it appears to be (Gilmore, 1973). As the child grows to adulthood, experience amply demonstrates that plans are sometimes thwarted, expectations are disappointed, and the unanticipated can strike at any time.

One response to such uncertainty is an attempt to guarantee safety. Extraordinary measures may be taken to ensure the avoidance of physical danger, psychological upset, or disappointment. The **obsessive-compulsive** personality style is an example of such certainty seeking, in which the person

Growing older requires both some new skills and a more graceful sense of self that continues to seek and find meaning.

follows highly ritualized and predictable life patterns. The result of such extreme safety seeking is usually a constriction of options, a limitation of possibilities. An inordinate need for safety has been described as symptomatic of poor mental health (Larson, 1978).

If this is so, then healthy adjustment requires a certain amount of risk taking. Adjustment involves change, and change involves uncertainty. To change is to act in the face of uncertainty. A fear of uncertainty thus can pose a substantial obstacle to change. The painful but tolerable present may be endured, rather than risking change and the possibility of going "out of the frying pan and into the fire." The ability to change, to adjust, requires dealing with uncertainty in a manner other than maintaining status quo and avoiding risk at all cost. Growth usually requires risk taking, and by definition risk taking holds the possibility of significant loss as well as significant gain.

Psychologist Ellen Siegelman (1983), in her book *Personal Risk*, describes seven steps involved in risk taking. The first three are awareness steps. First is awareness of negative feelings, which (as we have discussed in Chapter 3) serve to indicate the need for a change. Second is recognizing these negative feelings *as* a need for change and translating them into a goal. Awareness of negative feelings of loneliness (step 1) can be turned into a hopeful goal: "I want to spend more time with people and to feel closer to them." Resolving to pursue such a goal, however, usually leads to the third step, the experiencing of ambivalence, of anxiety about the risk involved in change. Some of the methods described in Chapter 8 may be helpful in forging ahead, getting past this stage.

The fourth step in Siegelman's description is to reduce the amount of risk through preparation. This can include acquiring important information, obtaining the help of others with needed expertise, practicing new coping skills, and asking for social support from friends or family. As a fifth step in preparation, she recommends a period of "incubation," letting the whole matter sit at least briefly, letting it go for a period of time.

Then comes the sixth step: taking the plunge. Having become aware of the need for change and the attached emotions, having prepared as much as is reasonable or possible, the time comes to take action. This is the step of commitment, where preparation becomes action. Finally comes the process of evaluation. What was the outcome? Was it worth the risk? How do you feel after having taken the plunge? Regardless of the outcome, reflect on your own courage and responsible decision making, which in themselves are characteristics worth developing.

In dealing with risk taking, we encounter another of Fowler's (1981) questions, listed at the beginning of this chapter: "What power or powers do you rely on and trust?" To have faith in someone or something is to act in spite of uncertainty. In the midst of a strange city, one may rely on a map or on directions from a friend to provide reliable guidance. In living, more generally, one places trust in certain persons, precepts, systems, or institutions, to provide reliable guidelines for pursuing the Good and avoiding threats to it. The choice of these guidelines, in which one places faith, is a key issue of meaning.

DEATH

Existentialists have always recognized death and fear of death as central issues of meaning. Physical death is the one totally reliable experience which comes to everyone. Death touches on every other meaning issue. It touches on quality of life in topics such as suicide and the right to die. The search for uniqueness is often a quest for contributions that will survive after one's own death. And death, of course, is the ultimate uncertainty, a possible outcome of risk taking or even of accident and chance.

Most people, before they die, must deal with the deaths of many others close to them. The death of parents and other family members, teachers and mentors, friends, or one's spouse, can evoke important questions of the meaning of one's life, and a redefinition of one's own identity. During the 1970s, there arose a strong mental health movement focusing "on death and dying." A key assumption of this movement was that by confronting death, including the reality of one's own death, it is possible to find new meaning and purpose

Death touches on every other issue of meaning.

in life (Kübler-Ross, 1969; Larson, 1978). The normal stages through which people pass in adjusting to death were described in Chapter 7 (see Box 7.1).

Specialists on the topic of death and dying emphasize to families of terminally ill patients the importance of telling the truth to one another in a gentle and caring way. Often when people face death, they lie, or loved ones lie to them, with everyone trying to protect everyone else. The consequence of such protection is that patients and their families are robbed of the intimacy that is possible in the final weeks or months of their lives. Sometimes such protection is rationalized as a way to maintain patients' hope. Hope, however, is just as possible when a person knows the prognosis, if that prognosis is presented as just one perspective, with the recognition that each person's circumstances are unique.

Dying people have much to teach others. It can be a privilege to listen to someone who is close to death, because she or he has a very different perspective on living, on what matters in life. Too many people move through their lives with very little awareness of its wonder. Through the eyes of one at the end of life, it is sometimes possible to glimpse the beauty and meaning of the present.

One possible positive outcome from confronting death is a greater intentionality with regard to how you use your time (Lakein, 1973). Suppose you knew for certain that you had only one year left to live. Suppose, further, that until the moment of your death, you would be fully healthy and that all of the necessary practical details of your death had been taken care of (e.g., making a will, planning your funeral, etc.) What would you do in the time remaining? What would be most important? What things, on which you now spend time, would you let go? What things, which you are not now doing, might you do? What, if anything, would you want to finish?

15.5 A MEDICAL STUDENT'S REFLECTION ON DEATH

The following reflection was written by a medical student shortly after she participated in the heart surgery of an infant. The poem was the student's attempt to make sense of her experience, to make meaning for herself. Poetry is the map for her journey of self-discovery. Others choose different kinds of maps.

THE MOON, SHE'S ARISING

The only child
to leave that room
bundled in a brightly patterned
flannel blanket,
and a nurse's warm arms,
was the one
we couldn't save.

When the infant
was brought in
we held a breath.
Four months old,
she was no larger
than a newborn.
Her heart stopped
before anesthesia
was hardly begun.

Oxygen by mask
and closed chest compressions
brought her back.
"Let's make this fast,"
The surgeon said,
as he pulled the knife
smoothly along her fourth rib.

A rapid attempt
to correct an aorta
misassembled by nature,
mishandled by God.
But twice more
during that morning's work
that feeble heart stopped.
We held a breath
and watched the monitor.

The surgeon's long, slender fingers,
wrapped surely around that tiny organ of love,
pumped rhythmically, knowingly.
We held a breath,
watched the clock,
and thought of our children at home.

"It's no good,"
he says.
Let her go,
inside our heads.
The clock stops,
The monitors off,
he closes the incision,
every movement with precision,
out of habit.

I watch those
breaths not taken

and think of
my daughter's warm
and vital body,
the magnificent geometry
of her perfect heart,
her strong, resilient vessels.

She tells me
that the full moon
doesn't have a man—
it has a rabbit.
That full moon,
she's arising—
just east of Corona,
a little north of Carrizozo.
Thank you, jesus, for that moon.

Kathryn Zerbach

The fact is that you *do* have a limited amount of lifetime left. The amount is unknown, but it is definitely limited. No one can save up time to use later. What if you were to live as if this were true? How would your priorities change? On what would you be spending more time, or less time?

■ MAPS FOR THE JOURNEY

The search for meaning can be facilitated in a variety of ways. There is no single tried-and-true method that works for everyone, or even for most people. Rather there are different avenues, maps for the journey, which people have employed in the search to find or make meaning for their lives. We will consider seven such maps: solitude, meditation, journal keeping, living in the "now," rituals and disciplines, social support, and living "as if."

SOLITUDE

Solitude, having time alone for reflection, is often an important first step on the search for meaning. Alone time opens up a space in which exploration can occur, and some of the other approaches discussed in the paragraphs that follow can be used.

Some individuals, in their search, have used extensive solitude. Some enter a monastery or other setting that offers a life-style with substantial solitary time, perhaps spending long periods in total silence. Less extreme measures can be very helpful, however, such as having a definite period of alone time every day. This is most likely to occur if it is planned for a designated time and place. In a family setting, this may require some advance arrangements with and help from the rest of the family. Others plan a period of solitude in the middle of each workday, to break the pace of working and allow time for rest and meditation.

Longer periods of solitude may also be useful, particularly at times of transition and personal reevaluation. In many areas, there are retreat centers that offer a place for extended solitude. Wilderness back-packing, camping, hiking, or cross-country skiing can also afford opportunities for getting things into perspective.

MEDITATION

Once you have arranged for some solitude, then what? One answer is to focus your attention, using any of a variety of skills which are usually termed "meditation."

The most popular form, **transcendental meditation (TM),** involves an "emptying of the mind" through a conscious focusing procedure. Thoughts are experienced as they enter consciousness, but are not held or focused upon. (Trying *not* to think about anything is a technique doomed to failure.) To provide a focus, those who practice TM usually use a *mantra*, a meaningless sound (such as "om") that is chanted first aloud, then silently. With time and practice, the meditator is able to empty her or his consciousness of thoughts and worries, and to experience a very restful state. A variety of physical and psychological benefits have been reported to accompany the practice of TM, including decreases in addictive behaviors (Aron & Aron, 1980) and healthful changes on physical dimensions such as heart rate, blood pressure, metabolism, and brain waves (Benson & Klipper, 1975). The basic components of transcendental meditation are described in Appendix B of this book.

Other meditation approaches seek not to empty the mind, but rather to explore inner consciousness. Typically these approaches, often called **transpersonal,** assume an inner wisdom with which the individual can establish contact. Carl Jung (1958) postulated the existence of a "collective unconscious," the residue of accumulated experience of humanity, to which an individual can obtain access. The founder of psychosynthesis, Roberto Assagioli (1971), similarly proposed a personality theory which included not only an unconscious, but also a higher consciousness. More recently, Emmons (1978) described a form of meditative therapy by which the individual seeks to induce a naturally occurring, drug-free altered state of consciousness in order to promote self-healing through contact with an "inner source."

JOURNAL KEEPING

Another approach, which has been used for centuries as a method for exploring meaning, is the keeping of a personal journal or diary. The reflections of a person in his or her own journal have often proven useful not only to the individual, but to others as well. A wide variety of personal journals have been published and widely read for their meaning-filled content, including those of Dag Hammarskjold (1964), Hugh Prather (1970), Anais Nin (1981), and Anne Frank (1953).

Journal keeping can be helpful in a variety of ways. The very process of writing down one's own experiences provides an opportunity to reexperience and reflect upon them. Progoff (1975), who introduced an intensive journal method for self-exploration, discussed the experience of wanting to investigate one's own meanings: "Many persons have already had experiences in which they have sensed the presence of an underlying reality in life, a reality which they have recognized as a personal source of meaning and strength. . . . Others missed their opportunity because they had so low an opinion of themselves that it did not occur to them that there could be depth and meaning in the experiences of their lives" (p. 10). Progoff's method involves a specific format for writing, reflecting, and responding within the journal. He recommended a loose-leaf notebook with dividers indicating specific topics. One

Transcendental Meditation
a mental discipline by which consciousness is emptied of ordinary content.

Transpersonal Psychology
a system of psychology that pursues phenomena that transcend and are accessible to all individuals, such as Jung's concept of a collective unconscious.

such topic, for example, is labeled "Intersections" and consists of the opportunity to elaborate on choices you have made, as well as the roads not taken which were alternatives to those choices. One such intersection for you was the decision to enroll in the psychology of adjustment as opposed to enrolling in some other course, or not enrolling at all. By exploring intersections such as this, you may reach greater self-understanding and meaning about your life. Journal keeping is also useful in identifying consistencies over time, the patterns in your tapestry. For example, one client who recorded her dreams in a journal was able to identify a recurring theme in the dreams which helped her to understand herself and her life better. Sometimes it is in examining one's life over a longer span of time that the patterns and meanings become apparent. The threads of your unique identity may weave together only after a period of confusion when there seems to be no cohesive whole.

> Fatima was the daughter of a prosperous spinner. She and her father were on a journey together trading the wares from their spinning business when a storm caused the ship on which they were traveling to wreck. Her father was killed, and Fatima was found, exhausted, on the shore, by a family of cloth-makers who took her in. She made a second life for herself with the cloth-makers, only to be abducted by a band of slave-traders, along with other captives. She was sold as a slave in Istanbul. A craftsman who built masts for ships purchased Fatima to work in his wood yard. Fatima worked hard and well, and was given her freedom. She became the trusted helper of the mast-builder, who sent her to sell the masts for a profit. That journey also ended in disaster in a typhoon off the coast of China. Fatima wept bitterly, feeling that her life was fraught with hardship; that no plans met success. Once again she picked herself up and walked inland. No one in China knew anything of Fatima or her troubles, but there was a Chinese legend which foretold the arrival of a foreign woman who would make a tent for the Emperor. No one in China yet had the skills for tentmaking, and thus, the fulfillment of the legend was anticipated with interest by the Emperor's people. The law was that any foreign woman must appear at court. So the people who found Fatima wandering inland took her immediately to the Emperor who asked her if she could make a tent. She said that she believed she could. She asked for rope, but there was none to be had, so she drew on her father's teachings as a spinner, and made rope. Then she asked for stout cloth, but the Chinese did not have a suitable kind, so she drew on her experience with the family of cloth-makers and wove it. Her life with the mast-builder contributed to constructing tent poles, and her travels had exposed her to the tents of many lands to serve as models. Fatima went to work constructing a tent for the Emperor, and soon produced one which pleased him greatly. In return he granted Fatima her wish: to settle in China, marry, and live in happiness, surrounded by her children. Fatima found her ultimate identity and happiness through the weaving together of what before had seemed to be the unrelated fragments of her life. (Adapted from Shah, 1967)

LIVING IN THE "NOW"

Several major systems of psychotherapy have emphasized living in the "now," focusing on whatever one is experiencing in the present. These include client-centered therapy (Rogers, 1951), gestalt therapy (Perls, 1969), and existential therapy (Yalom, 1980). All stress that a person can live too much in the past or future, in fantasy and self-deception. Such patterns pull the person away from experiencing the present, where reality, relationships, and meaning are to be found.

15.6 DREAMS: KEY, NOISE, OR ERASER?

You awaken in the middle of the night, startled by a dream. You were being chased—by what? By someone or something terrible. Your legs were like great weights, and you could hardly move. You struggled to get away, but it was like moving in slow motion, and the presence behind you was gaining on you. Then you felt the touch, and screamed yourself awake.

From where do such experiences come? What do they mean? For more than a century psychologists and psychiatrists have been puzzling and disagreeing over the significance of dreams.

Freud's classic position, introduced in the late 19th century, was that dreams represent "the royal road to the unconscious." In dreams, he believed, one sees some of the most direct expressions of unconscious material and wishes, emerging during the less guarded time of sleep. His system of psychoanalysis focused heavily on dreams and their interpretation, an emphasis that persists among modern analysts. Dreams, in this view, contain symbolically disguised but highly significant expressions of the inner person. Freud's student, Carl Jung, saw dreams as a window not only on the personal unconscious, but on a common, *collective* unconscious filled with themes and symbols shared by all of humanity. Other analysts have given less significance to dreams. Harry Stack Sullivan, for example, regarded dreams primarily as the release of frustrations from the day, rather than a key for unlocking the unconscious.

Much is known of the physiology of dreaming. Dreams occur primarily during what is called "REM" sleep, a stage that got its name from the rapid eye movements that accompany it. During REM sleep, the body relaxes, autonomic arousal fluctuates, and brain wave patterns resemble those of a drowsy state. The timing and frequency of dreams are affected by factors such as age, fatigue, and the use of alcohol and other drugs. REM dreams include nightmares, bad dreams that frighten and awaken the person. A very different experience known as "night terrors" involves very high autonomic arousal (fear) with no dream recalled, and occurs during deeper stages of sleep. Bed wetting also usually happens in deep sleep, and not during REM sleep.

During dreaming, the brain is active. Do these electrical patterns have meaning? It has not been possible thus far, at least, to link the *content* of dreams with specific patterns of electrical activity. Some experts regard dreams to be a kind of random firing of nerve cells, which remain active during sleep, since the brain never shuts down. The frontal lobes of the brain, which organize experience, struggle to make sense of and organize these random firings, yielding the often strange, even bizarre content of dreams. Within this view, dreams are meaningless—the mere idling of the brain when conscious perceptions are unavailable (Melnechuk, 1983). Other scientists have argued, not unlike Sullivan, that dreams represent a kind of house-cleaning in the brain, in which irrelevant material is being detected and erased (Crick & Mitchison, 1983). In this view, the *last* thing a person should do is try to remember and interpret the content of dreams!

What do you think? Are dreams something to be ignored—the background noise of an idling brain, or the discarded refuse of nightly cleaning? Or do they contain important secrets and keys to meaning and identity?

In the third act of Thornton Wilder's (1938) play *Our Town*, Emily, a character who has died while giving birth, returns to relive her twelfth birthday, which took place 14 years before. She is struck by how her parents look, so young and beautiful, but also by how everyone is preoccupied with her or his own life, and no one pays more than superficial attention to anyone else. The returned Emily observes this for awhile, and then, with mounting urgency says:

> "Oh, Mama, just look at me one minute as though you really saw me. Mama, fourteen years have gone by. I'm dead. You're a grandmother, Mama. I married George Gibbs, Mama. Wally's dead, too. Mama, his appendix burst on a camping trip to North Conway. We felt just terrible about it-don't you remember? But just for a moment now we're all together. Mama, just for a moment we're happy. Let's look at one another." (p. 123)

However, none of the other characters hear Emily, and they continue as before, emphasizing the aloneness, the missed chance at joy and relationship which only Emily can feel so poignantly.

Much has been said and written about the impossibly rapid pace of life today, which can keep one from enjoying simple pleasures (Toffler, 1970). Wilder, in his play, observed this more than 50 years ago. He pointed to that mysterious something which gives a quality to our lives, and which is so delicate that it can be easily trampled like a flower in our race to achieve whatever it is we are pursuing. With eyes only on the future, on the horizon, one is likely to miss the many wonders of the immediate moment. Meaning is to be found not only in recalling the past or imagining a hoped-for future, but also by experiencing the present, living in the now.

RITUALS AND DISCIPLINES

Another long-standing approach for capturing, expressing, and celebrating meaning is through rituals and disciplines. By **rituals** we mean the practice of a set rite, usually observed repeatedly, and often at prescribed times. All world religions have preserved and expressed their central precepts through specific rituals. Observance of such tranditional rituals serves to affirm the group's beliefs and common identity and to foster a sense of belonging and connectedness. Some rituals also serve to mark the transition from one phase of life to another. Among our society's common rituals are weddings, funerals, services of worship, celebrations of birthdays and anniversaries, retirement observances, and school proms and graduations. Certain life changes within our culture (e.g., divorce) may be more difficult because there is no official ritual by which society marks and affirms the transition.

In many societies, healing is also associated with established rituals. Among Indians of the American Southwest, the practice of sandpainting is a long-standing ritual. The healer reproduces from memory elaborate designs and pictures, laboriously "painting" them on the ground near the one who is ill, using fine colored sands. The designs and chants of these rituals are carefully prescribed, and must be conducted in accordance with tradition. When the ritual is ended, the beautiful and intricate sandpainting is destroyed, its purpose having been accomplished. Modern psychotherapies likewise contain many elements of ritual healing. The place, seating arrangements, and rules of conduct are all prescribed, and a variety of elements (e.g., degrees on the wall, furnishings of the office) ascribe healing powers to the therapist.

Disciplines, like rituals, are orderly behaviors, practiced repeatedly, in pursuit of meaning. Some examples are systematic study, meditation and prayer, fasting and other forms of planned and time-limited self-deprivation, martial arts (such as karate and judo), yoga, and tai-chi. Those who practice such disciplines over time often report the experiencing and discovery of ever

Ritual
a prescribed set of behaviors that is practiced repeatedly, with specific meaning or intention.

Discipline
an orderly practice that is followed for the purpose of developing self-control or meaning.

15.7   THE LITTLE PRINCE AND THE FOX

In his classic children's story, *The Little Prince*, Antoine de Saint-Exupery (1943) comments on the importance of rituals. It occurs through the interaction of the little prince with a fox, who wishes to be tamed:

"What must I do, to tame you?" asked the little prince.

"You must be very patient," replied the fox. "First you will sit down at a little distance from me—like that—in the grass. I shall look at you out of the corner of my eye, and you will say nothing. Words are the source of misunderstandings. But you will sit a little closer to me, every day . . ."

The next day the little prince came back.

"It would have been better to come back at the same hour," said the fox. "If, for example, you come at four o'clock in the afternoon, then at three o'clock I shall begin to be happy.

I shall feel happier and happier as the hour advances. At four o'clock, I shall already be worrying and jumping about. I shall show you how happy I am! But if you come at just any time, I shall never know at what hour my heart is to be ready to greet you . . . One must observe the proper rites . . ."

"What is a rite?" asked the little prince.

"Those also are actions too often neglected," said the fox. "They are what make one day different from other days, one hour from other hours. There is a rite, for example, among my hunters. Every Thursday they dance with the village girls. So Thursday is a wonderful day for me! I can take a walk as far as the vineyards. But if the hunters danced at just any time, every day would be like every other day" (pp. 67–68).

---

deeper levels of meaning, sometimes likened to peeling an onion. The removal of each layer reveals another beneath it.

SOCIAL SUPPORT

Still another route by which people pursue identity and meaning is through the use of social support. Friendships that endure over many years may provide a sense of continuity and safety, allowing the friends to share with each other their search for meaning. In developing his system of client-centered therapy, Carl Rogers demonstrated the value of empathic listening in helping another person to grow (Rogers et al., 1967; Truax & Carkhuff, 1967). Support from others may also facilitate change and the risk taking it requires. It is no coincidence that among Fowler's questions about meaning is, "With whom or what group do you share your most sacred and private hopes for your life and for the lives of those you love?"

Values and priorities are often worked out in interaction with others. Some groups are intentionally designed to facilitate clarification of personal values (Simon et al., 1985). Some educational institutions (such as Alverno College, a women's college in Milwaukee, Wisconsin) have built values exploration into their curriculum. One goal of the Alverno curriculum is to clarify and expand the student's moral reasoning. Moral development (Kohlberg, 1981) is seen as an important and often ignored aspect of a liberal arts education. One sample exercise from the Alverno curriculum is shown in Box 15.8.

15.8 | VALUING EXERCISE

1. Indicate two decisions you made in the last two weeks.
2. Cite one experience of satisfaction during the past two weeks.
3. Cite one experience of frustration during the past two weeks.
4. How did you spend your most recent leisure experience?
5. Define nonproductivity.
6. Identify one experience (anytime) in which you felt most alive.
7. Identify one goal you achieved during the past week.
8. College is . . .
9. The belief or attitude I most recently affirmed in public . . .
10. List two different activities in which you chose to participate this past week.

Using your answers to these questions as data about what you value, write a letter to your instructor in which you make explicit three of your values. Indicate how you know that they are your values and what roles they play in your life. Identify what you believe to be some of the sources of these values. Finally, rank or prioritize them. Which seem to be your most important or most central values?

Adapted from Alverno College conference on "Teaching Ethics: Incorporating Values into Professional and Liberal Studies," June 1985, Milwaukee, Wisconsin.

LIVING "AS IF"

One final example of meaning making might be called "living as if" (Miller, 1985a). It consists of living in a manner consistent with one's desired values and goals. It is acting, in the face of uncertainty, to move toward a chosen purpose.

People are often immobilized by waiting. "If my values and priorities were clearer" or "if my confidence were stronger" become rationalizations for not acting. One very consistent message from psychological research is that to *act* changes values, confidence, faith, relationships, and self-esteem. To wait for such things to change *before* taking action is to wait indefinitely. Taking action becomes a self-fulfilling prophecy; it changes perception and belief (Jones, 1977). To live as if something is already true is to take a step toward making it true.

C. S. Lewis (1960) advised:

> Do not waste time bothering whether you "love" your neighbor; act as if you did. As soon as we do this we find one of the great secrets. When you are behaving as if you loved someone, you will presently come to love him. If you

To live as if something is already true is to take a step toward making it true.

injure someone you dislike, you will find yourself disliking him more. If you do him a good turn, you will find yourself disliking him less. . . . Good and evil both increase at compound interest. This is why the little decisions you and I make every day are of such infinite importance. (p. 116)

The point here is that meaning is found in action, in living in accord with your values and ideals even when those are out of step with the behavior of others (or with your own past behavior). Values remain abstractions until they are enacted. Further, actions do speak louder than words; they create and strengthen values. To act is to take a step toward change.

There is a folk tale about a peasant who had a dreadfully ugly face. He liked a young village woman named Heather but was always afraid that, if he approached her, she would reject him because of his face. So he went to the city and paid a handsome price to have a perfect mask made—a mask of an attractive face. So marvelous a piece of work it was, no one could even tell he was wearing a mask. Even he forgot at times. A few days later he introduced himself to Heather, and they quickly became the best of friends. They would walk by the river or through the forest, talking about almost everything. He felt so happy, so strong, so accepted. Then one day, when it became clear that they were growing to love each other, he realized that he could not keep his secret forever. Sadly he said, "I have something that I must show you." They sat down beside a quiet lake, and slowly he pulled off his mask. Heather laughed a little and then said, "Well?" He was puzzled by her puzzlement. He leaned over the water to wash away the remainder of the actor's glue and was startled by his reflection. His old face was gone. The image in the water and the mask he held in his hand were one and the same. (from Miller, 1985a, p. 63)

These are only a few of the avenues which people use in the search for meaning. The search remains a uniquely individual one, a journey in which each person must find her or his way alone. Nevertheless it is possible to share that aloneness, to be companions on these individual journeys. To share one's aloneness is to celebrate one of the deepest forms of friendship.

■ SUMMARY

Like work and relationships, the search for meaning is a major adjustment challenge throughout the life cycle. Meaning and identity are often conveyed in the form of stories, both for individuals and for cultures. Three understandings of the source of meaning in human life are determinism, human agency, and transcendence. Central issues of meaning include quality of life, uniqueness, uncertainty, and death. A wide variety of tools or maps are available for use on the journey toward meaning. Those discussed in this chapter include solitude, meditation, journal keeping, living in the "now," rituals and disciplines, social support, and living "as if." Weaving the tapestry of meaning is an intensely individual process, which can also be shared.

■ QUESTIONS FOR THOUGHT

1. Give your own answers to Fowler's questions:
   What are you spending and being spent for?
   What commands and receives your best time, your best energy?
   What causes, dreams, goals, or institutions are you pouring out your life for?
   As you live your life, what power or powers do you fear or dread?
   What power or powers do you rely on and trust?
   To what or whom are you committed in life? In death?
   With whom or what group do you share your most sacred and private hopes for your life and for the lives of those you love?
   What *are* those most sacred hopes, those most compelling goals and purposes in your life?

2. When someone asks you who you are, how do you answer?

3. How do you answer when someone asks, "What do you do?"

4. Describe who you are without referring to any roles you play in society (occupation, group memberships) or relationships to other people (parent, spouse, etc.). Can you do it?

5. In what ways are you unique, special, irreplaceable?

6. In what ways do you deal with uncertainty or ambiguity? When you are faced with a situation or choice about which you are unsure, what do you do?

7. Who or what controls your life? How much choice do you think you have about who you will be, and what directions your life will take?

8. If you knew that you had only a few months to live, what would be your top priorities? How do these compare with how you are spending your time now?

9. How comfortable are you with being alone? Would you prefer to have more or less alone time in your life? What do you do when you are alone?

10. What are your favorite stories? What is it about these stories that make them your personal favorites?

appendix a

Seeking Help

■ WHY PEOPLE SEEK HELP

Every year, millions of Americans seek help with their personal problems. They buy books and magazines giving advice, make use of self-help groups, and consult a wide range of mental health professionals.

Why do people seek help? How do you know when getting help is necessary or appropriate? We suggest that there are four general reasons for seeking help:

1. You are troubled, but cannot identify the reason.
2. You think you know what your problem is but not how to solve it. You feel "stuck."
3. You know what your problem is, and even some ways in which it might be solved, but you cannot seem to carry out or stick to your own solutions.
4. You do not have a "problem" per se, but want to learn more about yourself, and about how to continue your personal growth process.

To help clarify each of these reasons for seeking help, here are four real-life examples.

1. *What's the matter with me?* Jennifer is frightened. She has been having strange experiences at night, usually as she is beginning to fall asleep or early in the morning. The first of these happened three years ago, when she awoke in her dorm room unable to move her body. She blinked her eyes to be sure that she was awake, because it was snowing in her room. She closed her eyes for awhile falling back into a dream, then awoke again to find that the snow had become deeper and was falling even harder. Still paralyzed, she fell back asleep and woke half an hour later to find everything back to normal. On two other occasions she has awakened, again completely unable to move, to find someone standing over her with a knife; once it was a person who had been dead for some time. At still other times she has awakened to find the entire room bathed in an eerie shade of pink or blue. Each time she has fallen back asleep and awakened in a normal state. On a few occasions during the day she has lost all control of herself and has fallen to the ground without warning, particularly when she has been feeling a strong emotion or has been laughing. Jennifer believes that she is going crazy.

2. *I don't know what to do.* Ken feels sad most of the time. He has a good job at a bank, is in good health, and has lots of friends. Still he can't seem to shake the feeling of being worthless and of his life being hopeless. Ever since his divorce, a year and a half ago, he has felt fatigued and anxious most of the time. Sometimes things have looked so dismal that he has thought about taking his own life. He's not sleeping well, either. He can never seem to get enough sleep, yet when he lies down in bed he finds thoughts racing through his head, keeping him awake. Since he rarely felt this way before or during his marriage, he is fairly sure that he's having trouble accepting his divorce and adjusting to it. When it comes to knowing what to do about it, however, he's at a complete loss. For quite a while he hung onto the hope that he and his ex-wife would be reconciled and reunited. Now she has remarried, and that hope is gone. Still, Ken goes on feeling down, day after day. "If I just knew what to do to get over this," he says, "I'd do it!"

3. *I can't seem to stick to it.* Marty knows that he drinks too much. He often wakes up with a hangover, and sometimes can't remember part of the night before. He doesn't think of himself as being an alcoholic, but he knows that his grades have suffered because of his drinking. In class he learned that the amount he drinks—about a six-pack a day, sometimes more—is enough to do

serious damage to his health and his brain. He has tried making resolutions to quit or cut down, but his social life is very tied up with drinking, and he finds himself bored or uncomfortable without alcohol. That, too, worries him. He knows that he needs to change his drinking, and deep down he wants to do it. So far, though, all of his efforts have failed. He just can't seem to stick to his resolutions.

4. *I want to know where I'm going.* Maria is fairly pleased with her life. Though she has some problems, none of them seem all that serious, and she feels like she can handle them. She is bothered, though, by a vague sense of emptiness, of something missing. She wonders if she knows who she really is, or if somehow she is missing her intended path in life. She feels happy and comfortable with her work, her friends, her family. Perhaps, she thinks, she is *too* comfortable. Does she have talents she should be developing in a different career direction? Is there something she should be *doing* with her life? In the midst of what seems a very fulfilling life, she is haunted by the question: "What does my life *mean?*"

Each of these four people came seeking professional help. They came for different reasons. Jennifer wanted desperately to find out what was happening to her, and what to do about it. (Incidentally, Jennifer's psychologist quickly identified that she was not crazy at all, but was suffering from symptoms of narcolepsy, a very treatable and reasonably harmless problem.) Ken understood that he was depressed and that it was tied somehow to his divorce, but he didn't have a clue as to how to escape from it. Marty recognized his problem and even knew what he needed to do about it, but sought help because he couldn't seem to stick to his plan. Maria was ready to take the next step in weaving her tapestry of meaning and was looking for some direction.

Just as there are many reasons for seeking help, there are many kinds of help available. We will begin with an examination of the kind of help that people most often choose: self-help.

■ SELF-HELP

In self-help approaches there is no formal outside "helper" who provides direction. Rather the person comes up with a helping strategy on her or his own and carries it out. One fascinating kind of research in psychology asks people how they have brought about change in themselves (Prochaska & DiClemente, 1983; Tough, 1982; Tuchfeld, 1981). The fact is that most people who change do so with no formal outside help whatsoever.

There are many kinds of self-help approaches. We can outline only a few of them here. One popular form, of course, is the self-help book. The shelves of any bookstore are stocked with dozens or even hundreds of volumes offering self-help advice. Although some self-help books have been demonstrated to be effective aids to self-change (Glasgow & Rosen, 1978), there is no quality-control process which guarantees that advice given in such books is either safe or effective (Rosen, 1976). Self-help materials are increasingly available in other forms such as audio- and videotapes and computer software. Though caution is wise, self-help resources may be useful in clarifying a problem area and in developing strategies for overcoming it.

Another time-honored self-help approach is the keeping of a personal journal or diary. In Chapter 5 we recommended self-monitoring of problem behaviors as a strategy for increasing awareness and self-control. More often, journal keeping has been used for personal reflection and exploration (Chapter 15). Jungian psychotherapist Ira Progoff (1975), for example, has developed an elaborate method for keeping a personal growth journal. Others use private meditation or prayer in a similar manner.

In many communities, a variety of courses and workshops are offered on themes related to self-help. Community colleges and continuing education centers often offer courses on assertiveness (Chapter 9), career development (Chapter 13), communication skills (Chapter 10), and addictive behaviors (Chapter 11). Local universities, hospitals, or professional groups may provide public workshops on topics such as coping with emotions, parenting skills, or divorce adjustment.

■ PARAPROFESSIONALS, PARTNERS, AND PEERS

There are many helpers besides those who are formally trained mental health professionals. Christensen and his colleagues (1978) have distinguished three different types of such helpers. (See Box 14.5 in Chapter 14.) *Paraprofessionals* are helpers who lack advanced professional degrees, but who have received specialized training in providing certain kinds of help. Like the more familiar "paramedic," they are competent to provide specific types of services, which should be offered under the supervision of a properly licensed or certified professional. Some clinics and colleges, for example, use paraprofessionals to offer low-cost services such as relaxation training, assertiveness or communication training, health education, or basic counseling and referral.

Many people turn for help or advice to members of their natural network of social support: their friends, family, or co-workers. Such support can have a stress-buffering or stress-reducing effect (Hunter & Riger, 1986). Christensen et al. (1978) refer to such untrained helpers as *partners.* Though not sharing the same immediate problem, these helping partners may be able to provide important support, advice, and perspectives. The Big Brother and Big Sister programs offered in many communities are another example of partners as helping agents.

Still another form of help with a long history is that of *peers* offering each other mutual aid. In this sense, peers are individuals who face similar problems, struggles, or challenges. Peer support groups have the potential to be powerful sources of help. A key benefit of discussing issues with others who are experiencing similar problems is the realization that you are not alone. By self-disclosure, mutually sharing what you are thinking and feeling with others, a sense of "universality" can develop (Yalom, 1975). Universality is the realization that you are not alone and that your problems are not unique; that others share your concerns.

Many self-help organizations are structured around the idea of peer counseling or mutual support among individuals facing similar problems. In many communities there are peer support programs for widows, parents without partners, people with terminal illnesses, the relatives of those who are severely ill, former mental patients, ex-prisoners, parents, children of alcoholics, and dozens of other groups. In the addictive behaviors (Chapter 11), peer self-help groups have a long tradition (Robinson, 1986). The most familiar of these are programs based on a set of principles known as the "Twelve Steps." Alcoholics Anonymous, Narcotics Anonymous, Overeaters Anonymous, Gamblers Anonymous, Al-Anon (for family and other loved ones of those suffering from addiction), and Emotions Anonymous are all Twelve Step programs. Membership in such organizations is free and open to anyone with a sincere desire to work on

A.1   THE TWELVE STEPS

The Twelve Steps have been described as principles, guidelines, or suggestions. They were first formulated by the two founders of Alcoholics Anonymous (1935) as steps for aiding their own recovery from alcoholism. Since then, the Twelve Steps have been studied and used by millions of members of self-help groups throughout the world. Though profoundly spiritual in tone, they are not tied to any particular religion, and the "God" to which they refer is very liberally interpreted as any "higher power" to which the individual can turn for help and guidance.

The Twelve Steps are slightly rephrased by each organization, depending upon the particular problem that unites its members. The following are the original Twelve Steps.

1. We admitted we were powerless over alcohol—that our lives had become unmanageable.
2. Came to believe that a Power greater than ourselves could restore us to sanity.
3. Made a decision to turn our will and our lives over to the care of God, as we understood Him.
4. Made a searching and fearless moral inventory of ourselves.
5. Admitted to God, to ourselves and to another human being the exact nature of our wrongs.
6. Were entirely ready to have God remove all these defects of character.
7. Humbly asked Him to remove our shortcomings.
8. Made a list of all persons we had harmed, and became willing to make amends to them all.
9. Made direct amends to such people whenever possible, except when to do so would injure them or others.
10. Continued to take personal inventory and when we were wrong, promptly admitted it.
11. Sought through prayer and meditation to improve our conscious contact with God, as we understood Him, praying only for knowledge of His will for us and the power to carry that out.
12. Having had a spiritual awakening as the result of these steps, we tried to carry this message to alcoholics, and to practice these principles in all our affairs.

The Twelve Steps reprinted with permission of Alcoholics Anonymous World Services, Inc.

their common problems. Members meet regularly, discussing the Twelve Steps and seeking to apply them to their own lives.

A remarkable nationwide network of peer support, known as Co-Counseling or Re-Evaluation Counseling, was founded by Harvey Jackins (1970). It is a form of peer counseling in which every participant regularly experiences being both "client" and "counselor" by taking turns in each role with a partner. First, a sixteen-week course teaches the basics. Students in a class for co-counseling pay a tuition fee, but thereafter, counsel with their classmates free. In co-counseling, students learn basic skills and rules for attending (looking at and listening to the client with a relaxed expression), discharge (physical release of emotional tension), and time limits (establishing length of turns and abiding by that time frame). The person in the counselor role does *not* give opinions, tell of similar problems, interpret, or give advice. The counselor role is defined as listener. The person in the client role is encouraged to give herself or himself credit and to develop "affirmations," positive self-statements that have personal meaning. If the person in the client role laughs or cries or shakes during her or his turn, it is considered discharge of physical or emotional tension, and the counselor lets the discharge happen with an attitude of interest and relaxed concern. In Re-Evaluation Counseling, emphasis is placed on carefully listening to each person's contribution, and validating her or his experience and options. Empathic listening to words and to nonverbal communication without interruption for the major portion of the client's turn is essential.

PROFESSIONAL HELP

Self-help groups and peer counseling can be very helpful, but they are not therapy. People with more serious psychological problems need the care of a professional.

Some people feel a stigma in seeking professional help. They may perceive it as an admission of personal weakness, or of being "sick" or "crazy." They may fear that if others find out, they will be judged as "maladjusted" and will be ridiculed or rejected. As discussed earlier, however, there are many reasons for seeking professional consultation. Psychology is increasingly recognized as a *health* profession, and therapy can be understood as pursuing many possible goals including prevention and personal growth as well as crisis intervention. Furthermore, there is nothing noble or admirable about avoiding proper health care, about trying to "tough out" a serious problem alone. Most people now recognize that it is foolish to avoid proper medical or dental care. The same is true when the problems being faced are psychological in nature.

FINDING PROFESSIONAL HELP

How does one locate a competent professional? One approach is to ask people you respect. You may ask for recommendations from a member of the clergy, your family physician, an attorney, or other professionals you know. Another approach is to call the office of your state psychological or medical association. Your community probably has a mental health clinic, and your campus may have a psychological clinic within the student health center. The academic department of psychology or psychiatry at your school might also supply you with a list of local or campus therapists. The dean of students at your college may have a referral list as well.

A somewhat more risky method is to consult the Yellow Pages of your telephone directory, which list therapists under various headings. To be listed under some of these headings (such as "Psychologists" or "Physicians"), a professional must be properly licensed or certified by the state. Other headings, however, are unrestricted. In some states, for example, *anyone* may advertise their services as a "counselor" or "therapist," regardless of their training and qualifications.

CHOOSING A THERAPIST

In choosing a therapist, it is important to find a good match, someone who seems right for you. If you spend a session with a therapist and leave feeling that you have not been listened to or understood, or if your values are at odds, perhaps you should try elsewhere.

It is your right to ask about the therapist's beliefs about treatment; for example, how long treatment can be expected to take, how much it will cost, and how he or she feels about values that are important to you. This is not to say that a therapist must share all your values, but if she or he views your basic values, religious beliefs, or sexual orientation as pathological, it may be best to find another therapist.

We are, in essence, recommending that you do some shopping before you decide on a therapist. This is much harder to do when you are feeling in crisis. That is one reason to establish a relationship with a therapist when you are feeling O.K., much as you might choose a family physician before you become ill. In this way, you are thinking preventively about your own mental health.

If you are in crisis, however, use crisis hotlines. They are usually listed inside the front cover of your telephone directory with names such as "crisis center," "rape crisis center," "center for victims of domestic violence," or "suicide prevention and crisis center." Call them if you need to, even if you feel embarrassed. It can be difficult to reach out for help, but it is well worth the risk.

How do you choose a therapist or a kind of therapy? There are at least five ways to choose, five factors to consider in making a decision. You may choose based on (1) therapeutic orientation, (2) qualifications, (3) contact, (4) your problem or concern, and (5) access. We will elaborate on these five criteria.

Therapeutic orientation means the professional's philosophy or basic views of therapy. In Chapter 1 we introduced four basic orientations: psychodynamic, behavioral, humanistic, and existential, although there are dozens of other specific therapeutic approaches. The therapist's orientation can influence in a major way the type of treatment you would receive. Some types of therapy are very *directive*, offering advice and giving homework assignments to do between sessions. Other therapies are more *nondirective*, allowing the client to explore his or her feelings freely with little or no guidance from the therapist. Therapeutic orientation often affects the *length* of treatment, with some favoring long courses of treatment while others emphasize brief consultation. It can also determine the mode of treatment, such as individual, couple, family, or group sessions.

Second, you may choose based on *qualifications* and training of the professional. Find out about her or his training and experience to do what you want her or him to do. A therapist should be properly *certified* or *licensed* by the state to practice her or his profession. If the person is not independently certified or licensed, find out who supervises his or her practice. If the practitioner gets no supervision, be skeptical. It is appropriate for you to ask about qualifications. If you get the impression that the therapist is offended by your questions, try someone else. It is here that different professions also become a consideration. *Clinical psychologists* (usually holding a Ph.D. degree) receive five or more years of graduate training focusing on principles of behavioral

A.2	HERE WE DIFFER/HERE WE AGREE How Useful Is Long-Term Therapy?

In this world of the quick fix, fast food, and high technology, I find myself very amused by those who promote "short-term" therapy as if it had just been invented. In fact, many old clinicians (in age and practice) like myself have been using brief therapy techniques for quite a while, whenever possible. Many people who come into therapy are suffering from a situational stress of some kind and use the therapist as an objective sounding board or problem solver. Once the crisis is past or a solution is found, these people happily leave therapy. These short-term therapy approaches seem to take care of many problems (though it is also true that people just change with time).

It also happens, however, that some people arrive in therapy because of a situational stress (such as a divorce) that turns out to be only a small part of a bigger, more generalized problem. These people are candidates for longer-term therapy. Why? The answer, in a somewhat oversimplified form, is that it has taken them years to get the way they are, and it is just plain unrealistic to think that six weeks of therapy will undo twenty years of life experiences. In fact, it is somewhat amazing to me that so much can be done in one or two *years* with some of these folks. (Even that would be called "short-term" therapy by some practitioners.) It is a testimony to the magnificent ability of the human brain to use language to accomplish genuinely impressive cognitive and mediational changes.

Some protest that long-term therapy isn't very cost-effective. One of the reasons why there isn't much worthwhile research demonstrating the efficacy of long-term therapy is that such research requires enormous amounts of time and money to conduct (in contrast, for example, to finding out how to help college students overcome snake phobias). It's very difficult to characterize and control the content of long-term therapy. There is also the important issue of what to measure, to decide whether change has occurred. Most of the measures used in treatment research, unfortunately, are either superficial or trivial (or both). Measuring true change is not easy. There just is no easy answer, no quick fix here either, since none of us know even the right questions to ask. How do you measure changes in the quality of life?

Don't get me wrong. Research can teach us a lot. We know from current research, for example, that both short- and long-term therapy reduce long-range medical costs. This is very measurable from hospital stays, physician visits, insurance claims, and the like. I'm just saying that capturing really significant personal change is difficult. And if you *could* measure change after short-term treatment, how would you ever know that it was due to the therapy, and not to different treatment the person received later, or to other life circumstances? —JMR

In any health care economy where it is profitable to provide treatment, there is a built-in temptation and tendency to give more treatment than is necessary. From a cost-effectiveness standpoint, the question is not whether long-term therapy helps, but rather how much is *enough*.

The fact is that many agencies and professionals offer unnecessarily lengthy, intensive, and expensive treatment. Dozens of well-controlled studies have compared the impact of longer with briefer treatment, or inpatient with outpatient care (e.g., Kiesler, 1982; Miller & Hester, 1986b). With impressive consistency, these studies have found no advantage for more extensive or intensive treatments. That is, the effectiveness of treatment is usually not increased by making it longer, more intensive, or more expensive. When differences in absolute impact have emerged, they have as often favored the less heroic intervention. In sum, there is, thus far, little persuasive scientific evidence that long-term therapy is superior overall to briefer interventions.

If one looks at *cost-effectiveness*, however, there are substantial differences. Inpatient hospital treatment of alcohol problems, for example, may cost ten times more than outpatient treatment. Although long-term and hospital-based treatments can be very profitable, there is thus far little basis for arguing that they are any more effective than briefer treatment.

I also view with some skepticism the argument that more expensive treatments produce a kind of "real change" that is lacking in other therapies, but that cannot be measured scientifically. Changes in many kinds of human problems can be measured with reasonable reliability. Although it can be expensive to conduct the research necessary to study the effectiveness of different approaches, it is far more expensive to go on offering costly unevaluated therapies.

I do not wish to argue that there is no place for long-term or hospital-based treatment. Likely there are certain types of problems or individuals who will benefit more from such treatment. Research thus far, however, suggests that we should proceed with caution. In an economy where health care costs are rising at an alarming rate, it is important to guard against the use of unnecessarily expensive approaches. If we fail to do so, the likely outcome will be further governmental regulation, which makes these treatments less available to all, including those who need them.

We should offer people who want help the very best that we have, in as cost-effective a way as possible, and then let them get on with their lives and their own natural change processes. We share the same concern—to help people overcome their obstacles and psychological problems. The question is: What are the most effective and cost-efficient ways of doing that?   —WRM

INTEGRATION

There are many types of therapy in this day and age. The right mode depends on the person, the problem, and the therapist. For some people, problems, and therapists, a relatively brief intervention will be sufficient. For others, a longer course of treatment is necessary. Debates in the abstract about the relative merits of longer versus shorter treatment are unlikely to yield definitive answers. Useful information is likely to emerge by asking *when* a longer or more intensive form of therapy is needed, for *whom*, offered in what kind of setting and by whom. In the interim, it seems prudent to begin with simpler and less expensive forms of treatment and reserve more extensive therapies for those who do not respond. Even here, the research question remains: Will longer treatment succeed where briefer therapy has failed? Research to answer such questions is indeed complex, but possible.

science, and learning various approaches to the psychological assessment and treatment of human problems. *Psychiatrists* are trained in general medicine (M.D. degree) and then specialize in the treatment of emotional problems. Because of their medical training, psychiatrists are permitted to prescribe medications and may be particularly helpful when physical health problems are involved. *Social workers*, *counselors*, and *psychiatric nurses* typically hold a masters degree in their respective fields and have been trained in counseling methods for helping people deal with life problems. Each profession is usually regulated by state laws, and the properly trained individual will be certified or licensed by the state in his or her chosen profession. Regardless of profession, however, the question of qualifications remains: What specific training, supervision, and experience has the person had that would prepare him or her to help with this particular problem?

Choosing based on personal *contact* is a third option, especially if you feel unable to choose based on orientation or qualifications. Simply make one appointment to meet the person and find out whether you can work together.

The particular *problem* or concern with which you want help is a fourth consideration, in that therapists often specialize or are particularly skilled in helping with particular problem areas. Certain problems limit the choice. For example, if your goal in entering therapy is to stop smoking, then your initial phone calls will be to professionals who specialize in smoking cessation. This consideration may be less definitive, however, when the issue is less clear-cut. If the problem area is not so clear ("I want to feel better"), it is often wise to consult first with a general counselor (at your student health center, for example), to clarify your goals and decide what might be most helpful.

A.3   ETHICAL PRINCIPLES OF PSYCHOLOGISTS

The American Psychological Association (APA) in 1981 adopted the following revised set of ethical standards for psychologists. These principles apply not only to psychologists, but also to students of psychology and to those who work under the supervision of psychologists. Acceptance of membership in the APA commits the psychologist to abide by this set of ethical principles. The preamble to the principles states that psychologists "are committed to increasing knowledge of human behavior and of people's understanding of themselves and others and to the utilization of such knowledge for the promotion of human welfare." Ten areas of ethical accountability are then outlined, based upon the "prime directive" of promoting human welfare. The following ethical principles are quoted directly from the 1981 statement of the American Psychological Association.

1. *Responsibility*. In providing services, psychologists maintain the highest standards of their profession. They accept responsibility for the consequences of their acts and make every effort to ensure that their services are used appropriately.

2. *Competence*. The maintenance of high standards of competence is a responsibility shared by all psychologists in the interest of the public and the profession as a whole. Psychologists recognize the boundaries of their competence and the limitations of their techniques. They only provide services and only use techniques for which they are qualified by training and experience. In those areas in which recognized standards do not yet exist, psychologists take whatever precautions are necessary to protect the welfare of their clients. They maintain knowledge of current scientific and professional information related to the services they render.

3. *Moral and legal standards*. Psychologists' moral and ethical standards of behavior are a personal matter to the same degree as they are for any other citizen, except as these may compromise the fulfillment of their professional responsibilities or reduce the public trust in psychology and psychologists. Regarding their own behavior, psychologists are sensitive to prevailing community standards and to the possible impact that conformity to or deviation from these standards may have upon the quality of their performance as psychologists. Psychologists are also aware of the possible impact of their public behavior upon the ability of colleagues to perform their professional duties.

4. *Public statements*. Public statements, announcements of services, advertising, and promotional activities of psychologists serve the purpose of helping the public make informed judgments and choices. Psychologists represent accurately and objectively their professional qualifications, affiliations, and functions, as well as those of the institutions or organizations with which they or the statements may be associated. In public statements providing psychological information or professional opinions or providing information about the availability of psychological products, publications, and services, psychologists base their statements on scientifically acceptable psychological findings and techniques with full recognition of the limits and uncertainties of such evidence.

5. *Confidentiality.* Psychologists have a primary obligation to respect the confidentiality of information obtained from persons in the course of their work as psychologists. They reveal such information to others only with the consent of the person or the person's legal representative, except in those unusual circumstances in which not to do so would result in clear danger to the person or to others. Where appropriate, psychologists inform their clients of the legal limits of confidentiality.

6. *Welfare of the consumer.* Psychologists respect the integrity and protect the welfare of the people and groups with whom they work. When conflicts of interest arise between clients and psychologists' employing institutions, psychologists clarify the nature and direction of their loyalties and responsibilities and keep all parties informed of their commitments. Psychologists fully inform consumers as to the purpose and nature of an evaluative, treatment, educational, or training procedure, and they freely acknowledge that clients, students, or participants in research have freedom of choice with regard to participation.

7. *Professional relationships.* Psychologists act with due regard for the needs, special competencies, and obligations of their colleagues in psychology and other professions. They respect the prerogatives and obligations of the institutions or organizations with which these other colleagues are associated.

8. *Assessment techniques.* In the development, publication, and utilization of psychological assessment techniques, psychologists make every effort to promote the welfare and best interests of the client. They guard against the misuse of assessment results. They respect the client's right to know the results, the interpretations made, and the bases for their conclusions and recommendations. Psychologists make every effort to maintain the security of tests and other assessment techniques within limits of legal mandates. They strive to ensure the appropriate use of assessment techniques by others.

9. *Research with human participants.* The decision to undertake research rests upon a considered judgment by the individual psychologist about how best to contribute to psychological science and human welfare. Having made the decision to conduct research, the psychologist considers alternative directions in which research energies and resources might be invested. On the basis of this consideration, the psychologist carries out the investigation with respect and concern for the dignity and welfare of the people who participate and with cognizance of federal and state regulations and professional standards governing the conduct of research with human participants.

10. *Care and use of animals.* An investigator of animal behavior strives to advance understanding of basic behavioral principles and/or to contribute to the improvement of human health and welfare. In seeking these ends, the investigator ensures the welfare of animals and treats them humanely. Laws and regulations notwithstanding, an animal's immediate protection depends upon the scientist's own conscience.

Reprinted with permission from "Ethical principles of psychologists," *American Psychologist, 36,* 1981, pp. 633–638.

Our fifth and final consideration in choosing a therapist has to do with *access.* Your campus or community may have limited resources from which to choose. Issues like location, confidentiality, and cost can limit your options. One couple was only willing to see a therapist in the evening, because the husband refused to take time off from work. Thus, their range of choices was limited to therapists who saw clients after five o'clock. Another woman had insurance that would pay only for sessions with a psychiatrist. Consequently her access to psychologists and counselors was limited. In asking about cost, find out whether there is a set charge per session, or whether fees are set on a "sliding scale" adjusted to ability to pay.

WHAT IS THERAPY ABOUT?

Therapy involves a special kind of relationship between two people. It is not a social relationship, in which the two people mutually chat about their lives. It is never a sexual relationship, regardless of the client's problem area. Rather it is a professional relationship in which you seek the consultation of a person with particular expertise. The nature of this relationship is carefully described in the code of ethics of the American Psychological Association, which defines the professional conduct of psychologists.

The exact content of therapy varies widely, but there are four stages that characterize most therapeutic consultation (Miller & Jackson, 1985). In the *clarification* phase, therapist and client begin to build their working therapeutic relationship, discuss the client's general life situation, and clarify the general goals of their work together. Not all therapy is directed toward change, for example. Sometimes the client is seeking help in making a choice or in sorting out a confusing life situation (Gilmore, 1973). In the *formulation* phase, the therapist helps the client to reach a basic understanding of the nature of the problem(s) or concern(s), and their possible causes. Some therapists draw up a formal written contract with their clients at this stage. In the *intervention* phase, which may be brief or prolonged, the client and therapist work together to discover and correct the causes of the client's problem(s) or concern(s). It is often useful, during this phase, to have an ongoing evaluation of progress. Finally, in the *termination* phase, they work toward an ending of the therapeutic relationship, preparing the client to continue the growth process on his or her own. This can include making plans for how to maintain or extend the gains that have been made during therapy. (Recognize the parallel to the natural stages of change, described in Chapter 5.) Sometimes arrangements are made for periodic follow-up visits. If satisfactory progress has not been made, this phase includes planning for referral, if desired, to another appropriate therapist.

■ SUMMARY

The potential sources of help for a psychological problem are many and varied, as are the reasons for seeking help. Many people accomplish significant change on their own, sometimes with the assistance of self-help resources such as books, workshops, classes, or journal keeping. Self-help groups and social support networks likewise have a long history. In choosing professional help, it is worthwhile to invest some time in exploring alternatives. The therapist's orientation and qualifications are important considerations. The possible choices may be narrowed somewhat by the particular problem for which help is being sought and by the accessibility of various forms of help. Personal contact with several possible helpers may be useful in finding a therapist with whom one can work comfortably and effectively. Therapy is a special kind of relationship in which one seeks professional consultation from a person with special qualifications to provide such help. A therapeutic relationship differs from other kinds of relationships, and is governed by a set of professional ethical standards.

appendix b

Learning to Relax

■ WHAT IS RELAXATION?

People have many different notions about relaxation. Some think of it as just doing nothing. Some associate it with a particular activity such as fishing, jogging, or talking with friends. For some, relaxation means comfort and competence in what one does—the ability to perform social or work tasks calmly and confidently.

People also vary in their attitudes about relaxation. Some wish they were more relaxed, more able to retain a peaceful serenity in their lives. Others view relaxation as wasteful, even sinful: to relax is to be lazy and unproductive.

There are also many ways in which people seek to relax. Some pursue relaxation by taking time out from ordinary activities for a nap, a break, a period of rest, meditation, a cup of coffee, or a vacation. Some seek relaxation through activities such as exercising, playing, or socializing. Some use alcohol, tobacco, or other drugs in an attempt to relax (Chapter 11), and physicians often prescribe medications such as muscle relaxants to help calm their patients.

Although "relaxation" can mean many things, we will use this term to refer to a relative *physiological state* that tends to be associated with subjective feelings of calm and well-being. This is a naturally occurring state, and one that a person can learn to induce and enhance in a variety of ways (Lichstein, 1988).

In Chapter 3 we discussed the autonomic nervous system (ANS) and its division into sympathetic and parasympathetic portions. Arousal of the sympathetic portion of the ANS produces physical changes in the body that are incompatible with relaxation: muscle tension, rapid heart rate, and rapid breathing. Parasympathetic arousal, by contrast, is associated with decreased heart rate, relaxed breathing, and decreased muscle tension. Research has also linked a variety of other physiological changes to the experience of relaxation. These include decreased blood pressure, lowered oxygen consumption, and changes in electrical activity patterns within the brain.

It is possible to induce such physiological changes through a variety of different, learnable approaches to relaxation (Benson & Klipper, 1975). These include progressive deep muscle relaxation, regulated breathing, meditation, self-talk, imagery methods, biofeedback, and self-hypnosis, all of which will be discussed briefly in this appendix. Other methods associated with physiological relaxation are the regular practice of zen, yoga, prayer, exercise, or massage.

■ PROGRESSIVE DEEP MUSCLE RELAXATION

The method most commonly used by psychologists for teaching relaxation is one that was introduced by Jacobson (1938). Called progressive deep muscle relaxation (PDMR) training, it involves a series of exercises designed to teach the person how to induce a physiological state of deep relaxation. Jacobson's original method was quite detailed and time consuming, requiring a period of months of instruction and practice. His methods have been adapted, however, into a much briefer form of PDMR that appears to be quite effective as a relaxation strategy (Rosen, 1977). This abbreviated PDMR is a common component in modern psychological treatment with both adults and children (Cautela & Groden, 1978).

The basic concept of the PDMR approach is that physiological relaxation (parasympathetic arousal) can be induced by relaxing the muscles. If one gains conscious control over the state of tension in one's muscles, then, it is possible to induce relaxation at will. Because muscular relaxation is incompatible with sympathetic ANS arousal, PDMR can be used to diminish anxiety states that are associated with sympathetic arousal. PDMR has also been found to be beneficial in decreasing tension headaches, overcoming insomnia and nightmares, and diminishing overall tension.

The method that Jacobson devised is based on a series of muscle tensing exercises. The idea is that by first tensing a muscle group, the person learns to feel where those muscles are and to recognize a state of tension in them. The tension is then released, and the person experiences the sensation of the muscle relaxing. Through repeated practice, Jacobson believed, the person could eventually learn how to cause the muscles to relax without having to go through the tensing-relaxing exercises.

Try this demonstration. Close your eyes (but read this paragraph first, of course!). Make a fist with your right hand and squeeze it tight. Feel the tension this creates, and notice in particular *where* the muscles are. You should be able to feel some tension in the muscles in your palm, your fingers, on the back of your hand, and up into your forearm. There is no need to tense so tightly that it hurts. Painful tensing will defeat the purpose of this exercise. Just tighten your fist enough to feel tension in your muscles. Hold the tension for about 10 seconds, then release it. Open your hand and fingers, and let the muscles relax. With your eyes still closed, study how the muscles feel as they change from tense to relaxed. Feel them release. After about 15 seconds, repeat the exercise by tensing your fist for about 10 seconds, then relaxing it. How do the muscles feel? Sensations of warmth, lightness, or heaviness are common.

This is the same procedure that is used with fifteen different muscle groups. The method is the same for each group. First tense the muscle group using the method described, hold and study the tension for about 10 seconds (but use your own pace), then let it go and study the muscles as they relax and change. Each muscle group is tightened and released twice, for emphasis.

To practice PDMR properly, you should find a quiet room with a comfortable place to sit. A recliner chair is perfect, but any surface that supports you firmly will do. Turn down the lights, sit back in the chair, close your eyes, and take a few slow, deep breaths. Then, one group at a time, progress slowly through the fifteen muscle groups. Box B.1 includes the groups and how to tighten them.

B.1   MUSCLE GROUP EXERCISES FOR PDMR

1. *Hands.* Tighten your right hand by making a fist and squeezing. Do this twice. Repeat with the left hand.

2. *Forearms and back of hands.* With your right arm resting on the chair and the back of your hand facing up, bend your hand at the wrist, pointing your fingers straight up. Study the tension this creates in the back of your hand and forearm. Repeat. Now do it with the left hand and arm.

3. *Biceps.* Flex the large muscles in your upper arm by trying to touch your right shoulder with your right fist, tightening the biceps. Repeat. Right arm first, then left.

4. *Shoulders.* Bring your shoulders up, as if to touch your ears with them. Repeat.

5. *Forehead.* Wrinkle up your forehead by bringing your eyebrows up as far as they will go. Repeat.

6. *Face.* Wrinkle your nose and close your eyes tightly. Repeat.

7. *Lips.* Press your lips tightly together. Repeat.

8. *Tongue.* Push your tongue into the roof of your mouth. Repeat.

9. *Neck.* Press your head against the back of the chair. Repeat.

10. *Chest.* Take a breath that is so deep you

can feel it stretch your chest muscles. Hold it. Release it slowly. Feel yourself relax as the air leaves your lungs. Repeat.

11. *Stomach.* Such in and tighten your abdomen, as though preparing to receive a punch in the stomach. Repeat.

12. *Back.* Arch your back away from the chair. Repeat.

13. *Legs and thighs.* Lift your legs up from the chair, holding them straight out in the air. Repeat.

14. *Calves.* Point your toes back toward your chest, creating tension in your lower legs. Repeat.

15. *Feet.* Curl your toes downward, as if digging them into sand. Feel the tension in your arches. Repeat.

Reprinted with permission. WR Miller & RF Muñoz (1982). *How To Control Your Drinking* (rev. ed.) (p. 86). Albuquerque: University of New Mexico Press.

After you have tensed and relaxed each of these muscle groups, with eyes still closed, notice how you feel. If you identify any particular muscles that still feel tense, find a way to tighten and then release them in the same manner. Remember never to create pain. The purpose is simply to teach you where the muscles are, and how they feel when they are tense and when they are relaxed.

This series of exercises, which normally requires twenty to forty minutes, is typically practiced at least three times a week (daily is better) for four to six weeks. Over this span of time, you may find that it becomes easier and easier to induce deep feelings of relaxation in your body. After four to six weeks of practice with the tensing-relaxing exercises, try inducing relaxation without first tensing the muscle groups. What seems to occur is learning how to release muscle tension without the exercises. The very skillful person who has practiced this method is able to release muscle tension throughout the body in a brief period of time.

When this level of skill has been achieved, PDMR can be used in a variety of ways. A short period of time can be set aside daily for relaxation, perhaps in the middle of the most hectic part of the day. It can be used at bedtime to facilitate sleep. Little reminders can be placed in the environment, to prompt you to check for muscle tension and to relax. A piece of tape on the face of your watch, or a colored dot on the speedometer or on the telephone, could serve as such reminders whenever you see them. PDMR can also be used as part of a program of systematic desensitization to overcome specific fears and anxieties (see Chapter 8).

■ REGULATED BREATHING

Patterns of breathing are closely associated with states of tension or relaxation. Many approaches to relaxation have used the conscious regulation of breathing as an aid. Tension is associated with rapid and shallow breathing. Relaxation, on the other hand, is promoted by deep, slow, calm breathing.

One simple demonstration of this is to close your eyes and take five deep breaths, inhaling, and exhaling at a slow and calm pace. What changes do you experience in your body? Maintaining this pattern of deep, slow, relaxed breathing can in itself have a calming effect.

A related pattern has been called deep sleep breathing. As the name suggests, this method simulates a pattern of breathing that is associated with deep sleep. Tension is associated with inhaling and holding the breath. (This, in fact, is one of the exercises used for tensing in PDMR.) In deep sleep breathing, you draw a deep breath and then release it with no pause between inhaling and exhaling. The pause comes after exhaling. Wait for your body to decide when to draw the next breath. Make no attempt to "wait as long as possible," because this can actually increase tension. Instead just exhale and then experience the natural pause between breaths. Your body will decide when to inhale. Some people experience this pattern of breathing as very restful and calming. It can be used in combination with other relaxation methods.

Patterned breathing can be used to accentuate other methods of relaxation. Breathing can, for example, be used in combination with the PDMR method by inhaling during muscle tensing, then exhaling at the point where muscle tension is released. Deep sleep breathing may amplify the relaxing effects of meditation.

■ MEDITATION

Drawing from teachings and research on transcendental meditation, Benson described a meditative technique which he termed "the relaxation response" (Benson & Klipper, 1975). He conceptualized the relaxation response as a naturally occurring altered state of consciousness, which can be induced through the practice of a relatively simple method. The four essential elements of this method, as described by Benson, are

1. *Find a quiet place.* Remove as many external sources of noise and distraction as possible (e.g., unplug the telephone).
2. *Find a comfortable position.* Choose a position that minimizes muscle tension and that you can maintain comfortably for at least twenty minutes without moving. The position should also be one that does not favor going to sleep. For this reason, lying down is not recommended.
3. *Choose something upon which to focus your attention.* In transcendental meditation this is a particular sound or *mantra*, such as the sound "om" or the word "one," which is chanted first aloud, then silently. It is also possible to fix attention by gazing at a particular object: a candle, a mountain, a symbol, a blank wall.
4. *Maintain a passive attitude.* Benson emphasizes this as the most crucial element of the relaxation response. Thoughts, memories, feelings, or images may drift into awareness, but they are not focused upon. Rather they are allowed to flow into and out of consciousness with no attempt either to hold them or to keep them out. Returning to a chanted mantra or another point of fixation may help to decrease focus on other elements of consciousness. Do not attempt to prevent thoughts from occurring, for this guarantees that they will occur. Do not evaluate yourself ("How well am I meditating?"). Rather maintain a *passive* attitude, fixing your attention on the sound or object you have chosen.

This approach to meditation is distinctly different from contemplation or reflection, in which the person focuses upon a certain thought, reading, or idea to discern its meaning. Rather this type of meditation seeks to *empty* consciousness. Contemplative and reflective forms of meditation can also be calming, however, and are preferred by some.

■ SELF-TALK

Throughout this book we have discussed the importance of self-talk in adjustment. The thought (T) element of the STORC approach also applies in learning relaxation. Simple self-instructions during the day ("Slow down, relax your muscles") can help to promote a calmer life-style. Identification and restructuring of anxiety-provoking thoughts (see Chapters 6 and 8) can help to eliminate a significant source of tension. A cognitive cue, such as the word "calm," can be repeated silently during relaxation practice, then used later to recapture feelings of relaxation. The point is that both tension and relaxation are influenced by self-talk.

■ IMAGERY METHODS

Another approach to relaxation involves the use of mental imagery. Proponents of *autogenic training,* for example, have employed a series of images that induce feelings of warmth or heaviness in the muscles (Luthe & Schultz, 1969). The arms might be imagined as two heavy sacks of flour. The hands might be warmed by imagining them immersed in warm water or sunshine.

Imagination of favorite places can also be used to aid in relaxation. Following PDMR, for example, it can be very enjoyable to rest for a period of time, experiencing deep relaxation, while imagining being in a special place. It might be an ocean beach, a forest, a mountaintop, the home of a friend or family member, a river bank, or a favorite city.

Through imagination it is also possible to enjoy fantasy experiences that are creative and calming. It is possible to float weightlessly on a cloud, visit a mountain treasure cave, explore underwater reefs, or fly as a seagull over the ocean.

■ SELF-HYPNOSIS

Many people think of hypnosis as losing control, as coming under the irresistible power of another person through a mysterious sleeplike trance. In fact, research suggests that hypnosis is nothing of the kind. Rather hypnotic "trance" is a wide-awake, voluntary, and natural altered state of consciousness, the achievement of which requires some skill and practice (Barber, 1969). In this sense, all hypnosis is self-hypnosis, even when it occurs with the assistance of instructions from a skilled helper.

In many ways, self-hypnosis is closely related to the process of meditation described earlier. It involves a focusing of attention, with a minimization of internal and external distractions. In self-hypnosis there is no loss of memory, and no loss of control. Instead self-hypnosis involves the skill of focusing one's attention and concentration.

A light and usually relaxing state of hypnosis can often be achieved by a few simple procedures. (If you find the experience at all frightening, don't use it. There are many other ways to relax.) Find a quiet room without external distractions, and assume a comfortable posture. Pick a spot upon which to focus your eyes. It might be a small mark on the wall, a corner where the ceiling meets two walls, a candle flame, almost anything. Stare intently at the spot while breathing deeply and calmly. As your eyes tire of holding this focus, allow your eyelids to close slowly. Continue breathing in a relaxed manner. Then imagine yourself at the top of a long staircase. The staircase has a banister, and the steps are very easy to descend. The staircase also curves slightly as you descend. Imagine yourself walking down the staircase slowly, step by step, and as you descend count backward from 40 to zero. Each step is one count, and when you reach zero you will be at the bottom.

This simple self-hypnosis procedure helps some people to feel very relaxed and peaceful. After reaching the bottom of the staircase, you may wish to use imagery just described to spend time in a favorite place or to explore a fantasy. Alternatively, you may simply use the "passive attitude" of meditation, enjoying the deeply restful state, or engage in prayer or contemplation. There is no danger of "getting stuck" in such a state. Even if you fall asleep, you will wake normally.

Neither is there any magic to "coming out" of a relaxed hypnotic state. Since you are never out of control, you merely decide to return your awareness back to your normal state. Some people like to reverse the process, counting forward from 1 to 10. Some give themselves a positive suggestion through self-talk such as, "Now I'm going to return my awareness to the room, and when I open my eyes I will feel relaxed, peaceful, and alert. I will keep this deep feeling of calm with me."

■ BIOFEEDBACK

One final approach to relaxation that is worth mentioning here is *biofeedback*. This involves the use of a monitoring device, usually an electronic instrument, which provides information (feedback) about one's physiological state. An electromyographic (EMG) monitoring device, for example, gives information about the state of tension in a muscle. Monitoring electrodes are placed on the skin above the muscle, and the instrument reads the tension level. An EMG biofeedback device then translates this information into a signal, such as a musical tone. As the muscle becomes more tense, the tone goes up in pitch, and as muscle tension decreases, the tone goes down in pitch.

Biofeedback, then, provides the person with information that is not ordinarily available to him or her, at least not in such a direct and immediate form. Research with biofeedback clearly indicates that most people, provided with this information, can gain conscious control over the state of tension in particular muscles. One commonly used muscle is located in the center of the forehead, where anxious tension is often reflected. When electrodes are placed on this muscle and feedback is provided, it is usually possible to relax (or tense, of course) the forehead. Decreased tension of the forehead has been reported to bring about a more generalized state of relaxation.

Muscle tension is not the only dimension that can be used in biofeedback. Another example is finger temperature. Tension and anxiety are often associated with cold hands, because of the effects of sympathtic arousal on the distribution of blood supply within the body. A finger temperature biofeedback device gives sensitive and immediate feedback about changes in warmth of the fingers. As temperature rises in the fingertips, the pitch of a musical tone may drop, for example. Given such feedback, many people are able to raise the temperature in their fingers. In addition to its relaxing effects, such biofeedback has also been found to be helpful in treating a variety of medical complaints, including migraine headaches and Raynaud's disease, a condition of painful coldness in the extremities.

■ THE CHOICE IS YOURS

No method of relaxation works for everybody. The methods we have outlined here are provided only as examples of approaches that have been found to be effective. Some people like the physical relaxation induced by PDMR, while others prefer the emptying of consciousness found through meditation. Imagery is a rich source for some, while others find it difficult to use and enjoy. If one method doesn't work for you, don't conclude that there is something wrong with you, or that you are "unable to relax." Rather try other approaches until you find one that is right for you.

appendix c

A Guide to More Effective Studying

■ A GUIDE TO MORE EFFECTIVE STUDYING

It happens every semester. Into our offices come a succession of students, one by one, saying things such as

"I really thought that I understood what I'd read, but I completely blew it on the last test. Tell me what I should do to study better."

"This course is really interesting to me, but it seems like I just can't learn the material."

"I can't seem to figure out what's going to be on the tests. I study hard, but when I get in there and look at the questions, it's like I've never seen the material before."

"I've been out of school for ten years, and I don't think I know how to study anymore. The other people in my classes seem to be keeping up, but I'm really out of practice."

"I can't believe the stupid mistakes that I made on the last test. I just get so nervous that I can't show you what I know."

All these students have the same sincere question: "What can I do?" We, like most educators, genuinely want to help. There *are* things that you can do to study more effectively, and these skills can be *learned*. Yet it takes time, often more time and attention than we can offer to so many individuals.

That's one reason why we have added this appendix on study skills. Worries and problems with studying are *very* common, though most students who come to us have the mistaken belief that their difficulties are unusual. We will explain some of the basic principles of effective studying, which can be applied successfully in your own study habits. In addition to applying the advice that we provide here, you probably have access to some helpful people on campus. Many professors are willing to take the time to help you improve your study skills. Special tutoring programs are often available. Many campuses have a special study skills center, office, or counselor to help students work on their study habits. If you are unsure of the resources available on your own campus, check with the office of the Dean of Students.

Most of the methods that we will discuss here are not new. They have been around for quite awhile, and have been tested in educational research. In one study, for example, Beneke and Harris (1972) evaluated the effectiveness of a study skills program consisting of many of the methods we will discuss here. Students who participated in the program *increased* their grade point average (GPA) by almost a full letter grade (from 2.5 to 3.4 on a 4.0-point scale) during the three semesters after they completed the program. In contrast, the GPA of students who did not participate in the program went *down* during the same three semesters. Students in another study reported greater efficiency in the use of their study time (Harris & Trujillo, 1975). There's a lot you can do to improve your own effectiveness in studying!

■ MOTIVATION

How much do you *want* to improve your study habits? It takes time and effort to learn how to study better. To study more effectively, you may have to give up some time that you are now spending on other things. The rewards for learn-

We wish to express our appreciation to Professor Mary B. Harris for providing us with training materials used in her research on study skills and for her feedback on this appendix.

ing how to study are *delayed*—they come much later, after you reap the benefits of a stronger education. The rewards for some of the things that can compete with studying (spending time with friends, relaxing, going out) can be much more immediate.

We recommend, therefore, that you take a few minutes to build your commitment to more effective studying. On a sheet of paper, make two lists. First, list for yourself the reasons why it is important for you to learn more effective study skills. What will be the short-term and long-term benefits to you of developing better study habits? When you have finished that, make a second list of the unpleasant things that happen when you don't study effectively. What are the short-term and long-term costs of *not* studying effectively?

■ WHAT'S THE PROBLEM?

People can have difficulty with studying and exams for a wide variety of reasons. A first step is to determine just where your present weaknesses lie and what new skills you need most. Having done this, you are in a better position to figure out what to do about them.

Box C.1 lists some of the most common problems that people have in relation to studying and exams. On each item, rate yourself on the scale from 1 (big problem) to 7 (no problem). The rest of this appendix is arranged to address each of the problems on this list. If one of the items is no problem for you, perhaps you will want to skip over that section in this appendix and focus on the sections dealing with items that are more problematic for you.

C.1	DIFFERENT TYPES OF STUDY PROBLEMS

An important first step in improving your study skills is to determine where the problem is. For each item in the following list, rate yourself on this seven-point scale:

1	2	3	4	5	6	7
BIG PROBLEM		NEED SOME IMPROVEMENT				NO PROBLEM

_____ 1. I don't take enough *time* for studying. I spend too much time doing other things and not enough time studying.

_____ 2. I don't take very good notes in class, and so when I study, my notes don't help me much.

_____ 3. I spend enough time in preparation, but I am not studying very well. I don't know how or what to study, and so I am not learning the material well enough.

_____ 4. I think I am learning the material when I study, but when I go in to take an examination I get so anxious that I freeze up and don't do well.

1. STUDY TIME

The first problem raised in Box C.1 is insufficient *time* devoted to studying. Good studying requires the devotion of significant amounts of time. One estimate is that you should study about two hours outside of class for every hour you are in class. If you are enrolled for twelve hours per week, then, you should be spending an additional twenty-four hours outside of classtime studying for these courses. Naturally, this is an average. Some classes require more time, some less. The point is that you have to *take* the time to study properly.

Here are some tips for increasing your study time. Regard this as a menu of possibilities, from which you can choose the strategies that are most effective and appropriate for you.

Self-monitoring.   Often it is helpful just to keep track of a behavior that you want to change. In Chapter 5 we called this self-monitoring. Start keeping track of the amount of time that you spend studying. If you are so inclined, make a daily chart or graph of the number of minutes you have spent studying. This will give you clear awareness of the amount of time you are devoting and also will serve as a record of your progress as you increase your study time.

Scheduling.   A simple approach is to set aside a regular block of time every day for studying. *Regular* study is likely to be much more effective in promoting long-term learning than is last-minute cramming. You may be aware that there are certain hours of the day that are your optimal study time, when you do your best studying and concentrating. Set these aside for studying, and avoid interruptions of that schedule. If you find it difficult to squeeze in study time because of a very full schedule, consider applying some of the time management strategies discussed in Chapter 13.

Reinforcement.   Behaviors that are followed by positive reinforcement are strengthened (Chapter 1). One way to increase study behavior, then, is to arrange for it to result in positive reinforcement. A simple application of this idea is that if you have two things to do, studying and something else that you would rather do, study *first* and then use the "something else" as a reinforcer for having studied. The arrangement is that you get to do the "something else" *only* if and when you have completed a certain amount of study time.

This implies that you should have a clear *goal* for the amount of study time you want to spend each day. As discussed in Chapter 5, two key ingredients for change are having a goal and having feedback of your progress toward that goal. The feedback can be provided by self-monitoring. The goal, however, is something you have to set. From your own experience, you may know the amount of time you can spend concentrating and studying effectively. Rather than forcing yourself to exceed this practical limit, it may be better to study in chunks of time about this size, taking small reinforcement breaks in between. If, for example, you can study very well for about thirty minutes but then your attention starts to wander, set a goal of working for thirty minutes before a break. When you have finished thirty minutes of study, take that break. (You may want to set a time limit on the break, too, so that you come back to studying as needed.) Your total study plan for a particular day might consist of four thirty-minute chunks. After you have completed those four chunks, you then can do the "something else" that you had planned as a reinforcer for meeting your goal. It may be helpful to draw up a clear contract for yourself, with explicit goals and plans for reinforcement (see Chapter 5).

You may find, too, that you can increase your "study tolerance" by gradually lengthening the chunks of time you spend studying. You may start out with twenty-minute chunks and gradually add five-minute segments to each chunk: 25, 30, 35, 40, and so on. You can experiment with this approach to determine how far you can expand your ability to do concentrated study in larger chunks. People differ widely in their ability to work for longer periods of time without a break, but it is also possible to increase your concentration tolerance. On the other hand, there's nothing wrong with studying in twenty-minute chunks if that is most effective for you.

Your Study Environment.   Some environmental planning can also be very helpful in making the most of your study time. The basic goal is to remove all the barriers to effective study. Find a place that is quiet and well lighted, and where distractions are minimal. If your own living space doesn't work, consider alternatives such as the library or an unused classroom. Your study place should be comfortable, though not so comfortable as to encourage sleeping. Sitting upright is a good protection against nodding off.

To enhance concentration, don't do anything in combination with studying. Don't listen to music, watch television, or eat while studying. Focus all your attention on the material to be learned. It is also wise to keep your study place as "pure" as possible. Designate a particular place to study, and don't do anything else there. That is your place to *study*. This helps you to connect this particular place with studying, minimizing other distracting associations. Remove as many barriers to studying as you can. Turn your study time into high-quality concentration time and save all other activities (including daydreaming) for other times and places.

2. EFFECTIVE NOTE TAKING

In most classes, taking good notes is a very important preparation for studying. A good set of notes allows you to recall and integrate the key information covered in class.

There are two opposite kinds of mistakes that students often make in note taking. One is to try to write down everything that the instructor says, like a human tape recorder. This seems more complete, but is immensely inefficient, and often interferes with your ability to hear and understand the material even the first time. The opposite mistake is to take very few, sparse notes. This allows more attention and participation in class, but often when it comes time to study your notes, it is difficult to remember what was presented. The best method for note taking is a compromise between these two extremes.

Capturing Organization.   A first key is to capture in your notes the instructor's *organization* of the material. A good set of notes looks like an *outline* of what the instructor taught. It distinguishes among the *main* points, minor subpoints, and examples. If you attempt to write down a lecture word for word, you are likely to miss the organization of the lecture. As a result, your notes will be a confusing mass of details and information, with no structure to help you organize and understand the material.

Often you can find clues as to the organization of a lecture in what the instructor says. A professor might say, for example, "There are four main reasons why this is so . . . ." This suggests that he or she is going to give a list of four subpoints in support of a major point that is being discussed. A lecturer's language may also indicate transitions from one topic to the next: "Now, the next point to consider is . . . ." An organized teacher will start off a lecture by describing the topic of the presentation, perhaps even with an overview of the main points to be covered. Some provide a written outline of the material to be covered, either in a handout or on the blackboard. Looking for clues such as these can help you to see the organization of the lecture.

If you find that you have difficulty detecting the outline of a lecture as you hear it, you have several options. One is to sit down soon after the lecture and reorganize your notes (see the upcoming discussion). A second, more time-consuming approach is to tape record the lecture and listen to it again for organization. A third option is to discuss the lecture with other students in the class, seeking the main points and organization. Still another possibility is to sit down with your professor and ask him or her to help you organize one day's notes into an outline.

Detecting the Main Points.

A key skill in finding the organization within a lecture is that of recognizing the main points and discriminating them from minor points, examples, and other less important remarks. Often within the lecture there are many clues as to which points are most important. The instructor may repeat a major point for emphasis or come back to it during a summary. There may be a direct indication such as, "The important thing to remember is that . . . ." Sometimes clues can be obtained from the instructor's tone of voice, placing stronger emphasis on key words or points. Professors may pause or slow down their pace when making major points.

You may also be able to detect major points by hearing a series of minor points. An instructor may give a series of reasons, examples, or explanations for an important point. When hearing such a series, ask yourself what major point these subpoints are intended to clarify. If it is not clear, don't be afraid to ask the instructor to explain how the points fit together. If it is unclear to you, it is very likely that other students are uncertain as well.

Whenever you hear a *main* point, write it down and mark it to indicate that it is an important point, perhaps with an asterisk (*). Don't try to write down everything said *about* the main point, but do record an example or important subpoints (as when a list of four is given).

Practical Tips.

Although the spiral-bound notebook is popular for note taking, some students find a loose-leaf three-ring binder to be more flexible and practical. Pages can then be reorganized or rewritten, and it is possible to take only a few sheets of notepaper to class rather than an entire notebook. Pencil or erasable pen is usually more practical than permanent ink in note taking.

Many students find it helpful to work out their own system for abbreviation and shorthand. Common terms within a field often have standard abbreviations (such as "S" for stimulus and "R" for response). Longer and frequently used words can often be shortened (for example, "pgy" for psychology or "psa" for psychoanalysis). If you use shorthand of this kind, keep a list of your abbreviations and their meanings handy inside the cover of your notebook. If, on rereading your notes, you find it confusing to encounter the abbreviations, it is wise to rewrite your notes after class without the shorthand.

Review Your Notes.

Another major mistake that students often make is to "turn the page" on their classroom notes, never reviewing them until just before a test. By that time you may have forgotten what many of your notes mean. For this reason, it is wise to spend some of your regular daily study time to review and perhaps rewrite your notes from the day. Rewriting and reorganizing may be particularly important if the class is taught by an instructor who is somewhat disorganized in his or her own presentation style.

First, give your notes for the day a "once over," reading them through quickly. Imagine that you are studying for an examination and you want to figure out what is important to know. Make sure you have written enough so that you could understand each major point later. Add more explanation or examples where your notes seem too brief. If your notes seem disorganized, rewrite them in an organized outline form.

When you have finished this step, close your notebook and see how many of the main points you can remember. Then reopen your notes and refresh your memory. Place a blank piece of paper over your notes, and slide it down each page, revealing one major point at a time. For each major point, see if you can give a good explanation of the point, remember subpoints, and give at least one example.

About a week later, review your notes again. This repeated review is a good way to learn material, and almost always works better than trying to cram it all into your head at the last minute.

3. A METHOD FOR EFFECTIVE STUDYING

Some students find that they take careful notes, read their assignments, and commit an adequate amount of time to studying, yet still aren't learning the material. They complain that there is such a large amount of information that they can't memorize it all or can't figure out what is important to know.

The fact is that memorization is a very *inefficient* way to study. The student who relies on this method tries to remember *everything*, because it might be on an exam. In a more challenging course, this strategy will prove very taxing and frustrating. Although memorization may work reasonably well during elementary and high school years, it is usually a disastrously inadequate way to approach learning in college.

One reason is that in many modern fields it is *impossible* to memorize everything. The volume of information is simply too large, and memorization results in a confusing mass of knowledge with few or no organizing guides. It would be like a university library card catalog that had cards for every book, but no system for filing them. The result would be mountains of accurate but useless information.

Another reason why memorization is inadequate in college is that new knowledge appears at an incredibly rapid rate in many fields. The student of medicine or psychology who simply memorizes material during his or her training will be outdated five years after graduation. Most professionals are responsible to keep up with new knowledge in their fields, and this cannot be accomplished with memorization.

The alternative to rote memorization is *learning how to learn*. To be sure, memory plays a very important role in learning. Without memory, there is no learning! We are saying, however, that learning at the university level involves much more than memorization. It requires some study and learning skills that you may not have developed before college.

Fortunately, psychologists have been working on this problem for a long time. A very good method, which was developed in the 1940s by Dr. Frances Robinson, has stood the test of time and has been shown to be effective in improving students' study habits. It was this method that was used in the research mentioned earlier (Beneke & Harris, 1972), where students increased their GPA by nearly a full letter grade. The method is called "SQ3R" (Robinson, 1970).

The name SQ3R, though it sounds like a futuristic robot, is designed to help you remember the five steps involved, which start with the letters S-Q-R-R-R. The steps are Surveying, Questioning, Reading, Reciting, and Reviewing. These steps are intended to be used as you approach new material to be learned, as when you study a textbook chapter.

Surveying.   Many students, when they open a new chapter, just plunge in and start reading paragraph after paragraph. This is an appropriate approach to a story or a novel, but it is not the best way to study college material. Instead you should start by getting the big picture, by understanding how the material you are going to study is organized.

The writers of textbooks usually take great care to organize their material clearly. In each of the chapters of this text, we have provided major headings and subheadings to describe and organize the material to be covered. Take a moment to glance back at Chapter 1, for example. The major heading, "Adjustment: Four Alternative Views" has four subheadings describing each of the alternatives: "Homeostasis," "Growth," "Learning," and "Choice." These are followed by an "Integration" subheading that suggests that we will attempt to put the four models together. Then comes another major heading, "Adjustment to What? Constructing Reality." This is followed by the major heading, "Personality Theories: How Psychologists Construct Reality," with the subheads "Some Limitations of Personality Theory" and "Four Major Personality Theories," announcing discussions of the psychodynamic, behavioral, humanistic, and existential approaches to personality. These four approaches correspond directly to the four alternative views of adjustment, presented earlier. The final major heading "Toward Self-understanding and Change" announces a major theme of this book, the psychology of change, and contains four subheadings that are key elements of change: "Awareness," "Acceptance," "Alternatives," and "Access." A summary concludes the chapter.

The purpose of surveying, the first step in SQ3R, is to gain an overview of what will be covered. This is accomplished by reading the major headings and subheadings of the chapter, as well as the chapter summary. This takes only a couple of minutes, but prepares you to receive and organize the material you will read. The main purpose of studying is not to memorize the contents of the chapter, but rather to understand how the material is organized and what the *main* points are. Surveying gives you a framework into which you can fit the points to be learned.

Suppose we were to begin handing you index cards, one at a time, with one word written on each card. Your instruction is to *organize* the cards. The first ten cards are EGG, GIRAFFE, CHEVROLET, NIXON, LIGHTBULB, PENCIL, NICARAGUA, PHYSICS, MARS, and CANDLE. We neglected, however, to tell you just *how* you are to organize the cards. You could go on receiving hundreds of cards, trying to figure out a good system for organizing them into categories. You might, for example, start off with categories for living and inanimate objects. Yet some objects are hard to classify clearly on this system (egg), and others are not objects at all (physics, Nicaragua). How many categories should there be? What are the really important dimensions on which to classify? Five hundred cards later you might have a system worked out, after several reorganizations. It is then that we tell you, "Oh! We wanted them in *alphabetical* order!"

It is best to get the lay of the land, to survey, before you start drawing a map. It is much easier to learn and handle *organized* information than masses of unorganized material.

Questioning.   You may be impatient to start reading, but there is a second important preparatory step: Q, Questioning. The trick here is to turn each major heading into one or more questions. The idea is to arouse your curiosity and to prepare you further to receive the information.

Again, from our Chapter 1, the chapter title might suggest the question, "What Is Adjustment?" Other major chapter headings could prompt these questions: "What *are* the four alternative ways to think about adjustment?" "To *what* do people adjust?" "How *do* psychologists view reality?" "What *are* the limitations of personality theory?" "What *are* four major personality theories?" "How *do* people change and develop self-understanding?"

This *questioning* stage helps to make you a more active participant in the learning process, rather than a passive reader. You develop questions to which you want answers. That is perhaps the best reason for learning!

Reading.   Now you are ready to start reading. You do so, however, with a specific purpose: to answer the questions that you formulated. Avoid the temptation just to plod along, waiting to reach the last assigned page. Instead, remember the organization that you discovered while surveying, and look for answers to the questions you are asking. As you reach each new major heading, renew your questions. What do you want to know from this section? Remember that your goal is *to learn*. Turn every heading into a question to be answered, before you begin reading the section underneath it. Try it!

You can even practice this method on other kinds of reading that you do. The headlines of newspapers are usually written to raise a question in the mind of the reader, enticing her or him to read the article underneath. Try the SQ steps before you read a magazine article, fliers you receive in the mail, even the back of a cereal box!

Reciting.   It is a very basic principle of memory: we remember best that which we rehearse. The song or poem heard once is quickly forgotten. The song or poem recited over and over may stay in memory for decades. Reading is *not* enough.

The word that Dr. Robinson used in her original method was "Recite." This is best done at the end of each section read. The basic method is to take notes on what you have just read, much as you might take notes on a lecture. Remember that what you should write down are the *main* points. A good way to do this is to record answers to the questions you raised by looking at the section headings. Write your answer in *outline* form, with the major point on the left margin, subpoints indented, and a few words or phrases under those, as needed.

It is best to do this from *memory*, to help fix the main points in your mind. Close the book, and make notes in your own words. Don't peek! Then check your notes against the book to see if you left out any important points.

Some students like to underline points in their textbook, either in pencil or with a colored transparent marker. We believe that the Reciting method is a much better approach to remembering key points, since it requires that you actively rehearse the information instead of passively underlining it. Students also tend to underline too much material in their books. If you do use underlining, practice restraint and underline only the major, most important points. Then use the Reciting method to reproduce the ideas in your own words.

Reviewing.   When you have finished a chapter or article using the first four steps of SQ3R, you will have a set of notes in your own words outlining the main points. Now it is time for a *review*. The method is the same as we discussed earlier for reviewing lecture notes. Cover up your notes and see how many of the major points you can recall. Then slide a blank piece of paper over each page of notes and pull it down to reveal the major points one at a time. For each point, try to recall the important subpoints. Pay attention to any new terms and their meaning. In the space of five minutes or so, you can have reviewed the entire chapter without having to reread it.

About a week later, repeat your review of your notes. First, see how many major points you can recall; then for each point as you uncover it, try to remember the important subpoints. Several brief periodic reviews of material will help more than one long cramming session just before an exam. When you review, keep it brief. Going longer than an hour is pushing the limit of useful review.

SQ3R with Friends.   It can be fun and very helpful to do portions of your studying with other people in your class. The Reciting and Reviewing steps in particular can be done well in a study group. Tell each other what you believe were the main points of the material studied. Ask each other questions about the material. Imagine that you were the instructor and had to write exam questions on this material. What questions would you write? How would you answer them?

4. TAKING EXAMINATIONS

Some students study well and know the material, but do poorly on some or all types of examinations. The term "test anxiety" has been used to describe this kind of difficulty. In fact, there can be a number of reasons for poor test performance despite conscientious studying. Lumping all these together as "test anxiety" can be misleading, since not all these problems involve anxiety. Likewise, as discussed in Chapter 8, anxiety itself is a very complicated phenomenon and is a term that covers a variety of different kinds of problems.

Anxiety, in the sense of arousal of the autonomic nervous system (see Chapter 3), is very common during exams. It is normal to feel somewhat anxious when being tested, and in fact a certain amount of arousal can improve test performance. Truly excessive arousal, however, can interfere with the person's ability to concentrate, recall, think, and answer questions. When excessive autonomic arousal is the problem, a variety of solutions can be effective. It can be useful to develop skills in physical relaxation or to use systematic desensitization to defuse fears of evaluation (Chapter 8). Certain medications can help temporarily to suppress arousal without interfering with performance. Be cautious using any medications, however, and consult with a physician. Your student health center may be able to help you consider a variety of solutions to excessive arousal during tests.

Concentration is a more common problem in test taking. As discussed in Chapter 8, "test-anxious" students are usually not more physically aroused than other students (Wine, 1971). Instead, they focus their attention differently. While most students are concentrating on answering the questions, test-anxious students are wasting time focusing on worries and self-defeating thoughts. The same appears to be true of math-anxious students (Tobias, 1978). A solution to this problem involves practice in stopping these irrelevant thoughts and immediately focusing attention back on the test (see Chapter 8).

Often, too, "test anxiety" involves a lack of important skills needed for studying and test taking. That is, the student is anxious with good reason: he or she has not learned how to study or to take tests. In this case, relieving the physical anxiety will not solve the problem. Sometimes the development of better study skills, as discussed, provides the student with greater self-confidence and diminishes the "test anxiety." For other students, specific test-taking skills are needed. Again, a campus Study Skills Center or other student service may be able to help. Box C.2 provides some examples of test-taking strategies that can be used. It may also be useful to have your specific abilities tested through a campus testing center. Your college entrance examination scores may provide clues to areas where you need additional strengthening of basic skills (vocabulary, math, etc.). An evaluation of your reading speed and comprehension may point to skills in need of further practice. The writing of essay examination answers at the college level requires advanced skills in expression and organization, rather than mere memorization and recall.

C.2 STRATEGIES FOR TAKING TESTS

1. *Prepare.* In studying for an examination, predict the kinds of questions that will be asked; then answer them. In a study group, write questions to ask each other. There is no remedy for being unprepared!

2. *Relax.* Before taking an exam, get adequate rest and allow a period of time for relaxing in preparation for the test.

3. *Focus.* If you are going to worry about a test, do it before or after. During the exam, focus all your attention on the test and don't waste time thinking about anything else.

4. *Survey.* Before beginning the exam, take a minute or two to look over the whole test to see how long it is, and how you should divide your time. Notice how much each question is worth, and be sure you get to those portions that count for the most points.

5. *Start with Strength.* Answer first the questions you know well. Skip over questions you don't know as well and come back to them if you have time. This will ensure that you answer the questions you know the best, and it will also help you to build confidence.

6. *Return to Other Questions.* Next return to the questions of which you are less certain. Read them carefully. Unless there is a penalty for guessing, try to give an answer for every question on an objective exam. On essay items, state at least a few points you may remember rather than leave it blank. Start with questions that count for the most points. Save the questions you know least for last.

7. *Recheck.* If time permits, go back through and recheck your work. Often points are missed because the question was not read clearly or because the student dropped out a key word or phrase in an essay answer. There is usually no reward for finishing early. Within the limits allowed, take all the time you need!

8. *Review.* After an exam has been graded, review it. When the exam is returned to you, check your answers (sometimes instructors make errors in scoring or adding). If the exam is not returned, ask to go over your exam during the instructor's office hours. Determine which questions you missed and why. Did you miss more questions of a certain kind, or based on material from a particular source (text, lectures)? Where did you lose the most points? What answer would have been correct, or have given you more points? Study the kinds of questions asked, and use this information in preparing for the next exam.

■ SUMMARY

Problems with studying and test taking are very common. It is important as a first step to understand the nature of the problem. Difficulties may be due to insufficient motivation and time devoted to studying, poor note-taking practices, ineffective study strategies, or test anxiety. Effective strategies for overcoming these difficulties are available.

Bibliography

ABRAMSON, L. Y., SELIGMAN, M. E. P., & TEASDALE, J. D. (1978). Learned helplessness in humans: Critique and reformulation. *Journal of Abnormal Psychology, 87*, 49–74.

ACKERMAN, N. J. (1984). *A theory of family systems.* New York: Gardner.

ADAMS, H. E., TOLLISON, C. D., & CARSON, T. P. (1981). Behavior therapy with sexual deviations. In S. M. Turner, K. S. Calhoun, & H. E. Adams (Eds.) *Handbook of clinical behavior therapy*, pp. 318–346. New York: John Wiley.

ADLER, A. (1923). *The practice and theory of individual psychology.* New York: Harcourt, Brace.

ADLER, A. (1931). *The case of Mrs. A: The diagnosis of a lifestyle.* London: C. W. Daniel.

ADLER, A. (1937). The significance of early recollections. *International Journal of Individual Psychology, 3*, 283–287.

AFTEL, M., & LAKOFF, R. T. (1985). *When talk is not cheap: How to find the right therapist when you don't know where to begin.* New York: Warner.

ALBERTI, R. E., & EMMONS, M. L. (1986). *Your perfect right: A guide to assertive living* (5th ed.). San Luis Obispo, CA: Impact.

Alcoholics Anonymous. (1955). *Alcoholics Anonymous: The story of how many thousands of men and women have recovered from alcoholism* (Rev. ed.). New York: Author.

ALDEN, L. (1988). Behavioral self-management controlled-drinking strategies in a context of secondary prevention. *Journal of Consulting and Clinical Psychology, 56*, 280–286.

ALPERSON, J. R. (1976). Gone with the wind: Role-reversed desensitization for a wind phobic client. *Behavior Therapy, 7*, 405–407.

Alverno College conference (1985, June). Teaching ethics: Incorporating values into professional and liberal studies. Milwaukee, WI: Author.

American Psychiatric Association. (1980). *Diagnostic and statistical manual of mental disorders* (3rd ed.). Washington, DC: Author.

American Psychiatric Association. (1987). *Diagnostic and statistical manual of mental disorders* (3rd ed., rev.). Washington, DC: Author.

American Psychological Association. (1981). Ethical principles of psychologists. *American Psychologist, 36* (6), 633–638.

American Psychological Association. (1983). *Publication Manual* (3rd ed.). Washington, DC: Author.

ANASTASI, A. (1976). *Psychological Testing* (4th ed.). New York: Macmillan.

ANDRASIK, F. (1986). Relaxation and biofeedback for chronic headaches. In A. D. Holzman & D. C. Turk (Eds.), *A handbook of psychological treatment approaches*, pp. 213–239. New York: Pergamon.

ANNIS, H. M., & DAVIS, C. S. (1989). Relapse prevention. In R. K. Hester & W. R. Miller (Eds.), *Handbook of alcoholism treatment: Effective alternatives*, pp. 170–182. Elmsford, NY: Pergamon.

ANSBACHER, H. L., & ANSBACHER, R. R. (1956). *The individual psychology of Alfred Adler.* New York: Harper & Row.

APPEL, C-P. (1986). From contemplation to determination: Contributions for cognitive psychology. In W. R. Miller & N. Heather (Eds.), *Treating addictive behaviors: Processes of change* (pp. 59–89). New York: Plenum.

APPLEYARD, D., & LINTELL, M. (1972). The environmental quality of city streets: The residents' viewpoint. *Journal of the American Institute of Planners, 38*, 84–101.

APTER, M. J. (1982). *The experience of motivation: The theory of psychological reversals.* London: Academic Press.

ARE, T. L. (1985). *The gospel for the clockaholic.* Valley Forge, PA: Judson.

ARKOWITZ, H., & MESSER, S. B. (Eds.). (1984). *Psychoanalytic therapy and behavior therapy: Is integration possible?* New York: Plenum.

ARON, A., & ARON, E. N. (1980). The transcendental meditation program's effect on addictive behaviors. *Addictive Behaviors, 5*, 3–12.

ARONSON, E. (1969). Some antecedents of interpersonal attraction. In W. J. Arnold & D. Levine (Eds.), *Nebraska Symposium on Motivation*, pp. 143–173. Lincoln, NE: University of Nebraska Press.

ASCH, S. E. (1946). Forming impressions of personality. *Journal of Abnormal and Social Psychology, 41*, 258–290.

ASCH, S. E. (1952). Effects of group pressure upon the modification and distortion of judgments. In G. E. Swanson, T. M. Newcomb, & E. L. Hartley (Eds.), *Readings in social psychology* (2nd ed.). New York: Holt.

ASCH, S. E. (1956). Studies of independence and conformity. 1. A minority of one against a unanimous majority. *Psychological Monographs, 70*, Whole No. 9.

ASIMOV, I. (1951). *Foundation.* Garden City, NY: Doubleday.

ASSAGIOLI, R. (1971). *Psychosynthesis.* New York: Viking.

Attorney General's Commission on Pornography. (1986). *Final Report.* Washington, DC: U.S. Department of Justice.

AUGSBERGER, D. W. (1979). *Anger and assertiveness in pastoral care.* Philadelphia: Fortress.

AVERILL, J. R. (1983). Studies on anger and aggression: Implications for theories of emotion. *American Psychologist, 38*, 1145–1160.

AX, A. F. (1953). The physiological differentiation between fear and anger in humans. *Psychosomatic Medicine, 15*, 433–442.

AZRIN, N. H., & BESALEL, V. A. (1980). *Finding a job.* Berkeley, CA: Ten Speed Press.

463

AZRIN, N. H., & BESALEL, V. A. (1982). *Job club counselor's manual: A behavioral approach to vocational counseling.* Austin, TX: Pro-Ed.

AZRIN, N. H., SISSON, R. W., MEYERS, R., & GODLEY, M. (1982). Alcoholism treatment by disulfiram and community reinforcement therapy. *Journal of Behavior Therapy and Experimental Psychiatry, 13,* 105–112.

BACHMAN, J. G., & O'MALLEY, P. M. (1977). Self-esteem in young men: A longitudinal analysis of the impact of educational and occupational attainment. *Journal of Personality and Social Psychology, 35,* 365–380.

BALTES, P. B., REESE, H. W., & LIPSETT, L. P. (1980). Life-span developmental psychology. In M. R. Rosenzweig & L. W. Porter (Eds.), *Annual Review of Psychology, 31,* 65–110.

BANDURA, A. (1973). *Aggression: A social learning analysis.* Englewood Cliffs, NJ: Prentice Hall.

BANDURA, A. (1982). The psychology of chance encounters and life paths. *American Psychologist, 37,* 747–755.

BANDURA, A., BLANCHARD, E. B., & RITTER, B. (1969). The relative efficacy of desensitization and modeling approaches for inducing behavioral, affective, and attributional changes. *Journal of Personality and Social Psychology, 13,* 173–199.

BANDURA, A., & CERVONE, D. (1983). Self-evaluative and self-efficacy mechanisms governing the motivational effects of goal systems. *Journal of Personality and Social Psychology, 45,* 1017–1028.

BANDURA, A., & MENLOVE, F. L. (1968). Factors determining vicarious extinction of avoidance behavior through symbolic modeling. *Journal of Personality and Social Psychology, 8,* 99–108.

BARBACH, L. G. (1975). *For yourself: The fulfillment of female sexuality.* Garden City, NY: Doubleday.

BARBACH, L. G., & AYRES, T. (1976). Group process for women with orgasmic difficulties. *Personnel and Guidance Journal, 54,* 389–391.

BARBER, T. X. (1969). *Hypnosis: A scientific approach.* New York: Van Nostrand Reinhold.

BARLOW, D. H., ABEL, G. G., & BLANCHARD, E. B. (1977). Gender identity change in a transsexual: An exorcism. *Archives of Sexual Behaviour, 6,* 387–395.

BARLOW, D. H., ABEL, G. G., & BLANCHARD, E. B. (1979). Gender identity change in transsexuals. *Archives of General Psychiatry, 36,* 1001–1007.

BARLOW, D. H., REYNOLDS, E. J., & AGRAS, W. S. (1973). Gender identity change in a transsexual. *Archives of General Psychiatry, 28,* 569–579.

BARNES, G. E. (1979). The alcoholic personality: A reanalysis of the literature. *Journal of Studies on Alcohol, 40,* 571–634.

BARRETT, K. (1982). Date rape: A campus epidemic? *Ms., 11* (3), 48–51.

BART, P. B. (1969). Why women's status changes in middle age: The turns of the social ferris wheel. *Sociological Symposium, 3,* 1–18.

BART, P. B. (1976). Depression in middle aged women. In S. Cox (Ed.), *Female psychology: The emerging self,* pp. 349–367. Chicago: Science Research Associates.

BARUTH, L. G., & ECKSTEIN, D. G. (1981). *Lifestyle: Theory, practice, and research.* Dubuque, IA: Kendall-Hunt.

BATESON, G., JACKSON, D., HALEY, H., & WEAKLAND, J. (1956). Toward a theory of schizophrenia. *Behavioral Science, 1,* 251–264.

BAUMRIND, D. (1967). Child care practices anteceding three patterns of preschool behavior. *Genetic Psychology Monographs, 75,* 43–88.

BECK, A. T. (1976). *Cognitive therapy and the emotional disorders.* New York: International Universities Press.

BECK, A. T., & YOUNG, J. E. (1978). College blues. *Psychology Today, 12*(4), 80–92.

BECKER, J. V., & ABEL, G. G. (1981). Behavioral treatment of victims of sexual assault. In S. M. Turner, K. S. Calhoun, & H. E. Adams (Eds.), *Handbook of clinical behavior therapy.* New York: John Wiley.

BELLIVEAU, F., and RICHTER, L. (1970). *Understanding human sexual inadequacy.* New York: Bantam.

BEM, S. L. (1974). The measurement of psychological androgyny. *Journal of Consulting and Clinical Psychology, 42,* 155–162.

BEM, S. L. (1985). Androgyny and gender schema theory: A conceptual and empirical integration. In T. B. Sonderegger (Ed.), *Nebraska Symposium on Motivation, 1984: Psychology and gender,* pp. 179–226. Lincoln: University of Nebraska Press.

BENBOW, C. P., & STANLEY, J. C. (1983). Sex differences in mathematical reasoning ability: More facts. *Science, 222,* 1029–1031.

BENEKE, W. M. & HARRIS, M. B. (1972). Teaching self-control of study behaviour. *Behavior Research and Therapy, 10,* 35–41.

BENSON, H. & KLIPPER, M. Z. (1975). *The relaxation response.* New York: William A. Morrow.

BERG, G., & SKUTLE, A. (1986). Early intervention with problem drinkers. In W. R. Miller & N. Heather (Eds.), *Treating addictive behaviors: Processes for change,* pp. 205–220. New York: Plenum.

BERGIN, A. E. (1980). Psychotherapy and religious values. *Journal of Consulting and Clinical Psychology, 48,* 95–105.

BERKOWITZ, L. (1962). *Aggression: A social psychological analysis.* New York: McGraw-Hill.

BERKOWITZ, L. (1983). Aversively stimulated aggression: Some parallels and differences in research with animals and humans. *American Psychologist, 38,* 1135–1144.

BERNE, E. (1964). *Games people play.* New York: Grove.

BLACK ELK. (1972). *Black Elk speaks.* Lincoln: University of Nebraska Press.

BLANCHARD, E. B., MARTIN, J. E., & DUBBERT, P. M. (Eds.) (1988). *Nondrug approaches to treating hypertension.* Elmsford, NY: Pergamon.

BLANEY, P. H. (1986). Affect and memory: A review. *Psychological Bulletin, 99,* 229–246.

BLECHMAN, E. A., McENROE, M. J., CARELLA, E. T., & AUDETTE, D. P. (1986). Childhood competence and depression. *Journal of Abnormal Psychology, 95,* 223–227.

BLUMENTHAL, J. A., BURG, M. M., BAREFOOT, J., WILLIAMS, R. B., HANEY, T., & ZIMET, G. (1987). Social support, type A behavior, and coronary artery disease. *Psychosomatic Medicine, 49,* 331–340.

BLUMSTEIN, P., & SCHWARTZ, P. (1983). *American couples.* New York: William A. Morrow.

BOBO, J. K., GILCHREST, L. D., SCHILLING, R. F., NOACH, B., & SCHINKE, S. P. (1987). Cigarette smoking cessation attempts by recovering alcoholics. *Addictive Behaviors, 12,* 209–215.

BODIN, A. M. (1981). The interactional view: Family therapy approaches of the Mental Research Institute. In A. S. Gurman & D. P. Kniskern (Eds.), *Handbook of family therapy,* pp. 267–309. New York: Brunner/Mazel.

BOGEN, J. E., & VOGEL, P. J. (1962). Cerebral commissurotomy in man: Preliminary case report. *Bulletin of the Los Angeles Neurological Society, 27,* 169.

BOLLES, R. N. (1986). *The new beginning quick job-hunting map,* (rev. ed.). Berkeley, CA: Ten Speed Press.

BOLLES, R. N. (1989). *What color is your parachute?* (rev. ed.) Berkeley, CA: Ten Speed Press.

BOOTZIN, R. R., & NICASSIO, P. M. (1978). Behavioral treatments for insomnia. *Progress in Behavior Modification, 6,* 1–45.

BOWER, G. H. (1981). Mood and memory. *American Psychologist, 36,* 129–148.

BREHM, S. S., & BREHM, J. W. (1981). *Psychological reactance: A theory of freedom and control.* New York: Academic Press.

BRIDGES, W. (1980). *Making sense of life's transitions: Strategies for coping with difficult, painful, and confusing times in your life.* Reading, MA: Addison-Wesley.

BROADBENT, D. W. (1971). *Decision and stress.* New York: Academic Press.

BROVERMAN, I. K., BROVERMAN, D. M., CLARKSON, F. E., ROSENKRANTZ, P. S., & VOGEL, S. R. (1970). Sex-role stereotypes and clinical judgments in mental health. *Journal of Consulting and Clinical Psychology, 34,* 1–7.

BROWN, R. A. (1980). Conventional education and controlled drinking education courses with convicted drunken drivers. *Behavior Therapy, 11,* 632–642.

BROWN, R. M. (1980). *Creative dislocations: The movement of grace.* Nashville, TN: Abingdon.

BROWN, S. A., GOLDMAN, M. S., INN, A., & ANDERSON, L. R. (1980). Expectations of reinforcement from alcohol: Their domain and relation to drinking patterns. *Journal of Consulting and Clinical Psychology, 48,* 419–426.

BROWNELL, K. D., MARLATT, G. A., LICHTENSTEIN, E., & WILSON, G. T. (1986). Understanding and preventing relapse. *American Psychologist, 41,* 765–782.

BUCK, K., & MILLER, W. R. (1981). Why does bibliotherapy work? A controlled study. In W. R. Miller (Chair), Effec-tiveness of bibliotherapy: Empirical research. Symposium at the annual meeting of the Association for Advancement of Behavior Therapy, Toronto.

BUCKHOUT, R. (1974). Eyewitness testimony. *Scientific American, 231*(6), 23–31.

BUHLER, C. & ALLEN, M. (1972). *Introduction to Humanistic Psychology.* Monterey, CA: Brooks/Cole.

BURGESS, A. W., & HOLMSTROM, L. L. (1974). Rape trauma syndrome. *American Journal of Psychiatry, 131,* 981–986.

BURNS, D. D. (1980). *Feeling good: The new mood therapy.* New York: William A. Morrow.

BURNS, D. D. (1980, November). The perfectionist's script for self-defeat. *Psychology Today,* 34–52.

BUSCAGLIA, L. (1972). *Love.* New York: Ballantine.

CAHOON, D. D. (1968). Symptom substitution and the behavior therapies: A reappraisal. *Psychological Bulletin, 69,* 149–156.

CAMP, B. W. (1977). Verbal mediation in young aggressive boys. *Journal of Abnormal Psychology, 86,* 145–153.

CAMPBELL, A., CONVERSE, P. E., & RODGERS, W. L. (1975). *The quality of American life.* Ann Arbor, MI: ISR Social Science Archive.

CAMPBELL, J., WATTS, A. W., & MILLER, D. L. (Eds.) (1988). *Myths, dreams, and religion.* Dallas, TX: Spring.

Can you rely on condoms? (1989, March). *Consumer Reports, 54* (3), 135–141.

CAPLAN, G. (1964). *Principles of preventive psychiatry.* New York: Basic Books.

CARLSMITH, J. M., & ANDERSON, C. A. (1979). Ambient temperature and the occurrence of collective violence: A new analysis. *Journal of Personality and Social Psychology, 37,* 337–344.

CASSELL, C. (1984). *Swept away: Why women fear their own sexuality.* New York: Simon & Schuster.

CAUTELA, J. R., & GRODEN, J. (1978). *Relaxation: A comprehensive manual for adults, children, and children with special needs.* Champaign, IL: Research Press.

CHANDLER, M. J. (1973). Egocentrism and antisocial behavior: The assessment and training of social perspective-taking skills. *Developmental Psychology, 9,* 326–332.

CHAPMAN, L. J., & CHAPMAN, J. P. (1967). Genesis of popular but erroneous psychodiagnostic observations. *Journal of Abnormal Psychology, 72,* 193–204.

CHESLER, P. (1971). Marriage and psychotherapy. In Radical Therapist Collective (Eds.), *The radical therapist,* pp. 172–183. New York: Ballantine.

CHESTERTON, G. K. (1910). *What's wrong with the world.* London: Cassell & Co.

CHODOROW, N. (1978). *The reproduction of mothering.* Berkeley: University of California Press.

CHRISTENSEN, A., ARKOWITZ, H., & ANDERSON, J. (1975). Practice dating as treatment for college dating inhibitions. *Behaviour Research and Therapy, 13,* 321–331.

CHRISTENSEN, A., MILLER, W. R., & MUÑOZ, R. F. (1978). Paraprofessionals, partners, peers, paraphernalia, and print:

Expanding mental health service delivery. *Professional Psychology, 9,* 249–270.

Clayton, P. J. (1979). The sequelae and nonsequelae of conjugal bereavement. *American Journal of Psychiatry, 136,* 1530–1534.

Clayton, P. J. (1982). Bereavement. In E. S. Paykel (Ed.), *Handbook of affective disorders.* New York: Guilford.

Cohen, S., Evans, G. W., Krantz, D. S., & Stokols, D. (1980). Physiological, motivational and cognitive effects of aircraft noise on children: Moving from the laboratory to the field. *American Psychologist, 35,* 231–243.

Cohen, S., Evans, G. W., Krantz, D. S., Stokols, D., & Kelly, S. (1981). Aircraft noise and children: Longitudinal and cross-sectional evidence on adaptation to noise and the effectiveness of noise abatement. *Journal of Personality and Social Psychology, 40,* 331–345.

Cohen, S., & Weinstein, N. (1981). Nonauditory effects of noise on behavior and health. *Journal of Social Issues, 37,* 36–70.

Collins, G. (1980). *Christian counseling.* Waco, TX: Word.

Collins, W. A. (1973). The effect of temporal separation between motivation, aggression and consequences: A developmental study. *Developmental Psychology, 8,* 215–221.

Collins, W. A., & Wiens, M. (1983). Cognitive processes in television viewing: Description and strategic implications. In M. Pressley & J. Levin (Eds.), *Cognitive strategy research: Educational applications.* New York: Springer-Verlag.

Cooper, T., Detre, T., & Weiss, S. M. (1981). Coronary prone behavior and coronary heart disease: A critical review. *Circulation, 63,* 1199–1215.

Coopersmith, S. (1968). Studies in self-esteem. *Scientific American, 218*(2), 96–106.

Coppen, A., Metcalfe, M., & Wood, K. (1982). Lithium. In E. S. Paykel (Ed.), *Handbook of affective disorders,* pp. 276–285. New York: Guilford.

Costello, R. M. (1975). Alcoholism treatment and evaluation: In search of methods. *International Journal of the Addictions, 10,* 251–275.

Costello, R. M., Biever, P., & Baillargeon, J. G. (1977). Alcoholism treatment programming: Historical trends and modern approaches. *Alcoholism: Clinical and Experimental Research, 1,* 2311–2318.

Crick, F., & Mitchison, G. (1983). The function of dream sleep. *Nature, 304,* 111–114.

Cummings, C., Gordon, J. R., & Marlatt, G. A. (1980). Relapse: Prevention and prediction. In W. R. Miller (Ed.), *The addictive behaviors: Treatment of alcoholism, drug abuse, smoking, and obesity,* pp. 291–321. New York: Pergamon Press.

Dalton, K. (1964). *The premenstrual syndrome.* Springfield, IL: Charles C Thomas.

Damasio, A. R., & Van Hoesen, G. W. (1983). Emotional disturbances associated with focal lesions of the limbic frontal lobe. In K. M. Heilman & P. Satz (Eds.), *Neuropsychology of human emotion,* pp. 85–110. New York: Guilford.

Davies, D. L. (1962). Normal drinking in recovered alcohol addicts. *Quarterly Journal of Studies on Alcohol, 23,* 94–104.

Davison, G. C., & Valins, S. (1969). Maintenance of self-attributed and drug-attributed behavior change. *Journal of Personality and Social Psychology, 11,* 25–33.

Deaux, D. (1976). Sex and the attribution process. In J. H. Harvey, W. J. Ickens, & R. F. Kidd (Eds.), *New directions in attribution research,* Vol. 1, pp. 335–352. New York: Halstead.

de Beauvoir, S. (1972). *Old Age.* New York: Penguin.

Deci, E. L. (1975). *Intrinsic motivation.* New York: Plenum.

Deci, E. L., & Ryan, R. M. (1985). *Intrinsic motivation and self-determination in human behavior.* New York: Plenum.

Delgado, J. M. R. (1963). Social rank and radio-stimulated aggressiveness in monkeys. *Journal of Nervous and Mental Disease, 144,* 383–390.

Dembroski, T. M., & Williams, R. B. (1989). Definition and assessment of coronary-prone behavior. In N. Schneiderman, P. Kaufmann, & S. M. Weiss (Eds.), *Handbook of research methods in cardiovascular behavioral medicine.* New York: Plenum.

Denmark, F., Russo, N. F., Frieze, I. H., & Sechzer, J. A. (1988). Guidelines for avoiding sexism in psychological research: A report of the ad hoc committee on nonsexist research. *American Psychologist, 43*(7), 582–585.

Denney, N. W., Field, J. K., & Quadagno, D. (1984). Sex differences in sexual needs and desires. *Archives of Sexual Behavior, 13*(3), 233–245.

de Saint-Exupery, A. (1943). *The little prince.* New York: Harcourt, Brace & World.

Diamant, L. (1987). *Male and female homosexuality: Psychological approaches.* Cambridge, MA: Hemisphere.

Dickens, C. (1984). *A Christmas carol.* New York: Penguin.

DiLoreto, A. O. (1971). *Comparative psychotherapy: An experimental analysis.* Chicago: Aldine-Atherton.

Dimond, R. E., Havens, R. A., & Jones, A. C. (1978). A conceptual framework for the practice of prescriptive eclecticism in psychotherapy. *American Psychologist, 33,* 239–248.

Dion, K. K., & Dion, K. L. (1975). Self-esteem and romantic love. *Journal of Personality, 43,* 39–57.

Dodge, K. A. (1980). Social cognition and children's aggressive behavior. *Child Development, 51,* 162–170.

Dodge, K. A. (1983). Behavioral antecedents of peer social status. *Child Development, 54,* 1386–1389.

Dodge, K. A., Coie, J. D., & Brakke, N. P. (1982). Behavioral patterns of socially rejected and neglected preadolescents: The roles of social approach and aggression. *Journal of Abnormal Child Psychology, 10,* 389–410.

Dodge, K. A., & Frame, C. L. (1982). Social cognitive biases and deficits in aggressive boys. *Child Development, 53,* 620–635.

Doherty, M. A. (1978). Sexual bias in personality theory. In L. W. Harmon, J. M. Birk, L. E. Fitzgerald, & M. F.

Tanney (Eds.), *Counseling women.* Monterey, CA: Brooks/Cole.

DOHERTY, W. J., McCABE, P., & RYDER, R. G. (1978). Marriage encounter: A critical appraisal. *Journal of Marriage and Family Counseling, 4,* 99–107.

DOLLARD, J., & MILLER, N. E. (1950). *Personality and psychotherapy: An analysis in terms of learning, thinking, and cultures.* New York: McGraw-Hill.

DONNERSTEIN, E., & WILSON, D. W. (1976). Effects of noise and perceived control on ongoing and subsequent aggressive behavior. *Journal of Personality and Social Psychology, 34,* 774–781.

DONOVAN, D. M., & MARLATT, G. A. (Eds.). (1988). *Assessment of addictive behaviors.* New York: Guilford.

DOUGLAS, V. (1983). Attentional and cognitive problems. In M. Rutter (Ed.), *Developmental neuropsychiatry,* pp. 280–329. New York: Guilford.

DUSH, D. M., HIRT, M. L., & SCHROEDER, H. (1983). Self-statement modification with adults: A meta-analysis. *Psychological Bulletin, 94,* 408–422.

DWECK, C. S., & ELLIOTT, E. S. (1983). Achievement motivation. In E. M. Hetherington (Ed.), *Handbook of child psychology, 4,* 643–691.

DWECK, C. S., & GOETZ, T. E. (1978). Attributions and learned helplessness. In J. H. Harvey, W. Ickens, & R. F. Kidd (Eds.). *New directions in attribution research,* Vol. 2, pp. 157–179. Hillsdale, NJ: Lawrence Erlbaum.

DZEICH, B. W., & WEINER, L. (1984). *The lecherous professor: Sexual harassment on campus.* Boston: Beacon.

EASTMAN, M. (1922). *The sense of humor.* New York: Charles Scribners.

ECCLES, J. S. & JACOBS, J. E. (1986). Social forces shape math attitudes and performance. *Signs, 11,* 367–389.

ELIADE, M. (1978). *The Forbidden Forest.* Notre Dame, IN: University of Notre Dame Press.

ELLENBERGER, H. F. (1972). The story of "Anna O.": A critical review with new data. *Journal of the History of the Behavior Sciences, 8,* 267–279.

ELLIS, A. (1970). *The essence of rational psychotherapy: A comprehensive approach to treatment.* New York: Institute for Rational Living.

ELLIS, A. (1973). *Humanistic psychotherapy: A rational-emotive approach.* New York: McGraw-Hill.

ELLIS, A. (1980). Psychotherapy and atheistic values: A response to A. E. Bergin's "Psychotherapy and religious values." *Journal of Consulting and Clinical Psychology, 48,* 635–639.

ELLIS, A. (1984). Rational-emotive therapy. In R. Corsini (Ed.), *Current Psychotherapies* (2nd ed.), pp. 196–238. Itasca, IL: F. E. Peacock.

ELLIS, A., & HARPER, R. (1975). *A new guide to rational living.* Englewood Cliffs, NJ: Prentice Hall.

ELLIS, H. C., & ASHBROOK, P. W. (1987). Resource allocation model of the effects of depressed mood states on memory. In K. Fiedler & J. Forgas (Eds.), *Affect, cognition, and social behavior.* Toronto: Hogrefe.

ELLIS, H. C., THOMAS, R. L., & RODRIGUEZ, I. A. (1984). Emotional mood states and memory: Elaborative encoding, semantic processing, and cognitive effort. *Journal of Experimental Psychology: Learning, Memory, and Cognition, 10,* 470–482.

EMMELKAMP, P. M. G., KUIPERS, A. C. M., & EGGERAAT, J. B. (1978). Cognitive modification vs. prolonged exposure *in vivo:* A comparison with agoraphobics as subjects. *Behaviour Research and Therapy, 16,* 33–41.

EMMELKAMP, P. M. G., & WESSELS, H. (1975). Flooding in imagination vs. flooding *in vivo:* A comparison with agoraphobics. *Behaviour Research and Therapy, 13,* 7–15.

EMMONS, M. L. (1978). *The inner source: A guide to meditative therapy.* San Luis Obispo, CA: Impact.

EMRICK, C. D. (1975). A review of psychologically oriented treatment of alcoholism. II. The relative effectiveness of different treatment approaches and the effectiveness of treatment versus no treatment. *Journal of Studies on Alcohol, 36,* 88–108.

EPSTEIN, S. (1973). The self-concept revisited: Or a theory of a theory. *American Psychologist, 28,* 404–416.

Equal Employment Opportunity Commission Guidelines on discrimination because of sex. (1980). *Federal Register, 45,* 74676–74677.

ERIKSON, E. (1959). Identity and the life cycle. *Psychological Issues,* Monograph 1. New York: International Universities Press.

ERIKSON, E. H. (1963). *Childhood and society* (2nd ed.). New York: W. W. Norton.

ERIKSON, E. H. (1968). *Identity: Youth and crisis.* New York: W. W. Norton.

ERON, L. D., WALDER, L. O., & LEFKOWITZ, M. M. (1971). *Learning of aggression in children.* Boston: Little, Brown.

EXNER, J. E. (1986). *The Rorschach: A comprehensive system, basic foundation,* Vol. 1. (2nd ed.). New York: John Wiley.

EYSENCK, H. J. (1953). *The structure of human personality.* New York: John Wiley.

FABE, M., & WIKLER, N. (1979). *Up against the clock: Career women speak on the choice to have children.* New York: Warner.

FARRELL, W. (1974). *The liberated man: Beyond masculinity: Freeing men and their relationships with women.* New York: Random House.

FESHBACH, N. D., & FESHBACH, S. (1969). The relationship between empathy and aggression in two age groups. *Developmental Psychology, 1,* 102–107.

FESHBACH, N. D., & FESHBACH, S. (1982). Empathy training and the regulation of aggression: Potentialities and limitations. *Academic Psychology Bulletin, 4,* 399–413.

FESHBACH, S. (1970). Aggression. In P. H. Mussen (Ed.), *Carmichael's manual of child psychology,* Vol. 2, pp. 159–259.

FEUERSTEIN, M., LABBE, E. E., & KUCZMIERCZYK, A. R. (1986). *Health psychology: A psychobiological perspective.* New York: Plenum.

FIEVE, R. (1976). *Mood swing.* New York: Bantam.

FINKELHOR, D. (1979). *Sexually victimized children.* New York: Free Press.

FINKELHOR, D. (1984). *Child sexual abuse: New theory and research.* New York: Free Press.

FINKELHOR, D., & BROWNE, A. (1985). The traumatic impact of child sexual abuse: A conceptualization. *American Journal of Orthopsychiatry, 55,* 530–543.

FISHMAN, P. M. (1983). Interaction: The work women do. In B. Thorne, C. Kramarae, & N. Henley (Eds.), *Language, gender and society,* pp. 89–101. Rowley, MA: Newbury House.

FISHWICK, M. (1974). *Parameters: Man-media mosaic.* Bowling Green, OH: Bowling Green University Press.

FORDYCE, W. E. (1976). *Behavioral methods for chronic pain and illness.* St. Louis: C. V. Mosby.

FORTMANN, S. P., HASKELL, W. L., WILLIAMS, P. T., VARADY, A. N., HULLEY, S. B., & FARQUHAR, J. W. (1986). Community surveillance of cardiovascular diseases in the Stanford five-city project: Methods and initial experience. *American Journal of Epidemiology, 123,* 656–669.

FOWLER, J. W. (1981). *Stages of faith: The psychology of human development and the quest for meaning.* New York: Harper & Row.

FOY, D. W., SIPPRELLE, R. C., RUEGER, D. B., & CARROLL, E. M. (1984). Etiology of posttraumatic stress disorder in Vietnam veterans: Analysis of premilitary, military, and combat exposure influences. *Journal of Consulting and Clinical Psychology, 52,* 79–87.

FRANK, A. (1953). *The diary of Anne Frank.* London: Vallentine, Mitchell.

FRANK, E., ANDERSON, C., & RUBINSTEIN, D. (1978). Frequency of sexual dysfunction in "normal" couples. *New England Journal of Medicine, 299,* 111–115.

FRANKENHAEUSER, M., & LUNDBERG, U. (1977). The influence of cognitive set on performance and arousal under different noise loads. *Motivation and Emotion, 1,* 139–149.

FRANKL, V. (1963). *Man's search for meaning.* Boston: Beacon Press.

FRANKLIN, D. (1987). The politics of masochism. *Psychology Today, 21*(1) 52–57.

FRAUENGLASS, M. H., & DIAZ, R. M. (1985). Self-regulatory functions of children's private speech: A critical analysis of recent challenges to Vygotsky's theory. *Developmental Psychology, 21,* 357–364.

FREEDMAN, R. R., & IANNI, P. (1986). Raynaud's disease. In K. A. Holroyd & T. L. Creer (Eds.), *Self-management of chronic disease: Handbook of clinical interventions and research,* pp. 473–501. New York: Academic Press.

FREUD, A. (1948). *The ego and the mechanisms of defence.* London: Hogarth.

FREUD, S. (1917). *Mourning and melancholia.* (Std ed.), Vol. 14, pp. 243–258. London: Hogarth.

FREUD, S. (1922). *Dreams and telepathy.* (Std ed.), Vol. 18, p. 215. London: Hogarth.

FREUD, S. (1933). *New introductory lectures on psychoanalysis.* New York: Morton.

FREUD, S. (1936). *The problem of anxiety.* New York: Psychoanalytic Quarterly Press.

FREUD, S. (1960). *Jokes and their relation to the unconscious.* New York: W. W. Norton.

FREUD, S. (1964). In J. Strachey (Ed.), *Standard edition of the complete psychological works of Sigmund Freud.* London: Hogarth.

FREUD, S. (1966). *Introductory lectures on psychoanalysis.* New York: Liveright.

FRIEDMAN, M., & ROSENMAN, R. H. (1974). *Type A behavior and your heart.* New York: Alfred A. Knopf.

FRIEDMAN, M., THORESEN, C. E., & GILL, J. J. (1981). Type A behavior: Its possible role, detection, and alteration in patients with ischemic heart disease. In J. W. Hurst (Ed.), *The heart: Update V.* Hightstown, NJ: McGraw-Hill.

FRIEDMAN, M., THORESEN, C. E., GILL, J. J., POWELL, L. H., ULMER, D., THOMPSON, L., PRICE, V. A., RABIN, D. D., BREALL, W. S., DIXON, T., LEVY, R., & BOURG, E. (1984). Alteration of Type A behavior and reduction in cardiac recurrences in post-myocardial infarction patients. *American Heart Journal, 108,* 237–247.

FRIEDMAN, M., THORESEN, C. E., GILL, J. J., ULMER, D., POWELL, L., PRICE, V. A., BROWN, B., THOMPSON, L., RABIN, D. D., BREALL, W. S., BOURG, E., LEVY, R., & DIXON, T. (1986). Alteration of type A behavior and its effect on cardiac recurrences in post-myocardial infarction patients: Summary results of the recurrent coronary prevention project. *American Heart Journal, 112,* 653–665.

FRODI, A., MACAULAY, J., & THOME, P. R. (1977). Are women always less aggressive than men? A review of the experimental literature. *Psychological Bulletin, 84,* 634–660.

FROMM, E. (1956). *The art of loving.* New York: Harper & Row.

FROMM, E. (1963). *Escape from freedom.* New York: Holt, Rinehart, and Winston.

FROST, R. (1949). Take something like a star. *Complete Poems.* NY: Holt, Rinehart & Winston.

GARFIELD, S. L., & BERGIN, A. E. (1986). *Handbook of psychotherapy and behavior change* (3rd ed.). New York: John Wiley.

GARMECZY, N., & TELLEGEN, A. (1984). Studies of stress-resistant children: Methods, variables, and preliminary findings. In F. J. Morrison, C. Lord, & D. P. Keating (Eds.), *Applied developmental psychology,* Vol. 1, pp. 231–287. New York: Academic Press.

GEEN, R., & O'NEAL, E. (1969). Activation of cue elicited aggression by general arousal. *Journal of Personality and Social Psychology, 11,* 289–292.

GEER, J. H., DAVISON, G. C., & GATCHEL, R. I. (1970). Reduction of stress in humans through nonveridical perceived control of aversive stimulation. *Journal of Personality and Social Psychology, 16,* 731–738.

GENDREAU, P., & ROSS, R. R. (1987). Revivification of rehabilitation: Evidence from the 1980s. *Justice Quarterly, 4,* 349–407.

GERBNER, G., GROSS, L., MORGAN, M., & SIGNORELLI, N. (1980). The mainstreaming of America. *Journal of Communication, 30,* 12–29.

GILBERT, R. K. (1988). The dynamics of inaction: Psychological factors inhibiting arms control activism. *American Psychologist, 43,* 755–764.

GILLIGAN, C. (1982). *In a different voice: Psychological theory and women's development.* Cambridge, MA: Harvard University Press.

GILMORE, S. K. (1973). *The counselor-in-training.* Englewood Cliffs, NJ: Prentice Hall.

GLASGOW, R. E., & ROSEN, G. M. (1978). Behavioral bibliotherapy: A review of self-help behavior therapy manuals. *Psychological Bulletin, 85,* 1–23.

GLASS, D. D., SINGER, J. E., & FRIEDMAN, L. N. (1969). Psychic cost of adaptation to an environmental stressor. *Journal of Personality and Social Psychology, 12,* 200–210.

GLASSER, W. (1976). *Positive addictions.* New York: Harper & Row.

GOLDBERG, L. R. (1974). Objective diagnostic tests and measures. *Annual Review of Psychology, 25,* 343–366.

GOLDING, W. (1962). *The lord of the flies.* New York: G. P. Putnam.

GOLDMAN, M. S., BROWN, S. A., & CHRISTIANSEN, B. A. (1987). Expectancy theory: Thinking about drinking. In H. T. Blane & K. E. Leonard (Eds.), *Psychological theories of drinking and alcoholism,* pp. 181–226. New York: Guilford.

GOODWIN, D. W. (1976). *Is alcoholism hereditary?* New York: Oxford University Press.

GOODWIN, D. W., & GUZE, S. B. (1979). *Psychiatric diagnosis.* New York: Oxford University Press.

GORDON, T. (1970). *Parent Effectiveness Training: The "no-lose" program for raising responsible children.* New York: Peter H. Wyden.

GORDON, W. C. (1989). *Learning and memory.* Pacific Grove, CA: Brooks/Cole.

GOTTMAN, J. M. (1979). *Marital interaction: Experimental investigations.* New York: Academic Press.

GOULD, R. (1972). The phases of adult life: A study in developmental psychology. *American Journal of Psychiatry, 129,* 5, 33–43.

GRANBERG, D., & GRANBERG, B. W. (1985). A search for gender differences on fertility-related attitudes: Questioning the relevance of sociobiology theory for understanding social psychological aspects of human reproduction. *Psychology of Women Quarterly, 9,* 431–438.

GREER, G. (1971). *The female eunuch.* New York: McGraw-Hill.

GRIFFITH, R. M. (1961). Rorschach water percepts: A study in conflicting results. *American Psychologist, 16,* 307–311.

GROSS, G., & EDWARDS, M. M. (1976). Alcohol dependence: Provisional description of a clinical syndrome. *British Medical Journal, 1,* 1058–1061.

GROSS, L. (1983). *How much is too much? The effects of social drinking.* New York: Random House.

GUERNEY, B. G., JR. (1977). *Relationship enhancement.* San Francisco: Jossey-Bass.

GURMAN, A. S., KNISKERN, D. P., & PINSOF, W. M. (1986). Research on the process and outcome of marital and family therapy. In S. L. Garfield & A. E. Bergin (Eds.), *Handbook of psychotherapy and behavior change* (3rd ed.), pp. 565–624. New York: John Wiley.

GUTTMAN, H. A. (1986). Epistemology, systems theories and the theory of family therapy. *American Journal of Family Therapy, 14,* 13–22.

HALES, S. (1979). A developmental theory of self-esteem based on competence and moral behavior. Paper presented at the Society for Research in Child Development Meetings, San Francisco, March 15–18.

HALEY, A. (1976). *Roots.* Garden City, NY: Doubleday.

HALEY, J. (1963). *Strategies of psychotherapy.* New York: Grune & Stratton.

HALL, E. T. (1966). *The hidden dimension.* Garden City, NY: Doubleday.

HALL, S. (1979). The abstinence phobia. In N. A. Krasnegor (Ed.), *Behavioral analysis and treatment of substance abuse.* Rockville, MD: National Institute on Drug Abuse.

HAMILTON, D. L. (1980). Cognitive representations of persons. In E. Higgins et al. (Eds.), *Social cognition: The Ontario Symposium on Personality and Social Psychology.* Hillsdale, NJ: Lawrence Erlbaum.

HAMILTON, D. L., & ZANNA, M. P. (1974). Context effects in impression formation: Changes in connotative meaning. *Journal of Personality and Social Psychology, 29,* 649–654.

HAMILTON, E. (1942). *Mythology.* New York: Little, Brown.

HAMMARSKJÖLD, D. (1964). *Markings.* New York: Alfred A. Knopf.

HANCOCK, E. (1981). Women's development in adult life. *Dissertation Abstracts International, 42,* 2504B (University Microfilms No. 8125485).

HANEY, C., BANKS, C., & ZIMBARDO, P. (1973). Interpersonal dynamics in a simulated prison. *International Journal of Criminology and Penology, 1,* 69–97.

HANKOFF, I. D. (1982). Suicide and attempted suicide. In E. S. Paykel (Ed.), *Handbook of affective disorders,* pp. 416–428. New York: Guilford.

HANSEN, J-I. C., & CAMPBELL, D. P. (1985). *Manual for the SVIB-SCII* (4th ed.). Palo Alto, CA: Consulting Psychologists Press.

HARE, R. D. (1970). *Psychopathy: Theory and research.* New York: John Wiley.

HARLOW, J. M. (1848). Passage of an iron through the head. *Boston Medical and Surgical Journal, 39,* 389–393.

HARLOW, J. M. (1868). Recovery from the passage of an iron bar through the head. *Massachusetts Medical Society Publication, 2,* 329–347.

HARRIS, G. M., & JOHNSON, S. B. (1983). Coping imagery and relaxation instructions in a covert modeling treatment for test anxiety. *Behavior Therapy, 14,* 144–157.

HARRIS, M. B., & TRUJILLO, A. E. (1975). Improving study

habits of junior high school students through self-management versus group discussion. *Journal of Counseling Psychology, 22,* 513–517.

HARRIS, T. A. (1967). *I'm OK-You're OK.* New York: Harper & Row.

HARTUP, W. W. (1974). Aggression in childhood: Developmental perspectives. *American Psychologist, 29,* 336–341.

HATCHER, R. A., STEWART, G. K., STEWART, F., GUEST, F., JOSEPHS, N., DALE, J. (1982). *Contraceptive Technology 1982–1983* (11th rev. ed.). New York: Irvington.

HAVIGHURST, R. J. (1972). *Developmental tasks and education.* New York: David McKay.

HEATH, R. G. (1963). Electrical self-stimulation of the brain in man. *American Journal of Psychiatry, 120,* 571–577.

HEATH, R. G. (Ed.). (1964). *The role of pleasure in behavior.* New York: Hoeber Medical Division, Harper & Row.

HEATHER, N., & ROBERTSON, I. H. (1981). *Controlled drinking.* London: Methuen.

HEBER, F. R. (1978). Sociocultural mental retardation: A longitudinal study. In D. G. Forgays (Ed.), *Primary prevention of psychopathology,* Vol. 2. Hanover, NH: University Press of New England.

HEIMAN, J., LoPICCOLO, L., & LoPICCOLO, J. (1978). *Becoming orgasmic: A sexual growth program for women.* Englewood Cliffs, NJ: Prentice Hall.

HEMIBERG, R. G., VERMILYEA, J. A., DODGE, C. S., BECKER, R. E., & BARLOW, D. H. (1986). Attributional style, depression, and anxiety: An evaluation of the specificity of depressive attributions. Manuscript submitted for publication, State University of New York at Albany.

HESTER, R. K., & MILLER, W. R. (Eds.) (1989). *Handbook of alcoholism treatment approaches: Effective alternatives.* Elmsford, NY: Pergamon.

HILGARD, E. (1978). Hypnosis and consciousness. *Human Nature, 1,* 42–51.

HILLERMAN, T. (1980). *People of darkness.* New York: Harper & Row.

HITE, S. (1976). *The Hite report: A national study of female sexuality.* New York: Dell.

HODGSON, R., & MILLER, P. (1982). *Self-watching: Addictions, habits, compulsions: What to do about them.* New York: Facts on File.

HOFLING, C. K., BROTZMAN, E., DALRYMPLE, S., GRAVES, N., & PIERCE, C. M. (1966). An experimental study in nurse-physician relationships. *Journal of Nervous and Mental Disease, 143,* 171–180.

HOLLON, S. D., & BECK, A. T. (1986). Cognitive and cognitive-behavioral therapies. In S. L. Garfield & A. E. Bergin (Eds.), *Handbook of psychotherapy and behavior change* (3rd ed.), pp. 443–482. New York: John Wiley.

HOLMES, T. H., & RAHE, R. H. (1967). The Social Readjustment Rating Scale. *Journal of Psychosomatic Research, 11,* 213–218.

HOLROYD, K. A. (1986). Recurrent headache. In K. A. Holroyd & T. L. Creer (Eds.), *Self-management of chronic disease: Handbook of clinical interventions and research,* pp. 373–413. New York: Academic Press.

HOLZMAN, A. D., TURK, D. C., & KERNS, R. D. (1986). The cognitive-behavioral approach to the management of chronic pain. In A. D. Holzman & D. C. Turk (Eds.), *A handbook of psychological treatment approaches,* pp. 31–50. New York: Pergamon.

HORNER, M. (1972). Toward an understanding of achievement-related conflicts in women. *Journal of Social Issues, 28,* 157–175.

HOUSEKNECHT, S. K. (1987). Voluntary childlessness. In M. B. Sussman & S. K. Steinmetz (Eds.), *Handbook of marriage and the family,* pp. 369–395. New York: Plenum.

HOWARD, G. S. (1989). *A tale of two stories: Excursions into a narrative approach to psychology.* Notre Dame, IN: University of Notre Dame Press.

HOWARD, G. S., & CONWAY, C. G. (1986). Can there be an empirical science of volitional action? *American Psychologist, 41,* 1241–1251.

HOWELL, W. H., & DIPBOYE, R. (1986). *Essentials of industrial organizational psychology* (3rd ed.). Chicago: Dorsey.

HUNT, W. A., BARNETT, L. W., & BRANCH, L. G. (1971). Relapse rates in addiction programs. *Journal of Clinical Psychology, 27,* 455–456.

HUNTER, A., & RIGER, S. (1986). The meaning of community in community mental health. *Journal of Community Psychology, 14,* 55–71.

HUXLEY, A. L. (1946). *Brave new world.* New York: Harper.

HYDE, H. S. (1985). *Half the human experience: The psychology of women.* Lexington, MA: D. C. Heath.

Institute of Medicine, National Academy of Sciences (1987). *Causes and consequences of alcohol problems.* Washington, DC: National Academy Press.

JACKINS, H. (1970). *Fundamentals of co-counseling manual for beginning classes in re-evaluation co-counseling.* Seattle: Personal Counselors.

JACKLIN C. N. (1989). Female and male: Issues of gender. *American Psychologist, 44,* 127–133.

JACOBSON, E. (1938). *Progressive relaxation.* Chicago: University of Chicago Press.

JACOBSON, N. E., & MARGOLIN, G. (1979). *Marital therapy.* New York: Brunner/Mazel.

JACOBSON, N. S. (1984). A component analysis of behavioral marital therapy: The relative effectiveness of behavior exchange and communication/problem-solving training. *Journal of Consulting and Clinical Psychology, 52,* 295–305.

JAMES, W. (1918). *The principles of psychology.* New York: Holt.

JANIS, I. L., & MANN, L. (1977). *Decision making.* New York: Free Press.

JANOV, A. (1970). *The primal scream.* New York: Dell.

JELLINEK, E. M. (1952). Phases of alcohol addiction. *Quarterly Journal of Studies on Alcohol, 13,* 673–684.

JENNI, M. A., & WOLLERSHEIM, J. P. (1979). Cognitive therapy, stress management, and the Type A behavior pattern. *Cognitive Therapy and Research, 3,* 61–73.

JESSOR, R. (1984). Adolescent development and behavioral health. In J. D. Matarazzo, S. M. Weiss, J. A. Herd, N. E. Miller, & S. M. Weiss (Eds.), *Behavioral health: A hand-*

book of health enhancement and disease prevention. New York: John Wiley.

JOHNSON, D. W. (1978). *Human relations and your career: A guide to interpersonal skills.* Englewood Cliffs, NJ: Prentice Hall.

JOHNSON, J. H., & McCUTCHEON, S. M. (1980). Assessing life stress in older children and adolescents: Preliminary findings with the Life Events Checklist. In I. G. Sarason & C. D. Spielberger (Eds.), *Stress and anxiety.* Washington, DC: Hemisphere.

JOHNSON, R. L., & SHRIER, D. K. (1985). Sexual victimization of boys. *Journal of Adolescent Health Care, 6,* 372–376.

JOHNSON, S. M. (1977). *First person singular: A guide to living the good life alone.* Philadelphia: J. B. Lippincott.

JOHNSON, S. M., WAHL, G., MARTIN, S., & JOHANSSEN, S. (1973). How deviant is the normal child: A behavioral analysis of the preschool child and his family. In R. D. Rubin, J. P. Brady, & J. D. Henderson (Eds.), *Advances in behavior therapy,* Vol. 4. New York: Academic Press.

JONES, E. E., & NISBETT, R. E. (1971). The actor and the observer: Divergent perceptions of the causes of behavior. In E. E. Jones, D. E. Kanouse, H. H. Kelley, R. E. Nisbett, S. Valins, & B. Weiner (Eds.), *Attribution: Perceiving the causes of behavior,* pp. 79–94. Morristown, NJ: General Learning Press.

JONES, L. S. (1986, December) Update on DSM-III(R). *Association for women in psychology newsletter.*

JONES, M. C. (1924). The elimination of children's fears. *Journal of Experimental Psychology, 7,* 382–390.

JONES, M. C. (1968). Personality correlates and antecedents of drinking patterns in adult males. *Journal of Consulting and Clinical Psychology, 32,* 2–12.

JONES, R. A. (1977). *Self-fulfilling prophecies: Social, psychological, and physiological effects of expectancies.* Hillsdale, NJ: Lawrence Erlbaum.

JUNG, C. G. (1958). Psychology and religion. In *The collected works of C. G. Jung.* New York: Bollingen.

KANFER, F. H., & GOLDSTEIN, A. P. (Eds.). (1986). *Helping people change* (3rd ed.). Elmsford, NY: Pergamon.

KANNER, A. D., COYNE, J. C., SCHAEFER, C., & LAZARUS, R. S. (1981). Comparison of two modes of stress measurement: Daily hassles and uplifts versus major life events. *Journal of Behavioral Medicine, 4,* 1–39.

KANTER, R. M. (1977). *Men and women of the corporation.* New York: Basic Books.

KAPLAN, A. G., & BEAN, J. P. (1976). *Beyond sex-role stereotypes: Readings toward a psychology of androgyny.* Boston: Little, Brown.

KAPLAN, H. S. (1974). *The new sex therapy: Active treatment of sexual dysfunctions.* New York: Brunner/Mazel.

KASS, D., STRAUSS, F. F., WEILL, E., GREIST, J. H., CHILES, J. A., & THURRELL, R. J. (1976). *Sex therapy at home.* NY: Simon & Schuster.

KATZ, J. H. (1985). The sociopolitical nature of counseling. *The Counseling Psychologist, 13,* 615–624.

KAZANTZAKIS, N. (1971). *Zorba the Greek.* New York: Simon & Schuster.

KAZDIN, A. E. (1982). Symptom substitution, generalization, and response covariation: Implications for psychotherapy outcome. *Psychological Bulletin, 91,* 349–365.

KEEN, S. (1988). The stories we live by. *Psychology Today, 22*(12), 42–47.

KEESEY, R. E. (1978). Set-points and body-weight revaluation. *Psychiatric Clinics of North America, 1,* 523–544.

KEESEY, R. E. (1986). A set-point theory of obesity. In K. D. Brownell & J. P. Foreyt (Eds.), *Handbook of eating disorders,* pp. 63–87. New York: Basic Books.

KELLEY, H. H., BERSCHEID, E., CHRISTENSEN, A., HARVEY, J. H., HUSTON, T. L., LEVINGER, G., McCLINTOCK, E., PEPLAU, L. A., & PETERSON, D. R. (Eds.) (1983). *Close relationships.* New York: W. H. Freeman.

KELLY, G. A. (1950). The warm-cold variable in first impressions of persons. *Journal of Personality, 18,* 431–439.

KELLY, G. A. (1955). *The psychology of personal constructs* (2 vols.). New York: W. W. Norton.

KIESLER, C. A. (1982). Mental hospitals and alternative care: Noninstitutionalization as potential public policy for mental patients. *American Psychologist, 37,* 349–360.

KINDER, B. N., PAPE, N. E., & WALFISH, S. (1980). Drug and alcohol education programs: A review of outcome studies. *International Journal of the Addictions, 15,* 1035–1054.

KINSEY, A. C., POMEROY, W. B., & MARTIN, C. E. (1948). *Sexual behavior in the human male.* Philadelphia: W. B. Saunders.

KINSEY, A. C., POMEROY, W. B., MARTIN, C. E., & GEBHARD, P. H. (1953). *Sexual behavior in the human female.* Philadelphia: W. B. Saunders.

KINZEL, A. F. (1970). Body buffer zone in violent prisoners. *American Journal of Psychiatry, 127,* 59–64.

KIRESUK, T., & SHERMAN, R. (1968). Goal attainment scaling: A general method for evaluating comprehensive community mental health programs. *Community Mental Health Journal, 4,* 443–453.

KIRKLAND, K., & HOLLANDSWORTH, J. G., JR. (1980). Effective test taking: Skills acquisition versus anxiety-reduction techniques. *Journal of Consulting and Clinical Psychology, 48,* 431–439.

KLAGSBRUN, F. (1985). *Married people.* New York: Bantam.

KLATSKY, A. L., FRIEDMAN, G. D., SIEGELAUB, A. B., & GERARD, M. J. (1977). Alcohol consumption among white, black, or Oriental men and women: Kaiser-Permanente multiphasic health examination data. *American Journal of Epidemiology, 105,* 311–323.

KLEIN, M. H. (1976). Feminist concepts of therapy outcome. *Psychotherapy: Theory, Research, and Practice, 13,* 89–95.

KLEINKE, C. L., & STANESKI, R. A. (1980). First impressions of female bust size. *Journal of Social Psychology, 110,* 123–134.

KLUCKHOHN, F. R., & STRODTBECK, F. L. (1961). *Variations in value orientations.* Evanston, IL: Row, Peterson.

KNAPP, T. J., DOWNS, D. L., & ALPERSON, J. R. (1976). Behavior therapy for insomnia: A review. *Behavior Therapy, 7,* 614–625.

KNEFELKAMP, L. L., WIDICK, C. C., & STROAD, B. (1978). Cognitive-developmental theory: A guide to counseling women. In L. W. Harmon, J. M. Birk, L. E. Fitzgerald, & M. F. Tanney (Eds.), *Counseling women.* Monterey, CA: Brooks/Cole.

KOBASA, S. C. (1979). Stressful life events, personality, and health: An inquiry into hardiness. *Journal of Personality and Social Psychology, 37,* 1–11.

KOBASA, S. C., MADDI, S. R., & ZOLA, M. A. (1983). Type A and hardiness. *Journal of Behavioral Medicine, 6,* 41–51.

KOBASA, S. C. O., & PUCCETTI, M. C. (1983). Personality and social resources in stress resistance. *Journal of Personality and Social Psychology, 45,* 839–850.

KOESKE, R. D. (1987). Premenstrual emotionality: Is biology destiny? In M. R. Walsh (Ed.), *The psychology of women: Ongoing debates,* pp. 137–146. New Haven, CT: Yale University Press.

KOHLBERG, L. (1967). Moral and religious education in the public schools: A developmental view. In T. R. Sizer (Ed.), *Religion and public education.* New York: Houghton Mifflin.

KOHLBERG, L. (1969). Stage and sequence: The cognitive-developmental approach to socialization. In D. A. Goslin (Ed.), *Handbook of socialization theory and research.* Chicago: Rand McNally.

KOHLBERG, L. (1981). *The philosophy of moral development,* Vol. 1. San Francisco: Harper & Row.

KOLB, D. A. (1984). *Experimental learning: Experience as the source of learning and development.* Englewood Cliffs, NJ: Prentice Hall.

KONECNI, V. (1975). The mediation of aggressive behavior: Arousal level vs. anger and cognitive labeling. *Journal of Personality and Social Psychology, 32,* 706–712.

KONECNI, V. J., LIBUSER, L., MORTON, H., & EBBESON, E. B. (1975). Effects of a violation of personal space on escape and helping responses. *Journal of Experimental Social Psychology, 11,* 288–299.

KOPEL, S., & ARKOWITZ, H. (1975). The role of attribution and self-perception in behavior change: Implications for behavior therapy. *Genetic Psychology Monographs, 92,* 175–212.

KOPP, C. B. (1982). Antecedents of self-regulation: A developmental perspective. *Developmental Psychology, 18,* 199–214.

KRUMBOLTZ, J. D., & KRUMBOLTZ, H. B. (1972). *Changing children's behavior.* Englewood Cliffs, NJ: Prentice Hall.

KÜBLER-ROSS, E. (1969). *On death and dying.* New York: Macmillan.

KUHN, T. S. (1970). *The structure of scientific revolutions* (rev. ed.). Chicago: University of Chicago Press.

LAFRAMBOISE, T. D. (1988). American Indian mental health policy. *American Psychologist, 43,* 388–397.

LAKEIN, A. (1973). *How to get control of your time and your life.* New York: Peter H. Wyden.

LANG, A. R., SEARLES, J., LAUERMAN, R., & ADESSON, V. (1980). Expectancy, alcohol, and sex guilt as determinants of interest in and reaction to sexual stimuli. *Journal of Abnormal Psychology, 89,* 644–653.

LANG, P. J. (1969). The mechanics of desensitization and the laboratory study of human fear. In C. M. Franks (Ed.), *Behavior therapy: Appraisal and status.* New York: McGraw-Hill.

LANG, P. J., & MELAMED, B. G. (1969). Avoidance conditioning therapy of an infant with chronic ruminative vomiting. *Journal of Abnormal Psychology, 74,* 1–8.

LARSON, B. (1978). *The meaning and mystery of being human.* Waco, TX: Word Books.

LAWRENCE, G. D. (1979). *People types and tiger stripes: A practical guide to learning styles.* Gainesville, FL: Center for Applications of Psychological Type.

LAZARUS, A. A. (1971). *Behavior therapy and beyond.* New York: McGraw-Hill.

LAZARUS, A., & FAY, A. (1975). *I can if I want to.* New York: Warner.

LEFCOURT, H. M. (1982). *Locus of control: Current trends in theory and research* (2nd ed.). Hillsdale, NJ: Lawrence Erlbaum.

LEFKOWITZ, M. M., ERON, L. D., WALDER, L. O., & HUESMANN, L. R. (1977). *Growing up to be violent.* New York: Pergamon.

LEHRMAN, N. (1971). *Masters and Johnson explained* (rev. ed.). New York: PEI Books.

LEONG, F. J. L. (1986). Counseling and psychotherapy with Asian-Americans: Review of the literature. *Journal of Counseling Psychology, 33,* 196–206.

LEVINE, R., CHEIN, I., & MURPHY, G. (1942). The relation of the intensity of a need to the amount of perception distortion: A preliminary report. *Journal of Psychology, 13,* 283–293.

LEVINGER, G. (1983). Development and change. In H. H. Kelley, E. Berscheid, A. Christensen, J. H. Harvey, T. L. Huston, G. Levinger, E. McClintock, L. A. Peplau, & D. R. Peterson, (Eds.). *Close relationships,* pp. 315–359. New York: W. H. Freeman.

LEVINSON, D. J., DARROW, C. M., KLEIN, E. G., LEVINSON, M. H., & MCKEE, B. (1974). The psychosocial development of men in early adulthood and the midlife transition. In D. F. Ricks, A. Thomas, & M. Roff (Eds.), *Life history research in psychopathology,* Vol. 3. Minneapolis: University of Minnesota Press.

LEWINSOHN, P. M. (1974). Clinical and theoretical aspects of depression. In K. S. Calhoun, H. E. Adams, & K. M. Mitchell (Eds.), *Innovative treatment methods in psychopathology,* pp. 63–102. New York: John Wiley.

LEWINSOHN, P. M., & AMENSON, C. S. (1978). Some relations between pleasant and unpleasant mood-related events and depression. *Journal of Abnormal Psychology, 87,* 644–654.

LEWINSOHN, P. M., HOBERMAN, H. M., & ROSENBAUM, M. (1988). A prospective study of risk factors for unipolar depression. *Journal of Abnormal Psychology, 97,* 251–264.

LEWINSOHN, P. M., MUÑOZ, R. F., YOUNGREN, M. A., & ZEISS, A. M. (1978). *Control your depression.* Englewood Cliffs, NJ: Prentice Hall.

LEWINSOHN, P. M., & ROSENBAUM, M. (1987). Recall of parental behavior by acute depressives, remitted depressives, and nondepressives. *Journal of Personality and Social Psychology, 52,* 611–619.

LEWIS, C. S. (1960). *Mere Christianity. New York: Macmillan.*

LEWIS, H. B. (1978). Psychology and gender. In E. Tobach & B. Rosoff (Eds.), *Genes and gender.* New York: Gordian Press.

LICHSTEIN, K. L. (1988). *Clinical relaxation strategies.* New York: John Wiley.

LICHTENSTEIN, E., & BROWN, R. A. (1980). Smoking cessation methods: Review and recommendations. In W. R. Miller (Ed.), *The addictive behaviors: Treatment of alcoholism, drug abuse, smoking, and obesity,* pp. 169–206. New York: Pergamon.

LIFTON, R. J. (1984). Beyond psychic numbing: A call to awareness. In B. H. Weston (Ed.), *Toward nuclear disarmament and global society: A search for alternatives,* pp. 111–122. Boulder, CO: Westview.

LIFTON, R. J., & FALK, R. (1982). *Indefensible weapons.* New York: Basic Books.

LIPMAN-BLUMEN, J. (1984). *Gender roles and power.* Englewood Cliffs, NJ: Prentice Hall.

LIPS, H. M. (1988). *Sex and gender: An Introduction.* Mountain View, CA: Mayfield.

LITMAN, G. K. (1986). Alcoholism survival: The prevention of relapse. In W. R. Miller & N. Heather (Eds.), *Treating addictive behaviors: Processes of change,* pp. 391–405. New York: Plenum.

LITTLE, K. B. (1968). Cultural variations in social schemata. *Journal of Personality and Social Psychology, 10,* 1–7.

LØBERG, T., & MILLER, W. R. (1986). Personality, cognitive, and neuropsychological dimensions of harmful alcohol consumption: A cross-national comparison of clinical samples. *Annals of the New York Academy of Sciences, 472,* 75–97.

LOBITZ, W. C., & LOPICCOLO, J. (1972). New methods in the behavioral treatment of sexual dysfunction. *Journal of Behavior Therapy and Experimental Psychiatry, 3,* 265–271.

LOCKE, E. A., SHAW, K. N., SAARI, L. M., & LATHAM, G. P. (1981). Goal setting and task performance: 1969–1980. *Psychological Bulletin, 90,* 125–152.

LONG, V. O. (1986). Relationship of masculinity to self-esteem and self-acceptance in female professionals, college students, clients, and victims of domestic violence. *Journal of Consulting and Clinical Psychology, 54,* 323–327.

LONG, V. O., & HEGGEN, C. H. (1988). Clergy perceptions of spiritual health for adults, men, and women. *Counseling and Values, 32,* 213–220.

LORENZ, K. (1966). *On aggression.* New York: Harcourt Brace Jovanovich.

LUDWICK-ROSENTHAL, R., & NEUFELD, R. W. J. (1988). Stress management during noxious medical procedures: An evaluative review of outcome studies. *Psychological Bulletin, 104,* 326–342.

LUDWIG, D. J., & MAEHR, M. L. (1967). Changes in self-concept and stated behavioral preferences. *Child Development, 38,* 453–467.

LUNDBERG, U. (1982). Psychophysiological arousal of performance and adjustment to stress. In H. W. Krohne & L. Laux (Eds.), *Achievement, stress, and anxiety,* pp. 75–91. Washington, DC: Hemisphere.

LURIA, A. R. (1961). *The role of speech in the regulation of normal and abnormal behavior.* New York: Liveright.

LURIA, A. R. (1973). *The working brain.* New York: Basic Books.

LUTHE, W., & SCHULTZ, J. H. (Eds.) (1969). *Autogenic therapy.* New York: Grune & Stratton.

LYLE, J. (1972). Television in daily life: Patterns of use. In E. A. Rubenstein, G. A. Comstock, & J. P. Murray (Eds.), *Television and social behavior: IV. Television in day-to-day life: Patterns of use.* Washington, DC: U.S. Government Printing Office.

MACCOBY, E., & JACKLIN, C. N. (1974). *The psychology of sex differences.* Palo Alto, CA: Stanford University Press.

MACCOBY, N., FARQUHAR, J. W., WOOD, P. D., & ALEXANDER, J. (1977). Reducing the risk of cardiovascular disease: Effects of a community-based campaign on knowledge and behavior. *Journal of Community Health, 3,* 100–114.

MACE, D. R. (1975). Marriage concepts for research. *The Family Coordinator, 24,* 171–173.

MACE, D. & MACE, V. (1974). *We can have better marriages if we really want them.* Nashville, TN: Abingdon.

MACKLIN, E. D. (1987). Nontraditional family forms. In M. B. Sussman & S. K. Steinmetz (Eds.), *Handbook of marriage and the family,* pp. 317–353. New York: Plenum.

MACY, J. R. (1983). *Despair and personal power in the nuclear age.* Philadelphia: New Society.

MAHLER, M. (1975). *The psychological birth of the human infant.* New York: Basic Books.

MAHONEY, M. J. (1974). *Cognition and behavior modification.* Cambridge, MA: Ballinger.

MAHONEY, M. J. (1979). *Self-change: Strategies for solving personal problems.* New York: W. W. Norton.

MAHONEY, M. J., & AVENER, M. (1977). Psychology of the elite athlete: An exploratory study. *Cognitive Therapy and Research, 1*(2), 135–141.

MANASTES, G., & CORSINI, R. (1982). *Individual psychology.* Itasca, IL: F. E. Peacock.

MARCIA, J. E. (1967). Ego identity status: Relationship to change in self-esteem, "general maladjustment," and authoritarianism. *Journal of Personality, 35,* 118–133.

MARKS, I. M. (1978). *Living with fear: Understanding and coping with anxiety.* New York: McGraw-Hill.

MARLATT, G. A. (1983). The controlled drinking controversy: A commentary. *American Psychologist, 38,* 1097–1110.

MARLATT, G. A., & GORDON, J. R. (Eds.). (1985). *Relapse prevention: Maintenance strategies in the treatment of addictive behaviors.* New York: Guilford.

MARLATT, G. A., KOSTURN, C. F., & LANG, A. R. (1975). Provocation to anger and opportunity for retaliation as determinants of alcohol consumption in social drinkers. *Journal of Abnormal Psychology, 84,* 652–659.

MARLATT, G. A., & ROHSENOW, D. J. (1980). Cognitive processes in alcohol use: Expectancy and the balanced placebo design. In N. K. Mello (Ed.), *Advances in substance abuse: Behavioral and biological research*, Vol. 1. Greenwich, CN: JAI Press.

MASLOW, A. H. (1954). *Motivation and personality.* New York: Harper.

MASLOW, A. H. (1968). *Toward a psychology of being.* New York: Van Nostrand.

MASLOW, A. H. (1971). *The farther reaches of human nature.* New York: Viking.

MASSON, J. M. (1984). *The assault on truth: Freud's suppression of the seduction theory.* New York: Farrar, Straus, & Giroux.

MASTERS, W. H., & JOHNSON, V. E. (1966). *Human sexual response.* Boston: Little, Brown.

MASTERS, W. H., & JOHNSON, V. E. (1970). *Human sexual inadequacy.* Boston: Little, Brown.

MATHENY, K. B., AYCOCK, D. W., PUGH, J. L., CURLETTE, W. L., & CANNELLA, K. A. S. (1986). Stress coping: A qualitative and quantitative synthesis with implications for treatment. *The Counseling Psychologist, 14*, 499–549.

MATHEWS, A., BANCROFT, J., WHITEHEAD, A., JACKMANN, A., JULIER, D., BANCROFT, J., GATH, D., & SHAW, P. (1976). The behavioural treatment of sexual inadequacy: A comparative study. *Behaviour Research and Therapy, 14*, 427–436.

MATHEWS, K. W., & CANON, L. K. (1975). Environmental noise level as a determinant of helping behavior. *Journal of Personality and Social Psychology, 32*, 571–577.

MATLIN, M. W. (1987). *The psychology of women.* New York: Holt, Rinehart, and Winston.

MATTHEWS, K. A., & HAYNES, S. G. (1986). Type A behavior pattern and coronary disease risk: Update and critical evaluation. *American Journal of Epidemiology, 123*, 923–960.

MAY, R. (1967). *Psychology and the human dilemma.* New York: Van Nostrand.

MAY, R. (1969). *Love and will.* New York: Dell.

MCCAULLEY, M. H. (1977). *The Myers longitudinal medical study.* Gainesville, FL: Center for Applications of Psychological Type.

MCCAULLEY, M. H. (1978). *Application of the Myers-Briggs Type indicator to medicine and other health professions.* Gainesville, FL: Center for Applications of Psychological Type.

MCCLELLAND, D. C., & ATKINSON, J. W. (1948). The projective expression of needs: I. The effect of different intensities of the hunger drive on perception. *Journal of Psychology, 25*, 205–222.

MCCORD, W., & MCCORD, J. (1962). A longitudinal study of the personality of alcoholics. In D. P. Pitman & C. R. Snyder (Eds.), *Society, culture, and drinking patterns.* New York: John Wiley.

MCGHEE, P. E. (1979). *Humor: Its origin and development.* San Francisco: W. H. Freeman.

MCGINNIS, K., & MCGINNIS, J. (1983). *Parenting for peace and justice.* Maryknoll, NY: Orbis.

MCGREGOR, D. (1960). *The human side of enterprise.* New York: McGraw-Hill.

MCINTYRE, M. S. (1980). The epidemiology and taxonomy of suicide. In M. S. McIntyre & C. R. Angle (Eds.), *Suicide attempts in children and youth*, pp. 1–23. New York: Harper & Row.

MCREYNOLDS, P. (1968). The assessment of anxiety: A survey of available techniques. In P. McReynolds (Ed.), *Advances in psychological assessment techniques*, Vol. 1, pp. 244–264. Palo Alto, CA: Science and Behavior Books.

MEAD, M. (1935). *Sex and temperament in three primitive societies.* New York: William A. Morrow.

MEECE, J. L., PARSONS, J. E., KACZALA, C. M., GOFF, S. B., & FUTTERMAN, R. (1982). Sex differences in math achievement: Toward a model of academic choice. *Psychological Bulletin, 91* (2), 324–348.

MEICHENBAUM, D. (1975). A self-instructional approach to stress management: A proposal for stress inoculation training. In I. Sarason & C. D. Spielberger (Eds.), *Stress and Anxiety*, Vol. 2, pp. 227–263. New York: John Wiley.

MEICHENBAUM, D. (1977). *Cognitive-behavior modification: An integrative approach.* New York: Plenum.

MELAMED, E. (1983). *Mirror, mirror: The terror of not being young.* New York: Linden.

MELNECHUK, T. (1983). The dream machine. *Psychology Today, 17*(11), 22–34.

MENNING, B. E. (1977). *Infertility: A guide for the childless couple.* Englewood Cliffs, NJ: Prentice Hall.

MENNINGER, K. (1968). *The crime of punishment.* New York: Viking.

MENNINGER, K. (1973). *Whatever became of sin?* New York: Hawthorne.

MESULAN, M. M. (1985). *Principles of behavioral neurology.* Philadelphia: F. A. Davis.

METALSKY, G. I., ABRAMSON, L. Y., SELIGMAN, M. E. P., SEMMEL, A., & PETERSON, C. (1982). Attributional styles and life events in the classroom: Vulnerability and invulnerability to depressive mood reactions. *Journal of Personality and Social Psychology, 43*, 612–617.

MILAM, J. R., & KETCHAM, K. (1983). *Under the influence: A guide to the myths and realities of alcoholism.* New York: Bantam.

MILGRAM, S. (1963). Behavioral study of obedience. *Journal of Abnormal and Social Psychology, 67*, 371–378.

MILGRAM, S. (1974). *Obedience to authority: An experimental view.* New York: Harper & Row.

MILL, J. (1869). *The analysis of the phenomena of the human mind.* 2nd. ed. Charlottesville, VA: Ibis.

MILL, J. S. (1865). An examination of Sir William Hamilton's philosophy. In J. M. Robson (Ed.), *Collected Works of John Stuart Mill.* Toronto: University of Toronto Press.

MILLER, B. F. (1987). *Encyclopedia and dictionary of medicine, nursing, and allied health* (4th ed.). Philadelphia: W. B. Saunders.

MILLER, D. R., & SOBELMAN, G. (1985). Models of the family: A critical review of alternatives. In L. L'Abate (Ed.), *The handbook of family psychology and therapy*, pp. 3–37. Homewood, IL: Dorsey.

MILLER, J. B. (1976). *Toward a new psychology of women.* Boston: Beacon.

MILLER, J. G. (1978). *Living systems.* New York: McGraw-Hill.

MILLER, R. R., & BALAZ, M. A. (1981). Differences in adaptiveness between classically conditioned responses and instrumentally acquired responses. In N. E. Spear & R. R. Miller (Eds.), *Information processing in animals: Memory mechanisms,* pp. 49–80. Hillsdale, NJ: Lawrence Erlbaum.

MILLER, W. R. (1976). Alcoholism scales and objective assessment methods: A review. *Psychological Bulletin, 83,* 649–674.

MILLER, W. R. (1978). Behavioral treatment of problem drinkers: A comparative outcome study of three controlled drinking therapies. *Journal of Consulting and Clinical Psychology, 46,* 74–86.

MILLER, W. R. (Ed.) (1980). *The addictive behaviors: Treatment of alcoholism, drug abuse, smoking, and obesity.* New York: Pergamon.

MILLER, W. R. (1983a). Controlled drinking: A history and critical review. *Journal of Studies on Alcohol, 44,* 68–83.

MILLER, W. R. (1983b). Motivational interviewing with problem drinkers. *Behavioural Psychotherapy, 11,* 147–172.

MILLER, W. R. (1985a). *Living as if: How positive faith can change your life.* Philadelphia: Westminster.

MILLER, W. R. (1985b). Motivation for treatment: A review with special emphasis on alcoholism. *Psychological Bulletin, 98,* 84–107.

MILLER, W. R. (1986). Haunted by the *Zeitgeist:* Reflections on contrasting treatment goals and concepts of alcoholism in Europe and the United States. *Annals of the New York Academy of Sciences, 472,* 110–129.

MILLER, W. R. (1988). Including clients' spiritual perspectives in cognitive-behavior therapy. In W. R. Miller & J. E. Martin (Eds.), *Behavior therapy and religion: Integrating spiritual and behavioral approaches to change,* pp. 43–55. Newbury Park, CA: Sage.

MILLER, W. R., & DANAHER, B. G. (1976). Maintenance in parent training. In J. D. Krumboltz & C. E. Thoresen (Eds.), *Counseling methods.* New York: Holt, Rinehart & Winston.

MILLER, W. R., & DIPILATO, M. (1983). Treatment of nightmares via relaxation and desensitization: A controlled evaluation. *Journal of Consulting and Clinical Psychology, 51,* 870–877.

MILLER, W. R., GRIBSKOV, C. J., & MORTELL, R. L. (1981). Effectiveness of a self-control manual for problem drinkers with and without therapist contact. *International Journal of the Addictions, 16,* 1247–1254.

MILLER, W. R., HEDRICK, K. E., & ORLOFSKY, D. R. (1982). The Helpful Responses Questionnaire: An objective instrument for measuring accurate empathy. Unpublished manuscript, University of New Mexico, Albuquerque.

MILLER, W. R., HEDRICK, K. E., & TAYLOR, C. A. (1983). Addictive behaviors and life problems before and after behavioral treatment of problem drinkers. *Addictive Behaviors, 8,* 403–412.

MILLER, W. R., & HESTER, R. K. (1980). Treating the problem drinker: Modern approaches. In W. R. Miller (Ed.), *The addictive behaviors: Treatment of alcoholism, drug abuse, smoking, and obesity,* pp. 11–141. New York: Pergamon.

MILLER, W. R., & HESTER, R. K. (1986a). The effectiveness of alcoholism treatment: What research reveals. In W. R. Miller & N. Heather (Eds.), *Treating addictive behaviors: Processes of change,* pp. 121–174. New York: Plenum.

MILLER, W. R., & HESTER, R. K. (1986b). Inpatient alcoholism treatment: Who benefits? *American Psychologist, 41,* 794–805.

MILLER, W. R., & JACKSON, K. A. (1985). *Practical psychology for pastors.* Englewood Cliffs, NJ: Prentice Hall.

MILLER, W. R., LECKMAN, A. L., & TINKCOM, M. (1989). *Long-term follow-up of behavioral self-control training.* Manuscript submitted for publication.

MILLER, W. R., & MARTIN, J. E. (Eds.). (1988). *Behavior therapy and religion: Integrating spiritual and behavioral approaches to change.* Newbury Park, CA: Sage.

MILLER, W. R., & MUÑOZ, R. F. (1982). *How to control your drinking,* (rev. ed.). Albuquerque: University of New Mexico Press.

MILLER, W. R., & PECHACEK, T. F. (1987). New roads: Assessing and treating psychological dependence. *Journal of Substance Abuse Treatment, 4,* 73–77.

MILLER, W. R., & SAUCEDO, C. F. (1983). Assessment of neuropsychological impairment and brain damage in problem drinkers. In C. J. Golden, J. A. Moses, Jr., J. A. Coffman, W. R. Miller, & F. D. Strider (Eds.), *Clinical neuropsychology: Interface with neurologic and psychiatric disorders,* pp. 141–195. New York: Grune & Stratton.

MILLER, W. R., & TAYLOR, C. A. (1980). Relative effectiveness of bibliotherapy, individual and group self-control training in the treatment of problem drinkers. *Addictive Behaviors, 5,* 13–24.

MILLER, W. R., TAYLOR, C. A., & WEST, J. C. (1980). Focused versus broad-spectrum behavior therapy for problem drinkers. *Journal of Consulting and Clinical Psychology, 48,* 590–601.

MILLET, K. (1970). *Sexual politics.* Garden City, NY: Doubleday.

MINDHAM, R. H. S. (1982). Tricyclic antidepressants and amine precursors. In E. S. Paykel (Ed.), *Handbook of affective disorders,* pp. 231–245. New York: Guilford.

MINUCHIN, S. (1974). *Families and family therapy.* Cambridge, MA: Harvard University Press.

MIRELS, H. L., & McPEEK, R. W. (1977). Self-advocacy and self-esteem. *Journal of Consulting and Clinical Psychology, 45,* 1132–1138.

MISCHEL, W., EBBESEN, E. B., & ZEISS, A. R. (1973). Selective attention to the self: Situational and dispositional determinants. *Journal of Personality and Social Psychology, 27,* 129–142.

MOODY, R. A., JR. (1975). *Life after life.* Covington, GA: Mockingbird Books.

MOORE-WEST, M., HARRINGTON, D. L., MENNIN, S. P., & KAUFMAN, A. (1986). Distress and attitudes toward the learning environment: Effects of a curriculum innovation. *Research in Medical Education: Proceedings of the 25th Annual Conference*, pp. 293–300. Washington, DC: Association of American Medical Colleges.

MOROKOFF, P. J. (1985). Effects of sex guilt, repression, sexual "arousability," and sexual experiences on female sexual arousal during erotica and fantasy. *Journal of Personality and Social Psychology, 49*, 177–187.

MOSHER, D. L. (1968). Measurement of guilt in females by self-report inventories. *Journal of Consulting and Clinical Psychology, 32* (6), 690–695.

MULLENER, N., & LAIRD, J. D. (1971). Some developmental changes in the organization of self-evaluations. *Developmental Psychology, 5*(2), 233–236.

MUNROE, R. L., & MUNROE, R. H. (1975). *Cross-cultural human development.* Belmont, CA: Wadsworth.

MYERS, I. B., & MYERS, P. B. (1980). *Gifts differing.* Palo Alto, CA: Consulting Psychologists Press.

MYERS, I. B., & MCCAULLEY, M. H. (1985). *Manual: A guide to the development and use of the Myers-Briggs Type Indicator.* Palo Alto, CA: Consulting Psychologists Press.

MYERS, R. E., & SPERRY, R. W. (1953). Interocular transfer of a visual form discrimination habit in cats after section of the optic chiasm and corpus callosum. *Anatomical Record, 175*, 351–352.

NAHAS, G. G., & FRICK, H. C., II. (Eds.) (1981). *Drug abuse in the modern world.* New York: Pergamon.

NAISBITT, J. (1984). *Megatrends: Ten new directions transforming our lives.* New York: Warner.

NAISBITT, J., & ABURDENE, P. (1985). *Re-inventing the corporation.* New York: Warner.

National Institute on Alcohol Abuse and Alcoholism (1987). *Alcohol and health: Sixth special report to the U.S. Congress.* Rockville, MD: U.S. Department of Health and Human Services.

NEAR, J. P. (1985). A discriminant analysis of plateaued versus nonplateaued managers. *Journal of Vocational Behavior, 26*, 177–188.

NEKI, J. S. (1976). An examination of the cultural relativism of dependence as a dynamic of social and therapeutic relationships. *British Journal of Medical Psychology, 49*, 1–22.

NELSON, J. W. (1976). *Your God is alive and well and appearing in popular culture.* Philadelphia: Westminster.

NEUGARTEN, B. L. (1976). Adaptation and the life cycle. *Counseling Psychologist, 6*, 16–20.

NEUGARTEN, B. L. (1979). Time, age and the life cycle. *American Journal of Psychiatry, 136*, 887–894.

NEUMANN, P. L. (1983, December). How to help a friend in tears. *Ms.*, 84–88.

NEWMAN, G. (1983). *Just and painful: A case for the corporal punishment of criminals.* London: Macmillan.

NEWMAN, J. E. (1984, December). Sex differences in conversational style: The use of questions and colour terms. Paper presented at the annual meeting of the Linguistic Society of America, Baltimore.

NGUYEN, T., HESLIN, R., & NGUYEN, M. L. (1975). The meanings of touch: Sex differences. *Journal of Communication, 25*(3), 92–103.

NIEBUHR, R. (1943). *The Serenity Prayer.*

NIN, A. (1981). *The diary of Anaïs Nin* (7 vols.). New York: Harcourt Brace Jovanovich.

NISBETT, R. E., & GORDON, A. (1967). Self-esteem and susceptibility to social influence. *Journal of Personality and Social Psychology, 5*, 268–276.

NISBETT, R. E., & SCHACHTER, S. (1966). Cognitive manipulation of pain. *Journal of Experimental Social Psychology 2*, 227–236.

NISBETT, R. E., & VALINS, S. (1971). Perceiving the causes of one's own behavior. In E. E. Jones, D. E. Kanouse, H. H. Kelley, R. E. Nisbett, S. Valins, & B. Weiner (Eds.), *Attribution: Perceiving the causes of behavior.* New York: General Learning Press.

NOBLE, E. P. (1973). Alcohol and adrenocortical function of animals and man. In P. G. Bourne & R. Fox (Eds.), *Alcoholism: Progress in research and treatment*, pp. 105–135. New York: Academic Press.

NORWOOD, R. (1985). *Women who love too much: When you keep wishing and hoping he'll change.* New York: Simon & Schuster.

NOTMAN, M. (1979). Midlife concerns of women: Implications of the menopause. *American Journal of Psychiatry, 136*, 1270–1273.

NOVACO, R. W. (1975). *Anger control: The development and evaluation of an experimental treatment.* Lexington, MA: D. C. Heath.

NOWICKI, S., & DUKE, M. P. (1974). A locus of control scale for college as well as non-college adults. *Journal of Personality Assessment, 38*, 136–137.

NUNES, E. V., FRANK, K. A., & KORNFELD, D. S. (1987). Psychologic treatment for the type A behavior pattern and for coronary heart disease: A meta-analysis of the literature. *Psychosomatic Medicine, 49*, 159–173.

NURNBERGER, J. I., & GERSHON, E. S. (1982). Genetics. In E. S. Paykel (Ed.), *Handbook of affective disorders*, pp. 126–145. New York: Guilford.

OATES, W. E. (1971). *Confessions of a workaholic.* Nashville, TN: Abingdon.

OATES, W. E. (1973). *The psychology of religion.* Waco, TX: Word Books.

OATES, W. E. (1978). *Workaholics, make laziness work for you!* Nashville, TN: Abingdon.

O'CONNELL, A. N., & RUSSO, N. F. (1983). *Models of achievement: Reflections of eminent women in psychology.* New York: Columbia University Press.

OLDS, J. (1958). Self-stimulation of the brain. *Science, 127*, 315–324.

O'LEARY, K. D., & WILSON, G. T. (1987). *Behavior therapy: Application and outcome* (2nd ed.). Englewood Cliffs, NJ: Prentice Hall.

OLLENDICK, T. H. (1986). Behavior therapy with children and adolescents. In S. L. Garfield & A. E. Bergin (Eds.), *Handbook of psychotherapy and behavior change* (3rd ed.), pp. 525–564. New York: John Wiley.

ORWELL, G. (1949). *1984*. New York: Harcourt, Brace.

OSGOOD, C. E., SUCI, G. J., & TANNENBAUM, P. H. (1981). *The measurement of meaning*. Urbana: University of Illinois Press.

OUCHI, W. G. (1981). *Theory Z: How American business can meet the Japanese challenge*. Reading, MA: Addison-Wesley.

PAGE, R. A. (1977). Noise and helping behavior. *Environment and Behavior, 9,* 311–335.

PARKE, R. D., & SLABY, R. G. (1983). The development of aggression. In E. M. Hetherington (Ed.), *Handbook of Child Psychology*, Vol. 4, *Socialization, personality and social development* (4th ed.), pp. 547–641. New York: John Wiley.

PATTERSON, G. R. (1971). Behavioral intervention procedures in the classroom and in the home. In A. E. Bergin & S. L. Garfield (Eds.), *Handbook of psychotherapy and behavior change: An empirical analysis*. New York: John Wiley.

PATTERSON, G. R. (1974). Intervention for boys with conduct problems: Multiple settings, treatments and criteria. *Journal of Consulting and Clinical Psychology, 42,* 471–481.

PATTERSON, G. R. (1976). The aggressive child: Victim and architect of a coercive system. In E. J. Mash, L. A. Hamerlynk, and L. C. Handy (Eds.), *Behavior modification and families*. New York: Brunner/Mazel.

PATTERSON, G. R. (1976). Some procedures for assessing changes in marital interaction patterns. *Oregon Research Institute Bulletin, 16*(7).

PATTERSON, G. R., COBB, J. A., & RAY, R. (1973). A social engineering technology for retraining the families of aggressive boys. In H. Adams & L. Unikel (Eds.), *Issues and trends in behavior therapy*. Springfield, IL: Charles C Thomas.

PATTERSON, G. R., LITTMAN, R. A., & BRICKER, W. (1967). Assertive behavior in children: A step toward a theory of aggression. *Monographs of the Society for Research in Child Development, 32* (Whole No. 5).

PATTERSON, G. R., & REID, J. B. (1970). Reciprocity and coercion: Two facets of social systems. In C. Neuringer & J. L. Michael (Eds.), *Behavior modification in clinical psychology*. New York: Appleton-Century Crofts.

PATTERSON, G. R., WEISS, R. L., & HOPS, H. (1976). Training of marital skills: Some problems and concepts. In H. Leitenberg (Ed.), *Handbook of behavior modification and behavior therapy*, pp. 242–254. Englewood Cliffs, NJ: Prentice Hall.

PAVLOV, I. P. (1927). *Conditioned reflexes*. London: Oxford.

PAYKEL, E. S. (1982). Life events and early environment. In E. S. Paykel (Ed.), *Handbook of affective disorders*. New York: Guilford.

PEABODY, D. (1967). Trait inferences: Evaluative and descriptive aspects. *Journal of Personality and Social Psychology Monographs, 7* (Whole No. 644).

PEABODY, D. (1984). Personality dimensions through trait inferences. *Journal of Personality and Social Psychology, 46,* 384–403.

PEABODY, D. (1987). Selecting representative trait adjectives. *Journal of Personality and Social Psychology, 52,* 59–71.

PEARL, D., BOUTHILET, L., & LZAR, S. J. (1982). *Television and behavior: Ten years of scientific progress and implications for the eighties*. Report by the Surgeon General on television and violence. Washington, DC: U.S. Government Printing Office.

PECK, M. S. (1978). *The road less traveled*. New York: Simon & Schuster.

PECK, M. S. (1987). *The different drummer: Community making and peace*. New York: Simon & Schuster.

PEELE, S. (1985). *The meaning of addiction: Compulsive experience and its interpretation*. Lexington, MA: Lexington Books.

PEELE, S. (1987). Why do controlled-drinking outcomes vary by investigator, by country and by era? Cultural conceptions of relapse and remission in alcoholism. *Drug and Alcohol Dependence, 20,* 1173–1201.

PEELE, S., & BRODSKY, A. (1975). *Love and addiction*. New York: Signet.

PELLETIER, K. R. (1977). *Mind as healer, mind as slayer: A holistic approach to preventing stress disorders*. New York: Delta.

PEPLAU, L. A. (1983). Roles and gender. In H. H. Kelley, E. Berscheid, A. Christensen, J. Harvey, & D. Peterson (Eds.), *Close relationships*, pp. 220–264. San Francisco: W. H. Freeman.

PEPLAU, L. A., & AMARO, H. (1982). Understanding lesbian relationships. In W. Paul, J. D. Weinrich, J. C. Gonsiorek, & M. E. Hotvedt (Eds.), *Homosexuality: Social, psychological, and biological issues*, pp. 233–247. Beverly Hills, CA: Sage.

PERLS, F. S. (1969). *Gestalt therapy verbatim*. Lafayette, CA: Real People Press.

PERRY, D. G., PERRY, L. C., & RASMUSSEN, P. (1986). Cognitive social learning mediators of aggression. *Child Development, 57,* 700–711.

PERRY, J. D., & WHIPPLE, B. (1981). Pelvic muscle strength of female ejaculators: Evidence in support of a new theory of orgasm. *Journal of Sex Research, 17,* 22–39.

PETER, L. J., & HULL, R. (1969). *The Peter principle: Why things always go wrong*. New York: William A. Morrow.

PETERS, S. D., WYATT, G. E., & FINKELHOR, D. (1986). Prevalence: A review of the research. In D. Finkelhor (Ed.), *A sourcebook on child sexual abuse*. Beverly Hills, CA: Sage.

PETERSON, C., & SELIGMAN, M. E. P. (1984). Causal explanations as a risk factor for depression: Theory and evidence. *Psychological Review, 91,* 347–374.

PETRIE, A. (1967). *Individuality in pain and suffering*. Chicago: University of Chicago Press.

PFEFFER, C. R. (1981). Suicidal behavior of children: A review with implications for research and practice. *American Journal of Psychiatry, 138,* 154–159.

PFEFFER, C. R. (1986). *The suicidal child*. New York: Guilford.

PHIFER, J. F., & MURRELL, S. A. (1986). Etiologic factors in the onset of depressive symptoms in older adults. *Journal of Abnormal Psychology, 95,* 282–291.

PIAGET, J. (1932). *The moral judgment of the child.* New York: Free Press.

PIETROPINTO, A. (1986). Survey analysis: Inhibited sexual desire. *Medical aspects of human sexuality, 20* (10), 46–49.

PLAS, J. M., & WALLSTON, B. S. (1983). Women oriented toward male dominated careers: Is the reference group male or female? *Journal of Counseling Psychology, 30,* 46–54.

PLUTCHIK, R. (1980). *Emotion: A psychoevolutionary synthesis.* New York: Harper & Row.

POLICH, J. M., ARMOR, D. J., & BRAIKER, H. B. (1981). *The course of alcoholism: Four years after treatment.* New York: John Wiley.

POPE, K. S., LEVENSON, H., & SCHOVER, L. R. (1979). Sexual intimacy in psychology training: Results and implications of a national survey. *American Psychologist, 34,* 682–689.

PRATHER, H. (1970). *Notes to myself.* Lafayette, CA: Real People Press.

PREMACK, D. (1965). Reinforcement theory. In D. Levine (Ed.), *Nebraska Symposium on Motivation: 1965,* pp. 123–180. Lincoln: University of Nebraska Press.

PROCHASKA, J. O. (1984). *Systems of psychotherapy: A transtheoretical analysis* (2nd ed.). Homewood, IL: Dorsey.

PROCHASKA, J. O., & DiCLEMENTE, C. (1982). Transtheoretical therapy: Toward a more integrative model of change. *Psychotherapy: Theory, Research and Practice, 19,* 276–288.

PROCHASKA, J. O., & DiCLEMENTE, C. (1983). Stages and processes of self-change of smoking: Toward an integrative model of change. *Journal of Consulting and Clinical Psychology, 51,* 390–395.

PROCHASKA, J. O., & DiCLEMENTE, C. (1984). *The transtheoretical approach: Crossing traditional boundaries of therapy.* Homewood, IL: Dow Jones-Irwin.

PROCHASKA, J. O., & DiCLEMENTE, C. C. (1986). Toward a comprehensive model of change. In W. R. Miller & N. Heather (Eds.), *Treating addictive behaviors: Processes of change,* pp. 3–27. New York: Plenum.

PROGOFF, I. (1975). *At a journal workshop: The basic text and guide for using the intensive journal.* New York: Dialogue House.

PROPST, R. (1980). The comparative efficacy of religious and nonreligious imagery for the treatment of mild depression in religious individuals. *Cognitive Therapy and Research, 4,* 167–178.

PRUYSER, P. W. (1976). *The minister as diagnostician.* Philadelphia: Westminster.

RADIN, J. J. (1978). An exploratory study of personality development during early adulthood, ages 23–29. Doctoral dissertation, University of Michigan, Ann Arbor.

RAMSEY, R. W. (1977). Behavioral approaches to bereavement. *Behaviour Research and Therapy, 15,* 131–135.

RANK, O. (1936). Life fear and death fear. In *Will therapy.* New York: Alfred A. Knopf.

RAPS, C. S., PETERSON, C., REINHARD, K. E., ABRAMSON, L. Y., & SELIGMAN, M. E. P. (1982). Attributional style among depressed patients. *Journal of Abnormal Psychology, 91,* 102–103.

REINISCH, J. M., SANDERS, S. A., & ZIEMBA-DAVIS, M. (1988). The study of sexual behavior in relation to the transmission of human immunodeficiency virus: Caveats and recommendations. *American Psychologist, 43* (11), 921–927.

REYNIS, L. A. (1987). *A woman's guide to the workplace.* (rev. ed.) Albuquerque: New Mexico Public Interest Research Group.

ROBERTS, W. R., PENK, W. E., GEARING, M. L., ROBINOWITZ, R., DOLAN, M. P., & PATTERSON, E. T. (1982). Interpersonal problems of Vietnam combat veterans with symptoms of posttraumatic stress disorder. *Journal of Abnormal Psychology, 91,* 444–450.

ROBINS, L. N., BATES, W. M., & O'NEAL, P. (1962). Adult drinking patterns of former problem children. In D. J. Pitman & C. R. Snyder (Eds.), *Society, culture, and drinking patterns.* New York: John Wiley.

ROBINSON, D. (1986). Mutual aid in the change process. In W. R. Miller & N. Heather (Eds.), *Treating addictive behaviors: Processes of change.* New York: Plenum.

ROBINSON, F. J. (1970). *Effective study* (4th ed.). New York: Harper & Row.

ROEHLING, P. V., SMITH, G. T., GOLDMAN, M. S., & CHRISTIANSEN, B. A. (1987). Alcohol expectancies predict adolescent drinking: A three-year longitudinal study. Paper presented at the annual meeting of the American Psychological Association, New York.

ROGERS, C. R. (1951). *Client-centered therapy: Its practice, implications and theory.* Boston: Houghton Mifflin.

ROGERS, C. R. (1957). The necessary and sufficient conditions of therapeutic personality change. *Journal of Consulting Psychology, 21,* 95–113.

ROGERS, C. R. (1959). A theory of therapy, personality and interpersonal relationships as developed in the client-centered framework. In S. Koch (Ed.), *Psychology: A Study of a Science,* Vol. 3. New York: McGraw-Hill.

ROGERS, C. R. (1961). *On becoming a person: A therapist's view of psychotherapy.* Boston: Houghton Mifflin.

ROGERS, C. R., GENDLIN, E. T., KIESLER, D. J., & TRUAX, C. B. (1967). *The therapeutic relationship and its impact: A study of psychotherapy with schizophrenics.* Madison: University of Wisconsin Press.

ROGERS, R. W. (1975). A protection motivation theory of fear appeals and attitude change. *Journal of Psychology, 91,* 93–114.

ROGERS, R. W., & MEWBORN, C. R. (1976). Fear appeals and attitude change: Effects of a threat's noxiousness, probability of occurrence, and the efficacy of coping responses. *Journal of Personality and Social Psychology, 34,* 54–61.

ROSEN, G. M. (1976a). *Don't be afraid.* Englewood Cliffs, NJ: Prentice-Hall.

ROSEN, G. M. (1976b). The development and use of nonprescription behavior therapies. *American Psychologist, 31*, 139–141.

ROSEN, G. M. (1977). *The relaxation book: An illustrated self-help program.* Englewood Cliffs, NJ: Prentice Hall.

ROSENBERG, S., & OLSHAN, K. (1970). Evaluative and descriptive aspects in personality perception. *Journal of Personality and Social Psychology, 16*, 619–626.

ROSENMAN, R. H., FRIEDMAN, M., STRAUS, R., WURM, M., JENKINS, C. D., & MESSINGER, H. B. (1966). Coronary heart disease in the western collaborative group study. *Journal of the American Medical Association, 195*, 130–136.

ROSEWATER, L. B., & WALKER, L. E. A. (Eds.) (1985). *Handbook of feminist therapy: Women's issues in psychotherapy.* New York: Springer.

ROSS, L. D., RODIN, J., & ZIMBARDO, P. G. (1969). Toward an attribution therapy: The reduction of fear through induced cognitive-emotional misattribution. *Journal of Personality and Social Psychology, 12*, 279–288.

ROTTER, J. B. (1954). *Social learning and clinical psychology.* Englewood Cliffs, NJ: Prentice Hall.

ROTTER, J. B. (1966). Generalized expectancies for internal versus external control of reinforcement. *Psychological Monographs, 80* (Whole No. 609).

ROTTER, J. B. (1971). External control and internal control. *Psychology Today, 5*, 37–59.

ROWLEDGE, L. R., BOND, M., & SCHRADLE, S. B. (1980). A few more baby steps: Reflections on social support, sexism, power, problem-solving, and prevention. Paper presented to the Oregon Psychological Association, November 15, 1980, Portland.

RUBIN, I. M. (1967). Increased self-acceptance: A means of reducing prejudice. *Journal of Personality and Social Psychology, 5*, 233–238.

RUBIN, Z. (1973). *Liking and loving: An invitation to social psychology.* New York: Holt, Rinehart and Winston.

RULE, B. G., & NESDALE, A. R. (1976). Emotional arousal and aggressive behavior. *Psychological Bulletin, 83*, 851–863.

RUSH, A. J., BECK, A. T., KOVACS, M., & HOLLON, S. (1977). Comparative efficacy of cognitive therapy and imipramine in the treatment of depressed outpatients. *Cognitive Therapy and Research, 1*, 17–37.

RUSH, F. (1980). *The best kept secret: Sexual abuse of children.* Englewood Cliffs, NJ: Prentice-Hall.

RUSSELL, B. (1930). *The conquest of happiness.* New York: Liveright.

RUTTER, M. (1984, March). Resilient children. *Psychology Today, 18*, 57–65.

SAAL, F. E., & KNIGHT, P. A. (1988). *Industrial/organizational psychology: Science and practice.* Pacific Grove, CA: Brooks/Cole.

SACHAR, E. J. (1982). Endocrine abnormalities in depression. In E. S. Paykel (Ed.), *Handbook of affective disorders,* pp. 191–201. New York: Guilford.

SACKHEIM, H. A., GUR, R. C., & SAUCY, M. (1978). Emotions are expressed more intensely on the left side of the face. *Science, 202*, 434–436.

SACKS, O. (1985). *The man who mistook his wife for a hat, and other clinical tales.* New York: Harper & Row.

SALTER, A. (1949). *Conditioned reflex therapy.* New York: Creative Age.

SANCHEZ-CRAIG, M., ANNIS, H. M., BORNET, A. R., & MACDONALD, K. R. (1984). Random assignment to abstinence and controlled drinking: Evaluation of a cognitive-behavioural program for problem drinkers. *Journal of Consulting and Clinical Psychology, 52*, 390–403.

SANFORD, R. H. (1936). The effects of abstinence from food upon imaginal processes: A preliminary experiment. *Journal of Psychology, 2*, 129–136.

SANFORD, W., HAWLEY, N. P., & MCGEE, E. (1984). Sexuality. In Boston Women's Health Book Collective (Eds.), *The new our bodies, ourselves.* New York: Simon & Schuster.

SANGIULIANO, I. (1980). *In her time.* New York: William A. Morrow.

SATIR, V. (1972). *Peoplemaking.* Palo Alto, CA: Science and Behavior Books.

SCHACHTER, S. (1971). Some extraordinary facts about obese humans and rats. *American Psychologist, 26*, 129–144.

SCHACHTER, S. (1977). Nicotine regulation in heavy and light smokers. *Journal of Experimental Psychology: General, 106*, 5–12.

SCHACHTER, S. (1978). Pharmacological and psychological determinants of smoking. *Annals of Internal Medicine, 88*, 104–114.

SCHACHTER, S., & SINGER, J. E. (1962). Cognitive, social, and physiological determinants of emotional state. *Psychological Review, 69*, 379–399.

SCHILLING, K. M., & FUEHRER, A. (1986, March 7). The politics of women's self-help. Paper presented at the Association for Women in Psychology conference. Oakland, CA.

SCHNEIDER, R. H., JULIUS, S., MOSS, G. E., DIELMAN, T. E., ZWEIFLER, A. J., & KARUNAS, R. (1987). New markers for type A behavior: Pupil size and platelet epinephrine. *Psychosomatic Medicine, 49*, 579–590.

SCHOVER, L. R. (1984). *Prime time: Sexual health for men over fifty.* New York: Harper & Row.

SCHRADLE, S. B., & DOUGHER, M. J. (1985). Social support as a mediator of stress: Theoretical and empirical issues. *Clinical Psychology Review, 5*, 641–661.

SCHULTZ, D. P., & SCHULTZ, S. E. (1986). *Psychology and industry today* (4th ed.). New York: Macmillan.

SEEMAN, T. E., & SYME, S. L. (1987). Social networks and coronary artery disease: A comparison of the structure and function of social relations as predictors of disease. *Psychosomatic Medicine, 49*, 341–354.

SELIGMAN, M. E. P. (1975). *Helplessness.* San Francisco: W. H. Freeman.

SELIGMAN, M. E. P., ABRAMSON, L. Y., SEMMELL, A., & VON BAEYER, C. (1979). Depressive attributional style. *Journal of Abnormal Psychology, 88*, 242–247.

SELIGMAN, M. E. P., CASTELLON, C., CACCIOLA, J., SCHULMAN, P., LUBORSKY, L., OLLOVE, M., & DOWNING, R. (1988). Explanatory style change during cognitive therapy for unipolar depression. *Journal of Abnormal Psychology, 97,* 13–18.

SELYE, H. (1974). *Stress without distress.* New York: Harper & Row.

SELYE, H. (1978). *The stress of life* (2nd ed.). New York: McGraw-Hill.

SEMANS, J. H. (1956). Premature ejaculation: A new approach. *Southern Medical Journal, 49,* 353–357.

Sex cools on campus. (1989, March). *Psychology today, 23*(2), 14.

SHAH, I. (1967). *Tales of the Dervishes.* London: Jonathan Cape.

SHANTZ, D. W. (1986). Conflict, aggression, and peer status: An observational study. *Child Development, 57,* 1322–1332.

SHAPIRO, D. H., JR. (1978). *Precision nirvana.* Englewood Cliffs, NJ: Prentice Hall.

SHAW, G. B. (1911). *Getting married* (Preface). New York: Brentano's.

SHEEHY, G. (1976). *Passages: Predictable crises of adult life.* New York: E. P. Dutton.

SHERIDAN, C. L., & KING, R. G., JR. (1972). Obedience to authority with an authentic victim. *Proceedings of the 80th Annual Convention of the American Psychological Association,* 165–166.

SHIPLER, D. K. (1983). *Russia: Broken idols, solemn dreams.* New York: Times Books.

SHOSTROM, E. L. (1966). *Personal Orientation Inventory Manual.* San Diego: Education and Industrial Testing Service.

SIEGELMAN, E. Y. (1983). *Personal risk.* New York: Harper & Row.

SIGALL, H., & GOULD, R. (1977). The effects of self-esteem and evaluator demandingness on effort expenditure. *Journal of Personality and Social Psychology, 35,* 12–20.

SILVER, L. B., DUBLIN, C. C., & LOURIE, R. S. (1969). Does violence breed violence? Contributions from a study of the child abuse syndrome. *American Journal of Psychiatry, 126,* 404–407.

SIMON, S. B. (1977). *Vulture: A modern allegory on the art of putting oneself down.* Allen, TX: Argus.

SIMON, S. B. (1978). *Negative criticism and what you can do about it.* Allen, TX: Argus.

SIMON, S. B., HOWE, L. W., & KIRSCHENBAUM, H. (1985). *Values clarification: A handbook of practical strategies for teachers and students.* New York: Dodd.

SKINNER, B. F. (1948). *Walden two.* New York: Macmillan.

SKINNER, B. F. (1953). *Science and human behavior.* New York: Macmillan.

SKINNER, B. F. (1961). *Cumulative record.* New York: Appleton.

SKINNER, B. F. (1971). *Beyond freedom and dignity.* New York: Bantam.

SKINNER, B. F., & VAUGHAN, M. E. (1985). *Enjoy old age.* New York: Warner.

SLOANE, R. B., STAPLES, F. R., CRISTOL, A. H., YORKSTON, N. J., & WHIPPLE, K. (1975). *Psychotherapy versus behavior therapy.* Cambridge, MA: Harvard University Press.

SMITH, G. T., ROEHLING, P. V., CHRISTIANSEN, B. A., & GOLDMAN, M. S. (1986). Alcohol expectancies predict early adolescent drinking: A longitudinal study. Paper presented at the annual meeting of the American Psychological Association, Washington, DC.

SMITH, R. E., & GREGORY, P. B. (1976). Covert sensitization by induced anxiety in the treatment of chronic alcoholism. *Psychological Reports, 41,* 92–94.

SOLLEY, C. M., & STAGNER, R. (1956). Effects of magnitude of temporal barriers, type of goal, and perception of self. *Journal of Experimental Psychology, 51,* 62–70.

SPENCER, H. (1855). *Principles of psychology.* Amersham, U.K.: Gregg International.

SPENDER, D. (1980). *Man made language.* London: Routledge & Kegan Paul.

SPIELBERGER, C. D. (Ed.). (1966a). *Anxiety: Current trends in theory and research.* New York: Academic Press.

SPIELBERGER, C. D. (1966b). Theory and research on anxiety. In C. D. Spielberger (Ed.), *Anxiety and behavior,* pp. 3–20. New York: Academic Press.

SPILKA, B., HOOD, R. W., & GORSUCH, R. L. (1985). *The psychology of religion: An empirical approach.* Englewood Cliffs, NJ: Prentice Hall.

SPRECHER, S. (1985). Sex differences in bases of power in dating relationships. *Sex Roles, 12,* 449–462.

SPRINGER, S. P., & DEUTSCH, G. (1981). *Left brain, right brain.* New York: W. H. Freeman.

STEENMAN, L. (1988, October 15). He's treated like a rock star wherever he goes. *American Way, 21*(20), 110.

STERN, D. (1977). *The first relationship: Infant and mother.* Cambridge, MA: Harvard University Press.

STERN, E. M. (Ed.). (1985). *Psychotherapy and the religiously committed patient.* New York: Haworth.

STERNBERG, R. (1986). A triangular theory of love. *Psychological Review, 93,* 119–135.

STERNGLANZ, S. H., & SERBIN, L. A. (1974). Sex role stereotyping in children's television programs. *Developmental Psychology, 10,* 710–715.

STEVENS-LONG, J. (1979). *Adult life: Developmental processes.* Los Angeles: Mayfield.

STEWART, W. A. (1977). A psychosocial study of the formation of the early adult life structure in women. *Dissertation Abstracts International, 38* (University Microfilms No. 1-B, 381–382).

STORMS, M. D., & NISBETT, R. E. (1970). Insomnia and the attribution process. *Journal of Personality and Social Psychology, 16,* 319–328.

STRICKLAND, B. R. (1988). Sex-related differences in health and illness. *Psychology of Women Quarterly, 12,* 381–399.

STROOP, J. R. (1935). Studies of interference in serial verbal reactions. *Journal of Experimental Psychology, 18,* 643–662.

STUART, R. B. (1974). Teaching facts about drugs: Pushing or preventing? *Journal of Educational Psychology, 66,* 189–201.

STUART, R. B. (1980). *Helping couples change.* Champaign, IL: Research Press.

SUE, D. W. (1977). Counseling the culturally different: A conceptual analysis. *Personnel and Guidance Journal, 55,* 422–425.

SUINN, R. M. (1982). Intervention with Type A behaviors. *Journal of Consulting and Clinical Psychology, 50,* 933–949.

SULLIVAN, H. S. (1953). *The interpersonal theory of psychiatry.* New York: W. W. Norton.

Surgeon General of the United States (1984). *The health consequences of smoking.* Washington, DC: U.S. Government Printing Office.

SWEENEY, P. D., Anderson, K., & Bailey, S. (1986). Attributional style in depression: A meta-analytic review. *Journal of Personality and Social Psychology, 50,* 974–991.

SZASZ, T. (1961). *The myth of mental illness: Foundations of a theory of personal conduct.* New York: Hoeber-Harper.

SZASZ, T. (1978). *The myth of psychotherapy: Mental healing as religion, rhetoric, and repression.* Garden City, NY: Anchor.

SZASZ, T. (1986). The case against suicide prevention. *American Psychologist, 41,* 806–812.

TABAKOFF, B., RITZMANN, R. F., RAJU, T. S., & DEITRICH, R. A. (1980). Characterization of acute and chronic tolerance in mice selected for inherent differences in sensitivity to ethanol. *Alcoholism: Clinical and Experimental Research, 4,* 70–73.

TAGESON, C. W. (1982). *Humanistic psychology: A synthesis.* Homewood, IL: Dorsey.

TARTER, R. E. (1981). Minimal brain dysfunction as an etiological predisposition to alcoholism. In R. Meyer, B. Glucek, J. O'Brien, T. Babor, J. Jaffe, & J. Stabereau (Eds.), *Evaluation of the alcoholic: Implications for research, theory, and treatment.* Rockville, MD: National Institute on Alcohol Abuse and Alcoholism.

TAVRIS, C. (1982). *Anger: The misunderstood emotion.* New York: Simon & Schuster.

TAVRIS, C., & WADE, C. (1984). *The longest war: Sex differences in perspective* (2nd ed.). San Diego: Harcourt Brace Jovanovich.

TAYLOR, F. W. (1911). *The principles of scientific management.* New York: Harper & Row.

TAYLOR, S. E. (1981). The interface of cognitive and social psychology. In J. H. Harvey (Ed.), *Cognition, social behavior, and the environment.* Hillsdale, NJ: Lawrence Erlbaum.

TAYLOR, S. E., & Crocker, J. (1980). Schematic bases of social information processing. In E. T. Higgins, P. Hermann, & M. P. Zanna (Eds.), *Social cognition: Cognitive structures and processes underlying person perception.* Hillsdale, NJ: Lawrence Erlbaum.

TEDERS, S. J., BLANCHARD, E. B., ANDRASIK, F., JURISH, S. E., NEFF, D. F., & ARENA, J. G. (1984). Relaxation training for tension headache: Comparative efficacy and cost-effectiveness of a minimal therapist contact versus a therapist-directed procedure. *Behavior Therapy, 15,* 59–70.

TENNOV, D. (1979). *Love and limerance.* New York: Stein & Day.

THOMAS, R. M. (1979). *Comparing theories of child development.* Belmont, CA: Wadsworth.

THORNHILL, R. (1981). Panorpa (Mecoptera: Panorpidae) scorpionflies: Systems for understanding resource-defense polygyny and alternative male reproductive efforts. *Annual Review of Ecological Systems, 12,* 355–386.

THORNHILL, R., & THORNHILL, N. W. (1983). Human rape: An evolutionary analysis. *Ethology and Sociobiology, 4,* 137–173.

THORNTON, C. C., GOTTHEIL, E., GELLENS, H. K., & ALTERMAN, A. I. (1977). Voluntary versus involuntary abstinence in the treatment of alcoholics. *Journal of Studies on Alcohol, 38*(9), 1740–1748.

THURMAN, C. W. (1983). Effects of a rational-emotive treatment program on Type A behavior among college students. *Journal of College Student Personnel, 24,* 417–422.

TILLICH, P. (1957). *Dynamics of faith.* New York: Harper.

TOBIAS, S. (1978) *Overcoming math anxiety.* Boston: Houghton Mifflin.

TOFFLER, A. (1970). *Future shock.* New York: Random House.

TOFFLER, A. (1980). *The third wave.* New York: William A. Morrow.

TOLMAN, E. C. (1932). *Purposive behavior in animals and men.* New York: Appleton.

TOTH, A. & TOTH, S. (1981). Group work with widows. In E. Howell & M. Bayes (Eds.), *Women and mental health.* New York: Basic Books.

TOUGH, A. (1982). *Intentional changes.* Chicago: Follett.

TRIANDIS, H. C., & DRAGUNS, J. G. (1980). *Handbook of cross-cultural psychology.* Vol. 6, *Psychopathology.* Boston: Allyn & Bacon.

TRUAX, C. B., & CARKHUFF, R. R. (1967). *Toward effective counseling and psychotherapy.* Chicago: Aldine.

TRUAX, C. B., & MITCHELL, K. M. (1971). Research on certain therapist interpersonal skills in relation to process and outcome. In A. E. Bergin and S. L. Garfield (Eds.), *Handbook of psychotherapy and behavior change.* pp. 299–344. NY: John Wiley.

TRULL, T. J., NIETZEL, M. T., & MAIN, A. (1988). The use of meta-analysis to assess the clinical significance of behavior therapy for agoraphobia. *Behavior Therapy, 19,* 527–538.

TSAI, M., FELDMAN-SUMMERS, S., & Edgar, M. (1979). Childhood molestation: Variables related to differential impacts on psychological functioning in adult women. *Journal of Abnormal Psychology, 88,* 407–417.

TUCHFELD, B. S. (1981). Spontaneous remission in alcoholics: Empirical observations and theoretical implications. *Journal of Studies on Alcohol, 42,* 626–641.

TUCKER, D. M., WATSON, R. T., & HERLMAN, K. M. (1977). Discrimination and evocation of affectively toned speech in patients with right parietal disease. *Neurology, 27,* 947–950.

TURNER, S. M., CALHOUN, K. S., & ADAMS, H. E. (Eds.) (1981). *Handbook of clinical behavior therapy.* New York: John Wiley.

ULRICH, R. S. (1983). View through a window may influence recovery from surgery. *Science, 224,* 420–421.

U.S. Office of Strategic Services. (1948). *The assessment of men: Selection of personnel for the Office of Strategic Services.* New York: Rinehart.

VAILLANT, G. E. (1975). Sociopathy as a human process: A viewpoint. *Archives of General Psychiatry, 32,* 178–183.

VAILLANT, G. (1977). *Adaptation to life.* Boston: Little, Brown.

VAILLANT, G. (1983). *The natural history of alcoholism: Causes, patterns, and paths to recovery.* Cambridge, MA: Harvard University Press.

VALINS, S. (1966). Cognitive effects of false heart-rate feedback. *Journal of Personality and Social Psychology, 4,* 400–408.

VALINS, S., & NISBETT, R. E. (1971). Attribution processes in the development and treatment of emotional disorders. In E. E. Jones, D. E. Kanouse, H. H. Kelley, R. E. Nisbett, S. Valins, & B. Weiner (Eds.), *Attribution: Perceiving the causes of behavior.* New York: General Learning Press.

VALINS, S., & RAY, A. (1967). Effects of cognitive desensitization on avoidance behavior. *Journal of Personality and Social Psychology, 7,* 345–350.

VALLE, S. K. (1981). Interpersonal functioning of alcoholism counselors and treatment outcome. *Journal of Studies on Alcohol, 42,* 783–790.

VAN GELDER, L. (1987). Cross-addiction: Surprising results of the *Ms* survey. *Ms., 15*(8), 44–47.

VELTEN, E. C. (1967). *The induction of elation and depression through the reading of structural sets of mood statements.* Unpublished doctoral dissertation, University of Southern California.

VELTEN, E. C. (1968). A laboratory task for induction of mood states. *Behavior Research and Therapy, 6,* 473–482.

VISHER, E. B., & VISHER, J. S. (1988). *Old loyalties, new ties: Therapeutic strategies with stepfamilies.* New York: Brunner/Mazel.

VOLBERG, R., & STEADMAN, H. (1988). Refining prevalence estimates of pathological gambling. *American Journal of Psychiatry, 145,* 502–505.

VON FRANZ, M.-L., & HILLMAN, J. (1979). *Jung's typology.* Irving, TX: Spring.

VYGOTSKY, L. S. (1962). *Thought and language.* Cambridge, MA: MIT Press.

VYGOTSKY, L. S. (1978). *Mind in society: The development of higher psychological processes.* Cambridge, MA: Harvard University Press.

WACHTEL, P. (1977). *Psychoanalysis and behavior therapy: Toward an integration.* New York: Basic Books.

WACHTEL, P. (Ed.). (1982). *Resistance: Psychodynamic and behavioral approaches.* New York: Plenum.

WADE, C. & TAVRIS, C. (1987). *Psychology.* New York: Harper & Row.

WAGONSELLER, B. R., & McDOWELL, R. L. (1979). *You and your child: A common sense approach to successful parenting.* Champaign, IL: Research Press.

WALK, R. D. (1981). *Perceptual development.* Monterey, CA: Brooks/Cole.

WALKER, A. (1982). *The color purple.* New York: Simon & Schuster.

WALKER, C. E. (1975). *Learn to relax: 13 ways to reduce tension.* Englewood Cliffs, NJ: Prentice Hall.

WALKER, L. E. A. (1985). Feminist therapy with victim/survivors of interpersonal violence. In L. B. Rosewater & L. E. A. Walker (Eds.), *Handbook of feminist therapy: Women's issues in psychotherapy,* pp. 203–214. New York: Springer.

WALLERSTEIN, J. S., & Blakeslee, S. (1989). *Second chances: Men, women, and children a decade after divorce.* New York: Ticknor & Fields.

WALLERSTEIN, J. S., & KELLY, J. B. (1980). *Surviving the breakup: How children and parents cope with divorce.* New York: Basic Books.

WARSHAW, R. (1988). *I never called it rape.* New York: Harper & Row.

WATERS, H. F., & MELAMUD, P. (1975). Drop that gun, Captain Video. *Newsweek, 85,* 81–82.

WATSON, J. B. (1925). *Behaviorism.* New York: W. W. NORTON.

WATSON, J. B. (1930). *Behaviorism.* New York: People's Institute.

WATSON, O. M., & GRAVES, T. D. (1966). Quantitative research in proxemic behavior. *American Anthropologist, 68,* 971–985.

WATTS, A. W. (1975). *Psychotherapy East and West.* New York: Random House.

WATTS, A. W. (1979). *The meaning of happiness: The quest for freedom of the spirit in modern psychology and the wisdom of the East.* New York: Harper & Row.

WATZLAWICK, P., WEAKLAND, J. H., & FISCH, R. (1974). *Change: Principles of problem formation and problem resolution.* New York: W. W. NORTON.

WEAVER, J. B., MASLAND, J. L., KHARAZMI, S., & ZILLMANN, D. (1985). Effect of alcoholic intoxication on the appreciation of different types of humor. *Journal of Personality and Social Psychology, 49,* 781–787.

WEEKES, C. (1972). *Peace from nervous suffering.* New York: Hawthorn.

WEIBE, D. J., & McCALLUM, D. M. (1986). Health practices and hardiness as mediators in the stress-illness relationship. *Health Psychology, 5,* 425–438.

WEIGLE, M. (1970). *The penitentes of the southwest.* Santa Fe, NM: Ancient City Press.

WEISSTEIN, N. (1971). Psychology constructs the female. In V. Gornick & B. Moran (Eds.), *Woman in sexist society:*

Studies in power and powerlessness. New York: Basic Books.

WELLS, G. L. & LOFTUS, E. F. (1984). *Eyewitness testimony: Psychological perspectives.* Cambridge, MA: Cambridge University Press.

WELLS-PARKER, E. MILLS, S., & SPENCER, B. (1983). Stress experiences and drinking histories of elderly drunken driving offenders. *Journal of Studies on Alcohol, 44,* 429–437.

WEST, C., & ZIMMERMAN, D. H. (1983). Small insults: A study of interruptions in cross-sex conversations between unacquainted persons. In B. Thorne, C. Kramarae, & N. Henley (Eds.), *Language, gender, and society,* pp. 103–117. Rowley, MA: Newbury House.

WESTERLUND, E. (1986). Freud on sexual trauma: An historical review of seduction and betrayal. *Psychology of Women Quarterly. 10,* 297–310.

WHELAN, E. W. (1976). *A baby? . . .Maybe: A guide to making the most fateful decision of your life.* New York: Bobbs-Merrill.

WHITE, R. (1975). *Lives in progress: A study of the natural growth of personality* (3rd ed.). New York: Holt, Rinehart and Winston.

WHITING, B., & EDWARDS, C. P. (1973). A cross-cultural analysis of sex differences in the behavior of children aged three through eleven. *Journal of Social Psychology, 91,* 177–188.

WIGGINS, J. S. (1973). *Personality and prediction.* Reading, MA: Addison-Wesley.

WIGGINS, J. S., WIGGINS, N., & CONGER, J. C. (1968). Correlates of heterosexual somatic preference. *Journal of Personality and Social Psychology, 10,* 82–90.

WILDER, T. (1938). *Our town.* New York: Coward McCann.

WILKINSON, D. A., & LeBRETON, S. (1986). Early indications of treatment outcome in multiple drug users. In W. R. Miller & N. Heather (Eds.), *Treating addictive behaviors: Processes of change,* pp. 239–261.

WILLIAMS, P. T., FORTMANN, S. P., FARQUHAR, J. W., VARADY, A., & MELLEN, S. (1981). A comparison of statistical methods for evaluating risk factor changes in community-based studies: An example from the Stanford three-community study. *Journal of Chronic Diseases, 34,* 565–571.

WILLIAMS, R. L. & LONG, J. D. (1983). *Toward a self-managed life style.* Boston: Houghton Mifflin.

WILSON, E. O. (1975). *Sociobiology: The new synthesis.* Cambridge, MA: Harvard University Press.

WILSON, G. T. (1980). Behavior therapy and the treatment of obesity. In W. R. Miller (Ed.), *The addictive behaviors: Treatment of alcoholism, drug abuse, smoking, and obesity,* pp. 207–237. New York: Pergamon.

WILSON, G. T., & LAWSON, D. M. (1976). Expectancies, alcohol, and sexual arousal in male social drinkers. *Journal of Abnormal Psychology, 85,* 587–594.

WINCZE, J. P. (1981). Sexual dysfunction (distress and dissatisfaction). In. S. M. Turner, K. S. Calhoun, &. H. E. Adams (Eds.), *Handbook of clinical behavior therapy.* New York: John Wiley.

WINE, J. (1971). Test anxiety and direction of attention. *Psychological Bulletin, 76,* 92–104.

WISE, R. A. (1984). Neural mechanisms of the reinforcing action of cocaine. In J. Grabowski (Ed.), *Cocaine: Pharmacology, effects, and treatment of abuse,* pp. 15–33. Rockville, MD: National Institute on Drug Abuse.

WISPE, L. G., & DRAMBAREAN, N. C. (1953). Physiological need, word frequency, and visual duration thresholds. *Journal of Experimental Psychology, 46,* 25–31.

WOLPE, J. (1958). *Psychotherapy by reciprocal inhibition.* Stanford, CA: Stanford University Press.

WOLPE, J. (1973). *The practice of behavior therapy* (2nd ed.). New York: Pergamon.

WOOD, C. (1986). The hostile heart. *Psychology Today, 20*(9), 10–12.

WOOLF, V. (1929). *A room of one's own.* New York: Harcourt, Brace & World.

WRIGHT, J., PERREAULT, R., & MATHIEU, M. (1977). The treatment of sexual dysfunction: A review. *Archives of General Psychiatry, 34,* 881–890.

WRIGHT, L. (1988). The Type A behavior pattern and coronary artery disease: Quest for the active ingredients and the elusive mechanism. *American Psychologist, 43,* 2–14.

WYLIE, R. C. (1979). *The self concept: Theory and research on selected topics,* Vol. 2. Lincoln: University of Nebraska Press.

YAHNE, C. E. (1984). The effects of a structured support group on the self-perceptions and goal attainment of women clients. *Dissertation Abstracts International, 46,* 321B (University Microfilms No. DA8501203).

YAHNE, C. E., & EDWARDS, W. S. (1989). Professional responsibility: More than medical ethics. Unpublished manuscript, University of New Mexico School of Medicine, Albuquerque.

YAHNE, C. E., & LONG, V. O. (1988). The use of support groups to raise self-esteem for women clients. *Journal of American College Health, 37*(2), 79–84.

YALOM, I. D. (1975). *The theory and practice of group psychotherapy.* New York: Basic Books.

YALOM, I. D. (1980). *Existential psychotherapy.* New York: Basic Books.

YARKIN, K. L., HARVEY, J. H., & BLOXOM, B. M. (1981). Cognitive sets, attribution, and social interaction. *Journal of Personality and Social Psychology, 41,* 243–252.

ZAHAVI, S., & ASHER, S. R. (1978). The effect of verbal instructions on preschool children's aggressive behavior. *Journal of School Psychology, 16,* 146–153.

ZEISS, R. A. (1977). Self-directed treatment for premature ejaculation: Preliminary case reports. *Journal of Behavior Therapy and Experimental Psychiatry, 8,* 87–91.

ZEISS, R. A. (1978). Self-directed treatment for premature ejaculation. *Journal of Consulting and Clinical Psychology, 6,* 1234–1241.

ZEISS, R., & ZEISS, A. (1978). *Prolong your pleasure.* New York: Pocket Books.

ZETTLE, R. D., & HAYES, S..C. (1982). Rule-governed behavior: A potential theoretical framework for cognitive-behavioral therapy. *Advances in Cognitive-Behavioral Research, 1,* 73–118.

ZILBERGELD, B. (1983). *The shrinking of America: Myths of psychological change.* Boston: Little, Brown.

ZILBERGELD, B., & ULLMAN, J. (1978). *Male sexuality: A guide to sexual fulfillment.* Boston: Little, Brown.

ZILLMANN, D. (1979). *Hostility and aggression.* Hillsdale, NJ: Lawrence Erlbaum.

ZILLMANN, D. (1984). Transfer of excitation in emotional behavior. In J. T. Cacioppo & R. E. Petty (Eds.), *Social psychophysiology: A sourcebook,* pp. 215–240. New York: Guilford.

ZIMBARDO, P. G. (1975). Transforming experimental research into advocacy for social change. In M. Deutsch & H. A. Hornstein (Eds.), *Applying social psychology.* Hillsdale, NJ: Lawrence Erlbaum.

ZIMBARDO, P. G. (1977). *Shyness: What it is, what to do about it.* Reading, MA: Addison-Wesley.

ZIMMERMAN, D. H., & WEST, C. (1975). Sex roles, interruptions and silences in converation. In B. Thorne & N. Henley (Eds.), *Language and sex: Differences and dominance,* pp. 105–129. Rowley, MA: Newbury House.

ZIS, A. P., & GOODWIN, F. K. (1982). The amine hypothesis. In E. S. Paykel (Ed.), *Handbook of affective disorders,* pp. 175–190. New York: Guilford Press.

ZISKIN, J. (1981). *Coping with psychiatric and psychological testimony* (3rd ed.). Marina del Rey, CA: Law & Psychology Press.

ZULLOW, H. M., Oettingen, G., Peterson, C., & Seligman, M. E. P. (1988). Pessimistic explanatory style in the historical record: CAVing LBJ, presidential candidates, and East versus West Berlin. *American Psychologist, 43,* 673–682.

■ PHOTO CREDITS

Glossary Index

The words in this glossary are defined specifically in relation to the psychology of adjustment. Many of these terms have other meanings outside of, or in other fields of, psychology.

Below are the glossary terms found in this text, followed by the page numbers on which they are defined.

Index

■ SUBJECT INDEX

Note: Bold face pages locate definitions